11/21

MASTER
of the Game

MASTER
of the Game

Henry Kissinger and the
Art of Middle East Diplomacy

MARTIN INDYK

A Council on Foreign Relations Book

ALFRED A. KNOPF New York
2021

THIS IS A BORZOI BOOK
PUBLISHED BY ALFRED A. KNOPF

www.aaknopf.com

Library of Congress Cataloging-in-Publication Data
Names: Indyk, Martin, author.
Title: Master of the game : Henry Kissinger and the art
of Middle East Diplomacy/ Martin Indyk.
Description: First edition. | New York :
Alfred A. Knopf, 2021. | Includes index.
Identifiers: LCCN 2021001578 (print) | LCCN 2021001579 (ebook) |
ISBN 9781101947548 (hardcover) | ISBN 9781101947555 (ebook)
Subjects: LCSH: Middle East—Foreign relations—United States. |
United States—Foreign relations—Middle East. | United States—
Foreign relations—1969–1974. | United States—Foreign relations—1974–1977. |
Kissinger, Henry, 1923– | Mediation, International. |
Arab-Israeli conflict—1973–1993. | Israel-Arab War, 1973.
Classification: LCC E183.8.M628 I53 2021 (print) |
LCC E183.8.M628 (ebook) | DDC 327.73056—dc23
LC record available at https://lccn.loc.gov/2021001578
LC ebook record available at https://lccn.loc.gov/2021001579

Maps (pages 339, 410, 527) copyright © David Lindroth, Inc.

Front-of-jacket photograph: Everett Collection / Alamy
Spine photograph: David Hume Kennerly White House photographs / photographs
selected for possible use in *Years of Renewal* [4 of 5] Image 27, Henry A. Kissinger
Papers, Part III (MS 2004). Manuscripts and Archives, Yale University.

Jacket design by Chip Kidd

Manufactured in the United States of America
First Edition

To
Stella and Mayzie Miller,
Ollie Indyk, and Harper Burt
in the hope that they too will pursue peace.

Contents

Contents

MASTER
of the Game

Prologue

Men become myths not by what they know, or even by what they achieve, but by the tasks they set for themselves.

—Henry Kissinger, *A World Restored*

Saturday, October 6, 1973, New York. The annual gathering of world leaders known as the UN General Assembly was convening in New York, snarling traffic and generating a seemingly endless ritual of speeches, speed dates, and receptions involving pooh-bahs and potentates from all corners of the earth.

For Henry Kissinger, it was an exciting moment. Two weeks earlier, in the ornate East Room of the White House, he had been sworn in as secretary of state by Chief Justice Warren Burger. His mother, Paula, had held a copy of the Old Testament; his father, Louis, his two children, Elizabeth and David, and Nancy Maginnes, his "occasional companion" (as *The New York Times* put it), had looked on with pride. The audience of some 250 friends and colleagues, including the actor Kirk Douglas, had given Kissinger a prolonged standing ovation. President Richard Nixon had introduced his new chief diplomat by noting that he was the first naturalized American to become secretary of state, and the first who didn't part his hair. That was Nixon's way of alluding to the fact that Kissinger was also the first Jewish secretary of state in the nation's history.

That particular Saturday also happened to be Yom Kippur, the Day of Atonement, the holiest day on the Jewish calendar, which Jews spend fasting and praying in penance for their sins. Kissinger had been raised in an Orthodox home, had been bar mitzvahed and married in Orthodox synagogues, and identified as a Jew.* However, he had experienced the horrors of the Holocaust

---

* As Kissinger told one of his biographers: "You cannot be part of a society that has suffered what the Jewish people have suffered for millennia without a strong sense of identification with it and

Henry Kissinger being sworn in as secretary of state by Chief Justice of the
Supreme Court Warren Burger on September 22, 1973, in the East Room
of the White House. His mother, Paula Kissinger, holds the family Bible.
President Richard Nixon bears witness. The audience included Kirk Douglas
and Kissinger's "occasional companion" Nancy Maginnes. Nixon noted that
Kissinger was the first American secretary of state who didn't part his hair.

as a teenager fleeing the Nazis and upon his return to Germany as a soldier in
the U.S. Army. He no longer believed in the concept of atonement to a just
and forgiving God. As he became more distant from his German Jewish past,
the practice of his religion would fall away completely.

One could forgive the new secretary for sleeping in on that first Saturday
morning in October. Friday had been unreasonably frenetic: he had met with
President Mobutu Sese Seko of Zaire, delivered a luncheon speech to Latin
American foreign ministers, and met, individually, with twelve other foreign
ministers. Among them were Israel's Abba Eban and Egypt's Mohammed el-
Zayyat, both of whom he agreed to meet again in November to engage in a
deeper dialogue about ameliorating the Arab-Israeli conflict.

That is why he was sleeping when, at 6:15 a.m., Joe Sisco, the assistant
secretary of state for Near Eastern and South Asian affairs, barged into the
baroque suite on the thirty-fifth floor of the Waldorf Astoria reserved for
American secretaries of state. Sisco, the son of Italian immigrants, was an officer in the Foreign Service who had the unusual distinction of rising to its top

---

sense of obligation to it [the Jewish faith]." See Niall Ferguson, *Kissinger, 1923–1968: The Idealist*
(New York: Penguin, 2015), 202.

ranks without ever having served abroad. They had started out as adversaries during Nixon's first term when Sisco reported to Kissinger's nemesis, Secretary of State William Rogers. Kissinger had nevertheless come to appreciate this lanky diplomat's tactical finesse, his indefatigability, his ebullience, and his Bugs Bunny smile.

Sisco wasn't smiling that morning. He brought alarming news from Kenneth Keating, the U.S. ambassador to Israel. Prime Minister Golda Meir had convoked an urgent meeting with Keating to warn the United States that coordinated Egyptian and Syrian offensives were expected to be launched against Israel in a matter of hours. Meir feared that there was some misunderstanding and wanted Kissinger to convey immediately to Moscow, Cairo, and Damascus that Israel had no intention of attacking its Arab neighbors. She also wanted him to know that she had decided not to preempt the expected Arab attack.

At 6:40 a.m., Kissinger called Soviet ambassador Anatoly Dobrynin, followed by the Israeli chargé d'affaires in Washington, the Egyptian foreign minister, and the Israeli foreign minister. At 8:29 a.m., he received a call from the Israeli chargé to inform him that, twenty minutes earlier, in coordinated attacks, Egyptian and Syrian forces had launched aerial bombardments of Israeli forces on the east bank of the Suez Canal and the Golan Heights.

At 8:35 a.m., Kissinger called General Alexander Haig, Nixon's chief of staff. In his deep, gravelly, German-accented voice, he asked Haig to convey to Nixon that "we may have a Middle East war going on today."

Thirteen days later, on October 19, 1973, with the war still raging and Israeli forces threatening both Damascus and Cairo, Kissinger embarked on a mission to Moscow and Tel Aviv to negotiate the cease-fire that would end that war and launch a new role for the United States as the broker of Arab-Israeli peace. It was a high-wire act. Richard Nixon was besieged by Watergate troubles and barely functioning. During the previous two weeks, Kissinger had managed to compartmentalize his crisis diplomacy, preventing the Watergate contagion from infecting and undermining his efforts. But as Nixon's troubles mounted, the danger grew. It culminated in superpower brinkmanship, in which Kissinger and Nixon's other advisers ordered a DEFCON 3 alert while the president was sleeping.

In this crisis, Kissinger skillfully maneuvered to secure four ambitious and somewhat contradictory objectives simultaneously: to ensure the victory of America's ally Israel over the Soviet-backed Egyptian and Syrian forces; to prevent a humiliating defeat of the Egyptian army so that its leader, President Anwar Sadat, would be able to enter peace negotiations with Israel with his dignity intact; to prove to the Arabs that only the United States could deliver results for them at the negotiating table; and to maintain the "détente" with Moscow, even as he worked to undermine the Soviet position of influence in the Middle East.

It was a virtuoso, though occasionally makeshift, performance that opened the way for Kissinger's diplomatic pirouette on the Middle Eastern stage. Over the next four years, that exertion—dubbed "shuttle diplomacy" because of the seemingly endless flights Kissinger made between Cairo, Jerusalem, Damascus, and other Arab capitals—produced three more agreements: two in the Sinai between Israel and Egypt, and a Golan Heights disengagement agreement between Israel and Syria. In all three cases, Israel ceded territory in return for stable, interim borders. In the process, Kissinger succeeded in laying the foundations for an American-led effort to resolve the Arab-Israeli conflict. It would lead two years later to the Israeli-Egyptian peace treaty, negotiated by President Carter, and eventually to the Israeli-Palestinian Oslo Accords and the Israeli-Jordanian peace treaty consummated under President Clinton.

Kissinger's performance was impressive for the vision, strategy, and deftness of America's chief diplomat. Time and again during those four years, Kissinger would combine his knowledge of history, his intuitive psychological

Israeli prime minister Benjamin Netanyahu shakes hands with Palestinian Authority president Yasir Arafat after signing the Wye River Memorandum on October 23, 1998, in the East Room of the White House. President Bill Clinton and King Hussein of Jordan bear witness. It would be the last Israeli-Palestinian peace agreement signed at the White House. King Hussein died of cancer a few months later.

skills, his sophisticated understanding of the complex balance of power in the Middle East, his willingness to take risks and improvise, and his Machiavellian ability to deploy the levers of influence bestowed upon him by immense American power to maneuver and manipulate the leaders of that troubled region toward peace. It was by no means a flawless performance, as we shall see. At times, he became blinkered by his pursuit of order and stability, missing both warning signs of war and openings for peace. At other times his success was at least as much the product of the ingenuity or risk-taking of his interlocutors than of his own brilliance. Nevertheless, if diplomacy is the art of moving political leaders to places they are reluctant to go, then Kissinger was the master of the game.

Friday, October 23, 1998, Washington, DC. Twenty-five years later, the negotiators and invited guests were filing into the same East Room of the White House where Henry Kissinger had been sworn in as the fifty-sixth secretary of state. They were there to witness the signing of the Wye River Memorandum by Israeli prime minister Benjamin Netanyahu and Palestine Liberation Organization chairman Yasir Arafat, presided over by an exasperated President Bill Clinton and a wan King Hussein of Jordan (he would die of cancer less than four months later).

The statesmen and diplomats in their dark suits were dwarfed by the grandeur of the room, with its cream-colored walls, oak parquet floors, and dramatic yellow silk curtains and valances, illuminated by three brilliant Bohemian crystal chandeliers. For this ceremonial signing, the riser with the podium and its presidential seal had been placed between the room's twin fireplaces with their Italian marble mantelpieces topped by massive gold-framed mirrors. On either side of the mirrors, full-length portraits of George and Martha Washington looked down at the audience. America's first president extended his right hand in welcome, but his left hand was firmly placed on his sword.

Abraham Lincoln, Franklin D. Roosevelt, and John F. Kennedy—presidents who had died in office—had lain in repose here. In this room, Lyndon B. Johnson had signed the Civil Rights Act of 1964, and Richard Nixon had given his farewell address to his staff. And here, twenty years earlier, building on Kissinger's handiwork, Anwar Sadat, Menachem Begin, and Jimmy Carter had signed the Camp David Accords (the framework for peace between Israel and Egypt) and then engaged in an iconic three-way handshake.

As the guests took their assigned seats to await the arrival of Clinton, Arafat, and Netanyahu, the scene was reminiscent of earlier occasions for Israeli-Palestinian signing ceremonies at the White House during Clinton's presidency. The first was for the Oslo Accords in September 1993, when

PLO chairman Yasir Arafat and Israeli prime minister Yitzhak Rabin shake
hands after the signing of the Oslo Accords on the White House lawn on
September 13, 1993. President Clinton's outstretched arms were meant to
symbolize the American embrace of this historic moment of reconciliation
between Israelis and Palestinians. Clinton chose a tie with a trumpet pattern
to symbolize the biblical trumpets that were blown by the Israelites to bring
the walls of Jericho down.

Yitzhak Rabin shook Yasir Arafat's hand on the South Lawn while Bill Clinton stood between them, arms outstretched before the world to symbolize
the American embrace of the peacemakers. The second, two years later, was
in this same East Room, when the two leaders returned to sign the Oslo II
Accord, which provided for Arafat to take control of some 27 percent of the
West Bank.

I participated in the first event as Clinton's Middle East adviser at the
National Security Council, and in the second as his ambassador to Israel. I
was present at this third White House event, three years later, as Madeleine
Albright's assistant secretary of state for Near Eastern affairs.

Arafat and Netanyahu were, at this point, unlikely peacemakers. The
peace process had survived the assassination of Yitzhak Rabin and the electoral
defeat of Shimon Peres, his diplomatic wingman, but this ceremony disguised
the serious jeopardy it was now in; just how serious would emerge two years
later, when the second Palestinian intifada erupted in Gaza and the West Bank.
It raged for five years, killing and maiming thousands on both sides and in the
process destroying the edifice of Israeli-Palestinian peace we had so painstakingly constructed.

The signs were there already in the exhaustion that President Clinton's peace team felt at that moment. It wasn't just the nine days and nights of tortuous negotiations at the Wye River plantation on the Eastern Shore of Maryland; it was also the eighteen months of laborious preparatory talks that it took just to get to this point. Finally, we had produced an agreement: Israel would yield 13 percent of its West Bank territory to the Palestinians in fulfillment of the redeployment requirements of the Oslo Accords. Yet because Netanyahu had agreed to concede that meager amount of territory, his coalition government would collapse soon after.

Little did we know that day that the Wye River Memorandum would turn out to be the last U.S.-brokered Israeli-Palestinian peace agreement.* More than twenty years have passed since then, and the chances for a resolution of the Israeli-Palestinian conflict seem, at best, to have receded far into the future, notwithstanding the efforts of the three presidents who succeeded Clinton.

Meanwhile, Iran's success in exploiting sectarian divisions in the Middle Eastern heartland, together with the terrorist operations of al-Qaeda and ISIS affiliates, helped cement relations between Israel and the Sunni Arab states, rendering the Palestinian issue all but irrelevant to their larger strategic concerns. The signing of the Abraham Accords in September 2020 gave expression to this new dynamic in the form of normalization of relations between Israel, the United Arab Emirates, and Bahrain. Sudan and Morocco would soon follow. Those accords broke the linkage between resolution of the Palestinian issue and normalization of relations with Arab states not directly involved in the conflict with Israel. They also aided in preventing Israel's annexation of significant parts of the West Bank, at least for a time, thereby helping to preserve the possibility of an independent Palestinian state. But beyond that, the accords did little to advance a resolution of the Israeli-Palestinian conflict.

The Trump administration actually made matters worse by proposing a peace deal that would have left the Palestinian entity as a heavily circumscribed enclave within Israeli territory. And the Abraham Accords enabled Netanyahu to argue that Israel could have peace with the Arab world without conceding anything to the Palestinians.

Meanwhile, the Palestinian polity has become so divided, politically between Fatah and Hamas, and geographically between the West Bank and Gaza, that its leaders find it impossible to negotiate meaningfully. In any case, few Palestinians believe that Israel will ever agree to an independent Palestinian state, and most Israelis, in turn, no longer believe they have a Palestinian partner for peace negotiations. For West Bank Palestinians, Israeli expansion

---

* In November 2005, Israel and the Palestinian Authority reached an Agreement on Movement and Access to facilitate the movement of goods and people into and out of Gaza, but that did not involve any Israeli withdrawal from Arab territory nor any Arab commitment to peace with Israel.

of existing settlements and legalization of outposts has already created a one-state reality under Israeli rule. And Donald Trump's recognition of Jerusalem as Israel's capital, his unwillingness to acknowledge Palestinian aspirations to a capital of their own in Arab East Jerusalem, and his plan's support for Israel's annexation of 30 percent of the West Bank and the 131 Israeli settlements embedded there, without Palestinian consent, only tarnished America's reputation as an honest broker.

Have the political challenges confronting Israeli and Arab leaders and the regional circumstances changed so dramatically that a resolution of the Israeli-Palestinian conflict is no longer important to them? Has the United States' influence in the region so waned that it lacks the leverage to practice effectively the kinds of diplomatic manipulations that generated earlier Arab-Israeli peace agreements? Has the United States lost the art of peacemaking in the Middle East?

If the answers were already emerging in 1998, they would become impossible to deny sixteen years later, when Secretary of State John Kerry made the last serious attempt to achieve a framework for a final Israeli-Palestinian peace agreement. I was involved in that endeavor as Kerry's special envoy for the negotiations. In meeting after meeting with Netanyahu and, separately, Palestinian president Mahmoud Abbas (Abu Mazen), both repeatedly ignored or rejected American entreaties. Regardless of our guile and determination, the United States seemed no longer capable of moving the two sides to peace.

The denouement came on March 16, 2014, when President Abbas arrived in Washington at President Barack Obama's invitation. For nine months, we had conferred with both sides and listened attentively as they articulated their requirements on the five core issues involved in ending the conflict: borders, security, refugees, Jerusalem, and mutual recognition. We had also used a secret back-channel negotiation between Yitzhak Molho, Netanyahu's counselor, Hussein Agha, a Lebanese academic based in London who was a close associate of Abu Mazen, and Dennis Ross, who had been the Middle East coordinator at the National Security Council (NSC) during Obama's first term. Dubbed the "London channel," it had been established several years before Kerry relaunched the front-channel negotiations, but its work dovetailed with our efforts to draft a framework agreement on final-status issues.

We had tried relentlessly to cajole the two sides into shifting their positions to bring them closer to each other. Now Obama had decided, on the urging of Netanyahu, to put forward detailed American "bridging" ideas that could help the parties move toward an agreement. The key challenge was to persuade Abu Mazen to respond to those ideas. If he did, we could go back to

Netanyahu and encourage him to reciprocate, moving them into the zone of a possible agreement.

To incentivize Abu Mazen to move toward Netanyahu on the issues critical to him—security, refugees, and recognition of Israel as a Jewish state—Obama decided to shift U.S. policy on Jerusalem. In May 2011, the president had already declared that the basis for defining the border between the Israeli and Palestinian states should be the pre-1967 Six-Day War lines (with mutually agreed-upon territorial adjustments). In preparation for Abu Mazen's visit, Obama decided to go one step further and define East Jerusalem as the place where the Palestinian state should have its capital. This change in policy was part of a balanced package of proposals that would also address all of Israel's needs, including recognition of Israel as a Jewish state and Jewish Jerusalem as Israel's capital.*

The evening before the Obama–Abu Mazen meeting, Kerry hosted the Palestinian president and his delegation at his Georgetown town house for an informal Chinese meal. Afterward, Kerry took Abu Mazen and Saeb Erekat, his chief negotiator, upstairs to his elegant sitting room to preview the detailed ideas that Obama would present to the Palestinian president in the Oval Office the next day. As Kerry emphasized the words "the borders should be based on the 1967 lines," a reiteration of Obama's commitment that the Palestinians had long insisted upon, jet lag caught up with Abu Mazen and he dozed off. Kerry paused, Erekat shuffled his papers and cleared his throat, and Abu Mazen awoke. Kerry then read the language on Jerusalem, with exaggerated emphasis: "East Jerusalem should be the capital of the Palestinian state." Abu Mazen responded with a harrumph.

The president fared no better the next morning in the Oval Office. When Obama explained his willingness to support the Palestinian claim to have Arab East Jerusalem as the capital of their state, Abu Mazen's only response was to ask for a few days to consult with his advisers. Obama left office more than two years later without ever receiving a response.

Three years later, when President Donald Trump recognized Jerusalem as the capital of Israel, he made no mention of Palestinian aspirations. And in his plan, all of Arab East Jerusalem, including the Old City and its holy sites, would come under Israeli sovereignty, leaving only two outlying Arab villages for a Palestinian capital.

---

* "Jewish Jerusalem" would include West Jerusalem and all the Jewish suburbs of East Jerusalem. In return, all the Arab suburbs of East Jerusalem would come under Palestinian sovereignty, as originally proposed in the Clinton Parameters of December 2000. Special arrangements would need to be agreed on for the Old City and the holy sites.

As president of the Palestinian Authority, Abu Mazen had nominal control over only 2.5 million West Bank Palestinians and a mere nine hundred square miles of land. He possessed no army and no natural resources. And yet he had no trouble refusing to respond to President Obama's offer of a significant shift in U.S. policy in the Palestinian direction on the signature issue of Jerusalem. Why? After nine months of negotiations, Abu Mazen had concluded that, whatever Obama might promise on East Jerusalem, the American ability to deliver on that, or any other commitment, was highly doubtful. He had good reason to feel that way. During the negotiations, the United States had stood by while Netanyahu humiliated him by repeatedly announcing new Israeli settlement building in the West Bank and East Jerusalem.

Presiding only nominally over a divided polity and facing a Palestinian public that no longer believed negotiations were a viable route to statehood, Abu Mazen was not willing to risk his tenuous hold on power by relying on American promises. That was especially so because, in accepting them as a basis for continuing the negotiations, his compromises would have been exposed and he feared that would trigger denunciation of him as a traitor by Palestinian critics. Instead of responding to the president, therefore, Abu Mazen exercised the ultimate power of the weak—he simply shut down.

Donald Trump fared no better. His Jerusalem decision drove the Palestinians to decry the United States as no longer a fair mediator. For the rest of his term, they refused to speak to any Trump administration officials. When he responded by cutting off all their aid, Abu Mazen simply dug in his heels.

The abiding lesson seemed clear: American willpower, ingenuity, and leverage were no longer sufficient to generate the necessary compromises between leaders on both sides who deeply distrusted each other and lacked the courage to make peace. Their people still preferred the two-state solution, but after decades of Palestinian terrorist attacks and Israeli settlement building, they no longer believed in the other side's desire to reconcile. Consequently, they no longer pressed their leaders to make peace.

Yet blaming both sides was far from a sufficient explanation. Something else was going on. It was manifest not only in the way Abu Mazen felt he could ignore Obama's offer or resist Trump's campaign of "maximum pressure," but also in the way Netanyahu, in front of a joint session of the U.S. Congress a year later, denounced the Iran nuclear deal that Obama and Kerry had negotiated. It seemed that the American superpower could be defied with impunity, even by its own partners in peacemaking.

It wasn't just Obama and Trump. Bill Clinton and George W. Bush, each in his own way, tried to resolve the Israeli-Palestinian conflict, and they too came up short. There was something about the practice of American peacemaking diplomacy in the Middle East that seemed fundamentally flawed, even if other factors contributed to the lack of success.

In seeking a better understanding of what has gone wrong, I found myself harking back to Kissinger's successful efforts to advance the peace process. By coincidence or *fortuna*, I had been present at the creation, more than forty years before, as an Australian graduate student living in Jerusalem when the October 1973 Yom Kippur War broke out. I would lie awake at night on a kibbutz near Gaza where I had volunteered my labor, heartsick at the casualties of a war I was convinced was unnecessary, fearing for Israel's ability to survive. I imagined I could hear the drone of the engines of the massive USAF C-5A Galaxies as they delivered a daily airlift of military supplies to a nearby air base, helping Israel turn the tide of battle. Later, I would listen to the BBC and Voice of America broadcasts that chronicled the efforts of Secretary of State Kissinger, already famous for his consummate diplomacy, as he flew to Moscow, Jerusalem, and Cairo to broker a cease-fire and then launch the negotiations that heralded the application of American diplomatic skills and influence to the task of ameliorating the Arab-Israeli conflict.

Living through the Yom Kippur War, and observing Kissinger's role in ending it, generated in me the unshakable conviction that the United States held the keys to peace in the Middle East. Understanding America's pivotal diplomatic role became essential to what then became my life's mission of helping to make peace. For more than forty years I have studied, written about, and participated in that effort. After my last attempt, as President Obama's envoy for the Israeli-Palestinian negotiations, I decided that if I was to come to terms with the experience, I needed to go back to when it first began and recount the story of Henry Kissinger's Middle East diplomacy. Perhaps there I would find some answers to the problems of Middle East peacemaking.

As Kissinger observed at the time, "The Middle East is an area of remarkable personalities, the last bastion where great men [and a woman] can come out of the desert and do unbelievable things." The characters in this story appear larger-than-life: Anwar Sadat, Golda Meir, Hafez al-Assad, King Hussein, King Faisal, Moshe Dayan, Shimon Peres, and Yitzhak Rabin have all become legends. Like other statesmen and women, they had their share of vanities, insecurities, and tragic flaws. But, as Kissinger recognized, "Men become myths not . . . by what they achieve, but by the tasks they set for themselves." All of them in their own ways had the courage to attempt to move their people toward peace. Sadat and Rabin gave their lives to the cause. In that respect, Henry Kissinger was fortunate to have capable partners who were willing to join his noble endeavor. No doubt their interactions with him elevated them on the world stage. But they, in turn, elevated Henry Kissinger and enabled his achievements.

To be sure, as the documents reveal, Kissinger made errors along the way, some with high human cost and others with strategic consequences that continue to impact peacemaking to this day. Had he taken Sadat seriously at the outset, he might have averted the Yom Kippur War. And had he enabled King Hussein of Jordan to regain a foothold in the West Bank when he had the opportunity to do so, the outcome of the most intractable dimension of the conflict—the Palestinian issue—might well have been dramatically different.

Unlike Kissinger's diplomacy in other regions of the world—such as his forlorn effort to back diplomacy with the application of force to end the war in Vietnam, his controversial covert undertaking to overthrow Salvador Allende in Chile, and his historic opening to China—his dealings in the Arab-Israeli arena had a uniquely personal dimension. As a Jewish survivor of the Holocaust who fled with his family from Nazi persecution in Germany to the freedom of the United States a year before the outbreak of World War II, his relationship with the Jewish state and its leaders was fraught and complicated.

Like Israeli prime minister Golda Meir, Kissinger was haunted by the Holocaust. By his own count, thirteen of his close family members and most of his classmates were killed by the Nazis.[*] In 2018, at the age of ninety-five, he was still referring to the shock of watching German soldiers enforcing a curfew in his hometown. "It was a traumatic experience that has never left me," he told Ed Luce of the *Financial Times*. The chaos of that era bred in him a profound insecurity that was compensated for only by his remarkable intellect and disguised by his self-deprecatory sense of humor. Although he rejected the idea that the Holocaust informed his political development, he readily volunteered that it gave him an emotional affinity with the fate of Israel.

Kissinger served a president who harbored anti-Semitic prejudices and taunted Kissinger about his Jewish identity—a humiliation that Kissinger did his best to abide. Once Kissinger became the Arab-Israeli peacemaker, however, his Jewishness became important to him in a different way. It gave him an opportunity to shape the Middle Eastern order he was creating in ways that would help preserve the Jewish state. He also discovered that his Jewishness was quite useful to this project. The Israeli leaders were mostly willing to treat him as a trusted member of their tribe, while Arab lead-

---

[*] The Kissinger biographer Niall Ferguson estimates that as many as thirty of Kissinger's relatives were killed by the Nazis. Kissinger estimates that 70 percent of his classmates were killed.

ers believed he would be more capable of delivering Israeli concessions. He was happy to exploit both perceptions to maximum effect. Nevertheless, he remained suspect in the eyes of some Arabs. He was also branded an "appeaser" and a "swindler" by some in Israel and the American Jewish community when he pressed Israel to concede territory to the Arabs. And yet, at critical junctures in his time at the pinnacle of U.S. power, Kissinger acted in little-recognized and unacknowledged ways to protect and help Israel—acts that had a profound and lasting impact, for better and for worse, on the Jewish state's future.

Unlike his successors, Kissinger did not have to deal with right-wing Israeli governments that were unwilling or unable to countenance ceding territory, especially in the West Bank. But the test of wills over peacemaking nevertheless brought confrontation in 1975 over the second Israeli-Egyptian agreement. There is much to learn about how the United States can succeed in persuading Israel to take calculated risks for peace from the way Kissinger handled that profound crisis in the relationship.

In researching and recounting Kissinger's Middle East negotiations, I have been aided by the fact that, as a member of President Clinton's peace team, I had the opportunity to engage intensively with three of the key actors involved—Yitzhak Rabin, King Hussein, and Syria's Hafez al-Assad. I walked in Kissinger's footsteps, participating in National Security Council meetings in the White House Situation Room where he convened the Washington Special Action Group (WSAG), and Oval Office appointments with Israeli and Arab leaders. I spent time in the palaces and prime ministers' offices that had once been Kissinger's hunting grounds. As special envoy for the Israeli-Palestinian negotiations, I even assumed a similar role, operating out of the same King David Hotel suite in Jerusalem. Though I would never compare my role to that which Kissinger played, I believe I came to understand what it was like for him.

During those sojourns at the King David Hotel, I was often accompanied by my wife, Gahl Hodges Burt, much as Nancy Kissinger would sojourn there with her husband during his shuttles. In an amazing twist of fate, four decades earlier, when Kissinger was pursuing his diplomatic derring-do and I was observing him as a student in Jerusalem, Gahl was his young secretary, traveling with him, making sure his eggs were cooked to his liking, bringing him his football scores, running interference with his celebrity girlfriends, ducking his tantrums, and transcribing many of the telephone conversations referred to in this story. In various ways, we have both been living with Henry Kissinger in our lives and minds ever since.

I have also had the opportunity to discuss these diplomatic case studies with Kissinger himself, in many long interviews and less formal conversations in his Park Avenue office and at his homes on the East River and in Kent, Connecticut. Even in his nineties, he had not forgotten many of the interactions that occurred four decades ago and the strategic calculations and geopolitical context that informed his decisions.

At an early stage in these conversations, I was appointed Obama's special envoy. When the news reached Kissinger, he called and asked in his baritone voice, "Is this just an excuse to avoid writing the book?" Taken aback, I responded that, on the contrary, I would be grateful if he would mentor me on the many challenges of my new appointment, drawing on his own experiences. In that way, I suggested, he would also help me write the book. "Are you free for lunch tomorrow?" he asked.

Much of this story has been told by Kissinger himself in his voluminous memoirs. Other players in this drama have also given their versions, some of them unpublished and accessed for the first time. Memoirs necessarily provide subjective accounts of what happened, but fortunately, almost all the American documents from that time are now accessible. And because Kissinger was himself a student of history, he made sure that, with only a few exceptions, his conversations were transcribed: National Security Council meetings, negotiations with foreign leaders, and telephone calls with the president and other officials. These provide a detailed historical record of Kissinger's Middle Eastern engagements. Although the Arab archives that exist remain closed to the public, the Israeli archives for that period are now open, providing fascinating insights into how Kissinger and his Israeli interlocutors managed to finagle each other.

Through those documents, my interviews with Kissinger, and the recounting of some of my own experiences, I have tried to take the reader into the rooms where he conducted his diplomacy to provide as accurate and vivid an account as possible of what transpired there as Arab and Israeli leaders, with Kissinger's help, struggled to find a way to move their nations from war to peace.

In one respect, this is a book of deep history about a period when the Middle East seemed set to move into a new era of accommodation. But it is also a story about the beginning of the American-led Middle East peace process told from my perspective as someone who was directly involved in what looks now to have been its denouement. I have tried to tell that story both as a historian poring over the records that preserve the memory of what happened, and as an actor in a master class, seeking to derive and apply the skills and lessons of Middle East peacemaking from the consummate diplomat. Along the way, I have tried to illuminate Kissinger's experiences with my own. These tangents are designed to provide a contemporary perspective on the historical events to help deepen the reader's understanding of the art of the Middle East deal as performed by one of its most skilled practitioners.

This is also a story about the rise of American influence in a region of once-vital interests. Kissinger's diplomacy ushered in the era of Pax Americana in the Middle East. It was a time when détente between the superpowers was taking hold and America's opening to China was stabilizing the international order, in no small measure because of Kissinger's foresight and endeavors. But it was also a time of retrenchment for the United States as a result of its defeat in Vietnam, when America's post–World War II dominance was ebbing and the consequences of overreach were being felt at home and abroad. And it was a time of leadership crisis, as Nixon became the first president to resign amid scandal. And yet, Kissinger was able to play a weak hand with such skill that the United States emerged dominant in the Middle East by dint of its peacemaking diplomacy rather than its deployment of war-making force.

At least that is the way it appeared to me as I embarked on this journey back to the origins of the American-led peace process. What I discovered along the way was that Kissinger's efforts were not just, or even primarily, about making peace between the Arabs and Israel. Rather, the gradual, step-by-step peace process that he developed became his primary mechanism for creating a new regional order in the Middle East that sidelined the Soviet Union in the midst of the Cold War and stabilized a turbulent region.

For Kissinger, promoting peace and creating order were symbiotic enterprises, two sides of the same coin. Most of the time his pursuit of peace disguised his preference for order. But there was no confusion in his mind. What might look on the face of it like diplomatic daring was informed by an innate conservatism. His experience fleeing the Holocaust had generated in him a relentless quest for order in his own life and in international affairs, and that in turn spawned his design for an American-led order in the Middle East. For him, peacemaking was a process designed to ameliorate conflicts between competing powers, not to end them. As we shall see, he would prove mightily resistant to more ambitious efforts to resolve the Arab-Israeli conflict because he feared that pursuing peace as an idealistic end state would jeopardize the stability that his order was designed to generate. Peace for Kissinger was a problem, not a solution. The desire for it needed to be manipulated to produce something more reliable, a stable order in a highly volatile part of the world. That Kissingerian Middle Eastern order would last for almost thirty years.

In this regard, he modeled his strategy and tactics after the European statesmen—Metternich, Castlereagh, and later Bismarck—who shaped and maintained the order in Europe for a century after the Napoleonic Wars until it came crashing down in 1914. Like the European leaders who came after Bismarck, most of the American policymakers who came after Kissinger knew neither Metternich nor the basic precepts of Kissinger's Middle Eastern order and would therefore often ignore them in favor of quixotic and grandiose efforts to end the region's conflicts, promote democracy, or overthrow regimes. As a consequence, Kissinger's order unraveled, causing immense human suffering and diminishing America's ability to influence events there.

It began with the failure of Clinton's striving for a final peace deal at Camp David in 2000, and the subsequent outbreak of the second Palestinian intifada at the end of his presidential term. Then, after 9/11, in an attempt to remake the Middle East in America's image, George W. Bush toppled Saddam Hussein and bogged the United States down in Iraq and Afghanistan in the longest wars in American history. In the process, he opened the gates of Babylon to an Iranian competitor for regional dominance while significantly reducing U.S. influence in the Arab-Israeli arena and exhausting the American people's appetite for foreign entanglements.

Obama's desire to be on the right side of history led him to support revolution in Egypt and regime change in Libya and Syria, compounding the turmoil. Syria's disintegration into a bitter civil war facilitated the return of Russia's military to the region, increasing its influence. Turkey too sought to fill the vacuum. At the same time, the withdrawal of U.S. forces from Iraq and Afghanistan, after the disastrous decade-long engagement in Iraq, further undermined America's once-dominant position and reduced its influence on Middle Eastern affairs in general, including on the Palestinian issue.

And then along came Donald Trump with his determination to accelerate America's military withdrawal from the Middle East, abrogating U.S. commitments in word and deed. Nevertheless, Trump too aspired to be the Middle East peacemaker. But his vanity project could not have been more different from Kissinger's purpose of creating a stable Middle Eastern order.

As the Middle East descends into a pre-Westphalian mode of failing states, religious wars, and ungoverned areas, the death knell is sounding for the American-led order in the Middle East that Kissinger created with his assiduous diplomacy. Little wonder that now, as the elder statesman of American foreign policy, he has harked back nostalgically to that earlier time:

> Once again, doctrines of violent intimidation challenge the hopes for world order. But when they are thwarted—and nothing less will do—there may come a moment similar to what led to the breakthroughs recounted here, when vision overcame reality.

I believe that moment will come again, although perhaps not in Kissinger's or my lifetime, when leaders in the mold of Sadat, Hussein, Meir, Rabin, and Begin will again pursue the vision of peace that, with American support, will enable them to build a new, more stable, and peaceful Middle Eastern reality. When that moment does come, it will be important to know what Henry Kissinger would have done with it.

PART I

Preparations

1

The Strategy

Policy may be based on knowledge but ... its conduct is an art.

—Henry Kissinger, *A World Restored*

M onday, *January 20, 1969, Washington, DC.* Henry Kissinger entered the White House as national security adviser on President Nixon's first day in office. At the time, he was seen by most observers as the obvious choice. Although at forty-five he seemed young and inexperienced with the ways of governing for such a weighty job, over the previous two decades he had established himself as a brilliant, incisive, and creative public intellectual with few peers in the realm of foreign policy expertise.

Three years after graduating with a PhD from Harvard, he had written a provocative policy study of U.S. nuclear strategy for the Council on Foreign Relations. In *Nuclear Weapons and Foreign Policy*, Kissinger argued that the United States needed to adopt a doctrine of "flexible response" to the threat of a Soviet nuclear strike, requiring the will and capability to fight limited nuclear wars. The idea of waging a limited nuclear war might seem crazy today, though at the time it was given serious consideration by policymakers. By unpacking the cruel dilemmas of the nuclear age and generating a grand strategy that wedded America's nuclear arsenal to its diplomatic purposes, Kissinger was catapulted into that elite club of nuclear strategists—Thomas Schelling, Herman Kahn, and Albert Wohlstetter among them—whose expertise was at a premium among Washington policymakers grappling with the challenges of the Cold War.[*]

---

[*] Put simply, Kissinger contended that it made no strategic sense to prepare only for all-out nuclear war given its potentially devastating consequences for humanity because that would have the effect of severely constraining America's ability to respond to Soviet aggression at levels below

The publication of that book, which became a best seller and the most widely read text on American strategy at the time, also launched Kissinger's career as a public policy intellectual. The Council on Foreign Relations study group where he generated and tested these ideas provided Kissinger with his first entrée into the American foreign policy elite.* But his preparation to be the highest foreign policy adviser in the land predated that experience.

Serving in Germany as an intelligence officer in the G-2 section of the 84th Infantry Division of the U.S. Army during and immediately after World War II, Kissinger gained valuable experience working in the vast bureaucracy of an army of occupation. As a bridge between the Germany of his birth and the America of his new life, that experience also did much to shape his personality. His personification of the trans-Atlantic relationship between the United States and postwar Germany gave him keen insight into the European pillar of the new world order that the United States was constructing after the vast destruction and disruption of the war. And his exposure, while still a graduate student, to what the Eisenhower administration labeled "psychological warfare" through his studies for the U.S. Army Operations Research Office also provided him with an understanding of the importance to policymaking of "discern[ing] the essence of a people's state of mind."

At that early stage in his career, he was already traveling to East Asia and gaining important exposure to the states of mind of the Japanese and Koreans. As a twenty-eight-year-old Harvard graduate student, he also set about assiduously building his own personal global network through the International Seminar, a two-month annual summer course for some forty promising young leaders from around the world, carefully selected and tutored by Kissinger.†

Similarly, he founded and edited a quarterly journal, *Confluence*, for which he invited European and American intellectuals to write on international affairs. This afforded him an opportunity to build a peer-group network of serious thinkers on foreign policy, some of them important American policymakers. That effort was enhanced when, a few years later, as a tenured

---

all-out war. Instead, the United States needed to prepare for the use of tactical nuclear weapons to be in a better position to deal with more limited Soviet challenges in local wars.
* The study group was chaired by Gordon Dean, former head of the Atomic Energy Commission, and included Paul Nitze, former director of policy planning in the State Department and author of NSC-68 (the National Security Council Paper that recommended preparation for the Cold War); Robert R. Bowie, then director of policy planning; David Rockefeller; and General James M. Gavin.
† Altogether, six hundred foreign students participated over the life of the International Seminar. Some of the participants went on to become leaders of their countries, including Japan's Yasuhiro Nakasone, France's Valéry Giscard d'Estaing, Turkey's Mustafa Bülent Ecevit, Belgium's Leo Tindemans, Malaysia's Mahathir bin Mohamad, and Israel's Yigal Allon.

Henry Kissinger at Harvard University, where he wrote his
PhD thesis on the nineteenth-century European order that
emerged after the Napoleonic Wars and kept the peace on the
Continent for almost one hundred years. It became his first
book, *A World Restored: Castlereagh, Metternich and the Problems
of Peace, 1812–1822*, published in 1957.

professor at Harvard, he directed the Defense Studies Program, a graduate
course to which he would invite Washington policymakers as guest lectur-
ers. He spent his summers traveling overseas, meeting and exchanging ideas
with senior government officials, businessmen, and intellectuals in Europe and
Asia. Those contacts enabled him to play a role in policymaking even before
he joined Nixon's administration.

By far his most important connection in this regard was Nelson Rockefeller, whom he met in 1955, when Rockefeller was an assistant to President
Eisenhower for foreign affairs. Rockefeller was so impressed that he appointed
Kissinger the director of his privately funded policy initiative, the Special Studies Project, whose purpose was to explore the critical challenges the United
States faced in the world. Kissinger oversaw a staff of some one hundred, conducted several expert advisory panels, and authored the project's report on
international security. That is where he first met Nancy Maginnes, the woman
he would eventually marry. After that stint, Rockefeller retained Kissinger as
a part-time consultant.

Advising one of the wealthiest scions of the white Protestant establishment provided Kissinger with schooling for high office and his entrée into
the political realm via a powerful patrician patron. In the process, he learned
how to cultivate the rich and mighty and the importance of flattery in achiev-

ing that purpose. In 1964, he had his first direct experience with the political fray, and his first exposure to American right-wing populism, when he joined Rockefeller's campaign against Barry Goldwater for the Republican presidential nomination.

Notwithstanding that critical Republican connection, Kissinger's first taste of policymaking came in the Democratic administration of John F. Kennedy, when he was hired as a part-time consultant by the president's national security adviser, McGeorge Bundy. It was the era of "the best and the brightest," when the new Bostonian president drew on his friends and their colleagues at Harvard to infuse his administration with intellectual heft. That provided a natural opening to the policymaking process for a young Harvard professor who had already found a place of distinction in the foreign policy elite.

Bundy, as the dean of the faculty at Harvard, had secured Kissinger his tenured position there, but he was wary of his protégé's brilliance and did his best to keep him at arm's length from the policy process. It was Kissinger's first exposure to White House bureaucratic politics, where a potentially influential player found himself co-opted but cut out. In 1979, he reflected on the frustrating experience on *The Dick Cavett Show*, noting that policymakers ask a consultant for his opinion for a variety of motives, "the least of which is that he wants to do what you are telling him."

In fact, much to Bundy's chagrin, Kissinger found another way to advise Kennedy, via his Harvard colleague and friend Arthur Schlesinger Jr. The Pulitzer Prize–winning historian had arranged Kissinger's appointment at the Council on Foreign Relations seven years earlier. Now operating as part of Kennedy's inner circle, Schlesinger would occasionally bring Kissinger into the Oval Office to brief the president, thereby providing a conduit to Kennedy for Kissinger's ideas about "flexible response," which Kennedy adopted during his confrontation over Berlin with Soviet premier Nikita Khrushchev. Kissinger was now directly impacting U.S. foreign policy. However, Kennedy's muted response to the building of the Berlin Wall proved to be too soft for Kissinger and this, together with Bundy's determination to thwart his influence, led him to part company with the Kennedy White House.

Kissinger subsequently became involved with the Johnson administration over the war in Vietnam. His first of three visits to the war-torn country took place in October 1965, at the invitation of Ambassador Henry Cabot Lodge (a Republican who had been Nixon's running mate against Kennedy in 1960). Kissinger quickly became convinced that a negotiated end to the war was the only way to extricate the United States from a futile commitment to a corrupt and feckless South Vietnamese regime. In 1967, using his international contacts, Kissinger tried his hand at Track II, unofficial back-channel diplomacy to help produce a negotiated outcome. The effort collapsed over Hanoi's insistence on an unconditional bombing halt prior to its entering negotiations, but not before Kissinger had been exposed to an intense policy debate in the White House with President Johnson, who reluctantly green-lighted Kissinger's mission. At the end of the meeting, in his inimitable style, LBJ leaned across the table and threatened Kissinger with castration if his recommended approach failed.

That experience seemed to feed Kissinger's appetite for policymaking. In 1968, he signed up again with Rockefeller's primary campaign for the Republican presidential nomination as his foreign policy adviser and speechwriter. When Nixon won the nomination, he resisted an invitation to join his foreign policy advisory board for the presidential campaign, preferring to keep his distance from his patron's rival, even as he promised to help "behind the scenes." He did just that.

By Nixon's account, Kissinger cautioned the Republican candidate to avoid offering new ideas or proposals that might be undercut by developments in the Vietnam negotiations Ambassador Averell Harriman was conducting in Paris on behalf of the Johnson administration. A few days later, according to Nixon, Kissinger told the campaign "that there is a better than even chance that Johnson will order a bombing halt at approximately mid-October."

Kissinger's information was based on briefings he had received on a trip to Paris in September 1968 from John Negroponte and Daniel Davidson, then junior staffers on Harriman's delegation. Both treated him as an insider because of the role he had played in the LBJ-sanctioned Track II negotiations.*

But in a demonstration of his political artistry, Kissinger was also providing briefings to the campaign of Hubert Humphrey. The Democratic presidential candidate later averred that, had he been elected, he too would have appointed Kissinger his national security adviser. It was a testament to the openness of the American policymaking process that a Jewish refugee from the Holocaust could so quickly rise to such prominence in foreign policy circles, where he found himself welcomed by both parties' presidential candidates for the brilliance of his ideas regardless of their delivery in heavily German-accented English.

As Kissinger observes in the opening to his three-volume account of his time as national security adviser and then secretary of state, "High office teaches

---

* In his memoirs, Nixon notes that "in the last days of the campaign . . . Kissinger was providing us with information about the bombing halt." In his memoirs, Kissinger says the campaign initiated contact with him. He told them that a bombing halt was highly probable just before the election, and he advised against making an issue of it. He says they checked that judgment "once or twice more during the campaign." See Richard Nixon, *RN: The Memoirs of Richard Nixon* (New York: Grosset & Dunlap, 1978), 340, and Henry Kissinger, *White House Years* (Boston: Little, Brown, 1979), 11.

decision making, not substance. It consumes intellectual capital; it does not create it."

Kissinger certainly entered Nixon's White House with a trunk load of intellectual capital. This included a deep appreciation for the importance of the historical context of international politics, and the mindsets of the leaders involved. But it did not encompass any particular knowledge of the complex history of the Middle East or the deep psychological traumas of its peoples. As a historian, he had not written anything about the region, notwithstanding its geopolitical importance as the crossroads to empire and as a locus of superpower competition. Amazingly, Kissinger's study of European history had not touched on the Ottoman Empire, and his peripatetic nature had not led him to visit any Arab capital, out of his concern that an American Jew might not be welcome there. Eisenhower's handling of the 1956 Suez crisis did gain his attention; he came away convinced that it was bad policy to weaken friends and help Soviet clients, and that State Department bureaucrats were to blame for that approach.

Ideologically, Kissinger shared the misgivings articulated by some American Jews of German origin about the Zionist project, though he did not take an active position on the issue. He was more like those German Jews who sought to assimilate into American society, much as they had tried to do in Germany. In his youth in Germany, he had been influenced by the attitudes of the Agudath Israel Orthodox Jewish organization that he joined along with his father. Agudath viewed the establishment of a Jewish state as heresy; according to their rabbis, that could occur only when the Messiah appeared. That attitude kept Kissinger from joining any Zionist youth movement. Intellectually, he also questioned whether a tiny Jewish state could possibly survive in such a hostile world of Arab states bent on its destruction. None of this amounted to an animus toward Israel; rather a concern, which Kissinger harbors to this day, that the survival of the small Jewish state, with its unique vulnerability to casualties, in a region hostile to its existence, could never be assured.

During his time at Harvard, he tutored at least two Arab students, one from Lebanon and the other from Saudi Arabia. With such limited exposure to the Arab world, he had developed a stereotypical perception of Arab leaders, believing that "the besetting difficulty is to determine at what point reality stops and intoxication with their own grandiloquent statements sets in, and at what point they are describing a strategy and at what point they are describing a dream."*

---

* In November 1973, Kissinger told King Hussein, "There is the Arab mentality which has a kind of romanticism about it. This is attractive, but it leads to impatience. An idea one day becomes a proposal the next day and a plan the next." See Memorandum of Conversation (Memcon hereafter) between Kissinger and King Hussein, November 8, 1973, KT00893, NSA.

By contrast, Kissinger made five trips to Israel, the first in 1962, at the invitation of Yigal Allon, then a rising Labor Party politician and hero of Israel's War of Independence, whom he had befriended when Allon was a student in his International Seminar at Harvard in 1957. He remembers meeting Israel's already legendary prime minister, David Ben-Gurion, and Shimon Peres, who was then deputy defense minister. He was impressed by the precariousness of Israel's existence, with a population at that time of only 2.3 million situated on a "splinter" of territory surrounded by much larger, hostile Arab states.

He returned a year later to deliver a lecture to the Israeli foreign ministry, where he caused some controversy by expressing the opinion that Soviet arms shipments to Arab countries were provocative—an early clue to what would subsequently become a fixation. A third trip took place in January 1965, when he met with Prime Minister Levi Eshkol and Peres, who was still deputy defense minister. He received extensive military briefings and came away very impressed by Yitzhak Rabin, who was then chief of staff of the Israel Defense Forces (IDF). He reported to the State Department that he believed Israel was already building nuclear weapons and that only an ironclad U.S. security guarantee could forestall this. His fourth visit was in the spring of 1967, a few months before the outbreak of the Six-Day War, when he met with Foreign Minister Abba Eban and discussed the need for a peace initiative. The fifth took place in January 1968, when he met Rabin again. The hero of the Six-Day War, Rabin was at the time preparing to assume his role as Israel's ambassador in Washington. Rabin remembers Kissinger warning that growing isolationism would reduce America's commitment to the fate of smaller Western nations like Israel.

Kissinger came away from those visits with the understanding that "peace in the Middle East was not only a physical necessity but a spiritual fulfillment." Nevertheless, it never occurred to him that someday he "might join the struggle for it." However, several ideas that he had developed in his research and writings would prove to be important for his subsequent approach to the Middle East in terms of both the ways in which he would successfully shape events and the misjudgments he would make along the way.

As a youth, his traumatic experience of Nazi chaos and arbitrary violence led him naturally to seek order in his own life. Maintaining order in the international system became the animating force in his writings; after entering office it would become the foundation stone of his strategy as a policymaker.

To preserve international order in his view required the maintenance of a stable balance of power. In his doctoral dissertation, which was subsequently published as *A World Restored* in 1957, Kissinger demonstrated how the post-Napoleonic nineteenth-century European order was maintained by an artful tending of the balance of power and the skillful manipulation of the antagonisms of competing forces to contain those who sought to disrupt it. That order, generated by the Congress of Vienna in 1814, produced one hundred years of relative stability without a continental war or a successful revolution. And that was what Kissinger sought to replicate in the Middle East when he had the opportunity.

From his studies, Kissinger understood that for the order to be sustainable it also had to be legitimate, meaning that all the major powers within the system had to be willing to adhere to a commonly accepted set of rules. Those rules would only be respected if they provided a sufficient sense of justice to a sufficient number of states. It did not require the satisfaction of all grievances, he wrote, "just an absence of the grievances that would motivate an effort to overthrow the order." As he observed in his seminal article on Bismarck, written in 1968:

> The stability of any international system depends on at least two factors: the degree to which its components feel secure and the extent to which they agree on the "justice" and "fairness" of existing arrangements. . . . Equilibrium is needed for stability; moral consensus is essential for spontaneity.*

Kissinger recognized that not every state in the system would be satisfied by a modicum of justice, which is why an equilibrium in the balance of power was the essential partner to a moral consensus that generated legitimacy. If the consensus was challenged by one or more of the states in the system, the balance of power needed to be there to enforce restraint so that the order could be preserved. A legitimate order, Kissinger argued, did not eliminate conflict, but it did limit its scope.

By the 1960s, Egypt's Gamal Abdel Nasser had emerged as a revolutionary leader seeking to disrupt the existing Middle Eastern order in much the way that Napoleon had posed a challenge to the European order of the eighteenth century. To contain Nasser and the Arab leaders who were influenced by him, Kissinger would seek to promote a balance of power tipped in favor of the regional defenders of the status quo: Israel in the Middle East heartland, and Saudi Arabia and Iran in the Persian Gulf. That balance would be bolstered by the détente he had in mind to develop with the Soviet Union, which would involve a joint superpower commitment to maintain stability in this volatile region.

Kissinger would come to recognize that the legitimacy of this Middle Eastern order was threatened as long as there was no credible effort to achieve a

---

* By "spontaneity" Kissinger meant that the states in the system did not have to be constantly forced to adhere to the rules of the game. Instead, they would do the right thing because of a "moral consensus."

modicum of justice for the Arab states that had lost vital territory to Israel in the 1967 Six-Day War. Nevertheless, as long as the equilibrium in the balance of power was maintained by the superpowers, he assumed that justice could be delayed.

As we shall see, he badly miscalculated, but when the Yom Kippur War broke out, he would spring into action with the confidence his study of the nineteenth-century European order provided. His objective would be to adjust the prewar arrangements in a way that would be accepted as more just and equitable by the Middle East's major players and would leave the United States in a better position to play the role of the predominant manipulator of the competing forces there. His mechanism for achieving this more legitimate equilibrium would be a process of Israeli withdrawal from Arab territory. That mechanism would become known as "the peace process," and its legitimizing principle would be found in UN Security Council (UNSC) Resolution 242, which provided for an exchange of territory for peace.*

In Kissinger's mind, however, the objective of the process would be to establish a more sustainable order rather than peace itself, because he did not believe in peace as an achievable or even desirable objective. In his own life, he had experienced the impact of Wilsonian idealism that sought a peace to end all wars but only succeeded in generating the appeasement that led to the rise of Nazism and Hitler's conquering of Europe. As he notes in his memoirs, "for most people in most periods of history, peace had been a precarious state and not the millennial disappearance of all tension." As we shall see, he would consistently shy away from aiming for peace treaties, instead seeking agreements that would give all sides a stake in preserving the existing order. As he told me decades later, "I never thought there could be a moment of universal reconciliation."

Kissinger's skepticism first found expression in the subtitle he chose for *A World Restored*. It was *Metternich, Castlereagh and the Problems of Peace*. The fact that after years of deep research and contemplation he concluded that peace was problematic would have a formative influence on his approach to peacemaking in the Middle East. On the first page of the introduction to *A World Restored*, Kissinger explains why. "[T]he attainment of peace," he writes, "is not as easy as the desire for it." He asserts that eras like the period he had studied turned out, paradoxically, to be most peaceful because the statesmen involved were least in search of peace. In his analysis, peace was abstract and

---

* UN Security Council Resolution 242 was adopted after the 1967 war. It laid out the principles that would need to be respected by both sides of the Arab-Israeli conflict in order to achieve peace. These principles included the unacceptability of the acquisition of territory by force. Israel was expected to withdraw from territories (not *the* territories) occupied in June 1967 in exchange for peace. However, until such an exchange could be negotiated it was accepted that Israel would remain in control of those occupied territories.

reversible. What mattered more was an absence of war, produced by the combination of "legitimacy" and "equilibrium." Clemens von Metternich, the foreign minister of the Austrian emperor Francis I, was one of his role models in this respect. While Metternich's emperor believed that "peace, lasting peace, is the most desirable goal of any decent man," what he sought was stability, not the realization of theoretical ideals.* And that is what Kissinger would seek too when he had the opportunity.

Kissinger also came into office with a keen appreciation for Immanuel Kant, the renowned German philosopher from the eighteenth-century Age of Enlightenment, who believed that peace was inevitable. But what Kissinger took away from Kant's essay "Perpetual Peace" was that conflict between states would lead *over time* to the exhaustion of their powers. Eventually, they would prefer peace to the misery of war. In other words, peacemaking was a gradual process that could not be rushed. Kant understood, as Kissinger noted, that "the root dilemma of our time is that if the quest for peace turns into the *sole* objective of policy, the fear of war becomes a weapon in the hands of the most ruthless; it produces moral disarmament." For Kissinger then, when it came to making peace, he would pursue it with caution, skepticism, and a process designed to buy enough time for exhaustion to set in. Equilibrium and legitimacy in the pursuit of order, and gradualism in the pursuit of peace, were the basic concepts of Kissinger's strategic approach to world affairs that he brought with him to the White House and eventually to the Middle East.

As we shall see, implementing the strategy would be harder than conceiving it. Indeed, had Kissinger been more sensitive to the shortfall in legitimacy that his design for a stable regional order was generating he just might have forestalled the 1973 Yom Kippur War with its devastating human toll.

By Nixon's account, his decision to appoint Kissinger as his closest foreign policy aide was an "uncharacteristically impulsive" one. He did not know the Harvard academic; indeed, he had met Kissinger only once before, and that was at a social gathering hosted by Clare Boothe Luce, wife of Henry Luce, the

---

* Kissinger's portrait of Metternich was the forerunner of his legendary depictions of the statesmen and politicians that he subsequently dealt with as secretary of state: "He was a Rococo figure, complex, finely carved, all surface, like an intricately cut prism. His face was delicate but without depth, his conversation brilliant but without ultimate seriousness. Equally at home in the salon and in the Cabinet, graceful and facile, he was the *beau-ideal* of the eighteenth-century aristocracy which justified itself not by its truth but by its existence." See Henry Kissinger, *A World Restored: Metternich, Castlereagh and the Problems of Peace, 1812–1822* (Brattleboro, VT: Echo Point Books and Media, 2013), 8–9.

publisher of *Time* magazine. She had served as a congresswoman from Connecticut and as Eisenhower's ambassador to Italy. Nixon's social awkwardness had precluded a serious conversation with Kissinger on that occasion. Nixon, however, had taken note of his seminal work on nuclear policy, for he took the trouble to write Kissinger a letter praising it (to which Kissinger did not respond). However, he was also aware that Kissinger had bad-mouthed him during the primary campaign when Kissinger had worked for Nelson Rockefeller, his political adversary.* And of course, Kissinger was Jewish, which on the face of it would seem to have been a problem for Nixon given his anti-Semitic stereotyping of Jews as conspiratorial and treacherous.

But in a perverse way, hiring someone with such a clear Jewish identity and Ivy League pedigree may have been part of the attraction, to demonstrate that now that Nixon had attained the highest office in the land he could co-opt and command the elites rather than just resent them. After one perfunctory interview, he offered Kissinger the job on December 27, 1968, in a meeting that took place in his transition offices in the swanky Pierre hotel in midtown Manhattan.

Nixon's version of his decision is straightforward and logical: he wanted to direct foreign policy from the White House; he knew Kissinger shared his outlook and his belief in "isolating and influencing the factors affecting worldwide balances of power." They agreed that policy needed to be "strong to be credible" and "credible to be successful." In particular, Vietnam policy needed to be rethought and put in its proper perspective as a short-term problem, NATO needed to be revitalized, and policy toward China needed to be reevaluated.

According to Nixon, Kissinger expressed delight with this agenda but noted that the president would need a national security apparatus capable not only of coordinating policy but also of developing policy options. That was exactly what Nixon had in mind: he would be the decision maker; the brilliant Kissinger would be the court Jew who developed the options for him. Nixon admitted that the combination of a grocer's son from Whittier, California, and a refugee from Hitler's Germany was "unlikely," but it was precisely their differences that in his view would make the partnership work.

Kissinger's account of his appointment also emphasizes their differences. He notes that he came from the other camp, whether that of Harvard academics, who viewed Nixon with disdain, or Nelson Rockefeller, who considered him an opportunist who lacked "the vision and idealism needed to shape the

* During the campaign, Kissinger was known to have railed against Nixon's "shallowness" and referred to him as a "hollow man" and "evil." After Nixon won the nomination, Kissinger expressed "grave doubts" in an interview with Emmett Hughes: "The man is of course a disaster. . . . Fortunately he can't be elected—or the whole country would be a disaster." He told many friends, "The man is unfit to be president." Nixon recounts that he chalked up all this talk to "politics." See Walter Isaacson, *Kissinger* (New York: Simon & Schuster, 1992), 127–28.

destiny of our nation." Nevertheless, Nixon was offering him the opportunity of a lifetime. Had he stayed in Germany, he would likely have followed in his father's footsteps and become a teacher at a gymnasium (high school), one of the more prestigious careers a Jew could aspire to in Germany. Instead, the president of the United States was offering him the chance to reshape world politics according to the vision he had so assiduously developed in his years as a scholar and teacher at Harvard. Notwithstanding the reservations he may have had about Nixon's personality, he could not refuse.

Kissinger also recounts that he and Nixon had a meeting of minds when it came to a common aversion to State Department bureaucrats with their preference for the status quo.* They agreed that foreign policy would be run out of the White House, and that Kissinger would develop a systematic approach in which policy would be related to the national interest and strategy would guide tactics rather than the reverse.

The two men also had a common set of personality traits. Both considered themselves to be outsiders; both were distrustful and deeply insecure, hungering for social acceptance. And, as Niall Ferguson, one of Kissinger's biographers, observes, "both were hypersensitive to slights, especially from those they considered establishment insiders."

Kissinger himself acknowledged to me, "While there was nothing I could do without Nixon, there was very little he could do without me." From working with Nixon in the White House, Kissinger came to see him as extraordinarily capable of understanding what needed to be done, but equally incapable of persuading other key actors to follow him because of his extreme awkwardness in dealing with people. Kissinger's indispensable role, he told me, was to articulate Nixon's concepts in a way that persuaded other policymakers as well as the public at large of the correctness of his vision.

Kissinger and Nixon also shared a sense of the gravity of the challenges to the international system for which they were assuming responsibility. In 1968, the United States was still adjusting to the reality that it could no longer dominate the international system yet had no choice but to lead that system to protect its interests. It was in many ways the worst of times. As Kissinger would later describe the situation:

> The Soviet Union had just occupied Czechoslovakia; there was no contact of any kind with China; India was aloof; hostilities were raging along the Suez Canal; and Vietnam was tearing the country apart.

---

* Nixon's aversion to the State Department came from his experience as vice president to Eisenhower, when he saw how its staff had manipulated and subverted the president. Kissinger's attitude had been shaped by his study of history: "Most great statesmen had been locked in permanent struggle with the experts in their foreign offices." See Kissinger, *White House Years*, 39.

Together, they would seek to reshape the world order by ending the war in Vietnam, establishing détente with the Soviet Union, strengthening NATO and trans-Atlantic relations, and, most consequentially, normalizing relations with China. Above all, the retrenchment involved in bringing the troops home from Vietnam required a more active diplomacy elsewhere to make up for the image of weakness in defeat.

When it came to the Middle East, however, Nixon's ambitions were modest. He was concerned from the outset that the Arab-Israeli conflict could draw the superpowers into a confrontation and he was therefore open to working with the Soviet Union to avoid that escalation. He was also keen for the United States to reestablish diplomatic relations with Egypt and other Arab countries that had been broken off in the aftermath of Israel's victory in the 1967 Six-Day War. Beyond that, Nixon saw no compelling strategic interest in making the Middle East a priority given the other more urgent issues on his agenda. He also saw no good reason to provoke a domestic political battle with Israel's supporters.*

An early indication that Nixon did not place a high priority on Middle East policy was his decision to leave that one issue exclusively to William Rogers, his choice for secretary of state, and Joe Sisco. As vice president during the Eisenhower administration, Nixon became a friend of Rogers, who was then serving as attorney general. Rogers had helped Nixon deal with a slush fund scandal that culminated in his famous Checkers speech in 1952.[†] Nixon respected and trusted Rogers, and he reassured Kissinger that this would work to their advantage since Rogers's "complete ignorance of foreign policy" would guarantee that Nixon's goal of directing policy from the White House would be preserved.

To achieve this, however, Nixon needed to give Rogers something to keep him occupied. Rogers was, as Nixon's legal counsel Leonard Garment observed, "a person of consequence in Washington, not content to play the part of diplomatic ornament." Nixon explains in his memoirs, somewhat disingenuously, "I felt that the Middle East required full-time and expert attention."

---

* Nixon sent that signal early on. Immediately after his election, in December 1968, he dispatched Governor William Scranton to the Middle East. Scranton declared from Jericho that it was important for the United States to be more "even-handed" so that it could "deal with all countries in the region and not necessarily espouse one." Stopping off in Rome on his way home, he announced that the new administration would draw up a peace plan for the Middle East. And for good measure, after briefing Nixon on his trip, Scranton repeated the objective of "even-handedness." That generated an uproar in Israel and from American Jewish leaders because the term implied that Israel would receive the same treatment as its Arab adversaries. Ronald Ziegler, the president-elect's spokesman, promptly distanced Nixon from Scranton's remarks. See "Scranton's View Draws Disapproval," *New York Times*, December 12, 1968.

† After Nixon left politics, for a short time both worked on legal matters in New York. Rogers worked at Dwight, Royall, Harris, Koegel & Caskey; Nixon worked at Mudge, Stern, Baldwin & Todd.

He told Kissinger, "You and I will have more than enough on our plate with Vietnam, SALT, the Soviets, Japan and Europe." He would soon add China to that list. Nixon also regarded dealing with the Middle East as a domestic political liability. Rogers would serve as the lightning rod, and if the political blowback from Congress and the American Jewish leadership became too strong, Nixon could disavow any involvement in Rogers's diplomacy, which he did on several occasions. Meanwhile, he could keep Kissinger focused on the issues Nixon really cared about.

Moreover, Nixon writes, "I felt that Kissinger's Jewish background would put him at a disadvantage during the delicate initial negotiations for the reopening of diplomatic relations with the Arab states."

In his memoirs, Kissinger confirms that Nixon "had his doubts as to whether my Jewish faith might warp my judgment." He notes that Nixon had excluded him from involvement in Middle East policy until late 1971 for that reason. For Kissinger, it was deeply problematic that his new boss would question his judgment on the Middle East and, by inference, his loyalty to America because of his ethnic identity. He was determined to overcome Nixon's ban.

Kissinger and Nixon on the Colonnade outside the Oval Office on September 16, 1972. Nixon wanted to exclude Kissinger from dealing with the Middle East because he believed that his Jewish faith would warp his judgment. Kissinger was determined to overcome the ban. The Jewish refugee from Germany and the small-town West Coast politician developed an effective partnership. "While there was nothing I could do without Nixon, there was very little he could do [in foreign policy] without me," said Kissinger.

The problem would be exacerbated by the anti-Semitic slurs Kissinger would have to endure from Nixon and the other aides who served him. As described by Leonard Garment, a fellow Jew on Nixon's staff, "Kissinger was treated at the White House as an exotic wunderkind—a character, an outsider. His colleagues' regard for him was genuine, but so were the endless gibes at his accent and style, and so were the railings against Jewish power that were part of the casual conversation among Nixon's inner circle. . . . Kissinger could never . . . shed his Jewishness."

Given the power and responsibility that Nixon had vested in him, Kissinger was clearly willing to live with the indignities of what he regarded as Nixon's "social anti-Semitism, the standard view that Jews are rich and tricky." He describes Nixon's stereotypical view of Jews as that of liberals who put loyalty to Israel above everything else. Notwithstanding this attitude, he was not the only Jew Nixon hired to be in his inner circle of advisers.[*] And Kissinger distinguished between the soft anti-Semitism he had to live with in the White House and the overt, vicious anti-Semitism he encountered among some in Nixon's cabinet and the WASP establishment.[†]

As Kissinger often remarked, "You cannot have thirteen members of your family perish in the Holocaust and not have that impact your identity." But he believed he had to present Jewish interests in the context of America's strategic interest, "not just Jewish destiny," and his policy recommendations were therefore cast in those terms.[‡]

He did worry about what non-Jews thought of Jews, and believed that American Jewish leaders were not sufficiently sensitive to that. It made him even more cautious and defensive when handling matters that affected the future of the Jewish people. Preserving Israel "was always a special concern of mine," he told me—and the events recounted in this book bear testament to that—but he understood that he had to disguise his support for Israel because he was under suspicion from the very beginning.

At times in Nixon's White House, he would go to some lengths to shield

---

[*] Leonard Garment was Nixon's legal counsel, William Safire was his lead speechwriter, and Arthur Burns was chairman of the Federal Reserve.

[†] The extent of Nixon's hostility to Jews was captured on an Oval Office tape in a discussion with John B. Connally, who was Nixon's treasury secretary. Nixon spoke of the untrustworthiness of "a terrible liberal Jewish clique" and vowed to cut down their numbers in his second administration. Connally encouraged him to do so. See George Lardner Jr., "Nixon Defended Envoy's Groping," *Washington Post*, March 1, 2002.

[‡] In a 2016 interview with the author, Kissinger explained, "You can't have lived at the edge of the Holocaust without having a responsibility. I've never denied that." In an interview with Dennis Ross, he explained that while he felt a common destiny with the Jewish people, his views carried weight to the extent that he was perceived as reflecting American strategy and not just Jewish destiny. "Whatever the influence we have had on the shaping of policies has been the degree to which we could convince those with whom we work of the nature of the global and the American strategic interest." See Indyk interview with Henry Kissinger, January 15, 2016, and "Dr. Henry Kissinger—Plenary with Ambassador Dennis Ross," Jewish People Policy Institute, June 7, 2015.

himself from the charge of dual loyalty, arranging the FBI's wiretapping of his Jewish staff as well as Jewish journalists in his entourage.* At other times, in conversations in the Oval Office, he would resort to taking a harder line against Jewish interests than Nixon himself, criticizing leaders in the American Jewish community. In one egregious case, he criticized the State Department for issuing a statement complaining about the Soviet government's treatment of its Jewish citizens: "The emigration of Jews from the Soviet Union is not an objective of American foreign policy," he said to Nixon. "And if they put Jews into gas chambers in the Soviet Union, it is not an American concern . . . [although it] may be a humanitarian concern."

Yet when it came to Middle East policy, Kissinger would adopt a strategic approach. His objective was clear: the promotion of an American-led Middle Eastern order based on partnerships with the status quo regional powers of the shah's Iran, Israel, and Egypt—the latter, after he had achieved its extraction from the Soviet camp.

In this way, he would reconcile his Jewish identity with America's national interests. And, in the process, he would help secure the existence of the Jewish state by providing a rationale for American support that he believed would be more enduring than the Judeo-Christian values Americans shared with Israel. As he explains in his memoirs, "Israel's security could be best preserved *by anchoring it to a strategic interest of the United States,* not to sentiments of individuals [emphasis added]." And that is exactly what he set about doing, in the process forging an alliance between the United States and Israel that has helped ensure Israel's survival in a hostile neighborhood long after he passed from the scene.

Rogers had been handed the Middle East mandate, but within three years Kissinger would succeed in wresting control from him in a bitter personal feud that would at times drive Nixon to distraction.† In the process, Kissinger systematically overcame, but never diminished, his boss's concerns about the effect of his Jewish identity.

---

* The wiretaps included the phones of Mort Halperin, Anthony Lake, and Helmut Sonnenfeldt from Kissinger's staff, and William Beecher, Henry Brandon, Marvin Kalb, and Joe Kraft from the media.

† Nixon's chief of staff, H. R. "Bob" Haldeman, records in his diaries repeated instances where Nixon would call him to complain about Kissinger's obsession with Rogers. Haldeman too grew tired of Kissinger's constant threats to resign if Rogers wasn't fired. However, he was basically sympathetic to Kissinger, recording that there was "some real merit" to Kissinger's concern about Rogers's loyalty. Whereas Nixon saw this as Kissinger maneuvering to get control of the Middle East file, Haldeman noted that "Rogers clearly maneuvers to clobber Henry." See H. R. Haldeman, *The Haldeman Diaries: Inside the Nixon White House* (New York: G. P. Putnam, 1994), 103, 145.

For Kissinger, however, the feud with Rogers was also an important learning experience. Driven by passions stirred by identity and ambition, he would discover how to approach the Middle East's politics and its vicissitudes, taking advantage of events there, his proximity to the president, and his understanding of Nixon's priorities and predilections to undermine and outmaneuver the secretary of state. No sooner had he succeeded in replacing Rogers than the Yom Kippur War erupted, but by then he had already developed a well-thought-out strategy for turning a profound crisis into a dramatic opening for U.S. peacemaking diplomacy.

2

Gaining Control

I got a trumpet, and I got a young wife, and I ain't got time to fool with none of the stuff you guys talking about.

—Louis Armstrong on the Arab-Israeli conflict, Cairo, 1961

A newly elected president inevitably resolves to do things differently from his predecessor, especially if he comes from the opposing party. He and his advisers instinctively treat the previous administration's policies as at best wrongheaded, at worst incompetent. In Nixon's case, Johnson's prosecution of the war in Vietnam had become a disaster in urgent need of fixing. Given that priority, and the importance Nixon attached to relations with the Soviet Union and China, it was not surprising that he would choose continuity in policy toward the Middle East, at least at the outset.

In the wake of the June 1967 Six-Day War, in which Israel had trounced its Arab adversaries and seized control of Egypt's Sinai Peninsula, Syria's Golan Heights, and the West Bank of the Jordan River, the Soviet Union had resupplied its Egyptian and Syrian allies with generous amounts of military materiel to secure its influence. This emboldened Egypt's Gamal Abdel Nasser, a leader of the Non-Aligned Movement and the promoter of pan-Arab nationalism, to resume hostilities with Israel.

In September 1968, Egypt launched artillery bombardments on Israeli military positions across the Suez Canal in the hope of forcing an Israeli retreat from that strategic waterway. This led to President Johnson's decision to balance the Soviet resupply effort by selling fifty F-4 Phantom strike aircraft—the most sophisticated aircraft in the U.S. arsenal—to Israel. That potentially escalatory move was offset by a decision to negotiate with the Soviet Union about advancing a more stable cease-fire and settlement of the Arab-Israeli conflict. The negotiations became known in Middle East peace process vernacular as the two-power talks.

At his first presidential press conference, Nixon signaled a deep concern about the need to "cool off" the situation in the Middle East, calling it a "powder keg, very explosive." Accordingly, Middle East policy was deliberated at an early meeting of his National Security Council, on February 1, 1969, attended by his principal foreign policy, defense, and intelligence advisers. Rogers led off with a proposal for an American initiative to pursue the two-power talks; he also recommended four-power talks that would add Britain and France to the mix. The purpose would be to seek agreement on a set of principles that would guide negotiations between the parties brokered by the United Nations' special envoy, Gunnar Jarring.*

The National Security Council meeting provided Kissinger with his first opportunity to opine officially on Middle East policy. In one of his early memos to Nixon, he criticized Rogers's position: if the two-power talks made progress, he said, the Soviet Union would get the credit with the Arabs, and if they failed, the United States would be blamed; in the four-power talks, given Soviet, French, and British support for the Arabs, the United States was likely to find itself isolated in its support of Israel. And implicit in the construct, said Kissinger, was the assumption that the United States would have to deliver Israel. "It meant that we were being asked to pressure an ally on behalf of countries which . . . had broken relations with us, pursued policies generally hostile to us, and were clients of Moscow," he argued.

Kissinger was appealing to the Cold War strategist in Nixon. But the president did not want to overrule his newly appointed secretary of state or rebuff the Soviet Union, with which he sought better relations. He was also about to travel to Europe for his first summit with France's president, Charles de Gaulle, whom he greatly admired for his manipulation of European affairs. So Kissinger proposed that the president should agree to both the two-power and four-power talks. It was, by his own subsequent admission, an attempt at slow-rolling the State Department by bogging them down in negotiations that were unlikely to go anywhere. But having received the green light from the president, Sisco and Rogers went galloping off with the Russians. In talks with Soviet ambassador to the United States Anatoly Dobrynin, Sisco attempted to achieve a joint set of principles, which included a commitment to "minimal changes" in Israel's borders that "should not reflect the weight of conquest."

---

* Jarring had been appointed by Secretary-General U Thant as the first special envoy for the Middle East peace process after the Six-Day War. He was a Swedish diplomat who had served as his country's permanent representative at the UN, followed by stints as ambassador in Washington and Moscow.

In the context of talks with the Soviet Union, Kissinger believed this last principle was a trap, even though it had previously been espoused by President Johnson. "We had already separated ourselves from Israel's position," Kissinger told the president, since Israel rejected the idea of only minor border rectifications—returning captured Arab territory—and insisted on direct negotiations with its Arab adversaries (direct negotiations were not mentioned in Sisco's offer to Dobrynin). The Soviets had shown no willingness to shift from the Arab demand of full withdrawal from all the territories occupied by Israel in the Six-Day War and rejected direct negotiations. This was the genesis of Kissinger's subsequent deep aversion to U.S. advocacy for Israel's return to the '67 borders, which he regarded as indefensible.

As he developed his understanding of the diplomatic dynamics of any negotiation of Arab-Israeli issues involving the Soviet Union, Kissinger was also discovering the intractability of the conflict. From his early encounters with the Egyptian foreign minister, Mahmoud Riad, and the Israeli foreign minister, Abba Eban, he came to understand just how far apart the parties were. This reinforced his view that American proposals, however well intentioned, were unlikely to bridge the gaps.

Nevertheless, because of Nixon's reluctance to overrule his secretary of state and his desire to continue LBJ's initiative, Kissinger could not persuade the president to prevent Rogers and Sisco from doubling down by making the American principles even more specific. However, when that too failed to elicit a shift in Moscow's position, Kissinger's argument was vindicated. It made little difference, though, because in the meantime the fighting between Israeli and Egyptian forces on the Suez Canal had escalated, providing a new justification for diplomatic activity to forestall the explosion that Nixon had feared from the outset.

In March 1969, emboldened by fresh, sophisticated arms supplies from the Soviet Union, Nasser formally announced the launching of the War of Attrition on the Suez Canal, followed by massive Egyptian artillery bombardments of Israeli positions there. By July, Israel began retaliating, using its air force to strike Egyptian positions on the west bank of the canal. In August, a deranged Australian set fire to the Al-Aqsa Mosque in Jerusalem—Islam's third-holiest site—provoking calls from Cairo and Riyadh for a jihad to liberate Jerusalem. Also, that month, an American airliner was hijacked to Damascus, and in September, King Idris of Libya was overthrown by young Nasserite officers led by an obscure colonel named Muammar Qaddafi.

In response to all this turmoil, some of it completely unrelated to Israel, Rogers sought permission from Nixon to present the Soviets with a more specific American endorsement of *full* Israeli withdrawal from the Sinai, con-

Henry Kissinger and Secretary of
State William Rogers at the White
House in January 1970. Kissinger
thought Rogers's approach to the
Middle East was wrongheaded, and he
sought to undermine and thwart him,
often with Nixon's help.

ditional on satisfactory security arrangements. Kissinger was beginning to recognize a pattern: in the face of growing strife, the State Department would
inevitably propose a new initiative for resolving the Arab-Israeli conflict,
claiming this would stave off a further decline in America's standing in the
Arab world. Kissinger would respond by arguing the opposite: that a diplomatic stalemate worked to America's advantage by convincing the Arabs that
their Soviet patron could not deliver political concessions from Israel via the
United States. But Rogers and Sisco had exclusive possession of the portfolio
and were determined to proceed as they saw fit.

Kissinger, however, was beginning to gain some traction with Nixon, who
was increasingly concerned with the potential advantage the Soviet Union
might gain in the Middle East given the current course of American diplomacy. By then, Nixon had begun to doubt his original premise of "linkage":
that cooperating with the Soviet Union in the Middle East or elsewhere could
be linked to reciprocal support from Moscow for American efforts in Vietnam.* He had also become more concerned about the domestic blowback all

---

* Kissinger and Nixon had sought to entice Moscow into pressuring Hanoi by secretly revealing
their bottom-line positions on withdrawal from Vietnam while withholding agreement to Strategic

this diplomatic activity was generating from Israel's vocal supporters on Capitol Hill and in the American Jewish community.

But that doubt was insufficient to enable Kissinger to constrain the ambitious endeavors of Rogers and Sisco.* So Kissinger began to develop another, more covert means of disrupting what he regarded as State's wrongheaded diplomacy.

Yitzhak Rabin was an Israeli war hero. As chief of staff of the IDF, he was responsible for their lightning victory over four Arab armies on three fronts in the Six-Day War. Rather than moving immediately into politics, the natural trajectory of successful Israeli generals then and now, Rabin had sought the post of Israel's ambassador in Washington, believing that the United States held the keys to Israel's economic, diplomatic, and military well-being. He presented his credentials to President Johnson early in 1968. The handsome Israeli general had tremendous cachet in a Washington that had become bogged down in its own war in Vietnam. This bought him easy entrée into the corridors of power on Capitol Hill, where he proved adept at mobilizing support for arms sales to Israel, culminating in Johnson's decision to sell Israel the fifty Phantoms. Four years later, he would demonstrate that he was no traditional diplomat by publicly endorsing Richard Nixon during his presidential reelection campaign.

Painfully shy and taciturn, Rabin was nevertheless a strategic thinker, like Kissinger. He had come to Washington convinced that the Soviet Union, through its arms supplies to the Arabs, was bent on the destruction of Israel. His agenda had two priorities: to secure the sophisticated weapons systems needed to counter the Soviet arms buildup on the Arab side, and to ensure that the United States would provide Israel with the political and diplomatic support it needed to exist in a hostile regional and international environment.

The arms relationship with the United States had only commenced in earnest in 1962, with President Kennedy's decision to provide Israel with Hawk surface-to-air missiles. The relationship with the United States in those days was a far cry from what it is today. In the crisis of June 1967, when Nasser

---

Arms Limitation Talks (SALT). But Moscow did not even deign to respond to the secret Vietnam initiative, and Nixon quietly dropped the idea of "linkage."

* In a eulogy for Sisco, Kissinger captured his irrepressible style: "He could wear down any objections by sheer persistence and outwork any aspirations to arbitrary decisions using three methods: (1) In crises, he would move himself physically as close to my office as circumstances permitted, preferably into the Situation Room, which had the added advantage of assuring his participation in all meetings. (2) From his office issued a seemingly endless array of policy proposals. Some say he offered more solutions than there were problems. But it kept me busy and cut down the time available for interfering in his concerns. (3) Finally, he knew that, in the end, strategy winds up as a cable, and he made certain that the process started with his draft." See Henry Kissinger, "Remarks at American Academy of Diplomacy Fifteenth Annual Diplomatic Awards Luncheon Honoring the Late Joseph Sisco," December 9, 2004, https://www.henryakissinger.com/remembrances/joseph-sisco.

evicted UN peacekeepers from the Sinai Peninsula and closed the Straits of Tiran to Israeli shipping, the Johnson administration had been unwilling to fulfill the written commitment of the Eisenhower administration to keep the Red Sea straits open. In the face of Nasser's threats to wipe out Israel and the mobilization of Egypt's armed forces, the closure of the straits was a clear casus belli. And yet LBJ had warned Foreign Minister Eban at the height of the crisis that Israel would be alone only if it acted alone. In other words, he opposed a preemptive Israeli strike.

France had been Israel's arms supplier in those days, but once Israel struck preemptively, de Gaulle imposed an arms embargo. The United States did too, suspending the delivery of already approved arms sales in the forlorn hope that the Soviet Union would do the same. These developments made Rabin, as the IDF chief of staff, acutely aware of the vulnerability of Israel's arms supplies, especially in the face of stepped-up Soviet supplies to its Arab adversaries.

Israel enjoyed a surge of support in the United States in the wake of its decision to take its fate into its own hands and the victory its armed forces had achieved in 1967. This provided an opening that Ambassador Rabin exploited to make sure the supply line remained open.

While he had developed good relations with Rogers and Sisco, Rabin was deeply troubled by their ideas for two- and four-power talks. To the Israeli government, that sounded like an imposed solution, which they feared most. In the wake of the 1967 war, Israel had found itself unexpectedly in control of the entire Sinai Peninsula, to the banks of the Suez Canal in the west and Sharm el-Sheikh in the south. The IDF had conquered East Jerusalem and taken control of the Old City with its Western Wall—the only remaining outer wall of the Second Temple that the Romans had destroyed in 70 CE, and the holiest place in Judaism. Israel had also taken control of the West Bank up to the Jordan River, the area of Judea and Samaria that was the land of the patriarchs, prophets, and judges of ancient Israel. And the IDF had occupied the Golan Heights, the mountain plateau above northern Israel from where Syrian forces had previously been able to harass Israeli farmers below. Suddenly, tiny Israel had gained room to breathe and control of territory that had once been the site of the ancient Jewish state.

After the war, in May 1968, Israeli Foreign Minister Eban accepted United Nations Security Council (UNSC) Resolution 242, with its call to exchange territories Israel occupied in the 1967 war in return for peace with its Arab neighbors. But the resolution also referred to the right of all states to live in peace within "secure and recognized borders." Israel interpreted that language as allowing significant adjustments to its borders. Given the government's makeup, which included the right-wing Herut Party under the leadership of Menachem Begin and the National Religious Party, Israel was certainly not willing to accept the minor border rectifications Rogers and Sisco had been promoting, let alone the full withdrawal from the Sinai for which Rogers was now seeking Nixon's approval.

From the Israeli perspective, the borders the Arabs might be prepared to recognize would not be secure and the borders that Israel considered secure would not be recognized by the Arabs. But if it had the political and military backing of the United States, Israel could afford to wait for the Arabs to come around to accepting Israel's existence and its requirement for major border adjustments. If, however, the United States adopted the Arab position of full withdrawal to the prewar borders, then Israel's ability to hold on to the occupied territories could be severely undermined.

Rabin was by no means averse to negotiations with Israel's Arab adversaries but, as he told Nixon when he first met him, "negotiations can only begin when Israel speaks from a position of strength and has concrete backing." His objective was to secure that backing from Washington. He well understood that Rogers and Sisco were his antagonists. His greatest fear was that they would succeed in getting the Soviets to join the United States in imposing an Israeli withdrawal to the 1967 lines, much as Eisenhower had done ten years earlier. In Rabin's view, "We were finished storming our way across Arab territory merely to pull back to the international border in return for nothing more than the promise of another round [of war] to come."

Rabin was therefore a natural interlocutor for Kissinger, right down to his own deep, gravelly voice. He was clearheaded, measured, and militarily precise about Israel's objectives and how to achieve them. A chain smoker, he developed a serious taste for Scotch whisky on the Washington cocktail circuit to overcome his shyness. When he spoke he could be blunt and dismissive. But, as Kissinger notes, "his integrity and analytical brilliance in cutting to the core of a problem were awesome."

Rabin was masterful at assessing the shifting balances of power in the Middle East and calculating how Israel, as a small state in a hostile neighborhood, could successfully navigate the dangerous shoals. He knew that Israel's newfound control of the Suez Canal—which had been shut down because of the 1967 war—now gave it geostrategic heft in the Cold War competition between the superpowers. That, combined with its recently demonstrated military prowess, had turned Israel into the dominant regional power in its neighborhood, and therefore an important factor in Kissinger's balance of power calculus.

Their first White House meeting took place on March 4, 1969. It was the beginning of a deep and consequential conversation in which each would help shape the other's strategy. Rabin's focus on Israel's security requirements rather than its territorial ambitions would be an approach that Kissinger would subsequently adopt as his negotiating strategy in the postwar peace negotiations. And Kissinger's focus on undermining the Soviet presence in the region would become the imperative that drove Rabin's geostrategic approach to Israel's regional challenges.*

Everything about the relationship that developed between Kissinger and Rabin was unconventional. Kissinger had the White House Signal Corps install a direct, secure phone line in Rabin's office in the Israeli embassy. They would meet secretly in the basement Map Room of the White House rather than in Kissinger's West Wing corner office, with its floor-to-ceiling windows through which the White House press corps could see whom Kissinger was meeting with on their way to and from the briefing room. Rabin would be escorted to the Map Room through the discreet East Wing entrance, far from the inquisitive eyes of the media.

The Map Room had originally been used as a billiards room, but during World War II it was converted to a situation room where President Roosevelt would be briefed on battles. Above the mantelpiece hung the last situation map prepared for Roosevelt on April 3, 1945 (he died nine days later). On the east wall, covering a case of world maps, hung a rare French map of the American colonies charted by Thomas Jefferson's father. Kissinger and Rabin would sit on the crimson-upholstered Chippendale chair and sofa that were positioned in front of the fireplace. Neither of them could possibly have imagined that twenty-four years later, President Clinton and PLO chairman Yasir Arafat would sit in the same chairs for their first meeting when Arafat came to the White House with Yitzhak Rabin for the signing ceremony of the Oslo Accords.

Their private rendezvous would normally take place on Saturday mornings, when the White House was deserted and the Israeli embassy was closed for Shabbat, a habit that Rabin would continue when he returned to Israel for meetings he wanted to keep private. When I was U.S. ambassador to Israel in the Clinton administration and Rabin was prime minister for the second time, he would invite me to meet him discreetly on Shabbat mornings at his Tel Aviv apartment, after his weekly tennis game.

After these Shabbat meetings, Rabin would summon Efraim Halevy, then his station chief, later the head of the Mossad, to a deserted embassy. There Halevy would transpose and transmit Rabin's reports via a secret Mossad communications channel directly to Simcha Dinitz, the director of Prime Minister

---

* During his time in Washington, Rabin would also be deeply influenced by James Jesus Angleton, the CIA's head of counterintelligence operations. Rabin had monthly luncheons with Angleton, who tutored him on the dangers of Soviet communism and the need for him "to keep the faith," especially when he became prime minister, as Angleton was convinced he would one day. Indyk interview with Efraim Halevy, January 29, 2020.

Meir's office, who would pass them immediately to her. In those reports, Kissinger was assigned the code name "Shaul"; Nixon's alias was "Robert." Just as Kissinger concealed these meetings from his State Department colleagues, so too did Meir and Rabin conceal them from Foreign Minister Abba Eban and the Israeli foreign ministry.

In the Clinton years, Rabin, now prime minister, would institute a similar procedure. His ambassador in Washington, Itamar Rabinovich, would transmit his reports directly to the prime minister's office, cutting out Shimon Peres, Rabin's foreign minister and bitter political rival.

For Kissinger and Rabin, this back channel would become an intimate forum to exchange views, coordinate strategy, and provide each other with sensitive intelligence material. Kissinger would routinely give Rabin the protocols of his meetings with foreign officials; Rabin would reciprocate with protocols or summaries of his prime minister's meetings with foreign leaders, especially from the communist East bloc.

Kissinger was careful to ensure that Nixon was aware of the back channel he had created. His boss was happy with it, partly because he admired Rabin and partly because, as long as the process remained covert, it avoided confrontation with his secretary of state, something he was constitutionally incapable of sustaining.

Kissinger used similar back-channel mechanisms for all his important endeavors in the White House. He records that the back-channel process on Vietnam began the day after Nixon's inauguration. He was soon to establish a back channel with the Soviet ambassador, Anatoly Dobrynin, for the management of relations with Moscow and the negotiation of the SALT agreements. The breakthrough with China was handled entirely out of the White House via a Pakistani back channel; Rogers only found out about Kissinger's trip to Beijing when he was already on the way. As Kissinger admits in his memoirs:

> Nixon distrusted State and wanted sensitive matters handled by the White House alone, but my presence made the two-channel procedures possible and I was quite willing to step into the breach. . . . The procedures so painful to Rogers were clearly instigated by Nixon; it is equally evident that I nurtured them.

When it came to the Middle East, the back channel with the Israeli ambassador would serve as an effective means of undermining the Rogers-Sisco initiatives. Kissinger recalls Nixon telling him, "Let them do what they want, as long as Rabin understands what we want."

The establishment of this White House back channel to Jerusalem, circumventing the State Department and the Israeli foreign ministry, would set a precedent that Kissinger was quick to maintain when Rabin was replaced by Simcha Dinitz in 1973. It became unnecessary, however, when Kissinger became secretary of state, since Kissinger retained his White House role as national security adviser. When Bill Clinton took office in January 1993, after Rabin had been reelected prime minister, the back channel was reactivated. As Clinton's Middle East adviser, I became the White House point of contact for Ambassador Rabinovich and Eitan Haber, Rabin's chief of staff.

When Ehud Barak became prime minister, he insisted on having a direct channel to Clinton himself to facilitate their intensive efforts to achieve a breakthrough to comprehensive peace. Clinton was so dedicated to the effort that the arrangement was fine with him, though it led Secretary of State Madeleine Albright to ask in exasperation, "What am I, chopped liver?"*

When Netanyahu became prime minister the second time in 2009, he chose his lawyer and close confidant Yitzhak Molho to serve as the back channel with Dennis Ross, who became Obama's Middle East coordinator on the National Security Council. At one point, Secretary of State Hillary Clinton became so frustrated with this circumvention that she asked me to go back to Israel for a third time as ambassador to open a channel for her with Netanyahu. I declined the honor because I was sure Netanyahu would prefer to conduct business directly with the White House.

When John Kerry became secretary of state, he was determined to do away with the back channel by establishing his own front channel with Netanyahu. Throughout his four years in office, no matter how strained the relationship, Kerry would maintain that channel, speaking on a secure phone to "Bibi" as often as three times a week, on occasion three times a day. It was a price Kerry was willing to pay to prevent Netanyahu from going behind his back to the White House.

In the Trump administration, Jared Kushner, the president's son-in-law, turned the back channel into a front channel by moving the peace process into the White House and cutting the State Department out of the game completely.

Kissinger's first opportunity to utilize the Rabin back channel was to plan for Israeli prime minister Golda Meir's introductory visit to the Nixon White House in September 1969. She was a stubborn, suspicious, and brittle leader

---

* When Ariel Sharon became prime minister, he used Dov "Dubi" Weisglass, his chief of staff, as the back channel to George W. Bush's national security adviser, Condoleezza Rice, circumventing Secretary of State Colin Powell. Ehud Olmert upheld the tradition when he became prime minister, using his chief of staff, Yoram "Turbo" Turbowitz, to communicate with Elliott Abrams, then the senior director for the Middle East on Bush's National Security Council, thereby circumventing Condoleezza Rice when she became secretary of state.

from the founding generation of Israelis, but with a compassionate core—the matriarch of her tribe. Nixon described her character as combining the qualities of "extreme toughness and extreme warmth."

Golda Meir had played an instrumental role in rebuilding the Jewish state, alongside David Ben-Gurion and his foreign minister, Moshe Sharett. As foreign minister, she had cultivated Israel's relations with Africa in an effort to leapfrog the ring of Arab hostility. She had also pioneered Israel's sub-rosa relationship with the kings of Jordan. Although she headed the socialist Labor Party, on security issues she was a hawk. Haunted by the Holocaust and deeply skeptical of Arab intentions, she was preoccupied with building Israel's military strength to ensure the survival of the Jewish state. As the prime minister of a fledgling nation that had suddenly emerged from the Six-Day War as the dominant regional power and, at the same time, as the leader of an unruly governing coalition reluctant to countenance talk of territorial withdrawal, Meir had become wedded to the status quo.

Born in Russia, she had migrated to the United States as a child and grew up in Milwaukee. In this regard, she shared a common experience with Kissinger and therefore a common insecurity, except her anxieties had become the expression of the Jewish nation's angst, conceived under threat in the aftermath of the Holocaust.

Kissinger describes his relationship with her as that of an especially favored nephew with a benevolent aunt, "so that even to admit the possibility of disagreement was a challenge to family hierarchy producing emotional outrage." In fact, she knew how to play on Kissinger's inherent sense of Jewish guilt and never hesitated to do so.[*]

For her unsentimental ambassador in Washington, this visit provided an opportunity to confirm the continued timely transfer of the Phantom aircraft that had already begun to arrive in July, and to ask for more. The Israel Air Force (IAF) was already pressing the Phantoms into service, using them to bomb Egyptian emplacements and air-defense systems on the west bank of the Suez Canal. The fear in the Israeli cabinet was that the United States would turn down further requests if Israel continued its military operations against Egypt.

In advance of Meir's Oval Office meeting with Nixon, Rabin consulted with both Kissinger and Sisco. From those talks, he reported to Meir that the National Security Council—a barely disguised reference to Kissinger—

---

[*] As Kissinger describes their relationship in his memoirs, "She seemed to feel that my Jewish religion obliged me to extend unqualified support to Israel—though, even then, she made sure to voice her complaints with the demeanor of an elderly aunt toward an obstreperous nephew." See Henry Kissinger, *Years of Renewal* (New York: Touchstone, 1999), 375.

believed that Israeli military operations against Egypt could generate "far-reaching results," especially the undermining of Nasser's standing, which in turn would weaken the Soviet position in the region. Israel's military operations were, according to Rabin's source, "the most encouraging breath of fresh air the American administration has enjoyed recently." Rabin then added his own less-than-diplomatic conclusion:

> A man would have to be blind, deaf and dumb not to sense how much the administration favors our military operations, and there is a growing likelihood that the United States would be interested in an escalation. . . . Thus, the willingness to supply us with additional arms depends more on stepping up our military activity against Egypt than reducing it.

It was the first time Kissinger had sought to deploy Israeli force to achieve the strategic objective of heightening Moscow's Middle Eastern dilemma. It would by no means be the last.

However, Rabin's other Washington interlocutors, particularly Joe Sisco, did not want an escalation of the fighting, especially because Israel was now using American-supplied bombers to inflict severe damage on Egypt. From their point of view, that would only further harm U.S. standing in the Arab world. They specifically rejected Kissinger's argument that the more Nasser was undermined, the weaker the Soviet position in the region would become. On the contrary, they believed that an escalation in the fighting would only increase Nasser's dependence on the Soviet Union and strengthen Moscow's regional standing.

Rabin also seemed to ignore the inherent danger that Rogers and Sisco would seek to link Israel's requests for arms sales to demands for more flexibility from Israel on the diplomatic front. Making diplomatic concessions to the Soviets and Arabs, as Rogers and Sisco were again planning to do, could well oblige the United States to pressure Israel to accept them. Nixon talked from time to time about imposing a solution on Israel for which arms supplies were an obvious lever. But Rabin was counting on Kissinger to make the argument against linkage. He knew from their conversations that Kissinger strongly believed such pressure would only benefit the Soviet Union.

This argument would be at the heart of an increasingly contentious debate between Kissinger and Rogers in which Kissinger would use Israeli military operations to advantage his case. As with the bombing of North Vietnam, Cambodia, and Laos, Kissinger believed the deployment of force—in this case Israeli proxy force—could be used to heighten the Soviet dilemma: Moscow could supply more arms to its Egyptian client to match American arms supplies and risk a superpower confrontation, or it could reduce the arms flow and increase Egyptian unhappiness with its superpower patron.

At that moment, another consideration factored into the arms supply relationship that favored both Israel's request and Kissinger's role in securing Nixon's approval for it. The United States had long been deeply concerned about Israel's nuclear program, fearing that if Israel crossed the nuclear weapons threshold it would spark a nightmarish nuclear arms race in the Middle East. David Ben-Gurion had used Israel's nuclear program as leverage on President Kennedy to secure the supply of sophisticated Hawk air-defense missile systems. In return, Levi Eshkol, Ben-Gurion's successor, had agreed to regular American inspections of Israel's newly declared nuclear reactor at Dimona, in Israel's Negev desert, supposedly to ensure its peaceful purposes. However, the Israelis had proven adept at managing those inspections to prevent the United States from discovering Dimona's real purpose as a plutonium factory for Israel's nuclear weapons program.

By the spring of 1969, Nixon's defense advisers had become alarmed that Israel's nuclear program was about to go critical. The initial concern was that Israel would roll out its weapons for public display, thereby triggering an Arab and Soviet reaction at a time of already high tension in the region. Defense Secretary Melvin Laird and Under Secretary of State Elliot Richardson had wanted to hold up scheduled deliveries of the Phantoms if the United States could not get adequate assurances about Israel's nuclear program. Kissinger had managed to get Nixon to veto this linkage to avoid a direct confrontation with the Israeli prime minister on her first visit. In return, he needed Rabin to get Meir in the one-on-one part of her meeting with Nixon to reassure him that Israel would make "no visible introduction of nuclear weapons or undertake a nuclear test program."

There is no declassified record of what transpired in that Oval Office conversation on September 26, 1969, but ever since then Israel has conducted its nuclear affairs cautiously and covertly according to a strict code of conduct. To this day, Israel refuses to acknowledge that it possesses nuclear weapons and U.S. officials scrupulously avoid any confirmation.* In return, the United States

* Avner Cohen and William Burr, at the National Security Archive, have pored over the documentary record on this issue. As they explain it: "As long as Israel kept the bomb invisible—no test, declaration, or any other act displaying nuclear capability—the United States could live with it. Over time, the tentative Nixon-Meir understanding became the foundation for a remarkable U.S.-Israeli deal, accompanied by a tacit but strict code of behavior to which both nations closely adhered." See Avner Cohen and William Burr, "The Untold Story of Israel's Bomb," *Washington Post*, April 30, 2006.

has avoided pressuring Israel to sign or come into compliance with the nuclear Non-Proliferation Treaty. This tacit compact was tested and ultimately reaffirmed in the Obama administration, even though President Obama placed such a high store on non-proliferation.[*]

This helps explain what is known of the outcome of the meeting between Nixon and Meir. Nixon sympathized with Israel's concerns and promised favorable consideration of her request for twenty-five more F-4 Phantoms and one hundred A-4 Skyhawks as well as $200 million a year in security assistance. As long as he was president, said Nixon, "Israel would never be weak militarily."

There was no explicit connection made by either side between Israel's nuclear policy of "ambiguity" and American arms supplies, but from that point on it was understood that to avoid Israel publicly going nuclear, its conventional strength would need to be maintained. Over time, this developed into an American commitment to maintain Israel's "qualitative military edge" over any possible coalition of forces in the region. As Rabin testifies in his memoirs, "The story of Kissinger's contribution to Israel's security has yet to be told. . . . Suffice it to say that it was of prime importance."

Rogers and Sisco pressed ahead even though there were clear indications that whatever State proposed would not be acceptable to either Israel or Egypt given the distance between their positions. Nixon was sure that nothing would come of their efforts, so he told Kissinger to avoid a needless confrontation with the secretary of state.

On December 9, 1969, Rogers decided to go public with a U.S. blueprint for Arab-Israeli peace. In a public address to the Galaxy Conference on Adult Education at the Shoreham Hotel in Washington, he laid out the principles for a "final and reciprocally binding accord" to establish a state of peace between Israel and Egypt, which included the determination that the "secure and recognized" border would be the previous international boundary.

Israel immediately rejected what became known as "the Rogers Plan." Nonetheless, the United States presented a parallel plan to the four-power

---

[*] Rose Gottemoeller, Obama's under secretary of state for arms control, told a non-proliferation conference in New York in May 2009 that Obama sought "universal adherence to the NPT—including by India, Israel, Iran and North Korea." Listing Israel in that company directly undermined the tacit agreement Kissinger had first arranged and subsequent administrations had honored. It did not take long for the Obama administration to revert to form and reaffirm the original understanding. See Mark Landler, "Israeli Leader to Meet Obama as U.S. Priorities Shift," *New York Times*, May 15, 2009, and Louis Charbonneau, "U.S. Wants Israel, India in Anti-Nuclear Arms Treaty," Reuters, May 5, 2009.

talks for an Israeli-Jordanian peace agreement. It was marginally more flexible on the territorial border between Jordan and Israel, allowing for "minor border rectifications," but it also spelled out a solution for shared control of Jerusalem and provided for an annual quota of Palestinian refugees to be repatriated to Israel (with the number to be negotiated).

The Israeli cabinet formally rejected both proposals on December 22, 1969, declaring that "Israel will not be sacrificed by any power or inter-power policy and will reject any attempt to impose a forced solution on her." Rabin was recalled to Jerusalem for consultations and sent back to Washington to mobilize the American Jewish community and launch an all-out campaign against the Rogers Plan on Capitol Hill and in the media.

Concerned by the political fallout, Nixon sent Attorney General John Mitchell and his counselor Leonard Garment to reassure the American Jewish leadership that "the Rogers Plan on the Middle East was aptly named and did not originate in the White House." This was particularly ironic given Nixon's repeated declarations to his advisers and to foreign leaders that he would not allow "domestic political considerations"—a euphemism for American Jews—to influence his policy toward the Middle East.[*]

Nixon and Kissinger also dispatched Garment to meet with Meir in New York, where she was about to embark on a tour of American Jewish communities. Their message startled Garment even though he was wise to the ways of Washington. "Tell her wherever she goes . . . ," Kissinger instructed him, "we want her to slam the hell out of Rogers and his plan."

Kissinger also arranged for Nixon to reassure Rabin in what was an unusual meeting since presidents do not normally meet with ambassadors, except when they present their credentials. Nixon expressed an understanding of Israel's concerns and reminded Rabin of his promise to provide for Israel's defense and economic needs. "In all matters connected with arms supplies . . . it would be better if you would approach Kissinger," he instructed the Israeli ambassador. Nixon had now vested Kissinger with control of the arms spigot, continuing the erosion of State's mandate on Middle East policy. Three years later, arms supplies would prove to be a crucial lever in his toolbox when he assumed the role of peace negotiator.

In the meantime, on December 23, the Soviet Union also officially rejected the Rogers proposals as "one-sided," despite the fact that they represented a

---

[*] For example, at the outset of his administration in February 1969, after reading a Middle East memo from the State Department referring to domestic politics, Nixon sent a written memo back that declared: "Under no circumstances will domestic political considerations have any bearing on the decisions I make with regard to the Mideast. The only consideration that will affect my decision on this policy will be the security interests of the United States." See Memo from Nixon to Rogers and Kissinger, February 22, 1969, FRUS 1969–1976:23, Doc. 9.

tilt toward Egypt and Jordan. Moscow urged its Arab clients to follow suit, though they needed little encouragement. Moscow's rejection rendered the Rogers Plan dead on arrival.

In Washington, a stumble by one part of the bureaucracy usually provides an opportunity for rivals to step in, claiming greater competence. The manifest and public failure of the Rogers Plan had come in the face of Kissinger's clear warnings to Nixon that the Soviet Union would not be persuaded to pressure Egypt by American concessions that distanced it from Israel. Not only had his analysis proven to be prescient, but Nixon now had to deal with the deleterious consequences of Rogers's initiative: a firestorm of criticism from Israel's supporters in the United States, and damage to America's credibility in the Middle East. However, Kissinger still hadn't found a way to overcome Nixon's reluctance to deprive Rogers of responsibility for the Middle East, even though in every other important area of foreign policy Nixon was already cutting him out.

Feeling betrayed by Rogers and Sisco and emboldened by a mandate from his government to go on the offensive against them in Washington, Rabin decided to step up his campaign in Jerusalem for more aggressive military action against Egypt. His argument fell on receptive ears given Meir's anger at Rogers. It certainly helped that he could again cite his sources as telling him to "hit them hard," this time arguing that influential elements in Washington wanted to see the U.S. strategy of bombing Hanoi to the negotiating table applied by proxy to Egypt. Moreover, he could cite the fact that a steady flow of ordnance for the bombing campaign was being provided by the Pentagon with authorization coming from the White House.[*]

As a direct consequence of Rabin's lobbying, in January 1970 Israel began deep penetration raids into Egypt, including attacks on the outskirts of Cairo, with the avowed dual purpose of pressing Nasser to end his War of Attrition and undermining his hold on his people. Just as with Nixon's bombing of Hanoi, it had the opposite effect, as Rogers and Sisco had predicted. Nasser made a secret visit to Moscow and threatened that if the Soviets failed to come to his aid he would resign. By March, to counter the Israeli offensive, Moscow began shipping fifty SA-3 surface-to-air missile systems with ten thousand Soviet personnel to man them, complemented by 120 MiG-21 fighters with Soviet pilots.

This dramatic injection of Soviet forces into the crucible of conflict in the Middle East would play to Kissinger's advantage in Washington's bureaucratic

---

[*] Eight thousand tons of ordnance were dropped on Egypt in the first four months of 1970. See Yaacov Bar-Simon-Tov, "The Myth of Strategic Bombing: Israeli Deep-Penetration Air Raids in the War of Attrition, 1969–1970," *Journal of Contemporary History* 19.3 (1984): 555.

politics because it now propelled the Middle East issue onto the superpower agenda—Kissinger's realm. It didn't take long before his own back channel to Dobrynin replaced the Sisco-Dobrynin front channel that had been the vehicle for the failed two-power talks.* Yet Kissinger would admit, "I was not in the dominant position."

Kissinger argued vehemently to Nixon that this Soviet move was unprecedented: never had the Soviet Union made such a military commitment to a non-communist country. In his view, it was essential and urgent that the United States stand up to the Soviets lest it be seen as accepting a Soviet combat role in the Middle East that would drastically change the political and military balances. Any future Israeli concessions, he argued, would be perceived as the consequence of Soviet military pressure.

Kissinger did not prevail. Nixon was preoccupied with the domestic backlash from his decision to invade Cambodia and was still hopeful for a positive U.S.-Soviet summit, so he took the path of least resistance: he endorsed a new Rogers initiative for an immediate cease-fire and negotiations under Jarring's auspices, accompanied by a decision to hold in abeyance Israel's request for the Phantoms and Skyhawks. In typical fashion, Nixon told Kissinger that he thought the new Rogers effort would fail. On March 18, 1970, he met with Rabin again and told him, "The moment Israel needs arms, approach me by way of Kissinger, and I'll find a way of overcoming the bureaucracy."

Kissinger did manage to convince Nixon it was imperative that he reverse the signal of weakness the State Department was sending. On June 26, 1970, at San Clemente—Nixon's "Western White House"—Kissinger directly challenged the Soviet military presence in Egypt. The purpose of his background briefing was to make the case for the invasion of Cambodia. But the first question was about the Middle East. Noting the danger there of superpower confrontation, Kissinger pointed to "a Soviet combat base in Egypt," which generated the danger that the eastern Mediterranean might become a Soviet lake. And then he said:

> We are trying to get a settlement in such a way that the moderate regimes
> are strengthened, and not the radical regimes. *We are trying to expel the
> Soviet military presence*, not so much the advisors, but the combat pilots and
> the combat personnel, before they become so firmly established. (Emphasis added.)

* One example of the way the game was playing out was that Rogers had decided to play on Kissinger's turf, just as Kissinger was playing on his. On June 2, for example, Rogers called Dobrynin into the State Department to present him with a démarche that had not been coordinated with the White House which in effect acquiesced to the Soviet combat presence in Egypt except in the immediate vicinity of the Suez Canal. See Henry Kissinger, *White House Years* (Boston: Little, Brown, 1979), 574.

Kissinger's use of the word "expel" unleashed a storm of criticism, not least from Rogers, who saw it as a deliberate attempt to sabotage his cease-fire initiative. Kissinger would later tell me that it was an unfortunate choice of words, a product of his inexperience with background briefings, which Nixon had previously banned him from giving because of his German accent. He emphasized, though, that he would not have used the word if Nixon had not been comfortable with the concept, which they had spent some time discussing before the briefing.

Four days later, in another background briefing, Kissinger tried to put the statement in context. Noting that he would have done better to use "a more waffling expression," he nevertheless declared that it was a fair estimate of what the United States was trying to achieve.

> I think the Soviets realize that if they expand their military presence the point will be reached where they must be challenged by the Israelis. The Israelis cannot permit themselves to sit there and strangle gradually. . . . Secondly, at some point of the Soviet presence in the Middle East there will be some indigenous Arab forces that will have their own reasons for not wanting to substitute one colonialism for another.

Kissinger would prove to be prescient on both counts. In the four days between the two briefings, it had already become obvious that the Soviets were moving their missile bases ever closer to the west bank of the Suez Canal under cover of Soviet air patrols. If they succeeded in deploying them there, they would jeopardize Israel's ability to use its air force to protect its ground forces, which had taken up static positions along the east bank of the canal. Israel therefore repeatedly attacked the missile systems, but without success, and lost several Phantoms in the process. Nixon responded with a public warning to the Soviets on July 1 that undid his notion of a quiet resupply of aircraft for Israel. Noting that Soviet arms supplies threatened to upset the balance of power in the region, he warned that once that happened, "We will do what is necessary to maintain Israel's strength vis-à-vis its neighbors."

On July 25 and 27, Soviet-piloted MiG-21s entered Israeli-controlled airspace over the Suez Canal and engaged Israeli aircraft there. On July 30, twelve MiGs engaged the IAF's Phantoms again. This time, in a daring move, the IAF pilots ambushed the Soviet-piloted MiGs and shot down four, killing three Soviet pilots. A week later, the Soviets organized a counter-ambush, shooting down two Israeli Mirage-IIICs.

We know how Kissinger felt about the incidents from an exchange that took place six months later, on December 11, 1970, when Defense Minister Moshe Dayan met with Kissinger in his White House office (the memoran-

Henry Kissinger in his White House office on August 6, 1970. He was the
first national security adviser to secure occupancy rights to this street-level
office in the front, northwest corner of the West Wing. It has remained the
national security adviser's office ever since.

dum of conversation exists only in the Israeli archives). By then Kissinger had
managed to secure occupancy rights to this large room on street level in the
front, northwest corner of the West Wing. With large French windows on the
northern and western sides, it was filled with natural light. The furniture was
Early American but on the walls, Kissinger had hung paintings by a New York
abstract colorist, a Russian social realist, and a Chinese scroll painter.

Dayan wanted to know how the United States would respond if Israel was
engaged in another confrontation with the Soviet Union over the Suez Canal.
Kissinger responded by asking facetiously whether the shooting down of the
Soviet MiGs had been an accident. Dayan described the calculation behind
his decision to "clear the airspace over the Canal," emphasizing that it was
no accident and he would do it again if the Soviets provoked him. Then he
pressed Kissinger to say how the United States would respond.

"Your only hope is to be very bold," he explained to Dayan. "They must
never think that you are wavering. . . . If from time to time you didn't give
them a brutal blow, they will wear you out." He added that he had been astonished that they hadn't also destroyed the Soviet SAM sites.

While Kissinger was encouraging audacious Israeli military action in the
service of his theory of how to heighten the Soviet dilemma, Rogers was still

pursuing his cease-fire initiative. To the great surprise of all, Nasser accepted it on July 22, 1970. Inevitably, the pressure was now on Israel to accept too, which it did on July 31, after receiving a forward-leaning letter of assurances from Nixon about final-status issues.*

In accepting the cease-fire, both sides appear to have been responding to the conditions on the battlefield. Israel was doing its best to prevent the movement of the SAM batteries into the canal zone, but its air force had so far failed at the attempt, in the process losing twenty-one aircraft between May and August 1970. Continuing the effort would cost them more aircraft as well as the risk of a greater confrontation with the Soviet Union. A cease-fire might achieve their purposes better. For its part, Egypt had more chance of moving up the SAM sites under the cover of a cease-fire than in the face of Israeli attacks. Notwithstanding the self-congratulatory mood in Washington, neither Cairo nor Jerusalem saw any other utility in the arrangement.

The cease-fire went into effect on August 7. Almost immediately the Egyptians and Soviets began moving their missiles into the area that had been designated as a thirty-kilometer-wide "standstill zone" on the Egyptian side of the canal. Rabin cried foul to Kissinger, but Rogers was not keen to see the cease-fire disintegrate before the talks began, and so refused to confirm Israel's claims of Soviet-Egyptian perfidy. Eventually, the violations would become so blatant that the State Department would have to admit they had been hoodwinked.† The cease-fire held, but peace negotiations never got off the ground.

The Soviets and the Egyptians had succeeded in providing protection for Egyptian forces on the west bank of the canal. And they had also managed to exploit the cease-fire to build up a formidable capability for protecting Egyptian forces should they try to assault Israeli positions on the east bank of the canal. Three years later, Israeli soldiers there would pay the ultimate price in the opening days of the Yom Kippur War because of the movement of those SAMs. This Soviet protection would provide the key enabler for the Egyptian General Staff to plan for war, which they now began to do.

For the time being, however, Meir and Rabin were content to take advan-

---

* In this case, Nixon's assurances were precedential: "Our position on withdrawal is that the final borders must be agreed upon by the parties by means of negotiations. . . . We will not press Israel to accept a solution to the refugee problem that will alter fundamentally the Jewish character of the State of Israel or jeopardize your security. We shall adhere strictly and firmly to the fundamental principle that there must be a peace agreement in which each of the parties undertakes reciprocal obligations to the other. No Israeli soldier should be withdrawn from the present lines until a binding contractual peace agreement satisfactory to you has been achieved." See Yitzhak Rabin, *The Rabin Memoirs* (Berkeley, CA: University of California Press, 1996), 179.
† By mid-October, more than thirty missile batteries had been moved into the canal zone, enabling the Egyptians to deploy five hundred to six hundred air-defense missiles on the front lines.

tage of blatant Soviet and Egyptian cheating to avoid negotiations and secure more arms.* For Kissinger, the Soviet actions served as further proof of his assertion that diplomacy in the absence of taking a firm stand against Soviet military moves was futile. The Soviets had succeeded in strengthening their position in Egypt, demonstrating their value as a patron of radical Arab regimes, and, in the process, shifting the regional balance of power in their favor. U.S. unwillingness to stand up to them was only encouraging them to be more audacious.

It took only one month for Kissinger to be vindicated again by another aggressive Soviet move, this time in Jordan. The crisis it provoked would give Kissinger the opportunity to deal the coup de grâce to Rogers's failing Middle East diplomacy.

---

* Nixon and Kissinger saw to it that Israel received an antimissile package of anti-radar electronic systems, Shrike air-to-ground missiles, and cluster bombs, as well as sixteen more Phantoms to provide enhanced capability for destroying the missile sites.

3

The Jordan Crisis

Our way of dealing with a crisis is to try to judge the crest of the crisis
and try to anticipate the events that are happening and thereby dominate them.

—Henry Kissinger to Golda Meir, May 1974

J ordan is a small Arab kingdom wedged between the more significant
regional powers of Israel, Syria, Iraq, and Saudi Arabia. In Kissinger's time,
it was ruled by King Hussein, a Hashemite emir whose grandfather had been
enthroned there by the British after the Hashemites had been evicted from the
Arabian Peninsula by the al-Saud clan at the end of World War I. Palestinians assassinated Hussein's grandfather in Jerusalem in 1951. A military coup
removed his cousin from the throne in neighboring Iraq in 1958. And in the
Six-Day War, Hussein lost half his kingdom and his control of the Al-Aqsa
Mosque in Jerusalem to Israel. During that war, some three hundred thousand
Palestinians from the West Bank had sought refuge in his country, joining
earlier waves of refugees; by 1970, they had become radicalized by the operations within Jordan of Palestinian militant organizations led by Yasir Arafat,
the leader of the PLO.

This growing challenge to the young king's authority—he was thirty-five at
the time—boiled over in September 1970. The more radical fedayeen (as the
Palestinian guerrillas were referred to in those days) sought to overthrow him,
hoping to draw on the support of Iraq, which had stationed seventeen thousand troops in Jordan, ostensibly to fight Israel. The Palestinians also looked
to neighboring Syria, whose tank brigades were camped just across the border.

Kissinger had been watching these events unfold for some time. In June
1970, he convened a National Security Council meeting in which Nixon
ordered contingency planning should Jordan seek U.S. support. To prepare

those contingencies, Kissinger used his coordinating authority as the president's national security adviser to convene and chair the Washington Special Action Group (WSAG), an interagency committee with high-level participation from all relevant national security departments.

On September 1, the Popular Front for the Liberation of Palestine (PFLP) ambushed Hussein on his way to the airport to pick up his daughter, Princess Alia. The king barely escaped with his life. Then between September 6 and 9, 1970, the PFLP hijacked four Western airliners and flew three of them to Jordan, holing up at Dawson's Field, a remote desert airstrip near Zarqa, northwest of Amman. This blatant act of air piracy and hostage taking on Jordanian territory posed a severe challenge to Hussein's authority. Hesitating at first but facing increasing pressure from his Bedouin generals to act, the king indicated to Washington that he was contemplating drastic measures and would likely need American help against Iraqi intervention.

Kissinger sprang into action, using the WSAG as his vehicle for managing the looming crisis. State might have control of the diplomatic process in the Middle East, but crisis management was the natural preserve of the national security adviser. Accordingly, Kissinger used the Jordan crisis to correct what he viewed as a dangerous deterioration in America's position in the region caused by the State Department.

The White House Situation Room complex comprises a series of small, wood-paneled meeting rooms crammed into the windowless basement of the West Wing. There, deliberations about war and peace take place. The policymakers at the table represent vast bureaucracies; the most powerful armed forces in the world; the intelligence community, with its formidable assets; and often seated at the head of the table, the president, as commander in chief. In times of crisis, the place is abuzz with uniformed officials and their civilian counterparts. It houses a communications hub manned by the U.S. military that keeps a twenty-four-hour watch on developments across the globe and provides immediate secure communications for White House officials to U.S. embassies and military bases.

Kissinger presided over WSAG meetings in the largest of the conference rooms. Nowadays, the wood panels there open to reveal large flat-screen televisions that provide direct secure videoconference connections to high-level officials wherever they may be traveling. Digital clocks with large red numbers give the local time in the places that are the subject of discussion. But during the Nixon administration, the facilities were cramped, stuffy, and unadorned. An imposing mahogany conference table all but filled the room. Large brown-leather swivel chairs were set at the table for the principals from the different departments; smaller chairs for their deputies or assistants lined three of the four walls.

Wednesday, September 9, 1970, Washington, DC. The national security adviser convened the WSAG in the Situation Room at 11:40 a.m. to discuss the crisis in Jordan. Among the participants was U. Alexis Johnson, the deputy secretary of state. Rogers had sent him to represent the State Department in his place, a clear sign that he did not intend to defer to Kissinger's leadership. Similarly, Deputy Secretary of Defense David Packard represented the Pentagon. Richard Helms, the director of the CIA, took his seat farther down the table, adjacent to the chairman of the Joint Chiefs of Staff, Admiral Thomas H. Moorer. Around the walls sat their assistants: Joe Sisco, Robert Pranger, Rodger P. Davies, and Lt. Gen. Melvin Zais.

Kissinger focused the meeting on the priority of protecting American lives. Over half the hostages were believed to be American, some of them dual American-Israeli citizens, and they might need to be rescued. The WSAG participants also had to prepare for the possibility of U.S. military intervention to support Hussein. In the meantime, some muscle flexing might help correct the perception in Moscow of weakness conveyed by Washington when it failed to react to Soviet moves in Egypt.

Kissinger knew Nixon loved to wave a big stick and keep America's adversaries guessing as to how he might use it. And he shared the president's belief that it was the only way to get Moscow's attention. Thus, the meeting resolved to send the Sixth Fleet's USS *Independence* carrier task force into the eastern Mediterranean and to move six C-130 aircraft to Incirlik Air Base in southeastern Turkey, in case an evacuation of the hostages became necessary.

Nixon and Kissinger were not on the same page, however, when it came to the question of military intervention in the Jordan crisis. Kissinger believed that with American forces stretched thin fighting wars in Southeast Asia and deterring Soviet adventurism in Europe, the United States could not sustain combat in the Middle East. He much preferred that neighboring Israel do the job, if necessary. Hussein had made clear that in extremis he was willing to take support from "any quarter." Thanks in part to American largesse, Israel was in a position to fly seven hundred sorties a day compared to the two hundred sorties the United States could launch from the aircraft carrier. And Israel had a strong army, capable of intervening in Jordan or Syria at a day's notice, compared to the weeks it would take the United States to move its ground forces into the region from Europe or the United States.

To Kissinger's surprise, the participants in the WSAG meeting agreed with him. Moorer told the meeting that intervention in Jordan would require four brigades, one from Germany and the other three from the United States, which Helms noted would leave no strategic reserve in the United States. "That scares the hell out of me," he declared. Moorer agreed that "it would be a very tenuous situation with no end in sight." Joe Sisco noted, "We would have to stay for some time, and . . . the moment we got out, the King would be in a much weaker position politically."

Usually, Washington's national security establishment would have been deeply reluctant to rely on Israel to protect American interests in the Arab world. They feared Nasser and other Arab radicals would use it to discredit U.S. intentions and undermine the conservative Arab monarchs who depended on America. Israeli intervention on behalf of Hussein could further delegitimize him in the eyes of his people and Arabs everywhere. But since he had raised the idea of Israeli involvement, and the U.S. alternative looked problematic, the WSAG reached a quick consensus on using Israeli forces "for an operation in support of King Hussein against the fedayeen and possibly the Iraqis."

When Kissinger informed Nixon of this conclusion, the president rejected the advice. He believed that Israeli intervention would undermine the king in the Arab world and among his subjects. He preferred to use American troops to counter any Iraqi or Syrian intervention, a show of American force that he believed would impress the Soviets.

Tuesday, September 15, 1970, Amman, Jordan. The fedayeen had now removed the hostages from the four airplanes and, in a made-for-television moment, blew up the planes. King Hussein decided he could no longer tolerate this challenge to his authority. He informed the U.S. ambassador, L. Dean Brown, that he had decided to move against the Palestinian guerrillas. According to Brown's cable to Washington, Hussein stressed that "depending on fedayeen reactions, he may need to call for U.S. *and Israeli* assistance [emphasis added]."

The WSAG meeting that night reached a consensus: Hussein would likely defeat the fedayeen, and if Iraq's troops intervened, Israel would probably act. In that event, the United States should stand aside but warn against Soviet intervention or retaliation against Israel. When Kissinger conveyed this to the president, his reaction was "vehement." He covered Kissinger's memo with "angry scribbled comments," reiterating that if the confrontation was unavoidable, he wanted American forces used. He warned Kissinger that he "opposed any Israeli military moves unless he specifically approved them in advance." Two days later, Golda Meir came to call on the president at the

White House on a previously scheduled visit. Nixon warned her against acting precipitously too.

Thursday, September 17, 1970, Washington, DC. After delaying for a day because the king received a warning from his sister-in-law's fortune-teller in London about the inauspiciousness of the date, Hussein's forces launched assaults on Palestinian positions in his capital. Fighting spread to the northern town of Irbid. At Kissinger's direction, the Joint Chiefs ordered the USS *Saratoga* carrier battle group to join the USS *Independence* off the Lebanese coast; a cruiser and fourteen destroyers accompanied them. The USS *John F. Kennedy* and the helicopter carrier USS *Guam* were ordered into the Mediterranean to provide a further show of force. An amphibious task force of twelve hundred Marines was placed on alert in position off Crete.

Nixon loved all that. In a phone call on the same day, he told Kissinger that if the Iraqi or Syrian forces moved, "we should use American air and knock the bejesus out of them." Nixon also wanted the ship movements to be out in the open: "I want them to know we're moving. . . . The wear and tear on the nerves between the Syrians and Iraqis is very important."

Kissinger assured him that the movements would be picked up by the press and by Soviet intelligence but argued that it was better not to announce it. Nixon, however, wanted to send a clear public signal. He went straight into a meeting at the *Chicago Tribune*, where he told the assembled journalists and broadcasters that if the Syrians or Iraqis intervened in Jordan, it would be preferable for the United States to stop them. He also warned that the Russians would pay dearly for moving their missiles up to the Suez Canal: "The Israelis are going to get five times as much as they would have if the missiles would not have moved," he promised. Noting that "we are embarking on a tougher policy in the Middle East," he warned that the United States was ready to intervene militarily if necessary.

Kissinger was unfazed when the U.S. Information Agency director, Frank Shakespeare (who had accompanied Nixon to the meeting with the press), informed him of Nixon's remarks. Kissinger joked that "the Secretary of State is going to have a bloody heart attack. . . . Those fools at State think I am putting him up to it."

Persuading Nixon to go with the option of Israeli intervention was not going to be any simpler than getting him to keep quiet about U.S. force movements. To Kissinger's surprise and delight, however, he now discovered when he consulted Rogers by phone on September 17 that the secretary of state favored the Israelis' taking the lead. "It's almost commanding," said Rogers. "It would help in preventing the Iraqis from having a hand in the government of Jordan. The King can give as the reason the Israelis are on his soil is because of the acts of the fedayeen. Third, if we are going to have any peace, Jordan and Israel will have to work together anyway." Kissinger could not have said it better. Then Rogers added an Arabist twist to his conclusion: "Also, what if we failed? For Israel to bail us out would be awful."

Saturday, September 19, 1970, Amman. After two days of fighting, the king was still far from securing Amman, and the fedayeen were putting up stiff resistance in the northern city of Irbid. At that point, the crisis suddenly worsened when two Syrian armored brigades engaged the Jordanian army across a broad front. The Syrians had deployed 150 tanks in the vicinity; 70 had now crossed the border and were heading for Irbid. Hussein feared they would advance from there southward toward his capital.

Because fighting in downtown Amman had cut off the U.S. embassy from the king's compound, Hussein was able to communicate only through a radio in the attic of his residence in the Hummar Palace that connected him with Bill Speares, the MI6 station chief in the British embassy. Speares conveyed to Washington the king's urgent request for assistance in coping with this large armored force, "even from Israelis." The situation in Amman had become chaotic. The king was isolated in his palace, unable to get accurate information about what was happening around him or in northern Jordan. He was dependent on U.S. intelligence, which was, in turn, dependent on Israeli reconnaissance missions to determine whether the Syrians were moving in additional forces.

Sunday, September 20, 1970, Washington, DC. The WSAG meeting that evening decided to take the Jordanian request for reconnaissance as justification for sending a carrier plane to Tel Aviv to look at the latest Israeli photos. That would send a signal to the Soviets of military coordination between the United States and Israel. Kissinger reinforced this signal with a strong démarche, which Sisco delivered to the Russian chargé d'affaires, Yuli Vorontsov. He demanded that Moscow impress upon Damascus the grave dangers that would ensue if its forces were not withdrawn from Jordan forthwith.

In advance of that day's meeting, Kissinger spoke on the phone with Nixon, who was spending the weekend at the presidential retreat at Camp David. Kissinger again raised the option of calling on the Israelis to act, explaining the limitations of American airstrikes and the danger of entrapment if U.S. forces went in on the ground. Nixon expressed concern about the Arab reaction if

Israel intervened, and emphasized the much stronger message it would send to the Russians if the United States were to act forcibly in this critical area. Kissinger, putting the onus on Rogers and Sisco, noted that State preferred the Israeli option. But then he added, disingenuously, "I am slightly more on your side on this than Sisco's." Seemingly attempting to reinforce Nixon's negative attitude and undercutting his own desired option, Kissinger played to Nixon's prejudices. He warned that if the Israelis went in, it would be "damned hard to get them out." Nixon agreed: "They would just occupy more territory, wouldn't they?"

But then Kissinger added a dose of flattery: "Your instinct about the Russians is usually remarkable." He was preparing to push Nixon's hot button. Duly noting that the intelligence was "not very reliable," Kissinger nevertheless said that it looked like the Russians had given the Syrians the green light. Ignoring the caveat, Nixon became animated. "[The Russians] say, Stir it up, boys; give them trouble; face them down," he imagined. "Well, we may have to come to the Israelis, but I just want to be sure that at this point—that's why I've been so strong on it—we don't leave any impression we might come to them, or they'll come in precipitously. We must not do it. It's got to be a very calculated thing," Nixon warned.

Kissinger was quick to exploit the opening. He assured Nixon that he was not egging the Israelis on, but they were capable of beating the Syrians "to a pulp," and there would be congressional support for their acting. Most important, he reminded Nixon of a fundamental imperative of his national security policy: it would avoid the United States' getting bogged down in another war. Nixon responded: "There is no question the Israelis going in is good . . . they not only have the air but they have got a helluva good ground punch, they could just put them in there and clean them out." Recognizing the limits of American power projection in the prevailing circumstances, the president was coming around.*

That evening, just before the WSAG convened again, Nixon instructed Kissinger that if there were to be a military intervention, it should not be by U.S. forces. The WSAG had already reached that conclusion, but it was reinforced by a message from King Hussein, via the British embassy, reporting that the Syrian forces had entered Irbid; Hussein now requested immediate airstrikes.

Sisco recommended that Kissinger call Rabin and convey the Jordanian

---

* Kissinger notes in his memoirs how he prepared for Nixon's "tendency toward impetuous declarations that he never expected to see implemented." In the Jordan crisis, he had two contingency plans prepared simultaneously: "one embodying the President's preference for unilateral American action; the other reflecting the WSAG consensus for the United States to hold the ring against outside intervention." See Kissinger, *White House Years*, 606.

request. After checking with Nixon, they made the call together. Rabin was in the ballroom at the New York Hilton with his prime minister where she was addressing a United Jewish Appeal (UJA) dinner. Speaking to Rabin on a telephone in the hotel kitchen, Kissinger conveyed the Jordanian request for Israeli airstrikes and asked Rabin to arrange reconnaissance to confirm the Syrian attack. Rabin wanted to know whether the United States endorsed the king's request. Sisco said they could discuss that later; first they needed to establish the seriousness of the situation. From what he had heard from Israel, Rabin said, it certainly looked serious.

At that moment, as if to underscore Rabin's point, an aide rushed another cable into Kissinger's office. Kissinger told Rabin he would call him back.

According to the cable, a desperate King Hussein had just reached Ambassador Brown and asked him to convey the following alarming message to the president:

Situation deteriorating dangerously following Syrian massive invasion. Northern forces disjointed. Irbid occupied. This having disastrous effect on tired troops in the capital and surroundings. After continuous action and shortage of supplies Military Governor and Commander in Chief advise I request immediate physical intervention both air and land as per the authorization of government to safeguard sovereignty, territorial integrity and independence of Jordan. Immediate air strikes on invading forces *from any quarter* plus air cover are imperative. Wish earliest word on length of time it may require your forces to land when requested which might be very soon. (Emphasis added.)

Kissinger and Sisco immediately called Rogers and asked his view on how they should respond to Rabin's question about the American attitude to an Israeli airstrike. Rogers was straightforward: "I don't think we have any choice. What it amounts to is Israel is just doing it now at the right time."

In the meantime, Nixon had returned from Camp David. Kissinger, with Sisco in tow, raced from his office in the West Wing into the residence to find the president. The Secret Service took them through the labyrinth of corridors in the basement of the White House, past the kitchen, to a nondescript white door, the entrance to a two-lane, state-of-the-art bowling alley.* While Nixon bowled, Kissinger explained the deterioration in the situation and the precariousness of the king's position. Pausing between frames, the president

---

* I traveled the same circuitous route with President Clinton's national security adviser Anthony Lake in 1993 to inform the president that we had received official word that Yasir Arafat would be attending the Oslo signing ceremony with Yitzhak Rabin.

gave him the go-ahead to inform Rabin that the United States would support the immediate use of Israeli airstrikes.

A few minutes later, as the call to Rabin was being put through, Nixon, dressed in his casual bowling outfit, strolled into Kissinger's office to listen in. Kissinger told the Israeli ambassador:

> We would look favorably on your actions and the president has asked me to tell you if you undertake such action we would of course make good on any materiel problems that might arise . . . and we are cognizant of the fact we would have to hold the situation under control vis-à-vis the Soviets.

Rabin said he would check with the prime minister. He called back to say that she looked favorably on the request. He also informed Kissinger that the IDF believed there was a massive Syrian force "in the area," and therefore airstrikes might not be enough. They agreed to await the reports from the imminent Israeli reconnaissance flights.

That is how the first known instance of U.S.-Israeli strategic cooperation took place. As Rabin would describe it twenty-six years later, a principle had been established. The United States had turned to Israel to protect a "viable" Arab kingdom from being overthrown by Soviet-backed radical Arab forces.

Monday, September 21, 1970, Washington, DC. Rabin called Kissinger early that morning to inform him that air reconnaissance indicated a massive Syrian force of some three hundred tanks at Irbid, but it had not yet moved south toward Amman. He confirmed the IDF's assessment that airstrikes alone would be insufficient to force the Syrians to withdraw from Jordanian territory.

Rabin now wanted to know the American attitude to the deployment of Israeli ground forces. Israeli airstrikes were one thing, but a ground invasion of Jordan had the potential to stir up the Arab world, perhaps force Nasser's intervention, and provoke the Soviets to take a stand. Rabin's question spurred a new round of consultations in Washington.

Nixon had anticipated this development more quickly than Kissinger. He immediately moved into commander-in-chief mode, dictating detailed instructions to Kissinger for Rabin, which he had scribbled on his ubiquitous yellow legal pad:

1. The operation must succeed;
2. Success diplomatically as well as militarily must be considered;
3. If it is militarily feasible, [the Israelis] must lean in the direction of

accomplishing a true air action alone in the first instance, having in
mind the fact that that might have a psychological impact which is
needed;

4. If, however, that proves to be militarily and overall inadequate, again
   what is necessary to achieve success would have our support;

5. The ground for the action on the ground, as distinguished from the
   air, must strictly be limited to Jordan.

Then Nixon added: "I've decided it. Don't ask anybody else. Tell [Rabin], Go!"

Nixon's green light fit with Kissinger's preference for assertive Israeli action.
But he knew that if the president didn't first consult with the secretaries of
state and defense on a matter of such import, they would blame Kissinger.
So, despite Nixon's reluctance to engage in face-to-face deliberations with his
advisers, Kissinger promptly convened a meeting for them with the president.

At the outset of that meeting, the CIA informed the principals that a Syrian spearhead was en route to Amman (that was wrong information). Rogers
expressed grave concern about an Israeli ground operation, believing it would
be disastrous for the king to be seen to be depending on Israel for his survival. Informed that it would take two days for Israel to mobilize its ground
forces, the president decided to ask Hussein whether he wanted Israeli ground
forces to intervene. In the meantime, he instructed Sisco to tell Rabin that he
agreed to Israeli ground action in principle, subject to determining the king's
view. That would have the advantage of green-lighting an Israeli mobilization,
which, together with the massing of American forces in the eastern Mediterranean, was bound to make an impression on Syria and its Soviet patron.

Kissinger and Rogers were clearly parting company on how to handle the
crisis. While Rogers was in favor of Israeli force if necessary, he suspected Kissinger was trying to force Nixon into a rash decision. After the meeting, Kissinger invited Rogers back to his office and offered an olive branch: Couldn't
they work together in this crisis rather than be at each other's throats? Rogers
was not buying: he accused Kissinger of withholding information from the
president.

If Rogers wanted a turf war, so be it. Kissinger immediately called Rabin.
He told him to be guarded in his response when Sisco briefed him: "The less
you say the better. . . . And then come in and see me. It's terribly important
that we know who says what to whom and I will give you guidelines on that."
Kissinger wanted Rabin to understand that their back channel was the official
channel: "You will have to follow my recommendations. . . . You will have to
assume what I tell you is in the interest of everybody."

Rabin agreed. He also reported that the Israeli cabinet had now made a formal decision to intervene, but that would require activation of a relatively large ground force, which could provoke a resumption of hostilities along the Suez Canal and possible Soviet involvement. Therefore, he had instructions to seek written assurances that the United States would prevent Soviet intervention and protect Israel from any international fallout from its invasion of Jordan at America's request.*

By the time Kissinger convened the WSAG again, at noon, the situation on the ground had been clarified. The Syrians had captured Irbid without a fight and were digging in around the city rather than advancing toward Amman. The Syrian Air Force had remained on the ground, and the Iraqis were avoiding military action. Hussein, however, was still calling for Israeli airstrikes and preparations for U.S. intervention.

In fulfillment of the Israeli cabinet's decision and to ready its forces for action, IDF reserves were mobilized, and two Israeli tank brigades were deployed on the Golan Heights, threatening the western flank of the Syrian forces and their lines of communication. In the meantime, Zaid al-Rifai—Hussein's national security adviser—told Ambassador Brown that "ground operations are fine in the area as long as they are *not* . . . in Jordan [emphasis added]." That was precisely the opposite of the position adopted by Nixon the night before. It was also something that Israel was unenthusiastic about, as Rabin explained to Sisco. In Rabin's view, the situation required an Israeli assault on the Jordanian city of Irbid, which was now in Syrian hands. Israeli intervention in Syria, as Rifai preferred, could precipitate Egyptian and Soviet reactions and might not be effective in forcing the Syrian tanks to withdraw from Jordan.†

---

* Rabin formally conveyed the following questions from the Israeli cabinet: (1) Will the United States make a formal request to Israel? (2) Will the king agree to request Israeli assistance and coordinate with Israel? (3) How will the United States prevent Soviet intervention? (4) Would the United States commit to protecting Israel from any international fallout, particularly a UN Security Council resolution that would demand immediate Israeli withdrawal? Rabin asked that the answers be given in a secret U.S.-Israeli memorandum of understanding. The answers to these questions came back a day later: (1) The United States had already indicated its agreement in principle to "the operation under discussion." (2) The United States had heard from the king's national security adviser that Israeli "ground operations are fine in the area as long as they are not . . . in Jordan." Israel should also ask the king, since a channel of communication had been established between him and Deputy Prime Minister Yigal Allon. (3) All the actions the United States has already taken "clearly imply a decision not to permit Soviet intervention against Israel in the conditions under consideration." (4) The United States undertook to defend Israel in international forums and veto a UNSC resolution that would seek to condemn Israel for "this act of self-defense." (5) The United States did not consider it necessary to put these understandings into a formal MOU. See Telegram from Department of State to Embassies in Jordan and Israel, September 22, 1970, FRUS 1969–1976:24, Doc. 311.
† The Israeli *note verbale*, delivered to Sisco by Rabin the morning of September 21, explicated the Israeli military plan. The note stated that Israel intended to act first by air attack and, if the Syrians failed to withdraw, to follow with a ground assault. Israel made clear that the Israeli military would attack Syrian forces in Jordan and make no attacks against Syrians in Syrian territory. See Minutes of WSAG Meeting, September 21, 1970, FRUS 1969–1976:24, Doc. 304.

The conversation between Rabin and Sisco about where Israel might intervene drove Kissinger wild. From his earlier exchange, he had understood from
Rabin, and had so informed the president, that the Israelis would be willing to
move into Syria. Now Rogers, based on a briefing from Sisco, was telling the
president that the Israelis were prepared to move into Jordan but not Syria.
Kissinger called Rabin and interrogated him about the conversation with Sisco
and then upbraided him:

> I want to get one thing clear. Did I understand you correctly when we
> talked this afternoon that if a major operation was carried out in Syria,
> from a military point of view, this was a feasible operation? You and I have
> to be meticulous in our understandings for this reason. What you tell me
> I report to the president. When another version is reported, my version
> must be the correct one. Otherwise there is no sense in my talking to you.

Notwithstanding this altercation, the IDF was now bolstering its mobilization by sending forces into the Beit Shean valley, across the border from Irbid.
According to the U.S. defense attaché in Israel, "present positioning of Israeli
forces would permit military intervention at almost any point in the Jordan
Valley or even from the Golan Heights."

Meanwhile, the American force buildup in the eastern Mediterranean was
proceeding apace and the Soviet Union seemed to be getting the message.*
Much to Nixon's and Kissinger's satisfaction, on Monday evening Dobrynin's
deputy, Yuli Vorontsov, rushed to the White House from the Soviet embassy
on Sixteenth Street—three blocks away—with a conciliatory message. In it,
Moscow declared that it was now pressing Damascus to withdraw its tanks
from Jordan, and politely requested that the United States also press Israel not
to intervene.

Kissinger deliberately did not respond. That evening, a dismayed Vorontsov
buttonholed Kissinger at a diplomatic reception at the Egyptian ambassador's
ornate Georgian residence in Kalorama. He claimed that Moscow was trying
to get the Syrians out of Jordan but wondered whether the United States would
accept it if the Syrians would just stop firing. Kissinger repeated the original
American demand within hearing of other dignitaries and members of the
press: Syrian tanks would have to make a complete withdrawal. Vorontsov then
urged Kissinger not to intervene with U.S. forces, warning that it would cause

---

* The entire Sixth Fleet—two carrier task forces with 140 aircraft—was off the Lebanese coast;
a twelve-hundred-strong Marine amphibious force was in position thirty-five hours away; a third
carrier task force and two more submarines would enter the Mediterranean in three days; a second
amphibious task force would follow a few days later; two airborne battalions were on alert in
Europe; and the lead elements of the 82nd Airborne Division were ready to depart Fort Bragg.

Washington great difficulty in the Arab world. He quickly added, disingenuously, that Moscow didn't care since its interests wouldn't be affected. "Then
you would win either way," Kissinger responded with his characteristic wit.

Tuesday, September 22, 1970, Amman. On the ground in Jordan, developments
were breaking in the king's direction. Although Hussein had not yet regained
control of his capital, he was emboldened to act by the explicit backing of the
United States and Israel. Taking advantage of the fact that the Syrian Air Force
had not intervened, he sent his modest air force into action against the Syrian
tanks, backed by Jordanian tanks he had deployed from Amman. By the time
the president met with his advisers at noon, the Syrians had lost some 120
tanks, most due to Jordanian military action, the rest to mechanical breakdown.

Meanwhile, a chastened Rabin had arrived in the West Wing to brief Kissinger ahead of his meeting with Sisco to deliver the Israeli cabinet's formal
reaction to the U.S. answers to its previous questions. They met in the Map
Room. According to Rabin's report to Meir of the meeting, Kissinger again
expressed his anger at the fact that Rabin was operating through multiple U.S.
channels instead of exclusively through him. He warned Rabin that the Israelis
needed to have more discipline because their existence was at stake. And they
should take the president at his word when he said he was committed to supporting Israel's operation.

Having secured the president's support for Israeli intervention, Kissinger
feared Rabin would inadvertently provide Rogers with the means to undermine Nixon's resolve. He also wanted to make sure that the back channel he
controlled remained the only channel between Nixon and Meir. Decades later,
he would still show his sensitivity, telling me it was "nonsense" that Rabin was
working with Sisco because the Israelis had "no use for Sisco."

Comparing that episode to my own experience across three administrations in
dealing with Israeli leaders and their ambassadors in Washington, I am struck
by how intimidated Rabin was by Kissinger's angry tongue-lashing. It would
happen again with Simcha Dinitz, his successor, during the Yom Kippur War.
Neither Rabin nor Dinitz was a wilting flower; they were both used to the
rough-and-tumble of Israeli politics. Rabin was a battle-hardened general. Yet
Kissinger's rage could put the fear of God in them. They were not the only
ones who experienced it. His staff would, on occasion, find their carefully prepared papers thrown back at them; once, he stomped on a paper prepared by
the mild-mannered and bookish Harold Saunders. As Saunders explained it,
his aides were willing to tolerate it because they understood they were engaged

in something highly consequential. In Rabin's case, Kissinger didn't hesitate to remind him that he was playing with the fate of his then-fledgling nation. An exaggeration to be sure, but one that Rabin could not ignore.

Over the years, as relations between the United States and Israel grew closer, Israeli behavior would continue to drive American policymakers to distraction. But American anger had a decreasing impact, as Israelis became more confident in their ability to stand up to their indulgent patron. After President Clinton's first meeting with Prime Minister Netanyahu in the White House in 1996, he asked his aides whether Netanyahu understood who the superpower was in the relationship.

In January 2014, Israel's defense minister, Moshe "Bogie" Ya'alon, accused Secretary of State Kerry of being "obsessive and messianic" in his efforts to promote Israeli-Palestinian peace, adding that he hoped Kerry would get a Nobel Prize "and leave us alone." Despite the ensuing furor in Washington, Ya'alon did not apologize and Netanyahu did not condemn his defense minister's remarks. When Kerry called Secretary of Defense Chuck Hagel to suggest he postpone Ya'alon's upcoming official visit to the Pentagon as a show of Obama administration displeasure, Hagel demurred. He had been roughed up by pro-Israel organizations in his confirmation hearings for being critical of Israel and was not about to poke the hornet's nest.*

Wednesday, September 23, 1970, Washington, DC. Kissinger organized a morning meeting of the NSC principals with the president to review the overnight developments. Helms reported that the three Syrian armored brigades had withdrawn from Jordan, two returning to barracks, the last one to the Syrian side of the border.

Nixon was quick to claim credit. "If the Syrians do, in fact, disengage it will be because of the strong posture taken by the United States," he told the NSC participants with some satisfaction. However, Rogers had little appetite for high-fiving. With the crisis apparently abating, he feared that since the IDF had mobilized, the Israelis would seize the opportunity to move into Jordan. He wanted Nixon to warn them not to intervene and to make clear that if they did, U.S. commitments would no longer be binding.

Rogers didn't realize Nixon had become fed up with his feud with Kissinger. The day before, he had confided to H. R. "Bob" Haldeman, his chief of staff, that he could not tolerate it any longer and that one or the other would

---

* Hagel was confirmed by a vote of 58 to 41 in the most hotly contested confirmation of a secretary of defense since the Senate declined in 1989 to confirm George H. W. Bush's nomination of Senator John Tower.

have to go. Now Rogers managed to provoke him into a defense of Israel. Nixon pointed out that it was Hussein who had requested Israeli assistance. Whatever Rogers conveyed to the Israelis needed to acknowledge that "they ha[d] acted responsibly and . . . ha[d], in effect, been responsive to a U.S. initiative," Nixon insisted. While the message should make clear that the United States no longer wanted unilateral Israeli action, it should also underscore "that we are grateful for Israeli cooperation," said Nixon.

Notwithstanding the president's explicit instructions, Rogers personally wrote a terse and abrasive message for Sisco to deliver to Rabin. Sisco, now cooperating with Kissinger, sent the draft to him for approval. Seizing an opening too good to resist, Kissinger fired off a memo to Nixon, noting the negative message and emphasizing Rogers's role in drafting it. Understanding where the president was coming from, Kissinger recommended an alternative text that expressed the U.S. government's appreciation for "the prompt and positive Israeli response to our approach," but noted that, in the changed circumstances, the previous assurances were no longer applicable. When Rogers heard about Nixon's approval of Kissinger's rewrite of his message, he rushed to the White House to confront Nixon, who was holed up in his Old Executive Office Building hideaway. Kissinger was incensed. As Haldeman noted in his diary that evening, "K built up a monumental head of steam, said he'd see this through and then had to leave, couldn't take more of this."

Nixon chose Kissinger's draft over Rogers's, and it was dutifully conveyed by Sisco to Rabin. Kissinger followed up with a phone call to convey an additional, personal message from Nixon to Meir: "The President will never forget Israel's role in preventing the deterioration in Jordan and in blocking the attempt to overthrow the regime there. . . . The United States is fortunate in having an ally like Israel in the Middle East. These events will be taken into account in all future developments."

Rabin notes in his memoirs that this was probably "the most far-reaching statement ever made by a president of the United States on the mutuality of the alliance between the two countries." Of course, by today's standards of pro-Israel rhetoric from American presidents, the statement is mild. But in those days, when Israel was still struggling to consolidate its relations with the United States, it represented a breakthrough: they were now "strategic allies." For an unsentimental general like Rabin, and for a student of history like Kissinger, that was a much sounder basis for the relationship than the shared democratic values that Israel had previously relied upon to justify American support for Israel.

Kissinger had good reason to be satisfied. Seldom do international crises end with the precise outcomes the policymaker intended. The United States had demonstrated its resolve. Nixon had pressured Moscow into securing the withdrawal of its Syrian proxy. King Hussein had preserved his throne with his authority strengthened. A wider war had been averted. Israel had proven its strategic value in maintaining stability in a volatile region of vital American interest, and the president had registered his appreciation. Even more satisfying for Kissinger, he had beaten Rogers on his home turf and brought Nixon around to adopt his geostrategic approach to the region.

Three years later, in a meeting in the Map Room with Simcha Dinitz, Rabin's successor as ambassador, Kissinger reminisced. "You remember the Jordanian crisis?" he asked nostalgically. "I've never seen so effective an example of crisis management. We worked well together."

4

A Failure of Imagination

I thought [Sadat] was a clown . . . We all used to think sending the Russians out was a dumb thing; he got nothing for it. In the whole context, it was not such a bad strategy.

—Henry Kissinger to Golda Meir, May 1974

T he 1970 Jordan crisis marked a turning point. Kissinger had won a decisive round in the bureaucratic battle he had been waging to wrest control of U.S. Middle East diplomacy from the secretary of state.* Now he and Rabin would use their Map Room conversations to consolidate a common understanding of the appropriate strategy for manipulating the new regional antagonisms the Jordan crisis had precipitated.

Six days after the Syrian tanks withdrew from Irbid, on September 28, 1970, Nasser died of a heart attack brought on by his efforts to negotiate a cease-fire between King Hussein and Yasir Arafat. This would prove highly consequential.

Nasser's vice president, Anwar Sadat, a little-known, unimpressive officer, succeeded him. Sadat had risen in the ranks of the Free Officers who toppled Egypt's King Farouk in 1952, mainly by avoiding projecting the threat generated by unbridled ambition. From humble origins in a small Nile delta village, he had quietly studied the attributes of leadership, modeling himself after Gandhi, Ataturk, and Hitler. A deeply religious man, he had been trained at Egypt's Royal Military Academy, imprisoned by the British for his anti-colonial activism, appointed by Nasser as a government minister, and named

---

* Following the denouement of the crisis, Rogers inevitably tried to promote the Jarring talks again, but he was soon thwarted by Israel's continued refusal to countenance a withdrawal to the 1967 border and Egypt's refusal to sign a peace agreement with Israel.

editor of one of the regime's newspapers before becoming president of the National Assembly and, in 1964, vice president.

When Nasser died, Sadat became Egypt's president by default. But nobody assumed he would be there for long given the much more powerful generals who aspired to the job. American intelligence assessments at the time described him "as a weak man." Elliot Richardson described him to Nixon as "Nasser's poodle" when he returned from representing the United States at the funeral. The CIA assessed his rule would last no longer than six months. The Israeli Military Intelligence Directorate's assessment, which was shared with senior American officials, including Kissinger, depicted Sadat as a dull-witted, narrow-minded opportunist, a demagogue, and a talentless boor. Kissinger viewed him with amusement. "For all we knew, he was a character out of *Aida*," he said, referring to Verdi's grand opera set in ancient Egypt.

Sadat would need time to establish and consolidate his authority. Indeed, it was not until May 1971 that he succeeded in outwitting these rival generals, dismissing and arresting them all in a bold, rapid, surprise move that would become the hallmark of Sadat's historic presidency.

In Syria, there was a new leader too. At the time of the Jordan crisis, Hafez al-Assad had been commander of the Syrian Air Force. His rival, Salah al-Jadid, deputy secretary of the Ba'ath Party, had ordered the tank brigades into Jordan in support of the Palestinian fedayeen. Assad, who had a mind like a computer capable of calculating the balance of power and drawing unsentimental conclusions, refused to commit the air force to the battle when he saw the buildup of Israeli tanks on Syria's border, forty kilometers from Damascus, and the massing of American forces in the ocean off neighboring Lebanon. Without air cover, Jadid felt obliged to order the prompt withdrawal of the Syrian tanks from Jordan.

In the aftermath of the crisis, Assad decided that Syria's deteriorating strategic circumstances required an end to the power vacuum in Damascus that had resulted from years of bitter rivalry with Jadid. In November 1970, Assad moved against him in a bloodless coup, emerging as Syria's undisputed ruler. That was vintage Assad: normally cautious and conservative, he—like Sadat—was nevertheless capable of decisive action when strategic circumstances required it.

Sadat and Assad were both Soviet clients and, in the aftermath of the Jordan crisis, that would dominate Kissinger's thinking about how to handle them. Having succeeded in gaining control over America's Middle East diplomacy, his strategy was to maintain the status quo not reach out to them. This paradox is explained by Kissinger in the first volume of his memoirs:

I was always opposed to comprehensive solutions that would be rejected by both parties and that could only serve Soviet ends by either demonstrating our impotence or being turned into a showcase of what could be exacted by Moscow's pressure. My aim was to produce a stalemate until Moscow urged compromise or until, even better, some moderate Arab regime decided that the route to progress was through Washington.

Kissinger was aided in this approach by four key partners—Rabin, Meir, Nixon, and Leonid Brezhnev, secretary-general of the Central Committee of the Communist Party of the Soviet Union. Each of them had their own reasons for aligning themselves with the maintenance of the status quo. Rabin shared Kissinger's strategic outlook and, as long as the arms kept flowing to Israel, had every reason to work with him. Indeed, Kissinger notes in the third volume of his memoirs, in recounting the subsequent acrimonious confrontation he had with Rabin during the negotiation of the Interim Agreement between Egypt and Israel in 1975 (which I deal with in detail in Part V), that when they eventually reconciled, Rabin said to him:

I have no doubt that you followed the strategy that was worked out in 1970–71, to deny the Arabs a military option and force them to a political option. We may have disagreements, but I never doubted you acted in the framework of the strategy.

Reminiscing about that period to the Israeli cabinet in May 1974, Kissinger recounted that he and Rabin had developed a joint strategy which made them "experts in wasting time."*

Meir was equally committed to this approach, but out of political rather than strategic calculations. A peace process with the Egyptians or Jordanians was bound to precipitate a coalition crisis in her government because it would lead, one way or another, to American demands that Israel retreat to the international boundary with Egypt, withdraw from most of the West Bank, and share Jerusalem with the Arabs. As long as the cease-fire held with Egypt, she had every incentive to maintain the status quo. Increasing the sense of frustration of the Soviet Union's Arab clients by ensuring a diplomatic stalemate suited her just fine.

Nixon for his part was keen to pursue a negotiated settlement in Vietnam,

---

* Further evidence of the close strategic coordination between Kissinger and Rabin came in April 1974, during a meeting between Kissinger and the Conference of Presidents of Major American Jewish Organizations, when Kissinger said to them, "Talk to Rabin; we had a deliberate strategy to create such frustration in the Arab world that they would turn against the Soviets. For five years, we worked on this." See Memcon between Kissinger, Max Fisher, et al., April 25, 1974, FRUS 1974–1976:26, Doc. 36.

the opening to China, and détente with the Soviet Union. Occasionally, he would evince interest in the idea that the two superpowers might impose a solution on the Arabs and Israelis, but that was usually in the run-up to the now annual U.S.-Soviet summits, when Brezhnev would insist they put the Middle East on the agenda. Since the Soviets were unwilling to break with their Arab clients or give the United States an opportunity to exploit disagreements between them, these moments of interest would prove ephemeral. Most of the time, Nixon's political calendar would now dominate his thinking. In mid-1971, for example, in response to an NSC memo that provided an overview of the situation in the Middle East, Nixon scrawled instructions to Kissinger to make sure the situation remained calm there until the November 1972 presidential election was over.

Brezhnev became a willing partner in this great stall because the status quo in the Middle East suited the Soviet leadership too. Moscow was in the process of consolidating its sphere of influence in the region by concluding formal friendship treaties with the three regional powers who dominated the Arab heartland: Egypt, Syria, and Iraq. After the 1967 war, U.S. influence in the Middle East had come to depend on peripheral non-Arab powers (Israel, Turkey, and Iran) and moderate but weak Arab monarchies (Saudi Arabia, Jordan, and Morocco). This division of influence served Moscow's interests.

As Kissinger had understood, any attempt to resolve the conflict would require the Soviets to compromise on the maximalist demands of their Arab clients. If they did that, they might well jeopardize their standing in the Arab world and provide an opening for the rival American superpower. On the other hand, if the Arabs went to war again with Israel, the Soviet Union might be dragged into a confrontation with the United States. For Moscow, both approaches were too risky, especially compared to the advantages of standing pat.

With these accomplices, reinforced by the intractability of the conflict itself, Kissinger would have little difficulty stalling. But doing nothing inevitably left a vacuum, which Rogers would still try to fill with some new initiative. So Kissinger had to invent new ways to impress Nixon enough to keep Rogers in the wings. As he told Rabin, "It depends on creating the illusion that something is being done while we all know in fact that nothing is being done."

For this purpose, he focused on a speech Sadat had made in February 1971, in which the new Egyptian leader, for the first time, had suggested an interim agreement involving a partial Israeli withdrawal from the Suez Canal, followed by its reopening. Kissinger had previously told Rabin that the United States did not want the Suez Canal opened because it would shorten the arms supply route from the Soviet Union to Vietnam. But now he began to contemplate the virtue of a gradual, incremental approach to resolving the Arab-Israeli conflict. Moving Egyptian and Israeli forces back from the canal would stabilize the situation; the canal could be reopened, from which both sides would benefit (assuming Egypt would allow Israeli shipping to pass through), thereby reinforcing the incentives to maintain stability; and it could "launch a process of negotiation that might ultimately lead to peace," as Kissinger would subsequently write. He had already concluded that success in resolving the Arab-Israeli conflict was only going to come in small steps, if at all.

Thus, the seed was planted in Kissinger's mind of how to conduct Arab-Israeli negotiations that stood in contrast to Rogers's quixotic efforts at a comprehensive solution. It was an idea that he would resurrect in the wake of the Yom Kippur War when he needed a more active diplomatic strategy. In the meantime, pursuing an agreement could help him stall, since it had no chance of producing a breakthrough.

Kissinger's opportunity to try his hand at this legerdemain came in July 1971. Kissinger calculated that the best way to achieve his "motion without movement" strategy was to explore his idea of a partial accord with the Soviets on the assumption that they would not be willing to moderate their position. If that were the case, he "intended to draw them into protracted and inconclusive negotiations until either they or some Arab country changed their position." The approach was reinforced when Soviet foreign minister Andrei Gromyko met Nixon in the White House in September 1971 and confirmed that this make-work activity, dubbed "exploratory discussions," would take place in the Kissinger-Dobrynin channel. Its real purpose, according to Kissinger, was "to give the Soviets an incentive to keep the Middle East calm over the next year— a strategy that would only magnify Egyptian restlessness with Soviet policy."

To maintain the illusion, Kissinger needed the Israelis to play along. This new cooperation found expression in a December 1971 White House meeting between Nixon and Meir, for whom the president had developed an unusual regard. Nixon agreed to declare the Rogers Plan "a dead letter as an operative U.S. position," meaning that he would no longer insist on Israel's withdrawal to the international border. This was a concession Meir had been seeking since Rogers had issued his plan, two years earlier. In return, she told Nixon she would be willing to consider a partial settlement in which Israel would withdraw its forces to the Gidi and Mitla Passes, the gateway to eastern Sinai, and allow Egyptian police—but not armed forces—to cross the canal. To lubricate this initiative, Israel would receive additional Phantoms and Skyhawks over the next two years. Nixon authorized Rogers and Sisco to conduct "proximity talks" between Egypt and Israel in a front channel, but "the real negotiations" would be conducted between Kissinger and Dobrynin, and Kissinger and Rabin, in the back channels. Consistent with his diplomatic style, Kissinger would also leave the door open for a third back channel with Egypt.

With the Soviet Union preoccupied with the India-Pakistan war in South Asia, the back-channel talks at first went nowhere. However, the Soviets were keen to show at the Moscow summit in May 1972 that Nixon and Brezhnev were doing something about the situation in the Middle East in the context of the formalization of the "Basic Principles" of their new era of détente. The implications for the Arab-Israeli conflict were manifest in these principles: the two superpowers declared they would do their utmost to avoid military confrontations, they recognized that efforts by either to obtain unilateral advantage at the expense of the other were inconsistent with the objective of reaching accommodation by peaceful means, and they declared their mutual support for a peaceful settlement and *military relaxation* in the Middle East. The meaning was clear to all. As Kissinger explained it, "The Soviets would not rock the boat and we would stick to our strategy of keeping the Middle East on ice."

Kissinger was intrigued by Soviet willingness to play along with his game, which was, after all, designed to drive them out of the Middle East. The way they had backed down during the Jordan crisis and were now willing to coop-erate in maintaining the status quo reinforced his assessment of the vulner-ability of the Soviet position in the Arab world. And this insight would in turn inform his approach in October 1973, when it became time to launch a serious initiative.

Kissinger's strategy seemed to be effective, but in fact he had forgotten a lesson he had taught others about nineteenth-century European history: the stability of any international system depended not just on the security of its members but also, as I noted earlier, on the degree to which they accepted the "jus-tice" and "fairness" of the existing arrangements. Kissinger failed to notice that there was one important leader in the Middle East order who was now frustrated by his sense of its injustice and unfairness.

Egypt was easily the largest and militarily most consequential state in the Arab world. But it was ruled by a leader whom the rest of the world did not take seriously. In 1971, Sadat tried to demonstrate his earnestness and sense of urgency by declaring that year to be Egypt's "year of decision." But despite his February 1971 diplomatic initiative for an interim agreement, and subsequent attempts by Rogers and Sisco to achieve diplomatic movement, Israel had only consolidated its hold on Egyptian territory. Moreover, his Soviet patron now delayed the supply of offensive weapons to the Egyptian army while shipping arms via Egypt to its Indian ally for its war with Pakistan. The year of decision had to be postponed, further undermining Sadat's credibility.

Domestically, Sadat was being driven to action by a stagnating economy and increasing social unrest. After he had arrested his rival generals, all of whom were pro-Soviet, he had to reassure Moscow by signing a Treaty of Friendship the same month, in the hope that would unlock Soviet arms supplies.

Kissinger understood these signals to be an indication of Sadat's growing impatience, but his conclusion was that American strategy had to "frustrate any Egyptian policy based on military threats and collusion with the Soviet Union." This only reinforced his determination "to slow down the process even further to demonstrate that Soviet threats and treaties could not be decisive."

Since Sadat was making no impression on Washington, he started pressing his Soviet ally. In April 1972, he met with Brezhnev in Moscow and secured Soviet agreement that his arms requests would be met after the Moscow summit but before November 1972, so that he would be able to negotiate from greater strength after the American elections. However, following the Moscow summit, with its alarming message about "military relaxation," he wrote to Brezhnev seeking reassurance about the fulfillment of the April agreement. Six weeks elapsed before the answer came. When it did, Brezhnev urged patience and emphasized the need to focus on building up morale in Egypt's armed forces. As Sadat subsequently explained to his people, if "military relaxation" took place while Israel was superior, "it would be a case of the stronger side dictating conditions to us. . . . They would say: We are staying where we are and that is all."

On July 18, 1972, Sadat responded with a dramatic but calculated move: he ordered the immediate removal from Egypt of some twenty thousand Soviet military advisers and experts. As Mohamed Hassanein Heikal, Sadat's confidant and the editor of Egypt's main state-owned daily, *Al-Ahram*, wrote at the time, "It was Egypt's responsibility to solve the problem of 'no war-no peace' by its own initiative." Whatever the superpowers might declare, Sadat intended to see to it that there would be no "military relaxation" in the Middle East unless Israel withdrew from the Egyptian territories it occupied in 1967.

Sadat's application of shock treatment to a powerful patron caught the world—including Washington and Jerusalem—by surprise. Since when does a weak power at war with its stronger neighbor bite the hand of its patron and thereby further weaken itself? As Kissinger later observed, "We grossly underestimated Sadat. . . . It never occurred to us that he might be clearing the decks for military action."

At the time, Sadat sought no short-term reward from the United States, because his focus was on Moscow. As he subsequently explained it to Kissinger, he wanted to be free of the Soviet advisers because he was concerned they would try to stop him from going to war. And he did not want them to get credit for the Egyptian army's achievements. He was also threatening the

Soviet position of influence in the Middle East to pressure them to release the arms Brezhnev had promised him. And it worked. Within six months, Moscow had reopened the arms spigot and Sadat could report to his people that he was completely satisfied with Soviet military support.*

Two years earlier, at San Clemente, Kissinger had contemplated what he would do when an Arab leader turned on his Soviet patron. "Then would come the moment for a major American initiative, if necessary urging new approaches on our Israeli friends," he recalls in his memoirs. But if the strategy of delay was working, and the Soviet position of influence in the region was eroding as a result, why change it, especially if to do so would require a painful confrontation with Israel in advance of the U.S. presidential elections? Thus, Kissinger's first reaction was to treat Sadat's expulsion decision as foolish: "If he had come to me before this had happened and told me about it, I should have felt obliged to give him something in exchange. But now I've got it all for nothing."

In fact, Sadat had tried to establish a dialogue with the White House in April 1972, four months before his eviction of the Soviet advisers. He utilized the relationship between his then intelligence chief, Ahmed Ismail, and the CIA's station chief in Cairo, Eugene Winfield Trone, to establish the communication channel. Trone was a Princeton-educated Republican; a Dulles-generation, bow-tie wearing, old-school spy. With the official cover of first secretary and consul, he worked out of the U.S. Interests Section, which was housed in the Spanish embassy, since formal diplomatic relations had been broken off by Nasser after the Six-Day War. Trone was a seasoned Arabist, having operated in Iraq, Lebanon, and Jordan in the tumultuous 1950s and '60s before being posted to Egypt in 1969. Trone conveyed Sadat's first message to Kissinger, in which the Egyptian president proposed that he secretly send an envoy to Washington. But Kissinger deliberately slow-rolled his response, taking a month to answer because "a measured pace fitted in with our strategy of creating in Egypt the maximum restlessness with the status quo." His message back to Sadat was to wait until after the Moscow summit.

On July 13, five days before Sadat's announcement of the Soviet expulsion, Trone conveyed another message to Kissinger, reiterating Sadat's desire to send a special envoy to Washington in the hope that the United States "would have something new to propose."

Any doubt about Sadat's interest in rebalancing his relationships with the

---

* High-level talks on the renewal of arms supplies began in Moscow in October 1972, resulting in the immediate supply of SA-6 missiles. They were followed by a new arms agreement signed by War Minister Ahmed Ismail in March 1973 that provided Scud missiles and anti-tank and anti-aircraft weapons. See Galia Golan, ed., *Yom Kippur and After: The Soviet Union and the Middle East Crisis* (Cambridge, UK: Cambridge University Press, 1977), 35–40.

superpowers should have been dispelled by the fact that two days after his expulsion announcement, Kissinger received yet another message from Sadat, encouraging him to come up with new ideas. In it, he expressed an interest in the very interim agreement along the Suez Canal that had intrigued Kissinger more than a year earlier, when Sadat had first publicly proposed it.

Nevertheless, Kissinger was determined to stick with his dilatory strategy. On July 29, he sent a message to Sadat inviting him to send an envoy to Washington, but to lower expectations, he noted that it would only be for "a detailed discussion of what is realistically achievable." In September 1972, Kissinger agreed to exploratory talks in strict secrecy. Sadat quickly responded by offering to send Hafez Ismail, his national security adviser, even suggesting specific dates in October. But Kissinger was preoccupied with the Vietnam negotiations, which took until January 1973, when the Paris Peace Accords were struck. Kissinger finally agreed to a February meeting with Ismail, promising that, with the Vietnam War settled, he would give the highest priority to the Middle East.

After waiting ten months for a meeting, it's unlikely that Sadat placed much store in that. And by February 1973, another consideration had entered Kissinger's calculus: Israel was scheduled to hold elections at the end of October 1973, and in the run-up to those elections, Meir had made it clear she was not interested in any discussion of withdrawal with the Arabs. The acceptance of the American cease-fire proposal in 1970 had led to the departure from her national unity government of Menachem Begin and his Gahal Party because Begin feared that the cease-fire would be followed by negotiations, which might lead to territorial concessions.* The prime minister's attitude reinforced Kissinger's approach of prolonging the stalemate to marginalize Soviet diplomacy. Even though Sisco had reported to Kissinger after his first meeting with Sadat that he had been deeply impressed by Sadat's desire for peace, his ability to put himself in the shoes of his Israeli adversary, and his flexibility on interim arrangements, Kissinger had no interest in the meeting. He told Rabin immediately beforehand, "My strategy with Ismail will be to say next to nothing, or to speak at such a level of generality that it doesn't mean anything."

The Israelis nevertheless feared that Kissinger would be seduced by the suave Egyptian envoy. In advance of the meeting, Rabin provided Kissinger with a fifteen-page dossier on Ismail prepared by the Israeli intelligence community. Its credibility had been bolstered by input from their top-level source in Cairo: Ashraf Marwan, the son-in-law of the late Gamal Abdel Nasser, who

---

* Gahal was an acronym for Gush Herut Liberal, a coalition bloc of Begin's Herut Party and the Liberal Party, headed by Yosef Sapir. In September 1973, in preparation for the upcoming elections, it morphed into the Likud, a consolidation of right-wing parties with Herut as the dominant core.

was a member of Sadat's inner circle (we shall hear more about him later). As Rabin reported to Meir after handing the file to Kissinger in a Map Room meeting: "Shaul" committed that he would not "take any position or commit himself to anything except for a philosophical discussion and a promise of continuing contacts in the future."

There was another factor behind Kissinger's complacency. By December 1972, the CIA's assessment was that "Israel's military superiority appeared unchallengeable. Sadat could not escape his dilemmas by launching an all-out military offensive since it was bound to fail." That played into Kissinger's strategy too. The expulsion of Soviet advisers had only seemed to buttress the stability of the equilibrium in the regional order that he was tending.

Ismail's meeting with Kissinger was finally set for February 25, 1973. By then, Nixon had been resoundingly reelected, winning a stunning 60.7 percent of the vote and sweeping every state except Massachusetts. With the signing of the Paris Peace Accords, Nixon had achieved the trifecta: normalization of relations with China generated by his historic visit to Beijing in 1972; détente with the Soviet Union, as evidenced in the 1972 Moscow summit; and now a peace agreement with Vietnam that would end America's troop deployments there. Kissinger's boss wanted to move on to the next big challenge, which he identified as peace in the Middle East.

Nixon viewed Kissinger's back-channel diplomacy as the best way to proceed. As he told Alexander Haig, whom he would soon appoint as his chief of staff, "We can't let State handle the Mideast; they'll screw it up." But the president's assessment of what needed to be done in Kissinger's channel had changed quite dramatically, and he continued to harbor doubts about whether his national security adviser was the man for the job. "I just can't see Henry doing it," he said to Haig. The president recounted that he had told Kissinger after the elections, "The time has now come that we've got to squeeze the old woman [Golda Meir]." He then expressed his concern that Kissinger's "blind spot" when it came to his Jewish identity had not dissipated: "He's totally attacking what the Jewish agenda wants. . . . He doesn't want to do anything with the Israelis except reassure them and get them more arms."

That was an astute appraisal of what his national security adviser was up to, though Kissinger would have been deeply upset by Nixon's suggestion that he was pursuing this strategy to serve Jewish interests rather than the American national interest. Indeed, it was the very strategy that Nixon had ordered him to pursue in the run-up to the November elections.

Nixon records in his memoirs that he "hit Henry hard" on the need to get something done in the Middle East in 1973, regardless of the upcoming Israeli elections. His view, like Kissinger's, was that an interim agreement was the only thing the Israelis would go for and that the Egyptians were simply going to have to accept it, "with the assurance that we will do the best we can to get a total settlement later." Nixon wanted Kissinger to try this approach out on Ismail.

Once more, it seemed Kissinger was going to have to shape the president's instincts to fit his strategy. He could do that only by appearing to take Ismail seriously, and by engaging the president in the process. So Kissinger arranged for Ismail to meet with Nixon before they began their deliberations. Ushering Sadat's envoy into the Oval Office would also serve the purpose of signaling to the Egyptian president that Nixon was paying attention to him, even though, as we shall see, he really wasn't.

In preparation for such Oval Office meetings, the national security adviser normally sends a briefing memo to the president together with talking points for his use. But Kissinger had developed a method that Nixon preferred: laying out three options for him to choose from. Kissinger would subsequently joke about the bureaucratic device of confronting the president with a choice between nuclear war, the present policy, or surrender, to ensure that he would choose the middle option. Kissinger knew his mark.

The first option Kissinger presented was to "stand back" and "let the two sides reflect further on their position." Nixon's vehement opposition to this "delay" option, even though he would subsequently embrace it, was evident in his response. Next to a sentence that argued for stalling until after the Israeli elections he scrawled, "K, Absolutely not. I have delayed through two elections & this year I am determined to move off dead center." Next to a sentence suggesting there was little danger in delay, he wrote with a vehement prescience: "I totally disagree. This thing is getting ready to blow."

The second option was the "interim settlement" approach the State Department was now focused on, which would leave the question of final borders for a later negotiation and would not preclude total withdrawal. By mentioning State, Kissinger knew he would evoke an immediate visceral reaction in Nixon.

The third option was to pursue privately (i.e., through Kissinger's back channel) "an understanding on the framework for an overall settlement." This would be in parallel to option two, which would be pursued more publicly. But, as Kissinger pointed out, it would depend on whether Israel could be persuaded to accept Egyptian sovereignty over "most of the Sinai" in return for security arrangements that would leave it in control at strategic points. It would also depend on whether Egypt could be persuaded to accept such qualifications on its sovereignty or, as Kissinger put it, whether the Egyptians were prepared to think pragmatically about a settlement.

Kissinger would have known that he couldn't persuade the president to take the first option, even though that was his preference. So he steered him to the third option, appealing to Nixon's fondness for back-channel negotiations and his preference for a comprehensive peace. It also ensured that the process would remain in Kissinger's hands. Not surprisingly, Nixon took the bait, noting in the margin: "The preferred track for action." But then he added a broadside at the bottom of the page: "We are now Israel's only major friend in the world. I have yet to see one iota of give on their part. . . . This is the time to get moving—and they must be told that firmly."

Friday, February 23, 1973, Washington, DC. The Oval Office meeting with Ismail was carefully choreographed. Nixon greeted Ismail without his national security adviser by his side. Kissinger entered the room only toward the end of the meeting, a ploy designed to enable him to inform Rogers and Sisco that he had been present for just a few minutes, thereby avoiding the standard protocol of inviting State Department representatives to the meeting.

Always courteous with foreign guests, Nixon went out of his way to express his high regard for the Egyptian people and his desire to normalize relations. Ismail responded in kind. Then Nixon asked the note takers to put down their pens—a tactic designed to emphasize the gravity of what he was about to say. He emphasized that the secret Kissinger-Ismail back channel would be the one he would rely on and then noted that "the big issue is between Egyptian sovereignty and Israeli security." He recommended that interim steps be considered because he did not believe it was possible to reach a full settlement all at once. Nevertheless, he recognized Ismail's concerns about the interim turning into the permanent and gave his word that his goal was an overall settlement. He recommended that Ismail discuss these issues with Dr. Kissinger and emphasized again that their conversations needed to be kept strictly private.

Secret back channels are quite common in Middle East diplomacy. Indeed, they can usually be taken as a sign of earnest intent because the participants tend to be envoys of the leaders themselves, rather than career diplomats from the foreign ministries. And their seriousness can be verified by the willingness of all sides involved to keep the existence of the channel secret from their own people as well as from the press. Indeed, it is rare for any Middle East agreement to be struck without a secret back channel laying the groundwork for it.

In 1977, for example, when Sadat wanted to test Israeli prime minister Menachem Begin's openness to full withdrawal from Sinai, he sent Deputy Prime Minister Hassan Tuhami to meet secretly with Moshe Dayan in

President Nixon meets Egyptian national security adviser Hafez Ismail in the Oval Office on February 23, 1973. Nixon told Ismail that the secret back channel with Kissinger was the one that he would rely on. Nixon introduced the idea of distinguishing between Egyptian sovereignty in Sinai and Israel's security deployments there. This meeting foreshadowed Kissinger's secret meetings with Ismail in Armonk, New York, in February 1973 and in Moulin Saint-Fargeau, Rochefort, France, in May 1973.

Morocco. Sadat's historic visit to address the Knesset in Jerusalem followed two months later.

When Peres and Rabin wanted to achieve an agreement with Yasir Arafat, they sent Uri Savir, the director general of Peres's foreign ministry, to participate in Track II meetings that were being held between Israeli academics and Palestinian officials in Oslo. No one from the prime minister's office, the defense ministry, or the foreign ministry, let alone Clinton's peace team, was aware of the official nature of those back-channel negotiations, which produced the Oslo Accords. Similarly, in 1994, Rabin negotiated the Israeli-Jordanian peace framework—known as the Washington Declaration—in a back channel with King Hussein that was kept secret from Shimon Peres, his foreign minister and partner in the pursuit of peace.

When the Iranians decided to get serious about negotiating a nuclear deal with the United States, in 2012 they sent envoys to secret meetings in Oman with Deputy Secretary of State Bill Burns and Vice President Biden's national security adviser, Jake Sullivan. This negotiation was conducted behind the backs of all the parties involved in the front-channel P5+1 talks with the Iranians, as well as Israel and America's Arab allies, who were furious when they found out just before the framework agreement was announced.

However, the existence of a secret back channel by no means guarantees a successful outcome. For that to occur, the sense of urgency needs to be reciprocated—at least by an openness and flexibility on the other side, and certainly by a common desire to reach an agreement. Otherwise, it ends up being a fishing expedition by one or both sides, to test the flexibility and seriousness of a putative negotiating partner, usually in circumstances where they have had no previous contact. And that's exactly what occurred when Kissinger met with Ismail.

Sunday, February 25, 1973, Armonk, New York. Because this meeting was being conducted behind the back of the State Department, the CIA arranged for the talks to take place in an elegant private residence in Armonk, a quiet, upscale suburb north of Manhattan.* It just happened to be adjacent to White Plains, where Nancy Maginnes, whom Kissinger was courting at the time and later married, lived.

The press referred to Ismail as "Sadat's Henry Kissinger," but he was in many ways the Laurel to Kissinger's Hardy. He was tall, lithe, and elegant in his dark, three-piece suit, with his receding hairline and thinning silver hair. His face bore the characteristics of his pharaonic ancestors: high forehead, broad nose, thick lips, and square jaw. Like much of Egypt's post-revolution elite, Ismail began his career in the army. He was trained at the British Staff College and served on the Egyptian General Staff before transitioning to under secretary in the foreign ministry. He had been ambassador to Great Britain, France, and Italy before being appointed by Sadat as his national security adviser in 1971. He was chosen for the job because he was a student of military history and a strategic thinker, like Kissinger. Sadat gave him one objective: to determine how to extract Egyptian territory from Israel's grasp.

Ismail brought four Egyptians with him to the Armonk rendezvous. Three were staffers, but the fourth was Dr. Muhammad Hafiz Ghanim, a senior official from the central committee of Egypt's ruling party, the Arab Socialist Union. Ghanim was a close political confidant of the Egyptian president; his presence signaled the seriousness with which Sadat viewed the encounter.

Kissinger, on the other hand, did not take the encounter seriously at all. His attitude is captured in the anecdote he shared with me many decades later. He recalled that at a certain point in the meeting Ismail informed him that if

---

* Mohamed Heikal records that the meeting took place at the home of Donald Kendall, the CEO of PepsiCo, in Connecticut. But the official minutes clearly show the meeting took place in Armonk. See Mohamed Heikal, *The Road to Ramadan* (London: Collins, 1975), 207.

the talks made progress, Sadat would like to invite Kissinger to Cairo to continue the conversation. Kissinger passed a note to his aide Peter Rodman in which he asked, "If that's the first prize, what's the second prize?"*

They began with an informal fireside chat in the living room. Kissinger noted Egypt's decision to expel the Soviet advisers. Ismail observed that the decision did not seem to have been recognized or reflected anywhere. Kissinger responded that it had been recognized; the question was how to reflect it. With that they adjourned to the dining room, where the two delegations sat across the table from each other. Notably missing from the American delegation was any State Department representative.

As the two delegations sat together in this suburban safe house, two hundred miles from his White House office, Kissinger repeatedly stressed the importance of keeping their meeting secret from the State Department. "The only Presidential messages that will have real weight are those I confirm in our channel," he emphasized. "As long as this process is going on, you will avoid other processes," Kissinger instructed. "Yes, I understand," Ismail responded, though it wouldn't take long for the Egyptians to break the commitment to secrecy, and for the State Department to find out about the meeting.†

Ismail then informed Kissinger that Egypt was "moving on its own," did not want the Soviet Union involved, and had told Moscow that "we don't want to talk about any paper." Kissinger's ears pricked up. "Oh really?" he responded.

For months, he had been shadowboxing with the Soviets about a joint paper that would form the basis for Arab-Israeli negotiations. Here was the first indication of what he had hoped and planned for: Egypt was evidently turning away from its Soviet patron toward the American benefactor of its Israeli adversary. Since the Israelis had been giving him a hard time about the document, he should have been happy to hear that the Egyptians were not interested in it.

Ismail did not hide that Sadat's purpose was to get the United States "to

---

* According to the protocol of the meeting, on the morning of the second day Ismail suggested that the next meeting be in Cairo: "I think it would be very important, because between now and the beginning of April we will be approaching more precise and fundamental questions and then it would be important that you come and see the President. Then you can come and see the President directly and get your answers directly that will be decided by him." See Memcon between Kissinger and Ismail, February 26, 1973, KT00682, NSA.

† Ismail briefed the Saudi intelligence chief, Kamal Adham, in detail about the meeting. He in turn briefed Joseph Greene, the head of the U.S. Interests Section in Cairo, who sent a detailed cable back to the State Department that painted Kissinger in a very negative light. This caused a crisis in relations between Kissinger and Sisco that was only resolved by bringing Sisco in to meet with the president. It also provoked a rebuke from Kissinger to Ismail, conveyed on April 11: "If tight security cannot be maintained, Dr. Kissinger will have to reconsider his own participation. Dr. Kissinger would appreciate categoric assurances on these points. Obviously, he can have no interest in discussions whose primary purpose is to establish a villain." See Back-Channel Message from Kissinger to Ismail, April 11, 1973, FRUS 1969–1976:25, Doc. 47.

deliver Israel." He accepted it would be difficult, that there would be a domestic political price to pay, but unless the United States was willing to shift from its "balance of power" approach—a gentle dig at Kissinger—and seek a just solution, a settlement would not be possible.

Kissinger was not about to abandon the approach that lay at the very heart of his Weltanschauung, so he responded by putting the monkey on Egypt's back: flexibility from Sadat was the prerequisite, he explained, because that would provide him with the means "to morally justify bringing pressure" on Israel.

Kissinger asserts in his memoirs that Sadat's basic purpose in dispatching Ismail to meet with him was to "maintain a deadlock without creating the warning of a crisis." Looking back, he claims that "Ismail presented what sounded to us like the standard Arab fare: total withdrawal to the 1967 borders with only vague assurances of Arab reciprocity." But the verbatim transcript of their ten hours of meetings over two days tells a different story.[*]

Ismail in fact demonstrated considerable interest in working with Kissinger to find a way forward. Beyond signaling that Sadat would not be influenced by Soviet calculations, he also made clear that Egypt would not wait for other Arab states to reach agreements with Israel. While the deal between Israel and Egypt was being completed, Ismail explained, "we can start the motors elsewhere for Jordan and Syria," but they could move at different speeds. That was a critically important indication of Egyptian seriousness, since maintaining Arab solidarity would have dictated that all Israel's Arab neighbors had to proceed at the same pace.[†] Kissinger would seize on it after the Yom Kippur War to negotiate Israeli-Egyptian agreements ahead of Syria and Jordan.

On the Palestinian issue, Ismail said Sadat would leave it to King Hussein to sort out the solution for the West Bank with the Palestinians; in Gaza, where Egypt had a more direct interest, it would be left to the United Nations and did not need to be part of the deal between Egypt and Israel. Moreover, if Jordan wanted to make territorial concessions to Israel or give the Israelis a corridor of control along the Jordan River, Egypt would not object. In other words, Egypt would support Jordanian flexibility in its negotiations with Israel.[‡]

---

[*] They met on Sunday, February 25, 1973, from 1:50 to 6:30 p.m. and again on Monday, February 26, from 10:25 a.m. to 3:35 p.m. See Memcon between Kissinger and Ismail, February 25, 1973, KT00681, NSA, and Memcon between Kissinger and Ismail, February 26, 1973, KT00682, NSA.
[†] To make sure Kissinger understood the significance of what Ismail was saying, Dr. Ghanim, who was a close adviser to Sadat, elaborated: "We believe it should be achieved by stages, by phases. And when we try to imagine the procedure, it can be either by *an Egyptian-Israeli peace settlement as a point of departure* or both a Jordan-Israel and Egypt-Israel settlement going together [emphasis added]." See Memcon between Kissinger and Ismail, February 25, 1973, KT00681, NSA.
[‡] Thirty years later, Secretary of State John Kerry would try to convince the Palestinian leader Mahmoud Abbas to accept the same idea of a long-term IDF corridor along the Jordan River

Jerusalem was different, Ismail explained. He introduced a principle that would be embraced by Israel and the United States at Camp David II in July 2000: "the Arab part of Jerusalem is Arab," meaning by implication that Egypt would recognize the Jewish parts of Jerusalem as Israel's. Kissinger admitted to Ismail that he had not yet developed an appreciation for the nuances of Arab-Israeli diplomacy. Perhaps that is why he made no attempt to explore these openings.*

They did discuss the idea that Nixon had raised of distinguishing between Israel's need for security and Egypt's need for sovereignty. As Dr. Ghanim, Sadat's confidant, elaborated: "We feel the basic obstacle to an Egyptian settlement is to find how to compromise, how to reconcile the needs of the security of Israel with our sovereignty over Arab land." If agreement could be reached on that, Ismail added, then it might be possible to reach agreement on some of the other elements and implement them in phases.

Kissinger seized that moment to explain that the security arrangements would need to leave an Israeli military presence in Sharm el-Sheikh (at the southern tip of the Sinai Peninsula, controlling access to the Red Sea) and at other strategic locations. Ismail responded that if the arrangements were "something reasonable . . . *we would be very open-minded about this* [emphasis added]." Kissinger suggested that the Israelis probably would push "unreasonable" security requirements. Ismail said they would consider even those. Then Kissinger sought to sum up that discussion by suggesting that the security arrangements could last until there was a full peace and then they could be eliminated. Ismail responded in the way diplomats do when they're willing to concede the other side's argument: "I can see the logic of it."

Reading the transcript of these meetings almost fifty years later, what struck me was the sense of urgency that Ismail and Ghanim expressed. Time and again they emphasized to Kissinger the need for "immediate movement" and "a quick tempo," their hope for progress "in the coming months" or "before the end of the coming year," the emphasis on "a quick and rapid solution," and the need "to move on very quickly." At the end of the first day's meeting, Ghanim wanted to make sure Kissinger had not missed that Sadat's clock was ticking. "I would like to stress the time factor once more, Dr. Kissinger," he said. "The big part of the settlement should be taken in 1973."

---

to meet a requirement of Israeli prime minister Benjamin Netanyahu. Despite the support of Jordan's King Abdullah for this concept, Abu Mazen rejected it.
* Kissinger told Ismail: "I was so ignorant of the Middle East question that when I heard someone mention the text of 242, I said I didn't think it had any operational meaning." See Henry Kissinger, *Years of Upheaval* (Boston: Little, Brown, 1982), 213–16.

Although Kissinger lacked familiarity with the ways of the Arab world, he should have recognized that Ghanim and Ismail were warning that Sadat was dissatisfied with the status quo and was clearly willing to show flexibility if Kissinger and Nixon would only launch a full-fledged initiative expeditiously. In the first day's meeting, Ismail noted ominously, "The whole situation in the area is pregnant with danger." He came back to the point in his concluding remarks in the second day's session: "We don't even exclude the possibility of a military clash. The two countries [are] under the strain of thirty months of cease-fire. . . . People sometimes get broken down by the immense pressures and demands."

The fact that Sadat was in a hurry should have alerted Kissinger to the opportunity in the offing. But since, as we have seen, he had no previous experience dealing with Middle Eastern leaders, he could not know the full import of what Sadat's envoys were saying. Authoritarian Arab leaders usually move at a much slower pace than Washington, rarely respect a deadline imposed from abroad, fear that haste will be taken as a sign of weakness, and usually want to haggle over the details. Their calculations are necessarily hard for American diplomats to divine, since they tend to keep their own counsel.

But there are moments when an Arab leader breaks the mold of anticipated behavior and acts in a surprising way. It usually occurs when he finds himself under great economic pressure and fears that his people will revolt. However, it can also occur when he feels his rule is threatened by other factors. He will then look around for a way out of the corner into which he feels circumstances are painting him.

Saddam Hussein's invasion of Kuwait in 1991 and Yasir Arafat's decision to sign the Oslo Accords in 1993 were both generated by intense economic pressures, as was Ayatollah Khamenei's decision in 2014 to endorse negotiations with the "great American Satan" to conclude a deal that would require Iran to mothball its nuclear program. Similarly, Hafez al-Assad's decision in 1999 to send his foreign minister to negotiate a peace agreement with Israeli prime minister Ehud Barak was a product of his declining health and his desire to stabilize Syria's external relations ahead of the succession of his son Bashar, whom he knew was not ready for prime time. He died six months later.

Expelling the Soviet personnel was a textbook example of the way a sense of urgency had led Sadat to do the unexpected. But it had failed to generate an American response. By the time Ismail met Kissinger, Sadat was under growing economic pressure. Workers had taken to the streets to demand bread and wages. He had promised his people action but seemed incapable of taking it. If the United States failed to move now, Ismail had warned Kissinger, the situation would not hold.

In his memorandum to the president reporting on this first meeting with Ismail, Kissinger did not miss the urgency. In fact, it was right there as the first subheading: "A. Urgency of An Overall Settlement." But he misunderstood its import. Instead of pointing out the significance of that urgency for American diplomacy, he chose to contrast it with the procedures Ismail had outlined, which he argued would take a long time to produce an agreement. Where he should have seen an opportunity, he found a contradiction.

Kissinger did provide Nixon with a summary of the main points of Ismail's approach, commenting that the flexibility Ismail had shown on security arrangements "could be quite significant." His bottom-line conclusions accentuated the positive, highlighting "new points of emphasis" that could be developed in further back-channel talks.* Nixon circled Kissinger's name on the memo and wrote, "Excellent job."

Given the promise Kissinger conveyed to Nixon at the time, it is odd that in his memoirs he presents an almost entirely negative account of the meeting. Ismail, he writes, had put forward "a polite ultimatum for terms beyond our capacity to fulfill."[†] The only hint of flexibility he conceded was Egypt's willingness to sign an agreement ahead of the other Arabs, but he immediately devalues this by noting that the other negotiations would need to be running by then and there would be no full peace until those negotiations were completed. In his recounting, Kissinger ignores the critical importance of what Ismail was conveying: Sadat was prepared to go ahead without the other Arabs. The significance of that approach would eventually become clear for all to see when Sadat signed a separate peace with Israel six years later. Kissinger himself recognized it at the time, which is why it is so odd that in his memoirs he should have turned this on its head, arguing that Ismail had proposed to give "the most intractable parties a veto," which was not what Ismail said or Sadat intended. Similarly, in his memoirs Kissinger makes no mention of Ismail's

---

* Kissinger's summary of these new points included a negotiating process that might stretch over some period; flexibility on security arrangements during the transitional period; acceptance of an interim period; a willingness to normalize relations with Israel, albeit at the end of the road; no objection to a Jordanian-Palestinian deal; and a role for the UN in resolving the Gaza Palestinian refugee issue. See Memo from Kissinger to Nixon, February 25–26, 1973, FRUS 1969–1976:25, Doc. 28.

† In the third volume of his memoirs, Kissinger also presents the Egyptian position as negative: "Ismail presented what sounded to us like the standard Arab fare: total Israeli withdrawal to the 1967 borders with only vague assurances of Arab reciprocity." See Henry Kissinger, *Years of Renewal* (New York: Touchstone, 1999), 354.

flexibility on the security arrangements, which at the time he highlighted in his memo to Nixon. Instead, he concludes that the talks "left us with little reason for optimism."

Could Kissinger's revisionist version of his encounter with Ismail be an implicit recognition that he had failed to follow his own prescription—that while "patience could be our weapon," once an Arab leader turned to the United States, we had "to move decisively to produce diplomatic progress"? Kissinger did not move decisively at that moment, not because he failed to recognize the opportunity, but rather because he became overwhelmed by a series of events that reinforced his now deeply ingrained preference for maintaining the status quo.

First came the Israeli reaction. Kissinger had transmitted a summary of the two meetings to Rabin, who was about to leave his post to launch a political career in Israel. Kissinger wanted to discuss with him the next step, which Nixon would have an opportunity to raise with Meir when she arrived in Washington a few days later. However, when Kissinger met with Rabin to prepare for Meir's visit on the day after his meetings with Ismail, Rabin was scornful. "It's the toughest Egyptian position we have ever had," he said.

When Rabin decided to be dismissive, it was an intimidating performance. I learned that firsthand after the summit meeting President Clinton held with Syria's Hafez al-Assad in Geneva in January 1994. By this stage, Assad was quite frail, suffering from congestive heart failure and diabetes. Prime Minister Rabin and a host of other Israelis had told us that if they were to take Assad seriously as a partner in peace negotiations, Clinton needed to get him to say that he was prepared for "normal, peaceful relations" with Israel (the same issue that Ismail and Kissinger had discussed twenty years earlier). In the press conference after their meeting, Assad said those magic words.

Elated, Dennis Ross and I flew directly to Israel to brief Rabin on the president's meeting. To our great surprise, Rabin was as scornful as when he had discussed the record of the Ismail meeting with Kissinger twenty-one years earlier. Assad's words on normalization were "nothing new," he told us. He turned to Uri Saguy, his director of military intelligence, and had him explain to the American novices, in a Talmudic exegesis worthy of a learned rabbi, that the Arabic words Assad had used connoted "usual" relations, not "normal" relations. (In fact, as we would later discover in the Israeli-Syrian negotiations at Shepherdstown, West Virginia, in 2000, there was no difference.) With a dismissive swing of his right arm, as if he were sweeping Assad's words off the table, he wiped the smiles off our faces.

Confronted by similar treatment, Kissinger reiterated the positive points in Ismail's presentations. When he got to the part about Egypt settling ahead of the other Arabs, Rabin responded, "That is nothing new." Kissinger had to defend himself: "It's new to me, but that doesn't make it new." When Kissinger explained Sadat's willingness to consider Israeli control of Sharm el-Sheikh, Rabin answered with words he must have known would bruise Kissinger's ego: "He said that to Sisco two years ago!"*

Exasperated, Kissinger told Rabin he would give him the full transcript, and then pivoted to Meir's upcoming visit. He warned that Nixon was looking for movement from her. "Long speeches about how the status quo is the best will not help you," he said, jabbing back at Rabin. The Israeli ambassador predictably turned the conversation to the issue of fighter jet deliveries and then summed up Israel's attitude: "Why do we need a new strategy?"

Rabin's dismissiveness in 1973, as in 1994, was generated by the same deep-seated Israeli fear that the United States, Israel's sole patron and protector, would embrace any sign of Arab moderation at Israel's expense. His concern was that American policymakers were naive and gullible, always ready to compensate Arab words of moderation with demands for tangible Israeli concessions. The only way to head off that expected pressure was to preempt it by devaluing any Arab reasonableness that American diplomacy might generate.

The same approach was adopted by Meir the next morning when she met with Kissinger. When foreign heads of government come to Washington on official visits, it is standard protocol for them to stay at Blair House, the president's guesthouse, an elegant complex of adjoining row houses situated across Pennsylvania Avenue from the White House. The national security adviser meets there with the foreign leader before the Oval Office meeting with the president to prepare the agenda.

As waiters in tuxedos and black bow ties cleared away the cream-colored, gold-rimmed breakfast porcelain with its presidential seals, Kissinger insisted that Meir show some movement on the terms for an agreement with the Egyptians when she met the president. He shared with her Nixon's view that Israeli "intransigence" was threatening Arab oil supplies and that he was growing impatient with Kissinger's "pandering" to them. The prime minister snapped. She denounced the Egyptians as plotting "to get us back to the '67 borders, then to the '47 borders, and then bring the Palestinians back, which means no more Israel."

Ignoring Kissinger's counsel to Rabin, Meir told the president in their meeting on March 1 that "we never had it so good" and dismissed the notion

---

* Contrary to his behavior at the time, Rabin would later admit in his memoirs, "Kissinger did not try to hide the fact that Ismail's statements pleased him and even I could not deny that the senior Egyptian representative had some interesting things to say." See Yigal Kipnis, *1973: The Road to War* (Washington, DC: Just World Books, 2013), 100.

that the Arabs had a military option. However, after several dispiriting meetings she had held with U.S. officials before that meeting, she worried that
Nixon would not grant Israel's arms requests and she would go home empty-
handed to an Israel that was entering election season.*

As a result, the night before her meeting with Nixon, she had agreed to
have Rabin convey to Kissinger that she was willing for him to explore with
Ismail the idea that "Israel would have to accept Egyptian sovereignty over
all of the Sinai but that Egypt, in turn, would have to accept an Israeli military presence in certain strategic positions such as Sharm el-Sheikh [emphasis
added]." That was surprisingly close to Ismail's position.

In the Oval Office meeting, she proposed that the effort with Egypt focus
on an interim agreement for disengagement from the Suez Canal. She told
Nixon that Israel would be willing to pull back to the Gidi and Mitla Passes in
the middle of the Sinai, a significantly larger withdrawal than she had previously been willing to countenance. She also said Egyptian police could cross
into the territory Israel evacuated.[†] However, she was categorical: that would
only be discussed after direct negotiations began. In the meantime, she was
willing to have Kissinger try to get agreement on some general principles in
the back channel with Ismail while Rogers and Sisco focused on the interim
agreement in front-channel talks.

The mere hint that arms deliveries might be held up had produced some
interesting Israeli flexibility. In return, not surprisingly, Meir pressed Nixon to
agree to a new schedule of delivery of thirty-six F-4 Phantoms and thirty A-4
Skyhawks over the next two years, and to assist with the production in Israel
of one hundred Kfir (supersonic Mirage) aircraft by granting GE licenses to
provide the engines. Since Meir had green-lighted Kissinger's back-channel
process with Ismail, Nixon concurred.

For one bright moment after the meeting, Kissinger and Nixon imagined
how they would proceed. Kissinger, in contrast to his own subsequent, jaundiced recollection, dared to dream: "If the Egyptians were willing to accept
fuzzy language on general principles, we'd be home free. . . . The Egyptians
are panting to get us involved, and they're willing to pay some price."

"Yeah, we've got to tell [the Israelis] we're not squeezing them, and then
squeeze 'em," said Nixon. As for the new aircraft, "We also say we weren't
linking anything, knowing damn well we will."

---

* The Israeli prime minister met with Deputy Secretary of State Kenneth Rush, followed by
Secretary of Defense Elliot Richardson, who both raised serious doubts about the need for and
timing of new aircraft sales to Israel. After these meetings she considered canceling her meeting
with Nixon and flying home.
† On this relatively minor issue, the gap was eminently closable. Ismail had spent some time
explaining to Kissinger that before 1967, there were no regular army forces in Sinai, but rather a
lightly armed "frontier force" that sounded roughly equivalent to Israel's border police.

President Nixon and Henry Kissinger meet with Israeli prime minister Golda Meir, Ambassador Yitzhak Rabin, and Meir's political secretary Simcha Dinitz in the Oval Office on March 1, 1973. Brent Scowcroft, Kissinger's deputy at the National Security Council, is on Rabin's right. Meir green-lighted a diplomatic initiative focused on an interim arrangement in the Sinai. Nixon agreed to provide Israel with thirty-six F-4 Phantom fighter jets and thirty A-4 Skyhawks. Nixon told Kissinger after the meeting, "Yeah, we've got to tell [the Israelis] we're not squeezing them, and then squeeze 'em."

A few days later, Kissinger received a report from the CIA station chief in Cairo that confirmed his assessment at the time of Egyptian tractability. Ismail had expressed his pleasure with the talks "in every respect." He promised to be more specific at the next meeting with Kissinger, which he hoped would be in April, but he wanted Kissinger to know that regarding the balance between sovereignty and security, "if Egyptian sovereignty over Sinai could be restored, practical security arrangements might be worked out."

However, Kissinger would soon discover that Meir, notwithstanding what she had offered Nixon, was not actually very flexible. On March 10, in the last meeting he would have with Rabin before the ambassador's return to Israel, Kissinger explained that Ismail's opening could result in Israel's being able to control strategic locations in Sinai for a prolonged period. But in return, "Egyptian sovereignty will remain in effect for all of Sinai." Kissinger asked him bluntly whether Israel would be willing to accept only minor changes to the international border. Rabin called Kissinger back the next day with Meir's negative response. She had pocketed the arms and gone back on her offer.

Before Kissinger had a chance to put "the squeeze" on Meir, however, an unforeseen event sabotaged the entire effort.

On March 14, in a front-page, above-the-fold story, *The New York Times* reported Nixon's provision of new, sophisticated aircraft to the Israelis. A week later, after Sadat had been roundly criticized in the Arab press for putting his faith in the Americans, Kissinger received a formal message from Ismail warning of "the gravity of the situation" and declaring that the aircraft deal would "preclude any progress towards the kind of peace hoped for."

On March 26, in a two-and-a-half-hour-long stem-winder speech before the Egyptian People's Assembly, Sadat declared the situation "very grave," saying that Egypt was entering "the stage of total confrontation." He chastised the United States for building up Israel's military superiority. He directly referenced Ismail's talks with Kissinger (so much for the secret back channel), complaining that Egypt was being asked to make further concessions while Washington was not willing to pressure Israel. And he rejected an interim agreement over the canal. However, even as he was excoriating the United States, Sadat publicly embraced the idea of balancing Egyptian sovereignty with Israel's security needs. Nevertheless, the lesson was clear: "We have to tell the world we are alive and capable of altering the status quo militarily and politically."

To make sure Kissinger got the message, on April 9, Sadat gave an exclusive interview to his favorite American journalist, *Newsweek* senior editor Arnaud de Borchgrave, who was close to the secretary of state. "Every door I have opened has been slammed in my face by Israel, with American blessings," Sadat bitterly complained. "The United States will be committing the gravest error in its history if it continues to believe we are crippled and can't take action. Everything in this country is now being mobilized . . . for the battle, which is now inevitable," he warned. And he bragged that the Russians "are providing us now with everything that's possible for them to supply."

With a sense of alarm, de Borchgrave called Kissinger as soon as he returned to Washington and asked urgently for a meeting. They had lunch at the Metropolitan Club, the dignified redoubt of the Washington establishment, situated two blocks from the White House. De Borchgrave recounted Sadat's unmistakable warning of war. According to de Borchgrave, Kissinger responded that he wasn't sure whether there would be a war, but if it happened, "we shall restore some equilibrium between the Arabs and Israelis, which is essential for a peace process." Rather than act to prevent it, Kissinger already seemed to be contemplating what he would do if Sadat made good on his threat of war.

There were several reasons for Kissinger's apparent indifference. One was the increasing concern in the White House over Watergate. The same day that *The New York Times* broke the story of the fighter aircraft sales to Israel, White House Counsel John Dean was summoned to appear before the Senate

Judiciary Committee; Dean had begun to cooperate with Watergate investigators. Nixon was increasingly distracted. He no longer had time to press Kissinger to pursue Middle East peacemaking.

In addition, the State Department had finally accepted reality and given up on its efforts to jump-start Egyptian-Israeli negotiations, at least for the time being. When Kissinger arranged for Sisco to meet with Nixon on April 13, to effect a reconciliation after the State Department erupted over the discovery of Kissinger's secret back-channel negotiations with Ismail, Sisco told Nixon that he now understood Henry was "bulwarking the ceasefire" and that he believed it could work for another eight months, until after the Israeli elections. As for Sadat's threats, Sisco told Nixon, "[Sadat] knows that if he exercises the military option, he's going to get clobbered." The new director of intelligence, James Schlesinger, told Kissinger that was the CIA's assessment as well.[*]

There was one more consideration: relations between the White House and the American Jewish community had at this point become badly strained by the dispute over Soviet Jewry. Kissinger and Nixon believed that cooperation with the Kremlin was the best way to secure the release of the hundreds of thousands of Jews who were being repressed in the Soviet Union. American Jews, spurred on by Senator Henry "Scoop" Jackson, believed the better way was to press Moscow to open the gates by leveraging the most-favored-nation trading status Nixon had promised Brezhnev. With another superpower summit looming in May, Nixon and Kissinger could not afford a diplomatic confrontation with Israel that might provoke even stronger opposition to the détente with the Soviet Union they were promoting. Indeed, Kissinger had already sought the help of the new Israeli ambassador, Simcha Dinitz, in calming down the American Jewish leadership.

Kissinger quietly shelved his idea of a back-channel negotiation. On April 11, he had his first meeting with Dinitz, a jovial, round-faced Israeli with a pencil mustache, thinning hair, and a Jewish joke for every occasion. The one he liked to tell about Kissinger was how he responded when Kissinger complained about all the demands the Israelis were making of him. Dinitz pointed out that Hebrew is not a requesting language, noting that Moses had descended from Mount Sinai with ten commandments, not ten requests. Kissinger responded that the trouble with Dinitz was that he thought he was Moses. Dinitz parried, "The trouble with you is that you think you are God!"

Dinitz was more than familiar with Kissinger's methodology. He had worked for Rabin as his minister of information at the embassy before return-

* Schlesinger wrote Kissinger that "given the weak Egyptian military capability against Israel, any military move by Sadat would be an act of desperation. We see no evidence that he is that desperate at present." See Memo from CIA Director to Kissinger, April 16, 1973, FRUS 1969–1976:25, Doc. 50.

ing to Israel to become political secretary to the prime minister, a post he had previously held in Meir's office when she was foreign minister. There was no one closer to her. He captures the mood of the time in his unpublished memoirs: "I left an overconfident Israel and arrived in a troubled America."

Kissinger summoned Dinitz to this first meeting in the Map Room even before he had presented his credentials to the president, signaling to the new Israeli ambassador that he intended to continue the tradition he had started with Rabin. He also explained that he was following the strategy agreed on with Rabin: "We are pushing nothing, we are wasting time. . . . I will take no initiatives. I will react in a slow-moving way. . . . I am not aiming at a Nobel Prize on the Middle East."

President George W. Bush used similar words with me in March 2001 when I talked to him in the Oval Office after his first meeting with Prime Minister Ariel Sharon. I was still the U.S. ambassador to Israel, kept on by Bush to help deal with the intifada that was raging at the time, and he wanted to explain to me why he wasn't going to take a peace initiative in the early days of his presidency: "There's nothing to be done because Arafat already rejected an offer that Sharon is not going to repeat. There's no Nobel Peace Prize to be had here."

Kissinger was not quite as blasé. "Just because it looks easy," Kissinger warned Dinitz, "does not mean it can be done indefinitely." He noted that he had been stringing the Russians and Egyptians along for months. "I can do it another month or two. . . . But then two things could happen," he remarked prophetically. "The Soviets could put tremendous pressure, or the Egyptians could start a war."

Dinitz dismissed Sadat's March 26 warning as "threats with an empty gun," an attempt to pressure the United States to pressure Israel. He noted that Israel's intelligence assessment was that Sadat had no prospect of going to war and had made no concrete preparations for it. That would turn out to be a gross underestimation, but it was one Kissinger and the U.S. intelligence community shared, in part because they had been informed that Israel had a highly placed agent in Sadat's inner circle and therefore would know whether his threats needed to be taken seriously.

Kissinger did warn Dinitz not to be complacent. Concerned about his upcoming second meeting with Ismail, which had now been scheduled for May, he urged the Israeli ambassador to give him something that could "gain more time." When Dinitz reported Kissinger's plea to Meir, however, her response was categorical. She instructed Dinitz to tell "Shaul" that she would not accept sovereignty in return for security and there would have to be substantial changes to the border with Egypt.

It was too late anyway. Sadat was already onto Kissinger's game. He needed to show his people—and the Israelis—that he could liberate Egyptian territory, and he no longer believed that diplomacy alone would achieve that outcome. On April 5, after he had given the *Newsweek* interview to de Borchgrave but before it was published, he secured a commitment from Qaddafi to transfer one of his newly minted Mirage jet squadrons to Egypt. Then he convoked a secret meeting with his ministers and requested approval for military action against Israel. As he told de Borchgrave, "The time has come for a shock." But Sadat had added something in that interview that was surely directed at Kissinger: "Diplomacy will continue before, during, and after the battle."

Sunday, May 20, 1973, Moulin Saint-Fargeau, Rochefort, France. The rendezvous with Ismail took place in a country villa owned by an American businessman in a small town on the outskirts of Paris. Kissinger described it as a French provincial farmhouse, with beamed ceilings, a rustic quaintness, and an extensive garden complete with waterfall. As for the first meeting in Armonk, New York, the CIA's Eugene Trone made all the arrangements.

By this time, Nixon's Watergate troubles had deepened. By the end of April, his chief of staff H. R. Haldeman, his adviser on domestic affairs John Ehrlichman, and his attorney general Richard Kleindienst had all resigned, and John Dean had been fired after providing damning testimony. Now Nixon's longtime political adviser and presidential campaign manager, Attorney General John Mitchell, had been indicted for influence peddling and had been forced to resign. Three days before Kissinger and Ismail's meeting, the Senate Watergate hearings opened, enthralling Americans as they revealed one shocking aspect of the cover-up after another. The appointment of the Watergate special prosecutor, Archibald Cox, was announced on the Friday before the meeting in France, and three days after, Nixon issued a statement admitting he had ordered a "wide-ranging" cover-up of the Watergate affair.

Kissinger had his own problems too. As he was en route to Paris, *The New York Times* revealed that he had been personally responsible for requesting the wiretapping of his own aides, including Helmut Sonnenfeldt, one of his closest advisers on the National Security Council. An unnamed source was quoted as explaining that Kissinger did it only to clear Sonnenfeldt of suspicion of leaking, since he was so brilliant that "in a very innocent way, a man like that can let things slip." Sonnenfeldt never forgave him.

Kissinger had actually come to Paris to engage Le Duc Tho, North Vietnam's chief negotiator, in an effort to shore up the cease-fire agreement they had signed four months earlier, which was being observed in the breach by both sides. In what became known as the War of the Flags, the North Vietnamese army and the army of the Republic of Vietnam had engaged in an effort to grab as much territory as possible. Within three weeks of Kissinger's declaring that peace was "at hand," there were already three thousand violations of the cease-fire. The meeting with his Egyptian counterpart in the French countryside may have been a welcome respite from dealing with the North Vietnamese, whom he had come to regard as "loathsome," but it was a distraction from his more urgent task.

The Egyptian and American delegations were different this time. As an indication that Sadat no longer placed much store in the meeting, his political adviser Dr. Ghanim was absent, replaced by a lesser official from the president's office. On this occasion the State Department was allowed into the room, represented by Alfred "Roy" Atherton Jr., Joe Sisco's genteel deputy.

Kissinger and Ismail met for only five hours. In an indication that they had no reason to continue the talks, they did not meet for a second day, even though Kissinger's schedule allowed for it. They quickly agreed that their only objective was to continue the conversation, and Ismail made a point of wanting to keep the channel open "in any circumstances." Kissinger brought up the talk of war emanating from Cairo and expressed his desire to "insulate this channel from whatever other measure you may plan to take," an indication that he did not dismiss the possibility of war and may indeed have been expecting it.

Ismail observed that the White House was still hesitating to put its weight behind the negotiations and the Israelis were not interested in a solution. This, he explained, left Egypt with the choice of an interim settlement that would in fact become the final settlement, or a final settlement that would require enormous Egyptian concessions. Since Egypt could accept neither, it was left, he argued, with accepting the status quo or going to war.

Ismail had come with a portfolio of grievances. Kissinger had nothing to offer him except explanations. He provided a lengthy exegesis on his own challenges: congressional opposition to détente with the Soviet Union, the preference of the Israelis for the status quo, and the Israeli elections in October. He did not mention Watergate. He then tried on his idea of an agreement that would be vague and ambiguous like UNSC Resolution 242. Ismail countered by suggesting a new UNSC resolution that would remove the ambiguities in that resolution.[*]

* The Egyptians formulated this resolution, took it to the UN Security Council in July, and gained the support of all the members of the council except the United States, which vetoed it. This confirmed Sadat's view that he could expect nothing from Washington unless he shook up

Demurring, Kissinger tried to persuade Ismail that the best way for Egypt to realize its ambition for an active American role was not through the Security Council, where the United States would have to defend Israel, but rather through a negotiation, where the United States could separate from Israel on specific issues. In such a setting, he indicated that American support for Egyptian conceptions "would be considerable" since America had "no interest in bringing about a change of frontier" in Sinai. Once the process of withdrawal began, the United States could use its influence to ensure its continuation, he assured Ismail.

Kissinger was in effect previewing the American-led diplomatic effort he would pursue in the wake of the war. His remarks to Ismail were indicative of how his exposure to the dynamics of Middle East diplomacy had now generated a negotiating strategy: movement toward full withdrawal in stages. And Ismail made clear in this meeting that Sadat was open to it. What Kissinger did not seem to realize, however, was that Sadat had now decided he could not enter that process until he had altered Kissinger's conviction that the status quo was preferable to a serious American engagement, at least until after the Israeli elections.

For now, Kissinger understood that war would destroy his time-buying efforts, so he warned Ismail against an Egyptian resort to military action. He argued that any war would "not bring about a change of physical control, and Egypt's situation would only worsen." This assessment revealed Kissinger's unfamiliarity with Egypt's newfound capacity to protect its forces with Soviet-supplied SAMs. He had watched them being emplaced by the Soviet Union on the west bank of the canal under the cover of the cease-fire the United States had negotiated back in 1970. But like the Israelis, he had failed to imagine the consequences.

Kissinger then resorted to a diplomatic maneuver he had used with some success in his negotiations with Le Duc Tho. After lunch, he took Ismail for a walk in the garden.

Such informal, off-the-record discussions can often be used effectively by diplomats to explore the flexibility of the other side or to convey a message too sensitive to be part of the official record of a meeting. Dealing with Libya as

---

the status quo. In his memoir, Ismail recounts Sadat's instructions, relayed to him on the eve of his departure for Paris, to seek an agreement with Kissinger on a UNSC resolution: "Our decision to present the issue to the Security Council is meant to pressure the United States, giving it a card to play in pushing Israel to change its position. Egypt is asking the United States to not veto the council's discussion and decision on the issue." See Mohammed Hafez Ismail, *Amn Miṣr al-qawmī fī 'aṣr al-taḥaddiyāt [Egyptian National Security in an Era of Challenges]* (Cairo: Ahram Center for Translation and Publishing, 1987), 273.

assistant secretary of state for Near Eastern affairs, I was tasked with opening a secret channel of negotiations with Muammar Qaddafi's chief of intelligence, Mussa Kussa, to secure cooperation over the prosecution of the Libyan perpetrators of the Pan Am flight 103 bombing and compensation for the families of the victims. Between the formal negotiating sessions, Mussa Kussa and I took a walk in the garden of the Lake Geneva villa provided by our host, Prince Bandar bin Sultan, then the Saudi ambassador to the United States. I complained to Kussa about the latest anti-American verbal broadside from Qaddafi. He told me that we should expect Qaddafi to continue to criticize us publicly, but he urged me to ignore it. Qaddafi, he said, had decided to normalize relations with the United States, and his advisers would "put our arms around him" to make sure he stayed true to that commitment. And Qaddafi did, surrendering the accused Libyans to the Scottish court, paying $1.5 billion to the families, and eventually relinquishing Libya's clandestine nuclear program.

Kissinger's walk in the garden with Ismail proved less productive. Despite the spring sunshine, the chirping birds, and the bursting colors of the flowers, Kissinger later recorded that Ismail conveyed only a sense of dread. Intriguingly, however, he also reminded Kissinger that Egypt would be willing to move ahead of Syria in any negotiation. Sadat and Syria's Hafez al-Assad at that moment were beginning to coordinate their plans for a surprise attack on Israel. Perhaps Ismail wanted Kissinger to remember, once the war broke out, that Egypt did not intend to stay in lockstep with Syria for long, which is what indeed transpired.

According to Trone, after bidding farewell to Kissinger, Ismail went back outside. Trone found him sitting by a stream beyond the garden, visibly shaken. Ismail told his CIA confidant that Kissinger had explained to him, "If you want us to intervene with Israel, you'll have to create a crisis. We only deal in crisis management." Ismail, according to Trone, had concluded that Kissinger wanted Egypt to start a war with Israel. Trone reported that he left the distraught Egyptian weeping.

Whatever unrecorded words were spoken, both Ismail and Kissinger understood that the game had run its course. They referred to the possibility of meeting again in June or July, but without any enthusiasm.* In his debrief to Dinitz, Kissinger observed, "This whole exercise is barren, and nothing can come of it."

The indications of war had already been mounting. At the beginning of May, Sadat had moved troops, artillery, and bridging equipment up to the canal,

---

* An attempt was made to set up a meeting in Spain in early September, but it never happened.

placed his army on high alert, and welcomed the arrival of two squadrons of aircraft from Libya and Iraq. Within a few days, Sadat ordered his forces to stand down, but the warning was unmistakable. Instead of heeding it, the Israelis, who had undertaken a partial mobilization in response, concluded that it was just another bluff and sent a message to Washington reinforcing the prevailing conception that Sadat wouldn't dare attack.

A few days before Kissinger's meeting with Ismail, King Hussein sent a message to the White House warning that the Egyptians might initiate action against the Israelis soon. Immediately after his meeting with Ismail, Kissinger received a memo from Ray Cline, who headed the State Department's Bureau of Intelligence and Research, providing his assessment "that the resumption of hostilities by autumn" would "become a better than even bet," unless there was a major, credible peace initiative.

Cline's memo, with its prediction that Sadat's purpose in going to war would be to shake up the status quo and force the superpowers to intervene, proved to be amazingly prescient.* His assessment was buttressed a few days later, when yet another message came in from King Hussein, warning that "the situation grows steadily worse and the eruption on a military basis appears to be *most imminent* [emphasis added]."

These portents led Kissinger to contemplate how to approach the issue at the Nixon-Brezhnev summit that would take place on June 22–23 in Washington and then at San Clemente. He explained to Nixon that Sadat was waiting to see whether the superpowers could produce pressure for an Israeli commitment to full withdrawal, but if there was no acceptable diplomatic movement, then "Sadat continues to hold out the resumption of hostilities as his only choice." Nonetheless, Kissinger's recommendation to Nixon was standard fare: he should reach agreement with Brezhnev on a general statement of principles that he thought could buy another year.

To prepare for that approach, he checked his draft with the Israelis to see what flexibility they might allow him. Dinitz came back with a clear-cut message from Meir: "You should know that Israel can only live with a paper that leaves us room for negotiations on substantial changes in borders—not on the basis of no changes or only minor rectifications." In other words, as Kissinger noted to Dinitz, "You would prefer no document, and the only document we can use is something you will be against."

---

* Cline wrote: "Although [Sadat] has no illusions that Egypt can defeat Israel militarily, he seems on the verge of concluding that only limited hostilities against Israel stand any real chance of breaking the negotiating stalemate by forcing the big powers to intervene with an imposed solution. . . . From Sadat's point of view, the overriding desideratum is some form of military action which can be sustained long enough, despite Israel's counterattacks, both to activate Washington and Moscow and to galvanize the other Arab states, especially the major oil producers, into anti-American moves." See Editorial Note, undated, FRUS 1969–1976:25, Doc. 68.

Brezhnev's behavior at the summit should have been taken as another warning. Six weeks earlier, in the preparatory meeting at Brezhnev's hunting lodge in Zavidovo, he had repeatedly warned Kissinger that war might break out during, or shortly after, his visit to the United States. But he had apparently forgotten to raise the issue with Nixon during their several days of conversation—an indication of just how low a priority it had become for both leaders. Then, in a surreal development at San Clemente on the last night of the summit, after all had retired, Brezhnev demanded to discuss the Middle East. The Secret Service had to rouse the president and his national security adviser from their beds for this late-night gathering, which took place in Nixon's study.

Brezhnev warned Nixon, "If there is no clarity about the principles, we will have difficulty keeping the military situation from flaring up." Nixon would later remember the urgency of Brezhnev's message: "Unless the Israelis do withdraw, the Egyptians and Syrians are going to attack, and they are going to do it soon."* The Soviet leader clearly had a sense of what was just beyond the horizon in the Middle East and at least wanted to be on record that he had warned his American counterparts. However, the proposal he pressed on them—a joint effort to impose full withdrawal on Israel—was a non-starter.

At the time, Nixon was too burdened by the deepening Watergate crisis to worry about a developing crisis in the Middle East. And Kissinger simply took the bizarre performance as an indication that Brezhnev recognized "that our ally [Israel] was militarily stronger and we held the diplomatic keys to a settlement."

When Secretary of State Rogers informed Nixon and Kissinger two weeks later of his intention to launch a new initiative to promote secret Israeli-Egyptian talks in Washington, Nixon had Haig turn it off immediately. Instead, Kissinger continued to pursue his desultory attempt to reach agreement with the Soviets on a statement of general principles. He told Dinitz on July 3, "We must give the illusion of movement and avoid a showdown." But even that was too much for Meir. She instructed Dinitz to tell "Shaul" that she wanted him to "disengage from this document," because it was essential that there be no statement of principles before Israel's elections.

Sadat now understood that his threat of war had become "inoperative" because the superpowers were treating Egypt and the Arabs "as still corpses." In August he concluded an agreement with Assad on a coordinated two-front

---

* In a letter Ray Cline wrote to Kissinger after the 1973 war reminding him of the May 31 warning he had sounded, Cline also noted that "our calculations would have crystallized earlier . . . if we had known about the exchanges you were having with the Russians. In retrospect, the evidence of Russian concern appears to have been the missing element in the picture." See Ray Cline, "Policy Without Intelligence," *Foreign Policy* 17 (Winter 1974–1975): 132.

surprise attack on Israel, and one with Saudi Arabia's King Faisal to finance Egypt's arms purchases and deploy the kingdom's oil resources in support of the war effort. By then the Soviet Union had provided Sadat with all the weapons he needed for the limited assault across the canal that he had now decided upon.

By September, getting nowhere with the Soviets on his general statement of principles, Kissinger began to feel uneasy about the way his "motion without movement" approach was beginning to lose all credibility. He decided to deploy his good friend Ardeshir Zahedi, the shah of Iran's ambassador in Washington. Zahedi met with Ismail in Geneva to test again Sadat's willingness to accept Kissinger's "step-by-step" approach. Zahedi returned with a positive response. However, Israel would have to accept the principle of full withdrawal from Sinai up front. That was something Kissinger already knew he could not convince Meir to do in advance of the Israeli elections, which were now scheduled for October 30. So he reverted to his other tactic of encouraging the Israelis to take their own initiative to create the impression of movement.

On September 10, he reminded Dinitz of the way he had inundated Le Duc Tho with five American papers in rapid succession that would have shown that if negotiations broke down it would have been because of Hanoi's intransigence. An Israeli initiative could work the same way, dramatizing the extremism of Arab demands. To emphasize that his objectives were minimal, he reminded Dinitz, "I'm not interested in the Nobel Peace Prize. . . . My strategy is to exhaust the Arabs." He pleaded with Dinitz to explain to Meir that "in a reasonable period after elections, we will have to respond to the question of how to continue the game without giving up any card which is vital to us."*

On September 28, eight days before the outbreak of war, Nixon and Kissinger were warned again by Soviet foreign minister Gromyko of the need to make a serious effort to find a solution. "We could all wake up one day and find there is a real conflagration in that area," he told them on a visit to Washington. Kissinger's advisers did not believe there was that much risk. As the Syrians and Egyptians began to deploy their troops in preparation for launching war and Moscow began to evacuate dependents from Cairo and Damascus, Ray Cline, who had warned back in May that by now there would be a better than even chance that Sadat would resort to war, assessed that "the political climate in the Arab states argues against a major Syrian military move against Israel at this time." And the defense attaché at the U.S. embassy in Tel Aviv

---

* On September 30, Dinitz came back with Meir's response: she would be willing to come to Washington in January 1974 to develop the new "common strategy" that Kissinger was proposing. See Cable from Dinitz to Meir, September 30, 1973, A-2/4996, ISA.

reported that "Israelis do not perceive a threat at this time from either Syria or Egypt." Five days later the Yom Kippur War broke out.

The Middle East equilibrium that Kissinger had worked so assiduously to maintain had suddenly, dramatically broken down. What went wrong? In his almost five years as Nixon's national security adviser, Kissinger had certainly mastered the art of Middle East diplomacy. He had set a clear long-term goal: expulsion of the Soviet Union from the Middle East. He had developed a seemingly effective strategy: promoting and utilizing Israel's military superiority combined with his own foot-dragging to heighten Egyptian frustration and the Soviet dilemma. He had used the Jordan crisis to persuade Nixon to view Israel as a strategic ally. He had prevailed in the bureaucratic battles with Rogers and systematically overcome the president's reservations about his ability to do the job in the Middle East. And he had effectively utilized diplomatic back channels to achieve his multiple purposes.

Yet in the end, Kissinger's practice of diplomacy in the Middle East failed to achieve either progress toward peace or the avoidance of war. He was unwilling to use the trust he had generated with Israel to persuade Meir to show greater flexibility. When he eventually extracted that flexibility from both sides, he was unwilling to follow through. He appears to have become so single-minded about maintaining the status quo that when Egypt turned away from the Soviet Union, he failed to take advantage of the opportunity he had explicitly called for and his strategy had helped generate.

It was a failure to recognize that, in his own way, Sadat was similar to the "revolutionary" Kissinger had written about in an essay on Bismarck five years before. Just as in the nineteenth-century European order, so too in the Middle Eastern order of the 1970s one actor could not tolerate a status quo that left his territory in his adversary's hands while the dominant power tilted the balance in his enemy's favor. Having exhausted the other possibilities, the revolutionary leader—in this case Sadat—decided to disrupt the order.

Above all, it was a failure of imagination. As a student of history, Kissinger had well understood and articulated the "tragic aspect of policymaking which lies precisely in its unavoidable component of conjecture," which he defined as "the need to gear actions to an assessment that cannot be proved true when it is made." He geared his own actions to an assessment that Sadat, whom he viewed as "a buffoon," could not resort to force, and if he did, he would find himself worse off. That was the prevailing wisdom in Jerusalem and Washington, reinforced by repeated intelligence assessments from the CIA, the Mossad, the Israeli Military Intelligence Directorate, and, with one exception, the State Department's Bureau of Intelligence and Research.

In embracing that assessment, however, Kissinger overlooked his own insight, "that the philosophical assumptions that one makes about the nature of reality, the nature of historical trends that one is facing" were bound to determine the practice of his diplomacy. He was too quick to accept the assumption that in the Middle East reality he encountered from the White House, a fundamental disruption of the status quo was not possible.

Kissinger treated Sadat like the nineteenth-century Austrian emperor treated Bismarck's revolutionary impulses as "overstating his case for bargaining purposes." Kissinger overlooked his earlier insight that "revolutionaries always start from a position of inferior physical strength; their victories are primarily triumphs of conception or of will." He misunderstood Sadat's psychological mindset and underestimated his ability to conceive of and execute a strategy that would completely upend Kissinger's own. Accordingly, he concluded that he only needed to adopt a strategy designed to maintain the prevailing order. He became so wedded to this construct that he missed the alarm bells Sadat and the Soviets rang loudly in his ear before Sadat set the house on fire. As Kissinger wrote in 1963:

> Each political leader has the choice between making the assessment which requires the least effort or making an assessment which requires more effort. If he makes the assessment that requires least effort, then as time goes on it may turn out he was wrong and then he will have to pay a heavy price.

Kissinger consciously chose an assessment of the situation that required the least effort on the part of American policymakers. Or did he? As we have seen, there were several indications that Kissinger recognized the potential for Sadat to go to war to disrupt the status quo. But he seems to have viewed this prospect with equanimity, and to assume that if there was a heavy price to pay, the United States would not be the one to pay it. As he told Arnaud de Borchgrave, only a war could disturb the equilibrium he had cultivated, but if it did, it would advantage the peacemaking that he was in any case intending to pursue after the upcoming Israeli elections. In a postwar conversation with Meir in May 1974, Kissinger admitted that a year earlier it had been possible to prevent war. He recounted his meetings with Ismail, joking about how he had toyed with him. He remembered how Ismail had warned him several times that if there were no diplomatic agreement there would be war. While he had kept a straight face, Kissinger told Meir he was laughing inside.

In a late-night reflective conversation with Syria's Hafez al-Assad in February 1974, Kissinger made a similar acknowledgment when Assad asked about his negotiations with Ismail. He told Assad he had been planning to launch a diplomatic initiative after the Israeli elections, "but it would have failed," he predicted. "I would have to say that military actions were necessary. I did not recommend them but . . ." His voice trailed off. He explained that success required the Arabs to have restored their dignity and the Israelis to have suffered a military setback. He told Assad, just as he was reported to have told Ismail in the garden at Moulin Saint-Fargeau, that only war would trigger an effective American diplomatic initiative.

This suggests that Kissinger was not so much oblivious to the warnings of war as he was willing to risk that outcome. He had done such a good job of maintaining the equilibrium that he had become wedded to it. His diplomacy was designed to avert war, but if it came anyway, he had calculated that the war would benefit his diplomacy. He would win either way. As he told President Gerald Ford, when he gave him his first Middle East briefing, "We didn't expect the October War." But wasn't it helpful? the new president asked. "We couldn't have done better if we had set the scenario," said Kissinger.

Kissinger knew from his study of history that the scope for diplomacy is greatest in a revolutionary period. Then "the old order is obviously disintegrating while the shape of its replacement is highly uncertain," he wrote in a 1966 essay. "Everything depends, therefore, on some conception of the future." Sadat's decision to go to war in October 1973 would force the disintegration of an order maintained by Israel's strength. But Kissinger was ready with his conception of a new order that would require an activist American diplomacy designed to overcome the intractability of the conflict and move the region toward peace.

Over the previous five years, Kissinger had developed that conception of the future based on a step-by-step form of diplomacy in which the first step would involve an Israeli withdrawal from the Suez Canal. He already knew that both Meir and Sadat were willing to accept his approach. The war he had not expected at that moment would now provide him with the opportunity to manipulate the antagonisms it would unleash to begin the construction of what he intended to be a new, more stable American-led order in the Middle East.

PART II

War and Peacemaking

5

Resupply

The test of a statesman, then, is his ability to recognize the real relationship of forces and to make his knowledge serve his ends.

—Henry Kissinger, *A World Restored*

The war that erupted on October 6, 1973, marked a profound turning point in the history of the region. It introduced an era of American-led peacemaking that had a transformational impact on the nature and dimensions of the Arab-Israeli conflict. It is a great irony that it would take a war in the Middle East to make peace, but that was Sadat's intention and Kissinger understood it. He sprang into action the moment he learned of the war's outbreak, recognizing immediately, instinctively, that it had created a plastic moment he could use to mold a new reality.

He had certainly received multiple warnings that war was imminent, but the U.S. intelligence community had told him not to worry. When Joe Sisco barged into Kissinger's Waldorf Astoria suite and informed his new boss of the war's onset, early in the morning of October 6, Kissinger was therefore surprised. But he was also well-prepared. His diplomacy had failed to prevent the war, but now he would make a prodigious effort to end it as quickly as possible—on terms that maximized America's role and leverage in the postwar diplomatic effort to make peace.

From the outset, Kissinger was engaged in a complex game of multilevel chess involving multiple objectives: to end the war quickly but in a way that facilitated peace negotiations, with the United States as the sole broker; to encourage Sadat's turn away from Moscow toward Washington, even though the United States was providing Israel the means to defeat the Egyptian army; to maintain détente with the Soviet Union, even though Moscow had been complicit in the war's outbreak; to prevent America's client, Israel, from being defeated by Soviet arms but also to prevent an Egyptian military humiliation that would have made it too weak to negotiate; to make Israel more pliant to American will but not so weak that it could not negotiate from a position of strength; and to counter the widespread perception that Nixon's Watergate troubles had crippled his administration's ability to conduct an effective foreign policy.

Kissinger had several sources of leverage at his disposal to achieve these outcomes. The United States was the most influential outside power because of its superpower status, its détente with the Soviet Union, its special influence with Israel, and its potential relationship with Egypt. Wielding that influence diplomatically would be critical to the achievement of a cease-fire and to the peace negotiations that Kissinger, and Nixon, were determined would follow. Wielding that influence militarily, by the alerting and deployment of U.S. forces, had proven important in the successful resolution of the 1970 Jordan crisis that would now serve as a template for this crisis.

Another source of leverage, as Kissinger had learned from dealing with Israel's arms requests, was the resupply of materiel to the IDF. That issue would take on great urgency because of the success of the Arabs' surprise attacks. A related source of leverage was Israel's military capabilities. Just as the threat of Israeli force had been essential to the maintenance of the old prewar equilibrium, the use of Israeli force would now become critical to his efforts to establish a new equilibrium. However, if Kissinger calibrated arms supplies to Israel to constrain its battlefield behavior, how could he expect to use Israeli force to back up his diplomacy? Modulating the decisions of an independent state facing an existential crisis would prove to be a complicated undertaking, as we shall see.

Kissinger utilized multiple channels of communication simultaneously: to Meir through Simcha Dinitz in Washington; to Sadat through Hafez Ismail in Cairo; to Brezhnev through Anatoly Dobrynin in Washington; and to Nixon through Alexander Haig, the newly appointed White House chief of staff. To coordinate the national security bureaucracy, Kissinger convened the WSAG—the Washington Special Action Group—usually once a day during the crisis, occasionally three times a day. And, in between, he was in daily touch with the president, Haig, Scowcroft, James Schlesinger (now the defense secretary), and a bevy of complaining senators. He even found a moment to flirt with Liza Minnelli. Amid it all, he was awarded the Nobel Peace Prize for his role in ending the war in Vietnam, which he learned about during one of the WSAG meetings.

His phone logs and meeting notes reveal a diplomat in perpetual motion. His adrenaline must have been constantly pumping, since he seems to have slept little during those two weeks. The strain showed in the unleashing of his legendary temper when his subordinates, or at one point even the president, tripped him up or slowed him down. But he mostly maintained his sense of humor, although at times self-deprecation gave way to self-praise, so proud was Professor Kissinger of the way Secretary of State Kissinger managed this crisis.

He took full advantage of the fact that Nixon was preoccupied with his Watergate woes. That enabled him to function in the president's place for most of the time, freeing up the energy he would normally have had to put into flattering and maneuvering his commander in chief. His ability to focus his talents on the crisis at hand rather than the enervating bureaucratic warfare of Nixon's first term was also advantaged by the absence of William Rogers, his bête noir for the previous four years, now that Kissinger had appropriated the seventh-floor secretary's suite at the State Department.

In short, it was the prime of Dr. Henry Kissinger.

Day one, Saturday, October 6, 1973. Because Kissinger was en route from New York, his NSC deputy, Brent Scowcroft, convened the first WSAG meeting on Saturday morning.

Scowcroft was no ordinary U.S. Air Force general. Born and raised as a Mormon in Utah, he had acquired a PhD in international relations from Columbia University and years of experience in strategic planning from working at USAF headquarters in the Pentagon. In 1970, he had become special assistant to the director of the Joint Chiefs of Staff; two years later, he was assigned to Nixon's White House as military assistant to the president, the officer responsible for carrying the "nuclear football." When Kissinger moved to the State Department but retained his position as national security adviser, he appointed Scowcroft as his deputy at the NSC. Subsequently Scowcroft would become Ford's national security adviser, and he later held the same position under President George H. W. Bush, where his quiet wisdom and efficient coordination of the bureaucracy made him the model for national security advisers who came after him.

Scowcroft had the task of minding the store and maintaining communication with Nixon and Haig for Kissinger when he was out of town. Unlike Haig, whose loyalty to Kissinger became suspect after he moved up the chain of command, Scowcroft always remained his loyal, if occasionally resentful, lieutenant. Thin, short, balding, and self-effacing, with a quick wit and a gentle touch, Scowcroft was the embodiment of politesse. He enjoyed working for Kissinger because they were both strategic thinkers. He appreciated and played to Henry's sense of humor and became his confidant in all things, including his complicated private life.

For example, soon after the Yom Kippur War, Elizabeth Taylor showed up in Kissinger's State Department outer office, a not-unusual event for the secretary of state, who enjoyed his celebrity status. However, Kissinger was about to marry Nancy Maginnes—who was the love of his life—and she was not likely to understand or appreciate the beautiful actress, who was between marriages, hanging out with Henry during office hours. He immediately called Brent, who came up with the "brilliant" idea of arranging for Ms. Taylor to be invited to Ambassador Zahedi's dinner that night, where she could talk to Henry in more appropriate circumstances. At Scowcroft's suggestion, Zahedi seated her next to Senator John Warner of Virginia, then one of Washington's most eligible bachelors; they married three years later.

At the WSAG meeting, Schlesinger was the first to speak. Like Kissinger, he was a Harvard graduate, although his PhD was in economics. Like Kissinger, he was also a nuclear expert and had served as chairman of Nixon's Atomic Energy Commission. And like Kissinger, he had been born to Jewish parents. However, while a graduate student, Schlesinger had become a Lutheran and had avoided any connection with Israel. Once Nixon appointed him secretary of defense in July 1973, it was inevitable that he would become Kissinger's rival. Tough, smart, and forthright, he was also admired for his administrative skills. President Ford fired him in 1975 because he disliked his arrogance and condescension, as well as his rumpled, casual appearance. Subsequently, he switched sides politically and was appointed by President Carter as his secretary of energy.

On that Saturday in the Situation Room, the only question Schlesinger wanted the WSAG to address was whether the United States would be willing to label the Israelis as "aggressors." He argued that they had concocted the whole crisis, creating an elaborate cover story of an Arab attack on the holiest day of the Jewish calendar. He conjured up the next step as an Israeli assault on Damascus: "If Israel moves and we fail to come down on them, we've had it!" he declared.

Other participants in that first meeting readily agreed. Admiral Moorer, the chairman of the Joint Chiefs of Staff, also feared Arab reaction: "If we give [the Israelis] a single item of equipment, we will have taken sides." Moorer had a distinguished record as a naval airman and the first commander in chief of both the Atlantic and then the Pacific Fleets. While he admired Israeli military prowess, he harbored a resentment over the Israeli attack on the USS *Liberty* intelligence ship during the 1967 Six-Day War. Officially the attack, which killed 34 American sailors and wounded 171, was treated as a case of mistaken identity. Moorer, however, believed it was "a wanton sneak attack" ordered by Moshe Dayan, the Israeli defense minister. Little wonder that he wanted to distance the United States from Israel in this new crisis.

Deputy Secretary of State Kenneth Rush was alarmed by the prospect of an Arab oil embargo and wanted to avoid taking sides. He summed up the consensus of the meeting by declaring, "The basic problem is how to limit the damage in the Arab world." In Kissinger's absence, the WSAG meeting captured the prevailing mood among Nixon's national security team: American interests in the Arab world, particularly the free flow of oil from the Persian Gulf, should not be jeopardized by siding with Israel in this new war.

Kissinger, by contrast, was already looking beyond the war to the opportunity it created for generating progress toward a political settlement. That would require a cease-fire, but to achieve one, Kissinger explained in a phone call to Haig from New York, "we cannot give the Soviets and the Arabs the impression that we are separating too far from the Israelis." His preoccupation was with superpower rivalry, and he foresaw precisely the dynamics that were about to unfold: If the Soviets were willing to be neutral, then the United States should be neutral too, he argued. But if they "go to the other side, we have to tilt" toward Israel. And if the Soviets should go all out in support of Egypt and Syria, "we had better be tough as nails." That was exactly the approach to securing a cease-fire he would adhere to throughout the coming crisis. However, once there was a cease-fire, he told Haig, "we should use this as a vehicle to get the diplomacy started. Now there is no longer an excuse for a delay." And that is precisely what he did too.

In what would prove to be a serious miscalculation, based on the prevailing view of Israeli military superiority, Kissinger estimated that by Monday evening (two days hence), the Israelis would succeed in pushing back the Egyptians and Syrians from any territory they might have gained in the opening stage of the war and would be advancing toward Cairo and Damascus. If that happened, Kissinger asserted to Haig, in language he knew Nixon would appreciate, "we have to come down hard on them to force them to give up" the additional territories.

To keep the Israelis content in the meantime, Kissinger called the Israeli deputy chief of mission, Mordechai Shalev, to tell him that Israel's urgent military resupply requests would be fulfilled on Monday. The Israeli defense attaché, Mordechai "Motta" Gur, a celebrated IDF general who had led the capture of Jerusalem in the Six-Day War, had already lodged a request with the Pentagon for supplies of ammunition, mortars, and Sidewinder air-to-air missiles. That evening, Kissinger convened the WSAG again to consider the Israeli arms request.

Every National Security Council meeting begins with an intelligence briefing. In this case, the CIA and Defense Intelligence Agency (DIA) assessments, as delivered by CIA director William Colby and Joint Chiefs chairman Moorer, were confident: it would take Israel two days to dislodge the Egyptians and push them back across the Suez Canal, maybe a little longer on the Golan Heights. On this basis, Kissinger saw no reason to respond quickly to the Israeli arms requests. Rush assured him that "they have no real shortages—they plan better than that." Schlesinger said that shipping anything would blow the U.S. image as an "honest broker." The WSAG minutes noted "any reply to the Israeli request for equipment would be delayed until Monday or Tuesday (October 8–9)."

Day two, Sunday, October 7, 1973. When the war broke out, Simcha Dinitz was in Jerusalem sitting shiva for his father, who had passed away two days earlier. Meir immediately sent him back to Washington with a single objective: "Get the tools we need urgently."

The prime minister had made a fateful decision on the morning of Yom Kippur to forgo a preemptive strike on the Egyptian and Syrian forces that she knew by then were about to launch simultaneous attacks. As she told her cabinet that evening, "We will need the assistance of the Americans with equipment and military supplies, as well as their political and diplomatic support. All these will not be given to us if the notion is that we started the war."

Kissinger had tutored Meir well on this subject over the previous two years. The explicit bargain they had struck was that Israel would maintain stability and deter Arab military action in return for the United States' providing Israel with the wherewithal to do so. The moment she realized Israel's deterrent had failed, she must have remembered Kissinger's admonishment: "Don't ever preempt! If you fire the first shot, you won't have a dogcatcher in this country supporting you. You won't have presidential support. You'll be alone, all alone."*

The first message Meir sent to Kissinger, delivered by Shalev on Sunday, because Dinitz was still en route, referred indirectly to that understanding to generate a sense of both obligation and guilt: "You know the reasons why we

---

* Kissinger used a similar formulation with Dayan when he visited Israel toward the end of the war. According to Dayan, at one point during the meeting with Meir and her ministers, Kissinger took him aside and whispered to him that "if you had started the war, then you wouldn't have received anything. Not even a hammer." Kissinger was more explicit in a meeting with the Israeli cabinet in May 1974: "I had told you years ago that I thought that almost under no circumstances should you attack first." See Shimon Golan, *War on Yom Kippur* [in Hebrew] (Jerusalem, Modan Publishing, 2013), 1240, and Memcon of After-Dinner Discussion with Israeli Leaders, May 2, 1974, KT01129, NSA.

took no preemptive action," she reminded Kissinger. "Our failure to take such action is the reason for our situation now." At that point, she did not know how grave Israel's situation was about to become. She simply asked Kissinger to hold off on any cease-fire demand for three to four days until the IDF could move from defense to counterattack. She also requested that an Israeli Boeing 747 cargo plane that was headed for New York be allowed to land at a U.S. Air Force base to pick up military equipment. Kissinger, underscoring his cease-fire calculus, responded that he would do his "utmost" to get her the time but thought it would be tough to do.

That meeting was followed promptly by a phone call from Abba Eban, Israel's foreign minister. He informed Kissinger that Egyptian forces had crossed the canal; Syrian armor had penetrated deep into the Golan, threatening northern Israel; and Mount Hermon had fallen. This was the first indication Kissinger received that Israel might be in trouble, and he responded sympathetically by calling Schlesinger and urging him to provide some of the military equipment Israel had requested. Schlesinger said they could provide some Sidewinders. Kissinger admonished him to keep it secret. He then checked this decision with Haig, explaining that "we must be on their side now so that they have something to lose afterward. . . . My profound conviction is that if we play this the hard way, it's the last time they're going to listen. If we kick them in the teeth, they have nothing to lose."

Briefed by Haig, Nixon called Kissinger to tell him that he agreed, but "we have to have in the back of our minds that we don't want to be so pro-Israel that the oil states . . . will break ranks" with the United States. Nixon, like Schlesinger and Rush, was concerned about oil. Kissinger, however, was somewhat blasé about the prospect of an Arab oil embargo, not because he was blind to the concern, but rather because he believed that his efforts to use the crisis to generate a political settlement would stay the oil producers' hands.

In the meantime, under pressure from Meir to get the arms flowing and anticipating there would be resistance in the administration because of America's oil interests, Dinitz had started to rally the troops. On Sunday night, he had already briefed leaders of the Jewish community and key senators, including Scoop Jackson, Walter Mondale, and Birch Bayh, on the urgency of Israel's requests.

That Sunday evening, Kissinger received a welcome message from his Egyptian counterpart, Hafez Ismail, via Eugene Trone in Cairo. Ismail had initiated the contact with the clear intention of signaling Sadat's war aims. The "basic objective," Ismail explained, remained the achievement of peace: "We do not intend to deepen the engagements or widen the confrontation."

The Egyptian back channel had come to life with a message that Kissinger viewed as amazing. He now understood that Sadat's war aims were limited, and that his ultimate objective was peace, not war, with Israel.* As he explained to the WSAG principals that Sunday evening, "My judgment is that [Sadat] will cross the Suez and just sit there."† He did not share with his colleagues the reason for his confidence. But he did explain his understanding of Egyptian thinking: "Their reasoning was that the Israelis have been arguing that the situation is calm and there is no reason to do anything." Perhaps reflecting his walk in the garden with Ismail at Moulin Saint-Fargeau, he concluded, "They knew we wouldn't do anything unless things were stirred up."

The message from Ismail had heightened Kissinger's sense of diplomatic opportunity. But to seize the moment, he would need to achieve a cease-fire on terms that would enable peace negotiations. Israel needed just enough time to recover territory lost, but not enough time to take more. "Our policy is to stop Israel at the cease-fire line" that had existed before the war's outbreak, and then launch peace negotiations, he told his WSAG colleagues. He estimated it would take Israel three days to push the Egyptians and Syrians back to that line. "The Arabs will scream that they are being deprived of their birthright, but by Thursday they will be on their knees begging us for a cease-fire," Kissinger assured them.

Just as in military planning for war, however, diplomatic strategy rarely survives the first encounter with a crisis. As Sunday progressed, it was fast becoming evident to Kissinger that Israel was not performing as expected. He put it down to the impact of the surprise attacks on two fronts. With the Arabs still advancing, the time was clearly not right to press for a cease-fire.

Dobrynin agreed. Kissinger had reached out to the Soviet ambassador on the first day of the war. After checking with Moscow, he came back with a clear message that the Soviet leaders wanted to cooperate with Nixon and Kissinger on a cease-fire but would not attempt to convince their Arab clients "to give back territory which belongs to them."

With Israel asking for more time and the Soviets unwilling to support a cease-fire, Kissinger had no choice but to wait for developments on the battlefield. In the meantime, since the Israelis were anxious to buy time for their counterattack, Kissinger asked Eban to help him stall in the UN Security Council, where a debate was about to take place, encouraging him to draw on his legendary eloquence to filibuster.

---

* In the message, Ismail also detailed Sadat's requirements for peace negotiations: Israel had to agree to withdraw from all occupied territories, Egypt would then participate in a peace conference with Israel under any suitable auspices, and within that context Egypt would agree to freedom of navigation through the Straits of Tiran guaranteed by an international presence.
† According to Ahmed Aboul Gheit, who was then on Hafez Ismail's staff, Ismail's message had been misinterpreted. Sadat was responding to entreaties not to use Scud missiles, which would have "deepened" the war, and not to pressure Jordan to enter the war, which would have "widened" it. Indyk interview with Ahmed Aboul Gheit, November 17, 2018.

Day three, Monday, October 8, 1973. On Monday, Meir sent Kissinger a request for forty Phantom aircraft and three hundred M60 tanks, the most sophisticated in the American arsenal, a clear indication that Israel had suffered heavy losses. But with Dinitz telling Kissinger that the situation looked "considerably better" because Israeli forces were attacking on both fronts, Kissinger felt no urgency to fulfill requests that were not likely to be needed until after the fighting had ended.

At 10:00 a.m., he met with the president and Haig and secured Nixon's agreement that all Israeli aircraft losses would be replaced. With such an assurance, Kissinger believed, Israel could throw everything it had into the battle knowing that it would be replenished after the war. Meir was grateful for the assurance but asked that at least some of the Phantom aircraft be delivered immediately. Kissinger complained accurately of strong bureaucratic resistance in the Pentagon but claimed credit for squeezing two Phantom replacements out of them. As for the ammunition, cluster bombs, and Sidewinder missiles, Kissinger told Dinitz that Israeli planes would be allowed to land at U.S. air bases, provided they had their tails painted over—an artifice invented by Kissinger in the hope of disguising the resupply effort.*

In the WSAG meeting chaired by Kissinger on Monday evening, Schlesinger argued vehemently against replacing Israel's losses. At that point, the Soviets had not started resupplying the Arabs, and he was concerned that an American effort would precipitate such action. But in the end, the consensus as confirmed by the WSAG meeting the next day was that the secret resupply of "consumables" (ammunition, missiles, ordnance, and the like) should proceed, while aircraft and tanks would be delayed until after the fighting ended.

Presenting himself as Israel's friend at court was clearly in keeping with Kissinger's strategy of giving the Israelis something to lose later when he needed leverage on them. On Monday, he asked Dinitz to tone down reports about success on the battlefield to ensure he could push through the resupply requests with the Pentagon foot-draggers. He urged Dinitz to provide updates exclusively to him so he could ensure that Nixon would be supportive of Israel. According to Dinitz's report to Meir, Kissinger also advised Israel to hit the Egyptians "fast and hard" and advance beyond the current lines as soon as possible. This would become a recurring theme—he would encourage the same offensive action on the Syrian front—because Kissinger was focused

---

* According to one account, Schlesinger had met with his top aides after Sunday's WSAG meeting and decided to reject Meir's request that Israeli planes be allowed to land at U.S. air bases to pick up ammunition and spare parts. See Marvin Kalb and Bernard Kalb, *Kissinger* (New York: Little, Brown, 1974), 465.

on gaining diplomatic leverage over the Arabs and their Soviet patron from Israeli battlefield successes. When the Arabs and Soviets called for a cease-fire, he would then use the leverage that came with Israel's dependence on U.S. arms supplies to stop the Israeli military in their tracks and thereby achieve the cease-fire on terms advantageous to the United States.

At the same time as he was encouraging the Israelis to attack Egyptian forces, Kissinger was reassuring Ismail that the United States would do everything possible to assist the contending parties to end the fighting. He told his Egyptian counterpart that he was ready personally to be actively involved in helping resolve the conflict.

However, this finely tuned carrot-and-stick approach to both warring parties could only be effective if Israel promptly turned the tide of battle.

Day four, Tuesday, October 9, 1973. Kissinger went to bed in his Kalorama town house on Monday night believing that, as he had told his WSAG colleagues earlier in the evening, "we are well-positioned." The president had called and reinforced his assessment. "Poor dumb Egyptians getting across the canal and all the bridges will be blown up. They'll cut them all off," Nixon declared with great assurance. The two agreed that their challenge would be to stop the Israelis. Nixon was adamant that they would not be allowed to hold on to their gains. With jowls shaking, he declared, "They can't do that to us again. They've done it to us for four years, but no more!"

But at 1:45 a.m. Kissinger was awoken by an urgent call from Dinitz, who had new battlefield intelligence and insisted on briefing him as early as possible in the morning. Betraying his anxiety, Dinitz called again at 3:00 a.m. and at 6:35 a.m. Kissinger was puzzled; by his reckoning, the battles should have been turning in Israel's favor by now.

Kissinger met Dinitz in the White House Map Room at 8:20 a.m. In a somber mood, the Israeli ambassador reported that the IDF had lost five hundred tanks and forty-nine aircraft, astonishing numbers. General Gur, the Israeli defense attaché, unfurled a map of the Sinai and showed Kissinger the Egyptian positions along the east bank of the canal to a depth of six or seven miles. Kissinger was dumbfounded. "Our strategy was to give you until Wednesday evening," he blurted out, "by which time I thought the whole Egyptian army would be wrecked. We expected a quick victory."

Dinitz asked to speak to Kissinger alone. As Kissinger recounted the meeting, Dinitz conveyed an appeal from Meir to arrange a clandestine meeting for her with the president so she could make a personal plea for the arms she felt Israel desperately needed. Kissinger was horrified; the request indicated that she was either in a panic or hoping to blackmail the president, or both.

He turned down the proposal immediately, without consulting Nixon, telling Dinitz that her absence from Israel at such a critical time would send a terrible signal to her people and Israel's adversaries alike.

Kissinger was just beginning to comprehend the dimensions of the psychological—as well as military—blow that Israel had received over the previous three days. Moshe Dayan, the most accomplished of Israel's warriors, had returned from the Egyptian and Syrian fronts on October 7 so dispirited that he feared for Israel's survival. He said he felt an anxiety he had never known. He told Meir and her cabinet that Israel would have to retreat to more defensible lines. What he feared most, he told the IDF chief of staff, General David "Dado" Elazar, was that "there won't be enough tanks and planes, there won't be enough trained personnel" for Israel to take on a mobilized Arab world. As one historian of the war noted, "the breadth of Dayan's strategic vision had become the depth of his despair."

Meir was so horrified at Dayan's report that she later admitted to think-

Israeli defense minister Moshe Dayan in the war room at Israel Defense Forces headquarters, Tel Aviv, on October 8, 1973. On Dayan's right are General Rehavam Ze'evi (assistant to the chief of staff), General Shmuel Gonen (commander, southern front), and General Uri Ben-Ari (deputy commander, southern front). The day before, Dayan had returned from the Syrian and Egyptian fronts so dispirited that he feared for Israel's survival. "The breadth of Dayan's strategic vision had become the depth of his despair," according to one historian of the Yom Kippur War.

ing of suicide rather than surrender. She had not shared her sense of disaster with either Washington or the Israeli public because she hoped, like Kissinger, that the tide of battle would turn. So far there had been a disastrous attempt to drive Egyptian forces back across the canal, a failed bid to retake Mount Hermon, and a successful but costly effort to hold back the Syrian forces from reaching the western edge of the Golan Heights.

As Dayan presented the situation to the cabinet early on Tuesday morning, there was no possibility of the IDF approaching the canal, let alone crossing it. The soldiers in the surrounded forts along the east bank would have to surrender. A fallback line of defense would need to be established at the Gidi and Mitla Passes in central Sinai, should retreat become necessary. In the meantime, everything possible had to be done to drive Syria out of the war, including bombing Damascus, before Iraqi and Jordanian forces joined in.

That was the context in which a resupply of U.S. arms became an existential necessity. Israel did not need more tanks and aircraft to prosecute the current battles. Rather, Dayan's despondency had convinced Meir that Israel's status had changed overnight from the dominant regional power that could, back in 1970, shoot down Soviet-piloted MiGs over the canal with equanimity, to a small, vulnerable state far outnumbered by newly capable enemies on its borders. While Kissinger was focused on securing a cease-fire in the current battle, Israel's decision makers were focused on what they now believed would be a long war for survival. Meir was the one to raise the idea of a personal appeal to Nixon for the arms they would need to fight the future battles. Shlomo Gazit, the prime minister's office director, left the cabinet room and called Dinitz, who woke Kissinger with the request for the urgent meeting.

At 9:40 a.m. Kissinger went from that alarming meeting with Dinitz to a principals-only meeting of the WSAG in the Situation Room. He reported that the Israelis had been calling all night asking for deliveries. "They are desperate and want help," he said dramatically. Their immediate need was for anti-tank ammunition and they were willing to paint over the tails of the El Al transport planes to come and pick it up. The prime minister wanted to plead her case personally with the president.

Kissinger's report was met with wall-to-wall skepticism. Schlesinger questioned how yesterday they were fine with receiving the anti-tank ammunition by the end of the month and now it was an emergency. Both CIA director William Colby and Kenneth Rush argued that the Israelis were just trying to lock the United States into replacing all their weapons and ensuring their long-term aircraft and tank requirements were met (an accurate perception).

Kissinger laid out the options: meet the Israeli requests, deny them, meet them partially, or obfuscate. He immediately ruled out the first option because it would "drive the Arabs wild." His colleagues agreed, arguing that it would also trigger a Soviet resupply effort and a Saudi oil embargo. Kissinger did note that the president's instinct was to give the Israelis everything. Kissinger preferred to discreetly provide the "consumables" now, and provide the aircraft and tanks on a timetable that would have them arrive after the cease-fire took hold. In the meantime, he asked Schlesinger to arrange to add a few additional aircraft to the mix. The objective of this fine-tuning, in Kissinger's assessment, was "a costly victory" for Israel "without a disaster" for Egypt. He was already aiming for a renewed equilibrium.

When they reviewed this approach with Nixon in the Oval Office at 4:45 p.m., he agreed to go ahead with the consumables but ordered that the mix of heavy equipment that would go later be augmented by the M60s that Meir had requested. When Nixon said, "If it gets hairy, we may need to do more," Kissinger quickly countered, "but not today."

In return, Nixon wanted Meir to keep Congress and the Jewish community off his back. But his Watergate woes were about to be compounded by the resignation of Vice President Spiro Agnew in a plea bargain over tax evasion when he had served as governor of Maryland. The Conference of Presidents of Major American Jewish Organizations had convened an emergency national convocation that morning with some five hundred Jewish leaders at the Shoreham Hotel in Cleveland Park, a Washington neighborhood. The Jewish leaders dispatched Max Fisher, the community's Republican éminence grise, to the White House to meet with Nixon. Fisher was a tall, bespectacled Detroit philanthropist who had made his fortune from gas stations. He had sad, knowing eyes, a long nose, thick lips, and a sparse comb-over that did nothing to disguise his bald pate. He prided himself on serving as a discreet back channel between Republican presidents and Israeli prime ministers, from Eisenhower to George H. W. Bush. On this occasion, he handed Nixon a letter from the Jewish organizational leadership that respectfully urged the president to help Israel. After Nixon read it, Fisher added a personal plea. "I've worked hard for you and I've never asked anything for myself," he reminded the president. "But I'm asking you now. Please send the Israelis what they need. You can't let them be destroyed."

The soft-spoken Fisher obviously had an impact on Nixon. In a subsequent meeting, the president said to Kissinger, "The Israelis must not be allowed to lose." He ordered him to identify tanks and planes in Europe on a contingency basis to ensure they would be ready to move if needed. Kissinger agreed and was quick to point out the diplomatic advantage of Nixon's political motivation. "We want to stick by Israel now, so they won't turn on you during the diplomatic phase," he responded.

At 6:10 p.m., Kissinger met Dinitz in the White House to provide him with the official response to Israel's urgent requests. He emphasized that Nixon had agreed to replace all of Israel's aircraft and tank losses, with a substantial number of M60 tanks included. That meant, he said, that the IDF could expend its arsenal now in the certain knowledge that it would all be replaced. Israel should pick up the consumables in its own planes with the insignia painted over. Except for five F-4 Phantom aircraft, which would be transferred immediately, the heavy equipment would come later. "If it should go very badly and there is an emergency," he said reassuringly, "we will get the tanks in, even if we have to do it with American planes."

Then Kissinger asked to meet with Dinitz privately. According to Dinitz's report to Gazit, Kissinger urged the Israelis to hit the Syrians "fast and hard" and not worry about replenishment. And then he choked up and told the Israeli ambassador, "As long as I'm here, I won't abandon Israel."

Kissinger was attempting to walk between the raindrops, but his chances of staying dry were rapidly diminishing. To shore up his politically vulnerable boss, he had asked Dinitz to call off the congressional dogs, but with the American Jewish community now mobilized, that was unlikely. He had assuaged the bureaucratic opposition with his parsimonious approach to resupply, but he was now receiving the first indications that the Soviets were mounting what would fast become a massive air- and sealift of weapons to the Syrians and Egyptians, which, as he had foreseen, would make his approach untenable. And his effort to conceal the American resupply effort wasn't working either. The Norfolk *Ledger-Star* reported the next morning that an Israeli 707 with its tail insignia covered with paper and masking tape was observed loading missiles at Naval Air Station Oceana at Virginia Beach.

General Aharon Yariv was a legend among Israelis. Born in Moscow in 1920, he had migrated to Palestine in 1935 and fought in the Haganah (Israel's pre-state army) as well as the Jewish brigade of the British army during World War II. In the IDF, he had served as director of military intelligence during and after the Six-Day War. He had retired in 1972 to prepare for a run for the Knesset in the upcoming elections. In the wake of the September 1972 Munich massacre, in which Black September Palestinian terrorists murdered eleven Israeli athletes during the Munich Olympic Games, Meir had recalled Yariv to serve as her counterterrorism adviser. She tasked him with overseeing Operation Wrath of God, in which Mossad agents hunted down and killed every Black September operative involved in the Munich attack.

In his role as director of military intelligence, Arele, as he had affectionately become known among Israelis, had established himself as an articulate and forceful spokesman for the IDF. He spoke perfect English from his days in the British army, albeit in a clipped, high-pitched, Latvian-accented voice.

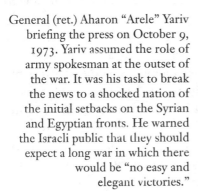

General (ret.) Aharon "Arele" Yariv briefing the press on October 9, 1973. Yariv assumed the role of army spokesman at the outset of the war. It was his task to break the news to a shocked nation of the initial setbacks on the Syrian and Egyptian fronts. He warned the Israeli public that they should expect a long war in which there would be "no easy and elegant victories."

When the war broke out, he was recalled to service as a special adviser to IDF chief of staff Elazar. In that capacity, on the evening of October 9, he found himself with the unenviable task of informing the Israeli public and the world of the Israeli army's battlefield setbacks.

I remember vividly that moment. A few days before, in the early afternoon of Yom Kippur, I had been listening in my Jerusalem apartment to rock music from a pirate radio station broadcasting from the John Lennon–financed "Peace Ship," off Israel's shores. Abie Nathan, the peace activist cum disk jockey, suddenly stopped the music and started broadcasting a personal appeal for peace. Moments later the air raid sirens sounded. If you've never heard one go off before, it scares the living daylights out of you. In this case, it drove all the inhabitants of our apartment bloc helter-skelter into the basement bomb shelter, except the new immigrants from Russia, who didn't know that every Israeli apartment block had one. As we sat there in the dank gloom, wondering what could possibly be going on, I tried to reassure my neighbors (including the Russians who had belatedly joined us) that the IDF had either launched a preemptive strike, or if the Arabs had attacked first, they would surely be quickly defeated. I was mouthing the prevailing wisdom among the Israeli public at the time, inculcated by the country's political and military echelons.

In the early days of the war, I had volunteered with the Jerusalem Municipality and had been assigned to a team of workers whose task was to clean out the air raid shelters that had accumulated rancid trash and stagnant water during the years when nobody in Israel believed they would ever be needed again. I labored with Palestinian municipal workers as we helped provide their Israeli "oppressors" with protection from the attacks of their Arab "liberators." Every hour, we would take a break to listen to the Kol Yisrael radio news bulletin. Since my Hebrew was rudimentary, I was dependent on my Israeli coworkers to translate. They would always cheerily report that the IDF either was on its way to Damascus or had just crossed the Suez Canal and was on its way to Cairo, or both.

In fact, for the first few days, the Israeli government had deliberately kept its people in the dark, partly for operational reasons, but mostly because the leadership feared that the effect on public morale would be as bad as the impact of the IDF's setbacks had been on their own. Israel is a small country. Back then, its population was only 3.3 million, and because the Israeli army depended on universal conscription and a large number of reserve divisions, just about every family had at least one member on the front lines or knew someone who did. As more and more families were informed of the deaths of their loved ones in battle, the news spread of major casualties.

From that first night on, Jerusalem was cloaked in the darkness of a total blackout. It was as if the city of peace had been covered with a death shroud. On the second night of the war, I joined other students at Jerusalem's city hall to register for work. As we entered the old sandstone British Mandate building, we passed a group of older men standing and praying in the shadows of the entrance. It took me a moment to realize that they had gathered a minyan to recite the Kaddish mourners' prayer for one of their sons who had died in the initial battles.*

That night, the French and the British announced they were blocking all arms supplies to Israel. Rumors started circulating that Jordan and Iraq were about to enter the war and the Saudis were about to impose an oil embargo. The sense of existential dread, always lurking in the dark corners of Jewish hearts, had become palpable. My student friends and I would anxiously watch the evening news, expecting to hear of victories from the two fronts. When we heard nothing of any significance for three evenings in a row, we began to realize something had gone seriously wrong. On this fourth evening, Tuesday, October 9, we watched Arele brief the Israeli nation.

His televised briefing preempted the nightly news. It took place at Tel Aviv's Beit Sokolov, the shabby journalists' club. Yariv stood before a cluster of microphones in front of a crowded room of Israeli and international journalists. Trim, short, and handsome, with a receding pompadour and brown-tinted,

---

* A minyan is a quorum of ten adult Jewish men (and women in Reform and Conservative congregations) needed for public prayer, especially for reciting the Kaddish.

large-frame spectacles that shaded his eyes, he was dressed in an open-neck, olive uniform, with the "falafel" and cross-swords insignia of an Israeli major general on his epaulettes, his shirt sleeves folded above his elbows, IDF-style. He clutched a long, thin cane, which he used to point out, on the two maps that stood on tripods behind him, the extent of Syrian and Egyptian penetration of Israel's front lines.

Yariv was at least able to show that on the Golan Heights the IDF had forced the Syrians back to the 1967 cease-fire line. However, Syrian forces had clearly been able to penetrate to the point where they might have descended into northern Israel had they not been repulsed by hastily mobilized Israeli reserve units.

In Sinai, the news was more shocking: The Bar-Lev line of Israeli forts along the Suez Canal had been overwhelmed by Egyptian forces, which had now taken up positions on a hundred-mile stretch along the east bank from Port Said in the north to Suez city at the tip of the Red Sea, in a strip three miles wide. The map showed that tank brigades of the Egyptian army had penetrated as far as seven miles east toward Israel. The best that Yariv could assert was that the IDF had managed to stabilize the Egyptian front. To an Israeli public that had grown used to lightning conquests, he warned, "[This war] is not going to be a short one. The people of Israel can expect no easy and elegant victories." Suddenly, Israelis went from a haughty and complacent conviction that their small country had become the superpower of the Middle East to a chastened and humbling fear that their very existence now hung in the balance.

Day five, Wednesday, October 10, 1973. Kissinger well understood the role in political decision making of the psychology of a people and its leaders. And as a Jew who had fled Nazi persecution, he had a particularly acute appreciation for Jewish insecurity. In a sense, he embodied it. Therefore, Kissinger quickly assimilated the implications of this psychological upheaval into his diplomatic calculus. In his discussions on Tuesday afternoon with Nixon, he had noted that the Israelis "have lost their invincibility and the Arabs have lost their sense of inferiority."

On Wednesday afternoon, in a presentation to the weekly senior staff meeting at the State Department, he noted that if it proved true that Israel had lost one thousand dead in the first five days of this war, that would be the proportional equivalent of twice as many casualties as America suffered in the entire eight years of the Vietnam War. This was going to be "a profoundly shocking experience to Israel." It had created a totally different strategic situation in the Middle East, improving the prospects for a permanent settlement, he explained. He would later argue that because of Israel's low tolerance for casualties, this war had made it more amenable to diplomatic solutions than it had been after its lightning victory in the Six-Day War. Then it had been impossible to discuss territorial concessions with its leaders. Now he assumed that when he needed Israel to accept a cease-fire it would have no choice but to do so, partly because of its losses, and partly because of its dependence on the United States.

Kissinger thought he had the resupply situation appropriately calibrated to ensure that Israel had the wherewithal to apply military pressure to its Arab adversaries while remaining on the "short leash" necessary to get it to accept the cease-fire. As for the cease-fire itself, the problem, as he articulated it in that same senior staff meeting, was that the only resolution that would command support in the Security Council was one that required a return by Israel to the 1967 lines. That was a resolution the United States would have to veto; otherwise it would be responsible for pressuring Israel to withdraw, and the Soviet Union would gain credit for the withdrawal with its Arab allies. But an American veto would alienate the Arabs. Conversely, Israel would be loath to accept a cease-fire in place until it had recovered lost territory. Were Israel to reject such a resolution, it might be subject to sanctions, which the United States would then have to veto or else face a domestic backlash for turning against an ally that had been subjected to aggression. Therefore, Kissinger explained to his staff, the resolution had to come in a suitable format and at the right moment, which was when the Israelis had taken back enough territory to regain their balance and the Arabs had lost enough territory to recognize it was time to call it quits. On Wednesday, he thought that it would still take "a hairy three or four days of juggling to do."

Kissinger had received a phone call from Dobrynin that morning conveying a message from Brezhnev to Nixon that, after difficult discussions with Syria and Egypt, the Soviet Union was now ready for a simple UNSC resolution that would call for a cease-fire in place. The Soviet Union would abstain, and the United States should as well. Dobrynin said the way to get Sadat to accept the cease-fire was for it to be seen to be coming from members of the Security Council other than the two superpowers. What Dobrynin did not reveal to Kissinger was that Sadat had refused Soviet entreaties to accept a cease-fire and Moscow was now depending on Security Council pressure to change his mind. Dobrynin had suggested that both superpowers abstain on the cease-fire resolution so that Moscow could avoid friction with Sadat. Kissinger, however, thought the idea of a Soviet abstention was designed to promote cooperation with Washington. That is why he downplayed the intelligence he had received that morning indicating many Soviet supply ships were steaming toward Egyptian and Syrian ports and a massive Soviet airlift seemed to be underway.*

Kissinger resolved to stall: he would limit the resupply to Israel to avoid an adverse Arab reaction, while slow-rolling deliberations over the cease-fire to buy Israel time to regain territory and apply military pressure to the Arabs. But with the Russians now beginning to openly resupply Egypt and Syria and encouraging other Arab states to lend their support to the war effort, he could not sustain this approach.† That was especially true because he knew Nixon would not be willing to endure congressional criticism in his weakened political state.

Kissinger was now in a bind of his own making. He was modulating the resupply to Israel but needed Israel's military pressure to secure Arab acceptance of the cease-fire. That required stalling Russia on the cease-fire resolution, even while welcoming its apparent desire to cooperate. By Wednesday evening, the elaborate system of leverage that Kissinger was attempting to deploy began to look like a Rube Goldberg device.

Fortunately for Kissinger, because of Vice President Agnew's resignation earlier on that Wednesday morning, he could tell Dobrynin that he would not have an answer for him until the next morning. Agnew's leaving office also made it possible to delay a meeting with Nixon, whom Kissinger had not yet informed that the Soviets were willing to work with him on a cease-fire resolution. He was holding out on his boss to buy time too, since he was sure that once Nixon knew, Kissinger would be ordered to secure an immediate cessation of hostilities.

At lunchtime, he called Schlesinger and asked him to be as forthcoming as possible on arms supplies with Dinitz if he saw him that day. He also asked the defense secretary to give him the credit for that, "before [he moved] in the other direction" of insisting that Israel accept a cease-fire in place.

In the afternoon, Scowcroft told Kissinger Dinitz was complaining that one-third of Israel's air force was out of commission and all he could get from the United States was an immediate replacement of five aircraft. Kissinger instructed Scowcroft to reassure Dinitz that there would be no joint U.S.-

* As the chairman of the Joint Chiefs conveyed it to Schlesinger on Wednesday morning, there were fifteen flights of AN-12s, which can carry about twenty-two tons of materiel each, heading for Syria and another twenty AN-22s, which can carry about forty tons of materiel, heading for Cairo. See Telephone Conversation (Telcon hereafter) between Schlesinger and Moorer, October 10, 1973, FRUS 1969–1976:25, Doc. 144.
† For example, Brezhnev sent a message to President Houari Boumediene, the militant leader of Algeria, urging the Algerian people to "use all means at their disposal and take all the required steps with a view to supporting Syria and Egypt in the difficult struggle imposed by the Israeli aggressor." See Bernard Gwertzman, "U.S. Says Moscow Bids Other Arabs Aid Egypt and Syria," *New York Times*, October 10, 1973.

Soviet cease-fire resolution yet. He asked Scowcroft to call Schlesinger to see whether he could spare some more aircraft.

That evening, Kissinger hosted Dinitz for the first time in his State Department office. The main sitting room had already been redecorated to suit his taste for modern art, with abstract expressionist paintings by Rothko and Pousette-Dart replacing the traditional Early American landscapes. He took Dinitz into his adjacent, more intimate study, with its view of the Lincoln Memorial and, across the river, the Pentagon.

Kissinger began by explaining that the president wanted to move forward with a cease-fire resolution, but he was managing to hold him off. Dinitz wasn't buying it. He angrily questioned why the United States was capitulating to Russian pressure when the Russians were resupplying the Arabs and he was struggling to get anything out of the Pentagon. He argued that a cease-fire now would leave the Egyptians on both sides of the canal and that would produce a victory for the Soviet Union. Kissinger told Dinitz that he agreed with his analysis, but he was the only one who thought that way. According to Dinitz's report to Jerusalem, Kissinger depicted himself as going up against "the entire administration."

When Kissinger subsequently reported on the meeting to Haig, he said that they would have to hold off the Russians for another twelve hours to allow Israel to improve its positions on the ground. In a discussion with Scowcroft that night, he revealed his anxiety. Scowcroft responded that if the Israelis did not "break out" on the battlefield in the next forty-eight hours, Kissinger would be faced with a choice between accepting a cease-fire resolution or mounting a massive resupply effort.

Day six, Thursday, October 11, 1973. The day started badly for the secretary of state. Still trying to buy more time to secure additional Israeli success on the battlefield, he had called Dobrynin late the night before. He claimed that because Zairean president Mobutu Sese Seko was visiting the White House that morning, he wouldn't have a response for him until the afternoon. To make up for the implausibility of that excuse, he complained about the substantial airlift of Soviet supplies going into Egypt and Syria. Describing it, diplomatically, as "[not] very helpful," he warned that the United States would have to respond by doing the same for Israel.

Kissinger's morning briefing included a press report that General Dayan had flown to the Syrian front on the Golan Heights and told correspondents there that the purpose of Israel's offensive was "to teach the Syrians that the same road that leads from Damascus to Tel Aviv also leads from Tel Aviv to Damascus." The briefing also contained an alarming piece of military intelligence: the Soviet Union had placed three of its airborne divisions on alert in Bulgaria. That, Kissinger assumed, was a direct response to the fact that the IDF, with his active encouragement, had now launched a tank offensive on the Golan and was advancing toward Damascus. It was one thing to apply military pressure on the Syrians—something which Kissinger keenly needed for his diplomacy to work—but it was another thing entirely to brag about it in public and threaten Damascus, as Dayan was now doing. That clearly had the potential to generate Soviet military intervention, the brightest of Kissinger's red lines, and it would unmask his stalling tactics to Dobrynin.

Kissinger now received a call from a furious Nixon. The president had gotten wind of Israeli embassy staff telling the press that he wasn't support-ing Israel. He ordered Kissinger to call Dinitz and tell him that the president would not tolerate it and would hold him personally responsible if it contin-ued. "If we hear any more stuff like this, I will have no choice domestically except to turn on them," he fulminated.

Kissinger picked up the hotline that connected him with Dinitz's office. Mordechai Shalev, his deputy, answered. He explained that the ambassador was in synagogue for the first day of the Jewish festival of Sukkot. Kissinger blew a fuse: "It is not very good for you on the one hand to ask me to slow down the UN and you get Dayan to say on radio and TV that you are heading for Damascus," he scolded Shalev. "What in the hell am I now going to tell the Russians? This looks like the most extreme form of collusion and bad faith. . . . For God's sake stay off the radio and TV," he demanded. Kissinger said the president was "beside himself," and cautioned that there would be "hell to pay" if Israeli diplomats did not stop bad-mouthing Nixon to the press.

There were problems on the resupply front as well. Israel had only seven transport planes available to pick up all the "consumables" that Kissinger had now committed to sending; they needed fifty. Israeli efforts to charter Ameri-can commercial aircraft were proving unsuccessful, since none of the airlines wanted to fly into an active war zone or risk Arab commercial retaliation. That Thursday afternoon, Kissinger ordered Scowcroft and Sisco to get the Penta-gon's Military Airlift Command to charter twenty American commercial air-craft to do the job.

Calculating that he could no longer hold Brezhnev and Nixon at bay, given Dayan's press statement, Kissinger decided he had better move ahead with the cease-fire resolution with all deliberate haste. With his radar always tuned for equilibrium, he found it now in the military situation on the two fronts: he assessed that Egyptian gains on the Sinai front would soon be balanced by Israeli gains on the Syrian front, at which point the cease-fire could go into effect.

He called Dinitz to inform him that he could stall Dobrynin no longer and that by Friday evening they would have to move on the cease-fire resolution in the Security Council. Dinitz was suitably contrite, saying that Meir would do her best to prevent a repeat of Dayan's press conference that morning. Kissinger made clear that he was talking only about the words, not the actions of the Israeli army. Dinitz confirmed that understanding. As to the cease-fire, Dinitz wanted to know whether there would be a "standstill" resolution. Kissinger confirmed that there would be and recommended an Israeli "yes, but" response, rather than a rejection.

Since the Russians had indicated they were going to abstain, and the United States would therefore do the same, Kissinger now approached the British to introduce the resolution. British prime minister Edward Heath saw an opportunity to play a more active role. He wanted to coordinate directly with the president and on Thursday evening asked to speak to him. Kissinger blocked the call because, as he told Scowcroft, "when I talked to the President, he was loaded." Heath went ahead on his own and ordered his ambassador in Cairo to discuss the cease-fire resolution directly with Sadat.

Carl von Clausewitz famously observed that "three quarters of the factors on which action in war is based are wrapped in a fog of greater or lesser uncertainty." Kissinger was fast discovering that his crisis diplomacy too was being impacted by a lack of real-time intelligence about what was happening on the Syrian and Egyptian fronts. Unlike the Soviets, who were able to operate their MiG-25 Foxbat spy planes out of Egyptian and Syrian air bases throughout the war, the United States was dependent on reports from American military attachés who were at least twenty-four hours behind in getting that information to Washington, or from the Israelis who were actively controlling the information flow to all quarters because they were in the midst of battle.*

Kissinger believed the best way to exploit a crisis to America's advantage was to try to anticipate events, judge the crest of the crisis, and, like a surfer, ride the wave as it swept all parties forward. But he couldn't do that without prompt and accurate intelligence. He knew from media reports that Israeli forces were advancing on the Syrian front, but he had no real-time information about what was happening in Sinai, or in the war rooms of the three combatants.

We now know that the Israeli cabinet had spent most of the previous day debating whether to launch an offensive on the northern front to take addi-

---

* Ray Cline, the director of intelligence and research at the State Department, complained about the lack of real-time intelligence in a meeting with Kissinger on October 23: "We did not have very good intelligence, and we didn't have nearly as much as the Russians had. And I think that is a very serious thing for the future. They had a great deal more to go on than we did." See Minutes of Kissinger's Staff Meeting, October 23, 1973, FRUS 1969–1976:25, Doc. 250.

tional territory beyond the 1967 cease-fire line and to advance on Damascus, only sixty kilometers from there. Informed by Dinitz that a cease-fire call was looming and understanding that they could not succeed in pushing the Egyptian forces back across the canal in the next forty-eight hours, Meir had decided to authorize the Syrian offensive. At the very least, she wanted more Syrian territory to bring to the bargaining table. The objective was not to capture Damascus but to advance close enough to threaten it. However, by nightfall on Thursday, after intense fighting and the loss of forty tanks, weary Israeli forces were still some forty-five kilometers short of Damascus.

The Israeli advance nevertheless forced the retreat of the Syrian 1st Armored Division and precipitated Assad's decision to sack its commander. He urgently appealed to Sadat to attack the Israeli forces in Sinai to relieve the pressure on Damascus. But such an attack directly contradicted the battle plan developed by Sadat's chief of staff, General Saad el-Shazli, which assumed that the Egyptian armed forces who had crossed the canal would stay put under the protective umbrella of the SAM batteries. Sadat decided he could not afford to be blamed for the occupation of Damascus. In an angry confrontation with his war minister, General Ahmed Ismail, on the evening of this Thursday, October 11, he ordered him to transfer two tank divisions across the canal to attack the Israeli tank formations in Sinai with the objective of reaching the Gidi and Mitla Passes in the center of the peninsula.

Meanwhile, in Tel Aviv, Elazar was urging the Israeli cabinet to accept a cease-fire in place "as a vital necessity." From his perspective, the offensive in the north would reach its peak the next day, Friday, October 12. In the south, he reported that Egyptian forces were digging in on the east bank under their SAM umbrella. The head of the Israeli Air Force, General Benny Peled, then provided the cabinet with a deliberately false assessment of disastrous aircraft losses leaving the IAF close to its red line of insufficient planes to provide ground support for a major Israeli offensive on the Egyptian front (in fact, the IAF was at 80 percent of operational strength for ground support).[*]

In these circumstances, Elazar argued that now was the optimal time for Israel to lock in the situation, rearm, and prepare for the next war rather than launch another costly and uncertain offensive against Egypt. He persuaded the cabinet to accept a cease-fire, partly because he expected that Israeli forces on the Golan would soon achieve their objective of threatening but not occupying Damascus, and partly because there seemed no good prospect of pushing the Egyptians back across the canal without taking even heavier casualties.

---

[*] Peled admitted later that his misleading assessment was designed to convince the cabinet to launch an attack across the canal. It had the opposite effect. See Golan, *War on Yom Kippur*, 753, and Abraham Rabinovich, *The Yom Kippur War: The Epic Encounter That Transformed the Middle East* (New York: Schocken Books, 2017), 345.

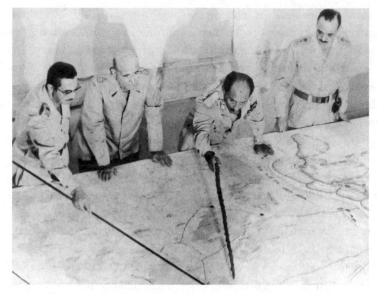

President Anwar Sadat at Egyptian military headquarters during
the October 1973 war, using his walking stick to plan for the land
offensive in Sinai that he ordered on October 11. On his left is
General Mohamed Abdel Ghani el-Gamasy, at that time the chief of
operations; on his right is War Minister General Ahmed Ismail and
Chief of Staff General Saad el-Shazli.

Elazar's recommendation was controversial because it meant leaving Sadat's
territorial gains intact and allowing him a substantial victory. In the middle of
these cabinet deliberations, Zvi Zamir, the Mossad chief, was called out of the
room. He returned with the news that Sadat had ordered a land offensive in
Sinai. That was a "make my day" moment for Elazar: a chance to hit Egypt's
tank divisions in open terrain where they would not enjoy SAM protection
from air attacks. He dropped his argument for the cease-fire. But now Dayan
made the case that if Sadat was ordering an offensive, there was no chance he
would agree to a cease-fire anyway. Therefore, they had nothing to lose and
a lot to gain by seeming to cooperate with Kissinger's diplomacy. Not for the
first or last time, the Israelis were gaming Kissinger as much as they thought he
was gaming them. Accordingly, Meir dispatched Eban, whom she had directed
to stay in New York to deal with Security Council deliberations, to Washington to tell Kissinger that Israel was now willing to accept a cease-fire in place.

Day seven, Friday, October 12, 1973. All Kissinger's careful calculations were
about to be upended. The Israeli plan on the northern front had been to
advance at first light on Tel Shams, a volcanic hill some thirty kilometers from

Damascus. However, as the Israeli tanks moved out, they suddenly discovered an enemy tank division kicking up a huge cloud of dust as it advanced across the plain in two columns from the southeast toward their exposed right flank. These were fresh Iraqi forces, totaling five hundred tanks, seven hundred armored personnel carriers (APCs), and thirty thousand men, equal to all the Israeli forces deployed on the Golan. The Israeli tanks had no choice but to turn and defend themselves. This stopped the Israeli advance on Damascus in its tracks.*

Kissinger knew none of this. When he briefed Nixon first thing that Friday morning, he explained that "today, diplomacy is going to begin moving," now that Israeli gains in Syria were about to offset their losses in Egypt. He planned to get the British to introduce the cease-fire resolution in the Security Council the next day. It would call for a cease-fire in place that would kick in twenty-four hours later. Nixon endorsed the plan, but he noted that the Israelis hadn't gained as much in Syria as he had expected and that it would probably take them weeks before "they can really start clobbering these people." Kissinger responded that international pressure would become unmanageable if they had to wait that long.

At this point, Kissinger had no idea that Sadat had ordered a new offensive. He was still assuming Israeli forces would be advancing to the outskirts of Damascus and that this would trigger Soviet pressure on Sadat to accept the cease-fire. He would then turn to the Israelis and insist that they too accept the cease-fire, creating the impression that the United States was responsible for getting the Israelis to stop their offensive. "For us to have gone in to have saved the Arabs' ass would have been perfect," he subsequently explained to his WSAG colleagues. Accordingly, he decided that his next move should be to send conciliatory signals to Sadat and Brezhnev to make clear he was ready to cooperate with them.

His message to Sadat was conveyed through the Ismail channel. In it, he committed the United States to do its utmost to play a useful role "both in ending current hostilities as well as in bringing a permanent peace based on justice." Emphasizing that he was expecting Sadat to seek an end to hostilities, he promised to treat any Egyptian peace proposal "with understanding and good will."

The signal to Moscow came in his first press conference since the war started. He praised Soviet moderation and restraint but warned that the airlift was not helpful and that there was a real danger of superpower confrontation. Nevertheless, he told the press that Soviet actions, as of then, "did not consti-

---

* The engagement with the Iraqi tanks stretched into October 13. By the end of the day, eighty Iraqi tanks had been destroyed but the Syrians were still managing to block the advance toward Tel Shams.

tute the irresponsibility that would threaten détente." Kissinger knew he was running the gauntlet of adverse American Jewish and congressional reaction to his soft message to Moscow in the face of its active encouragement and resupply of the Arabs. Indeed, a day later, he would be roundly denounced by Senator Jackson, who blamed Kissinger at a pro-Israel rally in Los Angeles for the deaths of hundreds of Israelis because the Soviets had been engaged in what Kissinger had dared to call a "moderate" airlift to the Arabs. But Kissinger was willing to pay that price to maintain Soviet cooperation in his cease-fire diplomacy.

What he did not realize until after the press conference was that the early indications of Soviet airborne divisions being placed on alert had now been confirmed, signifying that the closer the IDF got to Damascus, the more likely it would be to trigger Soviet military intervention. He had an opportunity to raise the matter with the Soviet ambassador when he hosted him for lunch in the secretary of state's elegant private dining room, with its Early American decor and Chippendale furniture, on the eighth floor of the State Department.

As they dined off the exclusive blue-rimmed, gold-trimmed china of the secretary of state, with its golden eagle emblem, they had a testy exchange. Although there is no record of the conversation, Kissinger remembers that he warned Dobrynin that the United States would not tolerate Soviet military intervention. Dobrynin called him later in the day to convey a threatening message from Moscow in return. Tel Aviv, Dobrynin declared, would not be spared if the Israeli advance on Damascus continued. Kissinger responded that if any Soviet aircraft appeared in the area, there would be direct American involvement.

Superpower tensions were clearly rising to a dangerous level. Having publicly defended Soviet behavior, Kissinger was now out on a limb of his own making. What he did not expect was a call he received from Dinitz that evening during which he learned that Meir wanted the cease-fire process to begin immediately and that Eban sought a meeting the next morning to negotiate the terms. Unaware of the Israeli calculus at that moment, Kissinger assumed they were responding to the Soviet threats. He counseled Dinitz, "Once you have been threatened, it is better to stick to your course."

Later that night, in his White House office, Kissinger complained to Dinitz, "I think the urgency will disappear if there are no [Israeli] military moves tomorrow." Dinitz was aware of the reasoning behind the cabinet's cease-fire decision, but his instructions were to secure the resupply. Despite Kissinger's promise of twenty chartered American commercial planes to transport the military consumables, not one had materialized. Unbeknownst to Kissinger, the Pentagon had been unwilling to use its authority to charter any commercial aircraft. And, following Kissinger's agreement with Schlesinger, the F-4 Phantoms had been dribbling out at only two a day, while Dinitz, according to Gazit's instructions prompted by Peled's misleading warning, was pressing for forty to arrive in the next two days.

Dinitz did what any smart ambassador would have done in the circumstances: he blamed the lack of a military offensive on the Golan on the shortage of materiel to carry it out. He then informed Kissinger that the Egyptians were transferring tanks and artillery across the canal in preparation for an offensive in the Sinai, leaving Kissinger to draw the conclusion that the IDF also lacked the means to counter that (even though, as we now know, the Israelis welcomed the opportunity that the offensive created to deal the Egyptian tank brigades a body blow).

Dinitz had good reason to exploit this opening. In a long-delayed meeting with Schlesinger and his military and civilian aides at the Pentagon earlier in the evening, he had been told by Schlesinger that "we have to keep a low profile—this is the President's decision. There are two planes a day, but then we have to watch every day for the Arab reaction." Then Schlesinger corrected himself, explaining the math to Dinitz: "So it is not necessarily two every day. It comes to an average of one and a half a day." Dinitz relayed this to Kissinger, adding, "We lost four days" with regard to the consumables. "So I have to tell you, on the authority of the Prime Minister, that the reason we changed our strategy is that we were depleted." Kissinger paused and then responded in his low, gravelly voice, "It's a disgrace."

Kissinger summoned Scowcroft, who confirmed Dinitz's account of Pentagon foot-dragging. Kissinger claimed that every night since Tuesday he had gone to bed believing that twenty planes had been authorized, "and the next morning I find they're not moving."[*] He instructed Scowcroft to get Schlesinger on the phone. While they waited, Dinitz made a pitch for a direct USAF airlift to Israel. Kissinger rejected that out of hand. Dinitz countered that there would be hell to pay in Congress and the Jewish community if there was no direct airlift. He had been holding them off, he claimed, but he could do it no longer. "I have no right, no historical right; we are dealing with the destiny of a people," Dinitz declared emotionally.

At that moment, Schlesinger came on the line. Kissinger explained the problem as he now understood it from Dinitz. "They are stopping their offensive in Syria because they can't move because of lack of supplies." To underscore the problem, he exaggerated one of Dinitz's talking points: "They are now in deep trouble in the Sinai." These battlefield developments would undermine his entire diplomatic game plan, he told Schlesinger, because the

---

[*] The State Department had tried and failed to charter commercial planes on Wednesday. On Thursday, Kissinger had told Scowcroft and Sisco to tell the Pentagon to use its powers to commandeer commercial flights. By Friday night, there were still no commercial charters.

Israelis would look impotent: "It can only work if they look as if they were gaining, not if they look as if they were losing."

Schlesinger needed to get his people in line, Kissinger fulminated. He blamed Deputy Secretary of Defense William Clements for deliberately sabotaging his efforts. He observed sarcastically that the wealthy Texas oil man, who had oversight responsibility for chartering the commercial transport, would just as soon send the materiel to the Arabs. A contrite Schlesinger suggested that they just load up the ten C-130s they were planning to give the Israelis and fly them straight to Israel. That suited Dinitz fine, but Kissinger still preferred that the Military Airlift Command use its authority to charter commercial airlines. Even though he wanted the supplies in Israel yesterday, he was still trying to conceal the process from the Arabs.

Then, with Dinitz still in the room, Kissinger picked up the phone to Alexander Haig: "Al, you know we are now having massive problems with the Israelis because the sons of bitches in Defense have been stalling for four days and not one airplane has moved." He explained that the lack of ammunition had halted the Israeli offensive on the Golan and they might collapse in the Sinai, adding, "You know what this does to the diplomatic scenario I described to you, which absolutely required an Israeli offensive." Kissinger asked Haig to call Clements directly "and throw the fear of God into him," and do it to Schlesinger too.

To salvage the situation, however, he still needed the Pentagon's cooperation. As soon as Dinitz departed the West Wing, Kissinger picked up the phone to Schlesinger again, this time to mollify him. Schlesinger asked why, if the Israelis were so desperate for ammunition, their military attaché, General Gur, hadn't mentioned this to his Pentagon colleagues. In fact, he said, Gur "has been perfectly relaxed about the [daily] supply. . . . They simply cannot be that short of ammo, Henry. It is impossible that . . . suddenly they've run out of it." Schlesinger was right. That same day, Israel's assistant defense minister, Tzvi Tzur, who had responsibility for logistics, briefed the Knesset Foreign Affairs and Defense Committee that there was no shortage of ammunition and that the tank and plane requirements were for future battles. Tzur assured the committee they were not at the point yet where shortages were affecting freedom of operations. Unaware of that reality, Kissinger and Schlesinger were in no position to dispute Dinitz's assertion. They now agreed that the best way forward was to send the ten C-130s directly to Israel, loaded with ammunition.*

* In this phone call, Kissinger and Schlesinger agreed that the delay had been for forty-eight hours. Kissinger noted that he was responsible for the first twenty-four hours, when State had failed to secure any commercial charters, and that Schlesinger was responsible for the last twenty-four hours, when Clements had failed to invoke military regulations to charter commercial aircraft. See Henry Kissinger, *Crisis: The Anatomy of Two Major Foreign Policy Crises* (New York: Simon & Schuster, 2003), 215–19.

The Israelis should also pick up materiel that was in the Azores, and "forced charters" should deliver the rest.

Day eight, Saturday, October 13, 1973. Nixon had been preoccupied for the previous twenty-four hours dealing with the aftermath of Agnew's resignation and the installation of Gerald Ford as his new vice president. During that same time frame, the U.S. Court of Appeals had ruled against him on the question of whether he needed to release the Oval Office tapes that would ultimately sink his presidency. As the judges noted in their ruling, the president "is not above the law's commands."

If the United States were to start a direct airlift into Israel, Nixon would have to approve it—especially because early on Saturday morning Schlesinger had told Kissinger that instead of ten C-130s, he had managed to secure three giant C-5A military cargo planes to transport the materiel to Israel. They would surely be noticed when they landed there. So, on Saturday morning, Kissinger and Scowcroft discussed the issue with the president. Schlesinger, Colby, and Admiral Moorer were also present.

There is no official record of that meeting.* Nixon gave his version four years later, in his famous interview with David Frost. According to the president, Kissinger presented the Pentagon proposal to send the three C-5As directly to Israel, explaining that "politically it would be, perhaps, dangerous for us to send a greater number and that it would destroy the chances for negotiations in the future if our profile was too high."

Nixon felt he understood politics better than his chief diplomat, and in circumstances like these, he always believed in the advantages of "going big." No doubt also weighing the domestic advantages of being resolute in support of Israel amid a constitutional crisis, he told Frost that he responded, "Look, Henry, we're gonna get just as much blame for sending three, if we send thirty, or a hundred, or whatever we've got, so send everything that flies. The main thing is *make it work* [emphasis added]!"

Suitably chastened, Kissinger in turn warned the WSAG immediately afterward that "the President said if there are any further delays in carrying out orders, we want the resignation of the officials involved." Schlesinger too had been shaken by the president's reprimand, fearing Nixon might fire him. He had earlier reported to Haig that he had investigated and found that his

---

* According to the Kalbs, the meeting took place at 10:30 a.m. on Saturday, October 13, 1973. In their version, Nixon asked why there was a delay in implementing his orders on resupply. Schlesinger explained the difficulty in chartering planes. Nixon exploded: "To hell with the charters. Get the supplies there with American military planes! Forget the Azores! Get moving!" See Kalb and Kalb, *Kissinger,* 477.

people had indeed dragged their feet.* He now asked Kissinger, "Where did we screw up?" Kissinger said the charters should have been mandated. "But we didn't know it was urgent," Clements responded defensively.

Clements had a point. If the Pentagon officials had understood that the president wanted "everything that flies" to go directly to Israel and that their jobs were on the line, they might well have acted differently. In fact, despite the rapidly evolving crisis, Kissinger had not convened the WSAG since Tuesday, October 9, four days earlier. That was the same day he had consulted Nixon about the resupply and left him with the impression that all the consumables Israel needed would be sent forthwith. Kissinger had coordinated closely with Schlesinger in the meantime, but he later admitted to Haig that he probably made a mistake in not convening the coordinating meetings daily. From then on, Kissinger convoked the WSAG almost every day until the crisis was over.

It seems clear in retrospect that Kissinger's initial concern with keeping the resupply low profile had combined with the Pentagon's fear of offending the Arabs and the logistical challenge of finding commercial charters to produce a three-day delay in the resupply effort. Kissinger now believed, wrongly, that the tardiness was responsible for his loss of military leverage and a too-early Israeli desire for a cease-fire. He lamented his predicament to the other principals: "Our problem is to get the war over in a way the Arabs have to come to us, and then [we] turn on the Israelis. If Israel feels we have let them down and the Arabs think they have done it themselves, we are sunk." He noted how the choreography was all bollixed up, saying, "We needed to get the stuff in when we needed an [Israeli] offensive. Now it is going in afterwards, when we want the diplomacy to work." He had put this concern more succinctly in a conversation with Haig earlier that morning: "The Israelis are slackening off when we need their pressure and when we want them to slacken off the stuff will be in there, and they will fight again."

Clements suggested that they should launch a massive airlift to recoup. He, like Nixon, now thought they were going to take public flak no matter the number of planes sent. "No, we will lose all our Arab friends," Kissinger rejoined. He suggested they use the C-5As until they could generate the charters, hoping that would provide enough materiel to get the Israelis back on the attack "without rupturing it with the Arabs." He resolved to explain it to Ismail in the Egyptian back channel as an exercise in restraint in the face of a massive Soviet resupply effort. Kissinger comforted himself with the thought of renewed leverage: "If the Arabs see that things will get worse if they don't get a cease-fire, we may be ok."

---

* The order from the Joint Chiefs of Staff to commence Military Airlift Command charters to move all Israeli-bound cargo was not even issued until 5:53 p.m. on Friday, October 12. See Minutes of WSAG Meeting, October 13, 1973, FRUS 1969-1976:25, Doc. 173, fn. 12.

Kissinger would discover that Sadat was operating according to a different logic. While he spent much of the day between White House meetings exchanging phone calls with Soviet and British diplomats about the timing of the cease-fire resolution, Egyptians were watching on their televisions the surrender of Fort Mezakh, the last Israeli position at the southernmost end of the Bar-Lev line. The sight of Israeli soldiers saluting the raising of the Egyptian flag had a powerful emotional impact. Egyptians poured into the streets of Cairo to celebrate their victory over the previously invincible Israelis. In the meantime, Arab states were sending reinforcements to both fronts and the Soviet airlift was continuing apace. Far from thinking that things would get worse for Egypt if there were no cease-fire, Sadat was busily transferring SAM batteries and the tanks of the Egyptian army's 4th and 21st Armored Divisions to the east bank of the canal in preparation for his attempt to take the Sinai passes.

The Soviet ambassador now told Sadat that Assad wanted a cease-fire, but when Sadat contacted Assad he denied it. As long as the Syrians were refusing to stop the war, Sadat felt he could not do so. In Dobrynin's words, it would prove to be "a gross political and strategic blunder." If Sadat had accepted the cease-fire offered by the British, to which the Israelis had already acquiesced, he would have locked in his victory and his territorial gains and the Israeli advance on Damascus could have been stopped.

Because it appeared to Kissinger as so obviously in Egypt's interests to have a cease-fire, he had assumed that the Soviets had Sadat on board. An hour before the WSAG meeting, however, Sir Alec Douglas-Home, the British foreign secretary, called to report that the British ambassador in Cairo had spoken to Sadat and he was still rejecting the cease-fire. Kissinger refused to believe it, so Douglas-Home sent his ambassador back to Sadat with the additional information that the Soviets were willing to abstain on the resolution. This so enraged Sadat that he threatened to get the Chinese to veto it. There would be no cease-fire until Israel agreed to withdraw from all of Sinai, Sadat declared.

At first, Kissinger treated this as a typical act of British perfidy. He could not understand why they had bothered to talk to Sadat if they knew the Soviet Union and the United States were behind the resolution. He had simply assumed that joint superpower action, combined with Israeli military pressure, would leave Sadat no choice but to accept it. After the war, in a conversation with Assad, he explained his naive operating assumption: "We went to the Soviets when we wanted something from the Arabs. Since Arab military equipment came from the Soviets, we thought you would do what the Soviets said."

He had similarly assumed that Sadat had no choice but to accept the rules of détente worked out with Moscow at the June 1972 summit. That assumption had helped drive Sadat to war; now it would fail to persuade him to end it. But Kissinger's belief in a superpower-determined order was so strong that he would not easily surrender his preconception. Instead, he abandoned the British for the always more reliable Australians, who happened to be serving on the Security Council. However, when he sought Soviet approval for the switch, he was surprised to discover from Dobrynin that Moscow rejected the idea, probably because by then they understood that Sadat's offensive was now underway in the Sinai. The scales slowly started falling from Kissinger's eyes. He concluded that the Soviets had been stringing him along to buy time for Sadat's offensive, just like he had been stringing them along to buy time for Israel's advance on Damascus.

Nobody likes to be taken for a sucker, especially not Kissinger after he had publicly defended Soviet behavior. That, combined with the delay in resupplying Israel, had already provoked Senator Jackson to call for an investigation of his handling of the crisis, a proposal that deeply offended him.

Kissinger consulted with Scowcroft. His instinct was to respond by "pouring stuff into Israel." Channeling Nixon, he noted, "We can't let Israel lose," because a victory for Soviet arms would lead to the end of détente. "Since we are going to be in a confrontation, we should go all out," he asserted. He asked Scowcroft to find out how long it would take to mobilize the 82nd Airborne, the U.S. Army's elite rapidly deployable infantry division. "I think those bastards only understand brutality," said Kissinger.

Not only was Kissinger mad, but he now vowed to get even. He decided to use what he perceived as the Soviet "bait and switch" to justify the American airlift that was already underway for very different reasons. He called Dobrynin and informed him that because Brezhnev had failed to deliver Sadat, Nixon no longer felt obliged to restrain the American resupply effort. Then he called Dobrynin back in the evening to say, "We will not under any circumstances let détente be used for unilateral advantage." He blamed the hardening of Sadat's attitude on the Soviet airlift: "You don't think we will accept a military setback in the Middle East. You can't believe it." Aiming to strike a stinging blow, he noted that he had been in direct touch with the Egyptians. Since the Soviets were unable or unwilling to produce a cease-fire, he asked, "Why do we have to deal with you on matters that depend on Sadat? Why not deal with Sadat directly?" And then he sounded an ominous note: "We are obviously on a collision course." He added, "The President is extremely agitated. We will not let ourselves be pressured." And he hung up.

The threats had their desired effect. According to Dobrynin, he and Kissinger spoke again late that evening and agreed that for the sake of preserving détente they should work together to develop a new cease-fire formula that would be more acceptable to Sadat. Instead of calling for a return to the 1967 lines, which he knew Israel would refuse, Kissinger proposed that UNSC Resolution 242 be invoked, with its more ambiguous formula for withdrawal from territories occupied in 1967. He expressed a willingness to insert a call for a peace conference, which would appeal to both Nixon and Brezhnev, and which he already knew would be acceptable to the Egyptians because Ismail had offered it in their first wartime communication. He insisted that this time the superpowers needed to cosponsor the new cease-fire resolution.

Kissinger declared that this was his best offer. He swore to Dobrynin that "the United States would accept nothing more even if it meant a clash with the Arabs and the Soviet Union."

Day nine, Sunday, October 14, 1973. As he explained it to Nixon and, subsequently to the WSAG on Sunday morning, he had adapted his formula for a cease-fire to the new circumstances: "We are working to link the cease-fire to a political outcome without saying specifically what the political outcome will be. . . . The strategy now diplomatically is to go for a cease-fire and maneuver to link it loosely to a permanent settlement. For pressure, we will begin a massive supply effort and stop it only with a cease-fire."

Kissinger formally conveyed the new cease-fire offer, which he had foreshadowed in his phone call the evening before, to Dobrynin. He added that the American airlift at this point was mostly consumables and only a little heavy equipment. But, he said, "we can . . . increase it considerably and include heavy equipment."

In fact, Schlesinger reported to the WSAG that six C-5As and twenty-two C-141s had either landed in Israel or were en route, ferrying sixteen hundred tons of supplies a day, at fifty tons an hour. In comparison, Colby reported that the total Soviet airlift, which had been ongoing for a week, amounted to three thousand tons. Eight F-4 Phantoms had also just landed in Israel, with another six on their way, and another eight in the Azores standing by. Twenty A-4 Skyhawks would also be delivered by leapfrogging them from aircraft carrier to aircraft carrier across the Atlantic and the Mediterranean. "This is the most dramatic airlift since 1948," Schlesinger declared with newfound enthusiasm. "We should strive for a major impact in the shortest period of time," said Kissinger.

He believed this would now provide the Israelis with the wherewithal to prosecute the war on both fronts. "Ideally," Kissinger explained to his colleagues, "Israel would win without exorbitant costs, and quickly. But we don't want Israel totally intractable." It fell to Schlesinger to articulate the new reality that Kissinger understood all too well: "I don't see how [the Israelis] can be. They have complete dependence on the United States."

Kissinger would later explain the strategy's other objectives to his senior staff: "We are trying to force the Soviets now into a more moderate stand and . . . convince the Arabs that if there is to be a settlement, they have to deal with us."

The new strategy made Kissinger's beleaguered boss feel like he was playing an important role. Twice that morning Nixon had reiterated to Kissinger the airlift order he had given him the day before. "Well at least I feel better," he admitted during the second phone call. "As I told Al, if I contribute anything to [the] discussion it is the business that don't fool around with three planes. By golly no matter how big they are, just go gung ho."

The C-5A Galaxy is one of the largest aircraft in the world, with a wingspan of more than 220 feet, a distinctive high T-tail, four jet engines each providing 43,000 pounds of thrust, 28 wheels on its landing gear, and a capacity to transport up to 130 tons of equipment some 4,800 miles. On the night of the eighth day of the war, six of these massive winged symbols of American might and commitment swooped in from the Mediterranean and touched down at Lod Airport.* Like the Berlin Airlift of 1948–49 they provided an immediate shot in the arm to an embattled and dispirited Israeli nation. Uzi Eilam, then the IDF's director of research and development, described his feeling as he stood on the tarmac and watched the first tank roll out of a C-5A's gigantic rear doors. "This boosted our morale tremendously," he remembered, "know[ing] that we had the support of the most important superpower."

In the adjacent Sinai desert, the IDF and the Egyptian army were engaged in a tank battle of epic proportions. More than four hundred Egyptian tanks pushed forward on Sunday at dawn in six separate thrusts toward Tasa, Baluza, and Sinai's Mitla and Gidi Passes. Their frontal assaults were met with the open arms of the IDF's tank brigades. By late afternoon in the desert, morning in Washington, two hundred Egyptian tanks had been destroyed; only twenty Israeli tanks were damaged and then quickly repaired. As Ariel Sharon, then a division commander in Sinai, put it, paraphrasing Julius Caesar's famous letter to the Roman Senate after his defeat of Pharnaces II in the Battle of Zela in 47 BCE, "They came, they were hit, and they started to run." It was, according to the Egyptian chief of staff, General Shazli, "our most calamitous day."

On the northern front the night before, Israeli paratroopers had finally managed to conquer Tel Shams, a hilltop dominating the plain that stretched

---

* Lod Airport was later renamed Ben Gurion Airport after Ben-Gurion's death at the end of 1973.

to Damascus. Israeli long-range artillery had then moved up. By Sunday evening, as Egyptian tanks were pulling back in the Sinai, Israeli artillery had deployed in positions from where they could shell the suburbs of Damascus and the Mezze military airport, a mere five miles from downtown. At that moment, however, the advancing IDF tanks were ordered to halt. With the goring of the Egyptian army in the Sinai, the IDF had decided to shift the focus of its efforts to the southern front.

That evening, Elazar briefed the cabinet on his plan to put forces across the canal. Elazar had visited the Sinai front the day before and found his troops ready with an answer for everything. "The repair shops are working, the tanks are fine, there's ammunition," he reported to his staff at the Kirya, the defense ministry compound in Tel Aviv. With the massive American airlift now underway, Elazar no longer had to worry about whether Israel would have the means to defend itself in future wars, the impetus for his recommendation to the cabinet to accept Kissinger's cease-fire proposal two days earlier. The airlift's morale boost had also made it easier for Meir and Dayan to support continuation of the war effort.

At half past midnight, on a motion introduced by the prime minister, Operation Stouthearted Men—the crossing to the west bank of the canal—was approved by the cabinet for execution on Monday evening, October 15. It would be the turning point in the war. At that cabinet meeting, Meir also ordered the transmission of instructions to Eban and Dinitz to inform Kissinger that Israel's earlier acceptance of a cease-fire in place was now moot. Just as Kissinger had feared, the Israelis were now intent on pursuing a military solution. Nevertheless, as a result of Israel's cabinet decision, Kissinger would also acquire the leverage over the Egyptians and Soviets he needed to persuade them to accept the cease-fire. Then, as he had foreshadowed, it would be Israel's turn.

6

Cease-Fire

Mr. President, this has been the best-run crisis since you have been in
the White House.

—Henry Kissinger to Richard Nixon, October 17, 1973

Day ten, Monday, October 15, 1973. It was a testament to Kissinger's creativ-
ity and stamina that he managed to recover so quickly from the demise
of his earlier strategy. The new one would prove to be more coherent, sustainable, and ultimately successful. The first positive sign came at 3:00 a.m., when
Dobrynin called to inform him that the Kremlin accepted his idea of linking
the cease-fire to a reaffirmation of UNSC Resolution 242 instead of the 1967
lines. The Soviets also volunteered to sell that formula to Sadat and Assad.

Now that they seemed back in harness, Kissinger would henceforth assert
that his initiative was made in Moscow. Because of Meir's aversion to any reference to withdrawal, however ambiguous, he wanted the Israelis to think the
Russians had cooked it up and that he had no choice but to reluctantly accept
it for the sake of preserving détente. It had the added advantage of answering
the domestic critics of détente by demonstrating that the Soviets were being
constructive.

Claiming that a proposal is somebody else's idea is a common practice in
Middle East diplomacy. As we shall see, Sadat preferred to have his concessions packaged as American proposals. When King Hussein and Yitzhak Rabin
decided to make peace, in 1994, they put the principles of their agreement into
a "Washington Declaration," which was announced by President Clinton. Shimon Peres was fond of presenting his ideas as American proposals, if he could
persuade his American interlocutors to embrace them. Peres's most brazen

effort was when he presented the Oslo Accords to Secretary of State Warren Christopher at Naval Air Station Point Mugu, California, in September 1993. Peres and Rabin had negotiated the agreements with the PLO behind the backs of Clinton and his peace team, but Peres then wanted the U.S. president to present them as his own. Although Clinton declined, he did offer to host the signing ceremony at the White House.

Similarly, in 2014, Prime Minister Netanyahu convinced Secretary of State John Kerry to put forward an American peace framework based on the ideas Netanyahu's negotiators had agreed on with a representative of Palestinian president Mahmoud Abbas in the so-called London channel. Netanyahu tried the same tactic, more successfully, with Jared Kushner, Trump's special envoy, who took Netanyahu's ideas about the shape of a final settlement with the Palestinians and recycled them as Trump's "Deal of the Century."

In all those instances, the local actors sought to put the weight of the United States behind their initiatives. In this case, Kissinger wanted to saddle Moscow with responsibility for helping to end the war and the blame for inserting UNSC 242 into the cease-fire resolution.

At the WSAG meeting on Monday morning, in response to this cooperative Soviet attitude, Kissinger called for muting anti-Soviet statements. But to incentivize Moscow's efforts with its Arab clients, he wanted to step up the pressure from the airlift and add a sealift component.[*] Schlesinger reported that three thousand tons of materiel had arrived in Israel or was in the pipeline. Every twenty-four hours, four C-5As and twelve C-141s were now landing in Israel. As Kissinger explained to his senior staff in a subsequent meeting, the only hope for a cease-fire was to convince the Soviets "that we could put in things faster than they could, and into hands perhaps able to use it more rapidly than their clients."

With the resupply functioning to his renewed satisfaction and the Israeli offensive about to get underway in Sinai, Kissinger wanted to make sure the airlift did not force Sadat into a renewed embrace of the Soviet Union. He reached out to Ismail via the back channel to explain that he had been left with no choice. He had held off for a week, but his effort had been undermined by the massive Soviet airlift and Sadat's refusal of the cease-fire that the Soviets had reported he would accept. In other words, the delay Kissinger had previously told the Israelis was due to the Pentagon, he now claimed credit for with the Egyptians. He noted that the United States was "emphasizing mostly consumables" in its resupply effort—a stretch Sadat would hardly find convincing

---

[*] The sealift actually ended up providing 74 percent of the resupplies, a total of 62,713 tons vs. the airlift of 22,497 tons. The airlift ended in mid-November 1973; the sealift continued until January 6, 1974. See Hearings Before a Subcommittee of the Committee on Appropriations on H.R. 14262 (Washington, DC: U.S. Government Printing Office, 1976), 440.

if he knew at that moment it included twenty Phantom jets and hundreds of M60 tanks. It would be terminated, Kissinger promised, as soon as a cease-fire was agreed upon. Kissinger then attempted to soften the blow with a solemn commitment "to make a major effort as soon as hostilities are terminated to assist in bringing a just and lasting peace to the Middle East."

Ismail responded the same day, emphasizing Sadat's desire to keep the back channel open and making clear that "no other party spoke in Egypt's name," thereby signaling that Sadat continued to maintain his independence from Moscow. However, he repeated Sadat's requirement for coupling a cease-fire with a complete Israeli withdrawal. He concluded by inviting Kissinger to Cairo.

Eight months earlier Kissinger had mocked that invitation when Ismail conveyed it in their first meeting in Armonk. Now he enthusiastically embraced it as a welcome signal of Egypt's desire for a new relationship with the United States.

Day eleven, Tuesday, October 16, 1973. By the time Kissinger arrived at the State Department on Tuesday morning, Ariel Sharon and his forces had managed to cross to the west bank of the canal—into "Africa," as the Israelis referred to it. The lead paratroop brigades were equipped with three hundred LAW anti-tank missiles delivered the day before by the American airlift. Fighting on the east bank around the location known as the Chinese Farm remained intense, delaying the establishment of a secure crossing for the Israeli tank divisions. Nevertheless, the war had clearly entered a new and decisive phase.

Kissinger now tried to crack open Sadat's insistence on an Israeli commitment to a full withdrawal before a cease-fire. He told Ismail bluntly that he could not deliver that. His tone was grave. "The Egyptian side . . . has an important decision to make. To insist on its maximum program means . . . possible jeopardy of all that has been achieved," he warned. American diplomacy, he lamented, could not be given its "full opportunity" unless it was preceded by a cease-fire. If Sadat were to accept the cease-fire in place without an Israeli commitment to full withdrawal, Kissinger guaranteed that the United States would engage itself fully to achieve "a real and just peace which *reconciles the principles of sovereignty and security* [emphasis added]." This was a purposeful harking back to the idea Nixon had raised when Ismail first came to Washington in February 1973. Next, Kissinger floated the cease-fire formula that he had just persuaded the Soviets to adopt: a cease-fire in place would be accompanied by negotiations aimed at achieving a settlement "in accordance with Security Council Resolution 242 in all of its parts, *including withdrawal of forces envisaged by that resolution* [emphasis added]."

In crafting this response to Ismail, Kissinger's ultimate objective was to remove Egypt from the Soviet orbit and place it in the American camp. It was ironic therefore, but testament to Kissinger's diplomatic skill in co-opting the Soviets, that Brezhnev was at the same time discussing with the Politburo in the Kremlin how they could lend him a hand.

During the crisis, Brezhnev had more real-time battlefield intelligence at his disposal than Kissinger. He understood better than Sadat the danger to Cairo that Sharon's daring intrusion across the canal now posed. He feared that Egypt's defeat would precipitate a collapse of the Soviet position in the Middle East. After a seven-hour Politburo debate, Brezhnev decided to urgently dispatch Premier Alexei Kosygin to Cairo to convince Sadat to embrace Kissinger's cease-fire formula. "Remind him that Cairo is not far from the canal," he said to Kosygin. To bolster Kosygin's credibility with Sadat, the Soviet airlift was accelerated, and he was empowered to promise whatever materiel Sadat needed. To persuade Sadat that he had nothing to lose by accepting the cease-fire, Kosygin carried a message from Brezhnev pledging that if the cease-fire did not lead to a full Israeli withdrawal, the Soviet Union would provide Sadat with the wherewithal "to finally expel the Israelis."

Here was the art of diplomacy on full display. As an American-supplied Israeli force was about to undermine Sadat's triumph in crossing the canal, Kissinger was offering Ismail a face-saving formula for a cease-fire that would preserve most of Egypt's achievements. He was also committing the United States to a full partnership in returning Egyptian sovereignty to Sinai. And America's Soviet adversary was intent on giving him a huge assist. The timing, the leverage, the diplomatic formula, the guarantee, and the superpower coordination had all been finely orchestrated by the conductor to achieve the desired result. The coda to this polyphony came in Kissinger's closing response to Ismail's twice-proffered invitation to visit Cairo: the secretary of state would be happy to do so, he wrote, once the cease-fire had been established.

Sadat was in no mood to listen. That evening, in his general's uniform, accompanied by his defense minister, Sadat led a victory parade in an open-air limousine through the streets of Cairo to the National Assembly. There he delivered a speech in which he ignored the Soviet airlift and addressed himself to President Nixon. In a direct response to Kissinger's cease-fire proposal, he warned that "Egypt was not ready to accept ambiguous promises or elastic phrases subject to all kinds of interpretation, which would only return the situation to stalemate." He repeated that he would only accept a cease-fire based on Israel's immediate withdrawal from all occupied territories.

Sadat went from the parliament to army headquarters, where he angrily overruled his chief of staff, who had advocated withdrawing forces from the east bank of the canal to deal with the Israeli intruders. Then he met with

Kosygin. According to the Russian account, Sadat explained that his goals were limited to breaking the myth of Israeli invincibility and jump-starting negotiations that would lead to Israel's complete withdrawal. Given his experience, he did not trust the cease-fire formula, believing it would only produce some minor withdrawals. What he needed, he told Kosygin, were guarantees from both superpowers that all Arab territory would be liberated.

Kosygin argued that the time had come to convert Egypt's military achievements into political gains. Full withdrawal would remain the ultimate objective, but the IDF's crossing of the canal lent urgency to a cease-fire which, Kosygin emphasized, the Soviet Union now strongly favored. Sadat remained unconvinced. He understood the Soviet view, correctly, as an indication that Moscow lacked confidence in the Egyptian army. And that was the lens through which he viewed Kosygin's entreaty. He dismissed the IDF's canal crossing as a political maneuver and asserted that the military situation was stable.

Meanwhile, in Washington at the WSAG meeting on Tuesday morning, Kissinger told his colleagues that he wanted the American airlift to be 25 percent ahead of the Soviet effort.* His objective was "to run the Soviets into the ground fast" to maximize their incentive for a quick settlement. He may have missed the irony of that moment: the United States was rushing supplies to its Israeli client to outstrip the Soviet effort and increase the pressure for a cease-fire, while the Soviet Union was rushing supplies to its Egyptian client to match the American effort and encourage Sadat to accept a cease-fire. The effort to end the war had generated a competition between the superpowers that would continue fueling it.

The ultimate irony, however, came a moment later. As Kissinger discussed the calibration of the military airlift with his WSAG colleagues, the Norwegian Nobel Committee in Oslo announced the award of its prestigious peace prize to the architects of the Paris Peace Accords, Le Duc Tho and Henry A. Kissinger. A staffer in the Situation Room interrupted the deliberations to bring Kissinger the Associated Press news bulletin that heralded the conferring of this ultimate diplomatic accolade. As Kissinger later recorded, he was embarrassed by the award because he was well aware of the precarious nature of the agreement he had struck with the Vietnamese; he also knew that Nixon would be deeply jealous. To make matters worse, Nixon's nomination for the prize was a matter of public record; Kissinger had been a dark-horse candidate.

Nixon was gracious when he called to congratulate Kissinger, but he still

---

* At that point, the Soviet airlift was delivering some 700 to 800 tons a day, and the U.S. airlift was bringing in 650 tons to Israel.

found a way to needle his adviser. The president suggested that he donate the prize money ($65,000 in those days, which is equivalent to $390,000 in current dollars) to the American Red Cross for disaster relief in Pakistan, Africa, and Nicaragua. "I would not put any in for Israel," Nixon cautioned. Kissinger responded defensively, "I never give to Israel."* Looking back, Kissinger subsequently recorded, he was prouder of what he would go on to accomplish in the Middle East than of what he'd accomplished in Vietnam.

Day twelve, Wednesday, October 17, 1973. Kissinger was in a waiting mode: waiting for the IDF to increase the military pressure on the Egyptian armed forces, waiting for Kosygin to return from Cairo, and waiting for Sadat to come around to accepting his cease-fire formula.

The first opportunity to soften up the Arabs came in a meeting he had arranged for Nixon with the foreign ministers of Saudi Arabia, Kuwait, Algeria, and Morocco. They had come to present their own principles for a settlement, but Nixon did his best to convince them that they should accept Kissinger's formula for a cease-fire in place.

Nixon felt it necessary to assure the Arab foreign ministers that his efforts "would not be affected by U.S. political considerations—ever!" He noted that some of his Arab friends had questioned whether they could trust Kissinger because of his Jewishness, but he promised them his secretary of state was committed to a fair and just settlement.

The foreign ministers clearly found this amusing. The Kuwaiti foreign minister, Sheikh Sabah al-Ahmad al-Jaber al-Sabah, assured the president that they had no problem working with his secretary of state, since they were Semites too. But for Kissinger it was an embarrassing reminder that, for the second time in twenty-four hours, the president had demonstrated his abiding doubt about his objectivity when it came to Israel.

Not only were the Arab diplomats unfazed by Kissinger's Jewishness, they also seemed unconcerned about the U.S. airlift to Israel. The Kuwaiti weakly inquired whether it was necessary. Neither in the meeting with Nixon nor in a follow-up meeting at the State Department with Kissinger did they mention the potential for an Arab oil embargo in response, even though three of the four foreign ministers were from the largest Arab oil-producing countries. This led Kissinger to conclude that there would be no oil cutoff. He spent his

---

* Kissinger used the money to establish a scholarship fund in the names of his parents, Paula and Louis Kissinger, for the children of American soldiers killed or missing in action in Indochina. When Saigon fell to the North Vietnamese in 1975, Kissinger returned the prize and the money, but the Nobel Committee refused to accept them. See Henry Kissinger, *Years of Upheaval* (Boston: Little, Brown, 1982), 373.

time with them explaining his cease-fire formula, securing assurances that they would support it. "I think we're going to get . . . a cease-fire within three or four days," he assured Nixon.

Kissinger had misjudged the ministers. "Did you see the Saudi Foreign Minister come out like a good little boy and say they had very fruitful talks with us?" he joked with his colleagues in the WSAG that afternoon. As if to demonstrate how badly he had underestimated them, that evening the Arab oil ministers announced a mandatory cut in oil exports to Western consumers by 5 percent a month until Israel was pressed to withdraw from all occupied territories. Saudi Arabia announced it was cutting its production by 10 percent.

Three days earlier, led by Kissinger's friend the shah of Iran, the OPEC oil ministers had raised the price of their oil from $3.01 to $5.12 per barrel, a hike of 70 percent. That should have been a wake-up call. By his own account, in the early years of the Nixon administration Kissinger had paid little attention to the indications of the structural shifts in the balance of power in the oil market. In those days, oil was treated as a domestic issue best left in the hands of the oil "majors," rather than a matter of national security.* Accordingly, Kissinger was not involved in formulating policy or in advising the companies, who had been steadily ceding control of oil production to the Arab oil states and Iran. That process coincided with a growing Western dependence on Arab oil production because alternative sources of supply, including American domestic production, were no longer capable of meeting growing demand. Circumstances had created a potent Arab oil weapon hiding in plain sight of Washington's policymakers.

Kissinger had received several private warnings from senior Saudi officials in April and June 1973.† In July, King Faisal had given interviews to *The Washington Post* and *The Christian Science Monitor* in which he said he was seriously considering blocking future increases in oil production because of all-out U.S. support for Israel. In September 1973, he warned in an interview with *Newsweek* that he might have to use the oil weapon. But, just as in the case of Sadat's voluble warnings of war, these threats of an oil embargo were not taken seriously in Washington. The experts pointed to the collapse of similar efforts

---

* Before the 1973 oil embargo, the "Seven Sisters" controlled 85 percent of the world's oil reserves. They included Gulf Oil, Standard Oil of California, Texaco, Standard Oil of New Jersey, and Standard Oil of New York.
† Saudi oil minister Ahmed Zaki Yamani met with American cabinet members in April 1973 and warned of a possible change in Saudi oil policy if the United States did not pressure Israel to withdraw to the 1967 borders. He issued similar warnings to Aramco's parent companies in May, June, and August. See Memcon between Yamani, Faisal, Kissinger, Saunders, April 17, 1973, FRUS 1969–1976:36, Doc. 176, and Juan de Onis, "Saudis Weighing Oil-Output Curbs," *New York Times*, August 20, 1973.

during the Six-Day War. Schlesinger dismissed Faisal's warnings as "little more than hot air."

When the war broke out on October 6, Sisco's deputy, Roy Atherton, in the first meeting of the WSAG, predicted an Arab oil embargo and Rush noted that there was no contingency plan in place to deal with it. But no action was taken except, as we have seen, to avoid visible acts of tangible support for Israel in the early days of the war.

After Nixon decided on the airlift, Kissinger had penned a letter to King Faisal on October 14, explaining the decision as the consequence of the massive Soviet airlift to the Arabs. According to Prince Fahd, the king's half brother and then interior minister, with whom Kissinger had also established a back channel, the letter offended the king because it assumed that Saudi Arabia "would be willing to associate itself with American support to Israel in the name of anti-communism." Kissinger nevertheless proceeded on the sunny assumption that the Saudis would take no drastic action. He told the WSAG on October 15, "We have had no indication up to now that they intend a cut-off." On October 16, CIA director Colby assured him that Faisal "is inclined to blow off emotionally about things, but he usually calms down."

While Kissinger was busy with the Arab foreign ministers, he asked Scowcroft to brief Dinitz on what he was cooking up with the Soviets. Scowcroft, following Kissinger's instructions, asserted that it was a Soviet idea to link the cease-fire to Resolution 242, but added that the United States was not opposed to it in principle. Dinitz asked whether that would mean a cease-fire in place; Scowcroft answered affirmatively.

Dinitz called Kissinger back later in the evening to convey Dayan's congratulations on the Nobel Peace Prize. He also reported that Dayan had just returned from the canal very happy with what he saw. "Our position is such that his feeling is we don't need to beg from anyone," Dinitz relayed. Kissinger was surprised by the cockiness that seemed to be returning to the Israeli posture. He responded by citing Nixon's view that a cease-fire linked to Resolution 242 would be "very hard to refuse."

That evening Kissinger called Eban in New York to seek his support for the resolution. He again claimed that the formula was a Soviet idea. He informed Eban that the United States and the Soviet Union would probably be cosponsors to avoid any unwanted amendments to the resolution. Eban dutifully cabled Meir in support of the reference to 242, a resolution which he had helped negotiate in 1967 and which Israel had formally accepted in 1970. But Eban was no fool. He also reported that it was his impression from his conversation with Kissinger that the United States had already conceded this point to the Soviet Union.

When Kissinger convened the principals in the afternoon he told them he was lining everyone up and waiting for Kosygin to return from Cairo. Once all the pieces were in place, however, he warned it would break quickly in the Security Council.

It had been a bloody day of fighting in Sinai. The Israelis were steadily widening the gap between Egypt's Second and Third Armies on the east bank of the canal to enable their tank divisions to cross safely to the other side. By Wednesday night, they had managed to transfer enough tank brigades to the west side that they were able to break out of their bridgehead. In the meantime, the Egyptian 25th Armored Division had suffered huge losses when it attempted to close the gap on the east bank.

The Soviet defense attaché, reviewing the battlefield intelligence, advised Kosygin that there was now a high risk of the IDF's speedy encirclement of the Egyptian Third Army. Kosygin tried again to persuade Sadat to accept the cease-fire, arguing that it was vital to preserve Arab interests and that any delay would simply advantage Israel. Sadat was still not convinced. He dismissed the Israeli operations as "a small episode, nonsense." Kissinger's leverage was not yet having its intended effect.

Day thirteen, Thursday, October 18, 1973. With the route to the canal now secured, the IDF started transferring three armored divisions across the waterway. General Avraham "Bren" Adan's division, which had crossed first, spent the day destroying the Egyptian SAM batteries that protected Egyptian forces from air attack.

Kosygin took reconnaissance photography of the Israeli advances in fierce battles on the west side of the canal to one last meeting with Sadat. But the Egyptian president was obdurate. "I'm sorry to disappoint you," he remembers saying to Kosygin, "but no threat will ever be posed to Cairo." Kosygin gave up and returned to Moscow. He reported to Brezhnev that Sadat had been "stubborn, persistent, adamant, and irresponsible."

Nevertheless, the deteriorating situation on the ground and the American resupply effort had taken their toll on Sadat. He records that at 1:30 a.m. in Cairo on October 19, after receiving a briefing from his generals, he cabled Assad to inform him that he had decided to accept a cease-fire. Assad was surprised; he was on the verge of launching a counteroffensive against the Israeli forces that threatened Damascus. He reluctantly acquiesced. Kissinger's leverage had finally delivered.

Two hours later, Dobrynin called Kissinger with Brezhnev's wording of a three-point draft cease-fire resolution.* Brezhnev's formulation included Kissinger's idea of substituting a reference to the 1967 lines with a reference to Resolution 242, but instead of calling for a complete Israeli withdrawal before the cease-fire, as Sadat had demanded, it now called for the *beginning* of one. Kissinger told Dobrynin that the United States would have a problem with that, but he let Nixon know "they are moving in our direction." He later told Scowcroft that two of Brezhnev's three points were "highly acceptable."

It was time to reach out to Ismail to prepare Egypt for his cease-fire endgame. That evening he sent his Egyptian counterpart a message repeating his idea of a cease-fire linked to a reaffirmation of Resolution 242. He praised Egypt's "strength and valor" and said its battlefield gains should not be jeopardized by prolonging the fighting. What was needed now, he argued, was "a prompt end to the hostilities in conditions that make possible a serious effort toward a fundamental settlement."

Next he needed to finalize the text with the Soviets. In a late-night conversation with Dobrynin, he proposed the idea of a meeting in Moscow to resolve the remaining differences directly with Brezhnev.† Kissinger believed that order in international affairs required a hierarchy of power in which, especially at times when peace hung in the balance, the interests of the superpowers needed to prevail. In the circumstances of October 1973, the best way to uphold that principle was to engage directly with the Soviet leadership, which is what Kissinger had resolved to do by seeking the invitation to Moscow.

In an international crisis, when the stakes are high and time is of the essence, face-to-face negotiations between the decision makers is a responsible, even necessary, course of action. Taking a midnight flight to Moscow to end a war also appealed to Kissinger's penchant for the dramatic. And it would help to separate Kissinger's crisis diplomacy from the deepening Watergate crisis.

In normal times, negotiations with the general secretary of the Central Committee of the Communist Party of the Soviet Union would be the president's rightful preserve. But these were not normal times. Kissinger expected

---

* The Soviet draft called for: (1) an immediate cease-fire in place; (2) followed by an immediate start to Israeli withdrawal "to the line in accordance with Resolution 242"; and (3) concurrent with the cease-fire, "appropriate consultations" between the two superpowers aimed at achieving an honorable peace.

† In the American documentation and Kissinger's accounts, there is no mention of him proposing that Brezhnev invite him. But Dobrynin records that when he proposed the idea to the Kremlin, he indicated that he was confident Kissinger would accept. In the Politburo, they were convinced it was Kissinger's idea. When I asked Kissinger, he said that Dobrynin's version was "basically correct." See Anatoly Dobrynin, *In Confidence: Moscow's Ambassador to Six Cold War Presidents* (New York: Crown, 1995), 290; Victor Israelyan, *Inside the Kremlin During the Yom Kippur War* (University Park, PA: Pennsylvania State University Press, 1995), 124; Indyk interview with Henry Kissinger, July 28, 2015.

Nixon in his embattled state to be particularly protective of his prerogatives. A personal invitation from Brezhnev might help.

Flying off to Moscow in the middle of the night would inevitably raise Israeli fears of an imposed cease-fire that would cut short its offensive. To calm them, he asserted that the purpose of his sudden trip was to buy Israel time. But the moment was fast approaching when Kissinger would need to bring the Israelis to heel. Just how much of a heavy lift he would have to undertake became evident that same evening when Dinitz brought Meir's response to his idea of introducing Resolution 242 into the cease-fire terms. "The very possibility of a mention of 242 lights up a red light for us," she said. She pointed out that the situation on the front provided "no reason for any speed up of the diplomatic moves." Revealing how little she knew of what Kissinger was up to, she argued that since so far there were "only feelers from the Soviet side," there was no reason "for undue haste."

This was precisely the problem Kissinger foresaw. With the airlift in full flight and the situation on the battlefield now developing in Israel's favor, the sense of urgency for a cease-fire the Israeli cabinet had felt six days earlier had evaporated, just when he would need it most.

Day fourteen, Friday, October 19, 1973. At 11:00 a.m. Dobrynin conveyed a message from Brezhnev to Nixon which asserted that "prompt and effective political decisions are needed." Brezhnev stressed that "now not only every day but every hour counts." Therefore, he invited Nixon to send "your closest associate Dr. Kissinger" to Moscow, saying that "it would be good if he could come tomorrow, October 20." Kissinger discussed the issue with Nixon and called Dobrynin back thirty minutes later to invite the Soviet ambassador, who had now become his cease-fire partner, to join him on his U.S. Air Force VIP aircraft, which would depart around midnight.* He explained that they would arrive at 9:00 p.m. on Saturday evening, so Kissinger would not be ready to negotiate until Sunday morning. He said that they shouldn't expect to conclude an agreement in one day.

Kissinger then reassured Dinitz that "the outcome cannot be implemented before we have discussed it with you." Nevertheless, the Israelis had their guard up. Meir asked Dinitz why Kissinger was going to Moscow. Eban wondered what his rush was, since the Russians were the ones that needed a cease-fire to protect their Egyptian client from military defeat. Meir feared he was

---

* Nixon accepted Kissinger's argument that the invitation would serve the purpose of keeping the issue out of the Security Council until the superpowers had shaped an agreeable outcome, discouraged Soviet bluster, and bought the Israelis another seventy-two hours.

about to capitulate to Soviet demands and wanted Dinitz to reiterate that the proposed Soviet cease-fire terms were completely unacceptable.

Notwithstanding her vehement opposition, Kissinger told Dinitz he should expect the president to accept the linking of the cease-fire to Resolution 242 and that the prime minister should find it in her heart to express appreciation because she would need him in the negotiations to come. It was a none-too-subtle warning, like the gun placed on the mantel in the first act of a murder drama. If the Israelis didn't want it to go off in the third act, he was implying, they had better be ready to accept his formula for the cease-fire resolution.

Day fifteen, Saturday, October 20, 1973. Kissinger departed Andrews Air Force Base on his USAF Boeing 707 at 12:30 a.m. En route, he received the unwelcome news that King Faisal had announced a total embargo of oil exports to the United States. Even though the announcement of the price hike and production cuts had rung alarm bells in Washington, nobody had thought to hold up Nixon's formal request to Congress the day before for $2.2 billion in supplementary assistance to Israel to pay for the military airlift. The news of that request gave King Faisal the justification to embargo Saudi Arabia's friend and ultimate protector. As Prince Fahd explained to Kissinger in an oral message three days later, "the embargo on oil for the United States will continue in force as long as Israel occupies Arab territory beyond its borders as they existed before the June 1967 war."

For the moment, Kissinger was too focused on his looming negotiations with Brezhnev to appreciate the significance of Faisal's decision. He dispatched a steady stream of cables from the plane with precise instructions to Scowcroft, whom he had left behind at the White House to manage the president, the bureaucracy, and the Israeli ambassador. Kissinger ordered that four Phantoms and ten Skyhawks be delivered each day, as well as ammunition and some helicopters. Keeping the rapid resupply going was not just to fatten up the Israelis before he demanded they comply with the terms of the cease-fire resolution he was about to finalize in Moscow. He also wanted to use it as leverage on the Soviets. As he explained to Scowcroft in the cable, "The negotiations I am about to undertake will be tough, and I will need to have some bargaining chips to give up should the occasion warrant."

His main leverage, however, would continue to come from Israeli military pressure. Recognizing that he did not have real-time visibility into the progress the IDF was making, he instructed Scowcroft to get Dinitz to report to him three times a day on the Israeli ground offensive and then dispatch that information immediately to him in Moscow. (Reflecting Israeli suspicions of what was afoot, Dinitz never called.)

Kissinger then sat with Sisco to work on the language of the resolution Brezhnev had supplied, inserting into the U.S. draft a sentence on the need for direct negotiations between the parties. That would vitiate the "joint auspices" for convening the negotiations that he would have to concede to the Soviets. He also calculated that Meir would appreciate it, since direct engagement with the Arabs was something Israel had long sought and the Arabs had long refused.

His work was interrupted by a distressing cable from Scowcroft informing him that the president had fired off a message to Brezhnev, without consulting Kissinger, announcing to the Soviet leader that "Dr. Kissinger speaks with my full authority and . . . the commitments that he may make in the course of your discussions have my complete support."

Normally, a diplomat engaged in high-level negotiations would welcome the clear-cut legitimation of his authority that Nixon had conferred on Kissinger in this message. But Kissinger "was horrified" by it, he recalls in his memoirs. Nixon's unilateral move, he feared, would deprive him of the ability to stall Brezhnev by claiming that he needed to consult with his president before reaching an agreement.

What really upset him, however, were the detailed instructions from Nixon that were transmitted to him two hours later. Kissinger had hoped to avoid this kind of presidential micromanagement by conjuring up the invitation to Moscow in the first place. Given that Nixon was at that moment finalizing details of his plan to fire Watergate special prosecutor Archibald Cox, the instructions show an unusual degree of presidential focus and clarity.

The president wanted to "go all out" to achieve a just settlement "now." Kissinger was instructed to tell Brezhnev that he had been right at San Clemente to warn about an imminent explosion, that four Arab-Israeli wars in twenty years was intolerable, and that the time had come for decisive action. Nixon wanted to work with Brezhnev to determine the proper course of action and "bring the necessary pressure on our respective friends."

Nixon was in effect ordering Kissinger to abandon his carefully constructed strategy for a cease-fire followed by American-led negotiations in favor of a full-fledged U.S.-Soviet attempt to impose a solution on the warring parties forthwith. Kissinger was furious. As he told Scowcroft, he regarded these instructions to be "unacceptable." They would "totally wreck what little bargaining leverage I still have." And if he failed to achieve the cease-fire and the war continued, he said, "the consequences will be incalculable." Here, in stark relief, lay the difference between Kissinger's and Nixon's approaches to Middle East peacemaking. It would prove to be the case with President Ford too. Kissinger would always look for the small, achievable, incremental step, whereas his bosses, hungry for dramatic diplomatic achievements, wanted to leap forward to the endgame.

For now, Kissinger decided simply to ignore the president's instructions. He would claim later that he had not received them before his first meeting with Brezhnev.* Of course, there was nothing to stop him from presenting Nixon's views in the second meeting, which took place the next day, but given the tumult in Washington by then, nobody bothered to make an issue out of Kissinger's noncompliance.† Kissinger explains in his memoirs what might otherwise have looked like insubordination. He believed Nixon expected him to delay implementing his "more exuberant directives." It was a way of "giving our President the opportunity to live out his fantasies" while Kissinger acted with the calculation that Nixon expected of his secretary of state.

At Brezhnev's insistence, the first meeting took place at 11:00 p.m. on Saturday night, despite Kissinger's best efforts to get some sleep. The Soviet leader received the American party in his large, drab, "communist-modern" office in the Politburo in the Kremlin. Kissinger couldn't help but notice the Soviet leader's huge desk with a telephone console "the shape and dimensions of a medium-sized organ." Brezhnev laid on dinner for Kissinger on his long rectangular conference table, adorned with cut-crystal glasses and ashtrays—Brezhnev was a heavy smoker. He greeted the American team in a blue jumpsuit.‡

Brezhnev was in a jovial mood, happy to point out, much to Kissinger's discomfort, that Nixon had fully authorized him, so they could conclude the deal on the spot. He was clearly in a hurry, which boded well for the negotiations even if not for Kissinger's dilatory intentions. Brezhnev bore down immediately on Kissinger's reaction to his cease-fire resolution draft. Kissinger responded that the first and third articles needed work but were broadly

---

* Scowcroft sent the instructions to Peter Rodman, with directions to put them in a sealed envelope and hand them to Kissinger's executive assistant, Larry Eagleburger. According to Kissinger's account in his memoirs, he read them only after he returned to the guesthouse following his first meeting with Brezhnev. If this is true, it would mean that Eagleburger did not deliver the presidential instructions to Kissinger during the two-hour interval between their landing and the meeting with Brezhnev, an unlikely dereliction of duty. See Kissinger, *Years of Upheaval*, 550–51.

† This was not the first time Kissinger had ignored Nixon's instructions when engaging the Soviet leadership. In April 1972, for example, when Nixon dispatched Kissinger to Moscow to prepare for the May summit, he instructed that the only item on Kissinger's agenda had to be Vietnam. As Stephen Sestanovich recounts, when Kissinger met with Brezhnev in the Kremlin, "he discussed whatever he pleased." See Stephen Sestanovich, *Maximalist: America in the World from Truman to Obama* (New York: Alfred A. Knopf, 2014), 181.

‡ Kissinger's team included Joe Sisco, Roy Atherton, Helmut Sonnenfeldt, Winston Lord, and Peter Rodman.

acceptable; the problem would be with the second article's insistence on linking the cease-fire to Israeli withdrawal.

Kissinger went to bed expecting that he would be able to conclude an
agreement on the morrow. However, to curb Nixon's enthusiasm for engagement, Kissinger instead predicted very tough negotiations ahead and only an
even chance of a breakthrough.

Kissinger need not have worried about further interference from his boss.
For on Saturday, October 20, 1973, Nixon was overwhelmed by a full-blown
constitutional crisis of his own making, precipitated by his firing of Archibald
Cox and the abolishment of his office. Nixon's attorney general, Elliot Rich-
ardson, then resigned in protest, and when his deputy, William Ruckelshaus,
refused to discharge Cox, Nixon fired him too. It went down in history as the
Saturday Night Massacre. In response, Democratic and Republican leaders on
Capitol Hill began to discuss impeachment.

Day sixteen, Sunday, October 21, 1973, Moscow. Kissinger awoke in the dreary
Soviet guest villa in the Lenin Hills overlooking the Moscow River to good
news from Cairo. He had sent a message to Ismail before leaving Washington
to inform him of his trip to Moscow and to repeat the U.S. commitment to a
diplomatic effort after a cease-fire had been achieved. The response he now
received signaled a breakthrough for his strategy of applied leverage. Ismail
said that Egypt was ready to accept a cease-fire in place, the convening of a
peace conference, and superpower guarantees of the cease-fire and the withdrawal of Israeli troops. In other words, Sadat was no longer insisting on Israeli
withdrawal before a cease-fire, and there was no mention of the 1967 lines.

Unbeknownst to Kissinger, Sadat had also summoned Soviet ambassador
Vladimir Vinogradov just after midnight, while Kissinger was breaking bread
with the Soviet leadership. His chief of staff, General Shazli, had just returned
from the front with the alarming news of Israeli advances on the west bank
of the canal and wanted to withdraw armored brigades from the east bank
immediately. Despite Shazli's emotional entreaties, Sadat said not a single rifle
or tank would be moved. Sadat would need the territorial gains for the forthcoming negotiations. Instead, he relieved Shazli of his command on the spot.
He then met with Ambassador Vinogradov and informed him that Egypt was
ready for a cease-fire. If Sadat was now in a hurry too, nothing stood in the
way of a quick agreement with Moscow and Cairo on the cease-fire terms. Kissinger no longer needed to stall in order to increase Israeli military pressure
on them.

The negotiating session with Brezhnev and Gromyko began on Sunday at
noon, back in Brezhnev's office in the Kremlin. They sat again on either side

Henry Kissinger and General Secretary Leonid Brezhnev in his
Kremlin office on October 21, 1973. Kissinger had sought an
invitation to Moscow to negotiate a U.S.-Soviet cease-fire resolution
to end the Yom Kippur War. The negotiations were concluded
quickly because of the pressure of Israel's military offensive on
Egyptian forces on the western side of the Suez Canal. Brezhnev
asked whether they should consult with Egypt and Israel before taking
the resolution to the UN Security Council. Kissinger said they should
go straight to the Security Council although he had promised Golda
Meir prior consultation.

of the long, polished, wooden conference table, last night's dinner settings
replaced by blotters and bottles of mineral water.

Brezhnev moved quickly to the question of how to proceed with the cease-
fire resolution. He asked whether they should consult with both warring sides
first or take the resolution straight to the UN Security Council and expect
them both to accept it. "In principle, if we reach agreement, then we should
submit it soon after to the Security Council to bring about an end to the hostilities," answered Kissinger. So much for the prior consultation he had promised Israel.

On the first point in the Soviet draft—the call for a cease-fire—Kissinger
wanted to make sure the language applied to all Arab combatants and that they
should stop "in the positions they now occupy." Brezhnev had no objection.
Ironically, it was the Israelis that Brezhnev and Kissinger should have been
worried about.

On the second point, Kissinger proposed substituting the Soviet call for
Israeli withdrawal with a call for the immediate implementation of Resolution
242 "in all of its parts," one of which referred to withdrawal. Kissinger said

that he had not discussed this with the Israelis (which was not accurate) but was ready to proceed anyway—a further indication that he did not intend to consult with them first.

On the third point, Kissinger proposed immediate, direct negotiations between the parties concerned under "appropriate auspices . . . aimed at establishing a just and durable peace."

Brezhnev responded by predicting that they would be having an early dinner that night. He too was ready to drop any direct call for Israeli withdrawal or any reference to the 1967 lines. Rather, 242's vague, ambiguous, and heavily qualified reference to Israeli withdrawal from territories occupied in 1967 would apply. Just as Kissinger had calculated, Israel's military pressure had worked wonders.

Seeking to secure the Soviet role in future peacemaking, Brezhnev did want a clearer understanding of what "joint auspices" would involve. He advocated that the United States and the Soviet Union should be "active" participants in the negotiations. Kissinger pointed out that the Israelis would violently object to active Soviet participation, and Brezhnev countered that the Arabs would object to active American participation. They settled on Kissinger's formulation that the negotiations would be conducted under their auspices and both would be involved "at crucial moments." Brezhnev interpreted that vague formulation to mean that they would both be involved in "the solution of all the key issues." Kissinger agreed, although, as we shall see, he had no intention of letting that happen.

Kissinger raised the issue of Israeli POWs, knowing that Meir would be concerned about it. They agreed that they would both press for an immediate exchange of all prisoners of war.

They arranged that their UN ambassadors would jointly call for a Security Council session to be convened at 9:00 p.m. New York time that evening, twelve hours after their meeting at the Kremlin concluded. The cease-fire would take effect another twelve hours from the time of the passage of the resolution. That meant there would be at least twenty-four hours between the Moscow agreement and the cease-fire called for in the resulting UNSC resolution.

Notably, for what would subsequently transpire, there was no discussion about how the cease-fire would be monitored. In the headiness generated by their newfound cooperation, both Brezhnev and Kissinger assumed that their two clients would have no choice but to accept the cease-fire.

The agreement took four hours to negotiate, including translation time—a record for U.S.-Soviet negotiations. Kissinger returned to the guesthouse to deal with the implementation arrangements. When he notified Scowcroft of the agreement and the text of the resolution at 7:30 p.m. Moscow time/12:30

p.m. Washington time, he instructed him not to communicate it to any-one, "especially Dinitz," until he had issued instructions to do so. Kissinger then met with the British, French, and Australian ambassadors in Moscow, informed them of the agreement, and asked their governments not to try to amend the text of the resolution in the Security Council if they wanted a quick end to hostilities.

He then issued instructions to Scowcroft to call in Dinitz, inform him of the cease-fire resolution, and hand him a letter from Nixon to Meir that Kissinger had drafted, urging her to see in the cessation of hostilities a considerable achievement for Israel: Israeli forces could hold on to their territorial gains; there would be direct Arab-Israeli negotiations for the first time since the 1948 armistice talks; and there was no reference to withdrawal, or to the 1967 lines, in the language of the resolution.

Confident that the Israelis would acquiesce, Kissinger took a nap. When he awoke, he was informed that his instructions had not been conveyed because of a communications snafu. Larry Eagleburger, then Kissinger's executive assistant, remembers his reaction: "I looked up to find [Kissinger] standing in the middle of the room with smoke issuing from nose, eyes, and ears."

Kissinger suspected the Russians were deliberately blocking his communications, but why would they want to disrupt the implementation of a cease-fire they now desperately sought? Scowcroft, though, received enough of Kissinger's cable to call in Dinitz and read him the text of the resolution, explaining that because of interference on the line his instructions were garbled. He called back an hour later with the rest of Kissinger's message about the advantages to Israel of the resolution, but he did not yet have in hand Kissinger's draft of the formal presidential request to the Israeli prime minister to accept the resolution.

Meir instructed Dinitz to complain to Scowcroft about the short time frame, especially because she would have to convene her cabinet to decide on whether to accept the cease-fire. That could not occur before midnight, given the time it would take for several of the ministers to travel from their homes in Jerusalem to the prime minister's office at the Kirya in Tel Aviv.

As she outlined to the cabinet her concerns about the contents of the resolution, the lack of consultation, and its rushed timing, she was suddenly interrupted by the arrival of General Elazar. He brought the welcome news that Mount Hermon in the Golan had been retaken after an intense battle. At 1:30 a.m. she finally received Nixon's letter asking her to accept the cease-fire resolution, which included a promise that he and Brezhnev would work for an immediate release of Israeli POWs. The letter noted that he would have preferred more time to consult, but the IDF was in a strong position, the resolution was good for Israel, and it made no sense to prolong the bloodletting.

While he did not yet know how the Arabs would react, the president hoped Israel would quickly accept the resolution. Fifteen minutes later, a message from Kissinger arrived, gilding the lily by emphasizing there would be direct negotiations, no call for Israeli withdrawal, and a minimum reference to 242, plus the UN would be kept out of the negotiations.

Meir's mood was exacerbated by a call she took during the cabinet deliberations from the British ambassador, who conveyed a message from Foreign Secretary Douglas-Home imploring her to accept the resolution. She concluded, correctly, that Kissinger had briefed the British before he had bothered to inform her. She told her fellow ministers that Kissinger had promised her before he had departed for Moscow that Israel would not be delivered a fait accompli, but now Israel could not alter, reject, or dismiss the cease-fire without damaging its relations with Washington, and if it did so, it would stop receiving arms from the only nation prepared to supply them. It could not even insist on conditioning the cease-fire on the return of Israeli prisoners of war, she said bitterly. "When there is no choice, then there is no choice. . . . We cannot reject the cease-fire," she argued.

Eban records that, despite the consternation and "rank[ling] in our hearts," his fellow ministers were positively disposed to the substance of the resolution: "The proposal being made to us kept our military victories intact and added an important political gain," i.e., direct negotiations. Eban felt that further fighting risked Soviet intervention, more Israeli casualties, and Egypt's humiliation. He notes, however, that the resolution made no provision for monitoring, "contrary to most UN ceasefire resolutions." Israel's chief diplomat well understood the resolution's weak point.

At 4:00 a.m. in Tel Aviv and 9:00 p.m. in New York, where the Security Council had already begun its deliberations, the Israeli cabinet voted unanimously to accept the cease-fire if Egypt and Syria did too. The cabinet also instructed Meir to seek a series of clarifications and assurances from the United States, a standard Israeli reflex whenever its leaders are pressured by Washington to make concessions to Arab adversaries they do not trust.[*]

Kissinger's resupply leverage had worked on them as surely as his military leverage had worked on the Egyptians and the Soviets, even though his decision not to consult with the Israelis left bitter feelings that would not be forgotten. Schlesinger had been right when he predicted that Israel's dependence on the massive American airlift would render pliable its recalcitrant

---

[*] In this case, the cabinet wanted assurances about the American interpretation of Resolution 242: that the cease-fire would apply to non-state actors, that there would be no interference with Israeli-bound shipping in the Red Sea, and that the resupply would continue on a par with the Soviet resupply of the Arabs. See Shimon Golan, *War on Yom Kippur* [in Hebrew] (Jerusalem, Modan Publishing, 2013), 1132.

prime minister. Kissinger had been right too in arguing from the outset that the United States had to stand with Israel in its moment of greatest need to be able to pry concessions out of it later. That was a lesson in patron-client influence that Kissinger would apply again two years later.

That night, the UN Security Council voted unanimously for Resolution 338, with the Israeli and Egyptian representatives expressing their acceptance and China absenting itself from the room in protest at what it viewed as U.S.-Soviet collusion. The cease-fire was set to go into effect on the battlefields of Egypt and Syria at 6:52 p.m. Monday evening, October 22, sixteen days after the beginning of the war. It was a triumph for Kissinger's diplomacy. But the crisis was far from over.

7

DEFCON 3

The Gods are offended by hubris. They resent the presumption that great events can be taken for granted. Historic changes such as we sought cannot be brought off by virtuoso performances; they must reflect an underlying reality.

—Henry Kissinger, *Years of Upheaval*

*D*ay *seventeen, Monday, October 22, 1973, Israel.* The sleek USAF Boeing 707 that would become Kissinger's workhorse while he was secretary of state arrived from Moscow at Israel's Lod Airport at 1:00 p.m. It taxied to a halt at a red carpet that stretched from the airplane stairs toward a speaker's podium surrounded by television cameras and a crowd of foreign press. At the foot of the stairs, waiting to greet Kissinger on his first visit to Israel since entering the Nixon administration, stood Abba Eban and his foreign ministry staff. Hundreds of Israelis had also gathered to view Kissinger's arrival and express appreciation to the representative of the country that recent experience had taught them was a true friend in need. As Kissinger emerged from the aircraft, they spontaneously broke into sustained applause. For Kissinger, it was "one of the most moving moments of my government service." The welcome did not reduce his apprehension. As he took Eban's extended hand, he said, "I expect Golda is mad at me."

The prime minister had decided to use the Mossad's facility at Herzliya, some eight miles up the coast from Tel Aviv, for the meeting with her special guest. The building there, known as the *midrasha*, became famous in later years as the guesthouse for clandestine visits to Israel by foreign leaders. Jordan's King Hussein was the most celebrated of them. Israelis in those days were an abstemious lot, but the Mossad stocked the living room with a full bar, including a selection of single malt whiskeys for the king's pleasure. The build-

Israeli foreign minister Abba Eban escorting Henry Kissinger from his plane at Israel's Lod International Airport on October 22, 1973. Kissinger received a hero's welcome from the assembled crowd of Israelis. He had flown in from Moscow after negotiating the cease-fire resolution with Brezhnev. As he stepped off the plane, his first words to Eban were "I expect Golda is mad at me."

ing resembled a flat-roofed California bungalow with floor-to-ceiling glass windows and sliding paneled doors. It was situated on a small hill, but grass-covered berms around the building prevented anyone from seeing in, or out.

As they sped across the coastal plain to their rendezvous with Meir, Kissinger noted to Eban that clearly not all Israelis were mad at him. He explained that Brezhnev had surprised him by accepting his formulations without warning, including the call for direct negotiations. Such sudden reversals were characteristic of totalitarian diplomacy, he claimed. He hoped Meir would see the overall result as a win in terms of the coming negotiations sufficient to overcome her chagrin about lack of consultation.

Meir and Kissinger spent the first fifteen minutes alone. According to Kissinger's account, she did not chastise him. Instead, she expressed concern about her nightmare scenario of a U.S.-Soviet deal to impose the 1967 borders on Israel, the very thing Nixon had instructed Kissinger to propose to Brezhnev. He discerned her underlying trepidation that in the upcoming negotiations Israel would have to give up territory, a fraught prospect for a politically weakened prime minister. Always sensitive to the mindset of the leaders with whom he dealt, Kissinger recognized the burden she carried. It was generated, he believed, by her inability to avert the war and all its casualties. "She was heartbroken not simply by the suffering but by her vision of what was ahead," he observed.

Once they were joined by note takers, Kissinger went into an elaborate explanation of why Resolution 242 was better for Israel than the alternatives he had managed to block. He claimed that it could have been a lot worse, since Brezhnev "had screamed for implementation of *all* UN Resolutions [emphasis added]" (that was a fiction). Meir sought his promise that the obscure language would truly result in direct negotiations. Reassured, she shifted her focus to the prisoners of war. Kissinger said he had solemn assurances that Gromyko and Brezhnev would speedily address the issue. In a poignant moment she blurted out, "I can't live with it. . . . How can I face the mothers and wives of these men?" Still emotional, she said, "I know what you did. Without you, I don't know where we would have been." The wayward nephew was forgiven, at least for the moment.

Meir noted that the IDF would have been in a better position with a few days' more fighting, and then asked what was meant by the resolution's call for a "standstill cease-fire." Could Israel rely on the Egyptians not to cheat, as they had done so blatantly in 1970? Surprisingly, given the way he had excoriated Rogers and Sisco for ignoring Egyptian violations in 1970, Kissinger admitted that he "hadn't thought it through." Meir noted that Egypt and Syria had not yet accepted the cease-fire. Kissinger responded by making her an offer she had not asked for but could hardly refuse: "You won't get violent protests from Washington if something happens during the night, while I'm flying. Nothing can happen in Washington until noon tomorrow," i.e., Tuesday. "If they don't stop, we won't," Meir declared. "Even if they do . . . ," Kissinger responded.

Kissinger was green-lighting another twenty-four hours of IDF activity *beyond* the cease-fire, which was due to go into effect at noon on Monday, Washington time.* He reiterated the signal to Eban in the car ride back to the airport, saying that he expected the cease-fire would come into effect "within a day or two."

At lunch, they were joined by Dayan, Eban, Yigal Allon (now Meir's deputy), and Kissinger's old friend Yitzhak Rabin, who had become her informal adviser. Dayan had a very clear agenda and was quite blunt about it: "I'd like not to stop." Then he asked whether there was any mechanism for deciding the cease-fire lines. "No. I think reality will determine it," Kissinger hinted. The conversation shifted to the prisoners of war, but Dayan brought it back to the cease-fire: "Our maneuvers on the Egyptian front were . . . very successful. You came too early." Kissinger ignored the gibe, but Dayan would not be denied. "There will be problems now with no line between the forces," he said.

---

* According to the Israeli record of this conversation, Kissinger said, "There won't be any complaints if the IDF advances this evening, it's normal that right after the start of the cease-fire, units continue to attack. If I'm still in the airplane, I will have an excuse." See Shimon Golan, *War on Yom Kippur* [in Hebrew] (Jerusalem, Modan Publishing, 2013).

Kissinger invoked his experience in Vietnam, where "everybody said it would be unmanageable—but it shook itself out very easily." Given that Hanoi and Saigon had ignored the standstill provisions of the Paris Peace Accords from the outset, he could only have come across as cavalier. Dayan explained to him that on the western side of the canal the battles were still raging. Kissinger changed the subject.

Over lunch, Dayan raised the idea of conquering Port Fuad, adjacent to Port Said at the northern end of the canal. Kissinger said he would not be opposed. Later he had second thoughts about Port Fuad, but he had signaled unmistakably that he would not object to the IDF continuing its advances.[*]

The generals entered the room to brief Kissinger on the military situation. Elazar explained that the war in the south was continuing apace and the Egyptian Third Army could soon be surrounded. Kissinger asked whether it could be resupplied. Elazar showed Kissinger on a map that the only route left open was around Jebel Attaka to the port of Adabiya, just south of Suez (see map on page 527). As Kissinger would subsequently recall, Elazar had told him "the exact location *and objectives* of their forces on the West Bank of the Suez Canal [emphasis added]."

He had earlier signaled Meir and Dayan that they could take another twenty-four hours, that there would be no monitors, and that he didn't care to establish where the Israeli lines were.[†] He had now asked Israel's generals whether they could cut off the Egyptian Third Army. While he may not have intended it, they understood that the United States would not stop them from doing so.

As Kissinger flew home, the Israelis moved to take advantage of the opening he had given them. In the hours before the cease-fire went into effect, General Haim Bar-Lev, who had been placed in command of the southern front, ordered all the forces on the western side of the canal to achieve territorial contiguity from Ismailia to Suez. General Adan sped with his tanks to the city of Suez and the canal; General Sharon ordered his forces to advance on Ismailia. They asked Bar-Lev what to do if the Egyptians reacted. He told them, "If they don't shoot at us, we won't shoot at them. If they open fire, of course, we'll respond."

---

[*] The discussion about Port Fuad does not appear in the American protocols of the meeting. However, it does appear in the Israeli version. Golda Meir refers to it again during a subsequent cease-fire discussion on October 26. She told the cabinet, "On the issue of Port Fuad, [Kissinger] told Moshe at the door, before he left the midrasha, that he wasn't opposed to it." See Golan, *War on Yom Kippur*, 1170–77, and Hagai Tzoref, ed., *Golda Meir: The Fourth Prime Minister, Selected Documents (1898–1978)* [in Hebrew] (Jerusalem: Israel State Archives, 2016), Doc. 164, 576.
[†] Meir confirmed that understanding to her cabinet on October 27: "[Kissinger] went to Moscow to arrange the cease-fire without any foundation, without a line." See Tzoref, ed., *Golda Meir*, Doc. 164, 576.

Day eighteen, Tuesday, October 23, 1973, Sinai. At 8:00 a.m., Elazar reported to Dayan that the Egyptians had opened fire, destroying nine Israeli tanks after the cease-fire went into effect. Elazar obtained Dayan's permission to inform Bar-Lev that his forces were free to act in the Egyptian Third Army's sector. That opened the way for the resumption of an all-out offensive. An hour after nightfall Adan's forces reached the outskirts of Suez city, the major logistical hub for provisioning the Egyptian Third Army. General Kalman Magen's division took control of the secondary road around Jebel Attaka to Adabiya, the one open road for resupplying the Third Army. Thirty thousand Egyptian soldiers were now surrounded and cut off by the IDF.

In Kissinger's memoirs, he admits that when he found out about Israel's military actions, he "had a sinking feeling that" he "may have emboldened them." To gain Israeli support for the cease-fire, he explains, he felt it was necessary to compensate them for the four hours lost by the communications snafu in Moscow. But, as the record shows, the Israeli cabinet had already accepted the cease-fire, and the Soviets and Egyptians had already capitulated.

When I asked Kissinger why he had winked at the Israelis when they had already agreed to the cease-fire, he said he had assumed the Israeli army would take a few more square kilometers in the north (where Dayan had indeed asked about taking Port Fuad). "It never occurred to me that it would make a huge strategic difference. I thought it would give them confidence that we had their security interests at heart. It was an emotional time. I thought Israel was going through a very hard period in which we would have to manage the negotiations. I was talking about something that would effect maybe a day or so. I didn't think that they would capture the entire Third Army."

Kissinger confirmed this in a subsequent argument with Meir when she came to Washington on November 1, 1973, after the cease-fire had gone into effect. "You gave me good military reports, but you didn't tell me what you intended," he told her. "I had no reason to think that another twelve more hours, twenty-four more hours, were decisive." Yet he had explicitly asked the Israeli chief of staff to show him how they could cut off the Egyptian Third Army and had given the IDF the time to do so. In a subsequent meeting with Dinitz, Scowcroft asked him why Israel hadn't cut off the Egyptian Third Army before accepting the cease-fire. Dinitz, looking at Kissinger, said Israel had bowed to American pressure. "With the hope that the Egyptians would open fire," Kissinger added, defensively, sounding as if he had been complicit.

There is another explanation, one that normally doesn't appear in the lexicon of diplomacy: guilt. For all the maneuvers and machinations that made Kissinger so effective, he was not just an unfeeling practitioner of realpolitik, especially when it came to dealing with Israel. He was at heart a sentimentalist. He had choked up when telling Dinitz earlier in the crisis that he would never let Israel down. He had told Meir before departing for Moscow that his purpose was to "buy time," and that Israel should keep fighting to improve its positions. And he had promised to consult Israel before concluding the cease-fire deal. Dinitz was so convinced that Kissinger would resist the Soviet insistence on a cease-fire until the IDF had finished the job that his parting gesture to Kissinger was to give him a handwritten note with an excerpt from the Old Testament book of Judges in which Gideon receives an injunction from God before he enters battle with the Midianites: "Go thou with that strength of thine and thou wilt help Israel."*

As we saw, Kissinger had been upset by Nixon's letter to Brezhnev authorizing him to do the deal on the spot precisely because it would confound his delaying tactics. But when he arrived in Moscow and discovered that his application of Israeli military pressure had succeeded beyond his expectations, he seized the moment to secure a cease-fire agreement with Brezhnev on favorable terms, rather than seek time to secure Israel's agreement, as he had promised.

From his study of the world order in the nineteenth century, Kissinger knew that the great powers of the Concert of Europe were able to maintain the peace for almost one hundred years in part by discounting the concerns of the lesser states. Brezhnev's Kremlin office hardly matched the grandeur of the Congress Hall of the Federal Chancellery on the Ballhausplatz in Vienna, where in 1815 the plenipotentiaries of the five European powers met to restore order to the Continent after Napoleon's defeat. Nevertheless, on both occasions, the representatives of the great powers operated on a shared assumption that, for the purposes of promoting peace, they could impose their will on smaller, dependent states. And in this case, they were right. Sadat had become desperate for the cease-fire, and the Israeli cabinet grudgingly accepted it.

Why, then, did Kissinger encourage Israel to ignore the cease-fire? Was it because he was uncomfortable with the way he had treated Israel by presenting it with a fait accompli and denying it a battlefield victory? Undoubtedly, the applause he received upon arrival from grateful Israeli citizens had gone some way toward assuaging his conscience. However, he was still on the defensive when he met with Meir. She wisely thanked him for all his support, and his heart went out to her. That was the context in which he decided to offer her

---

* A handwritten copy of the note was found in the Israeli archives. It is clearly a rough or pared-back translation of the Hebrew. The English version from the King James Bible is: [And the Lord looked upon Gideon, and said,] Go in this your might, and you shall save Israel [from the hand of the Midianites]. Judges 6:14.

more time, encouraged her to take advantage of it, hinted to Dayan that he was unconcerned by the potential for cease-fire violations, and discussed specific military objectives with the Israeli generals. He appeared to be thinking with his heart rather than his head.

Or was he? While Kissinger was aware of the perils of hubris, it was not impossible that the success of his virtuoso performance in Moscow had emboldened him to roll the dice. The same confidence that led him to present Meir with a fait accompli, believing she would have no choice but to accept the cease-fire terms, could have led him to encourage the Israelis to complete the job. Kissinger was certainly improvising, telling his Israeli interlocutors what they wanted to hear. He seemed so confident about his mastery of the game that he may have believed he could avoid or cope with the consequences, even if the Israeli advance contradicted what he had committed to others, in this case the general secretary of the Communist Party of the Soviet Union. Golda Meir sensed this about Kissinger. "He also has the principle that he doesn't need to solve everything ahead of time," she told her cabinet a week after their encounter in Israel, "because in any case, somehow it works out." It seems that guilt and hubris had combined to interfere with the careful calculations of the diplomat in chief, with unforeseen and dangerous consequences.

Kissinger landed at Andrews Air Force Base outside Washington at 3:00 a.m. and went straight home to bed. It was only when he awoke that he discovered the fighting had continued. Again lacking up-to-date information from the front, he was unaware of the implications of Israel's military advances, which he assumed were just "a few miles in the desert." But around 9:30 a.m., UN secretary-general Kurt Waldheim informed him that the Egyptians were seeking an emergency meeting of the Security Council because the Israelis were breaking the cease-fire. He quickly worked with Vorontsov, the Russian chargé d'affaires (Dobrynin had stayed on in Moscow), to introduce a new UNSC resolution. The draft called for an immediate cease-fire (at 7:00 a.m. on October 24, in Egypt and Israel), the return of forces to the positions they had held when the original cease-fire came into effect on October 22, and, this time, for the secretary-general to put observers in place to supervise the cease-fire.

This earned him a rebuke from Meir. In a message that Dinitz conveyed, she complained bitterly about the way Kissinger was treating Israel. If the resolution were passed, she warned, Israel would be forced to reject it. She could not tolerate a situation in which Egypt opens fire, Israel reacts, the Soviets threaten intervention, and the United States comes down on Israel, insisting they withdraw, causing a rupture in the U.S.-Israeli relationship.

Kissinger tried to calm her down by dismissing the resolution's call for a withdrawal to the pre-existing cease-fire lines, noting they were "indetermin-able." He suggested to Dinitz that the IDF make a token withdrawal of a few hundred yards in some area, which the United States would then declare had satisfied the requirements of the resolution. Dinitz responded acerbically that Israel was not going to withdraw from any place that was captured after an Arab attack.

As the fighting continued, Sadat became more anxious. He had received word that Israeli tanks were advancing on Cairo.* He called Brezhnev and demanded Soviet intervention. Then he ordered Ismail to send an urgent mes-sage to Kissinger requesting that the U.S. government immediately intervene to stop Israel from expanding its position on the western side of the canal. He followed up with a letter to Nixon—their first direct communication—formally requesting that the United States intervene, *"even if that necessitates the use of forces* [emphasis added]," to guarantee the implementation of the cease-fire resolution. He said it was only because of the U.S. and Soviet joint assurances that he had accepted the cease-fire resolution. Failure to fulfill those commit-ments would undermine his confidence in American guarantees, Sadat wrote.

Sadat's fear that Cairo was under Israeli threat had prompted Brezhnev to mobilize too. He took the unusual step of initiating a hotline message to Nixon at midday, where he too spoke of the United States and the Soviet Union as "guarantor-countries" of the cease-fire resolution. He proposed that they both take decisive measures to stop the violations of the cease-fire lest it damage their bilateral relations. To this, Kissinger had Nixon reply that the United States assumed full responsibility for a complete end to Israeli opera-tions and the Soviet Union should play a similar role with Egypt. Brezhnev responded two hours later with an assurance that Egypt was ready to end hostilities immediately if Israel did too. Kissinger received a similar commit-ment from Meir. Thus, as Resolution 339 passed unanimously that evening in the Security Council (with China abstaining), it seemed that both sides were finally ready to stand down.

That afternoon Kissinger told his State Department staff that "the events of the last two weeks have been on the whole a major success for the United States." The Arabs now understood that if they wanted a settlement, they had to turn to the United States, and the Israelis now realized that their "cockiness of supremacy is no longer possible," that they could no longer ignore U.S. insistence on a political process. He concluded, with surprising perspicacity given the way events were about to unfold, that the trick was "to end these

* The Soviet military attaché in Cairo had reported to Sadat that a reconnaissance patrol of four Israeli tanks had moved in the direction of Cairo, but they had subsequently pulled back. See Anatoly Dobrynin, *In Confidence: Moscow's Ambassador to Six Cold War Presidents* (New York: Crown, 1995), 295.

things in time, before one of the great powers feels it has to push in another batch of chips."

But the Israelis had not lost their cockiness. In her last message that evening, Meir had again rejected Kissinger's ploy of a withdrawal gesture. And during the day, while she was arguing with Kissinger, General Adan cut the water pipes across the canal and secured the IDF's stranglehold on Egypt's Third Army with the clear intention of forcing its surrender.

Day nineteen, Wednesday, October 24, 1973, Washington, DC. That morning Kissinger convened the WSAG for the first time since he had returned from his travels. In the meeting, he expounded on the way his diplomacy had given the United States the upper hand. He informed them that he had been "brutal" with Dinitz before this meeting to stop Israel's military activity, but he wanted to keep up the resupply effort "until we have a concrete proposal to put before [them]." He explained that "Israel knows it . . . would have lost this war except for us. . . . If we cut our diplomatic support, they're dead. They can't survive a joint U.S.-Soviet position in the Security Council. So, we have basically all the leverage we need." In a follow-up principals-only meeting that afternoon, he explained why nevertheless he needed the resupply to continue: "By December we will turn on them, but up to then we don't want to have the Jewish community on us for not being generous now."

Kissinger's confidence would soon dissolve as he came to realize that the gravity of the Israeli threat to the Egyptian Third Army had indeed provoked the Soviets to up the ante. The first indications came in urgent messages from both Sadat and Brezhnev, claiming they had "precise information" that the Israelis had resumed their attacks against the Third Army. Kissinger berated Dinitz for making Brezhnev "look like an idiot." He said the ambassador's claims that the Egyptian Third Army had broken the cease-fire lacked all credibility. "Don't tell me you're taking Cairo in order to prevent the breakout of the Third Army," Kissinger remarked sarcastically.

Looking for a way to escape Kissinger's wrath, Dinitz suggested that the United States send military attachés from Tel Aviv to observe whether Israel was respecting the cease-fire. Kissinger jumped at the offer because it enabled him to inform Sadat and Brezhnev that he had secured Israeli agreement to Sadat's proposal for "American ground observers." Sadat, of course, had asked for "forces," not "observers," but Kissinger had found a way to be partially responsive.* It would prove to be too clever by half.

---

* When Schlesinger questioned whether it was wise to give the Egyptians and the Soviets an excuse to send Soviet military observers too, Kissinger explained his thinking: "The Israelis tell us it is [quiet]; the Soviets are telling us it isn't." The U.S. military attachés would enable them to

Sadat immediately accepted Kissinger's offer and informed him that he was also "formally asking the Soviet Union to take similar action." In an attempt to lock in the superpowers, the wily Sadat then announced publicly that he was seeking a Security Council meeting to endorse the dispatch of American and Soviet "forces" to the Middle East. Sadat had taken Kissinger's proposal and used it to try to pressure Israel to release its grip on his army, but in the process, he had also crossed Kissinger's red line. As Kissinger would later observe, "We had not worked for years to reduce the Soviet military presence in Egypt only to cooperate in reintroducing it as the result of a UN resolution."

But the horse had bolted. By 7:00 p.m. that evening, Dobrynin was reporting to Kissinger that the Soviets would be voting in the Security Council for sending troops. Twenty minutes later he called back to inform him that the Politburo was so angry at what it regarded as Kissinger's perfidy in "allow[ing] the Israelis to do what they wanted" that they now sought to send troops to separate the armies and release the Israeli stranglehold. Kissinger responded ominously to Dobrynin, "If you want [a] confrontation, we will have to have one."

Kissinger immediately instructed John Scali, the U.S. permanent representative at the UN, to veto any resolution on dispatching troops. He then checked in with Haig to make sure he could say that the president was on board with confronting the Soviets if necessary. He noted to Haig that the Soviets were turning nasty: "They realize they were taken." Haig was sympathetic, so Kissinger said, "I think we have to be tough as nails now." "Sure we do, absolutely," Haig agreed. Kissinger added wistfully, "Of course if the Israelis had just stopped yesterday, we would be that much better off." Of course, if he hadn't encouraged them the day before, they might not have even started.

At 10:00 p.m., in what Admiral Moorer, the chairman of the Joint Chiefs of Staff, would later confide to his diary was a "pisswisher" of a message, Brezhnev threatened Nixon. The Soviet leader accused Israel of "brazenly challenging" both of them and urged Nixon to join him in urgently sending "Soviet and American military contingents" to Egypt to implement the cease-fire resolution. If the United States was unwilling to act jointly in this matter, he added, "I will say it straight. . . . We should be faced with the necessity urgently to consider the question of taking appropriate steps *unilaterally* [emphasis added]." The Soviet leader ended his hotline message with a demand for "an immediate and clear reply."

According to Dobrynin's subsequent account, this threat of Soviet military intervention was precipitated by their defense attaché in Cairo's reporting that

know what was actually going on. See Henry Kissinger, *Crisis: The Anatomy of Two Major Foreign Policy Crises* (New York: Simon & Schuster, 2003), 332.

the Third Army was about to be annihilated unless the cease-fire came into effect immediately. The Soviet embassy assessed that Sadat's regime was about to collapse. Sadat had insisted that if the United States was not prepared to join the Soviet Union in dispatching troops or observers, Moscow should be prepared to act separately.

The Politburo deliberations took on an air of crisis. Defense Minister Andrei Antonovich Grechko, supported by Soviet Presidium chairman Nikolai Podgorny, argued for an aggressive demonstration of military strength but was opposed by Premier Kosygin and Foreign Minister Gromyko. Brezhnev, according to Dobrynin's account, "also came out against any involvement of our troops in the conflict." He claims that the approved message was strongly worded "but did not contain any threat to act unilaterally." Somehow, the threat of intervention was inserted in the text of the message "as it reached Washington." Dobrynin said it was "anybody's guess" how that happened, but he thought it might have been because of a desperate appeal from Sadat.

The threat raised Kissinger's blood pressure. He called Dinitz and told him that the Israelis had better make some gesture. When Dinitz started arguing, he cut him off: "I don't have time for this!" He said the Soviets were about to put in forces to fight Israel; he wanted to know how the prime minister would have him respond.

Next, Kissinger called Dobrynin. Clearly worked up, he warned him not to take precipitous action because this was a matter of grave concern to the United States. "Don't you pressure us! I want to repeat again, don't pressure us!"

Consulting with Haig again, Kissinger urged that they "go to the mat on this." Haig wanted to know whether Kissinger had spoken to the president about it, a critical question given that Kissinger was preparing for a confrontation with the Soviet Union. Kissinger answered no. In a subsequent phone call, Kissinger asked Haig whether he should wake the president. This time Haig answered no. Kissinger records in his memoirs, "I knew what that meant. Haig thought the President was too distraught."

Kissinger called an urgent meeting of the national security principals for 10:40 p.m. that evening. During this war, WSAG meetings, with Kissinger in the chair, had been convened in the State Department. Haig, conscious of the importance of this particular gathering, urged Kissinger to move it to the White House Situation Room, to make it appear as though the president were actively involved in managing the crisis. They were joined by Schlesinger, Colby, Moorer, and Scowcroft. The only record of what transpired is the memo Moorer dictated after the meeting.

Kissinger began by circulating Brezhnev's messages and recounting the day's events. He reported that everything had been on track until suddenly the

Soviets had reversed themselves and issued this unmistakable threat. Kissinger noted the consequences should the United States go along with the Soviet proposal for a joint force: "Either we would be the tail to the Soviet kite in a joint power play against Israel, or we would end up clashing with Soviet forces in a country [i.e., Egypt] that was bound to share Soviet objectives regarding the cease-fire." He argued that they were looking at the demise of the strategy the United States had pursued for the last four years: drawing Egypt out of the Soviet orbit. Instead, the Soviet Union would emerge again as the dominant player in the Middle East.

Moorer then outlined the military indicators of what looked like a pre-meditated Soviet move: (1) seven Soviet airborne divisions were now on alert; (2) the Soviet airlift to Egypt and Syria had abruptly ended, freeing up air transport to lift troops to Egypt; and (3) a heavy sealift was underway, possibly transporting weapons to be used by the airborne divisions.* Moorer added that "the Middle East is the worst place in the world for the U.S. to get engaged in a war with the Soviets" given that its access was limited to one airfield (in Lajes, Portugal) between the United States and Israel.

Haig predicted that the Soviets would likely move at daylight, which was just a few hours away. He felt that the Kremlin was seizing on a weakened American president to reverse its loss of influence in the Middle East. Schlesinger believed the Soviets were using the Israeli cease-fire violation as an excuse to move their forces into the Middle East. Colby said that by placing major forces in Egypt, Moscow could recoup with the Arabs.

While Kissinger chaired this deliberation, he was also stepping out of the Situation Room to speak with Dobrynin, Dinitz, and Ismail. After hearing Haig's assessment that Soviet troops were about to move, he instructed Scowcroft to call Dobrynin to buy some time by demanding the Kremlin not take any precipitous unilateral actions before Nixon had an opportunity to respond to Brezhnev's tough message. Scowcroft was to warn Dobrynin of "the most serious consequences" if they acted.

At 11:20 p.m., Dinitz turned up at the White House with a response from the Israeli prime minister to Kissinger's demand that she do something. Meir proposed a reciprocal withdrawal: the IDF would withdraw from the west bank of the canal and the Egyptian armies would withdraw from the east bank. Kissinger knew Sadat would never agree to withdraw from the Egyptian territory he had just liberated in Sinai. He told Dinitz the proposal was a non-starter. It would not head off Soviet intervention and might even accelerate it.

Meanwhile, Kissinger continued to engage with his American counterparts

---

* According to Kissinger's account, there was an all-time high of eighty-five Soviet ships in the Mediterranean; twelve of them, including two amphibious ships, were headed for Alexandria. See Henry Kissinger, *Years of Upheaval* (Boston: Little, Brown, 1982), 584.

in what he termed "one of the more thoughtful discussions of my government service." He argued that the Soviet proposal would have to be rejected in a manner that would shock them into abandoning the unilateral move they were threatening. The principals agreed on a tough response. He circulated a draft authored by Helmut Sonnenfeldt, Kissinger's Russia hand. To make sure Brezhnev and the Politburo would not question U.S. resolve to stand up to Soviet military intervention at a time of domestic weakness, they then decided on a series of military deployments.

All U.S. forces worldwide, including the Strategic Air Command, were placed on DEFCON 3 alert.* This is the highest level of peacetime readiness. DEFCON 2 is for an imminent attack; DEFCON 1 is war. Moorer ordered the DEFCON 3 alert at 11:41 p.m. (although meant to be kept secret, it was on the newswires by 3:00 a.m.).

In Kissinger's view, that alert was still an inadequate signal. Channeling his inner Nixon, Kissinger told the group he had learned that "when you decide to use force, you must use plenty of it." Accordingly, they decided to transfer the *John F. Kennedy* carrier task force from west of Gibraltar to the Mediterranean, move the *Franklin D. Roosevelt* carrier task force from Sicily to join the *Independence* carrier task force south of Crete, order the two thousand marines of the Amphibious Ready Force based at Souda Bay in Crete to get underway, put the 82nd Airborne Division and all European-based U.S. forces on alert, and recall seventy-five B-52 strategic bombers from Guam. If for some reason the Soviets failed to pick up the DEFCON 3 worldwide alert, they were bound to pick up these more overt movements in the eastern Mediterranean and USAF's nuclear strike force.

At 11:55 p.m., Kissinger dispatched a message from Nixon to Sadat via the Ismail channel, making clear that the United States could not agree to the Soviet proposal for a joint force and that the result could be a superpower confrontation on Egyptian soil. It would also make it impossible, the message noted, for Kissinger to visit Cairo. Kissinger was trying to leverage Sadat's interest in American diplomatic intervention to counter his desire for Soviet-American military intervention.

Kissinger wanted to keep the Kremlin waiting on Nixon's written response

---

* The DEFCON alert system was created by the Joint Chiefs of Staff in 1959 to provide the U.S. military with a "uniform system of progressive readiness conditions." Five DEFCON levels were established. DEFCON 3 was code named "Round House." The first use of the system occurred in May 1960, in the wake of the U-2 crisis, after Soviet premier Nikita Khrushchev walked out of the Paris Summit. All commands were placed on DEFCON 3 out of concern that the Soviets might attack the United States or its European allies. See William Burr, ed., "Alerts, Crises, and DEFCONS," National Security Archive Briefing Book, Number 749, March 17, 2021, accessed here: https://nsarchive.gwu.edu/briefing-book/nuclear-vault/2021-03-17/alerts-crises-defcons?eType=EmailBlastContent&eId=96848c4f-ce71-460f-b3dc-8a8f440e0cc2.

to Brezhnev's threatening message until all the force movements had registered in Moscow. He had Scowcroft call Dobrynin at 1:45 a.m. to warn against
military intervention yet again and add that the principals still had several
more hours of deliberations ahead of them (which was not true; at that point
they were wrapping up). Nixon's response was only delivered by courier to
Dobrynin's office at the Soviet embassy on Sixteenth Street, across Lafayette
Park from the White House, at 5:40 a.m. on Thursday morning.*

The president's message endorsed the principle of joint superpower action
for peace but rejected Brezhnev's proposal for military intervention as "not
appropriate in the present circumstances." Nixon pointed out that the cease-
fire was holding, and promised the Soviet leader that the United States would
ensure Israel abided by it. Any violations by either side could be handled by
observer teams that would report to the UN Security Council. "In these circumstances," Nixon underscored, "we must view your suggestion of unilateral
action as a matter of the gravest concern involving incalculable consequences."
It would constitute a violation of the agreed-upon principles of détente, "which
would end all we have striven so hard to achieve."

At 2:09 a.m., as the principals meeting concluded, Kissinger called Dinitz
to inform him that the United States had dropped, for the time being, any
idea of an Israeli withdrawal to the cease-fire lines for fear that it would now
be seen as U.S. coercion of Israel in response to a Soviet threat. He invited
Dinitz to come to the White House to pick up a copy of Nixon's response to
Brezhnev and asked him in the meantime to get a military assessment of the
IDF's ability to "clean up" the Egyptian Third Army. Revealing his frustration
at Dinitz's previous dissembling about Israeli military activity, he added, "And
for God's sake, be honest with me!"

Kissinger received Dinitz in the West Wing lobby, the large reception room for visitors of the president and his senior staff, with its elaborate
eighteenth-century mahogany book cabinet centered along the south wall. On
either side of the cabinet were Early American sofas and chairs in rose-colored
upholstery. On the wall behind one of those sofas was a large, majestic, gold-
framed painting of *Washington Crossing the Delaware*, by Emanuel Leutze. On
the north wall, an outsize, circular, early-nineteenth-century gilt clock topped
with the head of a golden eagle marked the time with its large black hands. It
was 2:30 a.m.

Kissinger and Scowcroft walked up the narrow, creaky stairs from the Situation Room and sat with Dinitz under the painting of Washington. At that

* Although there was clearly great tension in the air during this meeting, Scowcroft recalled their
desire to play with Dobrynin by keeping him in suspense. Indyk interview with Brent Scowcroft,
October 20, 2015.

hour the symbolism was probably lost on them, but Sharon's crossing of the Suez Canal a week earlier had replicated Washington's passage across the Delaware on Christmas night, 1776.

Kissinger gave Dinitz a copy of Nixon's démarche to Brezhnev to convey to Meir. When she read it to the Israeli cabinet an hour later, the ministers were overwhelmed. Never in the short history of modern Israel had it received the contents of a crisis message that the U.S. president was sending to his Soviet counterpart *before* it was received in Moscow. During a tense, all-night, hand-wringing meeting, the Israeli ministers had worried that rather than standing up to the Soviet threat, Nixon would join Brezhnev in pressuring Israel to relinquish its grip. In his autobiography, Abba Eban recalls how "profoundly heartened and impressed" they were when they heard Nixon's message.

Kissinger explained to Dinitz that if Soviet forces landed in Cairo, it would take them four to five days to assemble and reach the Egyptian Third Army. During that time, he said, the first task for Israel would be to destroy the Third Army so that the United States and Israel would not have to stand against two Egyptian armies as well as Soviet forces. Dinitz believed this was achievable since the Third Army now lacked any air defenses. Kissinger wanted Israel to wait for a day after the Soviet forces began landing in Egypt so that the provocation would be clear. He also thought it possible the Egyptians, emboldened by the Soviet move, might attack in that time period, which would give the Israelis an even better justification for their assault.[*]

In a matter of hours, Kissinger had swung from pressing Israel to undertake a token withdrawal to ease the pressure on the Egyptian Third Army to encouraging Israel to plan for its destruction. When he had raised this idea in the principals meeting, Admiral Moorer had argued that it would be counterproductive, since the Soviets would then have all the excuses they needed to intervene. But as Moorer added in a postscript to his memorandum of the conversation, "We kept coming back to the $64,000 question: If the Soviets put 10,000 troops into Egypt, what do we do?" It would take the United States at least twice as long as the Soviet Union to put its own forces in place, and they would have none of the access advantages of the Soviet forces.[†] Just as in the 1970 Jordan crisis, they concluded that they would have to rely on the IDF.

In an era of retrenchment, Kissinger was looking to use Israeli force to compensate for the constraints on the use of American force. It would cer-

---

* Kissinger notes in his memoirs that he subsequently received a more detailed reply to his question of what it would take for the IDF to destroy the Egyptian Third Army: "It would take three or four more days of fighting along the entire front and the assurance of large quantities of modern equipment." See Kissinger, *Years of Upheaval*, 602.
† They would presumably have to off-load at Israel's Rephidim Air Base in the Sinai, seventy-seven miles from the front lines, whereas Soviet forces had access to Cairo West Air Base, a little more than half that distance from the front.

tainly have involved a high-stakes gamble, but Kissinger had already decided to signal that he was ready for a confrontation with Moscow if that's what Brezhnev wanted; to him, this was another move on the chessboard designed to check an advancing Soviet knight by moving a powerful Israeli rook. When I asked Kissinger about destroying rather than saving the Egyptian Third Army, he responded, "You know, we were determined; this was not the Obama administration."*

Much of the motivation for Kissinger's tough posture in this crisis stemmed from his fear that the Soviet Union had decided to take advantage of the fact that the United States had "no functional President." "They find a cripple in the White House and why shouldn't they go in there," he said to Haig before the meeting. In fact, while momentous decisions involving a high potential for superpower conflict were being made in Nixon's name and communicated to the Soviet leadership, the commander in chief was upstairs in his bedroom sleeping.

There is no indication that when Nixon's national security team decided to alert America's nuclear forces and respond to Brezhnev's threatening communication, they even considered waking the president. Just prior to convening the meeting at the White House at 10:20 p.m., Haig again asked Kissinger whether he had talked to the president. "No, I haven't. He would just start charging around," Kissinger responded. In his memoirs, Kissinger remembers Nixon's mood at that moment as "agitated and emotional"; Haig described him as "right on the verge."† Kissinger recounts how Nixon had called him earlier that evening to ask him to tell the congressional leadership about his indispensable role in this crisis. According to Kissinger, "he spoke of his political end, even his physical demise." He was a man "in the paralysis of an approaching nightmare."

When I asked Kissinger whether he had consulted with the president before making the DEFCON 3 decision, he deflected the responsibility. "Haig was going in and out of the meeting. I assume he was keeping the president informed," he told me. In his memoirs, Kissinger records that "I did not know what conversations Haig had had with Nixon in the early hours of the morn-

---

* Kissinger was referring to President Barack Obama's decision not to enforce his red line that the Assad regime crossed when it used chemical weapons in the Syrian town of Ghouta in August 2013.
† Scowcroft recalls that Nixon was "off the wall" that night. "He had had a very bad day." Eagleburger reported that he had received an account from Kissinger afterward of a "drunken Nixon," slurring his words and barely awake when Haig and Kissinger tried to speak to him in the first moments of the crisis. See Alistair Horne, *Kissinger 1973: The Crucial Year* (New York: Simon & Schuster, 2009), 302–303, and Roger Morris, *Haig: The General's Progress* (New York: Playboy Press, 1982), 257–59.

ing." Why hadn't he asked Haig? His answer to me said it all: "It was a very strange period."

Haig's account confirms that the last time he consulted the president was at 9:35 p.m. that evening, an hour before Kissinger convened the principals. He records that Nixon told him, "Words won't do the job. We've got to act." When he informed him that the principals would be meeting shortly, Nixon expressed no enthusiasm for attending the meeting. "You know what I want, Al; you handle the meeting," Haig remembered. He notes that this was consistent with Nixon's preference for making decisions in solitude. But he does not claim that, in his solitude, Nixon made any particular decision that night.*

That is hardly surprising. Congressman Peter Rodino had announced that same day that the House Judiciary Committee intended to proceed with an impeachment investigation. Nixon had already been instructed by the courts to hand over tapes he knew would incriminate him. And the Senate Republican leadership was publicly urging him to name a new special prosecutor who would undoubtedly recommend indicting him. Little wonder he had retreated to his bedroom in deep despair.

President Clinton went through a similar experience in December 1998. The final vote in the House Judiciary Committee on whether to impeach him for obstruction of justice, concealing evidence, and perjury in the case of his affair with Monica Lewinsky came a few hours after Clinton had departed Washington with his wife, daughter, and peace team on a Middle East mission to salvage the Wye River Memorandum, which Arafat and Netanyahu had signed in the East Room in October 1998. In the two months since then, the agreement had begun to unravel as both sides dragged their feet on implementation.

Although some in Washington were quick to criticize Clinton's trip to Gaza and Israel as an attempt to distract from his political travails, his purpose was to inaugurate Gaza International Airport and address a special convening of the Palestinian National Council (PNC) as an agreed-upon follow-on to the Wye accords. The visit was the brainchild of Natan Sharansky, the iconic Soviet Jewish émigré who served as minister for industry in the Netanyahu cabinet. At Wye, he had argued that the only way to convince Israelis that Palestinians were sincere about reconciliation was to have their representative

---

* According to a subsequent account provided to *The New York Times* by an anonymous senior White House source, Kissinger arrived at Haig's office at 10:30 p.m. (i.e., ten minutes before he convened the WSAG) to tell him about the Brezhnev ultimatum. Haig then went to see the president alone while Kissinger waited. "The President then gave General Haig specific instructions on what his senior advisers were to do without prejudging the specifics of their deliberations," the high official said. See Leslie Gelb, "Nixon Role in Foreign Policy Is Altered; Some Assert Kissinger Is Now in Charge," *New York Times*, December 24, 1973.

body renounce the clauses in their covenant that called for Israel's destruction. Arafat agreed to convene the PNC in Gaza for this purpose and invited Clinton to witness the event.

No American president had ever visited that tiny, poverty-stricken strip of land on the shores of the eastern Mediterranean, wedged between southwestern Israel and Egypt's Sinai Peninsula. It was quite a festive occasion on a brilliant Mediterranean winter afternoon when Clinton and Arafat cut the ribbon and opened the airport terminal. Two years later, during the second intifada, it was destroyed, and the airstrip torn up by IDF bulldozers in reprisal for a deadly Palestinian attack on Israeli soldiers. The hope of free movement for Palestinians that the airport symbolized was crushed into rubble.

That day in December 1998, however, Palestinian children in their school uniforms lined the route of Clinton's motorcade waving American and Palestinian paper flags. Huge flags also draped the terminal and control tower. After the ceremony, Clinton traveled the short distance from the airport to the Rashad Shawwa Cultural Center in Gaza City's upscale seaside suburb of Rimal by helicopter. Gathered in the hall were seven hundred Palestinian delegates from the PNC, the Palestinian Central Council, the PLO Executive Committee, and the Palestinian Legislative Council, as well as representatives from popular Palestinian institutions. At Arafat's invitation, they had journeyed from the West Bank, Jordan, and the far-flung Palestinian diaspora to amend the Palestinian National Covenant in the service of peace with Israel.

Just before the event began, Bruce Lindsey, Clinton's political aide, drew the president and the first lady aside. He informed them that key Republican congressmen whom Clinton had been counting on to vote against his impeachment when it came to the House floor were now deserting him. A grim-faced Lindsey judged that Clinton's impeachment appeared certain. The president turned to Hillary Clinton and said in alarm, "I'm in trouble."

The first lady took his arm and pulled him into the holding room, slamming the door shut in a way that made it clear that they were not to be disturbed. Fifteen minutes later, Clinton emerged with his chin up, his jaw clenched, and a determined look on his face, in contrast to the pensive, ashen, remote expression he had carried with him from Washington. He walked up to his peace team as we stood there and said, "Let's do it." As he joined Arafat onstage, the Palestinian delegates broke into a standing ovation so loud and prolonged that it should have washed away any apprehension Clinton might still be feeling.

Arafat, as the host, spoke first. He was in an ebullient mood, his protruding lower lip trembling in unison with the shaking index finger of his right hand, which he would raise from time to time to emphasize his point. Unlike his usual doctrinaire speeches, this one was poetic. He spoke of the "nearing, shining light" of an era of peace and freedom, which he labeled "the peace of the brave." He declared, "We will not go back to the ways before peace. And we will not allow or tolerate any violence or anyone to mess with the security of both sides, both sides, both sides." If only he had kept that commitment.

Arafat then asked the delegates to raise their hands in affirmation of the decisions of the PLO Executive Committee to nullify all the provisions of the covenant that ran contrary to Palestinian commitments to a peaceful solution and the renunciation of terror. With enthusiasm, an overwhelming majority of the Palestinian delegates rose from their seats and raised their hands. As they did so, Israeli TV cameras broadcast the proceedings to the Israeli public.

Then it was Clinton's turn. Given that his political survival as president hung in the balance at that moment, I had expected him to just read the speech we had prepared for him and get it over with. But he almost immediately strayed far from his text to preach an extemporaneous sermon on the need for each side in the conflict to understand the feelings of the other. He spoke empathetically about the Palestinian and Israeli children he had met on this trip whose fathers were either in Israeli prisons or had been killed by Palestinian violence. He noted that Palestinians and Israelis shared a history of oppression and dispossession. Both had felt their hearts turn to stone. "The time has come," he exhorted, "to sanctify your holy ground with genuine forgiveness and reconciliation."

Concluding his speech, Clinton closed his folder and, banging his hand on the table for emphasis, he put the onus on Palestinians and Israelis alike: "You and they must now determine what kind of peace you will have. Will it be grudging and mean-spirited and confining? Or will it be generous and open? . . . Will you begin to see each other's children in the way you see your own? Will they feel your pain, and will you understand theirs?" And then, as if he were channeling his late peace partner Yitzhak Rabin, he declared: "Enough. Enough of this gnashing of teeth. Let us join hands and proudly go forward together."

The whole hall rose in unison to applaud. I looked at the elderly Palestinian gentleman at the end of the row I was seated in and noticed tears streaming down his cheeks. As we moved to the side of the hall to join the other Americans in the president's party, I came upon a beaming first lady. I spontaneously embraced her and said, "He's an amazing man." Hillary laughed and said, "He certainly is!"

Clinton had an ability to compartmentalize in a way that Nixon's demons prevented him from mastering. This was no easy feat. The next morning, for example, in a meeting he hosted between Arafat and Netanyahu in which the two leaders squabbled, Dennis Ross, Clinton's special Middle East coordinator, noted that the president was writing on his yellow legal pad, "Focus on your job. Focus on your job. Focus on your job." Clinton managed to follow his own advice in a way that Nixon had become incapable of doing on that dramatic evening in October 1973. Both presidents rebelled against their fate, giving vent to their anger and resentment at the way the press and Congress treated them. But Nixon, deeply insecure and paranoid, brooded in isolation, avoiding human engagement. Clinton was insecure too, but he compensated for it by depending on human contact as his emotional prop. Although their transgressions were very different, Clinton was able to function effectively in the face of impeachment whereas Nixon had become paralyzed by it.

For months Nixon had been playing up his critical role in world affairs to distract the public and Congress from Watergate and to demonstrate his indispensability to the nation. It was ironic that at the very moment when he could have demonstrated how effective his leadership of the nation was in a superpower crisis, Nixon was missing in action.

That reality was hidden from the American public and the Soviets. In a press conference the next day Kissinger gave a precise "tick-tock" of the crisis from the inception of war on October 6. When he came to the previous night's events, he said, "The President at a special meeting of the National Security Council at 3 a.m. [ordered] certain precautionary measures to be taken by the United States." Kissinger acknowledged that the president had not participated in the deliberations with his national security team, but he claimed that Nixon had joined the meeting "after they had formed their judgment, that the measures taken—that he in fact ordered—were in the essential national interest." Nixon embellished this tall tale in his own press conference the next evening. Noting that he was responding to information that the Soviet Union was planning to send a very substantial force into the Middle East, "I ordered, shortly after midnight on Thursday morning, an alert for all American forces around the world." That was not true. In the early morning hours of October 25, the commander in chief was abed.[*]

Kissinger felt strongly that Nixon needed to be seen to be acting resolutely. If the truth were known, he feared the country could face great peril as its foreign adversaries sought to take advantage of the circumstances. That fear resulted in an overcompensation. Reflecting on their actions the night before, Kissinger asked Colby in a phone call on October 25 whether he thought they had overreacted. Colby responded that they may have gone a little far with the

---

[*] In his memoirs, Kissinger notes that Nixon was furious with the allegation that he had ordered the alert to ease his domestic difficulties. He points out that it was "an allegation [that Nixon] knew better than his critics to have been inherently impossible." In this way, Kissinger seems to be conceding that Nixon did not order the alert because he was incapable of doing so. See Kissinger, *Years of Upheaval*, 598.

worldwide alert, but "I don't think you had any choice. The Soviets may not have had the intention of going much further, but they sure sounded like it." Dobrynin claims that when he called Kissinger to complain angrily about the alert, Kissinger told him not to take it as a hostile act because it was "mostly determined by domestic considerations."

Ironically, recently declassified Soviet documents reveal that, far from seeking to exploit America's domestic political crisis, Brezhnev was going through his own physical and psychological breakdown at the very same moment as Nixon. He had apparently developed an addiction to sleeping pills that, when combined with vodka, of which he was known to consume copious quantities, left him unable to think straight.* The added pressure of the war in the Middle East had so exhausted him that, according to his daily schedule, on the afternoon of Monday, October 22, he had repaired to his dacha at Zavidovo and did not return to his office in the Kremlin until midday on October 25. Therefore, at the crucial moment on Wednesday, October 24, when, according to Dobrynin's account, the Politburo was formulating Brezhnev's ultimatum to Nixon, Brezhnev was as missing in action as Nixon. Brezhnev's schedule shows that "documents were sent to Zavidovo" on October 24, so it is possible the Politburo sought Brezhnev's sign-off on the letter to Nixon.† However, what now seems clear is that the aides on both sides were managing this superpower confrontation without either of the ultimate leaders engaging in the deliberations.

That meant Kissinger had misread Soviet calculations. Contrary to his assessment, the Politburo had no interest in engaging in a war in the Middle East at that moment. According to Dobrynin and Victor Israelyan, the foreign ministry official who participated in the Politburo deliberations, Soviet forces were no more ready than American forces for a large-scale intervention. That would have transformed the Arab-Israeli conflict into a superpower confrontation, which nobody in Moscow sought. Rather, the Soviet leadership felt betrayed by Kissinger, who had negotiated the cease-fire in Moscow and, in its view, then colluded with the Israelis to cut off the Egyptian Third Army. The

---

* Brezhnev's psychological condition at the time was attested to by KGB head Yuri Andropov, who wrote him on October 29, arguing that the United States and Israel were attempting "to tire us out, to exhaust us." He described a dynamic that had become routine during this crisis, in which Kissinger lulled them with sweet words about cooperation and joint action, which were then followed by urgent appeals from Sadat demanding immediate help. He believed this was all designed to disrupt the normal work of the leadership, "a kind of sabotage . . . creating over-exhaustion for all," especially for Brezhnev. See Library of Congress, Manuscript Division, Dmitri Antonovich Volkogonov papers, 1887–1995, mm97083838, Reel 16, Box 24, Folder 39, translated by Sergey Radchenko, https://digitalarchive.wilsoncenter.org/document/198187.
† Foreign ministry official Victor Israelyan's account of the crisis deliberations notes that on October 24, there was "a very conflicted psychological climate in the Kremlin." See Victor Israelyan, *Inside the Kremlin During the Yom Kippur War* (University Park, PA: Pennsylvania State University Press, 1995), 165.

intent of the threatening message to Nixon was to "frighten Washington and force it to take appropriate measures with Israel."

The Soviets detected the DEFCON 3 alert soon after Moorer's order was issued, but they decided not to respond to it by putting Soviet nuclear forces on alert. Instead, the military readiness of the Soviet fleet in the eastern Mediterranean was increased. The destroyers that shadowed the American ships were boosted by first-line missile-carrying warships, and the USS *John F. Kennedy* was shadowed by Soviet submarines as it made its way east.

When Nixon's message was received from the Soviet embassy early on the morning of October 25, the Politburo was satisfied by the sentence that provided reassurance that the United States would lean on Israel to ensure its full compliance with the cease-fire resolution. By threatening unilateral action, they had succeeded in sparing Egypt from humiliation. Accordingly, Brezhnev decided that the best response was no response at all.

Day twenty, Thursday, October 25, 1973, Washington, DC. At 8:00 a.m., Sadat answered the message Kissinger had sent him in Nixon's name the evening before. Because of the objections from Washington, Sadat explained that he had decided to forgo his request for the intervention of Soviet and American forces in favor of a UN-mandated international force, which by UN protocols precluded any contributions from permanent members of the Security Council, including the United States and the Soviet Union. Sadat informed Nixon that he had already ordered his ambassador in New York to introduce the resolution into the Security Council that morning.

This would not be the last time that Sadat saved Kissinger's bacon. But coming as it did in the midst of a superpower confrontation, it earned Sadat additional respect from the master diplomat, who had been prone to underestimate him. It also provided confirmation of Kissinger's most cherished outcome, as he would later observe: "It showed that Sadat was staking his future on American diplomatic support rather than Soviet military pressure."

Sadat's initiative ended the crisis almost as soon as it had started, for if Egypt no longer sought the intervention of American and Soviet forces, how could the Soviet Union insist? Kissinger briefed Nixon on what a victory the president had achieved (while he was sleeping!). He described the president as "clearheaded and crisp" that Thursday morning, when Kissinger detailed the decisions that had been made in his name the night before. Nixon ordered up briefings of congressional leaders and the press. He wanted to show everyone that he had been in command, and successful.

Kissinger decided to go before the press first, to play down the sense of crisis. Yet as the details of how close the United States had come to a nuclear confrontation began to sink into the American consciousness, the inevitable question was asked: Had Nixon blown up the crisis in order to distract attention from his Watergate woes? That too was ironic. Kissinger could hardly say Nixon had played no part in the decisions. So he went on the offensive. When Marvin Kalb, the CBS News diplomatic correspondent, asked Kissinger whether the alert might have been prompted by domestic circumstances, Kissinger let loose: "We are attempting to conduct the foreign policy of the United States with regard for what we owe not just to the electorate but to future generations. And it is a symptom of what is happening to our country that it could even be suggested that the United States would alert its forces for domestic reasons."

Day twenty-one, Friday, October 26, 1973, Washington, DC. With the cease-fire apparently holding, Kissinger was keen to launch his postwar peace diplomacy, an objective made even more alluring by a new message from Sadat on Friday morning saying that "in preparation for [Dr. Kissinger's] visit we are working out comprehensive proposals which we hope will provide a turning point toward a final peace settlement."

But before Kissinger could contemplate engaging with Sadat on peacemaking, he had to treat the source of the crisis: the parlous state of the Egyptian Third Army. As the day progressed, the situation at the front deteriorated. The Egyptians opened fire, apparently in an attempt to break out; the Israelis responded. This precipitated another plea for help from Sadat to Nixon, and from his foreign minister to Waldheim, threatening "desperate measures." Dobrynin notified Kissinger that a hotline message was on its way from Moscow, raising the specter of another superpower confrontation barely twenty-four hours after the last.

The immediate issue was humanitarian supplies of water, food, and medicine to both the Third Army soldiers and the citizens of Suez city, which was now besieged too. Having just been asked by Kissinger to prepare to destroy the Third Army, Israel was in no mood to consider saving it. From the perspective of the Israeli cabinet ministers who were confronting a looming election, there was still an opportunity to achieve a clear victory, if not by destroying the Third Army, then at least by forcing its surrender or retreat from the east bank of the canal. That would salvage Israel's self-image and help neutralize domestic criticism, now beginning to be voiced ever more emotionally, about the lack of preparation for the war and its conduct.

Kissinger's imperatives were the opposite. He was determined to rescue the Egyptian Third Army because he believed its surrender would shake Sadat's regime and regenerate a superpower crisis as Brezhnev threatened again to intervene to protect his Egyptian client. Moreover, he had sought to calibrate the outcome of the war to produce a new equilibrium in which neither side felt defeated and a chastened Israel and a grateful Egypt could enter American-mediated peace negotiations. That required the Third Army's survival. U.S. and Israeli objectives and the interests that underpinned them had seriously diverged.

Schlesinger and the Pentagon had an easy answer: the United States should either break the Israeli siege with its own resupply effort to the Third Army using USAF C-130s, or cut off the resupply to Israel. But Kissinger was not interested in confronting Israel militarily, nor in becoming the supplier to both sides of the conflict, nor in starting a fight with Israel's congressional supporters. This was a task for discreet diplomatic pressure on Israel.

Instead, the pressure on Kissinger mounted. Schlesinger kept demanding that the Israelis be cut off. Nixon, whom Kissinger was trying to keep from interfering, ordered him to press the Israelis "strongly." And then the president gave his evening press conference in which Kissinger felt he humiliated, even taunted, Brezhnev and negated his own carefully constructed effort to show the Soviet leader respect.

Nixon claimed the Soviet Union had been preparing to send "a very substantial force into the Middle East," labeling it "the most difficult crisis we have had since the Cuban missile crisis" and bragging that his toughness had produced Brezhnev's climbdown. His performance only confirmed Kissinger's view that Nixon's emotional state had made him unpredictable and even dangerous to the conduct of American foreign policy. "The crazy bastard really made a mess with the Russians," he said to Haig after the press conference, beseeching him to call Dobrynin and make amends in the name of the president.

Anxious about the potential for a new superpower confrontation, and worried about the prospect of an Egyptian collapse, Kissinger went to work on the Israelis. In a series of phone calls with Dinitz that began on the morning of October 26 and concluded late that night, Kissinger sought to persuade Meir to open a passage for convoys of food, water, and medical supplies. Having heard nothing back by early afternoon, he called Dinitz to warn him that Israel would face "irresistible pressure if you keep it up." To register an American red line, he declared, "You will not be permitted to capture that army. I am certain," and hung up. At 4:15 p.m., becoming increasingly impatient, he told Dinitz, "I don't want [Nixon] to say something you will regret" at the press conference that evening. He also informed Dinitz that there was a hotline message coming in from Moscow.

Dinitz dug in his heels: "We will not open up the pocket and release an army that came to destroy us. It has never happened in the history of war."

Kissinger knew something about the history of war. He answered acerbically, "Also, it has never happened that a small country is producing a world war in this manner. There is a limit beyond which you cannot push the president." Dinitz denied doing so. Exasperated, Kissinger said, "You play your game and you will see what happens."

Golda Meir was in no mood to accede to Kissinger's demands. Notwithstanding his solemn promise that the two superpowers would address the issue of prisoners of war, she had nothing yet to tell her demoralized people about their loved ones languishing in Egyptian and Syrian prisons. And the prospect of facing the voters' judgment in a looming election made her colleagues unwilling to accede to American demands.

Understanding her predicament, Kissinger tried to show Dinitz the way out. "Make a proposal to confuse the issue," he suggested. He would then recommend to the Egyptians that they enter discussions with the Israelis to resolve the matter. "I think you have a bargaining situation and you can get something for it," he said. However, he cautioned that the alternative was for him to take it to Nixon. "I guarantee . . . you will get a much worse answer," he said, threatening once again. The Security Council would be meeting at 9:00 p.m. that night to consider new Egyptian charges of Israeli breaches of the cease-fire. He needed an Israeli proposal before then "or you will get a condemnation on you." That was a shorthand way of saying the United States would not use its veto in the Security Council to block censure of Israel.

Three hours later, Dinitz called with a message from the cabinet proposing direct Israeli-Egyptian talks at the military level. Israel would offer Egypt something in these talks that was "neither surrender nor humiliation, but an honorable way out of their situation."

Kissinger was unimpressed by the vagueness of the proposal. The assumption that the Egyptians would be open to direct talks—something they had been refusing for twenty-five years, since the armistice talks of 1948—seemed a stretch to Kissinger, especially when Israel was in the process of humiliating them. He saw it as a further Israeli attempt to ignore the reality that they had no choice but to open the supply lines to the Third Army. Nevertheless, he transmitted the proposal to Hafez Ismail without embellishment, making clear he was not recommending Egypt accept it.

While Kissinger's exasperation deepened and his threats grew darker, Meir's anger mounted and her criticism became more personal. During one of the cabinet deliberations that day, she said to her colleagues that Kissinger lacked humility: "He thinks that his intelligence will be able to solve everything." In a phone call with Dinitz in which he reported to her that Kissinger had laughed at Israel's proposal for direct talks with Egypt, she questioned Kissinger's motivation: Was he attempting to put Israeli forces under siege? Seeking an excuse to put American forces into Sinai? Covering up a Soviet presence with the Third Army? She didn't understand him. When he visited Israel, he had suggested they take more Egyptian territory, she said. Now Israel was expected to pay the price in blood for doing so, "and that's the only price we're not willing to pay," she declared. She suggested Dinitz go behind Kissinger's back to Haig and Leonard Garment, Nixon's Jewish legal counsel, to inform them that Kissinger was opening the door to Egyptian military action against Israel and the entry of Soviet troops.

Dayan added to Meir's sense of betrayal by arguing that Kissinger's purpose was to show the Arabs that he was the only one who could deliver Israeli concessions, for which he would then demand an end to the oil embargo. He claimed that if Israel were to accede to Kissinger's request to open the road to the Third Army, it would lead to a demand to return to the October 22 lines. Meir argued to an already vexed cabinet that that could well lead to an American demand to withdraw to the 1967 lines.

Amid all this Israeli churning, the hotline message from Brezhnev arrived at the White House. It was Brezhnev's first written response to the DEFCON 3 alert, two days earlier. Believing it would strengthen his argument that the Israelis were risking a superpower confrontation, Kissinger had Scowcroft deliver it immediately to Dinitz. However, once he had a moment to read it, Kissinger discovered that his expectations had been confounded.

Brezhnev wrote that Israeli actions "jeopardize the interests of universal peace and are detrimental to the prestige of the Soviet Union and the United States." But then he said, "I must tell you frankly, that if the next few hours do not bring news that necessary measures have been taken . . . we will have the most serious doubts regarding the intentions of the American side." Brezhnev had blinked. He went on to ask politely that the United States bring its "effective and immediate" influence to bear on Israel to correct the situation.

As Kissinger later observed, "The cautious phrasing indicated that some important lessons had been learned." Just as in September 1970, when the Soviets pressed the Syrians to withdraw from Jordan, or in July 1972, when they acquiesced in Sadat's demand for the withdrawal of their military advisers from Egypt, or on October 18, 1973, when Brezhnev eagerly accepted Kissinger's cease-fire requirements, Soviet behavior in the Middle East was yet again characterized by an ultimate timidity in the face of American resolve.

This constituted good news for Kissinger's fundamental objective of stealing Egypt from the Kremlin's pocket, but it generated an immediate problem because it removed the threat of Soviet intervention as leverage on Israel. That was especially the case since he had already conveyed the text of Brezhnev's limp-wristed message to Dinitz. Given the urgency of the situation, the stakes for his Middle East strategy, and his weary conclusion that Israel "seemed to prefer being coerced to release its prey rather than relinquishing it voluntarily," Kissinger decided to issue an ultimatum.

Without checking with Nixon, Kissinger called Dinitz at 10:58 p.m. Speaking in the name of the president, he repeated that the United States would not allow the destruction of the Third Army. Requesting an answer by 8:00 a.m. the next morning, he demanded that Israel agree to provide non-military supplies to the Third Army and threatened that, if it failed to do so, the United States would join others in the Security Council to "enforce" Resolution 338 with its requirement that Israel withdraw to the October 22 lines (thereby letting the Third Army go free). In Security Council parlance, "enforce" has special meaning. Kissinger was indicating that the United States might go along with action under Chapter 7 of the UN Charter, which allows for the application of economic sanctions by all member states and legitimizes the use of force to deal with "threats to the peace, breaches of the peace, and acts of aggression." It was the diplomatic equivalent of the DEFCON 3 alert.

In the annals of U.S.-Israeli relations, the threat to remove American protection of Israel in the UN Security Council, where an automatic majority will almost always exist for condemnation of Israel, is rare. It happened during the Suez crisis in November 1956, and again in 1981, when Prime Minister Begin extended Israeli law to the Golan Heights. Four decades later, the threat would be deployed again by the Obama administration in a forlorn effort to persuade Israel to curb its settlement activity, which ran directly counter to long-standing U.S. policy. When the threat had no impact on Israeli behavior, Obama decided, in his final days in office, to abstain on a UNSC resolution condemning Israel's settlement policy. That resolution lacked the kind of enforcement mechanism Kissinger had threatened. It nevertheless provoked a firestorm in Israel and among its supporters in the United States, as well as an unprecedented last-minute effort by President-Elect Trump to thwart the decision of his predecessor, even while Obama still inhabited the Oval Office.

Wisely, Kissinger avoided this kind of public backlash by keeping the exchange with Dinitz private. Meir took the threat seriously enough to yield and agree to relieve the siege. As she explained to her cabinet colleagues, "It seems that [Nixon and Kissinger] are sitting under Brezhnev's and Sadat's threats. If we don't allow them this, they will do it themselves."

Nevertheless, she sent a scathing personal message to Kissinger, whom she well understood was responsible for Nixon's ultimatum. She informed him that she intended to report to her cabinet all that he had demanded of her "in order that Egypt may announce a victory for her aggression." Playing the role of victim, perfected over two millennia of Jewish suffering at the hands of tyrants, she said she harbored no illusions "that everything will be imposed on us by the two big powers." But that would not prevent her from proclaiming the bitter truth "that Israel is being punished not for its deeds but because of its size, and because it is on its own."

Kissinger was deeply offended. Hadn't he begged her to make some proposal that would have helped him defend against Soviet pressure? Hadn't he stalled the Egyptians and the Soviets for eighteen hours? Wouldn't the Egyptian Third Army remain trapped even after Israel allowed it some minimal supplies? He believed her response had been drafted to be leaked, as it surely would be after she shared it with her cabinet. And he knew her message would then be used to mobilize the pro-Israel community against him in Washington. Nixon might be full of bluster, but he would not have stood by Kissinger in those circumstances. He had his own problems.

Just as the prospect of a public confrontation with Israel loomed, Kissinger was yet again saved by Sadat.

Day twenty-two, Saturday, October 27, 1973. At 3:07 a.m., the White House Situation Room received a message from Hafez Ismail conveying Egypt's acceptance of Israel's offer of direct military talks. Ismail suggested a meeting between major generals, the highest-ranking officers in their armies. The location would be at Kilometer 101 on the Cairo-Suez road. The meeting should take place at 3:00 p.m. local time to discuss the implementation of UNSC Resolutions 338 and 339. It should be preceded by a complete cease-fire. The quid pro quo Ismail required was Israeli permission for just one convoy of non-military supplies for Suez city and the Third Army.

Kissinger called Dinitz in a state of disbelief. Describing it as a miracle, he urged Meir to accept Ismail's request. She acquiesced, in effect accepting her own offer for military-to-military talks. The Yom Kippur War was over. A new era of American-led peacemaking was about to begin.

As Kissinger wrote: "We had achieved our fundamental objectives: We had created the conditions for a diplomatic breakthrough. We had vindicated the security of our friends. We had prevented a victory of Soviet arms. We had maintained a relationship with key Arab countries and laid the basis for a dominant role in postwar diplomacy. And we had done all this in the midst of the gravest Constitutional domestic crisis of a century."

While Kissinger justifiably extolled the virtues of his diplomatic daring, it had come at a price. He did not mention the human toll of a war that might have been avoided if the same diplomacy that had ended it had been employed to try to make its outbreak unnecessary.* And now he would have to contend with the economic consequences of the Arab oil embargo, which would not have been deployed had there been no war. Nor did he mention the way he had green-lighted Israel's breaking of the cease-fire he had negotiated with Brezhnev, which had generated a superpower crisis that might well have ended very badly. And there was the dangerous precedent he and Nixon's other advisers had set by taking upon themselves the constitutional prerogatives of the commander in chief in a crisis that might have precipitated nuclear war.

Nevertheless, Kissinger had come out on top. In four years, he had gone from serving as national security adviser to secretary of state to "president for foreign policy," as some in the media now referred to him—an extraordinary feat. He had demonstrated the efficacy of backing his crisis diplomacy with the threat of American force and the use of Israeli force. He had shown that the United States could function effectively abroad despite a crisis at home that had incapacitated the president. And he had accomplished his primary long-term strategic goal in the Middle East of replacing the Soviet Union as the dominant outside player. He had emerged from the Yom Kippur War in the diplomatic catbird seat.

However, his personal relationship with Meir and the Israeli cabinet had suffered from the bruising encounter of the cease-fire endgame. He had gone to considerable, sometimes extraordinary, lengths to build a relationship of trust with them. But in this crisis, they had come to resent his manipulations. Israelis would not forget that he had snatched victory over the Egyptian Third Army away from them, even though, in the fullness of time, some would grudgingly admit that he had done them a service by preventing them from humiliating the first Arab leader to want to make peace with Israel.

The crisis had also been an important learning experience for Kissinger, who was still new to the ways of the Middle East. He had confirmed his intuition about the fundamental weakness of the Soviet position in the Arab world and his ability to build American influence there at Soviet expense. He had discovered how difficult and infuriating it would be to move stiff-necked Israeli leaders, with their complicated coalition politics, even when it was manifestly in their best interest. And he had come to appreciate the guile, ingenuity, and

---

* Israel's estimated losses were some 2,200 killed and some 5,600 wounded; the combined Arab armies' estimated losses were some 8,500 killed. See Kenneth Stein, *Heroic Diplomacy: Sadat, Kissinger, Carter, Begin and the Quest for Arab-Israeli Peace* (New York: Routledge, 1999), 91.

flexibility of Anwar Sadat, his new Egyptian partner in peacemaking. Sadat had broken the mold of expected behavior, earning Kissinger's respect and admiration and proving himself to be a reliable, if unpredictable companion for the journey they were about to embark upon together: Sadat in pursuit of peace, Kissinger in pursuit of a new American-led order, one that he intended to be more stable, peaceful, and durable than its predecessor.

PART III

The Road to Geneva

8

Golda's Inferno

I have never been in an Arab country and never had much dealings
with them. I frankly thought I could get through my term of office and
let someone else do it. To be honest, now that I have started, I will finish it and with enthusiasm.

—Henry Kissinger to Soviet foreign minister Andrei Gromyko

S*unday, October 28, 1973, Sinai.* There is a quiet stillness in the desert in the
early hours of the morning, when the temperature typically drops below
45 degrees Fahrenheit and the stars come out to illuminate the desert sands in
a soft, luminous light. The silence enveloped General Arele Yariv, as he stood
near a sign that marked Kilometer 110 on the highway from Cairo to Suez
city, providing him with a rare moment of solitude to contemplate his circumstances.* He had fulfilled the unenviable task the prime minister had given him
of explaining to Israelis, and the world, the extent of Egypt's gains in the war's
early days. Now she had tasked him with a no less weighty mission—to serve
as the Israeli head of the military-to-military talks that Kissinger had proposed
to Egypt on her initiative.

He approached this new rendezvous with a heavy but open heart. Earlier in
the day, he had toured the front lines and talked to the troops, who had unburdened themselves with the same tough questions the political echelon was facing back home: How had they been taken by surprise? Why were they so ill
prepared? Who was to be held accountable for the deaths of so many of their
friends? And the most pressing question of all: When were they going home?

---

* The meeting had been scheduled for earlier in the day but there had been a miscommunication.
Yariv was waiting at Kilometer 101, but el-Gamasy had been waiting at Kilometer 76. The
Egyptians then asked that the meeting be moved to Kilometer 110, which is where they met on
October 28. Subsequently, they would meet at Kilometer 101, which became the official location.

Yariv felt the burden of ensuring that the meeting with his Egyptian counterpart opened the possibility of moving from the cease-fire to political talks.
He swore to himself that whatever their disagreements, there would be no
misunderstandings. He was determined to be "resolute in the substance and
polite in my demeanor."

At fifty-two, General Mohamed Abdel Ghani el-Gamasy was the same age
as Yariv. A tall, lean, ramrod-straight Egyptian officer with a receding hairline,
a button nose, and a thick black mustache, he looked more like a character out
of a Tintin comic book than the chief of operations of the Egyptian armed
forces. Born into a merchant family in the same Nile delta governorate as
Sadat, he had entered Egypt's Royal Military Academy after high school and
dedicated himself to army life. Through the Nasser years, when military officers ruled Egypt, he had developed a healthy disregard for the involvement of
the Egyptian army in the politics of his country.

El-Gamasy had meticulously planned the retaking of the east bank of the
canal and earned well-deserved credit for the surprising success of the operation. Having spent his entire professional life fighting Israel, he accepted the
responsibility of initiating direct negotiations with Egypt's enemy with deep
misgivings. While he understood Sadat's logic in appointing the person who
was most familiar with the disposition and needs of Egypt's frontline forces, he
believed his job was to prepare to open the road to Suez and the Third Army
by force, rather than through the humiliating exercise of negotiating with the
Israeli enemy for access. He begged War Minister Ismail to replace him, but
when ordered to proceed, he saluted, in the stoic fashion of the professional
officer he prided himself on being.

As el-Gamasy moved through the Egyptian army's front lines, escorted by
UN observers and a detail of his own special forces, he was stopped by soldiers
who suspected they were deserters, "pushing their weapons into our faces and
demanding to know who we were and why we were proceeding in the direction of the enemy." He had neglected to bring a coat, so by the time he arrived
at the meeting he was shivering with cold.

For this hastily arranged first meeting, Israeli soldiers, whose scruffy improvisation was baked into their DNA, had strung a tarpaulin between a tank and
an armored car, placed a wooden table and camp chairs underneath, illuminated the site with field lamps, and surrounded it with four heavy machine
guns for protection. As el-Gamasy alighted from his jeep, he encountered a
line of Israeli officers with Yariv at its head. They exchanged salutes and then
el-Gamasy extended his hand. Grasping it, Yariv noticed the Egyptian general
was shivering and ordered his staff to provide windbreakers to the Egyptian
delegation. With both generals now clothed in the same khaki jackets, they
proceeded to take their seats under the dusty olive tarpaulin; it had become

impossible to distinguish which army each represented. After so many gore-filled days of death and destruction, the humanity of the moment was intensely moving for both.

The agenda for their meeting was the exchange of prisoners of war, the wounded first; the continued supply of food and water to the Egyptian Third Army and the remaining citizens of Suez (at this point, Israel had agreed to only one convoy of a hundred trucks); stabilization of the cease-fire; and relief of the implicit Egyptian blockade of the Bab el-Mandeb Strait at the entrance to the Red Sea.* Yet both generals were well aware of the larger issues at stake that informed their deliberations.

Yariv knew that el-Gamasy had to secure the relief of the Third Army; el-Gamasy knew that the Israelis could not long maintain the extended and vulnerable lines of communication of their reserve forces on the west bank of the canal.† To stabilize the cease-fire, both sides needed a separation of the two armies. From the Israeli perspective, the obvious answer was for the Egyptian forces to withdraw to the west bank of the canal and the Israelis to the east bank. But that would have meant a return to the status quo ante and the Egyptian army's relinquishment of its hard-won territorial gains on the east bank, something Sadat would never countenance.

El-Gamasy had a negotiating advantage in UNSC Resolution 339—the second cease-fire resolution, accepted by both sides—since it called for Israeli forces to return to the lines they held on October 22. That, as noted earlier, would have the effect of relieving the siege of the Third Army. But Yariv had an advantage too in that nobody (other than the IDF) could say for certain where the October 22 lines were, and the longer Israel delayed in complying with that demand, the more precarious the situation of the Third Army became.‡

In the early hours of the morning, each presented his opening position: Yariv proposed a "switching of fields" in which both sides would withdraw

---

* The Bab el-Mandeb (Gate of Tears) is a twenty-mile-wide strait located between Yemen on the Arabian Peninsula to the east, and Djibouti and Eritrea on the Horn of Africa to the west. It connects the Red Sea to the Gulf of Aden. Shipping passes through a 16.5-mile-wide channel on the western side. Cargo traveling to Israel's southern port of Eilat at the tip of the northeastern extension of the Red Sea had been threatened by the presence of two Egyptian frigates stationed in the strait during the war, even though they had not actually blocked any shipping bound for Israel.

† As el-Gamasy would observe subsequently, "The Israeli forces on the west bank of the canal changed from being a pressure point for us to becoming hostages which we could use to pressure Israel." See Mohamed Abdel Ghani El-Gamasy, *The October War: Memoirs of Field Marshal El-Gamasy of Egypt* [in Arabic] (Cairo: American University in Cairo Press, 1993), 302.

‡ In a candid moment, in a meeting with Kissinger in Washington on November 3, 1973, Yariv responded to Kissinger's direct question about where the IDF lines were before the October 22 cease-fire was supposed to go into effect. He said the IDF had already cut the Cairo-Suez road but had not yet cut the road to the south around Jebel Attaka. See Memcon between Kissinger and Meir, November 2, 1973, FRUS 1969–1976:25, Doc. 312.

their armies across the canal, leaving a twenty-kilometer buffer zone between them. El-Gamasy responded by requesting Israel fulfill UNSC Resolution 339 by withdrawing to the October 22 lines and, in the meantime, allow for a continual resupply of the Third Army and Suez city. At 4:30 a.m., they agreed to adjourn and meet again the next day.

As the Egyptian prepared to take his leave, he drew his Israeli counterpart aside and told him that he had a message for Yariv's prime minister from his president: "My highest authority wants peace . . . if Mrs. Meir wants peace."

Yariv and el-Gamasy quickly bonded. Yariv was determined to convince Meir and Dayan that they should open the road to non-military supplies to Suez and the Third Army, and he became frustrated with the Israeli cabinet, which seemed incapable of deciding on a strategy and sticking with it. Dayan especially angered Yariv because in those early days, he was under intense popular pressure to resign and therefore zigzagged between wanting to relieve the Third Army, to gain credit with the United States, and wanting to attack it, to gain credit with the Israeli public. Sadat, on the other hand, wanted to open the road in a hurry, and that gave el-Gamasy wide latitude.

The combination of frustration on one side and flexibility on the other generated an important sidebar conversation between the two generals in their third meeting, on October 30. El-Gamasy came to the meeting armed with two important humanitarian gestures. First, he handed over Dan Avidan, an Israeli officer who had been captured with his legs shattered in December 1969. Second, he expressed a willingness to exchange wounded prisoners *before* any Israeli withdrawal to the October 22 lines. To demonstrate his seriousness, he promised to provide the Red Cross with a full list of wounded Israeli POWs within two days. At a time when the Syrians were refusing to even acknowledge how many Israeli POWs they held, these Egyptian goodwill gestures made a strong impression in Jerusalem.

In their informal conversation, the generals broached the idea of a broader disengagement in lieu of the IDF's return to the October 22 lines. In their memoirs, each claims the other raised the idea, but they agree on its substance: an IDF withdrawal thirty to thirty-five kilometers east of the canal while Egyptian forces stayed in place, with the UN policing a buffer zone between the two armies. According to Yariv, el-Gamasy also indicated that he would be willing to discuss scaling back the Egyptian military presence on the east bank of the canal "from a division to a symbolic force."* As we shall see, these turned out to be the essential elements of the disengagement agreement Kissinger would succeed in brokering three months later. Conceptually, the

---

* This particular Egyptian offer emerged in Yariv's account to Kissinger of his talks with el-Gamasy. See Memcon between Kissinger and Meir, November 3, 1973, KT00886, NSA.

The negotiations at Kilometer 101 on November 14, 1973. General Yariv is on the left, wearing sunglasses. In the center holding a cigarette is the commander of the UN Emergency Force (UNEF), Lt. General Ensio Siilasvuo. Chief of Staff General el-Gamasy is on the right consulting a document.

generals had already reached an understanding, even though this was an informal conversation and they both took care to reserve their positions.

Meanwhile, in Washington, Kissinger had been ruminating on how he would play his much-strengthened hand. He had decided to make his first visit to the Arab world in the next few days, en route to Beijing for a previously scheduled visit. He was conscious that given the drama of the occasion and his celebrity status, the world's eyes would be upon him. He needed to produce results—what would later become known in the American diplomatic lexicon as "deliverables." In this regard, he was concerned that the Arabs, particularly Sadat, looked to him as some deus ex machina sent to deliver Israel. On the basis of limited exposure, he had concluded that it was in the Arab nature "to believe that some epic event or personality will miraculously transcend the humdrum mess that is the usual human condition." To fulfill such expectations would require him to overcome an Israeli intransigence that he understood, instinctively, had deepened because the war had left Israel isolated in the international arena and more heavily dependent on the United States. He worried that he would be forced by a weakened and impatient president, who was feeling the pressure of the Arab oil embargo, to reach for what Kissinger believed was an unattainable "comprehensive peace." He viewed that as dangerous because Arab radicals would set a maximalist agenda, the Soviet Union would become their lawyer, Sadat would lose control of his own decisions, and the Europeans would split from the United States, leaving it isolated in support of Israel.

Kissinger resolved to find a middle way: an achievable objective between Arab fantasies and Israeli fears. As he writes in his memoirs, "The statesman must weigh the rewards of success against the penalties of failure. And he is permitted only one guess . . . The statesman's errors are likely to be irrevocable." Conscious of the limits of his capabilities and the importance of demonstrating success for American diplomacy, he adopted a cautious, step-by-step approach that he had already conceptualized before the war. In that way, he would avoid overburdening the Israelis psychologically, reduce Arab expectations to reasonable proportions, and chalk up some early wins. In the process, he calculated that "each advance would build confidence and make further steps easier." It would also give Sadat and Meir time to adjust to their respective roles in the Middle East order he was intent on constructing.

His immediate challenge was to teach his Egyptian and Israeli interlocutors how to partner him in this diplomatic tango. Over the next four years, he would discover that they were far from willing to follow his lead, and the learning process would generate many awkward encounters.

Monday, October 29, 1973, Washington, DC. Sadat had no previous experience dealing with the United States, and Kissinger assumed he would need special tutoring, but he would quickly realize that Sadat seemed always to be ahead of him. Sadat understood that, with the onset of postwar diplomacy, he was now competing with Israel for American attention. He therefore resolved to get to Kissinger before Meir did. Immediately after the cease-fire took hold, Sadat dispatched Ismail Fahmy, then his minister of tourism, to Washington, uninvited.

Fahmy's departure from Cairo was on such short notice that there had been no time to swear him in as Egypt's new foreign minister.* Because of Sadat's sense of urgency, when Fahmy was greeted by Sisco at Andrews Air Force Base on Monday afternoon, he insisted on being taken directly to meet the secretary of state. Kissinger's willingness to adjust his schedule confirmed to Fahmy the importance the United States attached to its new relationship with Egypt.

Fahmy was an Egyptian career foreign service officer who had risen quickly

---

* Sadat had decided to appoint Fahmy as foreign minister before the war but, with the war raging, he could not remove his predecessor, Mohammed el-Zayyat. He had brought Fahmy into his cabinet as tourism minister instead, with the intention of appointing him after the war.

in the diplomatic corps because of his analytical and conceptual skills. He had come to Sadat's attention in 1972, when, as under secretary in the foreign ministry, he had argued publicly that Egypt needed to separate from the Soviet Union. Fahmy prided himself on his independence and willingness to speak truth to power. He had kept his distance from Nasser and his ruling clique of generals and therefore had only limited exposure to Sadat. But after Fahmy's public remarks, Sadat began to consult with him regularly, appreciating his candor and wiliness, and his anti-Soviet instincts.

Round-faced, balding, voluble, and irrepressible, Fahmy was proud and sensitive to any perceived slight. Kissinger dubbed him "the master of insinuating innuendo." Fahmy sported a congenial smile under a fulsome salt-and-pepper mustache. Like Hafez Ismail, he was an urbane Egyptian diplomat who had spent much of his career in Europe, where he had acquired a taste for Italian suits and Cuban cigars. Confident in his ability to deal with the superstar secretary of state, he had hastily formulated a proposal for proceeding toward peace, approved by Sadat.

Fahmy's ten-point framework for a settlement began with consolidation of the cease-fire through Israeli withdrawal to the October 22 lines. That would be followed by a second Israeli military withdrawal east of the mid-Sinai passes, and then a final withdrawal to the international border that would result in the termination of the state of belligerency (the Egyptians were not yet ready to accept the idea of a peace treaty with Israel). The whole process would be accompanied by a UN-convened peace conference for all parties to the conflict, including the Palestinians.*

As Fahmy pointed out when he gave the plan to Kissinger, it was a sequence rather than a package. In that sense, it coincided with Kissinger's own concept of "step-by-step," even though the steps contemplated by Sadat and Fahmy were quite a bit more ambitious than the ones Kissinger had in mind.

Notwithstanding the similarities in their diplomatic stratagems, and their matching egos, Fahmy did not trust Kissinger. He was quick to recognize his manipulative skills and insecurities. So when Kissinger expressed the hope that he would meet him planeside when he arrived in Cairo, Fahmy agreed to do so, provided Kissinger met him every time he landed at Andrews Air Force Base. Even though it was against protocol, Kissinger agreed, and kept his word.†

---

* The plan provided for an exchange of all prisoners of war after the first disengagement. UN forces would be stationed in a buffer zone between the two armies as the IDF made a second-phase withdrawal. The blockade of the Bab el-Mandeb Strait would then be lifted, and an operation to clear and open the Suez Canal would begin. A similar process of disengagement would be negotiated on the Israeli-Syrian front.

† Protocol requires only that an assistant secretary of state meet a visiting foreign minister at the airport as Sisco had done for Fahmy's first visit to Washington.

On one occasion, Kissinger was running late and asked the Andrews control tower to keep Fahmy's plane circling until he arrived. When he greeted Fahmy at the base of the stairs, the Egyptian foreign minister embraced and kissed him on both cheeks. In the process, Fahmy managed to burn a hole in Kissinger's cashmere overcoat with the cigar he was smoking. Kissinger was convinced that Fahmy did it purposely as payback for having to wait.

Fahmy believed that Kissinger was beholden to the Jewish lobby. He attributed Egypt's reversal of fortune in the war solely to Kissinger's decision to provide Israel with the weapons necessary to turn the tide of battle. In his memoirs, Fahmy writes that Kissinger might pretend to be the peacemaker and mediator, but "he was in fact always acting on behalf of Israel." Never having met Kissinger's meek and humble parents, he nevertheless claimed that they were "extremist, fanatic Jews."

In their first, impromptu meeting, Fahmy was too much the diplomat to let his jaundiced view of Kissinger show, and Kissinger was only interested in impressing him. It was more like a diplomatic pas de deux than a tango: Fahmy using flattery to win over the secretary of state, and Kissinger taking advantage of it to probe the Egyptian's flexibility.

Fahmy made clear that Egypt was now depending on Kissinger and the United States to deliver, but there would be no threats or pressure in the partnership Sadat sought. Repeating Ismail's words, Fahmy said the Palestinian cause would not hold Egypt back. Nor would Sadat accept a role for the Soviet Union.

Although he welcomed all this, Kissinger moved quickly to temper Fahmy's expectations. What mattered now, he said, was to secure a stable cease-fire, which would enable peace negotiations to take place in a calm atmosphere. This coincided precisely with Sadat's purpose and Fahmy's mission. Fahmy therefore cautiously began to reveal his hand: Sadat was ready to negotiate an exchange of POWs, starting with the wounded, and provide an assurance to the United States that there would only be non-military supplies in the convoys to the Third Army. In return, Sadat sought guarantees from the United States that the resupply would be ongoing rather than one time, and that Nixon would prevent Israel from attempting to destroy the Third Army.

Kissinger appreciated that an assurance from the Egyptian president that there would be no military supplies in the convoys could reduce Israeli concerns. On the POWs, Kissinger explained that the Israelis had only accepted the cease-fire because the Soviets had guaranteed their immediate release. Fahmy was shocked. Such a guarantee took away his bargaining card and suggested that the Soviet Union could speak for Egypt. He was quick to tell Kissinger that Sadat had made no such commitment and that only he spoke for Egypt.

They met again the next morning. Kissinger outlined an approach he had formulated based on what he had heard from Fahmy in their first meeting: The Israelis would return to the October 22 lines; UN-supervised, nonmilitary supplies would provision the Third Army; and after this initial Israeli withdrawal, POWs would be exchanged and the Bab el-Mandeb blockade lifted. Fahmy was broadly agreeable to this approach, with one exception: the permanent resupply of the Third Army had to come before the Israeli army's withdrawal to the October 22 line. He believed the details of this approach could be finalized between Sadat and Kissinger in Cairo and, at the end of that meeting, Kissinger would be able to announce the resumption of full diplomatic relations between Egypt and the United States. Kissinger had secured his first deliverable.

When Fahmy returned to his hotel he learned that Sadat, without consulting him, had instructed el-Gamasy to convey to Yariv that Egypt was ready for an immediate exchange of POWs. Fahmy also discovered that the ten-point negotiating framework he had drafted, and Sadat had agreed he would present to the Americans, had also been handed over by el-Gamasy to Yariv on Sadat's instructions.[*] If true, it meant the Israelis had received it before Fahmy had a chance to share it with Kissinger. He rushed over to the White House to brief Kissinger on the framework before they went into the Oval Office to meet with Nixon.

Kissinger saw the advantage in Fahmy's sequenced approach, and he too was horrified that el-Gamasy had apparently shown it to Yariv first. In a follow-up meeting with Fahmy the next day, he allowed that the plan "has some possibilities for progress in it." He returned the favor by agreeing to provide Fahmy with something he badly wanted: a written assurance that the United States would not allow Israel to undertake offensive action from its positions on the west bank of the canal.

For Nixon, the meeting with Fahmy was something he had been hoping for from the outset of his administration. He greeted him warmly, heaped praise on Sadat for Egypt's military achievements, and made clear that the United States was committed to pursuing Middle East peace. He then conveyed Kissinger's talking points on the need to consolidate the cease-fire first.

At that moment, Nixon was experiencing a mounting sense of siege because of the Watergate proceedings. The impeachment process had begun two days

[*] This appears to have been a miscommunication. There is no evidence that el-Gamasy shared Sadat's entire framework with Yariv. He did, however, share his ideas on the shape of disengagement, which was an important part of Sadat's framework.

Henry Kissinger greets Ismail Fahmy in his State Department office in Washington on October 29, 1973. After the war, Sadat was so keen to get to Kissinger before Mrs. Meir that there was no time to swear Fahmy in as Egypt's foreign minister before he departed for Washington. Fahmy was determined not to be taken in by Kissinger's charm and celebrity status even though they worked closely together. But he could not prevent Sadat from embracing "Henry," and referring to him as his friend and brother.

before in the House Judiciary Committee. The meeting with Fahmy was the message: notwithstanding the threat to his presidency, there he was, actively engaged in Middle East diplomacy. To underscore the point, Nixon escorted Fahmy to his car, an unusual gesture that was bound to attract the attention of the media. But the photograph of his vigorous handshake with Sadat's envoy was buried amid front-page coverage of his legal counsel's admission in court that two critical Watergate tapes had gone missing.

Wednesday, October 31, 1973, Washington, DC. That afternoon, Meir arrived in town, still smarting from her long-distance encounter with Kissinger. Now Israel's only ally in the world was consorting with its most important enemy. Others may have missed it, but she had taken note of the photo showing Nixon's embrace of Fahmy at the diplomatic entrance to the White House. The Israeli prime minister feared she was about to be jilted. Suffering from exhaustion and a severe bout of indigestion, she was nevertheless determined to set things straight by confronting Kissinger directly and, if necessary, going to Nixon. She had already mobilized Israel's congressional friends and the American Jewish community by letting it be known that Israel was being pressured unfairly.

Moshe Dayan sent that signal in a Knesset speech the day she departed Israel. He said Israel had been "forced" by the United States to allow a relief convoy through to the Egyptian Third Army. Dayan was responding to criticism from the opposition and from hundreds of protesters outside—mainly women and children bearing placards with messages such as "Where's My Daddy?"—who demanded to know why he was allowing the Egyptian Third Army to survive when Israeli POWs remained unaccounted for. "We had no choice," Dayan explained. "Anyone advocating we run the war in a state of rupture with the United States is advocating we can't possibly win." When Menachem Begin stood up to recount the bitterness he had encountered on a visit to frontline troops, Dayan responded, "I'm not sure the soldiers know it but the shells they are firing today were not in their possession a week ago."

Meir was determined to counteract the weakness inherent in Dayan's declaration of dependence on the United States. As she explained to the IDF General Staff on her return from this visit, "We cannot appear to be weak, because this could spell our end." She had also taken note of a vague reference to an "understanding" in Brezhnev's latest hotline message, which Kissinger had shared with her.* She wanted to know what Kissinger was cooking up behind her back with the Soviet Union.

Kissinger's objective was to prevent Meir from forcing the surrender of the Egyptian Third Army. His study of nineteenth-century European history had led him to appreciate the contrast between the respect with which Castlereagh and Metternich, the foreign ministers of Britain and Austria, treated France at the end of the Napoleonic Wars and the humiliation that Britain and France imposed on Germany at the end of the First World War. That informed his approach to Egypt's treatment at the end of the Yom Kippur War.

Metternich had recognized that another defeat for Napoleon would have taken the war to a level where it would have been impossible to limit the claims for reparations. The Treaty of Paris in 1814 dealt with the French enemy "so that he does not wish to attack again." Kissinger was determined now to adopt Metternich's approach and prevent Meir from inflicting defeat on Sadat. His purpose was a more stable Arab-Israeli equilibrium in which the task of statesmanship "is not to punish but to integrate."

From his study of history he also knew that "a small country's survival in a hostile world can turn on nuances not easily grasped by faraway nations with wider margins of safety." If Israel failed to follow his lead now, he believed its position would continue to erode and it would eventually be doomed, in turn

---

* Brezhnev's letter spoke three times of an unspecified "understanding" that the Soviet Union had reached with the United States. See Message from Brezhnev to Kissinger, October 24, 1973, FRUS 1969–1976:25, Doc. 262.

ruining his construction of the new American-led regional order. In his view, the success of his diplomacy and Israel's survival had become intertwined, making it imperative that Meir be persuaded to adopt the role of a European statesman like Metternich. This would prove to be a Herculean challenge, for Meir's knowledge of European history was informed by the Holocaust, not the Congress of Vienna, by Hitler's systematic attempt to exterminate the Jewish people rather than by Metternich's efforts to impose limitations on France's power while retaining its weight in the European balance. The confrontation that ensued was an epic battle between two very different conceptions of Israel's role in the new regional order that Kissinger was determined to shape.

Thursday, November 1, 1973, Washington, DC. The first meeting between Meir and Kissinger took place over breakfast at Blair House, ahead of the prime minister's meeting with the president later that morning. The two delegations sat across from each other in the elegant small dining room that looked out on a tree-lined inner courtyard as waiters served coffee from silver trays. Meir bluntly declared that she had come to Washington "because things had reached the stage where, beyond the issues of substance, things must be made clear." She demanded to know what was being discussed behind her back. "Do we get things after they're done? After it is worked out with other parties?" She could live with the war, but not with being told at late hours, "You have to do this." Adopting her default role of the victim, she demanded to know, "Are there plans for the negotiations?"

Meir believed she had good reason to suspect Kissinger. On the eve of her departure for Washington she had received an "eyes only" report from her Mossad chief, based on reporting from their best Egyptian source. Ashraf Marwan was an Egyptian official who had married Nasser's daughter and had, as a result, been brought into his father-in-law's presidential office as a low-paid gofer, carefully watched over by Sami Sharaf, Nasser's consigliere and gatekeeper. Nasser's and Sharaf's treatment of Marwan had made him miserable. Bent on revenge, in 1970, he had walked into the Israeli embassy in London and offered his services to the Mossad. He was assigned the code name "the Angel," but he had become known in Israeli intelligence circles as "the son-in-law."

When Sadat succeeded Nasser, Marwan demonstrated his value to the new president by providing him with the evidence that enabled him to thwart a coup by powerful, rival generals. This catapulted Marwan into the post of presidential secretary, where he had become an ever-present and trusted adviser. The Mossad now had an agent in Sadat's inner circle.

Marwan died in London in June 2007, when he was pushed off an apartment balcony. Yet he received a state funeral in Egypt. Whether Marwan was an Israeli spy or an Egyptian double agent remains an unresolved mystery. In Kissinger's day, however, "the Angel" was revered as the most important spy that the Mossad had yet recruited. He had played a pivotal role in providing Israel with a last-minute warning of the Egyptian surprise attack in October 1973 and therefore had achieved high credibility. He may well have been the source of Mossad chief Zamir's report to the cabinet on the fifth day of the war that Sadat had ordered a land offensive in Sinai.

The report Meir received provided an alarming account from Marwan of Kissinger's cease-fire negotiations with Brezhnev in Moscow. He claimed that Brezhnev had informed Sadat that the Soviet leader and Kissinger had agreed that after the cease-fire went into effect, they would together launch a superpower diplomatic initiative intended to push Israel back to the 1967 lines. That was Meir's worst nightmare. The Israelis had duly leaked to the *Washington Post* their belief that Kissinger had agreed on things with the Russians behind their backs. The story had appeared that morning.* Kissinger was unaware of Marwan's report. Indeed, it is unclear whether he knew Marwan was a Mossad agent since, as we shall see, he subsequently worked quite closely with him. But he had seen the story in the *Post* and used it now to attack her people for leaking untruths to the press. Nevertheless, her question had put him on the defensive because, while he had resisted any idea in Moscow of imposing a solution, he had indeed plotted out the negotiations with Fahmy the day before.

Kissinger responded to Meir's interrogation by threatening to walk away. If this was the way he was going to be treated after all that he had done for Israel, "as far as I'm concerned, after my trip I'm going to dissociate myself and have someone appointed to handle it." He insisted there was no secret deal with the Soviets, that he had gone to Moscow to buy Israel time, and that it was Meir who had failed to tell him what Israel's military plans were. He noted, with a touch of sarcasm, that it was "an unusual situation" for an army to be trapped after a cease-fire had gone into effect. And then he avowed that he was Israel's only friend, holding the Soviets and the Egyptians at bay, preventing the president from intervening, standing alone against the anti-Israel tsunami that was about to swamp Washington.

He attempted to steer the conversation back to substance. In his memoirs, he writes that once the United States became the mediator between the

---

* Joseph Kraft, a renowned foreign policy commentator, wrote in his column that morning that Meir was coming to Washington to find out from Nixon what Kissinger had failed to tell her about an agreement with the Russians. See Joseph Kraft, "Golda Meir's Mission in Washington," *The Washington Post*, November 1, 1973.

Arabs and Israel it would inevitably have to dissociate itself from Israel as it took Arab concerns into account. But he was also aware that if such distancing became a habit, "Israel was lost," as its numerous detractors sought to drive a wedge between the Jewish state and its sole protector. In his mind, the only way to prevent that was for the United States and Israel to coordinate their approaches in advance, so that the concessions Kissinger wrested from Israel would not break the Jewish state.

In this first effort at reeducating the Israeli prime minister, he suggested two approaches: Israel could offer to withdraw to an invented October 22 line, or agree to enter discussions on where the line was. The advantage of the first approach, an example of Kissingerian sleight of hand, was that the exchange of POWs could happen more rapidly, he explained. But Meir was in no mood to engage in this kind of coordination. At the mention of the hypersensitive POW issue, she exploded: "It's ridiculous. They start a war and lose, and they want us to hand it to them?"

Trying to make her understand the new reality, Kissinger countered by invoking her nightmare: "It won't take much to get the U.S. government to support a return to the 1967 borders." It would take even less for Nixon to insist Israel withdraw to the October 22 lines, he warned.

Then he revealed his view of the essentially manipulative nature of diplomacy: "My only problem is you are too honest. You are too uncomplicated. . . . You're too easy to isolate." He argued that if she accepted the principle of withdrawal to the October 22 lines, the line would then have to be established in negotiations with the Egyptians. "That will be hopelessly screwed up," he predicted. In the meantime, she would have to allow for non-military convoys to the Third Army, under UN supervision, and in return Israel would get its POWs.

Meir stated flatly, "I won't do it."

Meir had brought Yariv to Washington so that he could brief Kissinger on his Sinai desert meetings with el-Gamasy. At this point in their confrontation, Yariv intervened with an artful modification: combine the convoys, the POWs, the lifting of the blockade, and "an agreement that the October 22 line will be discussed *in the context of disengagement* [emphasis added]." That was a formula Kissinger would eventually embrace because it implied a larger Israeli withdrawal. But now Yariv made the innocent error of adding that, based on his discussions with el-Gamasy, he believed the Egyptians would accept it.

He triggered an indignant response from Kissinger: "That's irrelevant." Instead, he pressed for acceptance of the October 22 lines, noting acidly, "If you could live with it on October 22, you can live with it now."

That put Meir and Kissinger back on the merry-go-round for another ride. "Why should we live with it?" Meir asked. Kissinger responded that small states should prefer order over justice: "There is no sense in debating the issue of justice here. You're only three million. It is not the first time in the history of the Jews that unjust things have happened."

His belittling of Israel provoked her. She demanded to know, "Does this mean the Russians can bully us, like the Czechs?" (referring to the 1968 Soviet invasion of Czechoslovakia). She said Israel still enjoyed support in Congress, but Kissinger quickly knocked that down: "The Congress doesn't want American troops in the Middle East." He said Nixon's popularity rating had fallen to 30 percent and asked, "What difference is the Jewish vote?"

He then modified the proposal that he wanted her to offer: if the UN kept the road to Suez open in exchange for the swap of Egyptian and Israeli POWs, and if the Bab el-Mandeb blockade threatening Israel's oil supplies was ended, then Israel should be willing to discuss the October 22 lines. Meir wasn't listening. She still wanted to know why she had to accept "everything the Egyptians put to us." Kissinger responded again with an attempt to teach her about the real world of power politics: "If you take the absolutist position you've taken with me, you'll be confronted sooner or later with an imposition." He was invoking a code word for what she feared most: a superpower-imposed withdrawal to the 1967 lines. Meir dug in her heels, the natural reaction of a small power under pressure to yield on a vital interest: "We can say the October 22 lines, and not one truck. They can't have it both ways."

Kissinger was out of time, and patience. "You had better tell the President that I made a proposition to you, that it's very painful for you to accept and you'll probably be overthrown, but you'll present it to the government." The alternative, he warned her one last time, was to be forced back to the October 22 lines by a joint U.S.-Soviet UN resolution.

Wanting to avoid a confrontation with the president of the United States, which she knew would hurt her back home, Meir decided to concede. "There is not much difference between us," she said in a more conciliatory tone.

Kissinger saw his opening. He insisted she agree to UN control of the road. "All right," she responded, defeated. "For God's sake, don't make a proposal like this to the Egyptians this weekend," he warned Yariv, wanting to ensure that the small card he had managed to wrest from Meir's grip remained his alone to play in Cairo. "It would be better if you made an obnoxious proposal over the weekend, so I can go to them in Cairo with a big concession." With that, Kissinger took his leave, crossing Pennsylvania Avenue to report to Nixon ahead of his Oval Office meeting with the prime minister.

In a telephone conversation with Kissinger the day before, the president had been adamant that Meir was not going to get her way this time: "She's going to find a very tough problem when she walks into my office. . . . She doesn't have the cards any more, Henry." Even before the war, Nixon, as we've seen, had felt that Israel had to be pressured into moving toward peace. Now he was determined to make that point to Meir, but he would glove his iron fist in velvet.

She opened the meeting with a heartfelt expression of thanks to the president for the airlift of military supplies. She also expressed appreciation for the way he had shielded Israel from Soviet bullying. Reflecting Kissinger's influence, she conceded that Israel would not attempt to destroy the Egyptian Third Army but needed the return of POWs and a lifting of the Bab el-Mandeb blockade.

Nixon responded sympathetically to Meir's concern for Israeli POWs. But he gently admonished her, arguing that the war had demonstrated "that a policy of digging in, telling us to give you the arms and you will do the fighting, can't be the end." Nixon then succinctly made the case for Kissinger's step-by-step approach. The president assessed that each side wanted peace but at a cost the other side was not prepared to pay. "Lacking agreement on final terms, the danger is that you will agree on nothing else," he pointed out. "What we need to do is to develop a chain of events, to break the whole matter up and to move step-by-step. . . . You must not miss this opportunity," he said.

Without giving her a chance to respond, Nixon ran through the events of the war, emphasizing his role in ordering the massive airlift of arms to Israel. "I never believe in little plays where big issues are at stake," he bragged. He moved on to recounting the DEFCON 3 alert. Kissinger interrupted to remind him that once the Israeli army broke out, the Soviets pushed for an immediate cease-fire and that his trip to Moscow "was to gain Israel another forty-eight hours." Nixon said he had been prepared to go into a nuclear confrontation with the Soviets to prevent them from intervening against Israel. The net result was to leave the United States isolated; even the Europeans and Japanese had moved closer to the Soviet Union. Then he invoked the specter of the oil embargo, warning, "If this cease-fire breaks down and Europe and Japan freeze this winter, Israel will be in a hell of a spot."

It was a convincing prologue to the president's conclusion: "If hostilities break out over an unreasonable Israeli position, we are not going to lose our respect for Israel, but it will be difficult for us." He would do what he could, but she needed to understand "the problems I have in wanting to support Israel," he said. She shouldn't worry about the Soviets, Nixon explained, because "our strategy is to isolate them by working with them." It was the same for Egypt: "Our influence in Egypt is not anti-Israeli influence; it is in your interest that we have influence there." Therefore, he said, "you have to have some confidence in me and in Henry that we will do our best . . . when it comes to negotiations."

Henry Kissinger with President Nixon and Israeli prime minister Golda Meir outside the White House after their meeting in the Oval Office on November 1, 1973. Nixon warned Meir that if hostilities broke out again "we are not going to lose respect for Israel, but it will be difficult for us." The meeting was the beginning of a successful effort orchestrated by Kissinger to relieve Israel's siege of the Egyptian Third Army.

If Meir was stunned by the dire warning about the limits of U.S. support, she didn't show it. Instead, she said that Israel was committed to keeping the cease-fire. "And let non-military supplies through?" Nixon asked. Meir conceded, as long as POWs and the lifting of the blockade were in the mix. She urged him to leave it to the generals to discuss the October 22 line. Kissinger explained that accepting the line in principle got Israel off the hook "since we do not know where the line is." Nixon escorted her out to the Rose Garden for a photo opportunity and then to the limousine awaiting her outside the diplomatic entrance where *Newsweek* captured him saluting the prime minister as she departed.

But if Nixon and Kissinger thought they had cowed Meir into submission, they were sorely mistaken. In a public press conference, she said repeatedly to a skeptical press corps that there was no pressure from the Nixon administration. But in private meetings on the Hill, she took potshots at Kissinger, even suggesting to Senator John C. Stennis, chairman of the Senate Armed Services Committee, that the DEFCON 3 alert was contrived.

Kissinger's personal relationship with Meir deteriorated further that evening when he attended a dinner at the Israeli embassy in her honor. They sat next to each other in frosty silence. When the prime minister rose to speak, she complained that Israel's friends had deprived it of victory, and then sat down. Kissinger had to remind her to make a toast. He was so furious that he told Dinitz the next morning that he would not meet with her and that she should send Yariv over to continue the negotiations. She was just as angry with him and insisted that she was the only Israeli official he could meet with.

In a meeting with his WSAG colleagues that morning, Kissinger fulminated. "We did not go through four weeks of agony here to be hostage to a nation of two and a half million people; U.S. foreign policy will be determined by the United States, not by Israel," he declared. If they did not agree to withdraw to the October 22 lines, he swore that he would force them back. Anticipating Meir's visit to the Pentagon that afternoon, he encouraged Schlesinger and Clements to be "tougher than I am. Then I can play the good guy." Clements said they would be happy to play that role. Kissinger said they should keep the military supplies "flowing, but tell her there will be consequences if they don't cooperate."

But Schlesinger was hardly going to be the fall guy for Kissinger again, having already taken the brunt of the blame in the press for the resupply delay during the war. His meeting with Meir, according to Dinitz's report, was quite cordial. The closest he came to the harshness Kissinger had called for was to note that meeting Israel's military requirements would depend on "national policy," which by implication was out of his hands.

Kissinger's slow progress in moving Meir toward his objective created a problem for him with Fahmy, who had remained in Washington so that he could carry back to Sadat the fruits of Kissinger's labor. Kissinger tried to buy himself more time by saying that Meir would have to return to Israel and discuss the proposal with her cabinet. Fahmy insisted on the October 22 line, noting that the UN Security Council had already decided the matter. In exasperation, Kissinger responded, "There is [only] so much I can do in one day." "Does it mean she refused to return to the October 22 positions?" asked Fahmy. "We are not in a position now to get [that]," Kissinger admitted. "I hope you can settle this whole matter before you come to Egypt," warned Fahmy. "If not, you cannot accomplish anything."

Fear of failure was a powerful motivator for Kissinger. The next day, he met again with Fahmy and began to test a different proposition. Fahmy had brought him the welcome news that Sadat had decided to negotiate directly with Kissinger when he came to Cairo. He said Kissinger should be ready to talk about the larger issue of disengagement, rather than just focus on the cease-fire arrangements. This gave Kissinger the opening he needed.

"We have to avoid expending all of our efforts on a return to the October

Prime Minister Golda Meir and Secretary of State Henry Kissinger at Blair House in Washington, DC, on November 2, 1973. The dejected and distant stares on their faces were the harbinger of the battle royal they would have that evening as Kissinger tried to tutor her on the role that he needed Israel to play in the postwar American-led order he was seeking to construct.

22 position," he argued. That only mattered when it came to resupply for the Third Army. Did it make sense, he asked rhetorically, to have a massive brawl with Israel over the October 22 line, or would it be better to say, "To hell with this, let's tackle the bigger problem?" Surprisingly, Fahmy said he agreed with Kissinger and, more important, that Sadat did too.

To facilitate the change in approach, Kissinger gave Fahmy something to take home to Sadat in lieu of an agreement on the October 22 line: the written guarantee that the United States would prevent Israel from launching offensive military operations on the west bank of the canal.* For Fahmy, it represented proof of concept; he later claimed it was his most important achievement because it marked a turning point in U.S-Egyptian relations. In return, Fahmy told Kissinger in a phone call after their meeting that Sadat had given orders not to challenge a Liberian tanker that was traversing Bab el-Mandeb to deliver oil to Israel. Kissinger had what he needed for his next encounter with Meir, which took place at Blair House late in the evening of November 2.

---

* The letter from Kissinger to Sadat said, "In connection with any agreement between Egypt and Israel relating to implementation of Paragraph 1 of Security Council Resolution 338: The United States guarantees that it will do its utmost to prevent offensive military operations by Israeli forces on the West Bank against Egyptian forces while the Israeli forces are on the West Bank." See Memcon between Kissinger and Fahmy, November 2, 1973, FRUS 1969–1976:25, Doc. 311, fn. 1.

To underscore his anger with her, Kissinger had played hard to get all day. Finally, he took a call from Dinitz, who claimed that she had not said half the things that were being attributed to her, that she had come to Washington to deal directly with Kissinger, and that Kissinger should sit alone with her to resolve their personal differences. Kissinger relented.

Meir and Kissinger met alone in the sitting room at Blair House for a few minutes. A press photographer captured them at the beginning of their "four eyes" meeting, both looking grim-faced and tired. Kissinger had a distant stare; Meir looked down dejectedly. Uncharacteristically, neither would say a word to the press gaggle.

It was after 11:00 p.m. when their teams joined them. The growl of the lioness had noticeably subsided. Kissinger began the larger meeting by repeating to her advisers that he had been holding the Egyptians and the Russians at bay by promising that he would produce something on his visit to Cairo. If he didn't, Israel would face a UN Security Council resolution demanding its withdrawal to the October 22 line, and it could forget about the POWs. Then the oil pressure would mount, "someone will say slow down the arms," and the United States will have to join with the Russians in forcing Israel to open the road to the Egyptian Third Army without anything in return.

Yariv now revealed that el-Gamasy had drawn a map showing Egyptian and Israeli "beachheads" in Sinai, with a UN buffer zone in between. He said el-Gamasy had told him that the size of the Egyptian force on the east bank of the canal could be discussed. Here was confirmation for Kissinger of the broader disengagement that Fahmy had discussed with him earlier in the day. He allowed that he could discuss the proposal in Cairo "in an abstract way," but, he said, "It is absolutely imperative for me to know before I am in Cairo what you'll tell them."

Meir wasn't ready to buy el-Gamasy's proposal. "To me it's an absolutely impossible suggestion," she said, referring to the idea that Israel withdraw thirty kilometers and leave Egypt in possession of both sides of the canal. She wanted to return to her original proposal of both armies withdrawing to their respective banks. Exasperated, Kissinger explained again why Sadat could not accept giving up all his gains on the east bank as well as ten kilometers on the west bank. "He'll be overthrown," he declared.

Kissinger appealed to her as a co-conspirator working to get a better deal: "If you and we develop a degree of confidence . . . you can take an outrageous position and let us force you off it. Then we have a strategy." Israel was going to have to give up some territory eventually; that was just reality. But it would be better for her to allow him to produce that Israeli concession so that he could demonstrate his foundational proposition "that the Russians can give [the Egyptians] arms but only we can give them territory."

But for Meir, giving up territory to make Kissinger look good went against her most fundamental instincts as a pioneer in the Zionist movement. Later in the conversation he would try to put it in historical context. "You and we once worked out a strategy which was relatively painless," he recalled, referring to the prewar deal they had made to maintain the status quo through Israeli deterrence. "Now we have to work out one with a minimum of pain," he suggested, as if it would only involve some minor Israeli concessions. He tried again to drive home the larger point: "The strategy is to disagree with you and then get you to move to a pre-agreed position."

Kissinger then shifted back to the cease-fire consolidation that needed to be addressed now. Yariv explained that he had told his Egyptian counterpart that he would not get the October 22 line because it would put Israel in an inferior strategic position. El-Gamasy had accepted that "there is a difference between the road and the line," Yariv said. Israel could afford to give up the road if it held a line that controlled the area around the roads. If Kissinger tied the release of prisoners to the IDF's return to the October 22 line, Israel would be in the invidious position of having to choose between recovering its prisoners and relinquishing its strategic advantage. A better solution, he argued, would be to tie the prisoner release to the opening of the road, which Israel was prepared to concede as long as it didn't have to withdraw from its current line.

Kissinger grasped that Yariv's approach would enable him to offer Sadat a UN-controlled road through Israeli lines to Suez city and the Egyptian Third Army. Kissinger responded by giving Yariv the ultimate compliment: "You've now convinced me the line is more important than the road." He suggested they sleep on it and reconvene later that day. It was 12:45 a.m.

They reconvened on Saturday night at 10:45 p.m. at Blair House, after the Israelis had observed the Sabbath and Meir had consulted her cabinet. She began the meeting by announcing that instead of a UN-controlled road, the cabinet wanted "joint UN-Israeli supervision and inspection." Concurrently with the opening of the road, there should be an exchange of all wounded POWs and the lifting of the blockade at Bab el-Mandeb. Finally, "the question" of the October 22 line would be discussed between the two sides "in the framework of disengagement and separation of forces."

Kissinger asked what the significance of raising the October 22 line would be if Israel was proposing that it be done in the context of a broader disengagement of forces. Meir admitted, "It has none." Kissinger could hardly contain himself. "You and we are living in a different world," he said disdainfully. "In effect you're refusing to discuss the October 22 line." He predicted that Sadat would have no choice but to go to the Russians, and then he knew what Nixon would do: the United States would not stop the Russians. Yet again,

Kissinger warned of the danger of decoupling the United States from Israel and the need for a common strategy. That set Meir off again. "We didn't start the war," she said. Kissinger cut her off. "You didn't start the war, but you face the need for wise decisions to protect the survival of Israel."

The mention of Israel's survival upset her even more. With her voice shaking, she said, "You're saying we have no choice. . . . We have to accept the judgment of the United States . . . on what is best for us?" Kissinger said that was the reality. She turned melodramatic: "I'll call the cabinet and tell them we have to accept the U.S. position or see the destruction of Israel."

When Kissinger asked why she had gone back on the agreement he thought they had reached the previous night, she responded that she had come to understand that it would break her people. Kissinger objected to the notion that, by trying to develop an acceptable framework, he was attempting to "rape" Israel. Then he revealed his inner suspicion: "You're also—maybe deliberately—upsetting the strategy of trying to move the Egyptians away from the Russians. . . . Maybe it serves your purpose?"

Yariv tried again to move from the personal to the practical, arguing that he thought there was a good chance, based on his sidebar discussions with el-Gamasy, that the Egyptians would accept the Israeli offer of road access because they were preoccupied with the need for continuous resupply. Kissinger hoped he was right but made clear that, if not, the United States would have to support any move to ensure the survival of the Third Army. He pointed out to Meir that when he forced her to allow the first convoy through, the alternative had been much worse—a joint U.S.-Soviet force. "What we gained was some control over your destiny."

Like a dysfunctional family argument, this just set Meir off on her replay of the trauma of the night when Israel was presented with the U.S.-Soviet cease-fire fait accompli. "We put the transistor on the table," she recounted, referring to the way the Israeli cabinet heard the news of the cease-fire. "We are supposed to be the cabinet of a sovereign country. . . . Why ask us? Just tell us. We had a choice?" she asked, doling out a large helping of Jewish guilt. Defensively, Kissinger tried to explain yet again what happened in Moscow.

This last round had exhausted both of them. Since it was now past 1:00 a.m., Kissinger tried to sum up. First, he suggested that Yariv postpone his meeting with el-Gamasy until after his own visit to Cairo so there would be no danger that his effort would be preempted. Then they discussed the modalities of UN inspection for the continuous supplies, with Yariv conceding that Israel could live with inspections at the end of the road, as the goods were being off-loaded at the canal.

Kissinger agreed to present the Israeli formula on the October 22 line but warned again of the dire consequences if Sadat rejected it. He observed that the Egyptians would have a tactical choice to make: "to buy additional goodwill from the United States for a later round, or to test how much pressure there can be." He said he feared Sadat would run to the Russians (even though he knew that was highly unlikely from his discussions with Fahmy) and he would be unable to go to the Saudis and get the oil embargo lifted. He commented that his friend Governor Nelson Rockefeller had told him that New York was within two weeks of a blackout.* He predicted that within a week there would be a UN airlift of supplies to the Third Army.

Paraphrasing the title of the 1965 Hollywood comedy *Situation Hopeless—but Not Serious*, he added, the Israeli position was "hopeless, but not unreasonable." He promised to present it to Sadat "with conviction" but added that in his judgment, "there is next to no chance it will be accepted."

Kissinger was deploying his tactic of lowering expectations, which he used with both sides. Just as he wanted Sadat to believe that only he could deliver Israel, he wanted the Israelis to believe that he had pulled off a miracle if he were able to provide what they needed from Sadat.

As Kissinger departed Blair House, Meir summoned the senior embassy staff to provide a debrief of the meeting. Her face was "ashen white," the Mossad station chief, Efraim Halevy, recalls. She reported that she had been on the verge of bursting into tears, but she had restrained herself because she did not want to give Kissinger the satisfaction of seeing her cry. She went on to give such an emotional briefing that Halevy returned to the office shaken. He sat down and sent his boss, Mossad chief Zvi Zamir, a handwritten letter describing the immense psychological pressure that she was under.

Kissinger had wielded a rhetorical two-by-four to bludgeon Meir into understanding Israel's role in the postwar order, starting with relinquishing its chokehold on the Egyptian Third Army ahead of ceding control of Arab territory. At no point in his battle with Meir, however, did Kissinger hold out the promise that this process would lead to peace. It would instead reduce Israel's isolation, undermine Soviet regional influence, help lift the Arab oil embargo, and prevent the embargo from being reimposed. And if all that could be achieved under U.S. tutelage, he was trying to convince her, Israel's security would be better guaranteed than by the previous strategy of holding on to all the occupied territory.

* *The New York Times* carried a front-page story during Meir's visit reporting that the New York State Public Service Commission had ordered major utility companies to prepare emergency plans for a shutdown of schools, instituting curfews, and shutting down heat in New York City subways. See Francis X. Clines, "Curfews Hinted in Oil Shortage," *New York Times*, November 1, 1973.

Kissinger's challenge now was to convince Sadat of the role he needed Egypt to play in his scheme. On the tactical level, there was a reasonable chance that Sadat would accept the package he was putting together. The big challenge he faced was over the October 22 line, where he had failed to sell Meir on the idea of accepting the principle while dealing with the actual line later. But she had agreed to discuss the line in the context of a wider disengagement, and Fahmy had been open to, even encouraging of, the idea of substituting an argument about an invisible line for a larger disengagement.

As he turned in for the night and began to contemplate his first visit to the Arab world, he could at least be satisfied that the exchanges of the last four days, no matter how intensive, exhausting, and frustrating, had enabled him to achieve his purpose of "accumulating nuances for a long-term strategy." Notwithstanding the drama of the encounters with Meir—he later recounted that it was like a visit to Dante's Inferno—all the important actors were now ready to accept his step-by-step approach. Sadat appeared ready to perform his part in this American-led diplomatic drama. And Meir understood her role now too, even though she would continue to resist Kissinger's stage direction.

9

Henry of Arabia

The difference between great and ordinary leaders is less formal intellect than insight and courage. The great man understands the essence of a problem; the ordinary leader grasps only the symptoms.

—Henry Kissinger, *Years of Upheaval*

Monday, *November 5, 1973, Rabat.* At 9:15 a.m., the secretary of state's U.S. Air Force Boeing 707 took off in drizzling rain from Andrews Air Force Base bound for Rabat, Morocco. It would be the first stop in a nine-country, ten-day trip that would end in Japan, with stops in Tunisia, Egypt, Jordan, Saudi Arabia, Iran, Pakistan, and China.

This aircraft had first been commissioned as Air Force One in the days of the Kennedy administration. Its fuselage was painted with a distinctive robin's-egg-blue stripe atop its polished aluminum underbelly, a large American flag on its tail, and the words "United States of America" across the top of the fuselage. Two weeks after its inaugural flight, on November 22, 1963, it had flown President Kennedy to Dallas and had brought his coffin back to Washington accompanied by his widow, Jacqueline Kennedy. Vice President Lyndon Johnson had taken the presidential oath of office on this plane before it took off from Dallas.

It was also used by Nixon and Kissinger on their first visit to China in February 1972. After a new Boeing 707 replaced it as Air Force One in December 1972, it became Special Air Missions (SAM) 86970, the backup plane, available for Kissinger's travels as secretary of state. In Kissinger's day, Air Force Two was configured with a modest cabin just behind the cockpit that provided him with a bed, desk, and secure phone. Beyond that was a small "conference room" with a kidney-shaped table where Kissinger could consult with his

Henry Kissinger in his airborne office on Air Force Two, which he used for his shuttle diplomacy in the Middle East.

senior staff and brief the press. Behind those two cabins was a banquette that provided seating for the secretary's senior staff, and seats arranged on either side of fixed tables for the executive secretariat, who handled all incoming and outgoing cables as well as preparation of the secretary's briefing books. The area was a hive of activity and jocularity, the latter usually prompted by Joe Sisco, on Kissinger's Middle East voyages. He would quickly become the butt of Kissinger's deprecating humor.*

At the back of the plane, the traveling press were wedged into coach-sized seats. At least in the Clinton era, there was strict segregation of press and staff; none of us could wander back and talk to them. The press spokesman, occasionally with an area expert to help, was the only one to do so. Kissinger, however, would personally brief the press after each stop, barely disguised as "a senior official traveling with the secretary."

With him on this first journey into Arabia were his Middle East aides—Sisco, Hal Saunders, and Roy Atherton—and his personal staff, including Peter Rodman, L. Paul "Jerry" Bremer, Gahl Hodges, and Robert J. McCloskey, his press spokesman.

Accompanying Kissinger for the first time on his foreign travels was a press corps of fourteen reporters—including Marvin Kalb of CBS, Ted Koppel of

---

* *Time* correspondent John Mulliken reported that as the plane was landing in Rabat on this first trip, the Xerox copier broke loose and slid toward Sisco. Someone yelled, "Oh my God, stop it! We can't have more than one Joe Sisco on this trip." See "The World: Around the World with Henry," *Time*, November 19, 1973.

ABC, Richard Valeriani of NBC, Bernard Gwertzman of *The New York Times*, Marilyn Berger of *The Washington Post*, and Barry Schweid of the Associated Press—and three camera crews. Most of these journalists happened to be Jewish and were therefore, in Nixon's eyes, members of the media "cabal" that was determined to bring an end to his presidency. Nevertheless, dispatching them with Kissinger was a calculated move by the White House to generate positive headlines that might distract the public from the daily reports of Nixon's widening Watergate woes. It would also, however, serve to promote Kissinger's celebrity at the expense of his increasingly jealous boss and put even more pressure on him to deliver some breakthrough in the Arab-Israeli conflict.

Kissinger had a ready rapport with these journalists. He would dazzle them with his analytical insights and his historical analogies while feeding them the stories that suited his purposes. They were ready to indulge him because they felt they were reporting history in the making. Even though they knew they were often being spun, it still provided great copy. Kissinger later credited them with having a vested interest in the success of his missions, hoping that amid the drama of Watergate their country could still accomplish something

Henry Kissinger briefs the traveling press corps on his plane, en route from Alexandria to Tel Aviv. From left to right: Marilyn Berger (*The Washington Post*), Kissinger, Sisco, Barry Schweid (Associated Press), Bernard Kalb (CBS), Jerry Schechter (*Time*), Jim Anderson (Westinghouse Broadcasting), and Lars-Erik Nelson (Reuters). Directly across from Kissinger is Bernard Gwertzman (*The New York Times*). Crouching in the foreground is Richard Valeriani (NBC). Kissinger would brief the press on the plane after every stop as a "senior official traveling with the secretary of state."

of which they could be proud. From them he gained "moral support . . . at several crucial moments."

Morocco has the distinction of being the first country in the world to have established diplomatic relations with the United States, in 1786. Its leader when Kissinger visited was King Hassan II, forty-four, a diminutive, balding, olive-skinned man usually clad in an exquisite French silk suit, always puffing on a cigarette, which he held in his elegant fingers. Though he came across at first sight as a pocket-sized European dandy, he was a direct descendent of the Prophet Muhammad and therefore held a special leadership position in the Muslim world.

As the ruler of an Arab country located far from the epicenter of the Arab-Israeli conflict and separated by the Atlantic Ocean from the United States, Hassan II positioned himself as a bridge between the West and the Middle East. He served as an interpreter of the ways of the Arab world, and a mediator between its more radical leaders and the United States. He had a strong stake in Arab moderation and wanted to help lead the Arab world to peace with Israel. He was also motivated by the fact that he ruled over the largest Jewish community still residing in the Arab world. Many of the poorer members of this community had migrated to Israel in the two decades since the Jewish state had been established, but they maintained their allegiance to the king even from there.

I had the opportunity to conduct negotiations with Hassan II, two decades after Kissinger first set foot in Morocco, to persuade him to abandon a UN referendum and grant full autonomy to the Western Sahara. Our three meetings took place in his stunningly beautiful palace in Marrakesh, with its intricate, wood-carved stucco and Moroccan *zellij* tiles. After our final session with his cabinet ministers, sons, and aides, in which the king informed them of his adoption of the U.S. approach, he invited me alone into his private study. Exhausted by the effort and weighed down by the burden of his decision, he sought to ensure that the United States would not betray him.

For Arab rulers, personal trust is far more important than any words on paper, and he wanted to convey that he was investing his confidence in me. He proceeded to tell me the painful story of his upbringing. He had been taken from his mother at birth, an act of cruelty by his domineering father, Mohammed V, who had led Morocco's struggle for independence from France. A Moroccan Jewish nanny had substituted for Hassan II's mother as wet nurse and then guardian, providing his primary source of love and comfort as he grew up. Suckled by a Jewish mother's milk, he wanted me to know that he would always have a special place in his heart for the Jewish people.

Had Kissinger known that King Hassan viewed him through the same prism, it would have provided some reassurance to him as he nervously contemplated how a Jewish secretary of state would be received by Arab leaders. His purpose in stopping off in Morocco was to secure the king's support and guidance in advance of his meetings with Sadat and King Faisal of Saudi Arabia.

Hassan II was forthcoming. He accepted Kissinger's argument that it made no sense to waste valuable diplomatic capital on determining the October 22 line and that it was wiser to move directly to the broader disengagement of forces. He also sent a message to Sadat that "our chief impression [is] that if [Kissinger] gets into a commitment he will honor it. . . . You can put your trust in him." He undertook to send the same message to King Faisal of Saudi Arabia and dispatch his foreign minister to Arab capitals to convince them to give Kissinger a chance.

That endorsement came with a price tag. In preparation for his audience with the king, Kissinger had succumbed to his entreaties that the United States meet with the PLO. The king viewed the Palestinian umbrella organization, led by Yasir Arafat, as "the joker in the deck." He believed no Arab leader would act against the Palestinians, but if the United States won the PLO's confidence, then "no Arab nation would fail to follow." According to Kissinger's account, the king's appeals had begun in August 1973, before the Yom Kippur War, when Arafat had sought his help to begin a dialogue with the United States based on a purported willingness to accept Israel's existence. In September, the king had offered to host a meeting, and in October, during the war, Arafat had conveyed separately, through CIA channels in Beirut, where he then had his headquarters, that he was ready to participate in postwar negotiations with Israel.

Kissinger viewed this overture with a jaundiced eye given the PLO's antipathy toward Israel and King Hussein of Jordan. But, in contrast to subsequent American leaders, he was not prepared to let America's friends veto his contacts. His calculation was that a U.S.-PLO meeting could help create a supportive environment for moderate Arab leaders to join the American-mediated peace process. He knew that the PLO was a potential troublemaker, capable of disrupting the order he was constructing while it was still aborning. "We wanted it to be on its best behavior during the delicate early stages of our approach to Egypt and while we were seeking Saudi support," he writes in his memoirs.

The U.S.-PLO meeting took place in Rabat, two days before Kissinger's arrival. Kissinger sent Vernon Walters as his envoy. At the time, Walters was deputy director of the CIA; he went on to become the U.S. ambassador to the United Nations and then Germany. He was a more senior official than would

normally be sent to a first meeting with representatives of a terrorist organization responsible for the deaths of American diplomats.* But Kissinger trusted
Walters because he had helped establish secret meetings for him in France
with the North Vietnamese. Walters's counterpart in the meeting was Khalid
al-Hassan, a political deputy to Arafat and, along with his brother Hani, one of
the pioneers of the PLO's tentative efforts to reconcile with Israel.

Walters had a listening brief, except to make clear that the United
States would not countenance any effort to destroy Israel and would brook
no betrayal of King Hussein. But he also made clear that the United States
sought a comprehensive solution that would take account of peaceful Palestinian aspirations. For his part, al-Hassan emphasized the PLO's antipathy for
King Hussein and refusal ever to be governed by the Hashemites. The PLO's
ultimate objective was a secular democratic Palestine in place of Israel, he said,
but he conceded that was not a practical objective for the time being. Walters
thought he heard from al-Hassan some indirect willingness to recognize "an
Israeli state entity," based on the 1947 UN partition plan, but that was vague at
best. For both sides, the meeting was the message: Arafat was satisfied that he
now had a secret channel to Kissinger; the secretary of state was satisfied that
he had prevented "radical assaults on the early peace process."†

Tuesday, November 6, 1973, Cairo. Kissinger landed in Cairo a few minutes
before midnight. The city and its airport were still under a blackout, so it was
difficult for him to see what awaited him as he nervously peered through his
cabin's window. But once the media turned on their camera lights, he could
make out Foreign Minister Fahmy, as promised, at the foot of the airplane
stairs, along with a large and unruly press gaggle. Fahmy whisked him away in
his Mercedes limousine along the dark, deserted highway that cut a straight
line from the airport through the garden city of Heliopolis with its villas and
palaces of bygone majesty. The highway took a sharp right turn and headed
through Cairo's inner-city slums to the heart of the city and the Nile Hilton.

A Florida-style, modernist building with a utilitarian façade and crisp hori-
zontal lines, the Hilton was distinguished by a colorful mosaic that wrapped
around its mezzanine level. The first post–World War II international hotel in
the Arab world, it had become a stylish watering hole for the region's elite. The

---

* In March 1973, the PLO's Black September terrorist arm had attacked the Saudi embassy in
Khartoum, taking ten diplomats hostage. After Nixon announced that he would not pay blackmail
to terrorists, they murdered three of them, including Cleo Noel, the U.S. ambassador to Sudan,
and George Moore, the deputy chief of mission.
† After that meeting, Arafat's faction of the PLO—Fatah—ceased attacks on Americans. See
Henry Kissinger, *Years of Upheaval* (Boston: Little, Brown, 1982), 628–29, and Back-Channel
Message from Walters to Kissinger, November 4, 1973, FRUS 1969–1976:25, Doc. 318.

interior, according to a travel brochure of the time, was "quintessential 1950s Cairo with its lotus flower prints on fabrics and pharaonic-chic aesthetic." It fronted on the Nile, on the corniche that fringed the ancient river as it wended its way through the city. Behind the hotel was Tahrir Square, which would become famous in 2011 for the epic battles of the revolution that unseated President Hosni Mubarak and shook the foundations of the Arab world. To its north the hotel was flanked by the aging Museum of Egyptian Antiquities, which houses a stunning Tutankhamen collection; to its south were the imposing headquarters of the Arab League.

From his balcony, Kissinger could look down on the Nile, where feluccas docked on one bank and nightclub boats, their strands of decorative lights blacked out because of the war, on the other. For millennia, the Nile had flowed slowly and deliberately through Cairo toward its delta and the Mediterranean Sea. Notwithstanding the tension generated by the war and its uneasy aftermath, including the presence of Israeli tanks only fifty kilometers east of the city, the river created a sense of tranquility and permanence, the museum displayed the greatness of Egypt's ancient civilization, and the Arab League headquarters signaled that Cairo was, at that time, the unchallenged center of the modern Arab world.

At first, Kissinger seemed unimpressed. Daylight brought him the view of "a flat landscape divided by a muddy river," he writes in his memoirs. The main attribute of Egypt's stunning statues was, in his mind, their permanence, not the wonder of the ancient civilization they represented. But as he toured the museum, he began to appreciate the beatific, detached expressions of the massive statues, "as if the time allotted to mortals was irrelevant to their concerns."

As he walked back to the hotel across Tahrir Square, he could not help but be impressed by the teeming populace. In those days, some six million people inhabited Cairo, twice as many as in all of Israel. Kissinger contemplated Israel's dilemma: for the moment, it had military superiority, but time and numbers were on the Arab side. It gave him a new insight into why Meir had been so tense and rigid in their Washington encounters: The Arabs "could wait for the Israeli mistake that would prove fatal." It would reinforce his sense of Israel's impermanence in contrast to Egypt's five-thousand-year history.

The poverty of the masses he witnessed in the square should also have given him an appreciation of Sadat's predicament. Egypt's problems could only be alleviated by shifting resources from fighting a war to developing the economy. Western assistance had become imperative for the success of Sadat's cause and the survival of his regime. He knew it would only be forthcoming if he reconciled with Israel. Far from believing that time and numbers were on his side, Sadat had concluded that the numbers, in terms of Egypt's population growth, had turned time against him. Kissinger did not recognize it at that moment, but his diplomacy was about to benefit significantly from Sadat's sense of urgency, providing him with the necessary means to overcome Meir's inflexibility.

Sadat received Kissinger at his presidential office in the Tahra Palace in Heliopolis, situated halfway between the city center and the airport. The Italian architect Antonio Lasciac had designed this three-story edifice for the daughter of Khedive Ismail, who ruled Egypt in the 1860s and modernized its economy (though like later leaders of Egypt, he drove it into near bankruptcy). Built in the Italianate palazzo style with marble floors and alabaster ceilings, it reflected the European influence on Cairo's evolution that had begun with Napoleon's ill-fated invasion in 1798. It had become incongruous in the modern era of Egyptian military rule. Nevertheless, it remains the office of the Egyptian president to this day. It was here that Hosni Mubarak and Warren Christopher presided over the finalization of the Gaza-Jericho Agreement in May 1994, in a late-night negotiation with Yasir Arafat, Yitzhak Rabin, and Shimon Peres.

After ascending a magnificent marble staircase to the second floor, Kissinger again had to run the gauntlet of the Egyptian press gaggle outside Sadat's office before his host rescued him. Tall and swarthy, with a booming voice and a magnetic Eddie Murphy smile, Sadat had thrown his tailored military overcoat nonchalantly over his shoulders, in the Italian style of the palace itself. He welcomed his American visitor and swept him into his office for what turned out to be a three-hour meeting.

They sat together on a baroque, gilded settee upholstered in a large floral pattern, in front of tall windows shaded by sheer curtains to cut down the blinding Egyptian sunlight. Sadat was wearing a khaki military tunic with field marshal epaulets but no medals; Kissinger was in one of his dark Brooks Brothers suits with a black-and-white-striped tie. On the face of it, they were an odd couple: the American Jewish professor from the German town of Fürth and the revolutionary Arab general from the Egyptian rural village of Mit Abul-Kom. But they would form a deep friendship based on trust, mutual admiration, and the pursuit of a common vision of a more peaceful region.

For their first encounter, Sadat had decided they should meet alone, without note takers or translators.* Once the photographers had been shepherded out

---

* There is no official American record of the conversation, only Kissinger's recollections as captured in his report to Nixon, via Scowcroft. See Editorial Note, undated, FRUS 1969–1976:25, Doc. 324, and Kissinger, *Years of Upheaval*, 637–43. My account also draws on the versions related by several American journalists whom Kissinger briefed separately on the encounter. See Edward Sheehan, *The Arabs, Israelis, and Kissinger: A Secret History of American Diplomacy in the Middle East* (New York: Readers Digest Press, 1976), 48–51; Marvin Kalb and Bernard Kalb, *Kissinger* (New

Secretary of State Henry Kissinger meets President Sadat for the first time in the Tahra Palace, Heliopolis, on November 7, 1973. Kissinger would discover in this first meeting that he had been blessed with an Egyptian negotiating partner who was "free of the obsession with detail by which mediocre leaders think they are mastering events."

of his office, Sadat lit his signature pipe and launched into his pitch, pointing to a large map on the wall that portrayed the disengagement plan el-Gamasy had outlined to Yariv. Kissinger dodged that proposal for the moment, choosing instead to flatter Sadat. He asked how he had been so successful in the war.

As Sadat related his thoughts on that, Kissinger was impressed by his urbanity and charm. He felt that Sadat "seemed free of the obsession with detail by which mediocre leaders think they are mastering events." Indeed, as Sadat's daughter Camelia would later recount, her father taught her that "if details do not need attention, do not give them attention. Envision things and then calculate them. Understand a goal and then plan how to reach it." That was the essence of Kissinger's strategic approach too. But he was also a master of the details.

In a much calmer atmosphere than at his tutorial with Meir a few days earlier, Kissinger led Sadat through the precepts of his step-by-step approach, moving by stages without a guarantee of the final outcome. Would Sadat buy in? U.S. involvement in peacemaking required an Arab leader, said Kissinger, "willing to relate rhetoric to reality." The United States would not respond to pressure, nor reward clients of the Soviet Union, nor allow the defeat of

York: Little, Brown, 1974), 508–10; and Walter Isaacson, *Kissinger* (New York: Simon & Schuster, 1992), 540–41. Both Sadat and Fahmy gloss over the conversation in their biographies.

American allies with Soviet weapons. But if Egypt pursued its national interests, the United States was ready to cooperate, and if it would accept Israel, the
United States would help "allay reasonable Arab grievances."

Then followed Kissinger's customary exegesis on the constraints imposed
on him by domestic politics. Sadat should not expect him to be seen publicly
applying pressure on Israel, even though he and Nixon were determined to do
so in private. He knew from experience that the Israelis' instinctive response to
American pressure would be to dig in their heels and become more obstinate.
He explained that Israel "had never enjoyed the minimum attribute of sovereignty, acceptance by its neighbors." He urged Sadat to think about peacemaking with Israel as a psychological challenge rather than a diplomatic one.
Egypt, as the most influential Arab state, could make a critical contribution
by demonstrating a willingness to recognize Israel, and that would help the
United States obtain territorial concessions from Israel.

Kissinger proposed an Egyptian-American partnership. "Let's put aside
the irreconcilables for the moment," he urged Sadat. Instead, they should create together a negotiating dynamic that would build confidence on both sides.
"We must set in motion small agreements. We must proceed step-by-step," he
concluded.

Sadat took it all in, puffing on his pipe. Kissinger's argument was compelling, even attractive, because a new partnership with the United States was
exactly what Sadat had in mind. But Kissinger's approach didn't address his
immediate needs. "What about my Third Army? What about the October
22 line?" he asked. Kissinger launched into an argument he had been preparing since his discussions with Yariv and Fahmy in Washington. Sadat had two
choices. He could focus on the October 22 line in an effort to force Israel
back. But at best, that would only succeed in getting Israel to withdraw a few
kilometers on the west bank of the canal. The better course, in Kissinger's
view, was to ensure a continuous resupply of the Third Army and then, with
tensions defused, negotiate a disengagement agreement in which Israel would
withdraw into the Sinai, though not beyond the passes, which would have to
come later. Paradoxically, if Sadat focused on the broader disengagement, he
could achieve a faster Israeli withdrawal from the canal than if he insisted on
withdrawal to the October 22 line.

As Kissinger retells it, Sadat sat brooding in silence for several awkward
minutes. Then he astonished Kissinger. Instead of arguing or haggling, he
said that he agreed with Kissinger's analysis and his proposed procedure. He
was committed to turning his nation toward peace and he accepted that Israel
needed confidence to become his partner in this endeavor. Sadat noted, however, that Israel was occupying his land, so he needed reassurance too about
Israel's intentions. Nevertheless, he was prepared to accept Kissinger's strategy

if the United States guaranteed the continuous resupply of the Third Army. To give Kissinger's approach a chance, he was willing to defer the issue of the October 22 line.

Even though we have only Kissinger's testimony of the details of this meeting, he was undoubtedly persuasive. But Kissinger had been blessed with an Arab partner willing to do his bidding. Because of his own misstep, he had been forced to spend an inordinate amount of time arguing about the October 22 line, and suddenly Sadat had solved the problem. The monkey was now on Kissinger's back to deliver the wider solution, and he recognized the shrewdness of Sadat's move in that regard: "Since the course on which we had agreed depended on our exertions, [Sadat] would commit us more surely by a show of confidence in us than by haggling over technicalities."

Kissinger laid out the concept for the consolidation of the cease-fire generated from his conversations in Washington. Using the Yariv formula that he had spurned when he first heard it, he said that the *question* of the October 22 line would be discussed in the framework of an agreement on the disengagement of forces; Suez city and the Third Army would receive continuous nonmilitary supplies. To ensure this, the UN would take control of the Cairo-Suez road, Israeli officers would inspect the cargo at the canal, and as soon as the UN checkpoints on the road were established, there would be an exchange of all prisoners of war.

The issue Kissinger had been most concerned about—the timing of the POW exchange—turned out to be no problem at all. Sadat simply accepted Kissinger's proposal.* They also agreed to upgrade U.S.-Egyptian diplomatic relations to full-scale "interest sections" in Cairo and Washington headed by diplomats who would have the rank of ambassadors. That was one step short of full diplomatic relations, which Sadat promised would accompany the signing of the first disengagement agreement.

Kissinger was impressed, for it was the essence of statesmanship to set in motion a historical process rather than wrangle for marginal advantage. "From that meeting onward, I knew I was dealing with a great man," he writes in his memoirs.

Sadat seems to have been equally impressed. In his autobiography he writes, "The first hour made me feel I was dealing with an entirely new mentality, a new political method." He later told a leading Egyptian journalist that after this conversation he "became convinced that Kissinger is a man that

---

* As for the blockade at Bab el-Mandeb, Sadat explained that since he had never formally declared it, he could not now formally lift it. Instead, he offered a commitment to "ease" the blockade if Israel would conduct normal traffic through the strait and not make it a public matter. As Kissinger would subsequently observe, "The whole issue was a contribution to metaphysics, since we could find no evidence that any ships had ever actually been stopped in the first place." See Kissinger, *Years of Upheaval*, 642.

you can trust. He spoke logically, with a clear vision and a strategy rooted in clearly-defined characteristics." This was the face of the United States that he had always wanted to see, not that of Rogers. He informed his aides after the meeting that he was turning a new page in his relations with the United States, because it alone—not the Soviet Union—could impart momentum to the situation. He told them he had confidence in his new friend "Henry," who was sincere and would carry out what he promised. He felt as if they had known each other for years. It was, in Sadat's mind, the beginning of a beautiful friendship, a relationship of mutual understanding with the United States "crystallizing what we came to describe as the 'Peace Process.'"

With such a breakthrough in hand, logic dictated that Kissinger fly to Jerusalem to lock down the agreement. Even though a stop in Israel had not been part of his itinerary, he could have easily spent the night there en route to his next scheduled stop in Amman for an audience with King Hussein. But Kissinger did not want to offend the hypersensitive Fahmy, who had invited various Egyptian luminaries and ambassadors to dine with his celebrity guest. He also wanted to see the pyramids. So Kissinger dispatched Sisco and Saunders to brief the Israeli leadership, assuming that since he had secured 95 percent of what Meir had told him she needed, including the POWs, without having to worry about the October 22 line, there was no need for his presence there. He would later remark, "It proved that I did not yet know the Middle East."

That evening, at the Egyptian foreign minister's dinner table, he had his first exposure to Arab intellectuals, engaging in a lengthy exchange with Mohamed Hassanein Heikal, the legendary editor in chief of the state-controlled *Al-Ahram* newspaper and a celebrated confidant of both Nasser and Sadat (though Sadat would quickly tire of him). It earned him Heikal's seal of approval in his weekend column, which was read throughout the Arab world. In Heikal's view, Kissinger was "serious in his search for a solution." He judged that his Jewishness would "not restrict him," and that it might even give him immunity from American Jewish pressure groups (revealing his ignorance of the workings of the Israel lobby).

For Sisco and Saunders, this was the first time that American diplomats had reached agreement with an Arab country and then come to Israel to sell it. Over the many decades since then, the general reaction from Jerusalem has tended to be the same, regardless of the complexion of the coalition government in power or the nature of its prime minister. The first response is to devalue any concession made by the Arab side to reduce the expected pressure for a reciprocal Israeli gesture. The second is to engage in a Talmudic examination of every word in the text to reveal its hidden meaning and uncover the loophole or trapdoor that might represent a threat to the national interest, usually of existential dimensions. The third is to demand written assurances from the United States to codify Israel's interpretation of the text as the one that will prevail should any dispute arise. These assurances are usually presented in a U.S.-Israeli memorandum of understanding (MOU) that is supposed to be strictly confidential, but then the Israeli side inevitably leaks to provide political cover in the cabinet, Knesset, or public arena. "Israeli domestic politics combined with the insecurity of a nation denied legitimacy to produce a maddening, nitpicking style of negotiation," Kissinger once observed. It could not have stood in starker contrast with what he had just encountered in Cairo.

In her exchanges with Sisco, Meir objected to Israeli checkpoints being replaced by UN ones on the Cairo-Suez road, wanted to know who would control the road, and then insisted that "nothing must change on the road." She allowed how she was "full of suspicion" about the Bab el-Mandeb arrangements too. "I can't imagine that we can accept this," she declared. After several hours of this back-and-forth, Sisco asked her what he should convey to his boss. She responded, with a wry smile, "Give him my best and tell him this is a *fantastic* achievement."

Yet when she brought it to the cabinet the next morning, Meir faced new demands from her ministers. Since any attempt to change the wording of the agreement would open it up to Egyptian changes as well, Sisco and Saunders went to work with Yariv and produced a U.S.-Israeli MOU.* She wanted this MOU to be part of the agreement, which Kissinger refused, accepting instead that she could declare her interpretation to the Knesset and he would not contradict her. But that afternoon, in a hastily convened meeting at Kilometer 101 between Yariv and el-Gamasy, Yariv tried to get formal Egyptian acceptance of the Israeli interpretations. This generated a series of terse, long-distance exchanges between Fahmy, Meir, and Kissinger, who was traveling from Tehran to Islamabad. However, in both the Egyptian and Israeli messages to Kissinger there were clear indications that both sides were simply looking for his reassurance as they nervously approached the announcement of their first agreement.

Sunday, November 11, 1973, Sinai. Kissinger was in Beijing when the signing of the six-point cease-fire agreement by Yariv and el-Gamasy took place in the tent at Kilometer 101. General Ensio Siilasvuo, the commander of the UN Emergency Force (UNEF), presided over the ceremony in the presence of hundreds of journalists who had traveled from Cairo and Tel Aviv. There were no speeches or toasts. The orange soda bottles provided by the Israeli hosts

---

* The MOU clarified that adherence to the cease-fire "ruled out" the blockade of the Bab el-Mandeb Strait, and detailed the procedure for manning the checkpoints on the Cairo-Suez road, as well as other Israeli interpretations of the agreement that the United States was willing to accept.

remained unopened. Yariv alone issued a statement afterward that referred to the agreement as "the first step along the long and difficult road that leads to a settlement of the conflict between us and our neighbors and to peace with them."

Four days later, a Red Cross plane ferried twenty-six wounded Israeli POWs from Cairo to Tel Aviv, and another Red Cross plane transferred forty-four wounded Egyptians in the opposite direction, beginning the prisoner swap that was at the core of the prime minister's concerns. The Israeli soldiers were greeted at Lod Airport by Dayan and an enthusiastic crowd bearing flowers and welcome banners, one of which quoted the prophet Jeremiah: "Thy children shall return to their own land."

At the same time, UN forces took over the Israeli checkpoints on the Cairo-Suez road while Israeli forces signaled their continued control by deploying on top of the dunes alongside the road as the convoys passed. In a large, UN-controlled parking lot near the canal, Israeli officers inspected the unloaded supplies. Meanwhile, oil tankers from Iran resumed their uninterrupted passage to Israel's southern port of Eilat through the Bab el-Mandeb Strait.

For Kissinger, the agreement had proved the wisdom of focusing on a small initial step on the road from war to peace. To his delight, the credit he gained was out of proportion to the size of the step he had managed to get the Israelis and Egyptians to take. Premier Zhou Enlai, his Chinese host at the time the agreement was signed, branded him "the Middle East Cyclone." For the moment, Nixon was happy too: Haig cabled Kissinger that "the President is elated by your accomplishments. . . . You never fail to exceed our expectations."

Notwithstanding his efforts on Israel's behalf, Kissinger's methods had taken their toll on his reputation there. The realization that Israel was no longer master of its own fate—that it now had to make concessions to lubricate American diplomacy—had generated a resentment toward him that spread from the prime minister's office through the press to the Israeli public. "Never take your eyes off him," one Israeli official told *The New York Times*. "He's fast, he's shrewd, he's clever, but we realize he has his own goals to achieve and some of these may be at our expense." Because he had been so unexpectedly successful in moving Sadat to accept Israel's requirements, Meir was now convinced that he must have promised Sadat an Israeli withdrawal to the 1967 lines, just as she had earlier been convinced that he had made a similar commitment to Brezhnev to secure the cease-fire resolution. It was beyond her ken to accept that Sadat might give something for nothing.

Rather than worrying about what Kissinger had promised Sadat, Meir should have been focused on what he was going to say to the king of Saudi Arabia when he stopped off in Riyadh en route to Beijing. Ironically, while Kissinger's diplomacy had secured Israel's oil supply from Iran through the Bab el-Mandeb Strait, the United States was coping with a complete cutoff of oil from the Arab oil producers, including for the U.S. armed forces. The impact of the Arab oil embargo was now being felt across the world.

The Arab oil producers had explicitly linked their price hikes and production cuts to the policies of consumers toward the Arab-Israeli conflict. Europe and Japan had already reacted by breaking ranks with the United States. On November 6, while Kissinger was en route to Cairo, the nine foreign ministers of the European Economic Community—the precursor to the European Union—issued a communiqué calling on Israel to return to the October 22 lines. They also demanded the implementation of UNSC Resolution 242, noting that it required Israel to withdraw from territories occupied in 1967. The page-one headlines in the American press that week comingled news of Kissinger's meetings with Arab leaders with reports of fuel-conservation measures, a possible gasoline tax, a fifty-mile-per-hour speed limit on state roads, and portents of blackouts. Kissinger's intelligence briefings included dire warnings of panic in Europe and severe gasoline shortages in the Midwest and the northeastern United States, and the prospect of a grave energy crisis come winter, only a month away.

Kissinger had pointed to these pressures on the United States in his confrontation with Meir at Blair House a week earlier to underscore his argument that she needed to coordinate her concessions with him. But while he was using that specter as leverage, he was also putting up determined resistance to the linkage of the oil embargo to Israeli concessions, even though he received no credit in Israel for doing so.

Although he had not taken the warning signs seriously, he quickly came to understand that the embargo complicated his diplomacy. This had been driven home on October 23, when Prince Fahd had sent him an oral message that emphasized "the embargo on oil for the United States will continue in force as long as Israel occupies Arab territory beyond its borders as they existed before the June 1967 war." Just as he had reacted very badly when he thought the Soviets were threatening the United States with military intervention, his response to the Saudi move was to confront it. "We will break it," he said at his staff meeting on October 23.*

---

* On October 26, Kissinger expressed his deep frustration at the predicament to his staff. "I know what would have happened in the nineteenth century. But we can't do it. The idea that a Bedouin kingdom could hold up Western Europe and the United States would have been absolutely inconceivable. They would have landed, they would have divided up the oil fields, and they would

He insisted to Arab and European interlocutors alike that U.S. diplomacy could not be seen to be the product of Arab oil pressure because that would only invite more of the same. "If [the Saudis] inflict a cold winter on us, there will be less incentive for us to continue with diplomacy," he said. "We cannot operate under threat or blackmail" became his constant refrain. And since he had reached the firm judgment that the United States had neither the interest nor the ability to impose the 1967 lines on Israel, as opposed to persuading it to engage in a process of gradual withdrawal, he believed it unwise to encourage the Arabs to believe that it could. "I am not a prophet who can ride in from the desert on a white horse with a dramatic solution," he told oil company executives as he sought to enlist them in the effort to ground the Arabs in reality.

Similarly, he believed he was serving the interests of America's European and Japanese allies better by demonstrating that the United States would not be moved by their efforts to curry favor with the Arab oil producers. As he explained it to his senior staff, urging them not to engage in hand-wringing when he rigidly resisted pressure, "If we once get on the wicket that oil will be released as a result of progress made in negotiations, we are dead, because on that basis the Europeans and Soviets will outbid us at every stage." Instead, by establishing that the United States was impervious to pressure from its European allies, he believed the Arabs would, in turn, come to recognize the folly of pressing them.

Constrained by this calculus from bending to Saudi demands, Kissinger nevertheless needed to find a way to persuade King Faisal to lift the embargo because it was causing panic and division among America's allies and disruption to life in the United States as well. Moreover, an increasingly desperate Nixon imagined that ending the embargo would somehow provide for his political salvation. On the eve of Kissinger's audience with the Saudi king, in an address before Congress, the president had made a fanfare out of unveiling his "Project Independence" plan to deal with the energy crisis. Nixon pressed Kissinger to persuade King Faisal to end the embargo, but he emphasized through a message from Haig that, should Kissinger succeed, "[the President] hopes that progress made in this area could be announced by him from the White House after your return."

Thursday, November 8, 1973, Riyadh. Kissinger met with King Faisal at the Royal Palace. Everything about this encounter was in contrast to his meet-

---

have solved the problem." See Minutes of Kissinger's Staff Meeting, October 26, 1973, FRUS 1969–1976:36, Doc. 229.

ing with Sadat. Saudi Arabia's princes were glorified Bedouin tribal sheikhs. Their exposure to Western modernization had been recent and limited. Unlike Egypt, they had no ancient civilization to mold their society. In founding the modern state, Faisal's father, King Abdulaziz ibn Saud, had forged an alliance with Wahhabi clerics to secure his family's religious legitimacy. The clergy drew its inspiration from the strictest interpretation of the Prophet Muhammad's teachings, thereby ensuring that Saudi society still adhered to seventh-century norms. The vast oil wealth that would come to symbolize and transform their nation was still, in those days, mostly a mirage.

King Faisal embodied all the shrewdness generated by centuries of survival in the harsh desert environment. He was no newcomer to international affairs, having served as his father's foreign minister since 1930. He was the first Saudi prince to be exposed to the West, dispatched by his father to England in 1919, at the age of twelve. In 1943, he was dispatched again, this time to Washington, to meet with President Roosevelt and lay the foundations for the critical meeting between his father and the president on the USS *Quincy* two years later, which established the alliance between the United States and the Saudi kingdom.

Faisal was no stranger to conflict either. In the 1920s he had been commander of the siege of Jeddah, which led to the defeat and ouster of the Hashemites from the Hejaz and their relinquishment of custodianship of the holy mosques in Mecca and Medina.* As king, he had confronted a dire threat to his realm from Soviet-backed Arab radicalism. Recruiting the United States, Britain, and even Israel to his cause, Faisal had succeeded in bogging down Nasser in an unwinnable war in Yemen. At the same time, he sought to counter Pan-Arabism through the promotion of Pan-Islamism, establishing the Organization of the Islamic Conference and spreading the Wahhabi brand of puritanical Islam to the Muslim world through the funding of mosques and the export of Saudi clergy.

In 1962, President Kennedy convinced Faisal to embark on a gradual but deliberate process of modernization of the kingdom, including ending slavery and introducing television. By 1973, Faisal had transformed the kingdom from a weak, poor monarchy, its people vulnerable to the passions of Nasser's Pan-Arabism, to an increasingly prosperous, stable, modernizing ally of the United States. Nasser's defeat in Yemen and then against Israel in 1967 had opened the way for Faisal to assert himself in the Arab-Israeli arena. He championed the Palestinian cause, raising funds from Saudi citizens to aid Palestinian families and using the issue, particularly the need to liberate Jerusalem, to mobilize support for his efforts to spread the word of Wahhabi Islam.

---

* The Hejaz is the western region of Saudi Arabia that contains the port city of Jeddah and the holy cities of Mecca and Medina.

Secretary of State Kissinger and King Faisal of Saudi Arabia in Riyadh. King
Faisal lectured Kissinger on the Zionist-communist conspiracy, noting that
it was unfortunate "that among those of the Jewish faith there are those who
embraced Zionism." Nevertheless, he said that he would pray to God for the
success of Kissinger's "noble efforts."

During this period, when the Soviet Union was providing patronage to his
radical Arab enemies, Faisal did his best to connect the dots between communism and Zionism, printing and distributing *The Protocols of the Elders of Zion*,
the infamous fabrication about supposed Jewish plans to conquer the world, in
Arabic and other languages. Despite his anti-Jewish bent, he did not oppose
the existence of the Jewish state. He insisted that Israel relinquish its occupation of East Jerusalem, but in return he was willing to recognize Israel in its
pre-1967 borders. It should not have been surprising to the U.S. government,
then, that Faisal was prepared to lend Saudi Arabia's support to Sadat when
he heard of his plans for limited war against Israel to reclaim Arab territory.

The king hosted Kissinger in his *diwan*, a cavernous but sumptuous hall
where he received plaintiffs. Faisal's dour, unsmiling visage was an expression of his aloof and stern personality. His hooded eyelids, hook nose, and
protruding chin, barely disguised by a goatee, gave him an intimidating
appearance. He was dressed in traditional Saudi garb, a black ankle-length
thobe, or kaftan, covered by a gold-lined, white woolen cloak, matched by
a white keffiyeh headdress, topped by a double-banded golden agal, which
denoted royalty.

They sat in two large, adjacent chairs, deliberately positioned, it seemed, so that the king could avoid eye contact with his petitioner. The chairs were separated by a low side table upon which had been placed a 1950s-style ivory telephone, the ultimate symbol of modernity, even if it was twenty years out of date. The king's advisers sat along one side of the hall opposite Kissinger's team aligned on the other wall, at least twenty feet apart.

The differences between Kissinger and Faisal could not have been starker. A product of the European enlightenment, a German Jewish refugee from Nazi persecution, a leading American intellectual, and the high representative of the world's superpower was about to engage with a Bedouin, homeschooled, tribal sheikh. They did have one thing in common: they had both developed an oblique style of speech, Kissinger to impress and sometimes confuse his audience, Faisal to retain his distance and maneuvering room. Kissinger used ambiguity to disguise or bridge differences; Faisal used it to avoid making a commitment.* Among Clinton's peace team, we used to joke that you would rarely hear a direct "yes" or "no" from a Saudi interlocutor. Instead, for them a "yes" meant "maybe" and a "maybe" meant "no." As Kissinger notes in his memoirs, "We warily circled each other like wrestlers before a match, studying each other's moves without, in the end, ever going beyond this preliminary phase."

Kissinger was apprehensive about how he would be received, given his Jewish identity. In those years, Jews were strangers in Saudi Arabia. That had not always been the case. In the seventh century, when the Prophet Muhammad and his Islamic creed emerged, Jews were well established in the Arabian Peninsula as traders, craftsmen, and farmers. The "People of the Scripture" (Ahl al-Kitab), as they became known, were included in Muhammad's definition of the Islamic community (the Umma) and the teachings of the Torah were incorporated into the Koran. Along with Christians and Zoroastrians, the Jews were treated as Dhimmi, or protected people, because they too were regarded as the recipients of God's revelation.

Muhammad, however, had a falling out with the large and powerful Jewish community of Medina, which would not accept him as the Prophet. Those Jews who weren't killed in the ensuing confrontation were banished from the Hejaz. Some Jews remained in northern Arabia until the twelfth century, after which they too disappeared. For eight centuries the tribes of Arabia had no contact with Jews, unlike cosmopolitan Arabs in Egypt, Syria, and Iraq, where

---

* In his nineties, Kissinger would still resort to this tactic. For example, in 2018, Edward Luce, the American correspondent for the *Financial Times*, interviewed Kissinger and concluded: "Kissinger is to geopolitical clarity what Alan Greenspan was to monetary communication—an oracle whose insight is matched only by his indecipherability." See Edward Luce, "Henry Kissinger: 'We Are in a Very, Very Grave Period,'" *Financial Times*, July 20, 2018.

Jewish communities thrived well into the twentieth century. Jewish poets and writers from Arabia did leave a slight mark on Arabian culture. For example, to this day, the poems of Samaw'al (Samuel) ibn Adiya are taught in Saudi high schools; Jews also make cameo appearances in the folk tales of *One Thousand and One Nights*. But the absence of day-to-day contact with Jews created fertile ground for anti-Semitism, which sprouted and grew in Arabia, especially after the creation of the state of Israel.

Over dinner, as they sat at tables groaning with Bedouin dishes of lamb, rice, chicken, and yogurt, King Faisal launched into one of his favorite subjects, the Jewish-communist conspiracy to rule the world, which, he explained, was in the process of taking over the American government.

In September 1998, I was witness to a similar exchange when Crown Prince Abdullah, a younger half brother of Faisal's, treated President Clinton to a more modern version of this peculiarly Saudi obsession with Jewish conspiracy theories. During lunch in the Family Dining Room of the White House residence, the crown prince leaned across the table and, lowering his voice, told Clinton he had "information" that Monica Lewinsky was Jewish and part of a Mossad plot to bring the president down because of his efforts to help the Palestinians. He informed Clinton, in front of his mostly Jewish aides, that he intended to share this intelligence on the Hill when he met with senators who were at the time deliberating Clinton's impeachment.

Faisal's after-dinner conversation continued his Zionist-communist trope. If Israel withdrew from occupied Arab territories, that would "automatically lead to the shrinking of Communist influence in the area," Faisal expounded. Kissinger tried to deflect him by explaining that the airlift to Israel was required to prevent a victory for Soviet arms and therefore an increase in communist influence. He listed all the things the United States had since produced by pressuring Israel: the cease-fire, the resupply of the Egyptian Third Army, and now the stabilization agreement. Since pressure on Israel was precisely what Faisal wanted, that triggered another exposition of the conspiracy theory: Israel's aggression in 1967 had opened more avenues for the communists to advance their goal of stirring up trouble with the express purpose of toppling the Saudi royal regime, and Israel was still preparing the ground for their success, he claimed.

Looking at Kissinger around the corner of his keffiyeh, Faisal said it was unfortunate "that among those of the Jewish faith there are those who embraced Zionism." He noted that before the advent of Israel, relations between Jews and Arabs had been good. But "the intrigues and designs of Israel" had created all the problems. He claimed that at Yalta, Stalin alone insisted on a state for the Jews, and at the UN, the Soviets pushed for the creation of Israel, thereby revealing their intentions to use the Jewish state as their cat's paw.

The solution, Faisal reiterated, was "Israeli withdrawal from the occupied territories and allowing the Palestinians to go home." And after that, "a mixed Jewish-Moslem state" should be established in Palestine. "Start by having Israel withdraw," he counseled.

Thinking that Faisal's conspiratorial worldview would lead him to comprehend the power of the Jewish lobby, Kissinger tried to explain that an attempt to force Israel to withdraw would unleash the passions of its supporters in the United States. For Faisal, that just revealed their dual loyalties. As far as he was concerned, Israel was a liability to the United States.

Rather than respond, Kissinger tried to focus on what he and Nixon were doing to achieve a settlement. He emphasized that this effort would include Syria. To Kissinger's surprise, Faisal told him that he had been speaking to the Syrians and had learned definitively that Assad was anxious to meet with him. Kissinger explained that he was ready to do so, but this was part of a larger process that would take some time. Faisal wasn't buying. He said it could be done in weeks "to get rid of Communism once and for all."

Kissinger chose that moment to bring up the oil embargo, detailing the damage already done to the U.S. economy and the danger that, with the onset of winter, gas might have to be rationed and heating limited in American homes. He regretted that such an old friend would impose hardship on the United States; Faisal countered that he had suffered even more, claiming that the decision had caused him such "red hot anxiety" that he had almost had a nervous breakdown. That was why he wanted Kissinger to move quickly "so we can not only rescind the ban but increase our production." Increasing Saudi oil production was the key to reducing the pressure on prices, which was actually more important to the U.S. economy than the temporary interruption of supply.

But Kissinger was focused on lifting the embargo. He proposed that the king limit its application, asserting that if he did, Sadat would support the move. The answer, Faisal insisted, was for the United States to force Israel to withdraw. Kissinger tried to reason with him: that would just cause a domestic upheaval. In strict confidence, he told him that the airlift to Israel would be ended in the coming days. "That is something that should be," said Faisal disparagingly.

This foiled Kissinger's attempt to link the ending of the airlift to the easing of the oil embargo. Instead, he appealed to Faisal's shrewdness. He explained that if the king were not satisfied, he could always go back to imposing it again. Faisal responded by explaining that the embargo was a joint Arab decision and therefore he was not a free agent. He needed to have something in his hands to persuade his Arab brothers. For that, he said, "first I need speed; and second [I need you] to announce your position in favor of Israeli withdrawal." Kissinger explained that he couldn't do that before the negotiations even started and asked, instead, that Faisal consider whether what the United States had already done by saving the Egyptian Third Army, as well as what he promised he would soon do in ending the airlift to Israel, weren't enough to justify the easing of the embargo.

Faisal had clearly had enough of this exchange. But as he walked Kissinger to the door, a gesture in itself for the king, he spoke to him in English, expressing respect for Kissinger's "proven ability and wisdom." And then he said he would "pray to almighty God that he will continue to grant you success in all these noble efforts." In other words, Faisal was blessing Kissinger's diplomatic exertions and accepting his role, notwithstanding his Jewishness.

Kissinger's lack of success was announced to the world in a front-page, above-the-fold headline in *The New York Times* the next day: "Kissinger Fails to Sway Saudis from Oil Embargo." Beyond the negative headlines, however, Kissinger was discovering the subtlety of Faisal's diplomacy. Having taken a hard line in their audience, he then sent his aides to hint at a possible softening of the Saudi position.

Prince Fahd paid a late-night call on Kissinger at the guesthouse. Already in those days, Fahd had been identified as a friend of America at court; as king in the 1990s, he would vindicate this reputation by agreeing to host a vast American expeditionary force in Saudi Arabia for the purposes of evicting Saddam Hussein's army from neighboring Kuwait. Fahd wasted no time in reassuring Kissinger. Where Faisal was elliptical, Fahd was explicit. "We appreciate that things cannot be done overnight and have to be done step-by-step, but expeditiously," he said, adding a Saudi coda to Kissinger's concept. He volunteered to support Kissinger's effort to persuade Faisal to ease the embargo because "the thread of a solution" had now appeared.

Kissinger received a confirmation that Faisal was looking for a way to end the embargo when Omar Saqqaf, the Saudi minister of state for foreign affairs, arrived at the guesthouse to accompany his counterpart to the airport. He said Faisal needed some pretext to change his position. Saqqaf thought the opening of peace negotiations could provide that. To signal Saudi appreciation for Kissinger, Saqqaf walked him hand in hand to his plane. The headline may have been failure; the reality, as so often in diplomacy, was something more nuanced.

Knowing that King Faisal might lift the embargo at the launching of peace negotiations reinforced Kissinger's own instinct that the next step in his diplomatic endeavors needed to be a peace conference to provide the ceremonial opening for direct negotiations. He had promised it to Brezhnev in Moscow on October 21, and they had incorporated it into UNSC Resolution 338, the cease-fire resolution. Kissinger had done so because he understood that for his new regional order to be stable, an equilibrium in the balance of power was insufficient. The order also had to be accepted as legitimate by all the powers involved. Conference diplomacy was the mechanism the great powers had used to legitimize their reconstruction of the European order in the nineteenth century.

That is why he had raised the idea in Moscow. He also knew that the stability of his new Middle Eastern order would require the Soviet Union to play by the rules of the game. The only way to do that was to give them a stake in promoting peace rather than fueling war. But he was busily subverting their regional position of influence. He therefore needed to find a way to include them in the process without giving them the ability to interfere in it. As Nixon had told Meir, the United States was seeking to work against the Soviet Union by working with it. The conference, with its co-equal role for the Soviet Union alongside the United States, was one method for doing that.

Since that Moscow meeting, however, Kissinger had negotiated the cease-fire stabilization agreement between Israel and Egypt without any Soviet involvement. He now worried that, feeling cheated, Brezhnev would seek to undermine his peacemaking efforts. The Kremlin had been eerily quiet since the DEFCON 3 crisis, leading Kissinger to believe that the Soviets were somehow up to no good. The conference was a way now to provide them with the appearance of involvement—a reward for not disrupting his efforts.

Kissinger understood the dangers he was courting. The conference was useful to him only as a means of legitimizing the bilateral negotiations between Israel and Egypt that would be conducted by the United States alone. As he subsequently explained it, "The Geneva Conference was a way to get all the parties into harness for one symbolic act, thereby to enable each to pursue a separate course, at least for a while." Somehow, he had to maintain the conference façade as a trompe l'oeil, an optical illusion of depth when it was designed to function only as a flat surface.

Kissinger could rely on Meir and Sadat to ensure that the conference was so constrained that it would not interfere with their bilateral negotiations, even while it lent them an air of legitimacy. Sadat needed to show his fellow Arab belligerents, particularly the Syrians, that Egypt was not going its own way with the United States now that the war was over, even though that was exactly what he intended to do. Meir was not enamored of the idea of an international gathering because therein lay the ever-present danger of a ganging up on Israel. But Israel sought legitimacy for its existence as a state, so participation in a peace conference with its Arab neighbors and the superpowers was a way to manifest that. Perhaps the photos of Arabs sitting down with Israelis to talk peace for the first time in their history would even help in her imminent reelection campaign. However, when Kissinger raised it with her, she had a critical caveat: all the conference modalities—terms of reference, participants, agenda, even seating arrangements—had to be acceptable to Israel.

Thus when Fahmy had presented Kissinger with a six-point Egyptian framework for the peace conference before he departed Cairo on the morning of November 8, Kissinger was more than willing to embrace it.* But when Kissinger returned to Washington on November 17, after completing his travels in Asia, he discovered that the Egyptians were no longer on board with his carefully constructed concept. Awaiting him was a letter from Fahmy arguing that before there was any convening in Geneva, there needed to be a disengagement agreement negotiated between the generals in the desert. That didn't work for Kissinger: the United States had no role in the Kilometer 101 talks, the Soviets would not wait quietly in the wings if they too were given no part to play, and without a conference, how would he convince the Saudis to lift their embargo?

Fahmy was reflecting Sadat's sense of urgency to achieve, if not the larger Israeli withdrawal Kissinger had promised him in Cairo, then some initial withdrawal that would show his diplomacy was yielding results and would relieve the siege of his Third Army. Sadat was also nervous about the potential for the conference, with its Soviet and Arab participants, to impede and constrain his efforts to take advantage of the plasticity his war decision had generated. By contrast, he was impressed by the progress el-Gamasy and Yariv had made in their talks, especially in their side discussions on disengagement, which probably led him to believe that the Israelis were ready for a quick deal.

Kissinger ascribed Fahmy's about-face to his desire "to speed up the process without waiting for the complicated minuet leading to Geneva to be completed." Fearing the upending of his design, Kissinger decided to go around him and appeal to Hafez Ismail.

While the Ismail back channel had functioned well during the war, once Fahmy appeared in Washington, Kissinger had let it lapse. He tried to revive it now, as he explained to Ismail, to allow for the exploration of ideas "more difficult to discuss in formal government-to-government channels" (a thinly disguised denigration of his Fahmy channel). He wanted Ismail to explain to

---

* Fahmy wanted the conference to be under UN auspices with the United States and the Soviet Union as co-chairs. Only Egypt, Israel, Jordan, and Syria should be invited to the opening of the conference. Palestinian participation should be left until later. The conference should then break into bilateral committees to deal with disengagement in their first stages.

Sadat that "the peace conference is the place where U.S. influence can be most effectively used." He told Ismail that he particularly wanted to head off the floating of Sadat's ideas on disengagement in the Kilometer 101 talks: "I fear it will limit U.S. flexibility if these ideas are placed too soon in the public spotlight where they can be attacked before there is an opportunity to introduce them at the right moment in the negotiations."

Fahmy was deeply offended by Kissinger's ploy. In a meeting with Ambassador Hermann Eilts, the new high-level U.S. representative in Cairo, he irately emphasized that his proposal to Kissinger was not a personal view but rather "had been dictated on President Sadat's specific instructions and the President had gone over every word before it was approved." He demanded again that "some meaningful progress" be made on disengagement before the conference.

Caught red-handed by Fahmy, Kissinger reached for the section in the diplomat's handbook for such occasions titled "I Didn't Do It, and I Promise Not to Do It Again." He immediately instructed Eilts to seek a meeting with Fahmy to convey the message that it was Ismail, not he, who had suggested they reopen the private channel; that Kissinger of course had "total confidence" in Fahmy; that in the future he would not initiate any correspondence through the Ismail channel; and that he would instead rely on his friendship with Fahmy "to maintain close and frank communications." He added, however, that his views hadn't changed on the correctness of the original plan to make disengagement negotiations the first phase of the peace conference.

The tactic of picking the other side's more reasonable player to thwart or undermine an intransigent one is often used by American diplomats in the Middle East, but it rarely works. We deployed a similar tactic in July 1999, when President Clinton tried to engage with Mohammad Khatami, the newly elected, seemingly moderate president of Iran. Clinton decided to write to Khatami behind the back of Ayatollah Khamenei, the Supreme Leader who controlled the Islamic Revolutionary Guard Corps (IRGC) and the Ministry of Intelligence and Security (MOIS). We had good reason to believe these organizations were responsible for directing terrorist attacks against Americans. Clinton's letter was supposed to be delivered secretly to the new Iranian president by Yusuf bin Alawi, the Omani foreign minister, who was friends with Khatami.

Bin Alawi had set up a meeting with Khatami directly, emphasizing that he needed to meet with him alone. However, when he arrived at the presidential office he was met by his counterpart, Iranian foreign minister Kamal Kharrazi.

While he waited outside Khatami's office, bin Alawi sent a message to Khatami saying that it was imperative he meet with him alone. Nevertheless, when he entered Khatami's office, Kharrazi was there. Afterward, bin Alawi learned that, on Khatami's instructions, Kharrazi had provided a copy of Clinton's letter to the Supreme Leader. Our attempts to establish a discreet back channel had failed.*

President Trump's son-in-law and special envoy for Israeli-Palestinian peace negotiations, Jared Kushner, faced a similar rebuff in his efforts to find a moderate Saudi leader to support his peace plan. He worked successfully with then Deputy Crown Prince Mohammed bin Salman to arrange for President Trump's first trip abroad to a summit of world Muslim leaders in Riyadh in May 2017. It seemed natural therefore for Kushner to work with "MBS," as he became known in Washington, on his peace efforts, especially since the king's young, headstrong, and charming son was quick to disparage Palestinian claims and keen to get on with cooperation with Israel against the common enemy, Iran. Kushner therefore made the mistake of listening to MBS when he told him not to worry about moving the U.S. embassy in Israel to Jerusalem. There would be some initial negative Arab reaction, he said, but it would calm down in a couple of months. That proved true. However, when Trump moved the embassy and recognized Jerusalem as Israel's capital, Kushner learned that MBS did not speak for his father. King Salman was infuriated, summoning Arab leaders to an Arab League "Jerusalem summit" in Dhahran, Saudi Arabia, in April 2018, where he declared his fealty to the Palestinian cause and led the Arab League in a condemnation of Trump's decision.

To Kissinger's dismay, he could not control what happened in the makeshift tent at Kilometer 101 either. There Yariv and el-Gamasy had already succeeded, on their own, in reconciling the differing interpretations of the six-point agreement when it came to provisioning the Third Army and exchanging POWs. Then, on November 16, the day after the convoys started to roll toward Suez and the POW exchanges began, Yariv made a presentation to el-Gamasy of the general principles that he thought should apply to the disengagement negotiations.† El-Gamasy found these principles broadly acceptable. He responded by

---

* Like the PLO after the meeting with Vernon Walters in Morocco in November 1973, the MOIS and the IRGC stopped targeting Americans after bin Alawi's meeting with Khatami. They resumed after the U.S. invasion of Iraq in 2001. See Martin Indyk, *Innocent Abroad: An Intimate Account of American Peace Diplomacy in the Middle East* (New York: Simon & Schuster, 2009), 224–26.
† Yariv proposed that the lines should not be seen as a defeat for either side; they should be parallel and temporary but also militarily defensible; to contribute to an atmosphere of peace, normal life should be restored to the canal zone; and UNEF should patrol the buffer zone between the two lines.

proposing a three-phase Israeli withdrawal: first, to the October 22 line; then to the El-Arish–Ras Muhammed line to the east of the Sinai passes (150 kilometers east of Suez); and finally, to the international border. Yariv countered with an IDF withdrawal in one stage to positions east of the canal but short of the Sinai passes (thirty kilometers east of Suez), combined with a thinning out of Egyptian forces on the east bank and removal of their tanks, the opening of the Suez Canal to navigation, and the formal lifting of the blockade at Bab el-Mandeb.* (See map on page 527.)

El-Gamasy's proposal put the first line of IDF withdrawal to the east of the Sinai passes; Yariv's line was to their west. Other than that, the differences between them were not great. It's not surprising therefore that Sadat felt Kissinger's intervention could secure him a quick initial Israeli withdrawal before the Geneva Conference, with a more substantial Israeli withdrawal to be negotiated after the conference's opening.

Yariv, however, was out over his skis. For the next meeting, he was authorized by Meir and Dayan only to offer an IDF withdrawal five kilometers east of the canal in return for Egyptian forces withdrawing entirely from the east bank. That was an obvious non-starter. So when the Kilometer 101 talks reconvened on November 22 and the two generals presented their formal positions, there was a much wider gap than the Egyptians had expected. For the next three days they informally explored ways to overcome their differences.† According to el-Gamasy, however, Yariv finally admitted that he had not been authorized to discuss a meaningful withdrawal because his government was in no position to settle the matter until after elections, which had now been set for December 31. El-Gamasy asked one more time for Yariv to officially define Israel's position. Yariv was under instructions from Meir to say no to everything and propose instead that the negotiations be moved to Geneva. At that point, el-Gamasy ended the meeting, went to the press tent, and informed everyone there that the talks were stalemated. The next day, November 30, Sadat ordered the Kilometer 101 talks suspended.

Kissinger was well satisfied with this outcome. He confides in his memoirs that "the whole process tested our patience." Just like during the war, he had

---

* According to Yariv's account, el-Gamasy countered informally with the idea that Israel withdraw forty kilometers east of Suez while Egypt's forces would maintain a line ten kilometers east of the canal; UNEF would occupy the thirty-kilometer buffer in between. He then introduced the idea of mutual reduction of armor to reconcile Yariv's requirement for thinning out Egyptian forces on the east bank with Egyptian honor.
† At one point, on November 26, Yariv appears to have offered an Israeli withdrawal to the east of the Sinai passes if Egypt would minimize its forces on the west bank of the canal as well. This is according to a report from the United Nations, recounted in a memo from Saunders and Quandt to Kissinger. Kenneth Stein, who interviewed both el-Gamasy and Yariv, confirmed Yariv's offer. See Memo from Saunders and Quandt to Kissinger, December 3, 1973, FRUS 1969–1976:25, Doc. 371, and Kenneth Stein, *Heroic Diplomacy: Sadat, Kissinger, Carter, Begin and the Quest for Arab-Israeli Peace* (New York: Routledge, 1999), 110–11.

little accurate information about what was transpiring in the tent because there was no American official present.* In any case, from his perspective, nothing good could come of it. Either there would be a breakdown, casting doubt on the viability of his concept of a first step and raising the specter of a return to war, or there would be a breakthrough, in which case, who needed American intervention? His strategy for wooing Sadat required that the United States be the one to deliver Israeli concessions. In his mind, the conference had become the platform for achieving that purpose. Convening it would "defuse the situation and symbolize progress," he writes in his memoirs, and then he would "use its auspices to establish our central role."

Accordingly, he determined to sabotage the Kilometer 101 negotiations. He had to find a way to get the Egyptians to fall in with his game plan, so he turned to Meir, whom he could rely upon to block progress given her opposition to any withdrawal, especially in advance of her reelection bid. In a meeting in his State Department office on November 20, Kissinger recommended to Dinitz that Israel postpone the substantive discussions with the Egyptians over disengagement until the Geneva Conference. He communicated the same recommendation to Abba Eban when he met him on November 22. On November 25, Kissinger instructed Scowcroft to call Dinitz and read him the riot act over proposals he had heard that Yariv was making in the Kilometer 101 talks. Scowcroft should request instead that "the Israelis find ways to keep the talks going without making substantive proposals."

As Dinitz describes it in his memoirs, Kissinger "wanted all major political moves to take place under his direct supervision." On November 26, Dinitz informed Kissinger, "We have accepted your suggestion to delay the question of the separation of forces until the peace conference." Yariv would not break off the talks at Kilometer 101, "but these meetings will deal with purely local issues," Dinitz reported. Kissinger responded, "Very good."

That is the backstory to the failed negotiations. Yariv was deeply frustrated by the instructions he received, believing that he could have reached agreement with el-Gamasy. He was angry with Meir and Dayan because "they weren't even open to hearing [his] arguments" and repeatedly refused his requests to convene a discussion of his ideas with the cabinet. But Yariv was a good soldier and, by then, was undergoing a personal conversion from general to politician. Meir had offered Yariv a safe position on the Labor Party slate for the Knesset in the upcoming elections. To enable him to run, he was officially relieved of his military duties on November 23, while he was still negotiating with el-Gamasy as Israel's military representative.

---

* Kissinger's staff appears to have been relying on reports from the UN, which was receiving updates from General Siilasvuo, who had the advantage of being in the tent though not present for the informal discussions, which took place outside the tent.

Thursday, December 6, 1973, Washington, DC. Moshe Dayan shared Kissinger's aversion to the Kilometer 101 talks. He believed Yariv wanted to make a vital concession—the IDF's withdrawal from the west bank of the canal—in return for nothing of value to Israel. In his view, the withdrawal needed to be part of a political agreement involving the opening of the Suez Canal to commercial traffic and the termination of hostilities between Egypt and Israel. He believed those elements could only be achieved with U.S. mediation. Even though he had his reservations about Kissinger's manipulations, Dayan writes in his auto-biography, he "was not unmindful of his achievements."

With the airlift of arms ending and the sealift containing only replacement supplies, Dayan also wanted to make sure that Israel's future arms requirements would be met as part of a U.S.-mediated agreement. Just as Nixon imagined his political salvation would come through announcing the end of the oil embargo, Dayan hoped that working with Kissinger to broker a disengagement agreement might help stave off his political demise.[*]

On December 6, Dayan turned up in Washington to coordinate with Kissinger. Having forestalled progress before Geneva, Kissinger welcomed Dayan's visit as a way to lay the foundations for rapid movement immediately after. "It is important that you not give away crucial points too early," he counseled Dayan. "You must continue to look fierce and dangerous." He thought moving before Geneva would have been taken as a sign of weakness, and then the Arabs and the Soviets would have held out for further concessions.

"I am in a strange position," he admitted in a moment of candor. "Seems at one point I am pressing for movement and at another point I am asking you to slow down, but I think the timing is essential if we are to break this combination of pressures," he said, referring to the oil embargo, Arab and Soviet demands for Israeli withdrawal to the 1967 lines, and Sadat's demand for an early Sinai withdrawal.

"We have to discuss a strategy for next month," Kissinger suggested. "That is the only way we are going to survive together . . . [by] making a complex situation look as if we are running it," he concluded, sounding as if they were now as close as Rick Blaine and Captain Renault in the final scene of *Casablanca*. Dayan reiterated that it was up to Kissinger; Israel was ready to move when he was. Kissinger asked him to come back in the afternoon.

Dayan returned after meeting with Clements at the Pentagon, where he

---

[*] In the aftermath of the war, the public protests against Dayan, and a demand from a fellow cabinet minister for his resignation, had already led him twice to submit his resignation to Meir, which she refused. They both eventually resigned after the Agranat Commission investigation into the conduct of the Yom Kippur War submitted its interim report in April 1974.

had been told that the Defense Department had no problem fulfilling Israel's arms requests. Kissinger had wanted Clements to hold the line so that he
could take credit "for springing some things." But Clements, like Schlesinger,
was not willing to be portrayed as the bad cop. Instead, in his meeting with
Dayan, he pointed the finger at Kissinger, claiming it was "a political decision." In a well-practiced ploy, Kissinger called Scowcroft in front of Dayan
and instructed him to tell Clements that "the only way to make political progress is to increase our shipments to ensure [Israel's] security."

Dayan reciprocated with a tactic familiar to Kissinger: he offered his government's position and then his "personal" view. Officially, Israel was willing
to offer a one-kilometer withdrawal on the west bank in return for an Egyptian commitment to keep the cease-fire, including at Bab el-Mandeb. But he
wanted to plant an idea in Kissinger's mind about the larger concept of disengagement. He explained his own version of a staged process: a small separation of forces to stabilize the cease-fire to begin with, a larger disengagement
agreement with a UN buffer and demilitarized zones to follow, and then a final
peace treaty. Dayan was as skeptical as Kissinger about ever getting to the third
stage because it would have to deal with the Palestinian issue and Jerusalem.
But he wanted him to understand that Israeli withdrawal from the canal would
involve playing "our best card." Therefore, Israel had to get something of
value for it, "like assurances there will be no more fighting."

Not knowing the animus Dayan felt for Yariv's disengagement ideas, Kissinger responded by invoking what he now called "the Yariv plan" for three
zones, suggesting the same could be done on the Syrian front. Dayan persisted: "If we go back and accept the Yariv plan, what will they [the Egyptians]
be willing to give?" Dayan urged him to find out and also test whether Sadat
would be willing to sign a separate peace without Syria and Jordan. If the
answer was no, which he expected, then there wouldn't be a final peace deal
and that made it even more important to get something meaningful, in terms
of an end of hostilities, in the first or second stage.

Kissinger allowed that "this approach has possibilities." That was good
enough for Dayan, since he was already late for meetings with Israel's supporters on the Hill. Dayan ended the conversation by attempting to seal their
newfound partnership: "Any time you have any wild ideas just say so and I will
come over and we can discuss them." He sounded like an excited bro planning
a fraternity party. Kissinger was just as excited. He had found an equal in intellectual heft and conceptual thinking, a leader of global stature compared to
the provincialism of his prime minister. He would later describe Dayan as "a
brilliant manipulator," who at his best "had the most fertile and creative mind
of Israel's leaders."

Because Middle East diplomacy is a game of multilevel chess—Kissinger referred to it as a three-ring circus, but he was more of a grandmaster than a ringmaster—progress on one plane is often accompanied by setbacks on another, with the ever-present danger that the whole game will crater. While Kissinger could be satisfied that he now had the Israelis where he needed them to pull off his complex maneuver, he was still in danger of losing Sadat's cooperation.

Following the suspension of the Kilometer 101 talks, Egypt ratcheted up tensions with the objective of persuading Kissinger to press the Israelis to make a withdrawal before the Geneva Conference. The Egyptian army made it look like it was planning a resumption of hostilities. At the same time, Cairo threatened to enforce the blockade at Bab el-Mandeb and refer the whole matter to the UN Security Council.

Kissinger viewed the crisis atmosphere that the Egyptians now seemed intent on generating as a product of "hotheads" around Sadat, i.e., Fahmy. Nevertheless, he became sufficiently concerned that he drafted a letter from Nixon to Sadat urging him to stick with what he and Kissinger had agreed on during their Cairo meeting. Delivered by Eilts on December 1, the letter reiterated Kissinger's argument that the Kilometer 101 talks were not the place for real movement. "It is at the peace conference that the United States will be in a position to exercise our constructive influence," Kissinger asserted in the president's name.

Sadat was unpersuaded. He told Eilts that without a first-phase withdrawal, he might order Fahmy to denounce the negotiations at the conference and walk out. He beseeched Nixon to strengthen his position by lending America's weight to an early disengagement and threatened again that otherwise he would have no choice but to call on the United States and the Soviet Union to send forces.

Coming from Sadat, those words should have disturbed Kissinger. He had been wrong to assume that the complaints and threats were Fahmy's idea alone. Sadat was clearly under pressure to produce. Yet Kissinger was unmoved.

On December 10, Eilts reported that Fahmy had again complained about the lack of progress. Egypt was being criticized in the Arab world for failing to show results; radical Arabs were accusing Egypt of having gone soft; Sadat was losing face at home and abroad. This bellyaching too made little impression on Kissinger.

Why was he so determined to stay the course in the face of Sadat's obvious unhappiness, especially in circumstances where the Israelis were ready to accommodate Sadat's desire for an initial withdrawal? The explanation comes from Kissinger's engagement with Soviet ambassador Dobrynin.

If the Soviets had sought to exploit the breakdown in the Kilometer 101 negotiations to curry favor with Sadat, threaten UN Security Council action, and stoke tensions—all of which they could have easily done—it might have persuaded Kissinger to change course. But when he met with Dobrynin on November 30, he learned that the Soviets also wanted to defer disengagement until after the conference convened. Just as Kissinger had hoped, the Soviets preferred the role of co-chair of the peace conference to their traditional Middle Eastern role as patron of troublemakers. This Soviet stance effectively closed off Sadat's option of seeking Security Council or superpower intervention. Going back to war was not a realistic option either, given the IDF's proximity to Cairo and the backing he understood Israel would get from the United States if he did. Sadat had no choice but to accept Kissinger's preference.

So after Fahmy complained to Eilts in their December 10 meeting, he subtly pivoted to arguing that a "large or medium scale disengagement" must emerge from the first phase of the conference. The same day, Sadat responded to Nixon's importuning in a letter that also focused on what he expected to happen in Geneva, expressing the hope that "during the opening phase of the peace conference a major disengagement will promptly be effected."

Kissinger had prevailed. Egypt, Israel, and the Soviet Union were now all following his script, cooperating in laying the foundations for his American-led order via the Geneva Conference. That effort had required him to deliberately block progress in what might well have been a fruitful channel of Egyptian-Israeli negotiations. His NSC aides certainly thought so. Saunders and his deputy, William Quandt, had sent him a memo on December 3 that detailed the considerable progress made at the Kilometer 101 talks. They suggested that Kissinger encourage Yariv and el-Gamasy to return to the tent. He could then work out the final details of the disengagement on a Middle East trip and announce the agreement at Geneva, helping it "get off to an impressive start."

Kissinger, however, was wedded to convening the conference first. That would co-opt the Soviets and perhaps impress King Faisal enough to lift the oil embargo. The promise shown in the Kilometer 101 negotiations could still be exploited after the conference opening. The concepts developed there would still be applicable. But at the conference, the negotiations would be conducted under U.S. tutelage, and Kissinger would then be the broker of the deal. Moreover, the framework of the Geneva Conference would provide legitimacy for the enterprise that Egyptian and Israeli generals meeting alone in a tent in the desert could not.

We faced a similar dilemma during the Kerry-sponsored negotiations I participated in as U.S. special envoy in 2013. We had inherited the secret, London back-channel negotiation between authorized Israeli officials and an associate of Abu Mazen, the president of the Palestinian Authority. Kerry had then suc-ceeded in launching a more public, front-channel negotiation. Like Kissinger, we had a sense of urgency, in our case because there was a nine-month clock ticking on the formal negotiations. By then, we would have had to produce a breakthrough or at least show enough progress to justify an extension of time.

However, there was no such urgency on the informal track. The nego-tiators there had been working episodically for three years, coming together when their schedules allowed, with no deadline. Unlike Meir and Dayan, who saw the benefit in stalling the Kilometer 101 talks, Netanyahu insisted that the informal London rendezvous was the only place where he would allow prog-ress to be made, fearing that any concessions offered in the formal negotiations would be leaked by the Palestinians and embarrass him politically. Abu Mazen, as it transpired, was quite content to use the London channel to explore the extent of Netanyahu's concessions as long as he didn't have to make any of his own.

Kerry resolved that the only sensible way forward was to merge the two tracks, taking whatever had been agreed on in the back channel and using it as the basis for negotiations in the front channel. We therefore pressed the "London boys," as we called them, to finish the framework for the negotia-tions they had been working on, which they did in December 2013. With Netanyahu's agreement, we then used their work as the basis for the bridging ideas that Kerry proposed as principles to guide the final-status negotiations in the formal talks. In the process, much like Kissinger, we put an end to the informal talks. Whether they would have made more progress if we had left them to continue at their leisurely pace is conjecture. But in both cases the preference of the United States took precedence over the desire of the parties to be left alone to manage their negotiations themselves.

By contrast, the Oslo negotiations between Israel and the PLO, which took place in secret behind the back of the Clinton administration as we struggled to keep the formal negotiations going in Washington, did achieve a break-through.* The commitments each made to the other, however, were not bro-kered by the United States. While Clinton did his best symbolically to embrace and legitimize them at the signing ceremony on the South Lawn of the White House in September 1993, the United States could not hold the signatories' feet to the fire because the president had not been the mediator. In the end, the agreement broke down because each side observed its commitments in

---

* The formal negotiations were the outgrowth of the 1991 Madrid Conference, which like the 1973 Geneva Conference enabled Israel to have separate bilateral negotiations, in this case with Syria, Jordan, Lebanon, and the Palestinians. Because the PLO was not represented in the Israeli-Palestinian negotiations, Arafat ensured that they made no progress.

the breach, with the Palestinians tolerating, if not encouraging, terrorism and incitement, and the Israelis engaging in settlement building in territory supposedly reserved for the Palestinians.

Clinton tried to rebuild a more solid foundation in the Wye River agreement which codified each side's commitments in detail, but by then Rabin had been assassinated and his peace partner and successor, Shimon Peres, had been defeated by Netanyahu in elections. And when, at Wye, Clinton finally persuaded Netanyahu to yield 13 percent of the West Bank, his government collapsed. The step-by-step process agreed on in the Oslo Accords looked like it had been run into the ground. With the clock ticking on Clinton's presidency, he and the newly elected Israeli prime minister, Ehud Barak, decided to abandon Oslo's phased process in favor of negotiating a conflict-ending peace agreement. The failure to achieve a final-status agreement at Camp David and, subsequently, through the Clinton Parameters at the end of his administration, left Israelis and Palestinians mired in bloody conflict.

The lesson for American peacemaking mediation in the Arab-Israeli arena is that Arab and Israeli negotiators should be encouraged to engage directly and secretly when they can to explore ways to reconcile their differences. But when they achieve a conceptual foundation, the United States needs to enter the process, to provide the bridging formulas necessary to reach an agreement and then ensure its implementation.

That is not, however, sufficient to guarantee success. For that, there needs to be a sense of urgency, an ability to fulfill commitments entered into, and a level of trust between the parties. The United States can facilitate an agreement, but it cannot substitute for the commitment and follow-through of the parties themselves.

Legitimization of the process becomes important at that stage too, for secret agreements, secretly arrived at, need the support of the people on whose behalf those accords are made. They also need the embrace of outside actors, who can disrupt any fragile effort at reconciliation if they are excluded from the process but can help provide political cover for risk-taking by their involvement.

Fortunately for Kissinger, Yariv and el-Gamasy had laid the conceptual foundations for the disengagement agreement; Sadat had a burning sense of urgency; the Israelis had the will to fulfill their commitments; and, slowly but surely, with Kissinger's help, they were able to build trust in each other. As Kissinger observed, "the road to American mediation and the step-by-step approach was opening." The only missing piece was a framework to legitimize the process, to which Kissinger now turned his attention.

10

"A Time for Peace"

Nothing so warms the heart of a professional diplomat as the imminence of a major conference.

—Henry Kissinger, *Years of Upheaval*

Organizing a Middle East peace conference is an exercise in herding cats. Following the defeat of Saddam Hussein in the first Gulf War in 1991, it would take Secretary of State James Baker eight shuttle trips in as many months to convene the Madrid Peace Conference, which blessed the opening of direct negotiations between Israel and its Levantine Arab neighbors, Jordan, the Palestinians, Syria, and Lebanon. Henry Kissinger would have an easier time of it in 1973 because the urgency felt by the Arabs and Israelis was far greater. In the Gulf War they had not fought each other. Indeed, on the insistence of the United States, Israel had sat out the war even though it was assailed by Saddam Hussein's missiles. In the Yom Kippur War, the Syrian and Egyptian fronts were dangerously unstable. If Kissinger's cease-fire were to hold and American diplomacy given a chance to gain traction, he would have to separate the forces. To launch that process, he needed a quick convening of the Geneva Conference.

He had agreed with the Soviets to set December 18, 1973, as the date. Now he embarked on a second trip to the Middle East to secure the agreement of the key participants—Israel, Egypt, Syria, and Jordan—and to persuade King Faisal to lift the oil embargo when the conference convened.

In preparation, Kissinger had managed to get Dobrynin and Fahmy to agree that the conference would be held under the *auspices* of the United Nations and the *co-chairmanship* of the United States and the Soviet Union. But on December 10, when Kissinger had stopped off in Brussels for a NATO meeting en route to the Middle East, Dinitz informed Scowcroft that Israel would not participate if the talks were held under UN auspices. Inherently suspicious of the UN, with its automatic anti-Israel majority, Prime Minister Meir was unwilling to accept any UN role that might allow it to interfere in the postwar diplomacy.

The other sticky issue was Palestinian representation, something that would still plague Baker's efforts eighteen years later. Fahmy had originally accepted that the Palestinians could join the negotiations at a later stage and only "the question" of Palestinian participation need be discussed at the opening session of the conference. However, at an Arab League summit in Algiers on December 4, the Arab leaders had secretly resolved, in the presence of Yasir Arafat, that the PLO would henceforth be treated by the Arabs as "the sole representative of the Palestinian nation." Accordingly, following Fahmy's return to Cairo from Algiers, Egypt wanted "the timing" of Palestinian participation in the conference to be discussed at its first session, thereby making clear that the *principle* of Palestinian attendance had already been accepted by the other attendees.

Mrs. Meir vehemently rejected this proposition, insisting that there be no reference to Palestinian participation at all, and that Israel be given a veto over any additional participants.* It was difficult enough for her to contemplate territorial concessions to Egypt, Syria, and Jordan, but to include the Palestinians in the conference clearly implied that they would get a piece of territory too. That was a door she was determined not to open.

Thankfully, the Soviet ambassador to Egypt, Vladimir Vinogradov, whom Kissinger regarded as something of a jackass, managed to convince Fahmy to moderate his proposed language, returning the Palestinian participation issue back to a "question" and restricting the UN auspices to "convening" the conference rather than participating in it. Kissinger's wager that giving the Soviet Union a role at the conference would generate its cooperation was paying off.

Meir also made clear that Israel would only sit with the Syrians at the conference table if there had been an exchange of POWs, or at least an exchange of lists, before the convening took place. To assuage Israeli concerns on these and other issues, Sisco had worked with Dinitz on a draft U.S.-Israeli MOU; there were fourteen separate assurances.

But neither the assurances nor the language of the invitation proved acceptable to Meir. On December 13, she sent an oral note to Kissinger explaining

---

* At the Madrid Conference, Palestinians who were not identifiable members of the PLO were included in the Jordanian delegation. Once negotiations began in Washington, the Jordanians and Palestinians refused to enter the room with the Israelis unless they were treated as separate delegations. See Martin Indyk, *Innocent Abroad: An Intimate Account of American Peace Diplomacy in the Middle East* (New York: Simon & Schuster, 2009), 20.

that she could not accept the changes in the letter of invitation. She added, politely, that "while she had accepted faits accomplis before, she [was] not able to do so this time." Still smarting from her last experience of what she believed was Kissinger's collusion with Moscow, she would not be taken for granted again.

Kissinger was still sore too and responded to this démarche by having Nixon write her a letter that ended with an unmistakable threat: "I want to say to you in all solemnity, that if Israel now fails to take a favorable decision to participate . . . I will not be able to justify the support which I have consistently rendered in our mutual interests to your government. . . . I urge that you transmit promptly your favorable reply."

It is never a good idea to set up the American president to be rejected by a foreign leader. Should that leader refuse the demand, the president is then left with the Hobson's choice of giving up, in which case he looks like a paper tiger, or escalating the threat and engendering a confrontation. That was especially the case for Nixon now that his ability to exercise power was in serious dispute. Since Kissinger's diplomacy depended on being able to deliver Israel, generating a crisis over a minor matter was a mistake. Fortunately, Meir chose not to respond to Nixon's letter. Instead, she instructed Dinitz to seek out Haig while Kissinger was en route to the Middle East to check on the president's real feelings. According to Dinitz, Haig was cautious, recommending that Dinitz deal with Scowcroft, but if any difficulties arose, he should get in touch directly. Kissinger's favorite tactic of back-channeling had been deployed against him. Meir, like Fahmy, could play the game too.

They weren't the only ones. Involving the president at this moment of vulnerability triggered his urge to engage in his own peacemaking activity, without consulting his secretary of state. On December 13, while Kissinger was in the Middle East, Nixon met alone with Dobrynin in Washington.

When Kissinger found out later that evening, he dispatched an angry and emotional cable to Scowcroft arguing that the meeting had placed him in an impossible position at a most delicate moment: "The slightest miscalculation— the least slip—and we will be involved in a major foreign policy failure of the gravest sort." He demanded to know what Nixon had said to Dobrynin. "I urge you not to underestimate the seriousness of this cable," he warned Scowcroft.

Haig asked Nixon for a debrief of the meeting but was fobbed off by the president, who said he was just promoting U.S.-Soviet cooperation and had requested that Moscow exert its influence on Syria regarding the POW issue. What Kissinger didn't find out at the time was that the president had fulminated to Dobrynin about Israel and the Jews. According to Dobrynin, Nixon depicted them as dedicated to preventing any improvement in Soviet-

American relations. He claimed the Jewish lobby was encouraging Israel's intransigence while the American media, run "essentially by the same Jewish circles," was mounting a hostile campaign against him. Nixon was unsparing about Kissinger too. While acknowledging that Kissinger's Jewish roots made him less vulnerable to criticism from this cabal, the president told Dobrynin that Kissinger's instincts were "strongly to indulge Israel's nationalist sentiments." Kissinger was caught between a president who believed he was too close to Israel and an Israeli premier who thought he wasn't close enough.

Thursday, December 13, 1973, Al Qanater Al Khairiya, Egypt. Sadat again came to his rescue. This time they met at his weekend retreat, some twenty kilometers north of Cairo, at the point where the Nile divides into the Rosetta and Damietta branches, broadening the arteries of the nation as its lifeblood heads through the delta to the sea.

The presidential villa overlooked one of the twin barrages, dams that spanned both branches of the Nile, with their picturesque aqueduct-style arches. At one end of each of these dams, identical Ottoman towers had been constructed to disguise the wheelhouses that raised and lowered the heavy steel barriers that modulated the Nile's flow into the agriculturally rich delta region. They had been built in the 1860s by Muhammad Ali Pasha, the founder of modern Egypt. Like the pyramids at Giza, they evoked a bygone era of Egyptian grandeur, this one marking the industrialization of an ancient civilization.

The fertile flatlands between the two dams had been converted into parks and gardens where Egyptian families would picnic on weekends and holidays. Sadat's villa was located within these grounds, in a compound that contained ten acres of carefully manicured, verdant gardens dotted with palm trees and ficus and a swing set for Sadat's grandchildren. At the front and back of the yellow stucco mansion, pergolas supported by incongruous Greek columns provided shade to the second-floor terraces. Green shutters adorned the arched windows.

The centerpiece of the villa's gardens was an enormous ancient banyan fig tree whose expansive canopy was supported by four aerial roots that had long ago descended to earth to create sturdy trunks that buttressed the massive boughs extending from the main torso. In its shade, fanned by the cool breeze that blew off the nearby river, Sadat would sit and contemplate the slow-moving waters of the Nile tributary as they passed through the barrages on their way to the Mediterranean.

Kissinger's motorcade headed north from Cairo on a highway that ran adjacent to the river. It quickly narrowed to a two-lane road through crowded suburbs of dilapidated, redbrick apartment buildings. Steel rods poked through

Henry Kissinger is greeted by President Anwar Sadat at his weekend villa at
Al Qanater Al Khairiya, north of Cairo, on December 13, 1973. They agreed
on the terms for the Geneva Peace Conference and the principles for the
disengagement with Israel.

unfinished roofs, awaiting the next floors to be built when Cairo's rapidly
expanding population required it. On both sides of the road, mechanics
worked on broken-down pickup trucks next to bakeries displaying pita bread
in street stalls. Shish kebab was being grilled on makeshift street barbecues
along the way.

Kissinger's motorcade raced by, forcing rickety, donkey-drawn carts off the
road and leaving a swirl of Cairo's ubiquitous dust to settle on the bread trays.
If Kissinger had looked up from the papers he was reading, he would have
seen a desperately poor country. Egyptians had regained their pride, but they
otherwise remained mired in the misery that demography, aided by the incom-
petence and corruption of Nasser's regime, had bequeathed them.

The motorcade crossed the first barrage and headed through the gardens.
They turned south and drove along the Rosetta bank of the Nile toward the
Ottoman wheelhouse that marked the beginning of the second barrage. Just
before they reached it, they turned into the driveway of Sadat's villa, arriving
at the alabaster stairs that led to the first-floor terrace and the unadorned front
door.

As Kissinger alighted from his limousine, he noticed Sadat waiting for him
at the top of the stairs, dressed in his bespoke military uniform. He greeted
him warmly on the terrace in front of the press cameras and then led him into

a modest reception room across the hallway from his study. The room looked out on the Nile through two small, arched windows that were framed by bookshelves. A floor-to-ceiling relief map of Egypt adorned the wall of an adjacent sunroom. Kissinger and Sadat sat together across from the arched windows on a low French chaise longue. On the wall above their heads was a crude painting of the Aswan High Dam, a massive engineering project that the Soviets had just completed in Upper Egypt, at the other end of the Nile.

Once the media had been ushered out, Sadat moved to his tufted-leather rocking chair, lit his ubiquitous pipe, and launched into an attack on the Soviet Union. What triggered the diatribe was the recent rebuff he had suffered when he sought new arms supplies from Moscow to counter the U.S. resupply of Israel. Sadat made his intentions clear to Kissinger. He would reduce Egypt's reliance on the Soviet Union and depend instead on the United States. This would include denying the Soviets access to Egyptian bases and allowing the Soviet-Egyptian Friendship Treaty to lapse.

In return, he told Kissinger, he looked to the United States to use its influence with Israel to generate peace. He avowed that peace was his true aspiration, as long as it did not come at the expense of Egyptian territory. Sadat's determination to lead the Arab world to peace, rather than be constrained by its hostility toward Israel, had first been conveyed by Hafez Ismail when he met with Kissinger in February 1973. But coming from Sadat himself, the words had much greater weight. He told Kissinger that Egypt would attend the conference even if Syria stayed away. This was the first hint Kissinger had received of the possibility that Syria might not attend the conference, and it did not register with him. But he did not miss the signal that proud Egypt under Sadat's leadership would not be controlled or impeded by any other party.

Sadat wanted to make sure that the conference would not complicate Egypt's negotiation of a significant disengagement agreement with Israel. In his view, the Soviets would try to constrain him to win favor with their other, more recalcitrant Arab clients. Therefore, Sadat insisted that after the opening formalities, the conference break up into bilateral military working groups without the presence of the Soviet and American co-chairs. This conformed with Kissinger's own idea, originally expressed to Brezhnev in Moscow during the war, that the superpowers would only intervene in the "direct negotiations" between the parties should an impasse arise. And it allowed Kissinger to work his diplomatic magic with Sadat and the Israelis directly.

Once reassured on that count, Sadat was flexible when it came to the other issues in the invitation. So, Kissinger gingerly tested language on Palestinian participation that might overcome Meir's objections. Could "the question of additional participants" be discussed at the first stage of the conference, without a specific reference to the Palestinians? In his unique way, Sadat accepted the finesse and then went one step further: Kissinger could reassure Meir that he would not raise the Palestinian issue during the initial disengagement phase of the negotiations.

Clearly, Sadat was wary of what would happen at the conference with all these other actors present. He wanted Kissinger to understand Egypt would not be delayed by the Soviets, or the Syrians, or even the Palestinians.[*] Almost five decades before the crown prince of the United Arab Emirates would break the Arab consensus and normalize relations with Israel before a Palestinian peace deal had been agreed on, Sadat was ready to move ahead without them.

With the procedures for the conference seemingly ironed out, Kissinger returned the next morning to discuss the substance of the disengagement. Sadat said he was depending on Kissinger to introduce an American plan. Kissinger eschewed the idea. He knew the Israelis would view such an intervention as an attempt to impose a solution on them, which would in turn generate a domestic backlash in the United States. It would also give the Soviet Union and its more radical Arab clients a big American-branded target at which to take aim. His preferred approach was to massage the positions of the two sides until they were close enough to bridge with American proposals.

Kissinger therefore resorted to a conceptual discussion about the principles involved. In doing so, he drew on the Yariv negotiations with el-Gamasy, which he had just managed to stymie.[†] He was encouraged to hear that Sadat accepted the three elements developed in the Kilometer 101 talks: a "thinned out" Egyptian military presence on the east bank of the canal, an Israeli pullback to the eastern edge of the Sinai passes, and a UN buffer zone in between. Sadat went one step further, informing Kissinger that he would rebuild the canal cities and reopen the canal, including to Israeli cargoes. These were the very commitments Dayan had sought in his Washington strategy session with Kissinger as a means of ensuring that Sadat had a stake in keeping the peace. Sadat also offered to reduce the number of Egyptian divisions on the east bank of the canal from five to two and remove their armor. Through these unilateral concessions, Sadat had made it possible to organize the Geneva Conference on Kissinger's terms and agree at the same time to his conceptual framework for the disengagement negotiations. Now Kissinger had to bring the Israelis along.

---

[*] They also quickly agreed that the conference would last four to five days, devoted only to ceremonial and procedural matters, and then adjourn until after the Israeli elections. When they reconvened, bilateral subgroups would focus on disengagement negotiations, which would be completed by the end of January. See Editorial Note, undated, FRUS 1969–1976:25, Doc. 390, and Henry Kissinger, *Years of Upheaval* (Boston: Little, Brown, 1982), 767–70.

[†] In his memoirs, Kissinger concedes that the Kilometer 101 negotiations proved to have been helpful after all—"especially some of the Israeli ideas that Yariv had tried out with Gamasy." See Kissinger, *Years of Upheaval*, 772.

Before he engaged in hand-to-hand combat with the Israeli prime minister, though, he had a rendezvous in Riyadh to keep.

In the four weeks since his last encounter with King Faisal, Kissinger had developed a more comprehensive approach to the challenge posed by the Arab oil embargo, and the accompanying price hikes and production cuts. In that scheme, the Geneva Conference would serve as a high-profile alternative to the Arab oil producers' demand for an immediate Israeli withdrawal to the 1967 lines.

If Geneva was to serve as Kissinger's carrot with Faisal, talk of invading the oil fields became his stick. In the WSAG meeting on November 29, he explained this approach. "If we drop a hint now and then on what actions we might take in return, it might worry them a little," he said.* Schlesinger had already been signaling to the Saudis through the British that the Pentagon was developing a plan to send in airborne Marines to occupy the oil fields of Saudi Arabia, Kuwait, and Abu Dhabi "as a last resort." When he raised this in a meeting in the Map Room, Kissinger responded, "It is ridiculous that the civilized world is held up by eight million savages." That was frat-boy talk in the National Security Council, but it also revealed Kissinger's frustration at the idea that a group of small, weak countries could hold the American superpower hostage.

That was not the way things were meant to work in Kissinger's hierarchical world, where the strong prevailed over the weak. He noted to his colleagues that the Saudis might have a monopoly over oil, but the United States had a monopoly over political progress in the Arab-Israeli arena. He would not be blackmailed. If the Saudis wanted any kind of Israeli withdrawal, they would have to lift the embargo. In return, they would get a step-by-step process rather than the full withdrawal that Faisal was demanding and which, according to Kissinger's timetable, was years off, if it would ever happen.

By early December, there were clear indications that the Saudis were starting to get nervous about the hints of possible American resort to force. After the Arab League summit, Kamal Adham, one of the king's closest advisers, sent a message to Kissinger to explain that Faisal had been unable to shift his Arab brothers from insisting that Israeli withdrawals precede any relaxation of oil pressure. Nevertheless, most of the king's advisers, Adham confided, were now arguing that the embargo should be modified after the conference opened.

---

* Kissinger had been encouraged down this path by Colby and Saunders. In a memo, Saunders transmitted Colby's argument that a variety of channels should be used to convey to King Faisal that "the United States is contemplating serious action against Saudi Arabia." See Memo from Saunders to Kissinger, November 30, 1973, FRUS 1969–1976:36, Doc. 255.

Kissinger had the president respond with a letter to the king designed to lay the groundwork for his visit. Nixon warned that his efforts to make a big push on the peace process would be unsustainable if the embargo and production cuts were not suspended when the conference opened. The alternative, he wrote, was a confrontation, and the weakening of the Western economies, which Nixon argued would only strengthen the communists. He promised to achieve full implementation of UNSC Resolution 242 and appended his handwritten, "total personal commitment" to that objective.

The pressure campaign appeared to have its intended effect. Kissinger received a back-channel response from Prince Fahd offering to come to Washington to coordinate lifting the embargo before the Geneva Conference if the participants agreed on a "reasonable" agenda for negotiating Israel's withdrawal. There was a caveat, however: the decision to lift the embargo had to have the concurrence of Sadat, Assad, and Houari Boumediene, Algeria's president.

Therein lay the rub. Just before Kissinger departed on this second Middle East trip, the oil ministers of the Organization of Arab Petroleum Exporting Countries (OAPEC) convened in Kuwait and decided that only when a timetable was agreed upon for Israel's full withdrawal from occupied territories, *including Jerusalem*, would they resume oil production to pre-embargo levels. In another message to Kissinger, Fahd explained that the hard-line oil producers, led by Algeria, had vetoed Fahd's more moderate approach.

Kissinger had experienced his own taste of what that hard line was like when Saudi Arabia's oil minister, the flamboyant Ahmed Zaki Yamani, paid a visit to the State Department with his Algerian counterpart, Belaid Abdesselam, on December 5. The Algerian insisted that the United States had to secure full Israeli withdrawal from Syria as well as Egypt, deliver on the rights of the Palestinians, and resolve Jerusalem before anything could be done to increase oil production or lift the embargo.

Kissinger met Yamani again the next evening without the "radical Algerian," as Kissinger would later refer to Abdesselam. Yamani committed to lifting the embargo when the Israeli-Egyptian disengagement negotiations were completed. This was not what Kissinger had hoped for, but at least he had moved Faisal's advisers in his direction.

None of that would count for anything if he could not convince King Faisal but he now understood that Saudi Arabia's decision was hostage to the Arab oil hard-liners. Accordingly, en route to Cairo and Riyadh, Kissinger decided, like David of biblical times, to beard the lion in its den by traveling to Algiers to meet Boumediene, the legendary revolutionary leader of Algeria.

Both leaders clearly enjoyed the skirmish. Boumediene wanted to engage in a philosophical debate; Kissinger was happy to oblige. Kissinger won the encounter, at least judging by the results, since Boumediene agreed to upgrade diplomatic relations and sanctioned Kissinger's approach of putting disengagement first. The Algerian's requirement, however, was an effort by Kissinger on the Syrian front, after he concluded an agreement between Israel and Egypt. Assad was Boumediene's radical Arab ally. His desire to see Syrian interests served gave Kissinger the opening to link his efforts in Damascus to Algerian support for a prior lifting of the oil embargo.

Friday, December 14, 1973, Riyadh. With Boumediene on board, Kissinger was as armed as he could hope to be for his second encounter with the dour Saudi king. They met again in the king's *diwan* in the royal palace.

Kissinger began by emphasizing America's commitment to the overall objective of Israeli withdrawal, knowing that would appeal to Faisal. However, he explained that he was going to have to postpone the convening of the conference by three days to give himself time to work on the Israelis. Drawing Faisal into his confidence, Kissinger revealed that if he couldn't overcome Israeli objections, he would convene the conference without them.

Kissinger was right to judge that Faisal would appreciate this (even though Prince Nawwaf, who was at the meeting, later correctly questioned the point of the conference if Israel didn't show up).* But it provided the king with an opening to invoke the Zionist-communist alliance's interest in avoiding a resolution of the conflict. Kissinger quickly diverted him by detailing the procedures for convening the conference. That led Faisal to raise the need to mention the Palestinians in the invitation, an idea that Kissinger had just managed to convince Sadat to shelve. So, he shifted the focus to the disengagement ideas he had discussed with Sadat, emphasizing that he planned to apply the same conceptual template to the Syrian front.

Fortunately for Kissinger, Faisal was enough of a pragmatist to accept his step-by-step approach, but he added two requirements: the explicit goal needed to include the achievement of "the legitimate rights of the Palestinians to return to their homeland," and the execution of the steps needed to be "expeditious . . . so that we can bring the waters of friendship back into stream."

Kissinger responded that sweeping declarations would only result in domestic upheaval in the United States. He claimed, however, that his systematic efforts with Congress had already produced a shift in public opinion in support of the president's policy. But he feared this could be reversed if the oil

---

* Prince Nawwaf bin Abdulaziz, a half brother of King Faisal's, was serving as the king's special adviser on Gulf affairs at the time. He later went on to become head of Saudi Arabia's General Intelligence Agency.

embargo continued too long. Then it would look as if the United States was responding to pressure rather than acting out of its own interest, and public opinion would turn against the Arabs.

Better, Kissinger argued, to suspend the embargo, and if necessary, reimpose it at a later stage if Israel were the cause of a negotiating impasse. Conversely, if the embargo were maintained into the winter months and the new year, Nixon would be blamed for the hardships and that would reduce his authority to achieve what Faisal wanted. The situation, Kissinger concluded, would require Faisal to decide on the embargo "in the relatively near future."

With his interpreter noting that the king was weighing his words "very carefully," Faisal responded that, once he achieved the first disengagement, Kissinger should declare that this was but one step toward a withdrawal that would lead to the realization of Palestinian rights. "At the moment that is said," Faisal declared, "the faucets would open again."

Faisal had given Kissinger what he needed: a clear willingness to lift the embargo after an Israeli-Egyptian disengagement. The quid pro quo, however, was a statement that committed the United States to securing Palestinian rights to return to their homeland, and a total Israeli withdrawal. Kissinger responded that a vaguer formula, invoking UN Resolution 242, was more desirable "to keep our opponents divided." Faisal upped the ante: Jerusalem needed to be in the expression of the ultimate goal too, he insisted.

Kissinger stood his ground. "I never want to promise something which I cannot deliver," he said. He would, however, make clear that disengagement was just the first phase on the road to implementing Resolution 242, but, he added, "it would not be in our mutual interest if we were more explicit than that." He reminded Faisal, as he had at their first meeting, that the embargo was "a weapon that, once it is in its sheath, is not unavailable."

Faisal was unpersuaded, so Kissinger elaborated. If it looked like he was selling out Israel in response to Arab oil pressure, he wouldn't be able to make good on the private understandings he had reached with Sadat, thereby implying that Faisal would be undermining what he had already agreed upon with Egypt. However, he reassured Faisal, "I could conceive of a time when I might welcome a statement by Your Majesty threatening to reimpose the Arab oil embargo." In fact, Kissinger argued, it would help his efforts if the embargo were lifted in good faith and then reimposed in the event of Israeli intransigence.

In other words, in lieu of a sweeping public declaration on withdrawal, Kissinger was offering to corner Israel through a conspiratorial partnership with the Saudi king to threaten reimposition of the oil embargo once it had been lifted. Faisal loved it. "We are very grateful and cannot express our thanks enough for these sentiments," he told Kissinger. He added that "nothing would

please me more than to say that tomorrow morning we will lift the embargo."
However, from Faisal's point of view they should not approach their cooperation like a game of chess "where two adversaries work against each other."
Rather, he said, "it should be a situation where you strengthen my hand and I
strengthen yours." He concluded the meeting with a prayer that "we can move
ahead jointly together."

In three encounters over six weeks, Kissinger had managed to enter into secret
understandings with Meir, Sadat, and now King Faisal. To Meir, in Washington, he had promised to buy time through a partial withdrawal, thereby stav-
ing off the specter of full withdrawal. To Sadat and Faisal, he had promised a
significant Israeli withdrawal in Sinai, speedily arrived at, as the first phase in
a process that would lead to larger withdrawals later. It was a testament to his
diplomatic skills that by taking each of them into his confidence he had managed to enlist all of them in his cause, even though fulfilling his commitment
to one had the potential to cause tensions with the others.

While the Saudi and Egyptian leaders seemed willing to engage in this
game of diplomatic nuance, Kissinger was about to discover a Syrian leader
who was not.

Saturday, December 15, 1973, Damascus. The road Kissinger took to Damascus
was more prosaic than the romantic, biblical route taken by travelers in earlier
centuries. They had approached Damascus from the western Anti-Lebanon
Mountains and recounted seeing a shimmering mirage—a white city fringed
by a green oasis with the dry desert beyond stretching to the horizon. Mark
Twain had waxed lyrical about a city as old as man that "measures time not by
days and months and years, but by the empires she has seen rise and prosper
and crumble to ruin."

Kissinger's route from Damascus Airport allowed for no such view as he
sped along a dark, deserted highway in a government limousine, accompanied by a sour and cynical Abdel Halim Khaddam, the Syrian foreign minister.
What he noticed was the heavy security detail in his motorcade and the armed
sentinels, their backs turned to his car, posted every twenty feet along the side
of the road. Had he been allowed to tour the city, he would have observed
units of Assad's Defense Companies, the praetorian guards, located on most
street corners, and a tank brigade encamped between downtown Damascus
and the nearby presidential palace. Although the new front line with Israel
was only thirty kilometers to the southwest, these forces were there to protect
Assad's regime from other Syrians who might conspire to replace him.

Kissinger viewed this visit in transactional terms. If Sadat and King Faisal were to cooperate in his peace strategy, he had to find a way to buy off Assad's opposition to them moving forward. Egypt was like a jewel-encrusted Fabergé egg he sought to wrest from the Soviet grip. Syria was mere costume jewelry— Moscow's militant Arab ally could stay that way as long as it didn't obstruct his game plan.

Kissinger's meeting with Assad took place in the unadorned Al-Rawda residential palace, a five-story former hotel nestled in a leafy Damascus neighborhood on fashionable Abu Rummaneh Street. As Assad's translator described it, "palace" was a misnomer since it was in fact an old building that had "no design, no gardens, and absolutely no color." The exterior was pockmarked as a result of a gun battle that led to the deposing of President Amin al-Hafez in 1966. There was one balcony, which Assad would use to greet his supporters, especially after periodic elections in which he would routinely be returned to office with more than 99 percent of the vote.

Later Assad would move to an imposing gray marble palace on a high mountain perch overlooking Damascus. It was built by Lebanon's prime minister Rafic Hariri, a Saudi-financed construction tycoon who needed to pay homage to Assad because he was, at the time, the de facto ruler of Lebanon. The meetings we had with Assad in this palace in the 1990s took place in a vast room with massive floor-to-ceiling windows through which he could look down on his subjects in the city below. Assad would sit with his principal guest in two large square damascene lounge chairs with intricate mother-of-pearl inlays. Behind them on the wall was an elaborate Moroccan mandala.

By contrast, Kissinger's meetings took place in a rectangular salon with heavy velvet curtains covering up the windows, making the atmosphere dark and gloomy. As Kissinger described it to Meir, there was no air conditioner or fan, it felt like it was eighty-five degrees, and the door was locked. Assad would usually sit with him in two plain sofa chairs with dreary brown upholstery positioned under a large painting depicting the victory of Saladin over the Crusaders at the Battle of Hattin in 1187. Kissinger notes in his memoirs that Assad had explained to him that the painting symbolized the fate Israel would suffer sooner or later. However, the painting depicted the defeat of Western invaders at the hands of a Muslim army. As such, it expressed Assad's attitude toward Kissinger, as the representative of the latest Western power come to conquer Damascus, more than his uncompromising attitude toward Israel.

What Assad lacked in power he made up for with guile, and what he lacked in guile he compensated for with obduracy and pedantry. Kissinger perceived the gap between Assad's ambition to lead the Arab world and Syria's lack of power to do so, and he intended to exploit it. The challenge proved arduous. Assad considered anything less than a five-hour meeting too short to enable

Henry Kissinger's second meeting with Syrian president Hafez al-Assad in
Damascus, on January 20, 1974. Kissinger came to admire Assad for his "first-
class mind allied to a wicked sense of humor" but in their first meeting Assad
surprised him by indicating that he had no intention of attending the Geneva
Conference. Kissinger thought it spelled the end of his mission. Only afterward
did he realize that Assad had done him a favor by deciding not to attend.

him to wear down his Western interlocutor. James Baker branded it "bladder diplomacy." Warren Christopher, who believed in keeping strictly to his
schedule, had no patience for it and managed to offend Assad by looking at his
watch after two hours.

Kissinger observed that Assad's head seemed to rise straight from his neck.
The back and top of Assad's head were flat, creating a boxy profile, which
seemed to be a trait of Syrian Alawites. His cranium appeared oversized,
which, together with his gaunt cheeks, gave his head the shape of a lightbulb.
It contained a brain that operated like a computer, constantly calculating the
balance of power and calibrating his response accordingly. Like most Syrian
men at the time, he sported a bold black mustache, to signal his virility. His
eyes were small and piercing. By the 1990s, diabetes and a heart condition
had started to take its toll. Dementia set in toward the end of Clinton's second
term; he died in June 2000 at age sixty-nine. But in 1973, he was in his prime,
having overcome all political opposition and maintaining tight control of the
armed forces and security services.

Kissinger came to admire Assad for his "first-class mind allied to a wicked
sense of humor." In my experience, his sense of humor was always pointed;
behind any joke was a clear message he wanted to convey to his interlocutor.

Kissinger likened him to a riverboat gambler and marveled at his willingness to move to the edge of the precipice, even over it, to demonstrate that he had no further margin for maneuver. Kissinger was clearly intrigued by the challenge. But unlike Sadat, the leader of an ancient civilization who could afford grand gestures to curry favor with a new patron, Assad reluctantly and suspiciously doled out his concessions with a teaspoon. Kissinger reported to Nixon after this first meeting that he was "the toughest and least conciliatory Arab leader that I have met."

They approached their first encounter like sumo wrestlers searching for each other's vulnerabilities. Kissinger's nervousness generated a too-lengthy presentation designed to make it clear to Assad that the United States was ready to make a major effort toward peace, and that it was the only country that could produce results. He argued, as he had to his other Arab interlocutors, that domestic pressure from Israel's American supporters required him to proceed carefully, focusing on first steps rather than taking final positions. By the beginning of the year, however, he promised Assad he would begin to show his hand.

The first order of business, Kissinger explained, was to get the peace conference opened because that would provide "a legal front," "scenery and framework" for negotiations outside the conference. The next step was to get Israel to withdraw from the Suez Canal to the Mitla Pass, which would bring about "a great psychological change in the area." There should be a similar first-phase withdrawal from Syria, followed by discussion about the next phase. He asserted it would be harder with Syria because "the Israelis don't like you at all," Kissinger asked Assad for his reaction.

"The whole thing depends on the results of our talk today," Assad responded. "We are not dreaming about going to the conference," he said. "Even the delegation has not been formed." Kissinger was flummoxed: "We'd been told by the Soviets you had agreed to go to the conference. We had assumed you would be there. I didn't know the question was still open." Assad was quick to deny that he had agreed to anything with the Soviet Union. "This has never happened," he insisted. Kissinger was discovering that the Soviet Union was as popular with its Arab allies as a skunk at a picnic.

He continued with his own agenda nonetheless, attempting to secure Assad's support for postponing the issue of Palestinian participation in the conference. He nervously explained why they couldn't be represented in the first phase, how he had authorized contact with them but it had to be kept secret, and how Sadat had accepted invitation language that wouldn't even mention them by name.

Assad seemed bemused by all this. "Is it my turn to speak?" he asked sardonically. Noting that Kissinger had spoken like a professor "for fifty minutes," he said he was a military man and would therefore be brief (although brevity was not his style). He ticked off his points: Syria is not against the United States, even though it supports Israel; Syria is independent and non-aligned; it needs and wants a just peace; there can be no peace with justice unless the Palestinian question is settled; Syria is not against Jews, only Zionists. Finally, he added, with emphasis, "We cannot compromise one inch of territory."

While he understood that Kissinger believed "things require time," his view was that "when the United States tells Israel to go back it will do so without hesitation." Thus he wanted to know whether the conference would lead to a result similar to what happened in 1956 (when Eisenhower ordered Israel to withdraw from the Sinai).

As in his conversation with other Arab leaders, Kissinger would not promise full withdrawal, but he sought to reassure Assad that "our direction is clear." He explained his concept of a disengagement between Egypt and Israel and suggested that the idea of a partial withdrawal could be applied to the Golan.

Assad quickly rejected that idea, declaring that "disengagement should involve all of the Golan Heights." Kissinger countered that the Israelis would never accept it, so it would be better to focus on the area they occupied after the war began. Assad said withdrawal from what he referred to as "the pocket" of territory the Israeli army had occupied was worth nothing to him. And then he made his position on the conference clear: "There must be prior agreement on Syrian-Israeli disengagement, otherwise our attendance at the conference is without sense." But not wanting to send Kissinger away angry, he complimented him: "The general impression is that Dr. Kissinger is a serious man and keeps his promises."

Kissinger wasn't ready to give up. He said the Israelis had a precondition too: they would not participate in any disengagement discussion until Syria provided a list of Israeli POWs in its custody and allowed for the Red Cross to visit them.

Assad responded in characteristic style: "Why give up these cards? For what?" The POW lists would come only after agreement on disengagement. Then he explained the crux of the matter for him: "Beginning talks are a loss to us. Our people do not want talks. If we go to the conference without deciding things our losses would be very great." In other words, in Assad's universe, sitting with the hated "Zionists" at a conference, or across a negotiating table, was a costly concession. Assad had no intention of making it unless he was paid in advance with an Israeli withdrawal.

Facing an impasse, Kissinger attempted a sleight of hand: "When I was in Moscow, Brezhnev promised that you would release the POWs in a few days." Assad's response was akin to Fahmy's when Kissinger had made the same claim to him at their meeting in Washington. "I never talked on this subject with them," he said.

With all avenues seemingly blocked, an exasperated Kissinger asked Assad how he wanted to proceed.

The Syrian leader finally revealed his hand: "I prefer to reach prior agreement with you on where the line of disengagement is. This is just the way it was in the case of Egypt."

Since he was new to the rivalries inherent in Arab politics, Kissinger did not yet appreciate just how critical it was to Assad that he negotiate at least as good a deal as Sadat would get. Sadat had told Assad that Israel had already agreed to withdraw east of the passes in Sinai, a considerable exaggeration. So Assad wanted to know the depth of Israeli withdrawal on the Golan before the conference too.

Kissinger countered with an alternative approach: "I want to hear from Israel, then you should talk to the Israelis, then I can help."

Assad responded that it was Kissinger who should talk to the Israelis and then come back to confer with him. To draw Kissinger into his design, Assad suggested they look at a map of the Golan together. He pointed to the prewar October 6 line and the Israeli pocket beyond it, noting how short the distances were and how quickly Kissinger could resolve it. But Kissinger understood the game and declined to draw a line, arguing that Sadat had not insisted on it, and to do so with Syria would only disappoint Assad. Instead, he tried to bring Assad back to the modalities for the conference and the wording of the invitation. Assad was indifferent: "Anything you agree with the Egyptians on a text of a letter is all right with us."

Kissinger would later come to understand that Assad had just provided him with "a major breakthrough," since if Syria was uninterested in the details of the letter of invitation, he could finesse all the issues with Sadat and Meir. But at that moment he was too focused on persuading Assad to attend.

"If there is no conference," Kissinger now told Assad, "I will be discredited." Assad couldn't care less. He repeated that disengagement needed to be agreed upon before the conference. Kissinger said that was impossible. "In this case, Egypt and Jordan will go, and we will see what happens," Assad replied, sounding like Donald Trump.

Kissinger became plaintive: "How can we discuss disengagement on the Syrian-Israeli front if there is no [Israeli-Syrian] military working group at the Geneva Conference?" Assad's response was matter-of-fact: "In any event, agreement will be outside the conference." That is exactly what Kissinger himself had in mind but, at that moment, he seemed to forget that the only purpose of the conference was to provide window dressing for his negotiations. He insisted that Assad read a draft of the invitation letter. Assad put on his reading glasses and looked at it, noting that it was inaccurate because it listed Syria as one of the participants.

"If you don't agree to go to the conference," said Kissinger, "my Middle East mission would be a failure."

It would take Kissinger a few rounds with Assad to understand that Assad was immune to any feeling of guilt. But on this first occasion he tried to lay it on with a thick brush: "If there is no conference, I will not be able to do anything more. We will look ridiculous. . . . This would be a setback for months. . . . This will make us the laughingstock in the American press." Then, just as he had done earlier with Meir, he threatened to give up his efforts, saying, "I have tried to be helpful to the Arab people. If this is not possible, it is fine with me."

None of this made any impression on Assad. After six hours of these exchanges he wrapped up. "I'm sorry if you have failed," he said, accepting no responsibility. Kissinger now sought to salvage something for his trouble, suggesting that they maintain contact by establishing interest sections in each other's capitals. Assad readily agreed since engagement with the United States was what he wanted most. Kissinger asked how he should characterize their conversation to the press. Assad was happy for him to say "that we have had a frank and useful talk, and that we have agreed to maintain contact."

On reflection, Kissinger would realize he had achieved "somewhat more than we had hoped for." In the meantime, not wanting to admit defeat, he reported separately to Nixon and Meir that he believed Assad would probably go to Geneva and had just been engaging in hard bargaining.

To Sadat, he was more alarmist, expressing his fear that the conference would fail if Assad did not attend and "all the hopes we have had will be dissipated." Sadat's response calmed him. The Egyptian president was not about to have his peace strategy upset by his recalcitrant Syrian brother any more than he had been willing to pursue his war strategy on Assad's timetable. Sadat reassured Kissinger that he would stand by the agreement they had reached in Cairo: Egypt would "under all circumstances" go to the conference.

With the fear of failure removed, he came to see more clearly what Assad had been signaling him in his convoluted way. The terms for Assad's engagement in Kissinger's Middle East diplomacy were evident: Assad would negotiate an Israeli withdrawal through Kissinger, making his concessions to the United States, and it would be Kissinger's job to deliver the Israelis. By insisting he would not attend the conference, Assad had simplified Kissinger's immediate challenge. Now it was just a matter of convincing the Israeli prime minister.

Sunday, December 16, 1973, Jerusalem. Kissinger arrived in Israel in the evening, after stops in Lebanon and Jordan. The Lebanese were not invited to Geneva and King Hussein was happy to participate, especially now that Kissinger had ensured that the Palestinians would not be there in a separate delegation.

In contrast to his first arrival in Israel, this time Kissinger was greeted by rowdy demonstrators, their placards expressing the distrust that had developed in the minds of some Israelis: "America–Et Tu, Brute?" and "Kissinger Abandoned Formosa, Us Next?"

Mrs. Meir received him in her small Knesset office in Jerusalem for a private meeting, followed by dinner with her inner cabinet hosted by Abba Eban at his home. In the private meeting, there was none of the rancor of their earlier exchanges. That was in part because Kissinger had followed up Nixon's threatening letter with a softer one from the president informing her that the conference would be delayed by three days to give Kissinger an opportunity to discuss her concerns in person. She no longer needed to fear another fait accompli. Kissinger had recovered sufficiently from his traumatic moment in Damascus the night before too. He joked in the larger dinner meeting about Assad's flexibility on the modalities of a conference he had no intention of attending.

Kissinger reported to Meir on Sadat's forthcoming positions on all the disengagement issues. That should have been music to her ears, but she was still fixated on her original idea of symmetrical withdrawals (Israeli forces from the west bank and Egyptian forces from the east bank). Kissinger again rejected that as a non-starter. He said Sadat had indicated that a substantial Sinai disengagement would solve 90 percent of his problems, thereby implying that she would not have to face pressure for a full withdrawal after the first disengagement. And he was willing to reduce his forces on the east bank to two divisions. That, combined with a UN buffer zone separating the Israeli and Egyptian forces in Sinai, meant Sadat would not be able to resort to war before Israel had time to mobilize.

It is interesting that Kissinger cataloged these concessions rather than dramatizing them. This was the first time he had seen Meir since meeting with Sadat. He was in a unique position to convey to her his understanding of Sadat's motives and intentions; that was the essence of his role as mediator. Sadat had given him several important cards to play, designed to convince her of the seriousness of his peaceful intent, especially the personal message to her that he would not raise the Palestinian issue at Geneva, and his intention to rebuild the canal cities. Yet Kissinger conveyed them in a way that devalued Sadat's gestures and turned the conversation into a transactional engagement. Had he become so used to Israeli dismissals of Arab concessions that he thought it better to downplay them? As we shall see later, it was actually indicative of his own skepticism about Arab intentions and the dangers of depending on them.

So instead of selling the hope of peace to his Israeli interlocutors, he resorted to his well-practiced threats, reminding them that Israel's position was "very precarious." He asserted that he alone had managed to keep the wolf from Israel's door by what he described as charismatic "razzle-dazzle." But with the continuation of the energy crisis, Europe, Japan, and much of the U.S. government had already turned against Israel, and he claimed, with some justification, that Nixon was upset by what he viewed as Israeli intransigence. He revealed, however, that if they could make progress on disengagement, King Faisal would lift the embargo. Then explicitly contradicting what he had argued to the Saudi monarch, Kissinger told Meir that once the embargo had been lifted, the Arab oil producers would have difficulty reimposing it. And without the oil embargo, he reminded her, the Arabs would have less leverage to insist on the '67 lines. She seemed to accept his argument.

He then reported that Assad had refused to give him anything on the issue that mattered most to her—the Israeli POWs. The lists and visits would come only after an agreement on disengagement. Anything in advance of that was, in Assad's view, giving something for nothing. Kissinger then added his own assessment, which was either prescient or indicative of some undocumented understanding he had reached with Assad: the Syrian leader would give him the lists and visits at the beginning of the disengagement negotiation, and the prisoners would be returned to Israel at its end. As for the substance of a disengagement deal, his prediction too would prove quite accurate: "My judgment is that if you left that pocket that you took after October 6, and anything symbolic beyond October 6, even a kilometer or two, he'd almost certainly accept it."

Meir rejected any quid pro quo for the provision of a POW list and Red Cross visits, which the Geneva Convention and basic humanity required. She turned to the letter of invitation to the Geneva Conference. Not satisfied with the wording, she sought a written guarantee from the United States that the Palestinians "were out." Kissinger tried to assuage her by promising that as long as he was secretary of state, "you'll never be pressured by me to accept Arafat as a negotiating partner."

But he didn't feel obliged to go beyond that because, as he told her with a hint of menace, "I believe you can't afford not to go to the conference." She responded that Israel would attend, it just wouldn't go into the hall and sit with the Syrians unless the POW lists were forthcoming. Either way, Kissinger said, the Israelis needed to show up at Geneva; if they did not, the oil crisis would turn public opinion against them. This had become an all-purpose talking point—since he had also warned King Faisal that the embargo would turn the American public against Saudi Arabia. She softened: "I must say, taking out the Palestinians helps."

However, in the subsequent dinner with her colleagues, when Kissinger got back into arguing about the modalities of the conference, her sense of the unfairness of it all returned. "You are saying if a war breaks out, or the oil [embargo] is not lifted, we face being sanctioned . . . either by the UN or by the absence of an airlift," she observed. "Whether it is just or not, moral or not moral, you say anytime the talks break down [it will be] because we haven't accepted Egyptian or Syrian demands. . . . Is there any point at which the U.S. will say Israel is right?"

Kissinger reminded her of her own responsibility for Israel's current predicament. "Rightly or wrongly, the present perception is that Israel was excessively obstinate for six years and contributed to the October war," he said. "The starting of the war again would have disastrous consequences."

Meir gave up. The dinner concluded at 12:42 a.m. At 1:00 a.m., she convened her cabinet, which approved the letter of invitation and the U.S.-Israeli MOU without reservations.

Kissinger had succeeded in securing Israeli agreement to the modalities for convening the conference. The fact that he had done so on the eve of Israel's elections, when Meir and her cabinet were at their most skittish, was no mean feat. He was certainly aided by Israel's postwar dependence on the United States. But he had managed to manipulate their fears quite effectively.

In the annals of Middle East diplomacy, it is difficult to endow a ceremonial gathering, one that Kissinger purposely designed as window dressing for a negotiation that would take place elsewhere, with the attributes of a major diplomatic breakthrough. Yet his success stands in stark contrast with a similar effort his immediate successors in the Carter administration tried and failed rather spectacularly to execute.

I said earlier that every new American president tends to eschew the policies of his predecessor, especially if he hails from the alternative party. In Carter's case, the Middle East peace process he inherited was built on the solid foundation of Kissinger's step-by-step diplomacy. But Carter decided early on that the time had come to abandon that approach in favor of a comprehensive resolution of the Arab-Israeli conflict in all its dimensions, including the Palestinian problem. The vehicle he chose to launch his effort was a return to the conference at Geneva.

Rancor in the U.S.-Israeli relationship was inevitable, as it had been in Kissinger's time, made more so by the election of Menachem Begin's right-wing government in the first year of Carter's presidency. But Carter exacerbated the problem through public pronouncements that convinced Israel's American supporters that he was hell-bent on creating a Palestinian state that would threaten its existence. Unlike Kissinger, who went to great pains to convince Israelis that he was in their corner, Carter was deaf to their concerns.

Carter's determination to achieve a comprehensive solution via the Geneva Conference also required him to ensure Syria's attendance and Palestinian participation. Carter managed to persuade the Israelis to agree to Palestinian participation as part of a unified Arab delegation.* But Carter paid heavily for this Israeli concession in the form of agreement to a U.S.-Israeli working paper for Geneva. Kissinger had kept his assurances to Israel concerning the conference in a private side memorandum. Carter's public paper created the impression among his Arab interlocutors that he had caved to domestic pressure.

That impression was exacerbated by Carter's handling of the Soviet Union. One of Kissinger's most important objectives had been to sideline the Soviets from the negotiations. On Sadat's insistence, he had carefully constrained their role at the conference even while creating the illusion of their full involvement. Carter, however, in his headlong rush to convene the conference, was oblivious to Sadat's antipathy toward the Soviet Union.

Accordingly, in the effort to relaunch the Geneva Conference, Cyrus Vance, Carter's secretary of state, blithely negotiated a Joint U.S.-Soviet Communiqué that enunciated the principles of a comprehensive resolution of the conflict. Recall that this was an approach Kissinger had resisted when Brezhnev had pressed it on Nixon at their June 1973 summit, and again in October 1973, when Nixon had instructed Kissinger to pursue it with Brezhnev in Moscow.

Carter had no such reservations. But when the joint communiqué was released, it generated a firestorm of criticism in Washington and Jerusalem for bringing the Soviet Union back into the game. Four days later, in response to the domestic outcry, Vance and Dayan issued a joint U.S.-Israeli statement. In it, the U.S.-Soviet Joint Communiqué was dropped as a basis for the conduct of the Geneva Conference. For Carter and his advisers, the rush to Geneva had become an end in itself, and it had generated a monumental flip-flop which signaled that the United States lacked seriousness.

All of this had a profound impact on a dismayed Sadat. Carter was explicitly undoing the basic understanding he had developed with Kissinger. Worse still, in Carter's pursuit of Syrian participation in the conference, he had conceded that the Arabs would attend in a unified Arab delegation that would hand Assad a veto over Egypt's negotiations with Israel. This was something

---

* The Israelis accepted that the Palestinians could be PLO sympathizers from the West Bank and Gaza provided they were not "well known" (a reference to Arafat and his lieutenants).

Sadat would never countenance, as had been made clear as far back as Hafez Ismail's first meeting with Kissinger in February 1973, and again after Assad refused to go to Geneva in December.

Just as Sadat had repeatedly surprised Kissinger by his willingness to engage with Israel, so too did he now come up with a daring way out of the impasse created by Carter's diplomacy. Perhaps influenced by Kissinger's tutoring of him on the importance of treating the psychological dimension of the conflict, Sadat declared to the Egyptian National Assembly on November 9, 1977, that he was prepared to go "to the ends of the earth" for peace, even to Jerusalem to address the Israeli Knesset. Ten days later, he arrived in Israel.

Even that stunning, historic initiative was at first insufficient to turn Carter away from his determination to reconvene the Geneva Conference.* On November 30, eleven days after Sadat's Jerusalem visit, in his first public statement, Carter still called for "a comprehensive consultation at Geneva."

The best that could be said for Carter's conference diplomacy was that it drove Sadat to escape Geneva by going all the way to Jerusalem. That proved to be a huge contribution to peacemaking. But it was an unintended consequence that left the United States on the sidelines, looking awkward and foolish, rather than the master of the game that Kissinger had become with his successful convening of the Geneva Conference in December 1973.

Thursday, December 20, 1973, Geneva. Kissinger arrived in Geneva on a cold, misty winter's evening after two weeks on the road shuttling between Middle Eastern and European capitals. He was clearly in no hurry to go home to a Washington mired in Watergate afflictions. Besides, he had labored long and hard for this moment, and the historic role he was now playing in promoting Middle East peace was not lost on him. He described his mood as buoyant. The conference served his diplomatic purposes well.

There was the ceremonial pomp with accompanying media attention that heralded the beginning of peace negotiations. In that sense, it was reminiscent of the grand peace conferences that had marked the end of the Napoleonic Wars and the First and Second World Wars. The Vietnam peace negotiations had enjoyed no such validation; indeed, it is doubtful that Kissinger would have wanted any such adornment to a deal whose purpose was to allow for an ignominious American withdrawal. But Middle East peacemaking had a

---

* A few days before Sadat's visit to Jerusalem, Carter was actually thinking about publicly opposing it on the grounds that it would end any hope of a comprehensive agreement. Stuart Eizenstat, Carter's domestic policy adviser, relates a corridor conversation with Carter after Sadat's visit was announced in which he said, "Stu, I think I'm going to oppose Sadat's visit. It will be the end of any hope of a comprehensive peace." See Stuart E. Eizenstat, *President Carter: The White House Years* (New York: St. Martin's, 2018), 474.

unique and unanticipated cachet, not just for Kissinger personally, but for the United States as the creator of the postwar international order.

The symbolism of Arab and Israeli foreign ministers sitting together to speak of peace for the first time since Israel's creation, twenty-five years earlier, gave the conference an historic resonance. Four bitter and bloody Arab-Israeli wars had been fought in the interim. As the narrator in Ecclesiastes foretold, there had been "a time for war"; the Geneva Conference heralded that "a time for peace" had finally arrived.

And there was the legitimization of Kissinger's step-by-step diplomacy, which would now be formally endorsed by the Arabs, Israel, the two superpowers, and the United Nations—in effect the entire international community—through the vehicle of the conference. As he reported to Nixon at the end of the conference, "an institutionalized conference framework has been established, which, with careful nurturing, will keep the principal parties and the Soviets engaged, will keep the UN happy, and will help preserve the cease-fire." It was exactly the legitimization he had been seeking to bolster the Middle Eastern order he was building.

Little wonder then that he put aside his jaundiced view of peace and instead waxed lyrical about it. On arrival at Geneva Airport, he told the press that the lives and hopes of millions of people in the Middle East depended on the success of the conference. He noted that the region which had generated the three great Abrahamic faiths was now challenged to produce another act of faith: "that hatred can give way to reconciliation, that peace can become our purpose, compromise our method, and hope our inspiration."

The opening event took place in the Council Chamber of the Palais des Nations, the imposing complex of art deco buildings on the shore of Lake Geneva that hosted the alternate headquarters of the United Nations (officially known as UNOG, the United Nations Office at Geneva). The Palais, originally constructed to house the League of Nations, was completed in 1938.

The chamber had served as the meeting place of the League's thirteen-member Council. A large mezzanine gallery that could seat five hundred observers looked down on the desks and red leather chairs. Five majestic three-story-high windows framed a picturesque view of Lake Geneva and Mont Blanc. On this occasion, however, their heavy curtains were drawn shut. The walls and ceiling were adorned with massive, imposing, yellow realist murals depicting human progress. One mural portrayed the folly of war, another the triumph of hope in the form of a woman in a flowing white robe standing atop two massive cannons holding a baby aloft. The mural on the ceiling was titled

The opening session of the Geneva Conference on December 21, 1973. Sitting at the center of each table (from left to right) were Zaid al-Rifai, Jordanian national security adviser; Henry Kissinger; Egyptian foreign minister Ismail Fahmy; UN secretary general Kurt Waldheim; Israeli foreign minister Abba Eban; and Soviet foreign minister Andrei Gromyko. The empty table was for the Syrians, to indicate that they were still welcome even though Assad had decided not to send a delegation.

The Lesson of Salamanca and depicted five half-naked men joining hands in a muscular clasp, symbolizing the replacement of conflict with cooperation.

Unfortunately, there was no such clasp between the six delegations seated underneath this mural. They barely could bring themselves to shake hands. Fahmy was in a particularly picayune mood, brought on by Syria's absence. He had struggled hard to convince Assad to attend, even traveling to Damascus to negotiate modalities with him, only to discover that Assad had conjured up a new precondition: that after the opening plenary session, the disengagement negotiations should take place in a military committee of the whole. That would give Syria a veto over Egypt's disengagement negotiations with Israel, something Fahmy's boss would not tolerate.

In Syria's absence, Fahmy was determined to show the Arab world at Geneva that Egypt was not rushing to embrace Israel. Thus, at the last moment, he objected to being seated next to Israel, as alphabetical order would have required. He preferred that Eban be seated next to the empty Syrian chair, apparently to symbolize Israel's isolation, something which Eban found unacceptable. With the other participants waiting and the world's media looking down on an empty chamber, the opening was delayed some forty minutes while Kissinger's team scrambled to resolve the problem. Taking advantage of Soviet interest in a smooth event that would showcase their presence, Kissinger persuaded Gromyko to change places so that Eban would be on his right and the empty Syrian chair on the Russian's left. Meanwhile Kissinger would sit between Fahmy and Zaid al-Rifai, the Jordanian national security adviser, signifying America's new status in the Arab world, while Kurt Waldheim would separate the Egyptian and Israeli foreign ministers, just as the UN was destined to separate the Israeli and Egyptian forces in Sinai. But even that arrangement did not suffice. Fahmy insisted that he not enter the room with Eban, so Kissinger and Gromyko escorted the Israeli into the room through one set of bronze doors while Waldheim escorted the Jordanian and the Egyptian through another.

Fahmy and Rifai gave strident opening speeches blaming Israel's "militaristic and expansionist" policies for the continued conflict and calling for an end to its "warlike acts and aggression." They declared their willingness to make peace with Israel but only on condition that their maximalist demands for total Israeli withdrawal, the liberation of Arab Jerusalem, and the exercise of a Palestinian right to self-determination were met. Rifai, who by this time was in regular clandestine contact with Israel's leaders, even questioned what Israel was doing in the Arab region as a foreign and hostile "stranger in our homeland."

Eban, with his Oxford don's aristocratic eloquence, captured Israel's alternative narrative: the conflict arose from an Arab "total denial" of Israel's right to exist and a "mentality and ideology which produced the gas chambers and gallows of Auschwitz." He professed that Israel had come to terms with Arab nationalism but wondered whether the Arabs could ever accept Israel "as an organic part of its texture and memory." Nevertheless, Eban saw in this assembly a "mutual understanding of the sterility of war" and a common mandate to seek peace. Not so for the absent Syrians, however. He decried their violation of human decencies and their contravention of the Geneva Convention in their refusal to provide an accounting for the Israeli POWs.

Eban had expected his speech would be the last word, but Fahmy was determined not to allow that. He asked for the floor again and proceeded to provide an acerbic rebuttal of Eban's presentation. He portrayed Israel as the international outlaw, the denier of Palestinian rights, and the repeated aggressor and perpetrator of atrocities.

Kissinger's speech was the only one to rise to the occasion. While his personal experience and his study of European history had made him skeptical of peace as an end state, he embraced it on this occasion as a *process* of "correcting the conditions" which generated conflict. That process would have to relate "the imperative of withdrawals to the necessities of security, the requirement of guarantees to the sovereignty of parties, the hopes of the displaced to the realities now existing." That was an elegant way to describe the principles that would have to be reconciled. Five decades later, they remain the basis for the unresolved Israeli-Palestinian conflict.

While Kissinger promised an unflagging American effort, he cautioned that in the end it was up to the Arabs and Israelis. "Peace . . . cannot last unless it rests on the consent of the parties," he declared, noting that such a moral consensus required "arrangements so just that no one wishes to overthrow them."

Sounding like the Harvard professor of history he had been in an earlier life, he explained to this audience of diplomats that all peacemaking efforts had to address the overriding problem of how to relate "the sense of individual justice to the common good." The challenge, as he now defined it, was to recognize that there is justice on all sides, "but there is a greater justice still in finding a truth which merges all aspirations in the realization of a common humanity." To legitimize this utilitarian approach, he summoned the memory of his Jewish education to quote the sage Hillel: "If I am not for myself, who is for me, but if I am for myself alone, who am I?" Their challenge, he concluded, was "to muster the insight and courage to put an end to the conflict between peoples who have so often ennobled mankind."

PART IV

The Peace Negotiations

11

The Sinai Disengagement

The great man has a vision of the future that enables him to put obsta-
cles in perspective; the ordinary leader turns pebbles in the road into
boulders.

—Henry Kissinger, *Years of Upheaval*

N ow came the hard part: negotiating the agreements that would put the
Arabs and Israelis on the road to peace. The accolades Kissinger had
accumulated for his cease-fire and conference diplomacy would be worth little
if he could not quickly conclude the disengagement agreement he had promised Sadat. For that, he needed Nixon's backing and Israel's cooperation.

Kissinger's triumphant return to Washington was overshadowed by Watergate and the oil embargo. On December 19, 1973, Melvin Laird, Nixon's
former secretary of defense and now his domestic policy adviser, announced
that he would be leaving the White House, declaring that a House vote on
the president's impeachment would be "a healthy thing." General Motors
announced plans to lay off eighty-six thousand workers because of the oil crisis. On December 23, the shah of Iran declared that the Gulf oil producers
would once more hike the price of oil, this time more than doubling it, from
$5.12 to $11.65 a barrel. Libya, Nigeria, and Indonesia followed suit a few
days later. This dramatic increase in energy costs would soon drive the global
economy into a deep recession.

In Kissinger's absence, Nixon had become even more unpredictable. During a dinner conversation at the White House, Senator Barry Goldwater later
recalled, the president was erratic and distracted, at times speaking nonsense:
"I asked myself whether I was witnessing a slow-motion collapse of Nixon's
mental balance."

Kissinger's immediate problem was that the president was exercising his prerogative to interfere. While he was away, Nixon had attempted to link his request to Congress for $2.2 billion for the Israeli arms resupply to Meir's willingness to make concessions in the negotiations. Although Nixon had been wanting to do this for some time, and Kissinger would later use military assistance for the same purpose, to apply that leverage now risked upending Kissinger's carefully developed effort to generate Israeli flexibility just when it was succeeding.

Kissinger had headed off Nixon by arguing it would jeopardize the convening of the Geneva Conference. Once back in Washington, he worked with Haig to thwart the president's intentions while he sought credit from Dinitz for doing so. He showed Dinitz a daily briefing he had prepared for Nixon on which the president had scribbled that if war were to resume, regardless of the reason, "the Israelis would have to do it alone." Later, he warned the Israeli ambassador yet again that Nixon was anti-Semitic and surrounded by oil men who cared only about Arab interests. He reminded him that he was Israel's only true friend in Washington, adding that Schlesinger had backed Nixon's anti-Israel initiative.

Managing Nixon had also become more challenging because the positive media attention Kissinger received in the wake of his high-profile success at Geneva was heightening the president's jealousy. On December 24, *The New York Times* ran a front-page analysis by Leslie Gelb, then its diplomatic correspondent, headlined, "Nixon Role in Foreign Policy Is Altered; Some Assert Kissinger Is Now in Charge." *Time*'s headline on the same day was "The Superstar on His Own." The article noted that Kissinger had long been viewed as "the second most powerful man in the U.S.," but now "he is the one figure of stature remaining in the ruins . . . of Richard Nixon's stricken administration." Seeking to gain from Kissinger's glory, Nixon insisted that he accompany him to the Western White House at San Clemente over the New Year's break to demonstrate that they were coordinating on Middle East diplomacy. While Kissinger put on a positive face with the White House press corps, "I left San Clemente very depressed," he confided to Haig on his return to Washington. "I am beginning to wonder how long this is manageable."

Kissinger's spirits were lifted by a visit from Moshe Dayan. Three weeks earlier, in Jerusalem, he had prepared the ground for this engagement with the swashbuckling Israeli general. At their dinner at Eban's residence, he had enunciated two principles that he thought should assuage Israeli security concerns: Egyptian forces on the east bank of the canal should be insufficient to launch an attack, and the UN buffer zone should be enough of a barrier to give Israel time to mobilize should the Egyptians decide to cross the canal with their main forces. These basic principles of limited forces and demilitarized zones would come to be applied in all subsequent Arab-Israeli security arrangements.

Kissinger had then painted a broader picture of the strategic value of what he was pursuing. A disengagement agreement was a way to get the oil embargo lifted and avoid "talking about what everyone else wants to talk about, namely the 1967 borders."* He noted that Sadat was going easy on them. He was not linking the disengagement to a permanent settlement and was not threatening to return to a war in which the whole world would gang up on Israel. He explained that Sadat's malleability derived from his sense of urgency and his vanity: "He wants to ride in an open car into Suez City." The Israelis should take advantage of it.

Dayan felt that the first withdrawal would be the most important. "We will have made a major concession and he would get a major advantage." Israel had to get something worthwhile in return, he argued.

Dayan had then asked whether Kissinger wanted Soviet troops in the UN force. "I think the presence of Soviet forces in any guise whatsoever are a disaster," Kissinger answered. Later in the conversation, Allon raised the idea of Soviet aid in clearing the canal of sunken ships from the 1967 war. American army engineers would clear the canal, Kissinger responded indignantly. "If there is a disengagement agreement, I want it clearly to be the product of Sadat's moderate course . . . and ignoring the Russians."

He needn't have worried. Mentioning the Soviets stirred Meir's paranoia. She complained that Sadat will get what he wants, Israel will concede for promises that will not be kept, and then the world will start pressing again. Only next time, Israel will be fighting with a great disadvantage and the world will say, "a plague on the House of Israel," she said. "This is the first step towards 1967." It was all so unfair. "[I]n this world you paint . . . the aggressor and the victim are in the same position—except the aggressor has oil."

Instead of arguing with her, Kissinger had pointed out that if her scenario came to pass she would need U.S. protection, and the only way to ensure that was to create an obligation by helping to make his diplomacy successful.

Dayan had then suggested a gradual process that would minimize the prospects for the perfidy she feared. First there had to be "a normalization process" of repopulating the canal cities and turning the canal into a civilian waterway; that would be a safeguard of Egypt's peaceful intentions. He allowed that Sadat seemed to have this in mind. But he didn't want Israel to be cheated, like it was

---

* In a meeting with Jewish leaders after he returned from this trip, Kissinger was as explicit: "At present there is no U.S. position on secure borders. There won't be, as long as it is humanly possible. Our strategy is to postpone the question. Is it conceivable? Frankly, I can't say it is not." See Memcon between Kissinger and Jewish Leaders, December 27, 1973, KT00974, NSA.

in 1970. He therefore wanted this normalization process completed before the next phase of negotiations lest it be used as a bargaining tool.

Kissinger embraced Dayan's elaboration of his step-by-step process. He suggested that Sadat should make those commitments to the United States as well, because, if he reneged, "then we can say we've been tricked too." He had then reiterated his time-buying strategy, which "gives us a chance to quiet down the hysteria and break the cycle." This time, she had agreed with him.

That was before Geneva. Since then, Meir had been reelected prime minister, albeit with a narrower margin of seats.* With a renewed mandate but an official inquiry into the conduct of the war hanging over her head, she now needed to bring the troops home. She moved with surprising speed, persuading the interim Israeli cabinet to endorse the proposal Dayan had outlined to Kissinger in that earlier meeting in Jerusalem.

Friday, January 4, 1974, Washington, DC. When Dayan came calling on Kissinger in Washington on January 4, he presented him with a fully formed, cabinet-approved Israeli proposal. Dayan confidently predicted there would be no problem passing an agreement on this basis in the new Knesset. Compared to the teeth-pulling exercises Kissinger had gone through with the Israelis over the previous three months, this initiative was welcome indeed.

Kissinger summarized the disengagement of forces proposal Dayan presented to him in a memorandum to Nixon after their meeting:

- Israel would withdraw all its forces presently west of the Suez Canal behind a main Israeli defense line which would be about thirty kilometers east of the canal, at the western end of the Mitla and Gidi Passes;
- The Egyptian Second and Third Armies would retain, with slight modification, the line they presently held, which ran about eight to ten kilometers east of the canal;
- The Egyptian armies would be substantially thinned out east of the canal to create an additional six-to-ten-kilometer-wide forward zone containing only light Egyptian weapons; the same would apply on the Israeli side;
- Moving eastward, there would be about a ten-kilometer demilitarized buffer zone supervised by the UN force;

---

* The ruling Labor Party lost six seats and the newly constituted right-wing Likud Party, under Menachem Begin, gained eight. Yitzhak Rabin entered the government as minister of labor, Arele Yariv was appointed minister of information, and Ariel Sharon entered the Knesset as a leading member of the opposition Likud Party.

- In addition, the Israelis would be willing to move their artillery and anti-aircraft weapons far enough eastward so that only their own forces were covered, provided the Egyptians were willing to do the same, westward.

Dayan's proposal, with its thirty-kilometer Israeli withdrawal from the east bank of the canal, was in fact similar to the informal proposal Yariv had made to el-Gamasy in the Kilometer 101 talks two months earlier but had then withdrawn, ironically, because of Dayan's opposition. Kissinger's response was enthusiastic. "It's a good proposal," he observed. And then, like a professor encouraging a bright student, he praised it as "intellectually respectable . . . very ingenious and basically fair." He would happily present it to Sadat.

But Dayan wasn't finished. He listed all Israel's requirements in return, including two items that would become all too familiar in subsequent negotiations: an Egyptian commitment to non-belligerency (Dayan called it "the first step of peace"), and a long-term understanding on arms supplies from the United States. Listening attentively, Kissinger assessed that the one problem area would be Dayan's demand that all Egyptian tanks be withdrawn from the east bank of the canal. Sadat would put Egypt's interest first over broader Arab concerns, but he could not be left looking like a traitor, neither to his people nor to the Arab world. A ban on tanks on reclaimed Egyptian territory would make him vulnerable to that charge. Kissinger suggested a token number of fifty tanks so that Sadat could say there were no absolute disqualifications.

Kissinger then warned that it would be difficult to get an end-of-belligerency statement at this stage. As for a more stable arms supply pipeline, Kissinger said he would discuss it with Schlesinger, clinging to his threadbare artifice that the Pentagon was responsible for such decisions.

As they wrapped up their discussion, Kissinger asked whether Dayan could come back for another meeting the next day; he did not want the Egyptians to think they had reached agreement without a struggle. With that in mind, he urged Dayan to tell the press that they had discussed only ideas and principles, not details. To make sure the Egyptians got the message, Kissinger escorted Dayan down to the ground floor and the press gaggle outside the C Street entrance to the State Department. Two celebrities basking in the attention of the media: the handsome Israeli war hero with his iconic black eyepatch and winning smile standing next to the Harvard professor turned super-diplomat. As the journalists stuck their microphones and tape recorders in his face, Kissinger said they had made good progress but would meet again tomorrow for a second round. Sticking to the ploy, Dayan said he had come to discuss only "general concepts."

Kissinger had another reason for bringing Dayan back the next day. In

Henry Kissinger and Israeli defense minister Moshe Dayan after a meeting
at the State Department on March 30, 1974. At an earlier gaggle outside the
State Department on January 4, 1974, Dayan told the press that Israel was now
in a position to formulate concrete proposals. That was part of an elaborate
ruse. In fact, Dayan had brought a cabinet-approved, detailed proposal to
Washington, but Kissinger didn't want the Egyptians to know that.

Geneva, the Egyptian-Israeli military working group had now met three
times, but he did not want to leave the negotiations to the generals meeting
there, much like his aversion to the Kilometer 101 talks. Given what Dayan
had brought him, and what he had previously discussed with Sadat, it was
clear that the gaps had substantially narrowed. As he would report to Nixon,
the Israelis had "now come 85 percent of the way to the Egyptian position on
disengagement, and this without any demands for reciprocity."

Why not close the gap himself? It was, after all, the appropriate role for a
secretary of state to intervene in negotiations when the differences between the
parties were bridgeable and all that remained was for the leaders to make the
final, albeit difficult, compromises. He knew that dealing with Sadat directly
would lend itself to the Egyptian's "propensity for the sudden stroke," as he
would subsequently write.

Kissinger therefore decided he would engage with Sadat and Meir directly
and conclude the disengagement agreement as quickly as possible. That would
have the additional benefit of removing him from Washington and proximity
to a president who was in meltdown. In his memoirs, he disarmingly admits,
"[N]o doubt there was an element of vanity involved on my side as well."
But how to maneuver it so that it would look like he was being invited by the

parties rather than seeking to intervene? And how to convince Nixon that he should let him go so soon after he had just returned triumphant?

The next morning, Kissinger again met with Dayan, this time in Kissinger's seventh-floor, windowless conference room. A large Queen Anne mahogany conference table with an inlaid green leather top filled most of the space in this elegant, wood-paneled room, its walls adorned with tasteful Audubon prints. Across from the secretary of state's customary seat at the center of the table were two outsized, heavy mahogany doors with shiny brass fittings that opened onto a light-filled gallery which ran the length of the executive offices on the seventh floor, displaying grave-looking portraits of earlier secretaries of state.

Twenty years later, on the afternoon of September 13, 1993, Yasir Arafat had sat in front of those closed doors across the table from Secretary of State Warren Christopher after the Oslo signing ceremony on the South Lawn of the White House. It would be the only visit the PLO chairman ever made to the State Department. It was a memorable occasion, not only because the seventh floor had probably never hosted a leader like Arafat before, but also because, during the discussion, the large doors started creaking and then suddenly, with a bang, blew open. As staff from the Protocol Office quickly closed them, Christopher apologized to Arafat. But a few minutes later, it happened again. It was as if there were some ghost of a secretary of state past who couldn't believe Arafat was in his conference room and had resolved to burst out of there.

In the second meeting with Dayan, Kissinger praised the Israeli proposal again as "a tremendous step." He particularly appreciated the way the plan created a series of firebreaks and cleverly preserved the defensive capabilities of both sides while weakening their offensive capabilities. He cautioned that because they were not negotiating a peace agreement based on a final border, he would have to be careful how he presented Israel's demand for limits on weapons on Egyptian sovereign territory, but he had already adopted Sadat's idea: Egyptian commitments could be made to the U.S. president, who would then convey them to Israel.

Kissinger still saw a potential problem in Israel's demands for no Egyptian tanks and strictly limited forces on the east bank of the canal. The principle he thought he could sell to Sadat was that the number should be insufficient to launch an attack without reinforcement. However, he noted, with a reopened canal and normalized life behind the Egyptian forces in Sinai and the demilitarized zone ahead of them, "it will be extremely difficult [for Egypt] to then start pouring troops across." Israel could afford to show some flexibility on the force limitations, he argued.

Kissinger now sought to obliquely introduce the idea that he would be the one to conduct this negotiation with Sadat and the Israeli cabinet. Just as he sought an invitation from Brezhnev back in October to make the flight to Moscow that produced the cease-fire agreement, he now needed invitations from Israel and Egypt to justify launching this effort to a jealous boss. So he engaged in a coy exercise with Dayan, outlining three suboptimal ways of proceeding, concluding with his preferred option of pitching Dayan's ideas directly to Sadat.* Dayan immediately agreed that Kissinger should be the one to take them to Sadat.

Like a skillful fly fisherman playing his catch, Kissinger wanted to make sure Dayan was completely hooked. He reassured him that his approach would be to present Israel's proposal "in the way which gives the maximum chance he'll accept it as it is." But he would need some leeway: "I, however, cannot go to Cairo if I have to say take it or leave it. You don't have to give me a fallback position, but if I go back to Tel Aviv, I have to have some assurance it won't be rejected." He needed to be able to say to Sadat, if he responded with something reasonable, that he would at least present it to Meir.

Kissinger was fully aware of the dangers he was courting by committing himself to this form of negotiation. He wanted Dayan to understand that by asking him to go, asking him to invest the credibility he had built with Sadat, Israel was also taking on responsibility for his success. He then said sarcastically, "I know it is a stupid question for me to ask in advance if [Meir] will change her position, particularly since flexibility is her outstanding trait." Kissinger was putting Dayan on notice that he expected a flexible Israeli response if Sadat made a reasonable counterproposal.

After an almost two-hour review of Dayan's proposal, Kissinger left the room to take a phone call. On his way back in, an aide handed him a cable that had just arrived from Geneva summarizing the UN's report of that day's meeting of the Egyptian-Israeli military working group. According to the cable, "great progress had been made in Geneva." Since nothing was supposed to be happening in Geneva, this was unwelcome news for Kissinger.

As Kissinger now reported to Dayan, General Motta Gur had outlined an Israeli proposal to his Egyptian counterpart: "the main Egyptian force would be withdrawn to the West bank of the canal and the main Israeli force to a line 35km east of the canal." Kissinger threw the cable down on the table and shouted, "That's the goddamn plan!"

Dayan tried to explain it away as Gur just presenting some "models," or examples. Kissinger wasn't buying it.† He had experienced this freelancing

---

* The three suboptimal options were: a formal Israeli presentation to the Egyptian-Israeli military working group in Geneva, a presentation by Ambassador Eilts to Sadat in Cairo, or a meeting between Dayan and Sadat at Kilometer 101.
† In a subsequent conversation with Dinitz, Kissinger tried to make sense of what Gur had done. Dinitz explained that Gur was just "playing with models" of possible disengagement. Kissinger was unconvinced: "As a diplomat, why should you play with models when you have no intention

before in Yariv's exchanges with el-Gamasy. Gur was detailing to an Egyptian general in Geneva the formal Israeli government proposal that Dayan was at that very moment discussing with Kissinger. And instead of a thirty-kilometer withdrawal, Gur had offered thirty-five kilometers, which would have put Israeli forces at the eastern end of the passes. That was precisely what Sadat wanted and Dayan had rejected.

Kissinger was incredulous. "On the very day we discuss this, he tables your proposal?" If Kissinger now turned up in Cairo with the same plan, he would appear to be Israel's lawyer. "Sadat will say, Send me Gur. I don't need you." Caustically, he asked, "What is my achievement? That I got Dayan to agree with his subordinate?" He needed to be able to show that the Israeli plan he presented was the product of American pressure, not Israeli largesse. Suitably contrite, Dayan accepted Kissinger's insistence that they say publicly that Israel had made no proposal.

Together they went downstairs to the C Street lobby and again faced the press gaggle. Kissinger explained that Dayan had come to discuss some "general ideas," the American side had responded with some ideas of its own, and now Dayan would return to Israel to confer with his cabinet "and formulate some proposals for formal consideration in Geneva." Dayan played along, saying that he thought Israel was now in a position "to form concrete proposals."

With terms of engagement now clearly established with the Israeli side, Kissinger had to persuade Sadat to invite him and convince Nixon to agree to let him go. Sadat was easy. Kissinger sent him a message, via Ambassador Eilts in Cairo, offering to visit him to reach a rapid agreement. Since Sadat was as much of a showman as Kissinger, and in even more of a hurry, he replied on January 8, urging Kissinger to come immediately. He would meet him at his winter retreat in the upper Nile city of Aswan.

Now to convince Nixon. Kissinger knew the president wanted to be able to show that his administration was still capable of foreign policy achievements, but he also wanted—and in his beleaguered state, needed—to be seen as the one who was delivering them. Since by now Kissinger well understood his boss's jealousy, he tried to prepare the ground carefully.

On January 6, in the upbeat report to Nixon of his meetings with Dayan, he noted that the Israelis "have urged me to take the plan to Cairo immediately."*

---

of using them?" Dinitz then gave the real reason: "He did it because Dayan was away, and he thought he would go one step further." See Telcon between Dinitz and Kissinger, January 8, 1974, KA11828, NSA.
* Kissinger subsequently turned this account into folklore, telling his senior staff at the end of the Egyptian-Israeli disengagement negotiations that Dayan had asked whether he would be willing to go out and make the presentation to Sadat, "because they despaired of being able to present

He then painted a picture of a host of possible negative developments if he did not try for a breakthrough in the next ten days, and why a quick agreement was necessary to get the oil embargo lifted. He was trying to lead Nixon to his own conclusion that he should dispatch him to the Middle East again.

Nixon, however, was too distracted, so Kissinger asked Haig to raise the idea with him directly. Kissinger had warned Haig previously that the proposal to have him travel to Cairo and Jerusalem would probably drive Nixon "into orbit," but Haig reassured him that he could manage it. The same evening, in a phone call with the president, Kissinger buttered him up by pointing to the stories in that day's press, particularly *The Washington Post*, which had run the headline: "Nixon Seen in Firm Control." Nixon responded by talking about the weather in San Clemente.

On January 8, after Sadat had urged Kissinger to visit, Kissinger asked Haig to persuade Nixon to let him go, even authorizing Haig to give Nixon "a terminal date for my tenure" if he would allow him to wrap up the disengagement agreement. Haig should also tell Nixon that Kissinger would stage it so the president would be the one to announce the Egyptian-Israeli agreement, and also the lifting of the oil embargo that Kissinger expected to accompany it. Growing increasingly nervous as he waited for a response, he confided to Scowcroft, "If [the president] refuses it, I will certainly resign."

At 3:05 p.m., Haig called back with Nixon's approval. Indeed, the president thought the sooner Kissinger went, the better. Haig added his own encouragement: "I think you ought to leave very, very quickly, Henry," that is, before Nixon changed his mind.

Kissinger's anxiety would subsequently prove justified. Six days later, in the middle of his shuttling between Egypt and Israel, Scowcroft and Haig sent him a message urging him to fly back to Washington to receive some well-publicized instructions from Nixon to demonstrate presidential involvement. The harebrained scheme could well have been triggered by the need for a distraction from the news on January 15 that an eighteen-minute erasure on one critical tape that Nixon had handed over to the Watergate special prosecutor was not caused by an accidental pressing of the wrong button on the tape recorder. It appeared to be a deliberate effort to destroy subpoenaed evidence. By then, however, Kissinger was able to argue to Haig that his whole effort would be jeopardized if he had to return home before concluding the deal.[*]

---

it in a manner that would open any possibility for negotiation." See Minutes of Kissinger's Staff Meeting, January 21, 1974, KT01007, NSA.

[*] Kissinger was so concerned over Nixon's erratic behavior and his newfound penchant for going behind Kissinger's back that on his flight home from Israel after the successful conclusion of this shuttle, he asked Dinitz, who was accompanying him, to provide him with any intelligence Israel had on Nixon's communications with Arab leaders, particularly King Faisal. See Addendum to Kissinger-Dinitz Plane Conversation Report, January 21, 1974, A-7/7060, ISA.

Kissinger still had to make sure everything was lined up with Sadat and the Israelis, especially because the Egyptians had briefed the Soviets on the Gur "model," and Dobrynin was now asking him whether it was true that the Israelis had offered to withdraw *forty-five kilometers* into the Sinai! Kissinger sent instructions to Eilts to dissemble to Sadat, telling him the Israelis had put nothing on the table. Then he met with Dinitz to ensure that the Israelis exercised some discipline in what they said to the press about there being no concrete proposal. He suggested he would spend an extra day in Israel to make it look like he was having a hard time securing something concrete from Meir and getting her cabinet to approve it.

On January 10, he summoned Ashraf Ghorbal, the Egyptian ambassador designate, to brief him on his upcoming trip. With a straight face, he explained that the meetings with Dayan had not gone well. Dayan had not presented a firm plan because the Israeli cabinet was deeply divided. Therefore, he wanted to visit Sadat to discuss the issues with him and better arm himself "to confront the Israelis."

Kissinger maintained this artifice all the way through the subsequent negotiations. He told the press on the eve of his departure from Washington for Aswan that he was not carrying his own or Israeli proposals to Sadat but "if the Israeli cabinet" decided "on a concrete proposal" after his stop in Israel, he was ready to take it back to Egypt. En route to Aswan, "a senior official" told the traveling press corps that Sadat (not Dayan) had come up with some concrete ideas, which was why Kissinger was focused on getting Israel to generate "a formal proposal of her own." His talks with Dayan, the source explained, had revealed some difficulties in reconciling their positions, so Dayan had suggested he come to Israel to talk to the Israeli cabinet.

Consistent with this fiction, on January 12, after a late-night meeting in Jerusalem, Kissinger and Abba Eban announced to the press that their teams would work through the night on a concrete proposal. According to *The New York Times*, "Mr. Kissinger persuaded the Israelis to quicken their efforts to agree on a specific disengagement position." On January 13, the Israeli cabinet was reported to have approved a specific proposal for Kissinger to take back to Sadat. It just happened to be the same proposal that the cabinet had already approved before Dayan brought it to Washington on January 4. At midnight on January 16, after the disengagement agreement had been accepted by both sides, Kissinger outlined the history of the negotiations to the press. It was Dayan, he explained, who had suggested he come out to the Middle East and Sadat who had raised some ideas for the disengagement. Only then, he claimed, did the Israeli cabinet develop a proposal that formed the basis for the negotiations. The explanation had now entered into the annals of diplomatic history as folklore.

In 1612, Sir Henry Wotton, a diplomat and man of letters in Jacobean England, noted in a friend's guestbook that "an ambassador is an honest man sent to lie abroad for the commonwealth." This quote has since become a cliché, suggesting that dissembling is an essential gambit in the diplomat's attaché case. Thus, Kissinger's elaborate ploy should not be taken as unusual, even though the lengths to which he went were exaggerated, and predictably failed to fool the Egyptians. Kissinger's anxiety had made the matter more complicated than it needed to be. But his maneuvering reveals how far he felt he needed to go to set himself up for success in these negotiations. Whereas during the October crisis he had been forced to improvise, this time he was determined to leave nothing to chance, even if candor and truth became the casualties.

Friday, January 11, 1974, Aswan. Kissinger scheduled a nighttime arrival in Aswan in the hope that he could get a good night's sleep before meeting Sadat the next morning. But just as in October, when he was forced to have a midnight rendezvous with Brezhnev, he discovered that Sadat was impatient to see him too. Fahmy greeted him at the deserted military airport and whisked him away to Sadat's villa.

In those days, Aswan was a sleepy resort town renowned for its mild winter weather. It was located at the first cataract (or rapids) of the Nile, about four hundred miles south of Cairo. Unlike the rest of this majestic river, which flowed unimpeded northward to the delta and the Mediterranean Sea, the section at Aswan was strewn with boulders, rocky outcrops, and small islands that made the river impassable. It marked the southern frontier of the Egyptian empire in ancient times. Three thousand years ago, Aswan's granite quarries had provided the massive stones that were floated down the Nile and used to build the pharaohs' temples, statues, and obelisks at Edfu and Luxor. In more modern times, the British had built a dam just above the cataract to control the floodwaters of the Nile and enhance downstream irrigation. In the 1960s, Soviet engineers had constructed a much larger dam farther upstream, creating a vast lake and generating hydroelectricity to power Egypt's economic development. The Aswan High Dam, as it became known, symbolized the modernization of Egypt under Nasser's regime, the hinge between its glorious ancient past and its hopeful future. According to a sign at the observation point in broken English, it was "the Egyptian challenge against the silent nature."

It also symbolized Egypt's turn away from the United States and toward the Soviet Union during the Eisenhower administration. Piqued by Nasser's anti-colonialist antics, in July 1956, Secretary of State John Foster Dulles had abruptly canceled U.S. financing for the dam. Nasser turned to the Soviet Union, and First Secretary Nikita Khrushchev stepped into the breach, marking the moment when Russia penetrated the Middle East for the first time. The Aswan High Dam was completed in 1970. A huge, ugly monument was then erected at its eastern end to symbolize the friendship of the Soviet and Egyptian peoples. Two years later, Sadat evicted the Soviet military advisers, beginning the process of Egypt's decoupling from the Soviet Union and its eventual move into the American camp.

As president, Sadat chose to spend his winters in Aswan, which he appreciated for its beauty, climate, mystic atmosphere, and connection to the pharaohs of ancient Egypt. In earlier years, Aga Khan III had sojourned there and became so fond of the place that he erected a large mausoleum in the adjacent desert, where he was buried. Sadat's gray stone, flat-roofed villa was on a bluff overlooking the British dam in a development of similar drab houses that was built in the 1960s, when the town was dominated by the Russian presence. The presidential villa, covered with jasmine and rhododendron, was situated in gardens of palm, fig, and mango trees where a white gazebo afforded a shaded view across the cataract to the town. Below the bluff was a complex of military warehouses. On the other side of the road was a small mosque, where Sadat would pray. To the north, the distant skyline was interrupted by the nine-story New Cataract Hotel, a banal, Soviet-style edifice built to accommodate the Russian engineers who had worked on the dam. That is where Kissinger would spend an uncomfortable night.

Sadat greeted Kissinger in his elegant, fawn, double-breasted field marshal's uniform with golden epaulets. "Welcome! Welcome!" his voice boomed, notwithstanding the bronchitis from which he was recovering. He swept Kissinger into his study, which looked out on the gardens and the Nile beyond. The Empire-style settee on which they sat was upholstered in ivory silk damask, and a box of cigars lay open on the coffee table in front of them. Kissinger noted that, oddly, the settee faced away from the window. Diaphanous curtains concealed the bucolic view.

Once the camera crews had been ushered out, Sadat wasted no time in saying that, now that the opening ceremony of the Geneva Conference was over, there was no point in returning there to run the gauntlet of potential Soviet and Syrian interference. He was particularly agitated at that moment by criticism he was fielding from Damascus and other radical Arab capitals, and by pressure from Moscow to include the Soviets in the negotiations. To underscore his aversion to the Geneva Conference, he insisted that when they reached an agreement, it should be signed by Egyptian and Israeli generals at Kilometer 101, even though that negotiating forum had been replaced by the Egyptian-Israeli military working group in Geneva. He clearly wanted his disengagement agreement, and he wanted it now. He invited Kissinger to stay in the region to wrap up the negotiations.

Kissinger was more than happy to embrace this idea, since that had been his intention anyway. Although he had reassured Soviet ambassador Dobrynin on the eve of his departure that he would feed the results of his trip into Geneva for detailed negotiations, and said the same thing to the traveling press, he had also confided to Haig that he had no desire "to let the Russians hack at it" because that would surely produce a stalemate. In that conversation, he had expressly raised the idea that he would undertake what Sisco had referred to as "a shuttle." Haig had warned him he could end up "getting caught in a vise" and then he would own the failure.

The danger was ameliorated by Sadat's willingness to set a deadline for the effort. Sadat wanted the agreement wrapped up by January 18, only a week away, before he embarked on a scheduled trip to Arab capitals. Kissinger knew that setting such a time limit would put pressure on Sadat to be as flexible as possible, and since he had already concluded that the gaps were bridgeable, he decided on the spot to accept Sadat's challenge. Sadat sweetened the deal by saying that if they succeeded, he would use his travels in the Arab world to promote the lifting of the oil embargo. And if he prevailed on his Arab brothers, he promised Kissinger he would give Nixon the credit. The idea of "shuttle diplomacy" was conceived on that balmy evening in Aswan.

There is a proverb in the Koran that Assad would often cite to us to justify his dilatory tactics, that "haste is of the devil." Indeed, a sense of urgency is often absent in Arab-Israeli negotiations. When one or both sides are in no hurry, there tends to be little the United States can do to change their calculations. That is certainly true of the current prolonged impasse in Israeli-Palestinian negotiations. But it has been so long since any of the parties evinced a sense of urgency that it is easy to forget that urgency can often emerge just when it is least expected. This is especially so in the Arab world, where political currents run deep and are often not discernible to the Western observer. However, once one or both parties decide that time is not on their side, negotiations inevitably speed up as previously intransigent positions yield to greater flexibility on one side, which then puts pressure on the other side to respond.

Such was the case with Arafat in the 1993 Oslo negotiations. His situation had become parlous because of his ill-advised siding with Saddam Hussein in the Gulf War. Once Kuwait had been liberated, Palestinian workers were expelled from there and from most other Gulf Arab states too. This precipitated a massive decline in PLO revenues, since Gulf governments had been collecting taxes from Palestinian workers and remitting them to the PLO.

Arafat was forced to close some of his "embassies" and curtail subsidies to his followers, which were the lifeblood of his patronage system. At that moment of desperation, Yitzhak Rabin threw Arafat a lifeline in the form of the Oslo Accords, which he promptly grasped. Rabin too was in a hurry, having promised his people an agreement in his first year in office.

Similarly, when Assad was coming to the end of his life, in December 1999, he suddenly informed Secretary of State Madeleine Albright that he wanted to conclude a peace deal with Israel and insisted that it be done "quickly." That was a word we had never expected to hear from Assad. He had been informed seven years earlier by Bill Clinton and Warren Christopher that Rabin was willing to accept his demand for full withdrawal from the Golan Heights provided he met Israel's requirements. After Rabin's assassination, the same offer had been made to Assad by three successive Israeli prime ministers: Shimon Peres, Benjamin Netanyahu, and Ehud Barak. Assad had made that requirement a sine qua non of his negotiating position, and yet once it was met, he responded with a range of additional demands, which had the effect of bogging down the negotiations and enabling both Arafat and King Hussein to cut their own deals with Israel ahead of him. But knowing his time was short, Assad suddenly developed a sense of urgency and dispatched his foreign minister, Farouk al-Shara, to Washington for an unprecedented meeting with Israeli prime minister Ehud Barak. Shara's instructions were to conclude the deal by accepting Israel's reasonable requirements for security arrangements and the normalization of relations. In the end, we missed the agreement because Barak initially balked at Assad's territorial requirements and when he was eventually ready to agree to them, it was too late. Approaching his death, Assad shifted focus to securing the succession for his son, Bashar.

For American diplomats, a sense of urgency by one or both sides is an essential ingredient in success. Once manifested, the moment needs to be seized and fully exploited until an agreement is achieved, which is exactly what Kissinger did with Sadat and what Clinton and his peace team, of which I was a part, failed to do with Assad and Barak.

In the days before Kissinger's arrival in Aswan in January 1974, Ismail Fahmy had argued to Sadat that he had no reason to be in a hurry. He assessed, correctly, that U.S. relations with Egypt were the key to the success of Kissinger's strategy of reducing Soviet influence in the region, splitting the Arabs, lifting the oil embargo, and preserving Israel's interests. Given that Sadat held such high cards, Fahmy advised him to "play the game of nations" by pitting one superpower against the other while waiting for the pressure of the oil embargo to mount on the United States and the weight of a prolonged mobilization to wear down Israel's requirements. He recommended that Sadat tell Kissinger to go home and return in a month. Sadat humored Fahmy, but when Kissinger arrived, Sadat met with him alone, much to Fahmy's dismay, and set the one-week deadline for the agreement without even hearing Israel's disengagement proposal.*

Kissinger awoke the next morning to a picturesque view of cerulean waters and golden sands framed by palm trees and dotted by feluccas with their white sails loosened to catch the breeze off the Nile. The scene resembled a Raoul Dufy painting *Regatta at Cowes.* In the foreground, the island of Elephantine dominated the landscape, with its ancient Temple of Khnum, the ram-headed god of the cataract. Settlement there dated back three thousand years. Aramaic papyri indicated a Jewish community presence on the island around 500 BCE. On the distant desert horizon stood the Aga Khan's mausoleum in splendid relief. Kissinger joked that his staff should go out there and measure its dimensions so that he could build one for himself.

It was Sadat's habit to work late into the night and sleep in, which afforded Kissinger some rare time for sightseeing. His Egyptian hosts insisted on taking him to visit the Aswan High Dam first. That was of decidedly limited interest to Kissinger, but he understood Sadat's purpose: he wanted to show that he was replacing Egypt's Soviet patron with an American. Next his guides took him on a short boat cruise to the beautiful, romantic Temple of Isis, the godess of life, death, and resurrection.

Over lunch at the villa, Kissinger explained to Sadat that he was pressing Israel to come forward with a proposal that he would bring back to Aswan. He outlined the three principal issues he believed would need to be resolved: the disengagement line, the armament limitations, and the assurances and understandings that would need to accompany these military redeployments.

Kissinger chose not to raise Dayan's requirement of an "end to belligerency," reflecting his belief that it was a bridge too far. This would remain Kissinger's consistent position throughout his negotiations with Israel, Egypt, and Syria over the next three years. It reflected his firm conviction that the Arabs were not yet ready to reconcile with Israel and that he therefore needed to proceed with his small steps until they were.

Sensitive to Arab criticism, Sadat confirmed Kissinger's assessment by insisting that the agreement contain no political dimensions. Anything even vaguely political would have to be handled in side-understandings between the

---

* Fahmy later explained Sadat's rejection of his advice as an indication that Sadat's state of mind had been adversely impacted by the Israeli military counteroffensive, which had destroyed his confidence and rendered him willing to make unnecessary concessions. He claimed that Sadat's "eagerness to sign with the Americans" damaged Egypt and the entire Arab cause. See Ismail Fahmy, *Negotiating for Peace in the Middle East* (Abingdon, UK: Routledge, 1983), 58–59.

United States and Egypt, with Washington conveying them in secret to Jerusalem. Sadat's desire to maintain the impression of a strictly military accord was another reason for his desire to have generals sign it at Kilometer 101.

On the issue of the line, Sadat still insisted on leaving Israel in control only of the eastern end of the passes, as Kissinger had reported to the Israelis on his last visit to Jerusalem. On force limitations, Sadat said he could not go below two divisions on the east bank of the canal and was not prepared to accept limitations on their armaments. He was, however, ready to provide assurances regarding Israeli shipping transiting through Bab el-Mandeb and Israeli cargoes through the canal, once opened.

As a sign that he was determined to prevent anything from interfering with a quick agreement, Sadat again promised Kissinger he would not raise the Palestinian issue during the disengagement phase. However, he wanted to be sure that after he had secured Egypt's deal, Kissinger would then devote attention to securing an Israeli-Syrian disengagement. The Israeli-Egyptian deal would put pressure on Assad to negotiate with Israel, and once engaged, he could not then attack Sadat for the deal he had made. Sadat was therefore enthusiastic about Kissinger's idea of stopping off in Damascus after he had concluded the agreement to indicate that he was ready to do the same on the Syrian track. For Kissinger, this provided another reason for optimism. As he subsequently reported to the Israelis, "There is no doubt in my mind that Sadat will not wait for the Syrians to accept a plan he considers domestically bearable for himself."

Saturday, January 12, 1974, Jerusalem. Kissinger arrived in Israel at the end of Shabbat and helicoptered to Jerusalem. When he entered the lobby of the King David Hotel, he found it filled with American tourists waiting for him to arrive. To his delight, they greeted him by singing "Hevenu Shalom Aleichem" (We Bring Peace to You).

The King David is an iconic six-story hotel designed with strict symmetry and built in auburn Jerusalem limestone on a hill in West Jerusalem across from the Old City. It opened in 1931 and at first was famous for its sumptuous art deco furnishings and the royalty that frequented it. While serving as the headquarters for the British Mandate, the hotel gained international notoriety in 1946, when its southwest corner was demolished by a bomb planted by terrorists from Menachem Begin's Irgun. Ninety-one people died and forty-five were wounded. Subsequently, its broad terrace overlooking the walls of the Old City was memorialized in a scene from the movie *Exodus* in which Paul Newman as Ari Ben Canaan and Eva Marie Saint as Kitty Fremont had a rendezvous there.

Ensconced on the sixth floor in the presidential suite, Kissinger was treated to a stunning view of Jerusalem's Old City. Stretching across the panorama in front of him were its Ottoman crenellated ramparts, the Jaffa Gate, and the Tower of David, where General Edmund Allenby had proclaimed the Allied capture of Jerusalem during World War I. On the right, he could see Mount Zion, with its Dormition Abbey, and the sites of the Last Supper and King David's tomb. Beyond lay the rooftops and domes of the Armenian and Jewish quarters. In the far distance, he could discern the tower of the Church of the Holy Sepulcher in the Christian quarter, where Jesus Christ is believed to have been buried, and the Mount of Olives, from where he is believed to have ascended to Heaven. Hidden from Kissinger's view, on the slopes of the valley between Mount Zion and the Mount of Olives, was the Temple Mount, known to Muslims as the Haram al-Sharif (Noble Sanctuary), whose Western Wall is the holiest place in Judaism and whose Al-Aqsa Mosque is the third-holiest site in Islam.

The spirituality of this holy city, home to the three Abrahamic faiths, was palpable. And his sumptuous suite stood in stark contrast to his Soviet-style hotel room in Aswan. He resolved that if he was going to have to shuttle between Middle Eastern leaders, he would overnight at the King David in Jerusalem whenever possible.

Mrs. Meir was suffering from shingles and was not well enough to par-

Henry Kissinger takes in the panoramic view of the Old City of Jerusalem from his sixth-floor suite at the King David Hotel. He resolved on the spot that if he was going to have to shuttle between Middle Eastern leaders, he would overnight at the King David in Jerusalem whenever possible.

ticipate in his meetings, so Kissinger paid a courtesy call on her at the prime
minister's residence. Located a few blocks from the King David on the corner
of Balfour and Smolenskin Streets in the tony neighborhood of Rehavia, the
Bauhaus-style residence is on a plot of land too small even to have a garden. It
stands in stark contrast to the grandiose palaces of the leaders of Israel's Arab
neighbors, an expression of Israel's hardscrabble socialist origins that lingers
even though the country has long since grown rich on the talent of its people.
No prime minister has dared to suggest that a larger residence might be more
suitable for the leader of the most powerful country in the Middle East. The
modest abode had an L-shaped living and dining area that opened out onto
an inner courtyard. The prime minister's small, book-lined study, where Meir
met with Kissinger, was behind pocket doors.

Kissinger found her in fine sardonic form, questioning Sadat's honesty
and Assad's humanity. He told her that he had not raised the Israeli proposal
with Sadat, claiming that he spent his time instead "producing anxiety" over
whether he could deliver from the Israelis what Sadat expected. "He wants it
fast. He wants it done while I am here," Kissinger said.

He reported that Sadat had accepted his proposal that the limitations on
Egyptian armaments and deployments would be expressed in a letter from
Sadat to the U.S. president rather than in the agreement with Israel. Sadat
was also willing to accede to free passage for Israel-bound ships through Bab
el-Mandeb. However, in Kissinger's assessment, Sadat was unlikely to agree to
less than two divisions on the east bank or restrictions on SAM deployments.
Signaling that she would not easily accept his assessment of the limits of Sadat's
flexibility, Meir reminded him that he had underestimated Sadat before.

Kissinger returned to the King David for dinner with Allon, Dayan, Eban,
and the others on the Israeli team in the black wood-paneled Olive Room on
the basement level of the hotel. There his Israeli interlocutors stressed that
withdrawal to the eastern end of the passes, or even to the middle peaks, was
out of the question. They wanted to reserve that concession for a final peace
agreement. Kissinger did not press them because he sensed that he could persuade Sadat to concede the passes given his sense of urgency. And if the Israelis
were reserving their biggest territorial concessions for a final peace deal, they
could not complain if Sadat likewise reserved his political concessions, like
ending belligerency.

They then discussed whether to present Sadat with an Israeli map showing
their proposed line of withdrawal or something less. Kissinger was familiar
enough with Sadat's negotiating style that he decided it made sense to go with
their bottom line since Sadat, unlike Assad, did not believe in haggling. In
the end they settled on Kissinger's presenting two maps to Sadat, one offering a twenty-kilometer withdrawal in which Egypt would cede some of its

hard-won territory to UN control, and another reflecting the thirty-kilometer withdrawal that Dayan had first offered Kissinger in Washington. But they knew that he intended to spend little time with Sadat on the first map, except as a prop to bolster the impression that he had persuaded the Israelis to make a better offer.

On Sunday morning, after the cabinet had endorsed Dayan's proposal a second time, Kissinger sat down again with his Israeli interlocutors, who brought along General Elazar. Kissinger first treated them to a lesson on his role as mediator. He would not serve as "Israel's lawyer," arguing their case for them to Sadat. Instead, for the sake of his credibility, he would make clear that the proposal was Israeli, not American, and provide Sadat with his interpretation of Israeli thinking and his judgment on what changes might be acceptable and what would be out of the question. Then, in the same way, he would bring back Sadat's counteroffer for their consideration.

As Elazar briefed him on the Egyptian order of battle, Kissinger understood for the first time that Sadat had deployed 50 percent of his army on the east bank of the canal, including 70,000 infantry, 200 artillery pieces, and 720 tanks. How would he convince Sadat to order most of those forces back across the canal from territory they had liberated? And how could he exclude whole categories of weapons such as tanks and artillery from the east bank, as the Israelis were now insisting upon as part of the price for their withdrawal? "It's a massive movement and it's hard to justify as a unilateral decision," said Kissinger, knowing that was what Sadat would need to do lest he be seen as conceding to an Israeli demand. "His problem," he noted, "is what orders he has to give to his military and how he will look to them." He reassured the Israelis that, from the many hours he had spent with Sadat, he was convinced that he genuinely wanted a settlement. The question was "whether his domestic situation permits him to do what you think you require for your domestic situation."

Kissinger had captured the conundrum for would-be Middle East peacemakers: how to help Israeli and Arab leaders overcome the formidable domestic constraints to peacemaking. An Israeli leader's political limitations are so visible that American negotiators often wind up paying greater attention to them. Israel is a vibrant, some would say too vibrant, multiparty democracy in which the prime minister must cobble together a coalition government by making compromises to a host of small parties representing special-interest groups. President Clinton, a political junkie, was fascinated by the internecine maneuvering, making it his business to understand the fine points of Israeli religious party politics.

The domestic constraints on authoritarian Arab leaders, by contrast, are harder to discern because there is little visible internal debate. Their rubber-stamp parliaments and state-controlled press slavishly adhere to the leader's line. Sham elections, if they are held, usually produce 98 percent victories for the leader. Only at moments of extreme frustration, when the people defy the all-pervasive security services and take to the streets in protest, do outsiders gain a sense of the real state of public opinion. But that does not make the domestic constraints any less real for Arab leaders. Indeed, because they do not rule by consent of the governed and are quick to suppress dissent, they have no accurate means of gauging the views of their people. Consequently, they fear their publics more than Israeli leaders do theirs.

This problem has been exacerbated over many decades by their use of Israel as a means of distracting their people from their day-to-day woes. Because railing against the "Zionist entity" and "the Yahudis" reinforced popular antagonism toward the Israeli enemy, making peace required leaders to turn their people around. Sadat did this quite successfully through an Egyptian version of Franklin D. Roosevelt's fireside chats, aided by his ability to play on Egypt-first sentiments in the face of his Arab critics. When he chose to, Arafat was able to draw on his legitimacy as the Palestinian leader who had used violence to put his people's cause on the map to speak to them of the "peace of the brave." Even Assad, who had for decades fed his people a steady diet of anti-Zionist vituperation, when he eventually decided to make peace with Israel, began to educate them through billboards and speeches by his deputies to Ba'ath Party officials.*

None of this, however, makes the American peacemaker's conundrum any easier. In an environment of enmity, Israeli leaders find it very difficult to convince their people to make tangible concessions of territory to Arab neighbors whom they deeply distrust. When such concessions involve strategic real estate like the Sinai passes or the Golan Heights, or a biblical birthright like Judea and Samaria (the West Bank), the task becomes even more daunting. Similarly, Arab leaders require great courage to stand up to the inevitable accusations of their rivals for leadership in the Arab world that they are betraying the Arab or the Palestinian cause. Sadat and Rabin paid with their lives for daring to break the mold of conflict, both assassinated by their own citizens.

There is little that American leaders can do to help with public opinion. Clinton's spring 1996 intervention in Israeli politics to boost Shimon Peres

---

* Billboards across Damascus proclaimed, "We fought with dignity, we will make peace with dignity." Editorials explained Assad's "strategic choice" for peace. He also sent his foreign minister, Farouk al-Shara, to address the Revolutionary Council of the ruling Ba'ath Party and explain why Assad had decided to make peace. See Martin Indyk, *Innocent Abroad: An Intimate Account of American Peace Diplomacy in the Middle East* (New York: Simon & Schuster, 2009), 279.

probably only contributed to his electoral defeat to Benjamin Netanyahu. Clinton's speech in Gaza in December 1998 made little lasting difference to Israeli and Palestinian attitudes. Obama's attempt to win over the Muslim world through his Cairo speech in June 2009 alienated the Israeli public, which made it impossible for him to fulfill the promises he made to the Arabs about resolving the Israeli-Palestinian conflict, which in turn ended up alienating most of them as well.

Often the best a mediator can do is to sensitize each leader to the other's constraints and suggest ways they might help each other. But this is a heavy lift, since to make a public gesture to the other side usually requires reciprocation, otherwise the leader will be attacked for giving something and getting nothing in return.

The Oslo process was designed to build confidence through a series of interim steps and gradual Israeli military withdrawals over a five-year period. At the end of that process, both sides were meant to be more willing to undertake the difficult compromises involved in resolving the complex, emotional final-status issues such as Jerusalem and refugees. Instead, the Palestinians continued to commit acts of terror and violence against Israeli citizens and Israel continued to build settlements on territory supposedly reserved for the Palestinians. At the end of the interim period, instead of peace, they begat the second intifada, whose explosive violence raged for five years and destroyed all trust between the two sides. Kissinger understood this intuitively. Writing more than a decade before Oslo, he noted that "confidence is a precious commodity. Once plundered, it must grow again organically; it cannot be restored simply by an act of will or on the claim of national security."

Fortunately for Kissinger, in Sadat and Meir he was dealing with two strong leaders who could bring their people along when it came to digesting the small first step of an interim disengagement agreement. That underscored his wisdom in designing a process which did not require huge acts of courageous statesmanship. His sensitivity to the domestic constraints that impacted the political calculations of both leaders was an essential ingredient in his success. But, as we shall see, it would later reinforce his innate caution at a time when his Arab and Israeli interlocutors were willing to take bigger risks.

By early evening on January 13, when Kissinger met with Eban in his suite at the King David, he had already formulated his approach to this conundrum. He suggested that Israel might have to allow Sadat a small face-saving number of tanks remaining on the east bank, perhaps fifty to seventy-five. He said he would stand fast on the line of withdrawal, and he considered the Israeli political requirements reasonable as starting positions.* But, he argued, they needed to be ready for flexibility on the banning of whole categories of heavy weapons because he expected Sadat to reject it. He urged Eban, not the most persuasive of interlocutors with his harder-line colleagues, to explain that the consequences of failure meant more pressure on Israel. Eban allowed that there was some flexibility on troop numbers but not on tanks, or the line. "You know even our doves say they will reject it if there are any tanks," Eban emphasized.

Kissinger helicoptered to Dayan's residence in Zahala, a Tel Aviv neighborhood developed especially for IDF officers (Zahal is the Hebrew acronym for IDF). Dayan's backyard, where he had planned to host a garden party for Kissinger, had become infamous for the ancient archaeological artifacts he displayed there, some acquired by questionable means. For this occasion, Dayan had gathered a who's who of Israel's business, cultural, and religious elite as well as some West Bank mayors and senior army officers. Rain had forced them all inside, where excited guests mobbed Kissinger and some sought his autograph. At one point, General Elazar entered the room with a large map portfolio. Dayan took them both into his small study to show Kissinger the two maps of the line of withdrawal the IDF had prepared for his artifice. When Kissinger emerged, he looked pleased. He was actually bemused by Dayan's and Elazar's ingenuity and pride in producing a map he had no intention of selling to Sadat.

At 8:15 p.m., Kissinger was airborne again, headed back to Aswan with the maps and the Israeli proposal that he had taken so much care to prepare and package. It had taken relentless verbal bludgeoning and blandishments, threats of isolation, and offers to conspire to move the Israelis to concede that they had to give up hard-won Arab territory. Now he had an offer from them that he believed he could convince Sadat to accept.

Monday, January 14, 1974, Aswan. At 10:00 a.m., Sadat met Kissinger in the gazebo in the backyard of his villa, wearing a heavy double-breasted military overcoat despite the warmth of a glorious day. After a few minutes, he took Kissinger inside so that he could view the maps. Kissinger wasted little time with the first map, especially after Sadat, as predicted, rejected the idea of ceding any Egyptian territory, even to UN control. Instead, he focused on Israel's

---

* The Israeli proposal demanded explicit assurances that Sadat would clear the canal, rebuild the canal cities, permit Israeli shipping through the canal, and end the state of belligerency. Kissinger had already made clear that the first two requirements were achievable, the third would have to start with Israeli cargoes through the canal, and the fourth was something he would not even attempt.

insistence that its army stay on the western side of the Sinai passes. He claimed again that the Israeli cabinet was divided and having difficulty reaching agreement. While that might have seemed plausible, given the normally divisive nature of Israeli politics, as we know, it was untrue.

As he explained the other elements of the Israeli proposal, Sadat, who had no mind for details, interrupted him and asked if Fahmy and el-Gamasy could join them. They adjourned to the dining room where, for the first time, Kissinger and his aides sat across the table from Sadat and his advisers. Kissinger updated the others on their conversation, claiming that he, rather than Sadat, had rejected the first Israeli map. He maintained that the Israelis had wanted him to present the map and then come back to them, but he had refused. "I couldn't face Sadat with this proposal."

He showed the Egyptians the second map and told them that, in his opinion, the line of withdrawal depicted there was in fact Israel's bottom line. Sadat in turn insisted that he could not retreat from any Egyptian territory his army had liberated from Israel, and he could not accept the southern part of the line, which would have to be adjusted at Ras Sudar at the southern end of the canal.

Wanting them to believe he was on their side, Kissinger argued that they had the right to expect the line to be straightened in the south and he would strongly urge it when he returned to Israel. In this way, he distracted them from arguing about the passes, which he judged he had to deliver for Israel.

As for Egyptian troops on the east bank, he claimed to have told the Israelis that their demand for only three battalions was impossible. "That's right," said Sadat, taking his pipe out of his mouth in order to nod vigorously. When Kissinger outlined the artillery restrictions, it was el-Gamasy's turn: "Impossible!" Kissinger was quick to agree. "Quite right," Sadat added with emphasis.

After asserting with a straight face that the Israeli proposal had "caused us unbelievable anguish to produce," Kissinger provided his judgment: the number of battalions should be increased (though he was careful not to say by how many). Then he ticked off Israel's other requirements, which Sadat rejected as "ridiculous" because they were "political issues." Having adopted the same negative posture as his aides, Sadat suggested they form working committees to go over the details. But, realizing that would quickly lead to stalemate, he thought better of the idea. First, he said, he had to reach agreement with Kissinger on the principles, which would then guide the committees' work.

Sadat had provided Kissinger with an opening to separate him from his advisers again. They adjourned to the study. Back on the ivory-colored settee, Kissinger drew on the same tactic he had used to good effect in November to persuade Sadat to go for a large disengagement rather than insist on the October 22 line. Knowing Sadat was in a hurry, he suggested that he had to decide how fast he wanted to move. A prolonged negotiation might produce a better agreement. He could mobilize pressure on Israel to improve the details. But Sadat ran the risk that other events would intervene. The Soviets would be looking to undermine the whole negotiation by proposing a better deal since they bore no responsibility for delivering it, Arab radicals would side with their Soviet patron, and divisions in the Israeli cabinet could lead to extended haggling. In any case, in his judgment, he did not believe there was any chance that Israel would agree to vacate the passes in the first phase of disengagement.

Sadat sat silently, puffing on his pipe. Then he wondered out loud why the Israelis would seek to humiliate el-Gamasy. He noted that if he wanted to attack, he could put hundreds of tanks across the canal in one night, and if he didn't, it made no difference how many tanks were on the east bank. Kissinger explained that the Israelis needed to show they secured something in return for what would in fact be a unilateral withdrawal.

Then after another silent interval of several more minutes, which seemed like an age to Kissinger, Sadat suddenly made his move. As Kissinger would later relate it to the Israelis, Sadat said, "Let's go fast. You tell me very fairly what the Israelis say they cannot accept. But," he said, "I cannot accept everything."

Kissinger reiterated that the line of withdrawal was unchangeable. Just like that, Sadat conceded that the Israelis could stay on the west side of the passes. However, he could not accept the idea that Egypt's main line of defense was on the canal and that the land Egypt had captured on the east bank was treated as a forward zone. He had a creative solution: there should be only two lines—the Egyptian line and the Israeli line—with the UN buffer zone between them. Force limitations should be described by distances from those lines.

He wanted to keep ten battalions across the canal (the Israelis proposed two or three), but he would accept whatever Kissinger could deliver. He insisted his tanks be kept on the east bank, but he would again leave it to Kissinger to define the number. Kissinger said the best he could do would be fifty, but "thirty would be safer." Refusing to haggle, Sadat said he would accept any number as long as the agreement upheld the principle that Egyptian forces were not barred from Egyptian territory.

Sadat was deploying a typical tactic of the bazaar. "You decide what's a fair price," says the merchant to his customer, appearing to put his faith in the better angels of the buyer's nature and making him look mean-spirited if he does not reciprocate. By putting himself in Kissinger's hands, Sadat was in effect committing the mediator to achieve a reasonable outcome for him, but also giving him the means to clinch the deal. It was, in Kissinger's view, "vintage Sadat, brave and calculating, at once trusting and devious."

Sadat had one caveat: none of this could be expressed in a direct commitment to Israel. He suggested that Kissinger formulate it as an American proposal that both sides could then accept. He was willing to express his intentions in a letter to Nixon that included passage of Israeli cargoes through Bab el-Mandeb and the Suez Canal. He would reopen the canal and rebuild the cities, but this had to be seen as his own decision, not as a concession to Israel. He would provide Kissinger with oral assurances about that and about demobilization of his soldiers, as long as Israel demobilized too. He ruled out an end to the state of belligerency, and Kissinger accepted that with equanimity.

Sadat had just done Kissinger a huge favor. Focusing on the big picture, he was ready to settle for a thirty-kilometer withdrawal of Israeli forces, limitations on his armaments and forces, and the necessary assurances to Israel, provided they were presented as sovereign Egyptian decisions. Acceptance of these reduced the outstanding issues to the size of forces and the deployment of their armaments within the zones.

However, while Kissinger was savoring Sadat's largesse in the study, el-Gamasy and Fahmy were working themselves into a lather in the dining room as they dissected the Israeli proposal with Sisco and Rodman. Fahmy portrayed the Israeli proposal as an effort "to guarantee their safety and diminish our safety. It's useless," he said. El-Gamasy expressed his frustration too. With such force restrictions, "we can do better with police than with these three battalions!"

After their meeting, Kissinger and Sadat reentered the dining room. At Sadat's request, Kissinger summarized their understandings and announced that they had decided to move quickly. The working groups would convene to draw up the documents and Kissinger would return to Israel that evening.

In his summary, Kissinger had purposely skirted the actual limitations on forces within the zones, simply noting that he knew Sadat's thinking on those issues. They would be left blank in the draft documents, leaving it to Sadat to break the unwelcome news to his unhappy advisers of what he had just agreed to with Kissinger. Vagueness had become a momentary virtue.

Fahmy and el-Gamasy were fuming. Sadat had repudiated his chief diplomat's advice and, in Fahmy's view, damaged both Egypt and the Arab cause. Fahmy would eventually resign in November 1977, when Sadat announced his decision to travel to Jerusalem. But his disillusionment with Sadat began that day in Aswan. As noted earlier, he already had a jaundiced view of Kissinger, but this experience in Aswan also convinced him of Kissinger's "rather insidious and devious style"; according to Fahmy, he was not the honest broker he claimed to be. Fahmy understood that there was little he could do once his leader had made up his mind, so he resolved to do his best to prevent Kissinger from inserting any political language in the agreement on Israel's behalf, "and particularly nothing that departed from the basic Arab position concerning peace with Israel."

El-Gamasy's problem stemmed from his sense of responsibility as the head of Egypt's armed forces. Sadat had already made it clear that he intended to use his chief of staff, who had become a hero to his soldiers and the Egyptian people, to legitimize the disengagement deal. According to Kissinger, Sadat had called el-Gamasy into their first meeting in Aswan and informed him, "Dr. Kissinger and I have agreed on how to proceed to an agreement." And then he issued a direct order: "You, Gamasy, will sign it!" El-Gamasy had tried to persuade Sadat to replace him with General Ahmed Ismail who, as minister of war, was better placed to assume responsibility. But Sadat would hear nothing of it. For now, el-Gamasy would salute and bear it; later Sadat would reward his loyalty by promoting him to minister of war.

It took the American team three hours to prepare the two draft documents. During that time, Kissinger and Fahmy sunned themselves on the terrace of the Old Cataract Hotel, a grand British colonial edifice that had grown shabby and fallen into disrepair, eclipsed by its new, gauche Soviet sister. As they sat there in full view of the press, they chatted and joked as if they were the best of friends.

When the drafts were ready for their consideration, they sat with el-Gamasy and their advisers in the cavernous dining room in the New Cataract Hotel with its two-story-high windows looking across the hotel swimming pool to Elephantine. The documents were short and straightforward, each

Henry Kissinger and Egyptian foreign minister Ismail Fahmy sun themselves on the terrace of the Old Cataract Hotel in Aswan, Egypt, on January 15, 1974, while they wait for their teams to prepare the draft documents for the Sinai disengagement agreement.

some two pages of double-spaced type, the first labeled "An Egyptian-Israeli Disengagement of Forces," the second labeled "U.S. Proposal."

Scrutinizing the first document, Fahmy demanded that the words "refrain from . . . belligerent actions" be removed from the first paragraph. He was determined to avoid anything that might look like "end of belligerency." Kissinger had warned the Israelis that this was a bridge too far for a military disengagement agreement, so he accepted Fahmy's deletion.

While this calmed Fahmy down, el-Gamasy remained visibly agitated. He wanted to avoid anything in the Israeli-Egyptian agreement that would indicate Egypt had accepted specific arms limitations. Fahmy suggested instead language that would provide a cover: "Egypt will regroup its forces on the eastern side." Kissinger was happy to go along with such wordsmithing if it would help the bitter medicine go down.

The second document proved easier to agree on because it left all the force limitation numbers blank. El-Gamasy objected to the distance of the SAMs on the west bank from the Egyptian front line because it would reduce their ability to protect Egyptian forces. He suggested the zones should be no-fly zones for both air forces.

Kissinger knew he couldn't sell that to the Israelis, but rather than argue with el-Gamasy, he said he would discuss it with Sadat. The implication that Kissinger could go over his head to appeal to a higher authority offended the proud officer. As the meeting concluded, he walked out in a huff, noting ominously that he couldn't justify the agreement on military grounds.

When Kissinger returned to the villa to take his leave of Sadat, he found him no longer interested in the redrafted documents. El-Gamasy had briefed him on their meeting at the hotel and registered his strong objections to the force limitations, but Sadat had already made up his mind. Kissinger knew Egypt's requirements; he should do his best to achieve them, he said.

To give him an additional incentive, Sadat told Kissinger that he intended to remove Soviet Foxbat reconnaissance planes from Egyptian soil. Instead, surveillance of the agreement could be carried out by American reconnaissance aircraft flying over Egyptian territory at irregular intervals. He again promised to terminate the Soviet-Egyptian Friendship Treaty in two years (which he did). And in a gesture of personal confidence in Kissinger, he asked him to provide an American surveillance expert to ensure the Soviets were no longer able to bug his office.

All that not only whet Kissinger's competitive appetite, it also would remove a Soviet intelligence advantage that had handicapped his decision making during the war and its aftermath. Beyond the details of the disengagement agreement, Sadat was reminding Kissinger of the strategic value of his decision to shift from the Soviet to the American camp. Kissinger understood his intention. He was "luring America into pressing Israel for concessions." But this was not by adopting an intransigent posture; rather it was by acting with a generosity of spirit.

Monday, January 14, 1974, Jerusalem. As Kissinger and his team departed Aswan on Air Force Two, the effervescent Joe Sisco donned his shaggy yellow golf cardigan and sauntered back to the press cabin where, mimicking a flight steward, he hailed the American journalists with a greeting that would go down in history. "Welcome aboard the Egyptian-Israeli shuttle!"*

Kissinger arrived back in Israel at 11:00 p.m. that night, to be greeted by a violent rainstorm. The weather in the Holy Land is normally temperate, but because of its location on the eastern shore of the Mediterranean, winter storms tend to be biblical in their proportions. When it rains, it pours and the wind comes whistling in from the sea, while the thunder rolls on like waves. In Jerusalem, nestled in the mountains, it often snows too.

Unable to take a helicopter to Jerusalem, Kissinger rode up the mountain by car, briefing Eban on the forty-five-minute drive from the newly named Ben Gurion Airport, past the monastery and British fort at Latrun, where a decisive battle during Israel's War of Independence had been fought, through Bab el-Wad, the gates to the steep valley where the road ascends through the mountains to Jerusalem. At the King David, they were joined by Dinitz in Kissinger's sixth-floor suite. To his delight, the Israelis did not respond to his briefing with their usual wrangling. Instead, they expressed astonishment at the progress he had made. Dinitz was especially surprised to hear that Sadat had insisted on only thirty tanks on the east bank.

As expected, Allon and Dayan subjected him to a detailed cross-examination when he met them and the other team members in the cabinet room at the prime minister's office, located on the western side of Jerusalem. The building was an unadorned, sandy limestone rectangular box, only three floors high. It was part of a compound of characterless government buildings. The cabinet room is situated on the second floor, adjacent to the prime minister's private office. It has since been renovated with tan leather boardroom chairs flanking a large, yellow maple wood conference table. In those days, Israel's socialist origins dictated more austere furnishings. For security reasons, the windows were

* In February 1974, Kissinger appointed Sisco his under secretary of state for policy, the number three position in the State Department. By then Sisco had already become his principal adviser on Middle East policy. Three months earlier he had discussed the appointment with Scowcroft. Both agreed that Sisco was not suitable for the job. "I just don't consider him steady enough," said Kissinger. "What worries me is if I go off on trips and Sisco is here alone, I would hate to think what he would do." Kissinger dealt with his anxiety by taking Sisco on all his Middle East trips. See Telcon between Kissinger and Scowcroft, November 25, 1973, KA11645, NSA.

high above eye level, allowing Jerusalem's golden light to enter but obscuring the halcyon views across the valley to Mount Herzl, where Israel's founders and fallen soldiers are buried.

Kissinger gave the ministers a lawyerly account of Sadat's reactions to Israel's requirements. He also gave a fanciful version of what had transpired on the force limitation issue, designed to portray Kissinger as bargaining hard for Israel's requirements. He claimed that in the morning Sadat had insisted on one and a half divisions, but by evening Kissinger had managed to reduce his requirements to ten battalions. He ran through el-Gamasy's objections, avowing that his "explosions" were genuine. He related how el-Gamasy had tried to wash his hands of responsibility for the agreement.

He explained that Sadat considered it inconceivable that there could be no tanks on the east bank given their importance to the infantry that would remain there. It was a question of morale, not military force. Kissinger claimed Sadat had started at two hundred and then offered one hundred and then said that the absolute minimum was thirty. He depicted himself as negotiating Sadat down even though, as we know, Sadat was content to let Kissinger decide the number, as long as it wasn't zero.

He enunciated Sadat's idea that only artillery that could reach Israel's line should be excluded from the east bank. That allowed for howitzers that had a maximum range of twelve kilometers to stay there. In return, Sadat wanted Israeli artillery withdrawn thirty kilometers from Israel's forward line.

"He wants his artillery to cover his forces but does not give us the privilege," Dayan objected. Kissinger corrected him. Sadat had accepted the principle that both sides could cover their own forward line but not reach the other's forward line. "Your 155s can cover your forward line from the range of eighteen kilometers," Kissinger parried. Impressed by Kissinger's mastery of the details of artillery ranges, Dayan conceded, "You are right, Mr. Secretary."

Allon objected to Sadat's requirement that ten battalions be left on the east bank. Kissinger said Sadat would accept nine but not five. He added, "Eight, I don't know. It has to be something he can say is a division." Kissinger had cleverly inserted the number he felt he needed that came close to what the Israelis wanted but was not a major climbdown for Sadat.

Kissinger then read out loud the two agreements and ran through the side understandings. "I will take back anything you want me to, but I have the impression that we are at the outer edge of what is possible," he warned them as he concluded his presentation.

Dayan wanted to understand the rationale for Sadat's demand for an adjustment of the line in the south. Kissinger explained that Sadat regarded it as too close to Suez and that he needed to be able to say he hadn't just accepted the Israeli line. Kissinger recommended they consider it, bearing in mind that "thirty tanks and some adjustment to this line is of extreme psychological importance to him."

Allon asked whether Sadat had sought assurances on the "ultimate settlement." Kissinger insisted that the only assurance Sadat sought was on the implementation of the agreement. He allowed that Sadat could be engaged in deception and that after the disengagement he might go back to the Russians "and start screaming for the 1967 borders," but he hadn't prepared the ground for that and it didn't fit with his declared aversion to Geneva.

In summing up, Kissinger noted with deliberate understatement, "I personally don't consider this proposal all that disadvantageous to you." Not wanting to look like they were easy customers, the Israelis were sparing in their praise. They left it to Eban to comment, "You didn't waste your time."

When they reconvened for lunch at Eban's home, three hours later, however, the attitude was quite different. Allon opened the discussion by praising Kissinger for "achieving great progress," and declared that they saw "no reason why there cannot be a signing at Kilometer 101 on Friday." Dayan said that Elazar was at headquarters considering what they could do about the line in the south.

On forces, Allon said that officially Kissinger should offer Sadat six battalions, but unofficially they would accept eight. As for tanks, "we accept the number of thirty tanks, and not one more," Allon said, making it sound like a huge concession. Kissinger couldn't help a note of sarcasm, "You think you can handle that?" But, as he observes in his memoirs, "with this, everything fell into place."

They turned to the emotional issue of the Israeli POWs in Syrian custody. As the Israeli ministers began to contemplate selling the agreement to the Knesset and the Israeli public, they sought to link the release of the remaining eighty-six Egyptian POWs they still held to receiving the Israeli POW list from Syria. He argued that Israel had to decide what was more important, domestic public opinion or a strategic breakthrough. He pointed out the absurdity of their position: "For years, you have complained that the Egyptians don't care about prisoners; now you get an Egyptian leader who does care, and you won't do it?" Dayan said the Knesset would not accept it. "Then it will fail," Kissinger said. Dayan suggested Kissinger discuss it with Meir, since she would be the one who would have to defend the agreement in the Knesset.

When he entered her Balfour Street residence later in the evening, the prime minister greeted him with her ultimate compliment, "You did well." Kissinger returned the kudos: "Every time you give me a proposal that I consider outrageous, he [Sadat] accepts it."

It didn't take long, however, for her skeptical side to assert itself. She asked Kissinger whether he thought Sadat was acting in good faith. Looking back over forty-five years of Egyptian adherence to its peace treaty with Israel, it is easy to dismiss this question as an indication of Meir's suspicious nature. But remember that she and Israel were still suffering from the trauma of the October surprise. Nasser had deceived them in 1970 when he moved the SAM missiles up to the canal zone, an act of cheating for which Israeli soldiers and pilots had just paid a severe price. Now Sadat had fooled them by launching a war they did not see coming. Even though her hubris was to blame for that, since Sadat had warned her enough times, it nevertheless made her doubly wary of his craftiness.

Kissinger's response to her question is interesting. He allowed that he wasn't sure. Unlike Meir, he now had the advantage of many hours of dialogue with Sadat. He was about to become the beneficiary of Sadat's trust in him and his generosity of spirit, which would be manifested in the breakthrough he was engineering. And Sadat had already demonstrated his anti-Soviet, pro-American bona fides by restricting the role of the Geneva Conference with its Soviet cosponsorship. He was about to throw out the Soviet Foxbats that provided them with valuable intelligence. He even offered to delay the reopening of the Suez Canal if that would better serve American interests.

And yet Kissinger had his doubts. Her question seems to have forced the high-wire trapeze artist to look down and realize the precariousness of his situation. Driven by his own insecurities and history's lessons about diplomatic betrayals, he was riven by concerns about Arab intentions and the fear of Israeli vulnerability. Hence his cautious, step-by-step strategy, and his allergy to comprehensive peace solutions. If Sadat's gestures turned out to be part of an elaborate ruse, Kissinger would suffer the consequences in terms of his reputation and his claim to be Israel's protector. The United States would be exposed as unreliable at a moment of acute vulnerability brought on by Watergate and the demise in Vietnam.

Still he offered Meir reassurance. Sadat had confided in him that he was contemplating high-level secret political contacts with Israel.* And there was the conversation over lunch in Aswan when Sadat had said, "I really want to make peace with Israel." But, he told her, Sadat has his doubts too. "Does Israel really want a moderate leader of a strong Egypt or a fanatic leader of a weak Egypt?" he had wondered.

She was quick to answer, "We don't want a weak Egypt. We want Egypt developing." She noted that opening the canal and rebuilding the cities there

---

* The first known secret contacts took place some three years later, when Sadat sent Hassan Tuhami to meet with Dayan in Morocco, a meeting that paved the way for Sadat's visit to Jerusalem.

were the best guarantee of Sadat's peaceful intent. Kissinger responded that Sadat was ready to give him a pledge in that regard which he would then convey to her as an American assurance. He said Sadat had asked for a written guarantee that if he rebuilt the cities Israel wouldn't bomb them, which was another indication of his intent.

Slowly but surely, Kissinger was generating an indirect exchange between the two leaders that would help build confidence in the intentions of each toward the other and thereby reduce his own exposure as well.

Kissinger reminded her that he was in Israel's corner, fighting to break the Arab coalition, divide the Euro-Japanese-Russian coalition that wanted to pressure Israel, and lift the oil embargo "without mentioning the 1967 frontiers." Later in the conversation he would say, "What I am proudest of is getting all this without saying anything about the next step." The guarantee against Sadat's duplicity lay in limiting Israel's risk. That was the essence of Kissinger's gradualist approach.

They then turned to the Israeli POWs in Syria. Meir was clearly worried about the way the families were seeking to link their loved ones' fate to the release of Egyptian prisoners. But she accepted the logic of Kissinger's argument against linking the agreement to the POWs. Despite her shingles, her shoulders were still broad enough to take on this burden of leadership.

This conversation represented a turning point in their relationship. Perhaps her illness had softened her, or the need to reach an agreement that would bring reservists and POWs home had rendered her more flexible. But there is no doubt that Kissinger's power of persuasion had helped convince her of the necessity of ceding some territory.

Wednesday, January 16, 1974, Jerusalem–Aswan. At 8:30 a.m., Allon, Dayan, and Eban met Kissinger again in the cabinet room at the prime minister's office. Dayan opened by showing Kissinger the adjustment to the line in southern Sinai that Sadat had requested.* Dayan said that he had to overrule Elazar's objections. Clearly el-Gamasy was not the only general who was discomfited by the political decisions that were being made.

Kissinger then read out loud the entire Israeli-amended draft. As he read, he noticed that the ministers had reinserted language Fahmy had previously insisted on removing, substituting the word "hostile" for the word "belligerent." Kissinger made clear he would not insist on including the word "hostile" if Sadat objected.

---

* The IDF would move off a promontory and deploy two kilometers southward so that Israeli forces would be out of sight of Suez city.

He predicted "massive problems" with the Israeli language on artillery.* He pointed out that Sadat had already accepted the twenty-five-kilometer range limitations for SAMs but noted the Israelis were still insisting on thirty kilometers. He warned that Sadat might not want to overrule el-Gamasy again.

The Israeli language also stipulated that there would be no more than seven thousand Egyptian troops in Sinai. Kissinger wanted to know where that number came from. Dayan explained that the cabinet wanted a specific ceiling of troop numbers rather than just the number of battalions. This would become a classic problem in Arab-Israeli negotiations. Where the Arabs wanted vagueness to protect themselves from criticism for making too many concessions to Israel, the Israelis wanted specificity to protect themselves from what they feared would be deception.

Kissinger then went through Israel's wish list of nine separate assurances that would make up the accompanying U.S.-Israeli MOU.† The Israeli approach to assurances could be taken as a barometer of Israeli trust of Kissinger. In the Sinai II Agreement, which Kissinger negotiated in 1975, there were twenty-five separate assurances that Israel sought from the United States.

The last assurance Israel asked for this time was an American commitment "to make every effort to be fully responsive on *a continuing and long-term basis* to Israel's military requirements [emphasis added]." As down payment on this commitment, Israel wanted $200 million in economic assistance and a $500 million arms package.‡ An additional $700 million in aid would require a presidential determination. Kissinger was confident he could get it if he returned home with an agreement. If so, Kissinger would be establishing the precedent that tied Israeli concessions in the peace process to long-term infusions of military assistance, including advanced weapons systems, to reduce the risks Israel was undertaking.

Notwithstanding their belt-and-suspenders approach, Kissinger could see that he had what he needed from the Israelis: agreement to thirty tanks and eight battalions on the east bank of the canal, an adjustment of the line in Egypt's favor, and no insistence on an end to the state of belligerency. The

---

* The Israeli version declared that there could be no more than thirty tanks, no artillery except anti-tank guns, no weapons capable of interfering with the other party's flights over its own territory, and no fixed installations for missile sites; and the entire force of each party should not exceed seven thousand men (i.e., eight battalions of 875 men each, roughly the size of an Israeli battalion). In addition, in areas thirty kilometers on either side of the Egyptian and Israeli lines, there would be no weapons that could reach the other line, and no SAMs.
† The Israelis sought assurances on passage of Israeli cargoes through Bab el-Mandeb and the canal, the opening of the canal and the rebuilding of the cities and towns alongside it, the demobilization of Egyptian forces, a U.S. veto of any attempt by the UN Security Council to withdraw the UN monitoring forces, and a commitment to conduct aerial reconnaissance to ensure compliance with the agreement.
‡ The request included four hundred tanks and eight hundred APCs, as well as advanced weapons systems, including Lance mobile short-range ballistic missiles.

problem remained the restrictions on artillery and SAMs, but on these issues, he hoped he could rely on Sadat's sense of urgency to overcome el-Gamasy's objections.

Kissinger informed the Israeli ministers that he hoped to reach agreement with Sadat and return to Jerusalem the same night (i.e., Wednesday), announce the agreement simultaneously in Washington, Aswan, and Jerusalem on Thursday, and have it signed at Kilometer 101 on Friday. The Israelis were now so close to achieving their goals that the desire for agreement, and the accompanying demobilization of the Israeli reserve soldiers, eclipsed their penchant for endless negotiating.

Kissinger arrived in Aswan in the early afternoon. Fahmy picked him up at the military terminal and took him straight to Sadat's villa. Kissinger and Sadat repaired to his study, leaving Fahmy and el-Gamasy in the garden to cool their heels in the company of Sisco and Saunders.

Kissinger revealed the concessions he had secured from the Israelis, describing how he had wrestled them up from forty-five hundred to seven thousand men in eight battalions and salvaged thirty tanks too. He said the Israelis were immovable on the thirty-kilometer limit for the SAM deployments, even though Sadat had insisted on twenty-five kilometers. According to Kissinger's account, Sadat told him he would eventually accept the Israeli demand, but because el-Gamasy was so upset about it, he wanted him to try once more with the Israelis. If he failed, Sadat would not let the agreement collapse because of that.

Revealing one's fallback position to the mediator naturally removes his incentive to secure the original requirement. This was certainly true for Kissinger, no matter how grateful he was for Sadat's flexibility. It was a goodwill gesture on Sadat's part, but it also meant that whatever he gained in the big picture, in terms of promoting his relationship with the United States, he would end up paying for in concessions on these smaller details.

Sadat's preference in any case was to leave el-Gamasy and Fahmy to deal with the details, so Kissinger again repaired to the ugly dining room with the beautiful view in the New Cataract Hotel, where they awaited him. Their mood was already sour but quickly turned foul when they read the new version of the two documents.

Fahmy first addressed the letter that Nixon would write to Sadat outlining his understanding that Sadat intended to clear the canal and resume "normal economic activities in the area." In return, Fahmy wanted a U.S. guarantee that Israel would not attack the canal cities. Kissinger countered with an "assurance." Fahmy accepted.

Fahmy objected to any reference to Israeli ships in the assurance Sadat would give Nixon about free passage through the Bab el-Mandeb Strait. He preferred a generic assurance to apply to all ships. Kissinger knew that Israel would object but he let it ride for the moment.

As Kissinger had predicted, Fahmy objected to the word "hostile" in the first paragraph of the disengagement agreement, asserting that it was "belligerency" in another guise. Kissinger offered to change it to "paramilitary" if Fahmy would agree to keep the reference to Israeli ships and cargoes in Sadat's letter to Nixon. Fahmy conceded. Kissinger had given up something he knew he could not get for something he really needed.

Now it was el-Gamasy's turn. He objected to the specific exclusion of Egyptian artillery from the east bank because it would expose his infantry remaining there. Kissinger promised to argue for howitzers and mortars on the east bank.

El-Gamasy turned to the issue of SAM redeployments. He had wanted to deploy them fifteen kilometers west of the Egyptian line. Kissinger laughed and said the Israelis were insisting on forty. El-Gamasy thought Kissinger was laughing at his concerns and turned surly. "I think I will leave my job after I sign this," he said with wounded pride. Fahmy rushed to his defense: "I would prefer no agreement, politically speaking. And he can't face his people in the army."

El-Gamasy drew a map for Kissinger showing the canal and the Egyptian forward line ten kilometers to the east. The maximum range for the SAMs was thirty kilometers, but the effective range was twenty-four, he explained. If they had to stay thirty kilometers back, there would only be partial coverage for the Egyptian forces on the east bank. "We can explain it to our civilians by any means but not to our armed forces," said el-Gamasy with a downcast gaze. "It is suicide," Fahmy quickly added.

Noting that Sadat had asked him to press the Israelis for twenty-five kilometers, Kissinger said, "I tried and couldn't. But I can try again." El-Gamasy became emotionally wrought by the tension between duty to his president and loyalty to his men: "I don't want to sign this alone. I am a representative of the armed forces." As he mentioned his cherished soldiers whom he had led across the canal in battle, he became overwhelmed by his emotions. He excused himself.

As el-Gamasy records in his memoirs, it was the unfairness of it all that set him off. He could not believe that Sadat had accepted only seven thousand troops and thirty tanks on the east bank. "You're giving Israel what would guarantee the security of its forces and denying us everything that would safeguard our forces," he remembers telling Kissinger. He rejected the numbers. "I do not approve this, and I cannot as chief of staff of the armed forces justify it to our forces," he declared angrily. He felt humiliated that Sadat had not bothered to consult him before accepting. "I left the meeting room angry, with tears in my eyes," he writes.

Fahmy was deeply affected by the sight of Egypt's most senior general crying. "You have to help him with the army," he beseeched Kissinger. "It is becoming very dangerous. . . . Even if the President approves this, he will find it very hard with the army later on," Fahmy said gravely. But Kissinger knew what Fahmy did not: that Sadat had already accepted twenty-five kilometers if Kissinger could not persuade the Israelis to accept more.

Having mastered his emotions, el-Gamasy returned to the table. Kissinger tried to flatter him by calling him "an honorable man," but el-Gamasy was not appeased. Kissinger knew that Dayan would accept howitzers on the east bank. "What do you consider more important," he asked, "the howitzers or the twenty-five kilometers?" El-Gamasy tried again for thirty kilometers but Kissinger was insistent: "Thirty kilometers I cannot get. Twenty-five kilometers, I will try." In reply, el-Gamasy told Kissinger he needed the 122 mm howitzers.

Now that he had el-Gamasy where he needed him, Kissinger offered reassurance. He noted that if Egypt wanted to return to war, it would take only four hours to move five divisions under SAM and artillery cover across the canal. "This is no basic handicap to you; it is just an irritation," he argued. "The major objective is to establish a climate of trust," he said, trying to persuade el-Gamasy and Fahmy to look at the bigger picture. "If you look at Israeli history, never have they gone back . . . under Arab military pressure and Arab political pressure: this is an enormous psychological change."

The idea that Egypt should make concessions to treat Israel's psychoses provoked Fahmy's prickly side. He declared that from the Egyptian point of view all these concessions to Israel's insecurities were "nonsense!" Sadat was only doing it to build his relationship with the United States; Kissinger had a responsibility to reciprocate. "We sign with the United States, and don't forget this," he said archly, his voice rising. "The U.S. and Egypt, *not* Israel and Egypt [emphasis added]."

Fortunately for Kissinger, Sadat did not share the attitudes of his advisers. When he returned to the villa, he learned that Sadat had already been briefed on their outbursts and was determined to distance himself from them. "My army!" said Sadat. "First I had trouble convincing them to go to war. Now I have trouble persuading them to make peace." He encouraged Kissinger to do the best he could with the Israelis. And then he sought to address the very psychological dimensions that his foreign minister had just derisively dismissed.

He wanted Kissinger to tell Meir that even though she had conceded his right to deploy the thirty tanks on the east bank of the canal, he would not exercise it. He wanted the Israelis and his own generals and diplomats to understand that he had no intention of going back to war. Kissinger's astonishment at that goodwill gesture was compounded by Sadat's next move. He asked him to take a personal message to the Israeli prime minister, designed specifically to address her doubts about his intentions:

> You must take my word seriously. When I made my initiative in 1971, I meant it. When I threatened war, I meant it. When I talk of peace now, I mean it. We never have had contact before. We now have the services of Dr. Kissinger. Let us use him and talk to each other through him.

With all his back-channel experience, Kissinger had never imagined it might be possible to set up a back channel between Sadat and Meir. Yet again, Sadat was ahead of him.

After only seven hours on the ground in Aswan, Kissinger's shuttle took off again for Tel Aviv. From the plane, he sent a message to Nixon via Scowcroft reporting that "we are on the verge of an agreement." He outlined the plan for a simultaneous announcement that he recommended the president make on the next day, Thursday, January 17, at 3:00 p.m., Washington time. The agreement itself, he confidently predicted, would be signed by the Egyptian and Israeli chiefs of staff on January 18 at Kilometer 101.

Thursday, January 17, 1974, Jerusalem. Eban and Dinitz were too excited to wait until the morning for the debrief, so they went to Kissinger's suite at the King David at midnight and stayed there for two hours going over the Egyptian responses. Kissinger barely got four hours' sleep. When he awoke, he was presented with a serene sight through the panoramic windows. The roofs and walls of the Old City and the valley below were blanketed by a foot of snow, giving silent expression to the peace he was seeking to build. Unable to travel to the prime minister's office, Dayan arranged military transportation to bring the ministers and the chief of staff to him. At 9:30 a.m. they convened in his suite, sitting around the black lacquered dining room table, with the snow-covered backdrop of the Old City for inspiration.

Kissinger began by reporting on his conversation with Sadat, including the Egyptian president's message to the Israeli prime minister. Sadat had also promised to raise the issue of the Israeli POW lists when he traveled to Damascus to explain the agreement. Kissinger then revealed Sadat's bold gesture "to keep thirty [tanks] until the disengagement is completed, and then remove them [from the east bank]." He told them of el-Gamasy's anger but noted that Sadat was prepared to take the responsibility. He conveyed Sadat's promise to start clearing the canal the day the IDF completed its redeployment from the west bank and estimated it would take four to six months (it took eighteen months to reopen the canal). Sadat was also willing to undertake a substantial demobilization if Israel did too.

Kissinger then ran through the details of road openings, force redeployment timetables, and prisoner exchanges. Finally, he brought out the redrafted disengagement agreement and pointed out the word change in paragraph A from "hostile" to "paramilitary." Allon asked his team whether there was any objection. "It is better than nothing," said Dayan. And that was the end of the Israeli attempt to insert some expression of non-belligerency in the agreement. Kissinger should have savored the moment. The issue would prove to be his nemesis the next time it came up in Israeli-Egyptian negotiations.

Turning to the U.S. proposal, he said that Sadat had accepted the number of troops the Israeli cabinet had insisted upon. He said it had produced "an absolute uproar" from el-Gamasy because it was humiliating and demoralizing for his soldiers. He raised el-Gamasy's need for the howitzers. Dayan responded constructively, suggesting they specify a range of no more than twelve kilometers. With that agreed, Kissinger gave up on his promise to Sadat to try for twenty-five kilometers for the SAMs.

Now Dayan wanted to insert numerical and range limits on the howitzers he had just traded. As they argued, Kissinger became more exasperated. "Thirty guns won't change the course of history," he said. Allon then introduced the idea of a "package deal": eight batteries of howitzers for a thirty-kilometer limit on the SAMs.

Kissinger had what he needed. It gave him an opening to make a point about generosity of spirit. "The experience they have with you is that you really try to squeeze everything out of them," he chided. "Try giving them 10 percent more than they ask for, on one occasion," he gingerly suggested. He noted that if Sadat was engaged in a con game and broke the agreement, he would now be breaking a host of pledges to the United States as well. Kissinger again asserted that Sadat was genuinely interested in peace. His proof: "He never raised the question of the 1967 borders."

I have dwelled here on the give-and-take of the negotiations, the trade-offs that Kissinger fashioned, and the methodology he deployed to highlight his skill at manipulating both his interlocutors and the texts of the agreements.

In the process, Kissinger developed a negotiator's handbook for mediating between Israelis and Arabs. As he subsequently explained to his staff, he learned to avoid acting as the lawyer for one side or the other, presenting a maximalist position and then settling for less, creating the impression that he had been sent by the other side to extract a maximum concession. That would leave one side wondering whether he had secured everything the other side was prepared to yield. He would therefore present only one position, and if that was not acceptable, he would ask for a counterproposal and, in that way, get the two sides to make concessions to each other.

He also found that he could facilitate the negotiations by interpreting to both sides what the other side really had in mind but couldn't articulate in their proposals. And the United States could, where necessary, also come up with an "American proposal" that the two sides could accept because they were making a concession to the United States and not to the other side.

To do all that, Kissinger had to master the minutiae of military deployments, terrain, weapons ranges, and the like. Over the years of American-led Arab-Israeli negotiations, it became a well-worn technique of both sides to drag the American mediators, including the president, down into the weeds, where they had the advantage of local knowledge. It also served to level the playing field, since the United States could not wield its immense power advantage on every little detail. It is a testament to Kissinger's negotiating skill that he could master the details as surely as the local players and then fashion trade-offs acceptable to both sides.

As the Israelis prepared for the final cabinet meeting to approve the agreement, Kissinger went with Dinitz to see Meir. He was relieved to hear that she would chair the cabinet deliberations despite her illness, since he felt he could rely on her to squelch any attempt to reopen the agreement. When he delivered Sadat's personal message, her minimalistic response was, "It is a good thing." When he told her that Sadat would not deploy the thirty tanks on the east bank, she said, "We shall see."

Her skepticism led him to recount all the reasons he thought Sadat was sincere, emphasizing the things that he calculated would assuage her doubts. "He never, even privately, tried to ask me about the 1967 borders," he repeated. "The Palestinians he mentioned only for ten minutes. Jerusalem he never mentioned." She seemed unmoved. When he noted Sadat's promise not to interfere with Israeli flights down the Red Sea he finally said, "That is important," showing her particular interest as the pioneer of Israel's relations with Africa. "I keep asking, Why is he doing this?" she wondered out loud, giving expression to her distrust.

They agreed to meet on the morrow, when she would sign the agreement and give him a response to Sadat's message. Two hours later, upon her recommendation, the Israeli cabinet approved the agreement. And two hours after that, at 7:00 p.m. in Aswan and Jerusalem, Sadat initialed the U.S. proposal. At 10:00 p.m. in Israel, 3:00 p.m. in Washington, Nixon stepped before the cameras in the White House to announce that Egypt and Israel, with the assistance of the United States, had reached agreement on the disengagement of their forces.

When Kissinger briefed the traveling press at midnight on January 17, he was described as "far from jubilant" and he looked fatigued. "There's one thing that keeps you going," he told TV interviewer Dick Cavett in 1979, "which is you know there's nothing more important that you can be doing." That had an exhilarating effect, he said. "My letdown occurred not during the negotiations where I could do with three to four hours of sleep for long stretches of time. I usually was in a state of depression or letdown after what the public considered a great success," he admitted. "I was really both physically and emotionally drained, partly because I knew that whatever you solve in foreign policy is not final." On that night in Jerusalem, Kissinger knew he had taken only the first step toward resolving the Arab-Israeli conflict, since he had purposely designed it that way.

Earlier in the evening, he had allowed himself a moment of celebration with Eban and Dinitz and the American team in his King David suite. They joked at Sisco's expense as he popped the champagne cork and managed to hit the ceiling with it while spilling champagne all over the Persian carpet. Nevertheless, Kissinger's toast was laced with uncertainty. Were they at a fork in the road, he asked rhetorically, or was this just an episode in a long journey that might eventually lead to peace?

The long days and nights of negotiations, the lack of sleep, the punishing travel back and forth between Aswan and Jerusalem, and the constant pressure to be on his game as he coaxed and cajoled the two sides closer to agreement had taken their toll. But the fruits of victory would come soon enough, and they would do away with that nagging fear that, like his predecessor in 1970, he was being fooled by the Egyptians.

Friday, January 18, 1974, Jerusalem. Kissinger's first stop the next morning was at the prime minister's Jerusalem residence to pick up the American proposal she had signed. The rancor of their earlier meetings had long since vanished, but here for the first time Meir praised him to the assembled press. "I sincerely and honestly believe that you have made history this week. I want to tell you, on behalf of the people of Israel, how much we appreciate it," she said with a sincerity that moved him deeply.

He would later record that at that moment he felt "a deep tenderness toward her" and respect for her willingness to embrace a negotiating process "against which all her instincts rebelled." He could reasonably claim credit for that conversion, which had not been easy. He reciprocated with words that touched on his own Jewish identity: "No people have suffered more for the past generation than the people of Israel. No people have more cause to wish for peace." But peace wasn't just for Israelis and Jews. Kissinger hoped that peace would come to the wider region so that "all the talents and energy of all of its peoples can be devoted to the paths of construction."

Once the press had been shown the door, Meir gave him a message to take back to Sadat. She began by expressing how deeply conscious she was of the significance of the message from Egypt's leader and how much satisfaction it gave her to be able to converse with him in this way. She promised her best efforts to establish trust between them in order to achieve peace. She wanted him to know that she too meant it and was prepared to direct all her energies toward that goal. She then sang the intermediary's praises. "It is indeed extremely fortunate that we have Dr. Kissinger whom we both trust and who is prepared to give of his wisdom and talents in the cause of peace," she wrote. This private testimony was vital, for without trust, the mediator cannot function effectively, and without trust there can be no resolution of conflict.

Kissinger delivered Meir's message to Sadat in his Aswan study a few hours later, after Sadat had signed the U.S. proposal. As Sadat finished reading her words, an aide entered the room to tell them that el-Gamasy and Elazar had just signed the disengagement agreement at Kilometer 101. Sadat took off his glasses, folded the message, put it in the vest pocket of his winter uniform, walked over, and kissed Kissinger on both cheeks. If Kissinger was startled by that, he was even more surprised when Sadat said, "I am today taking off my military uniform. I never expect to wear it again except for ceremonial occasions. Tell her that is the answer to her letter."

Five hundred miles away, at Kilometer 101, the engagement between the generals was almost as surprising, given el-Gamasy's angry reaction to the force limitations two days earlier and the fact that three months before that they had led opposing armies in a ferocious war. The Israelis had done little to spruce up the olive-colored tent since the signing of the six-point cease-fire agreement there on November 11. The battered U-shaped table was still covered in tattered gray felt, complemented by the same old slatted wood folding chairs.

It was enough for el-Gamasy that he had to sign the agreement; he wanted no photograph to capture the moment for posterity. The 150 members of the press were kept outside the tent. From there they were able to watch as the two military delegations walked from their respective tents to the main tent between two lines formed by a UNEF honor guard in field uniforms and blue helmets, rifles held across their chests. As soon as the delegations entered the tent, el-Gamasy and Elazar saluted each other and took their assigned seats. The two chiefs of staff signed the agreement and initialed the maps, which had been placed in red leather binders in front of them by Harold Saunders, representing the United States. The Soviet Union went unrepresented.

El-Gamasy then read out a set of six principles that he proposed to guide the implementation of the disengagement.* Elazar could not have been more gracious in his response. He smiled as el-Gamasy finished reading from his notes and responded that it was a good omen that both sides had similar ideas about the implementation. He agreed with el-Gamasy that it was important to get off to a good start and said that Israel had no other interest than to honor the agreement in spirit and letter in order to improve the atmosphere for future agreements.

El-Gamasy asked whether the IDF could complete the withdrawal in a shorter time frame; Elazar said he would do his best. In return, he asked that talks about handing over the Israeli dead bodies start as quickly as possible. El-Gamasy agreed. Coffee was served. Fifty minutes after entering the tent, the two generals departed. El-Gamasy avoided the press; Elazar simply told them that the agreement benefited both sides and represented the first step toward a better future.

Six thousand miles away, the Council Chamber in Geneva's Palais des Nations stood empty and silent. Notwithstanding Kissinger's promise to Dobrynin on the eve of the shuttle that he would feed the results back into the Geneva process, Sadat had made sure to kill that idea. He even recalled the Egyptian military delegation to make sure there was no possibility of anything happening there (he would soon recall his ambassador too). The Israelis had little to gain from a return to Geneva since they had no diplomatic relations with the Soviet Union, so Meir raised no objection to its abandonment. The one who should have cared was Kissinger.

Why had he put so much effort into convening the Geneva Conference if it meant so little to him that he would forsake it at the first opportunity? Wouldn't it have been wiser to go through the motions of another ceremonial convening to bless his diplomatic achievement and give the Soviets a face-

---

* The principles were strict observance of the cease-fire; disengagement carried out in three phases, with Israeli withdrawal completed in the first fifteen days, and redeployment of both Israeli and Egyptian armies to the agreed-upon lines to take place in the next fifteen days; Israeli withdrawal to start from south to north so that the Cairo–Suez road would be handed over in the first three days, which would allow for the redeployment of the two Egyptian armies; UNEF operation during all phases of the agreement; no destruction of infrastructure as Israel withdrew; and continued meetings at the chief of staff level as appropriate.

IDF chief of staff General David "Dado" Elazar discusses the implementation of the Israel-Egypt Disengagement Agreement at Kilometer 101 on January 18, 1974, with chief of staff of the Egyptian armed forces General Mohamed Abdel Ghani el-Gamasy (back to the camera). UN Emergency Force commander Lt. General Ensio Siilasvuo is on the right at the center table (wearing glasses). The map of the disengagement lines is on the table in front of el-Gamasy.

saving claim to some legitimizing role? Even though the Russians had no part whatsoever in the effort to convene the 1991 Madrid Conference, Secretary of State James Baker made sure that Soviet leader Mikhail Gorbachev had a cameo role as the co-chair. Similarly, the Russians played no part in the Oslo Accords, but Bill Clinton gave Foreign Minister Andrei Kozyrev a place of honor on the podium at the signing ceremony. We did the same for Kozyrev at the signing ceremony for the Israeli-Jordanian peace treaty.

Not Kissinger. He had resolved to freeze the Soviets out of any role. Kissinger had kept Dobrynin briefed in general terms through Scowcroft while he shuttled between Aswan and Jerusalem. Fahmy had been doing the same, spending four days in Moscow after the agreement was signed to assuage the Russians' anger with Sadat.

All week, Kissinger had been receiving reports that the Russians were embittered by their exclusion. The announcement of the agreement and the signing at Kilometer 101 represented the last straw. Brezhnev wrote to Nixon complaining that the United States had broken the understanding that Soviet and American representatives would play an active role in the negotiations. Moscow began to put out the word that Kissinger was sabotaging Geneva, that Sadat's hand would have been strengthened if he had brought the Soviet Union into the game, and that the end result was a victory for Israel.

Normally, this would have concerned Kissinger enough to pay the Soviets some lip service, but he did not believe that was necessary. Instead of briefing Gromyko or Dobrynin himself once the deal was done, he had Scowcroft do it. And when Brezhnev proposed to Nixon that Kissinger meet with Gromyko in Geneva to discuss Soviet grievances, he fobbed him off with a meeting between Ellsworth Bunker, at that stage the U.S. representative in Geneva, and his Soviet counterpart.

Kissinger subsequently explained that he was not going to jeopardize the prospects of the disengagement by raising the specter of a Soviet-American condominium, but it is unlikely that a Soviet role at the signing ceremony after the deal had been concluded would have had that effect. Certainly, their role in the opening ceremony at Geneva ran a much greater risk of the appearance of a superpower condominium, and yet he had managed that perception without difficulty.

He had conceived Geneva "to keep the Soviet Union from running away with the process by developing too many initiatives of their own." In that regard, he had succeeded. He and Sadat were the ones running away with the process, leaving the Soviets in their dust. Moreover, he had correctly taken the measure of the Soviets in calculating that there was little they could do to slow him down or trip him up. But given that he was already eyeing the next disengagement agreement, with Syria's Assad, who was closer to Moscow than Sadat, it was unusual for him to snub them so visibly.

Kissinger's burgeoning relationship with Sadat was the decisive factor. Having ignored Sadat in 1972, when he evicted the Soviet military advisers, Kissinger was determined not to disregard his concerns again now that they had become partners in the common cause of marginalizing the Soviets in the Middle East. Looking back two months later, he allowed that he should have invited Gromyko to a signing ceremony in Geneva. "I think it was a mistake not to. The Egyptians would not have liked it, but it would have cost us nothing," he told Abba Eban in a reflective moment.

Notwithstanding Soviet unhappiness, the agreement generated a positive feeling in Egypt and Israel. The media in Cairo gave it high marks. The Egyptians were seen to have made considerable gains by removal of the Israeli bridgehead on the west bank that was "like a pistol pointed at the heart of Egypt." The fact that Israel had withdrawn from the canal into the Sinai as a result of diplomacy rather than war was seen as a milestone. The liberation of the Egyptian Third Army and the lifting of the sieges on the canal cities were welcomed in Cairo as great achievements. El-Gamasy had told Kissinger that it would be possible to mask the force limitations to the Egyptian people, and so it was. The Egyptian press was instructed to place the emphasis on the fact that almost all of Israel's heavy weapons would be moved east of the Sinai passes; no mention was made in the government-controlled media of the reciprocal movement of Egyptian forces west of the canal. If the Egyptian army was upset by the restrictions, there was no indication of it in the public arena. The soldiers just seemed happy to be going home.

Sadat had set the tone for the Egyptian press. After his last meeting with Kissinger on Friday afternoon in Aswan, Sadat had escorted Kissinger from the gazebo through the garden to his waiting limousine. There, in front of the cameras, he put his hands on Kissinger's shoulders and said slowly with emphasis, "Mr. Secretary you are not only my friend; you are also my brother." And then he kissed him on both cheeks.

Similarly, *The New York Times* correspondent in Israel reported that "the widespread initial reaction here is that Israel got a good deal." The shrinking of Egyptian forces on the east bank was seen as a major benefit in stabilizing the cease-fire and giving Israel a defensible front line. The reopening of the canal and freedom of passage through Bab el-Mandeb were treated as a bonus. Only Ariel Sharon seemed to object to giving up the pocket he had fought so hard to secure on the west bank. Most Israelis never expected to hold on to it. The most hopeful aspect of the agreement for many was that it just might indicate that Egypt, their largest and militarily most powerful neighbor, was turning away from war toward the peaceful pursuit of economic development.

Kissinger had managed to satisfy the needs and aspirations of both sides. It boosted his reputation mightily. In Israel, he had been viewed with great suspicion, in part because he was pressuring them, and in part because he was perceived as manipulative. With Meir, Dayan, and Eban now going out of their way to praise his efforts, the Israeli public began to soften their views too.[*] As the *Times* reporter put it, "Rightly or wrongly, the Israelis are convinced that he has played straight with them and fairly represented their views to the other side." On his last day in Jerusalem, he was greeted by a cartoon in *The Jerusalem Post* depicting him as an angel of peace sitting atop a silenced cannon. Contrast that with a cartoon in *Maariv*, the Israeli evening newspaper, at the outset of the shuttle, showing an Israeli soldier running headlong for an air raid shelter with the caption reading, "Kissinger's coming!"

---

[*] Meir convened the editors of the major Israeli newspapers to tell them she thought they were being unfair to Kissinger and to ask them to tone down their criticism. Similarly, Dayan publicly and privately praised Kissinger's negotiating methods. He said that no previous intermediary was as good in trying to reach an Arab-Israeli settlement. Eban told the press when he announced the breakthrough that there was "no pressure, no arm-twisting. It was an exemplary exercise in international conciliation." See Bernard Gwertzman, "Reporter's Notebook: The Active Life on Kissinger's Shuttle in the Middle East," *New York Times*, January 16, 1974, and Terence Smith, "Eban Terms Agreement with Syria Now Possible," *New York Times*, January 18, 1974.

Compared to the subsequent signing ceremonies that marked the transition from war to peace between Israel and its Arab and Palestinian neighbors, this first one, with its dispersed signing events in Jerusalem, Aswan, and Kilometer 101, was modest at best. Yet because it was the first ever Arab-Israeli agreement, its humble trappings belied its significance. As Kissinger was fond of pointing out to Israelis and Egyptians alike, it marked the first time in the history of the Arab-Israeli conflict that Israel would withdraw from Arab territory as the result of a negotiated agreement with an Arab government. It was the first time too that Israel would put its faith in Arab intentions rather than its own military power. And it was the first time that Israelis were prepared to test the proposition that by giving up territory they could become more, not less, secure.

It was also a first for the Arab world. Egypt, its natural leader as the largest and militarily most powerful Arab state, had just entered into an agreement with Israel that involved regaining territory through diplomacy rather than the use of force. While the political aspects of the military disengagement were disguised as unilateral acts or commitments to the United States, they were nevertheless groundbreaking.

And it was a first for the United States, which had brokered the agreement and taken on active responsibility for the fulfillment of the commitments that were made to it by both sides, as well as for further steps to resolve the wider Arab-Israeli conflict. Because it was negotiated by the United States without the involvement of other external parties, it heralded the coming of the Pax Americana, a new, U.S.-dominated regional order based on Washington's leadership in resolving one of the region's most persistent and bloody conflicts.

Kissinger earned the accolades he received for orchestrating this signal achievement. Yet he could not have achieved the agreement without a major assist from Anwar Sadat. By launching the war, limiting its objectives, and then pivoting to diplomacy, the Egyptian leader had created a plastic moment for Kissinger to exploit. By turning away from the Soviet Union and toward the United States, Sadat had provided Kissinger with the strategic incentive to play his role. By putting his trust in Kissinger, refusing to haggle, and embracing his psychological approach to treating Israeli insecurities, he empowered his efforts. And by his courageous determination to break the mold of conflict and pursue peace with his enemy in unconventional and creative ways, he facilitated and boosted Kissinger's diplomatic stratagem. At times it was difficult to determine who was the pupil and who the teacher in their relationship. But they developed a symbiosis that served them both well.

The Israeli leadership also played a critical role in Kissinger's success. They provided the military pressure that enabled him to achieve the initial cease-fire, and Yariv and Dayan provided the conceptual framework that Kissinger utilized to achieve the disengagement. Although he had to drag Meir kicking and screaming to the conclusion that it was in Israel's interests to allow the Egyptian Third Army to survive, her agreement to do so opened the way for his role as peacemaker. And in the end her willingness to suspend her disbelief and persuade her coalition government to give up territory for an agreement demonstrated a courage that matched Sadat's. Kissinger had succeeded in buying time to test the peaceful intentions of Israel's Arab neighbors. And he had fashioned the foundation stone of his new American-led order in the Middle East.

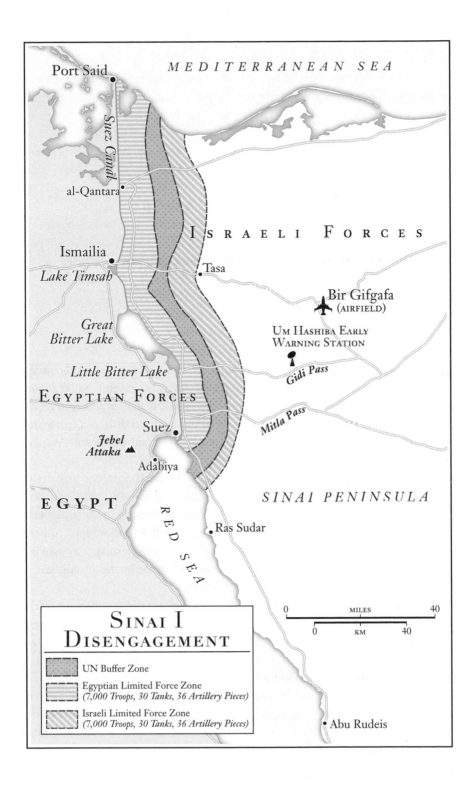

MEDITERRANEAN SEA

Port Said

Suez Canal

al-Qantara

ISRAELI FORCES

Ismailia

Lake Timsah

Tasa

Bir Gifgafa
(AIRFIELD)

UM HASHIBA EARLY
WARNING STATION

Great
Bitter Lake

Gidi Pass

Little Bitter Lake

EGYPTIAN FORCES

Mitla Pass

Suez

Jebel
Attaka

Adabiya

SINAI PENINSULA

EGYPT

RED SEA

Ras Sudar

MILES
0   40

KM
0   40

SINAI I
DISENGAGEMENT

UN Buffer Zone

Egyptian Limited Force Zone
(7,000 Troops, 30 Tanks, 36 Artillery Pieces)

Israeli Limited Force Zone
(7,000 Troops, 30 Tanks, 36 Artillery Pieces)

Abu Rudeis

12

"Ploughing the Ocean"

You can't make war in the Middle East without Egypt. You can't make peace without Syria.

—Henry Kissinger

Sadat had lubricated Kissinger's diplomacy with grand gestures and concessions. Kissinger now needed to return the favor by helping Sadat secure Syrian cover for his daring engagement with Israel, which would relieve the incoming fire he was taking from the Arab world—a good deal of it instigated by Damascus. An Israeli-Syrian disengagement agreement would rob Assad of his ability to criticize Sadat.

For Meir, a negotiation with Syria would facilitate the urgent priority of accounting for the Israeli POWs in Syrian hands and achieving their release. Bringing Israeli troops home from the northern front was also a pressing need, because the Syrians were exacting a daily casualty toll as they sought to keep the military pressure on Israel to withdraw. Winter in the Golan was proving bitter and miserable for Israeli reservists, fueling the growing discontent at home with the prime minister and her government.

Co-opting Syria would also help Kissinger shore up the foundations of the order he was building. As he told Meir and Dayan, "Unless something happens with Syria, there is no way to keep the process going." It would also facilitate the lifting of the oil embargo. Gas lines in the United States, indications that the American and global economies were slowing, and deepening differences with the Europeans and Japanese over how to deal with the crisis combined to make that an imperative. The decision was in the hands of the Saudis and the Algerians, who had made it clear that they needed a Syrian disengagement deal to justify lifting the embargo.

All roads, therefore, led to Damascus.

Sunday, January 20, 1974, Damascus. The first time Kissinger had visited Damascus, a month earlier, Assad had surprised him with his decision not to attend the Geneva Conference. This time, Kissinger was more confident of his assumptions. With the ink still drying on the Israeli-Egyptian disengagement agreement, he expected to find Assad keen to apply a similar process to the Golan, thereby removing Israeli forces from the Damascus environs.

Kissinger's objective was tactical and transactional. He hoped that Assad might turn on Moscow, but taking Syria out of the Soviet orbit was not a necessary part of the architecture of his new Middle Eastern order. Syria had little strategic value to the United States compared to Egypt. The empty Syrian chair at the Geneva Conference symbolized that reality.

Assad knew his leverage was limited but would never let that show to his interlocutors. He had been forced to accept the cease-fire before he was ready because Sadat had gone ahead without him. His biographer, the British journalist Patrick Seale, recounts that Assad was bitterly disappointed by what he viewed as Sadat's betrayal. Similarly, in the war's aftermath, Sadat had refused to be held up by Assad's desire to proceed in tandem. After Sadat's disengagement agreement with Israel had been announced, Assad had called Sadat in Aswan. "Do you understand the meaning of what you are doing?" he asked angrily. "It means Israel will move to our front every tank and gun it has in Sinai." Militarily, he now felt he faced Israel alone. Diplomatically, he shrewdly assessed Kissinger's purpose. "Assad wanted a united front against Israel," Kissinger told me decades later, "and I was breaking it up." If he succeeded, it would leave Syria weakened and isolated. But Assad also understood that Kissinger needed him to bolster Sadat and reinforce the perception that only the United States could deliver for the Arabs.

Like Sadat, Assad had become disillusioned with the Soviet Union. Given American leverage over Israel, he might as well explore what he could get for going along. Assad also wanted to move the Israeli army away from Damascus, but he did his best to disguise that vulnerability. He maintained to Kissinger that the U.S.-Soviet cease-fire agreement negotiated by Kissinger had robbed him of the opportunity to destroy the Israeli salient.

A military man who had spent most of the previous three years as president preparing for war, Assad was provincial in his outlook and experience. He had never visited the West. He was conscious of Kissinger's celebrity status on the world stage and flattered by his presence in Damascus, which elevated Syria's importance and enhanced its regional role. Assad was willing at least to test whether investing his trust in Kissinger could yield results. He was also keen to learn from him, a challenge that the professor in Kissinger welcomed, starting most of his meetings with an extensive tour d'horizon, touching on China's perspective on world order, the Vietnam peace negotiations, relations between Congress and the presidency, and other topical issues. They found a natural affinity for each other notwithstanding their competing objectives.

From the outset, it was a match of wits and guile unlike any other in Kissinger's experience as secretary of state. Assad's digressive style had been developed in long-winded Ba'ath Party meetings, but he had discovered that wearing down his interlocutor could provide a psychological advantage. Kissinger was determined to yield no quarter on that score. His bladder might not hold out, but his store of intellectual energy was more than a match for Assad's. In fact, he was charmed by the Syrian leader. He told Joe Kraft, a *Washington Post* columnist, that he viewed him as "a man of superb intelligence, great sense of humor, really quite attractive, and I found him to be a man of his word."

While Assad showed every sign of being charmed by Kissinger in return, he viewed him through the prism of radical Arab nationalism. What Kissinger told him in their early meetings about the challenges he faced in the United States from those who controlled "the financial capital and means of communication," not to speak of the Congress, only served to reinforce Assad's prejudices against Jews. Kissinger invoked these forces to justify his go-slow, step-by-step process. But it served to plant the idea in Assad's mind that the Jewish lobby was behind Watergate and that its ultimate purpose was to prevent Nixon from imposing a comprehensive peace settlement on Israel. Yet instead of identifying Kissinger as part of that supposed cabal, Assad found his Jewishness disarming.

Their encounter on January 20 had been preceded by an angry meeting between Sadat and Assad the day before. Sadat had coordinated his visit to Damascus with Kissinger in the belief that he could help soften up Assad before Kissinger met with him. That proved a major miscalculation. It gave Assad an opportunity to signal to the Arab world in an unmistakable way that he was in no hurry to embrace Sadat's agreement with Israel.

In an act designed to humiliate Sadat, Assad confined him to an airport conference room, barring the president of mighty Egypt from entering Damascus. In a nine-hour exchange, he accused Sadat of "duplicity and backstabbing," and of "leaving the battle" by agreeing to disengage his troops. It was Egypt, not Sadat, that mattered to the Syrian people, he told him, to take him down a peg. He wanted to know why Sadat was in such a hurry and why he had committed to reopening the canal. Sadat dissembled, claiming he had not promised to do so. That enraged Assad. He argued that by abandoning military pressure on Israel, Sadat had weakened both Egypt's and Syria's negotiating position. He beseeched Sadat to retain at least one point of friction with the Israelis that would enable him to threaten a return to war. Sadat agreed, but Assad no longer believed him.

Syrian foreign minister Abdel Halim Khaddam, a Ba'ath Party hard-liner, would escort Kissinger to and from the airport every time he visited Damascus, just as Fahmy and Eban would do. On this occasion, as they sped down the deserted highway, Kissinger observed to Khaddam that Sadat must have traveled the same road a day earlier. Khaddam responded: "We didn't let that pimp into Damascus!"

By contrast, Assad's approach to Kissinger was warm and welcoming. He served him a late lunch in what passed for his presidential palace, a courtesy denied other American secretaries of state who would follow in Kissinger's footsteps. In subsequent years, diabetes and a heart condition forced Assad to so restrict his diet that he no longer dined with his American guests for fear they would perceive his physical weakness.

For the first ninety minutes, Assad railed against Sadat's duplicity. Kissinger tried to focus the conversation on the future by offering to negotiate the same kind of disengagement agreement with Syria as he had just achieved with Egypt. He did his riff about the opposition he faced from the American Jewish lobby and pro-Israel senators like Scoop Jackson. Notwithstanding, he offered to focus on persuading Israel to withdraw from the pocket it had taken during the war, as well as two positions on Mount Hermon it had occupied after the October 22 cease-fire. Then Kissinger put the Golan Heights town of Quneitra on the table, arguing that it would be a great achievement if he could succeed in wresting it too from Israel's grip.

Before 1967, Quneitra had served as the capital of the Golan. Established in the Ottoman era as a way station on the caravan route to Damascus from the east, it had never been much more than a small market town and military garrison of twenty thousand people. Captured by the Israelis in the Six-Day War, it had become a ghost town, with many of its buildings flattened or gutted. Sadat had put the idea in Kissinger's head that Quneitra could serve as the key to a Golan solution. When Kissinger raised the subject now, Assad upped the ante. He said that when the Golan was in Syrian hands there were 163 villages there and a population of 170,000. He could not take back only Quneitra; many other villages on the Golan would also need to be included.

Assad then told Kissinger that before Geneva, when Sadat had told him there would be prior agreement on the disengagement lines, he had prepared three options, ranging from an Israeli retreat from half of the Golan to a full withdrawal from the plateau. He showed those to Kissinger on a large map that was perched on an easel in a corner of the room. Kissinger told him frankly that, based on his preliminary discussions with Israel's leadership, they would almost certainly reject all of Assad's options. Assad said if that were the case, he was willing to develop a further proposal. Kissinger took note that the Syrian president seemed so keen to engage that he was prepared to bargain with himself.

Not wanting to reveal his own eagerness, Kissinger digressed into process, suggesting that Israelis and Syrians could discuss all these issues in a military committee, like the Israeli-Egyptian military negotiations that had taken place at Kilometer 101 and subsequently in Geneva. True to form, Assad was unwilling to have Syrian officials sit with Israelis separately but agreed to send a Syrian representative to the Egyptian-Israeli military working group. He stressed, however, that he wanted Kissinger personally to conduct the negotiations just as he had on the Egyptian track.

Kissinger asked Assad what he could tell Meir about the Israeli POWs. Assad replied that she had "no reason to have any anxiety"; no prisoners had been killed. However, when Kissinger asked how many Israelis Syria was holding, Assad demurred. "Once efforts have progressed, we will agree with you on giving a suitable number," he explained, as if the number of POWs were negotiable.

Kissinger proposed that he stop off in Israel on his way home to brief the leadership there on these discussions. He would invite Dayan to Washington within two weeks to seek a formal Israeli response, and then Assad should send an envoy to follow up. Assad was satisfied with this procedure and, to Kissinger's relief, agreed that he could tell the press that their talks had been "constructive." "The essential thing," Khaddam told Kissinger on the way back to the airport, "is that you have put yourself inside the problem."

The "problem" was about to become seriously complicated by political developments in Israel. Meir was now engaged in a laborious effort to cobble together a new coalition government. The National Religious Party (NRP), hitherto her stalwart coalition partner, had come under the influence of a young guard of zealous settlers—the Gush Emunim (Bloc of the Faithful)—who fervently opposed any ceding of territory in the West Bank or the Golan. It took her two months of arduous negotiations to bring the NRP into the new government.

In the meantime, Dayan had become the target of vocal criticism and mounting public protests from demobilized reservists who blamed him for the disaster of the war, particularly the high casualties among their comrades in its early days. At a funeral ceremony for fallen soldiers, bereaved parents spat on his car while he was sitting in it. He reacted by refusing to serve in any role in Meir's new government. When Kissinger arrived at Ben Gurion Airport on his way home from Damascus on January 20, Dayan left it to Allon and Eban to convey the Israeli government's position that until and unless Assad provided a list of the Israeli POWs in Syrian possession and allowed the Red Cross to visit them, it would not enter any negotiations with Syria.

Given the political turmoil, Meir was in no position at that moment to add a negotiation with the hated Syrians over the treasured Golan to her basket of troubles. It looked like the Syrian disengagement process was stuck at the starting gate.

Returning to Washington, Kissinger went to work to try to create some room to maneuver. He first asked Sadat to send a message imploring Meir to negotiate with Syria to prevent Egypt's isolation. Then, in a series of phone calls and meetings with Dinitz in the last week of January, they managed to cobble together a convoluted series of parallel steps to overcome the impasse: first Assad would tell Kissinger how many Israeli prisoners Syria was holding; then Dayan would come to Washington with an Israeli disengagement proposal (like he had for the Sinai disengagement); then Assad would convey the list of Israeli POWs and allow the Red Cross to visit them, and Kissinger would in turn transmit the Israeli proposal to Damascus.

Kissinger persuaded both Assad and Meir to accept this approach. To jumpstart the sequence, he informed Dinitz on February 7 that he had received a message from the Syrian chargé d'affaires in Washington that there were sixty-five Israeli prisoners in Syrian custody. Dinitz reciprocated by informing Kissinger that Dayan would come to the United States at the beginning of March to discuss the Israeli proposal with Kissinger. So far, so good.

Kissinger was unpleasantly surprised to learn, however, that the Saudis and Algerians had begun to waver on lifting the oil embargo. He had been led to believe, because of his conversations in Saudi Arabia, Algeria, and Egypt on his earlier visits, that the Arab oil producers would lift their embargo once he had concluded the Egyptian-Israeli disengagement agreement and had begun negotiations with Syria. He had told Nixon that he had a solemn assurance from King Faisal to that effect. On that basis, the president had signaled in his State of the Union address to Congress on January 30, 1974, that the embargo was likely to be lifted shortly.* Nixon's credibility was now on the line just when he was engaged in an epic battle with Watergate special prosecutor Leon Jaworski about whether to hand over the incriminating tapes of his Oval Office conversations.

On February 12, Assad traveled to Algiers to meet Boumediene, Sadat,

---

* Nixon told the joint session of Congress, "I can announce tonight that I have been assured . . . that an urgent meeting will be called in the immediate future to discuss the lifting of the oil embargo." See "The Address on the State of the Union," *Public Papers: Nixon, 1974* (Ann Arbor, MI: University of Michigan Library, 2005), 47–55.

and King Faisal. Kissinger had primed all three Arab leaders to press Assad
to hand over the list of Israeli POWs to jump-start the Golan disengagement
negotiations, which they all wanted. But Assad told them now that he could
give up the list only if they would maintain the oil embargo until he reached
agreement with Israel. Notwithstanding their commitments to Kissinger, they
agreed to do so and dispatched the Egyptian and Saudi foreign ministers to
Washington to explain their backsliding.

Kissinger well understood the game the Arab leaders were playing. He told
Nixon that if they let Boumediene and Faisal get away with this renege, "every
time we promise something and deliver it, then they [will] ask for a new promise and a new delivery." Nixon could surely relate to that pitfall since, much to
his dismay, he was experiencing it with Congress over Watergate.

Kissinger had learned from his negotiations with the Vietnamese and the
Soviets how to deliver a tough message. The Arabs were child's play by comparison. He met Fahmy and Saudi minister of state Omar Saqqaf upon their
arrival at Andrews Air Force Base and wasted no time with pleasantries. He
knew that as personal envoys they would lose face with their leaders if they
went home without delivering their message directly to the president. So he
told them there would be no meeting with Nixon and no U.S. effort to pursue
the disengagement negotiations with Syria unless they dropped the linkage
between a Syrian-Israeli disengagement and the lifting of the embargo.

Nixon and Kissinger were bluffing. They cared mightily about getting the
embargo lifted. As the president told Kissinger at the time, "That's the only
thing the country is interested in." But Kissinger convinced him to simply
ignore the embargo because "the more we build it up the less we are going to
get it [lifted]." They should make it clear to the Arabs that they didn't even
want to discuss it.

Fahmy was his covert ally in this process because Sadat had promised Kissinger he would help get the embargo lifted. So Kissinger met with Saqqaf
and Fahmy separately, to play one off against the other. When they were both
ushered into the Oval Office on Tuesday, February 19, he then preempted
them by outlining to the president a three-point agreement that he claimed
they both supported: instead of linking the lifting of the oil embargo to an
agreement, it would be lifted *unconditionally* at the next meeting of the Arab
oil ministers in two weeks' time; the United States would commit to using its
"best influence" to achieve an Israeli-Syrian disengagement agreement; and
Nixon would send Kissinger to the Middle East to get the talks started.

Saqqaf objected. "I find it very hard not to link the three," he emphasized.
The embargo "is not going to be lifted without something else happening,"
he told Nixon.

"That is not the way I understood it," Kissinger interrupted, his voice rising. He insisted that all he could be expected to do on his next trip was to start the negotiations, not conclude them. Nixon then weighed in, emphasizing that "we will not link anything at all." On the other hand, the president argued, lifting the embargo would help American efforts to achieve what the Arabs wanted—an Israeli withdrawal on the Golan.*

Siding with Kissinger, Fahmy told Nixon that Assad understood that he would not get a disengagement agreement before the oil ministers' meeting. "What you have said is adequate and there will be no problem," he reassured the president, undercutting his Saudi brother. "We are not asking you to pay anything."

Nixon responded with his tough-guy routine, assuring them he had been "direct and firm" with Mrs. Meir and would continue to be so.

Lacking Egyptian support, Saqqaf folded. "This is what I wanted to hear," he said.

Kissinger had managed to rob Assad of two cards before the negotiations had even begun in earnest. Instead of working with Syria against Israel and the United States, Egypt was now working with the United States to move Assad toward Israel. And instead of helping Assad with the leverage of the oil embargo, the Saudis had now agreed to lift it before he had achieved his purposes.

Assad, however, still had the Israeli POWs. Dinitz made clear to Kissinger on February 17 that if Assad wanted negotiations, the number of POWs would not suffice; he was going to have to provide the actual list of names beforehand. Dinitz was quite comfortable with the idea of Kissinger going to the region to start the talks. However, the Israeli ambassador warned, "If before you go, there is no visible advance on prisoners, it will look in the press as if there is pressure on Israel."

Kissinger responded tartly, "Golda will get what she asks for."

Sure enough, the day after the Saudi foreign minister had folded in front of Nixon, the Syrian chargé d'affaires, Sabah Kabbani, brought Kissinger the list of names of the Israeli POWs together with a promise from Assad that the Red Cross visits could start in nine days' time. How could Kissinger have been so confident of this outcome? Eight days later, when Kissinger handed over the list to Meir, the explanation emerged. Kissinger told her, in strictest confidence, that Sadat had persuaded Assad to hand over the list in return for

---

* Kissinger also conveyed that message to Assad on February 5, though in more positive terms, promising to make a major effort on disengagement, but only once the oil embargo question was resolved. And he had Nixon assure the Saudi ambassador that he would continue to work for a settlement but added, "My efforts . . . will be seriously jeopardized if the embargo is an issue." See Telegram from Department of State to U.S. Interests Section in Syria, February 5, 1974, FRUS 1969–1976:26, Doc. 21, and Memcon between Nixon and Saudi ambassador Ibrahim al-Sowayel, February 7, 1974, FRUS 1969–1976:36, Doc. 309.

Kissinger asking the shah of Iran "to start military action against Iraq to draw Iraqi troops away from the Syrians."

Indeed, on February 4, Iraq announced that Iranian tanks and armored infantry supported by artillery had crossed the Iraqi border and killed ten Iraqi soldiers. The clashes continued until a major eruption of fighting occurred on February 10, in which twenty-three Iraqis and seventy Iranians were reportedly killed. After this incident, Iraqi news sources complained about Iranian troops massing on the border and Iranian fighter aircraft repeatedly breaching Iraqi airspace. The clashes continued for another month. Soon after, Saddam Hussein withdrew the Iraqi tank division that had been deployed to Syria at the outset of the Yom Kippur War; remaining in Syria after the war, it had posed a threat to Assad's regime.

Wondrous are the ways of the Middle East. Kissinger and Sadat had pulled off a triple bank shot. Assad understood the game. Much later, he would tell Clinton's peace team, "If you take one step towards us, we will take two steps towards you."* Kissinger had taken a step by diverting Saddam Hussein's attention from his border with Syria to his border with Iran. Assad had reciprocated by providing the Israeli POW list.† Kissinger's American-led Middle Eastern order was beginning to function the way he had hoped: Egypt and Iran, two regional partners of the United States, were working together to deter Iraq, a destabilizing, Soviet-backed power, and bolster the efficacy of the peace process as the mechanism for promoting his design.

In preparing for these negotiations, Kissinger handled the Soviet Union less effectively, and it would come back to haunt him throughout the process. Because Kissinger had excluded them from the Egyptian-Israeli disengagement negotiations, Brezhnev was determined to prevent a second humiliation. In a meeting Nixon and Kissinger held with Gromyko in Washington on February 4, Gromyko complained at length about the way the United States had

---

* In 1993, Secretary of State Warren Christopher persuaded Assad to allow the remaining fifteen hundred Jews to leave Syria by giving Kuwait permission to provide him with three used Boeing 727 commercial jets for the Syrian Arab Airlines fleet. At the time, Syria was on the State Department list of state sponsors of terrorism, and therefore no country could provide it with American aircraft without a waiver.

† In addition to the border clashes in mid-February, the United States also stepped up its military support for the Iraqi Kurds, which enabled the Kurds to tie down two-thirds of the Iraqi army. According to Kissinger's memoirs, by the spring of 1974, the United States was supplying $8 million a year in military equipment to the Kurds, while the shah increased his support to $75 million a year. One explicit objective of the covert operation was "to keep the present Iraqi government tied down." When I asked Kissinger about this gambit forty-five years later, he did not remember the details. But he said about his friend the shah of Iran, "I was certainly capable of encouraging him to exercise military pressure." See Henry Kissinger, *Years of Renewal* (New York: Touchstone, 1999), 589, and Indyk interview with Henry Kissinger, July 23, 2019.

circumvented and breached their understanding about "joint auspices," acted unilaterally contrary to repeated assurances, and had sacrificed the long-term relationship with the Soviet Union to gain short-term advantage in the Middle East.

"I accept your criticism," Nixon told Gromyko. "There was an impression in our press that the United States was trying to make this a one-man show," he said, taking a side swipe at Kissinger for his celebrity treatment in the American media. Gently throwing Kissinger under the bus, he assured Gromyko that he did not want to jeopardize relations with the Soviet Union "by any failure on our part to consult about the Middle East."

For Kissinger, the challenge was to restore the illusion of Soviet partnership in the Middle East while continuing to pursue his strategic objective of denying Moscow any meaningful role there. He had hoped to do that by accommodating the Soviets' interest in relations with the United States in other areas to deter them from interfering in his Middle East peacemaking efforts. But now congressional opposition to most-favored-nation treatment for Soviet exports to the United States was undermining that strategy. So, in a follow-up luncheon at the Soviet embassy, over repeated shots of vodka, Kissinger promised "when appropriate" to coordinate with Gromyko on the Syrian-Israeli negotiations. Gromyko understood that the diplomatic code words "when appropriate" effectively meant "never," so he insisted on daily consultations to coordinate their efforts. Kissinger said, "All right," but they both knew he had no intention of fulfilling that commitment.

Soviet unhappiness gave Assad a potential source of leverage over the United States. In the Cold War, a time of intense Soviet-American rivalry, playing one superpower off against the other was a well-honed tactic of smaller non-aligned states that had something both stronger powers desired. Nasser had developed this tactic into an art form. Sadat had deliberately eschewed this approach, abandoning his relationship with the Soviet Union to ingratiate himself with the United States and thereby oblige it to help Egypt. But Assad's relationship with Moscow was still quite good; the Soviets had cut off the arms resupply pipeline to Egypt, but the materiel was still flowing to Syria. And because the Soviets were losing their position in Egypt, their relationship with Syria became even more important to them.

Yet when Kissinger wrote Assad after his meetings with Gromyko to inquire in mock innocence whether the Syrian leader thought U.S.-Soviet coordination was "desirable and practical," he was surprised and gratified by the subtlety of his response. Assad had no objection to coordination with Moscow, he wrote back, but he "lacked the data to suggest a practical plan to achieve it." He wanted to make sure, however, that Kissinger had not shared with Gromyko his acceptance of Kissinger's reciprocal steps to jump-start the negotiations with Israel. Kissinger understood from this exchange that Assad was not coordinating with Moscow and had no interest in joint Soviet-American action. In Kissinger's view, Assad had decided at that point "that we were overwhelmingly strong. He must have seen the many opportunities that the Soviet Union had to intervene, and they didn't do it." Like Sadat, Assad had decided to put his eggs in Kissinger's basket.

Kissinger had now set the table for the Israeli-Syrian disengagement negotiations. It was the first of four hard-won breakthroughs that would eventually produce an agreement. It would prove to be a dispiriting, frustrating, and exhausting endeavor, one that would require all the manipulative skill and strength of will that Kissinger could muster. It was a challenge that would put him out on the frontier of American diplomacy without any serious backing from the president, who was by now completely preoccupied with fending off his imminent impeachment. It was a role he relished, "the cowboy who rides all alone into the town . . . with his horse and nothing else. Maybe even without a pistol, since he doesn't shoot," he told the legendary Italian interviewer Oriana Fallaci in November 1972. "This amazing, romantic character suits me precisely because to be alone has always been part of my . . . technique."

Tuesday, February 26, 1974, Damascus. The lone cowboy began his fateful journey with a quick trip to Damascus and Jerusalem to fulfill his part of the new bargain with the Arab oil producers, deliver the POW list to Meir, and open the disengagement negotiations with Assad. Meir was in no position to engage in a substantive discussion about the politically sensitive Golan Heights at this stage because she was still in the process of forming her government. To compound her difficulties, on the eve of Kissinger's departure, Dayan announced that he would not serve in her new government. Under these circumstances, Kissinger dared not delve too much into the substance with Assad. He resolved to take his time.

When Kissinger arrived, Assad was hosting Romanian president Nicolae Ceausescu at an official dinner. Consequently, the meeting in Assad's "palace" began at midnight; it continued until 3:25 a.m.

Assad's first concern was procedural. He again insisted upon Kissinger's shuttling between Damascus and Jerusalem; the military working group in Geneva would be left to deal with technical issues once agreement had been reached. This suited Kissinger just fine.

Not ready to broach substantive issues, Kissinger stayed focused on process. He proposed to Assad that he take the POW list to Israel and start a discussion there about ideas for disengagement on the Golan. He would let the Israelis develop their approach while he met with King Faisal and President

Sadat. Then he would return to Damascus to report to Assad. Following that, both sides should send senior officials to Washington to discuss the differences between them, and Kissinger would then devise some American ideas to help bridge the gaps. He would in the meantime "organize" public opinion in the United States and Israel to reduce opposition to the deal. Only then would he come to Damascus again to try to reach agreement.

Assad found all this quite confusing. What mattered to him was Kissinger's direct involvement. Kissinger said he could not spend all his time in the Middle East, to which Assad gave a typically Syrian-centric response. "There is no more important event in the world right now," he claimed in all seriousness.

They agreed to meet on the morrow and Kissinger departed for the Diyafa Palace, a government guesthouse up the road from Assad's office. From the balcony of this two-story building, Nasser had announced the ill-fated union of Egypt and Syria in 1958. Kissinger was accommodated in the bedroom Nasser had used on that occasion because, according to one of his biographers, Assad wanted to remind him of his pan-Arab credentials.

He fell fast asleep in Nasser's bed only to be awoken thirty minutes later by the muezzin's early morning call to prayer blaring from a nearby mosque. Kissinger stormed into the staff room in his boxer shorts, demanding that they turn off "that goddam noise." As he remarked sardonically to Assad when they met a few hours later, "I said my prayers at 4:30 this morning . . . like everyone else did."

Lack of sleep had ill prepared Kissinger for his second meeting with Assad. It began amicably enough, with Assad agreeing to send an envoy to Washington for consultations after the Israelis had visited. Kissinger asked what Assad would tell Gromyko, who was arriving in Damascus the next day. Assad said he would inform the Russian that after Kissinger brought him an Israeli proposal, the details would be discussed in the Egyptian-Israeli military working group in Geneva. This flummoxed Kissinger. A few hours earlier, Assad had made clear that he was not prepared to discuss anything in that committee. "I may not understand the full complexity of the Syrian mind," Kissinger said. Assad asked what he would prefer him to tell Gromyko. Kissinger said he should "keep it confused." Assad laughed and said he would be guided by Kissinger since he was an expert at that.

They turned again to process. Kissinger warned that he was having a hard time winning over Israeli and American public opinion. Assad bridled at the idea that he should be sensitive to the other side's public opinion; he had enough trouble with his own. He decided to lay down a marker in characteristic Syrian style.

"If they give a plan . . . that they will only go back to the October 6 line, we will reject it immediately," he warned, referring to the pre–Yom Kippur War cease-fire line. He would not be willing to leave the impression that "the sole result of war is to get back only newly-lost territory." Kissinger cautioned that rejecting the first Israeli proposal, even though it was bound to be inadequate, would be a grave mistake. Assad insisted on his red line. If the Israeli proposal did not include withdrawal from territory beyond the October 6 line, "I can say now that we will not discuss it." Drawing on an Arab proverb, he explained that it would be "equivalent to ploughing the ocean."

Assad claimed he was in no hurry. "If there are no results, we will go on fighting," he explained nonchalantly, as if endless war was a natural condition for Syria. "It is not necessary to extract our right today; we can get it tomorrow." Then he revealed his suspicion of what Kissinger was plotting. "Israel wants to retain the Golan and . . . deceive the world into thinking there's a negotiation going on. It would not be useful for us to help them deceive the world."

Kissinger knew that in their opening move, the Israelis were unlikely to offer anything like withdrawal to the October 6 line, let alone territory beyond it. He also knew that if Assad responded by blowing up the talks before the mid-March oil ministers' meeting, the chances of their deciding to lift the embargo would significantly diminish. But instead of trying to placate Assad, Kissinger decided to take umbrage. He said he was not willing to respond to a Syrian ultimatum. Moreover, he had not volunteered to come to Damascus; he had responded to the request of *four* heads of government! "Either I am permitted to work in my way, or I don't work at all," he said.

Assad took this calmly, explaining that it was all about his public opinion: "If we start from a dead point, the people will not be with us. We would lose a lot." Kissinger argued that what mattered was to get the Israelis to step back. Just withdrawing from territory Israel occupied in the last war "would damage us psychologically," Assad retorted. The psychologist in Kissinger could well have argued that gaining back territory that Assad had lost because of the war he had started could be presented as an achievement to his people, especially since it would remove a tangible threat to the citizens of Damascus. Instead, he accused Assad of wanting the result without the negotiation. "On the contrary," Assad responded, "I am giving what I have without any result." He was referring to the gesture he had made by giving Kissinger the list of Israeli POWs. The Israelis had been worried about their prisoners; "there is no more cause for them to worry," said Assad.

This was an important moment in the negotiations. Assad had attempted to intimidate Kissinger and he had stood his ground, earning the Syrian leader's respect (later Assad would even apologize). I witnessed a similar encounter twenty years later between Assad and Warren Christopher over the same issue—the extent of Israeli withdrawal. Christopher went to Damascus in August 1993 with something Assad dearly wanted and could not have dreamed of getting during Kissinger's negotiations: an Israeli commitment by then prime minister Yitzhak Rabin to full withdrawal from the Golan Heights. Instead of expressing satisfaction, Assad demanded to know whether Rabin had any other territorial demands, putting the secretary of state on the defensive. Rather than stand his ground, as Kissinger had done, Christopher said he would go back and ask Rabin. When he did so, Rabin caviled. He had already agreed to full withdrawal; what more did Assad want? According to Itamar Rabinovich, Rabin's negotiator on the Syrian track, it was at that moment that Rabin decided to go behind Christopher's back and do the Oslo deal with Arafat instead.

Wednesday, February 27, 1974, Jerusalem. Assad was right in arguing that he had given Kissinger something of value for the Israelis. Four hours later, when Kissinger handed over the POW list to Meir in her Jerusalem office, she was overwhelmed with relief. Dinitz writes in his memoirs that she took the list and held it close to her heart, "as if she was embracing the prisoners themselves." He notes that tears were falling from her eyes, and his weren't dry either.

After studying the list intently, even though it was in Arabic, and noting that it did indeed include sixty-five names, Meir called in Elazar, the IDF chief of staff. This hardened Israeli officer, like General el-Gamasy when thinking about his troops, choked up too as he expressed his appreciation to Kissinger in a hoarse voice, and then rushed out to inform the families. Later that evening, Meir opened the meeting between Kissinger and her cabinet colleagues by thanking him warmly: "To us it means more than we can say. . . . This is a great thing that you have done."

Trust is a vital commodity in any negotiation, especially for a diplomat seeking to mediate between two bitter adversaries. What Kissinger had done would not be forgotten by the Israelis. He took advantage of this moment of goodwill to persuade the Israelis that they would have to offer more than the October 6 line.

When he had broached that idea with Allon a few weeks earlier, the deputy prime minister had told him there would be no withdrawal beyond the October 6 line "under any circumstances," so he knew this would be no easy sell. On the Golan, the IDF was not exposed militarily in the way its flanks had been on the west bank of the Suez Canal. Secured through hard-won battles, the Golan pocket now held by the Israeli forces enabled their artillery to threaten Damascus. Withdrawal ran the risk of putting Israeli towns and villages nestled below the Golan Heights in range of Syrian artillery, reversing the balance of deterrence.

Kissinger began by deploying his "sky is falling" warnings, confiding to Meir that he feared Assad wanted to blow up the negotiations before they had barely started and rally the Arabs to his side. With Gromyko in the region and the Arab oil ministers soon to meet, he argued, tensions were rising. Meir was unmoved. Dayan, who at this stage was still in the outgoing cabinet even though he had insisted that he would not be part of a new government, suggested the Egyptian deal, with its limited-forces zones, UN buffer, and civilian repopulation, could be replicated on the Syrian front. However, he viewed it as a one-sided deal in which Israel paid and Assad gained. "It's all about how deep we shall withdraw," he argued. "We get absolutely nothing in return."

Kissinger begged to differ: a radical Arab state would be signing an agreement with Israel; that would remove the pressure on Egypt and help it honor its deal with Israel, the cause of moderation in the Arab world would be further legitimized, and Soviet efforts to undermine the process would be thwarted. Syria, he argued in summing up his case, "is the key to a moderate evolution." And then he made a by now familiar point: an agreement would buy Israel time to stave off international pressure. And in any case, Israel would only be giving up a small piece of territory. He emphasized that he was only looking for a symbolic move beyond the October 6 line. A withdrawal beyond Quneitra, he argued as he casually introduced the idea for the first time, would produce Syrian flexibility on thinning out forces too.

When Kissinger accentuated the positive in this way, he was so much more effective with the Israelis than when he played Jeremiah. But then Kissinger made an unforced error, one that would come back to plague this negotiation. In making his case for withdrawal, he volunteered that he was not suggesting that any Israeli settlements on the Golan be withdrawn. That, he explained, set a limit on how far the Israelis could be expected to withdraw. "If your real position is the one traced by the settlements then you don't give up anything by giving up the line between the settlements and the October 6 line," he contended.

Kissinger subsequently admitted that at this early stage he wasn't aware of the exact location of the settlements and the terrain around them, things that he would become painfully familiar with later. He was right to assume that it would prove impossible to get the Israelis to withdraw any settlement on the Golan merely for a military disengagement agreement with the Syrians, but to concede that principle for the sake of a talking point about how little the Israelis would have to give up was to make a major concession early on for no gain. It conceded the legitimacy of settlements in Arab-occupied territory at a time when, as he would later discover, Israel's generals—Dayan, Allon, and newly installed IDF chief of staff Motta Gur—were basing their requirements on Israel's security needs, not on the location of the Golan settlements.*

Nevertheless, they railed against the injustice of it all. Allon reminded Kissinger that Assad started the war and therefore had no justification in demanding a change in the demarcation line. Kissinger agreed that the Syrians didn't deserve it but urged them to look at the wider geopolitical context. The strategic objective, he explained, should be to isolate Syria. Proving prescient beyond anything he could have imagined at the time, he said that he envisaged the line of Israeli withdrawal would be "the final line."

"Our strategy," he concluded, speaking as if he were one of them, "is to keep [the Arabs] separated, to keep them moving . . . to keep the Russians out, and to keep the Europeans intimidated." But to achieve all that, Israel would have to give up territory on the Golan Heights. He left them to think about it, promising to return in a few days.

Thursday, February 28, 1974, Giza. After a morning session with the Israelis, Kissinger flew to Cairo for a late lunch with Sadat. They met at the presidential rest house at Giza, which afforded a stunning view of the nearby pyramids, the timeless testament to the expansive vision and extraordinary engineering skills of the ancient Egyptians. Kissinger had told Assad that he merely intended a courtesy call on Sadat to give the Israelis time to reflect on their proposal. His real purpose was to consult with his co-conspirator in the effort to move the reluctant Israelis and Syrians into an agreement.

Kissinger and Sadat had adapted to this challenge like two concert pianists joining together to perform a complex Schubert duet. They had bonded during the Sinai disengagement negotiations, when each gained an appreciation for the other's manipulative skills and daring. Their common antipathy for the Soviet Union and commitment to moving the Middle East in a more peaceful direction had provided the glue.

True to his promise to Meir to take off his uniform, Sadat met Kissinger dressed in an elegant pin-striped suit. Sadat's wife, Jehan, had organized a family lunch and invited a special guest to join them, Dr. Ashraf Marwan, Sadat's presidential secretary and Israel's premier spy.

Marwan had become as indispensable to Sadat as to the Israelis and his presence at this family lunch indicated his trusted status. Notwithstanding his reputation for corruption, Sadat used him as his personal emissary to his Arab

---

* The Golan settlers in those days were mostly Labor supporters in contrast to the ideologically driven West Bank settlers of Gush Emunim. They were unlikely to oppose being moved back from the disengagement line.

counterparts, including Muammar Qaddafi, Hafez al-Assad, and King Faisal. Kissinger had encountered him during the Sinai disengagement negotiations when Sadat asked for American help with his physical security once he had decided to split with the Russians. The CIA assumed responsibility for training Sadat's personal security detail, providing its personnel with weapons and surveillance equipment. Marwan became Sadat's liaison with the CIA for this purpose.

Marwan's reports went directly to the desks of Meir and Dayan, which meant they had an independent though not necessarily reliable means of checking what Kissinger was telling Sadat about his negotiations. Since it was one of Kissinger's diplomatic tactics to tell different things to his different interlocutors, Marwan's reports to the Israelis of the debriefings he received from Sadat after his meetings with Kissinger fed their suspicions of him.

The Israelis also had a way of checking what Kissinger was telling Assad because of their ability to intercept the Syrian reports of Assad's meetings. Only in this case, Dayan revealed it to Kissinger during the Syrian-Israeli negotiations by reading from the transcripts. While Kissinger was well aware at the time that Israel had high-level sources in Cairo, it is unclear whether he

Henry Kissinger and President Sadat meet the press after lunch at Sadat's rest house next to the pyramids at Giza on February 28, 1974. True to his promise to Prime Minister Meir, Sadat no longer wore his uniform. He was accompanied by his presidential secretary, Ashraf Marwan, seen here walking behind Kissinger. Marwan was a trusted confidant of Sadat, but he was also Israel's most valuable spy.

knew Marwan, with whom he was working on sensitive security issues, was an Israeli spy.

Over lunch with the Sadats it emerged that the Egyptian president was still smarting from his humiliation at Damascus Airport. He dismissed Assad as a "merchant" and his Ba'ath Party colleagues as in the pay of outside powers. (Marwan must have enjoyed that irony.) He spoke of the need to isolate Assad and bring him to his knees and explained how he was working on Boumediene toward that end.

Together, Kissinger and Sadat decided that the zone of a possible Israeli-Syrian agreement required a line of Israeli withdrawal a little, but not too much, beyond the October 6 line. Quneitra, Sadat explained, was enough of a prize for Assad to use to convince his people to support the agreement. Conveniently, that outcome would protect Sadat's interests by ensuring that Assad could not claim he secured a better deal than Egypt.

They assigned Marwan the task of moving Assad. Sadat had already sent him to Damascus in the run-up to the Geneva Conference to try to persuade Assad to attend. Indeed, it was from Marwan that Assad received Sadat's misleading assurance that Israel's line of withdrawal on the Golan would be defined before the Geneva Conference convened. This time, Marwan would accompany War Minister Ismail and Chief of Staff el-Gamasy to Damascus.

After lunch, Kissinger and Sadat briefed these Egyptian officials. Kissinger explained that he would need a few weeks to bring the Israelis around to the line he had just agreed on with Sadat; Ismail and el-Gamasy's mission was to help persuade Assad to accept it. Meanwhile, he would press the Israelis to give up the pocket they had acquired during the war, as well as Quneitra. Sadat warned his men not to tell Assad that he would get Quneitra. Kissinger agreed; at this stage, he just needed them to act as independent validators of his claim that he could get the Israelis to withdraw to the October 6 line, but they should make clear that anything beyond that would be much more difficult.

Sadat and Kissinger agreed on how to work the Israelis. Kissinger would convey to Meir that Sadat was ready to establish an intelligence liaison with the Mossad and did not expect Israel to give up any Golan settlements. More significantly, as Kissinger subsequently relayed to Meir, "Sadat said if you could get a small strip beyond [Quneitra] . . . he could stay out of the war and would take a public position in support of that offer."

Friday, March 1, 1974, Herzliya–Damascus. Kissinger met with Prime Minister Meir on Friday morning at the Mossad guesthouse. En route, he received word from Damascus that the Red Cross visits to the Israeli POWs had begun. That set a positive tone for his meetings with the Israelis. He first reported privately to Meir on his meeting with Sadat. Even if Assad didn't accept some territory beyond the October 6 line, he said, just offering it would keep Egypt out of the next war, which wouldn't be a bad outcome for Israel.

Meir told him that going beyond the October 6 line would be "dynamite" in Israel. That came as no surprise to Kissinger, but he knew she was thereby acknowledging that withdrawing to the October 6 line would not be explosive. Kissinger said he just needed to get the process started and buy a month's time to get the oil embargo lifted.

Meir then brought Kissinger into the conference room to meet with all her advisers. He explained that Sadat sought a Syrian-Israeli agreement to prevent Assad from creating mischief in the Arab world, enable Egypt to pursue constructive policies toward Israel, and eliminate a war started by the Syrians that could drag Egypt in. To achieve all that would require Israel to offer Assad "some kilometers" beyond the October 6 line, he said. Otherwise, Sadat "would probably be forced into a war even if he thinks the Syrians are unreasonable."

Kissinger left the Israelis to ponder what they would have to give to get a Syrian deal and headed for Damascus, where he met with Assad for four hours. Assad said he had received a message from Sadat, "but then you know all about that," letting Kissinger know he was onto him. Kissinger professed ignorance. Assad expressed his disdain for Sadat, describing the letter that Marwan had brought him as "full of verbiage." But Assad was pleased by one part of the letter: Sadat had written that Kissinger had "guaranteed" he would get the October 6 line, and that if Assad were patient he might get back Quneitra too. So much for the message Sadat was supposed to have sent about how much effort it would take Kissinger to get the October 6 line and his admonition to his officials not to tell Assad about Quneitra yet.

Kissinger responded that he wasn't in a position to guarantee anything. Regardless of what Sadat had written, it was going to be a heavy lift to get the Israelis just to accept the October 6 line.

Assad was fond of quoting another Arab proverb about stealing the grapes from the vineyard rather than fighting with the guard at the winery's gate. And that's how he now proceeded. He told Kissinger he had full confidence in him. And then he inquired ever so politely what Kissinger had in mind about the line. Resorting to his trademark obfuscation, Kissinger said Assad could realize "some distance" beyond the October 6 line. Assad said he wouldn't consider anything less than ten kilometers; that would allow most villagers to return home and reduce the vulnerability of towns that were overlooked by hills.

Kissinger—and Assad—knew that ten kilometers was well beyond anything he could hope to extract from the Israelis, so he changed the subject. Whom would Assad send to Washington? The answer: Chief of Intelligence General Hikmat Shihabi. Kissinger took that as a sign of seriousness, since Shihabi was Assad's most trusted confidant.

Assad returned to the line of withdrawal question. "What is now envisaged will do us no good; yet what we want does not seem achievable. What is the solution?" It would require changes in both sides' positions, Kissinger answered.

In contrast to his attitude in their last meeting, Assad allowed that there would have to be adjustments to his demands. He still wanted to know the depth of the line Kissinger had in mind. "I have thought that some kilometers beyond Quneitra might be possible, but I was just thinking out loud," Kissinger said.

Amazingly, this casual offer of "Quneitra plus" now appeared to mollify Assad. "I have confidence in you," he said. "I proceed from the premise that if withdrawal beyond the October 6 line is conceptually feasible, it can be done," he added constructively. He explained that in Arabic "some" means between three to nine kilometers; Kissinger said that in English it was closer to three, but his interest was in getting the maximum for Assad.

"I believe you," he said. "Can I hope that you will expend all possible efforts to realize the minimum I am seeking?" he inquired diplomatically. "I will make a maximum effort to get all that is attainable," Kissinger said obliquely, but he now knew that Assad would probably settle for around three kilometers.

Kissinger had succeeded in moving Assad into the zone. Of course, Assad, like Sadat, had just put the burden on Kissinger's shoulders. But he had moved from obduracy to flexibility and placed himself in Kissinger's hands.

Kissinger was still wary. As he told the Israelis, mixing his metaphors, "One of the maddening things in dealing with the Syrians is that you have a rational conversation for four hours and then some gear strips and they are off to the races." Kissinger's challenge now was to move the Israelis into the zone too. For that, he would have to await Dayan's arrival in Washington.

Saturday, March 2, 1974, Riyadh. In the meantime, the oil embargo needed to be dealt with. Before returning to Washington, Kissinger flew to Riyadh for another rendezvous with royalty. When he reported to King Faisal on Saqqaf's conversation with Nixon about lifting the embargo, the king surprised him by saying the separation of forces on the Golan had to come first. "Once that is done," Faisal explained, "it will remove the last obstacle."

Kissinger found it difficult to contain himself. That was the precondition he thought he had persuaded Saqqaf to drop when he was in Washington. He told Faisal that Nixon would never have agreed to send him to the region if he knew of that requirement. But Faisal had come under heavy pressure in the meantime from Assad not to rob him of his leverage over the Americans. The king explained to Kissinger that it wasn't just up to him. Although he would do his utmost, another Israeli withdrawal would "remove the arguments from the hands of those who . . . do not want to go along with lifting the embargo." He was referring to Qaddafi and Boumediene, as well as Assad.

Kissinger responded that it was beneath America's dignity to be pressured by its friends in this way. Faisal said it caused him much pain too. They continued in this vein until Faisal tired of the conversation. As he stood up to end the meeting he said, "Let us hope the difficulties will end soon." And then he blessed Kissinger's efforts and said he would pray to God "for your success."

Saqqaf was elated. He subsequently told Kissinger it was one of the best meetings he had witnessed with the king. "The King usually looks down when he talks to you; this time he is looking straight ahead. Usually, he sits there picking lint off his robe; this time he didn't," Saqqaf explained. He said Kissinger should be happy because the king committed to lifting the embargo. But, Kissinger protested, the king had told him he wouldn't lift the embargo. "That proves it," responded Saqqaf. "He thought you would leak it and therefore couldn't tell you."

Strange are the ways of the "Magic Kingdom." Faisal had just engaged in an elaborate ploy to balance the demands of the radical Arab states against the insistence of his American great-power protector. In front of Kissinger and Faisal's courtiers, some of whom would undoubtedly report to Assad, he had to appear to be in Syria's corner. But in fact, as his enigmatic closing blessing indicated, he intended to help the United States.

Sure enough, after a series of meetings that began in Cairo on March 11, then shifted to Tripoli, and culminated in Vienna on March 18, the Arab oil ministers announced that "because of continued U.S. efforts toward peace in the Middle East," they had decided to lift the embargo.

The Syrian and Libyan oil ministers had managed to drag out the decision for three days, but in the end all the other oil ministers, including the Algerian, decided to go along with Saudi Arabia's insistence that the embargo had achieved its purpose because it had persuaded the United States and Europe to adopt "a new dimension" toward the Arab-Israeli conflict. As a face-saving device for the Syrians, the Algerians proposed the decision be revisited at a June 1 meeting. But Sheikh Yamani, the Saudi oil minister, made it clear to the press that Saudi Arabia would not cooperate in reimposing the embargo then and, to speed the lifting, would immediately send one million barrels of oil to the United States. The decision was presented as "a provisional lifting," but Kissinger had been right when he had assessed months earlier that once lifted it would not be reimposed.

Kissinger had broken the back of the oil embargo. Abandoned by his best friends, the lesson for Assad was clear—he had better find a way to work with the United States or he'd be left alone with the Soviet Union, which was now busily hedging by arming his archenemy, Saddam Hussein.

If the force was now with Henry of Arabia, as *Time* magazine had taken to calling him, it made little impression in Jerusalem, where the political crisis had deepened. Dayan's refusal to join Meir's government had precipitated her resignation in frustration. A bevy of beseeching Labor Party colleagues then managed to change her mind. Dayan eventually changed his mind too, so that by March 10, the new government was finally formed. But Dayan was reluctant to come to Washington. As Dinitz explained it to Kissinger on March 14, any Israeli government that discusses giving up territory beyond the October 6 line "would be a dead duck tomorrow." Facing rising demonstrations against him at home, Dayan was not keen to fuel the fire by serving as the poster child for Golan concessions in Washington. When Eban came calling on Kissinger on March 19, he warned him that even though the new cabinet had by then decided to send Dayan on March 29, he would not be coming with a line west of the October 6 line. If the Syrians insisted on it, said Eban, they would only be inviting a counterproposal of a line *east* of it!

In Washington, the difficulties were mounting too. On the day of the oil ministers' announcement, federal district court judge John J. Sirica ordered evidence from the grand jury investigating Watergate be handed to the House Judiciary Committee, thereby providing a turbo boost to the impeachment proceedings.

The next day, Senator James L. Buckley, a conservative Republican legislator from New York who had been Nixon's staunchest defender, publicly called on the president to resign rather than confront the nation with a searing, televised trial. It was the harbinger of the Republican defections that would eventually force Nixon from office.

Watergate was undermining the president's authority just when Kissinger needed it to conduct effective Middle East diplomacy. It was also making his boss more difficult to constrain. When Kissinger reported to him on the Arab oil ministers' decision, Nixon used it as an opportunity to berate him about his step-by-step strategy. With his jowls shaking, he cautioned Kissinger against allowing the Israelis to think they could just dig in again now that the Arab oil pressure was off. "This is one thing we're going to do though, Henry. Let's understand that. There is going to be a permanent settlement," he declared.

Then there were the Soviets. On March 26, Kissinger flew to Moscow to prepare for a Brezhnev-Nixon summit under circumstances—including disappointment about congressional foot-dragging on improved trading terms, complications in the nuclear arms talks, and above all, Soviet discontent with Kissinger's Middle East pirouette—that ensured he would receive a frosty reception. He later referred to his experience in the Kremlin as "a four-hour brawl." Brezhnev demanded that Geneva be reconvened and that the disengagement negotiations take place there in the Egyptian-Israeli military working group with Soviet participation. He accused Kissinger of violating their understanding and told him to inform Nixon that if the United States continued to act separately, superpower relations would be adversely affected.

Kissinger refused to reconvene Geneva, instead repeating his offer of regular meetings with Gromyko to keep each other informed of their separate activities. That triggered an accusation from Gromyko that Kissinger was proposing "a semblance of participation" whereas in fact he intended to treat the Soviet Union as an outside observer. Brezhnev concluded ominously that in that case he considered himself "free to act at one's own discretion."

Shaken by this dressing-down, Kissinger quickly checked with Sadat and Assad. Predictably, Sadat was adamantly against reconvening Geneva, even dispatching Fahmy to Washington to make sure Nixon would signal "a red light to the Soviet Union." Assad surprised him yet again. He insisted that Kissinger stick with the agreed-upon procedure and go to Geneva only after agreement was reached. As Kissinger notes in his memoirs, "The President of Syria, remarkably, had chosen to negotiate without his principal ally."

Kissinger understood, however, that Assad's position was making it even more incumbent on him to deliver. He was discovering that in weakness and dependency there is also negotiating strength. As he explained to Dayan when he finally came to visit him in Washington, from the Soviets' perspective Syria had become "the hinge." They wanted to see Assad's efforts fail so that it could produce "a disintegration of our role in the Middle East . . . and the destruction of Sadat." To keep the Soviets out, he needed to be able to say to Assad that "with us you get something, without us you get nothing." That gave Assad some indirect purchase on Israel too.

Friday, March 29, 1974, Washington, DC. Though a reluctant envoy, Dayan had nevertheless prepared meticulously for his mission, consulting with the IDF General Staff and northern commanders as well as the Golan settlers.

He had also conducted repeated survey patrols along the length of the line. From these Golan excursions, he concluded that militarily Israel could afford to withdraw from Quneitra, the very thing that Kissinger needed to lubricate his diplomacy. But Dayan was not authorized to tell Kissinger that. Because of their experience with him in the Sinai negotiations, Meir and her advisers— who now included Yitzhak Rabin, Shimon Peres, and Arele Yariv, since they had joined her new cabinet—believed they had to start by offering the minimum. Kissinger had tutored them on hanging tough at first so that he could be the one to show the Arabs that only the United States could deliver Israel. Now he would discover that he had taught them too well.

They met in Kissinger's seventh-floor conference room before adjourning to his eighth-floor dining room for lunch. Dayan wasted no time in laying out his concept of the disengagement agreement, following closely the model of the Egyptian agreement. As in the Egyptian model, Dayan wanted Syrian civilians to return to their villages, but because the distances were much smaller, he suggested that some of them would need to be in the UN buffer zone. He offered as well to hand over to UN control Syrian positions on Mount Hermon that Israel had captured during the war.

Then he rolled open the map, and Kissinger blanched. As Eban had warned, the line was well *east* of the October 6 line, with Israel proposing to hold on to one-third of the pocket it had captured in the last war. "[T]hese lines are impossible," Kissinger said. If he presented the map to the Syrians, "war will break out; we will be discredited; Egypt will be discredited." He wanted Dayan to report back to the Israeli cabinet Kissinger's strong conviction that it would be very dangerous for him to present this line to Syrian intelligence chief Shihabi, whose visit had already been scheduled for two weeks hence. In Kissinger's view, the sky was about to fall again. Therefore, to avoid disaster, it was incumbent on Israel to accept his "Quneitra plus" formula. Bound by the Israeli cabinet decision, Dayan stuck to his brief.

Dayan's real concern on this visit was arms supplies, not lines on a map. When he reconvened with Kissinger on Saturday morning, he made the case for strengthening Israel in the years to come by allowing access to America's most sophisticated aircraft and conventional weapons, particularly the F-16 (at the time, the newest fighter aircraft in the U.S. arsenal). Kissinger and Schlesinger had earlier agreed to put the brakes on consideration of new Israeli arms requests so that Kissinger could use them as sweeteners. When Dayan expressed his concern about the delays, Kissinger seized the opening. If the negotiations are moving forward, he explained to Dayan, "Scowcroft . . . can say we need these to help you move." (Scowcroft had taken over Kissinger's role of shepherding Israel's arms requests through the bureaucracy.)

Kissinger then called Haig, in Dayan's presence, emulating his phone call in front of Dinitz at the height of the military resupply crisis during the Yom Kippur War. He explained to Haig that Dayan needed to go home as the man who produced "because that will help us in the subsequent talks." Following the script, Haig responded, "We'll just put the arm on [Schlesinger]." Kissinger promised Dayan he too would lobby Schlesinger. However, the best time to secure next-generation aircraft would be "when we complete the Syrian disengagement." Allowing how this might look like blackmail, he claimed that it was the only way to get the Pentagon to agree to it. The territory-for-arms linkage had become explicit.

Their meeting was interrupted by a secretary reminding Kissinger that he had to leave for his next meeting. Kissinger hurriedly bid Dayan farewell and took his private elevator to the eighth floor, where friends and family were waiting in the reception rooms for a celebratory lunch.* That afternoon, he and Nancy Maginnes were driven to the private office of Judge Francis E. Thomas Jr. in Arlington, Virginia, where they were married in a four-minute ceremony. They then departed for a short honeymoon in Acapulco.

Dayan saw Schlesinger on Monday morning. By the afternoon, he had a commitment from the Pentagon for two hundred more tanks and five hundred APCs, just as Kissinger had promised. Dayan understood the quid pro quo. In a private conversation with Kissinger after their first meeting on Friday, Dayan had discussed how to move the cabinet to his personal position on Quneitra. Dayan suggested Kissinger write Meir a letter explaining the consequences of presenting an inadequate line to the Syrians; Kissinger agreed and had Larry Eagleburger discuss the language with Dayan before he departed Washington.

On April 3, he dispatched the letter to Meir that he had approved while on his honeymoon. Writing with what he called "a heavy heart," he told her that the Israeli proposal had no chance of being accepted by the Syrians and, in his honest judgment, would lead to the outbreak of another war. To avoid certain doom, she needed to produce an Israeli proposal to withdraw beyond Quneitra, one that need not include Israeli settlements. Probably following Dayan's advice, he did not end this lamentation with the usual threat of a loss of American support. Instead, he praised her courage, asked her to reconsider, and gently sought her permission to offer the Syrian envoy "some hope that we can expect a further progression of your views by the time I come to the area."

The letter arrived on the prime minister's desk amid yet another Israeli political crisis. On April 1, the Agranat Commission, which was investigating

---

* The guests included Nancy Maginnes; Kissinger's two children, David and Elizabeth; his close aide Winston Lord and his wife, Bette Bao Lord; the celebrated columnist Joseph Alsop and his wife, Susan Mary; Larry Eagleburger; Brent Scowcroft; and State Department legal adviser Carlyle Maw.

the events that led to the Yom Kippur War, had issued its interim report and generated a political earthquake. It found the IDF chief of staff, Dado Elazar, and the head of military intelligence, Eli Zeira, directly responsible for the errors committed on the eve of the war and recommended they both resign. This was bad enough news for Kissinger, since he had come to greatly appreciate the quiet charm and intelligence of Elazar and was expecting to rely on him for the Golan negotiations. But when the chief of staff resigned, he pointed the finger at the defense minister, arguing that he was the one who had the authority and responsibility to make decisions in all military matters before the war. The public was already upset with Dayan, but now it became infuriated that he was let off the hook and the popular Dado was made the scapegoat. The outrage engulfed Meir too. Even though the Agranat Commission had not dealt with political culpability, she could not live with the idea that Elazar would be the one to take the fall. On April 10, she resigned, this time warning her Labor Party acolytes not to appeal her decision. They didn't. For a moment, it looked as if there would be a prolonged hiatus because of an Israeli election.

Instead of calling an election, however, the Labor Party nominated Yitzhak Rabin to form a government in Meir's place. Rabin, of course, was Kissinger's old friend with whom he had developed a common strategic vision for a Middle East free of Soviet influence. Under the Israeli system, Meir would stay in place at the head of a caretaker government, with Dayan by her side, fully empowered to make decisions until Rabin could form a government endorsed by a majority of the Knesset. It was an additional benefit that Rabin and Shimon Peres, his soon-to-be defense minister, had already joined Meir and Dayan on the other side of the table for the disengagement deliberations with Kissinger and his advisers, ensuring continuity. Disaster had been averted.

One of Meir's first acts as caretaker prime minister was to reject Kissinger's letter of doom by writing that the hard-line proposal presented by Dayan in Washington "reflects the position of the Israeli government."

Saturday, April 13, 1974, Washington, DC. Assad's envoy, General Hikmat Shihabi, came calling on Kissinger in his State Department office to discuss the Israeli proposal. Ahead of the meeting, Assad had written Kissinger that Shihabi was "not coming in a confrontational mood." Two days before their rendezvous, however, a suicide squad of three gunmen from the PFLP General Command, a Marxist Palestinian terrorist group, had crossed from Lebanon into the northern border town of Kiryat Shmona and killed eighteen Israeli civilians, including nine children, in an apartment building. Israel had responded by raiding six villages on the Lebanese side of the border and blowing up more than twenty houses, taking care to avoid casualties.

As he prepared to receive Shihabi, Kissinger learned of the Israeli retaliation, and of a flare-up in fighting on the Golan provoked by a Syrian attempt to retake a position on the crest of Mount Hermon. At the same time, intelligence reports showed that Brezhnev was showering Assad with additional tanks and aircraft. It was an inauspicious setting for this critical consultation.

In his memoirs, Kissinger describes Shihabi as fiercely proud, a little insecure, and eager for acceptance and recognition. I had the opportunity to engage with Shihabi when he came to Washington again in December 1994, this time as chief of staff of the Syrian army, to meet with Ehud Barak, then his IDF counterpart. He had by then become Assad's most trusted military adviser, a critical Sunni mainstay of the Alawite minority regime, sporting a rose gold Audemars Piguet watch as a trapping of his high office. In our meetings, he displayed none of the insecurity that Kissinger noticed. Probably because he was in the presence of Israelis, he came across as stiff and reserved. But there was an aura of intelligence, gravitas, and integrity about him. During a coffee break, he discreetly took Itamar Rabinovich, Israel's ambassador to Washington, aside and spoke just one sentence to him. "Tell your prime minister we want to make peace." It was the identical message that el-Gamasy had conveyed to Yariv, twenty years earlier, at their first encounter in the desert.

Before Kissinger showed Shihabi the Israeli map that Dayan had brought to Washington, he attempted to soften its negative impact by explaining that in the Sinai negotiations he had only been able to shift the Israelis to where he had needed them to be in the last days before agreement. Shihabi expressed concern about how long this would take. Kissinger said he was willing to make another trip to the region at the end of the month to speed up the process, and shuttle back and forth between Damascus and Jerusalem for as long as necessary to get the deal done.

Kissinger claimed that the Israelis had originally offered half the pocket and now, thanks to his efforts, Dayan was offering a line farther back, "almost to the October 6 line." He recounted what he had told Dayan: that even if Israel withdrew to the October 6 line, it would be insufficient for Assad. And he noted that he had written a strong letter to the Israeli prime minister making the same point. Kissinger then defined the zone of a possible agreement: "I will achieve the maximum line that is possible, and it will have to be beyond the October 6 line, and it has to include Quneitra." Only then did he reveal Dayan's map.

Shihabi's first reaction was to beg him not to show it to Assad. "It's not disengagement; it's a relinquishment of sovereignty!" Kissinger reassured him that it was just the starting point; he would put great pressure on the Israelis to achieve an endpoint beyond the October 6 line. Shihabi agreed that "some settlement along these lines can be reached."

This was hardly the reaction Kissinger had expected, and it proved what he had begun to suspect: Assad needed the disengagement. "What remains to be done when I come out to the Middle East," he now explained to Shihabi, "is to move the line and to agree on the disposition of forces." He made it sound easy. But when Shihabi unfurled his map it became clear that closing the gap between the Israeli-preferred line and the Syrian one was going to be no simple task. Shihabi's line was only a little different from the one Assad had shown him in Damascus; the only adjustment was in Syria's favor to encompass two large villages that had been split by Assad's line. The Syrian forces line was at least five kilometers west of Quneitra; the suggested Israeli forces line was another five kilometers beyond that.

Shihabi allowed for the principle of Israel remaining on the Golan "on a temporary basis." Little did the Syrians know then that "temporary" would come to mean more than forty-five years. His map also allowed for a three-to-six-kilometer-wide buffer zone between the Israeli and Syrian forces where civilians would return under Syrian civil administration and international observers could move freely. Dayan had proposed the identical idea.

Conceptually, the two sides were quite close, but territorially they were at least twelve kilometers apart. Closing that gap would prove to be a prodigious challenge. Kissinger was now late for lunch at the Soviet embassy with Gromyko, who happened to be in town. He sent Shihabi off with a reassuring message for Assad that such meetings with his Soviet counterpart were purely symbolic. "We will negotiate with President Assad directly, not through another country," he promised.

As soon as Shihabi left town, Kissinger had to deal with the fallout from the Kiryat Shmona terrorist attack. Lebanon had referred the Israeli retaliatory raids on its southern villages to the UN Security Council, where a resolution condemning Israel was drafted by America's allies. It contained a specific reference to the terrorist attack on Kiryat Shmona as justification for Israel's retaliation. Inexplicably, the draft the State Department sent back to the U.S. Mission to the UN retained the condemnation but removed the justification. At the last minute, perhaps realizing the now unbalanced nature of the resolution, the U.S. delegate tried to insert a censure of the Palestinian terrorists. When that attempt failed, instead of abstaining or vetoing the resolution as it would normally do, the United States voted for it.

That was an uncharacteristic misstep on Kissinger's part, one that would cost him dearly in the eyes of the Israeli public at a time of deep insecurity and high emotional stress. He had always positioned himself as their savior from a hostile world if they followed his game plan. He had told Assad that he needed to prepare Israeli public opinion for Golan concessions. Instead, he had now managed to raise doubts in their minds about his reliability. Two weeks later, while he was shuttling between Jerusalem and Damascus, the opposition Likud Party organized a four-thousand-strong demonstration against him and denounced his efforts to pressure Israel to withdraw on the Golan. The days of adoring crowds greeting him at Ben Gurion Airport were over.

Something similar occurred with John Kerry when, as Obama's secretary of state, he gave an unscripted speech at the Munich Security Conference in 2014 in which he warned Israel that it was in danger of becoming an "apartheid state" if it didn't make peace with the Palestinians. The Israeli media reported his remarks as a threat. This one poorly phrased statement did much to turn a politician who prided himself on a perfect voting record on Israel during twenty-eight years in the Senate into an antagonist in the eyes of many Israelis.

Herein lies a fundamental dilemma of American diplomacy toward Israel: a too-heavy hand can generate a backlash in public opinion that makes wresting concessions more difficult, but a too-indulgent approach makes it all too easy for Israeli leaders to deflect demands for compromise. The way to resolve the quandary was best expressed by Samuel Lewis, a U.S. ambassador to Israel in the Carter and Reagan administrations. He called it "the arm around Israel" technique, in which the U.S. president or secretary of state needed to put a reassuring arm around the Israeli prime minister's shoulders, and then nudge him or her forward in the U.S.-preferred direction.

In Kissinger's case, he knew he had made a tactical mistake, generated by his desire "to accumulate capital in the Arab world" ahead of his shuttle. "Wisdom most certainly eluded us on this occasion" is the way he put it disarmingly in his memoirs. He was so concerned about how Shihabi's report might be received in Damascus at that moment, and the need to ensure Saudi and Algerian encouragement to moderate Assad's demands, that he failed to consider Israel's concerns. Now when Kissinger tried to put a reassuring arm around the Israelis, they knew it was intended to pressure them to compromise, and they resisted. It was an important lesson: the United States gains more credit with the Arabs when it delivers tangible Israeli concessions than when it joins in condemning Israel.

President Joe Biden demonstrated the efficacy of this approach when he put his arm around Prime Minister Netanyahu during the May 2021 outbreak of fighting between Israel and Hamas. Notwithstanding the demands of his progressive Democratic base and efforts in the UN Security Council to insist that Israel cease fire, Biden first blocked Security Council action for a week before pressing Netanyahu to end the bombing campaign. The Israeli prime minister complied in twenty-four hours.

———

Thursday, May 2, 1974, Jerusalem. When Kissinger arrived in Israel for the start of the Israel-Syria shuttle, Meir scolded him about the UNSC resolution. She asked how it was possible that Israel was condemned "and the words Kiryat Shmona were not even mentioned?" Why was it always Israel that paid the bill? she wanted to know. Eighteen Israelis had been killed, including women and children, "and we're condemned, and the United States votes for it?" Kissinger claimed that Nixon had ordered him to vote for the resolution.

When they discussed the negotiations with Syria, she said she had asked the new chief of staff, General Motta Gur, to draw up a map. That name filled Kissinger with dread. Wasn't he the general who had spilled the beans about Israel's Sinai proposal to his Egyptian counterpart in Geneva? The prime minister said Gur felt Israel could be more generous in the southern Golan in an area they referred to as Rephidim (Al Rafeed, see map p. 410). Gur, however, was inflexible about Quneitra and the hills that surrounded it. But, she added, if "Assad is willing to be reasonable, I will be prepared to urge the cabinet to give the eastern part of Quneitra." Kissinger responded that every Arab he had talked to had told him Assad had to have all of Quneitra. Moreover, if her unwillingness to yield led to his failure, it would damage his ability to manage matters for Israel's benefit.

Personalizing the issue after his UN gaffe was hardly likely to convince her to be more responsive. Quneitra never meant anything to Assad, she said, and there wasn't a single member of her cabinet who thought Israel should give it up to an aggressor who had started two wars and was still firing on Israeli forces on the Golan.

Don't waste your time trying to convince your cabinet to give half of Quneitra, he retorted. The result would be the failure of his mission and trouble from the Soviets, plus he would not be able to line up the Gulf Arabs to ensure the oil embargo was lifted. Sadat would look like a fool for relying on the United States and would have to turn in a more aggressive direction, there would be constant escalation on the Golan, and what Nixon would do then was unpredictable. The recitation of the litany of woes had become tedious, but he never tired of repeating them to the Israelis, believing that he needed the verbal equivalent of a battering ram to weaken their psychological defenses.

It was a mistake to have made the trip, he said: "It is one thing to fail in Washington; it is another thing to come out here and put my prestige on the line." He wondered how he could explain that Israel had to hold on to Quneitra "to defend settlements when no one accepts your right to defend these . . . settlements. They will see it as a policy of annexation. We will regret this."

With that they adjourned to the cabinet room, where all Meir's advisers awaited them. This time, as she took her seat, she was flanked by Rabin and

Allon. General Gur began the meeting by showing Kissinger his map and explaining why the line of hills west of Quneitra were the last line of defense before the terrain started to slope down to the Jezreel Valley. In the southern Golan, he explained, the plateau had little military value, so Israel could make concessions there. But any move to the west in the central Golan would bring the Syrians right into the settlements. To defend them, Gur maintained, Israel had to retain the hills.

Kissinger could barely contain himself. He repeated his shopworn catalog of consequences. Then, belittling Gur's narrow military focus, he explained that it was not about a line of defense, but rather about the wider geopolitical consequences for Israel. Looking at Rabin, he recalled how together they had devised a strategy for generating Arab frustration with Soviet support until the Arabs eventually turned to the United States, "and we would thereby gain jointly the capacity to determine the pace of events." Now Gur's withdrawal line was jeopardizing what that strategy had achieved "by proving that those who followed the United States were following a policy of illusion and that those who stayed with the Soviet Union were right all along."

Again addressing Gur, he said that if the Arabs turned back to war, the Lajes Air Base might not be available this time to resupply the Israeli army. Then he switched to a conspiratorial air. His strategy, he reminded them, had been to prevent Israel from having to deal with final-status issues. He had successfully segmented the process into a set of individual small steps that Israel's political system could withstand. But that was all endangered. "If now this negotiation fails," he said, "and it is certain to fail with this map, it will move back to international forums." If he were to use Gur's argument there that Israel needed the territory to defend the settlements, "we would immediately have raised the issue of the 1967 borders." Having played his trump card—the specter of the 1967 borders—he returned to the map. "The location of one particular row of hills on the Golan Heights is not decisive in my view," he said.

He had missed Gur's point: He was making a military argument for the retention not of Quneitra but rather of the hills around it. Gur was as committed to finding a solution with Syria as Elazar, his predecessor, had been with Egypt. But he had made a mistake in his presentation. The hills, not the settlements, were essential to Israel's line of defense on the Golan. The settlements could be moved. But, as Gur had explained at the beginning of his briefing, there was no natural defense barrier for Israel on the Golan to the west of the hills. If he had stuck with that security justification, he would have armed Kissinger with a stronger case. Instead, Kissinger now thought it was all about convincing Assad that the hills were necessary to defend settlements that from Assad's point of view had no business being there in the first place.

Meir sprang to Gur's defense. If Israel were to withdraw and the Syrians went back to war, "how will we live with ourselves?" she asked. She pointed out that since the cease-fire, Israel had lost forty-two dead and 118 wounded. Kissinger himself had said that Assad's real intention was to destroy Israel. She wondered if she held out against withdrawal, whether it might be a better way to save Israeli lives.

Kissinger responded with a professorial lecture on the tragic aspect of statesmanship and the problem of conjecture: one could never know whether the course not taken would produce a better result. Nevertheless, there was compensation for risk-taking, he argued. It came in the form of territory for time: "Some price has to be paid for the time we are trying to gain." The minimal payment in his judgment was Quneitra plus a small strip beyond the October 6 line. That at least would be enough to put off another war by securing the support of Egypt and Algeria, thereby isolating Syria. He then asked them to reconsider. He would come back to Israel on Sunday after he had visited Assad and then consulted with Sadat.

Reflecting on these meetings in his memoirs, Kissinger remembers that he found himself delivering a seminar on the structure of international order, acting more as a psychological adviser than a mediator. He saw himself painstakingly molding the thinking of both sides to prepare them for the necessary compromises. As he had done in the Israeli-Egyptian negotiations, he was also training them to assume their roles in promoting and protecting the Middle Eastern order he was fashioning.

They agreed to resume the conversation again after dinner at Abba Eban's residence. But in this meeting the Israelis wanted to discuss all the other elements of a possible agreement.* Kissinger responded that if he could secure agreement on the line, the other issues would fall into place more easily.

As they walked out of Eban's residence, Kissinger pulled Dayan aside and asked if he could meet with him privately. Dayan checked with Meir, who agreed that he should take the meeting but make clear that he was offering Kissinger his personal views. She was using Dayan to explore how far she would need to go to assuage Kissinger.

Dayan writes in his autobiography that by this time, midnight in Jerusalem, he was almost dropping from fatigue, but "Kissinger appeared as sprightly as ever." In this unusual late-night rendezvous in Kissinger's King David suite, Dayan began by suggesting they forget everything that had been said about Quneitra in the previous meeting. He then laid out his plan in precise detail. Israel would hand over Quneitra to the UN. The Syrians could rebuild the

---

* The other elements included the role of UN forces, the limited-forces zones, the POWs, and the problem of Palestinian terrorists operating from Syrian territory.

town, but no Syrian forces could be there. Israel's military positions would be on the hills to the west of the town.

Could the UN buffer zone extend two kilometers west of Quneitra? Kissinger asked deftly. Perhaps, said Dayan, if there was some quid pro quo from the Syrians. He said personally he didn't have a problem with Syria taking back territory beyond the October 6 line, provided they didn't move their military positions forward. But he made clear that none of his cabinet colleagues agreed.

Dayan was now in the zone. Assuming he could convince Meir, Kissinger had what he needed for the moment. "This is the first thing I have heard that would not be humiliating," he said.

When Kissinger met with the prime minister at her residence the next morning, she signaled that she supported what Dayan had offered. Kissinger assured her he would not raise Dayan's proposal with Assad but would present it first to Sadat as his own idea, asking whether he would support it, "if I can sell this in Israel."

Both were in reflective moods. Meir lamented that she couldn't live with herself for what had happened in the war. Kissinger said that he too was thinking of resigning because of the way that Congress and liberal intellectuals were coming after him. Then he reprised his understanding of Dayan's concept: by squeezing the UN buffer zone, the Syrian line could be moved farther forward while the Israeli line would stay where Gur had wanted it. Kissinger thought he could sell that to Assad. She emphasized that to win Knesset approval of this kind of withdrawal, she would need to present a package deal that included arms supplies and economic assistance, and a real cease-fire. Kissinger said he understood.

Saturday, May 4, 1974, Damascus–Alexandria. The Syrians were happy to have Kissinger back in Damascus and keen to make a show of it. Foreign Minister Khaddam organized a high-profile official luncheon for Kissinger at the Orient Club, a favorite haunt of the regime's military officers and politicians. With its elaborate red-and-gold velvet brocade wallpaper and chandeliers, it looked like an upscale bordello and indeed normally provided a late-night milieu for card players and belly dancers. But this Saturday afternoon it had been commandeered to put the new relationship with the United States on public display, a gesture not repeated for any subsequent secretary of state.

Once back in the presidential palace, Kissinger explained to Assad that he had received an Israeli map, but it was the same as the one Dayan had presented to him in Washington. (Actually, Gur's map gave half of Quneitra and all of the area of Rephidim back to Syria, a lot more than Dayan brought to Washington.) He said he was working on the Israelis to improve their offer and would come back to Damascus in two days after discussing it again in Jerusalem.

Kissinger and Assad had an amicable conversation about the other aspects of the deal.* But then Kissinger did something inexplicable. He showed Assad Gur's map. Noting that Assad's line was unacceptable to the Israelis, he said he had made clear Gur's line was unacceptable to Assad. "If my line is unacceptable, we won't reach an agreement," said Assad. Calling the Israelis "bad guys" and insisting that he would not allow them "to continue to insult us in this way," he said he would not accept "one meter less than the line we have set down."

Urging Assad to be patient, Kissinger said that the United States would not support a policy of Israeli expansion. "The word Israel is synonymous with expansion," Assad responded. He declared that "without American help the Israelis could not send such an insulting map." In the face of this verbal onslaught, Kissinger claimed that the Israelis had already withdrawn the map, which begged the question of why he had bothered to present it.

In the course of twenty-four hours, Kissinger had been chastised by both Meir and Assad. As his aircraft winged its way down the Mediterranean coast that evening, a chastened Kissinger looked forward to an easier engagement with Sadat. He landed in Alexandria, Egypt's second city. Founded in ancient times by Alexander the Great, it had been the capital of Egypt for one millennium, and an important center of Hellenistic civilization, housing the Great Library with its massive collection of papyrus scrolls. Foreign Minister Fahmy escorted him to the Ma'amura rest house, the summer residence of the Egyptian presidency, located on a Mediterranean beach on the eastern side of the city.

To lubricate the conversation, Kissinger began by outlining a $180 million arms package for Egypt, in addition to the equipment Marwan was receiving from the CIA for the presidential security detail. The list included bombs; torpedoes; TOW, Maverick, and Walleye missiles; twenty-four Huey B helicopters; and sixteen F-4 Phantom aircraft. There was no possible way that Congress would approve such a list, so Kissinger suggested a false-flag operation in which the weapons would be sold to Saudi Arabia and passed on to Egypt. Kissinger cautioned Sadat about letting other Arab leaders know about this new arms relationship because if it leaked, "it would lead to my political destruction in America." And it surely would have, given that six months

---

* On military clashes, Assad said he was ready to calm things down if the Israelis did too. They discussed prisoner exchanges, limited-forces zones, and a UN buffer zone with lightly armed observers. Like Kissinger, Assad wanted to exclude Russian forces.

earlier Egypt had launched a war on Israel. In fact, it would take years for Kissinger's package to be delivered, but the list served as an informal letter of intent at a time when the Soviet Union had cut off arms supplies to Egypt. Sadat expressed immense satisfaction; Fahmy records that he didn't believe a word of it.*

Now Kissinger presented Dayan's Quneitra plan as his own idea, asking Sadat not to mention it yet to Assad. He showed him a satellite photo of Quneitra, explaining how a substantial part of the town could be returned to the Syrians. He noted that Dayan wanted the Syrians to withdraw their forces some two kilometers from their current lines, and Israel needed to retain the hills around Quneitra to protect the settlements.

Sadat gave him one-word responses for each idea: "Inconceivable!" and "Insane!" He reported on Field Marshal Ismail's most recent conversation with Assad in which the Syrian leader had insisted on territory beyond the October 6 line. Nevertheless, Sadat thought the affair could be managed if the Syrians received Quneitra in full and something beyond it. Anything like that, Sadat swore, would enable him to support it "100 percent" and secure Arab support.

Sadat asked whether Israel's military line would move back. Kissinger drew on Dayan's concept in response. Sadat grew more enthusiastic: "With this concept, I think you will have it."

They agreed to dispatch Harold Saunders and Marwan to brief the leadership in Saudi Arabia, Kuwait, and Algeria, sending a deliberate signal of Egyptian-American partnership. Kissinger, meanwhile, would visit King Hussein in Amman.

Monday, May 6, 1974, Jerusalem. Kissinger returned from Amman in the evening and met with Meir at the prime minister's office because hunger-striking protesters had camped outside her residence. They were waving placards that urged her not to give up Quneitra. A ghost town that few Israelis or Arabs could previously have located on a map had suddenly assumed cosmic importance for both sides. Such is the nature of the Arab-Israeli conflict that what one party wants immediately becomes unacceptable to the other.

This time they convened in the cabinet room at the prime minister's office.

---

* In his memoirs, Fahmy provides an account of this conversation in which he says that Kissinger promised the development of a three-phased arms relationship with Egypt, in which Egypt would first pay for all its arms, then 50 percent, and then when Congress had time to see the value of the relationship, 100 percent of the cost would be provided by military assistance from the United States. See Ismail Fahmy, *Negotiating for Peace in the Middle East* (Abingdon, UK: Routledge, 1983), 123–24.

As part of their negotiating tactics, the Israeli cabinet had approved in Kissinger's absence a map that fell far short of his expectations. It divided Quneitra into two parts under UN supervision: the area east of the main road would be under Syrian civil administration; west of the road would be under Israeli civil administration. Kissinger said this map would be totally rejected by the Saudis and the Egyptians; they would be willing to press Assad only if he were offered all of Quneitra. Even the United States would have difficulty supporting the new Israeli design, he said.

Dayan pointed to the fact that Israeli forces would be west of Quneitra, as Kissinger had demanded. Kissinger insisted that Israel had to relinquish all of Quneitra. They went around and around on this point until finally Gur said that while they had to keep the hills, they could move back between them. Dayan agreed that there could be a "sagging line" between the hills. "Excellent," Kissinger responded. As he observes in his memoirs, "Once the Israelis had moved their defense line west of Quneitra it was clear that the negotiations would not break down over lesser issues." He explains that "in diplomacy, the first advance is crucial."

Excited now, Kissinger stood up and summarized: they should prepare a map that showed the Israeli military line and the Syrian military line with Israel keeping its strongholds on the hills. But, he told them, "make [the line] look as straight as you can and as deep as you can." Allon complained that Kissinger was expecting Israel to make one concession after another. Kissinger reminded him of how far they had come: "If six months ago I would have told you that by May all you'd be talking about . . . is one kilometer from the October 6 line, you would have been very grateful." He thought there would be a good chance he could sell this line "if it just didn't look so unbelievably crooked." Couldn't they consider giving up one of the strongholds to straighten the line? he asked brazenly. Dayan responded, "We shall see what we can do tomorrow." Dayan was willing to show flexibility about arrangements around Quneitra too. It was as if the two of them were playing off a choreographed script designed to move the rest of the Israeli cabinet toward what was needed.

The room fell silent. Kissinger couldn't help himself. Instead of praising their flexibility he joked, "Don't think you have made an enormous concession to us!" The prime minister insisted on the last word. "This is a *great* concession [emphasis added]," she insisted, though she surely knew that was a stretch.

Kissinger told them he could now see enough light at the end of the tunnel to wrap up the agreement in about a week's time, on May 14. That left the impression that the Israelis had now made all the necessary concessions, thereby inadvertently laying the groundwork for a donnybrook when he had to come back to them for more.

But he had made progress. This was confirmed in a surprising way by Gromyko when they met on May 7 in Cyprus. Based on his visit to Damascus two days earlier, Gromyko confirmed that Assad's principal concern was Quneitra and if he regained it, the negotiations had a chance of succeeding. Kissinger reported to Nixon that night that for once Gromyko had not complained about exclusion or shown any intention of disrupting the negotiations, as long as the Soviet Union would be in on the "finalization" of the agreement at Geneva. Kissinger had rediscovered the usefulness of Geneva to keep the Soviets in line.

Kissinger's optimism was reinforced in a meeting with Meir, Dayan, and Gur upon his return from Cyprus. As they reviewed the Israeli map, Gur explained that they had moved the line west in the whole northern valley, as well as giving up the forward positions on Mount Hermon. Kissinger had asked for one stronghold; Gur had given him three and had extended the buffer zone to all the surrounding villages. Kissinger wanted to straighten the line. This drew a retort from Dayan: "[Gur] is really stretching himself. . . . I honestly think nothing more can be done. . . . We have reached the limit." If that were the case, Kissinger responded, then they should draw up "a less good map" that he could present to Assad. Then, when he rejected it, Kissinger could promise to try to get him more.* "There is a pathetic quality to these Arabs," he observed, "a sort of machismo." Assad had to show that he could outdo Sadat. So, Kissinger recommended the new map leave out the concessions on Mount Hermon in the north and Rephidim in the south. "I could say you insist now on holding Hermon but I have given you an ultimatum—if you don't mind," Kissinger concluded.

They didn't mind but having given at the office, Meir now wanted to ensure Israel received its reward from the United States. They agreed to discuss her arms requests in the morning before Kissinger departed for Damascus.

Wednesday, May 8, 1974, Jerusalem–Damascus. When they reconvened, Meir said Israel would need 750 new planes and some 1,400 additional tanks in the next decade given continued Soviet arms supplies to the Arabs. Now that he had squeezed meaningful territorial concessions from the Israelis, Kissinger responded positively. The IDF also wanted Pershing and Lance missiles. Kis-

---

* To back up his argument, Kissinger reported on Saunders's session with Rashad Pharaon, a Syrian adviser to King Faisal who served as his liaison to Assad. Pharaon had emphasized to Saunders and Marwan the importance of placing Quneitra under Syrian administration and claimed that Assad would be isolated in the Arab world if he did not accept it. The Kuwaiti emir said in that event he would cut off funding to Syria.

singer knew the Pershings would be problematic because they could carry a nuclear warhead and would therefore face opposition from the Pentagon and State Department. Perhaps the United States could help Israel develop its own missiles, he suggested. That would involve fewer approvals on the American side. Here was the first indication that Kissinger was thinking about easing the perennial political problems of American arms supplies to Israel by boosting its indigenous missile production capabilities.

Meir wanted assurances about what the next steps would be after the Israeli–Syrian disengagement. The focus should be on Egypt, Kissinger responded unhesitatingly: "If we can get Egypt out of [the conflict], Syria is isolated, and we can just delay and delay." As he explains in his memoirs, the Israelis were coming around to appreciate that "time could be an ally and it was worth a few kilometers on the Golan." There it was again: territory for time.

He tried to reassure her about what he referred to as his nightmare, which was hers too: international pressure to return to the 1967 borders. In a one-on-one meeting the day before he had assured her that he would not ask her to give up all the Golan, just the minimum necessary to buy off Assad. Now he added that "no Arab ever had me affirm the 1967 borders; no Arab ever will." She seized on this opening to press him for a letter of assurance that the United States would not expect Israel to come down from the Golan Heights. Knowing such a commitment would torpedo his nascent relationship with Assad should it leak, as it was bound to do given the nature of Israeli politics, Kissinger demurred. Instead, he said, "I give you my personal assurance I support Israel's presence on the Golan Heights." She knew a personal assurance was operative only while Kissinger remained in office, but she let it suffice for the moment. They agreed to meet again that evening when Kissinger returned from Damascus.

Kissinger's objective in his third meeting with Assad on this shuttle was to get him to accept the idea that the line of Israeli withdrawal was going to fall short of what he had been demanding. In a four-hour conversation over lunch at the presidential palace, he now prepared the ground by explaining how hard it would be to move the Israelis back on the Golan because they were comfortable there, threatening Damascus. He argued that the principle of Israeli withdrawal counted far more than the extent of it. There was only so far he could push the Israelis without raising a general uproar in the United States.

Assad's moods were always difficult to predict. That was especially true in December 1998, for example, when he told us he was ready for peace with Israel and wanted to conclude it quickly. Now, whether it was due to Kissinger's wiles or a letter that Assad had just received from Sadat praising his success in convincing Israel to withdraw to the October 6 line, Assad responded with rare openness and sincerity.* Referencing his offensive behavior in their last stand-off, Assad explained the challenge of bringing his people along because they "have been nurtured over twenty-six years on hatred [and] can't be swayed overnight by our changing courses." Later in the conversation he noted that he might face demonstrations, the nightmare of all Arab autocrats. "I fear our people," he explained in a moment of uncommon candor.

Assad noted that "we are all human—we all have our impulsive reactions to things." But in unheard-of self-criticism, he noted that the role of a leader is "to restrain ourselves and analyze and take steps in our own interest." Kissinger nodded his head in agreement. Then Assad surprised him with his conclusion: "A just peace is in the interest of our people." Sounding more like John Lennon singing "Imagine" than the Lion of Damascus, the moniker Assad had earned in the Arab world for his fiery pan-Arab nationalism, he said, "Seriously, we wish that peace will reign all over the world, and that competition will be peaceful."

This was getting a bit much for Kissinger, who was even more skeptical of the notion of world peace than he was of Arab-Israeli peace. He gingerly turned the conversation to where things stood in the negotiations, hoping that Assad would not get "too angry." He told him that what he was about to show him wasn't enough and he vowed to get more, though it would be difficult. He then unveiled the map that he had conjured up with Gur and Dayan, pointing out that the Israelis had now agreed to withdraw to the October 6 line everywhere except Mount Hermon (in reality, of course, they had agreed to withdraw from Mount Hermon too). He said he would insist that they give up the post–October 6 positions on the mountain and withdraw farther at other points along the line.

Assad studied the map and calmly made four observations: There is no return beyond the October 6 line. There is no straight parallel line. They keep posts on Mount Hermon they occupied after the cease-fire. They didn't give back Quneitra; they divided it. He then expanded on the importance of taking control of the town so that civilians could return. That wouldn't be possible if it were surrounded by Israel. And then, amazingly, he signaled flexibility: "We would only agree to a line *near the line* we have indicated. . . . First, we want a straight line [emphasis added]." In critiquing the Israeli proposal, he had implicitly laid out a set of reasonable requirements.

Now Kissinger had Assad in the zone.

---

* After seeing Sadat on May 10, Kissinger recounted to the Israelis that Sadat had told him about this letter, in which he had written to Assad, "You have had a tremendous diplomatic achievement." See Memcon between Kissinger, Meir, et al., May 10, 1974, KT01156, NSA.

"For the first time, I think we have a chance for an agreement," Kissinger excitedly told Meir in recounting this exchange. "He talked to me like he wanted an agreement and he wanted it next week, and with me, and to get the Russians out." He assessed that "we've got it in the range of a rational solution."

This was the moment, Kissinger would recall forty-five years later, when he thought Assad might convert to a peacemaker in the Sadat mold. Confirmation for this assessment came in an exchange with General Shihabi and Foreign Minister Khaddam at Damascus Airport before he departed for Israel. In the VIP waiting room, while Khaddam was called away to take a phone call, Shihabi too spoke of peace with Israel. Echoing Assad's concern about a public backlash, he said it would take a little time to prepare the Syrian people. But Assad was ready now to make a big effort with the disengagement line if Kissinger could bring him something he could accept.

From this point on, the challenge would prove to be in the details of the deal. This was brought home to Kissinger when Khaddam returned to the VIP lounge from his phone call—with the Syrian president, as it turned out. Assad had one more requirement that he wanted Khaddam to convey before Kissinger departed Damascus: his only interest in Quneitra was to resettle civilians there, and for that *he needed the hills that surrounded it.*

Kissinger knew that was unachievable, given what Gur had told him about the importance of the hills to the security of the nearby Israeli settlements. He said that to Khaddam and Shihabi. This did nothing to dampen Kissinger's enthusiasm, however, for he believed that Assad's tarmac afterthought was just an attempt to get something more, rather than a deal-breaking demand. He would soon discover that he underestimated the problem those hills would present.

Nevertheless, Kissinger had managed again to persuade Assad that his interests were better served by pursuing an agreement under American auspices rather than a prolonged conflict with Israel dependent on Soviet largesse. This suspicious Syrian leader had decided to put his trust in Kissinger and take the plunge with him into the waters of Arab-Israeli reconciliation.

13

Breakthrough

A secretary of state who undertakes too many journeys that lead nowhere depreciates his own coin.

—Henry Kissinger, *Years of Upheaval*

Wednesday, May 8, 1974, Herzliya. "It was the best meeting we have had," Kissinger recounted excitedly to Meir when they met at the Mossad's guesthouse. With thousands of demonstrators congregating that evening in Jerusalem to protest any return of Golan territory, the prime minister had decided to move the meeting to Herzliya. She brought twenty-one ministers and staff with her. Kissinger was happy to have a large audience for the good news he brought from Damascus. Up to now, he reminded them, he had been focused on minimizing the fallout from failed negotiations. For the first time, he believed agreement was possible.

Putting the burden on the Israelis' shoulders, Kissinger said that Assad indicated he was ready to make a real effort, "but you have to make it possible for him." Kissinger recounted the story of the airport conversation, adding that he did not expect Israel to concede the hills around Quneitra. He would, however, need a straightening of the line, as many villages as possible, and all of Quneitra under Syrian civilian administration.

Kissinger knew that any sign of progress with the other side would be greeted unenthusiastically by the Israelis, since they saw it as the prelude to pressure on them to make more concessions. However, Kissinger did not expect that the pushback would come from Dayan, his collaborator.

Carrying Kissinger's water in the cabinet deliberations was dangerous for Dayan given his precarious standing with the Israeli public, and he had become troubled by what he viewed as Kissinger's "salami tactics." Dayan had two basic principles on which he would not budge: to retain the hills that dominated

Quneitra, because they were an essential part of a defensible military line; and not to disturb or leave vulnerable the existing Israeli settlements. He sensed Kissinger, in his enthusiasm to make a deal, was coming too close to those red lines, so he warned him off. "I see no chance for any changes . . . even non-significant changes in the line of the map that we drew last night," Dayan said.

Kissinger put them on notice that they were going to have to reciprocate Assad's moderation. He would give them three days to reconsider their position. He wasn't going to run back and forth "debating the theology of security that both sides have." Either the Syrians would accept the Israeli requirement, "or you are going to have to change your position," and if neither side was prepared to budge, then "we have to have a hiatus." Kissinger added, "If by Monday night there isn't either an agreement in principle, or an imminent agreement in principle, I am going home."

The threat to walk out of a negotiation is an effective tactic only if it is based on a calculation that the costs involved in walking away are less than the potential benefits of concluding the deal. If not, then the threat becomes a bluff that, if called, undermines the credibility of the party making the threat. In September 1978, at Camp David I, for example, Israeli prime minister Menachem Begin was the only one who could afford to walk away from the summit and not suffer serious damage. Indeed, he would have been welcomed home as a hero for not relinquishing the Sinai. Conversely, both Sadat and President Carter would have done serious damage to themselves politically if they failed to secure the return of the Sinai to Egypt and the accompanying peace deal. Begin could threaten to walk and they could not, and Begin therefore secured the better deal, breaking the linkage between Egypt and the West Bank, conceding only autonomy for the Palestinians, and committing to a mere three-month settlement freeze.

Similarly, in July 2000 at Camp David II, Arafat was the only one able to walk away, once he had driven the negotiations to focus on Jerusalem. At that point, he could return a hero to his people for not conceding sovereignty over the Haram al-Sharif and Al-Aqsa Mosque. If he did that, President Clinton and Prime Minister Barak would be left without the deal they were increasingly desperate to achieve, given that time was running out for both of them. (Clinton's second term was about to expire; Barak no longer had majority support in the Knesset.)

At the Wye River negotiations in October 1998, Prime Minister Netanyahu threatened to walk out, adding to the drama by ordering up his motorcade and instructing his team to pack their bags and line them up on the lawn outside their lodgings. We assumed he was bluffing because if he left just as the negotiations were climaxing, he would have to explain to his people and a wider international audience why he was walking away from the peace process. Putting the bags out was a sure sign he was bluffing, since if he was going to leave, he would have done so without the drama, especially when we discovered that some of the bags were empty. We therefore told him that if he wanted to depart, we would help him do it. A day of intensive negotiations ensued, with the Israeli bags sitting on the grass. In the evening, when the Israeli spokesman told the Israeli media that Netanyahu was still threatening to walk, we refused to negotiate with his team under the threat of a public ultimatum, much like Kissinger had done with the Saudis over the oil embargo. Bibi sent his staff to apologize; the agreement was concluded the next day.

So it was with Kissinger's threat to end his efforts. To be sure, his Israeli and Syrian interlocutors would not have been happy to relinquish the high-level attention the United States was paying to their problem. But they could afford the consequences more than he could. The Israelis were absorbing daily casualties from Syrian artillery bombardments, but they were perfectly willing to stay put on the outskirts of Damascus. Similarly, Assad could live with the consequences of no deal with his Zionist adversary, which would alleviate the risk of stirring up public animosity.

Kissinger, however, could not easily return to Washington without an agreement. Nixon was counting on him to help salvage his presidency and pave the way for what he hoped would be a triumphal visit to Middle Eastern capitals. Sadat begged him to keep at it too, fearing that if Kissinger ended the shuttle without an agreement, the Arab world would consider Sadat's bet on American diplomacy a failure. It would also tarnish Kissinger's record of diplomatic success, rendering him vulnerable to the growing domestic criticism of his foreign policy and exposing him to the danger of being sucked into the Watergate vortex because of wiretapping charges.

He could have pressed the Israelis to accept the basic deal he was forging; instead, he gave them three days to think about it. His threat to go home was therefore the equivalent of putting luggage out on the Wye River plantation's lawn, and the Israelis knew it.

The Jerusalem–Damascus shuttle lasted for thirty days, an unprecedented amount of time for any official to be on the road, let alone the secretary of state who had responsibility for running the world's affairs. Given the president's preoccupation with his political survival, there was effectively nobody at home to manage U.S. foreign policy for that period. The media chalked it up to Kissinger's immense dedication to peacemaking, as evidenced by his willingness to devote so much energy to the details of a complex and frustrating deal. But other areas of the world suffered from the lack of high-level American attention. For example, during that period, India tested its first nuclear weapon and

Germany was plunged into a political crisis over spy allegations that brought down Chancellor Willy Brandt. In Washington, Senator Scoop Jackson used Kissinger's absence from the arena to rally support for his amendment to legislation granting most-favored-nation status to the Soviet Union that would link it to the exit of Soviet Jews. This amendment would shake the very foundations of Kissinger's U.S.-Soviet détente by denying Moscow the economic benefits of cooperating with the United States.

There's no doubt that the disengagement negotiations benefited greatly from Kissinger's unique high-level attention. The deliberate pace of his diplomacy better acclimated both sides to the concessions they would have to make than an attempt to force it down their throats. But it disguised another reality: Kissinger was in no hurry to go home to Watergate Washington.*

Friday, May 10, 1974, Giza. Sadat hosted the secretary of state for lunch on the terrace of his villa overlooking the pyramids. When Kissinger showed him the map and pointed out the Mount Hermon positions that Israel was now prepared to relinquish, Sadat said, "This is a very big achievement," repeating these words three times in the course of their conversation.

It didn't take long, though, for Fahmy to raise the Quneitra hills. Kissinger explained why it would be impossible to move the Israelis off them. A huge battle over two kilometers wasn't worth it, in his judgment. Sadat agreed that "the time is not right." Kissinger suggested that the Israelis could be on the hills, but without arms to threaten the returning Syrian inhabitants of Quneitra. "Very good!" Sadat responded effusively. He said he would send Assad a message urging him to seize the opportunity. They should both tell Assad not to push things to the point of explosion in Israel. "I tell you, Henry, this map, as it is, is approved by the Arabs. . . . More than that would be much better. But this is very solid ground," said Sadat.

Fahmy encouraged Kissinger to try for more. "If you straighten the line around Quneitra, it's like baksheesh. That is the Syrian way," he explained. Any tourist visiting Cairo would know that baksheesh is also the Egyptian way, but Kissinger ignored the put-down of Assad. He cautioned them that it would be very hard to get the hills demilitarized and extract another kilometer of withdrawal from the Israelis on top of that. He was already holding up tank deliveries and other materiel, blaming the delay on Pentagon inefficiency. He would have to issue an ultimatum and threaten to cut off aid to Israel to get them to move further.

* From the outbreak of the Yom Kippur War in October 1973 until Nixon's resignation ten months later, Kissinger made six trips to the Middle East, visited twenty-eight countries, and traveled 196,000 miles. See Walter Isaacson, *Kissinger* (New York: Simon & Schuster, 1992), 595.

The prospects for that looked even more unlikely by that evening as Kissinger learned that more Republicans in Congress were deserting the president, leading him to conclude that Nixon was in the "terminal phase of his presidency." This meant that Nixon's threats were likely to have little impact on the Israelis.* That concern was quickly eclipsed by Israeli news reports that revealed Meir's concessions on the line and on Mount Hermon, which Kissinger had been concealing from Assad. He had hoped to present them to the Syrians as the fruits of efforts by Sadat and King Faisal. Instead, the leaks made him look duplicitous. He was furious.

When Kissinger vented to the Israeli team during their meeting at the prime minister's office on May 11, after his return from Cairo, they defended the leaks as part of the democratic process. Dayan was unapologetic. He explained that, having provided the map to Kissinger, he was obliged to provide it to the Knesset Foreign Affairs and Defense Committee. The committee members, along with much of Israel at that point, were opposed to the withdrawal, so naturally one of them leaked it. Kissinger was hardly in a position to complain.

As he summarized the challenge in his report to Nixon that evening, the agreement would now depend on whether Israel would be willing to give up all of Quneitra and a one-kilometer UN buffer zone around it, and whether Syria would accept continued Israeli control of three hills to the west of Quneitra.

Sunday, May 12, 1974, Damascus–Jerusalem. Returning to Damascus the next morning, Kissinger found Assad was still in a positive mood. He unveiled the new Israeli map, which he had previously held back. Assad observed that the line around Quneitra had not changed. "It's difficult to fall in love with this map," Assad joked. Kissinger responded that it represented the first time the Israelis had offered to move beyond the October 6 line. Assad repeated his position that the line needed to be straightened to include more villages, and the hills around Quneitra needed to be in Syrian hands. He noted that the Israelis had now agreed to move 1.5 kilometers beyond the October 6 line; he insisted on another 1.5 kilometers.

At this point, Shihabi entered the room accompanied by two new interlocutors, Mustafa Tlass, the Syrian defense minister, and General Naji Jamil, the

---

* On May 7, Senate Republican leader Hugh Scott had denounced the transcripts of the Watergate tapes as "deplorable, disgusting, shabby performances." Congressman John Rhodes, the leader of the Republicans in the House, had called on Nixon to resign. On May 9, Republican Senator Richard Schweiker of Pennsylvania joined the growing chorus of those calling for Nixon's resignation. The press reported that Washington was rife with rumors that the president was on the verge of resigning. See Christopher Lydon, "Senator Brands Conduct as 'Immoral'; G.O.P. Leader in House Is Also Critical," *New York Times*, May 8, 1974.

air force chief of staff. Widening the circle of generals involved in the negotiations was Assad's way of generating broader support in his armed forces. Kissinger took it as a good omen, but he also understood that Assad would want to show them he was fighting for every inch.

Kissinger recounted the limits on what was achievable, adding a U.S. guarantee that there would be no Israeli harassment of returning villagers. He also committed to pressing Israel on other villages along the line. He agreed that the settlements were "inexcusable," but he admitted that he could not mobilize enough American pressure to move them.

Assad responded, "I appreciate your difficulty." Nevertheless, he insisted that the hills were inseparable from Quneitra. Kissinger said that was unobtainable.

"If hills are their passion an agreement is impossible," Assad responded. On the other hand, "the moment the Israelis dispense with the principle of the hills . . ." Kissinger cut him off by saying he did not believe he could deliver on Assad's requirement. Nevertheless, Assad was not ready to give up. He was even willing to have Kissinger tell the press that their talks were "making progress and dealing with concrete issues." And as an unusual goodwill gesture to Meir, he even provided Kissinger with the names of three Israelis who had been captured by the Syrians in recent clashes on the Golan.

When Kissinger briefed the Israelis late on the evening of May 12, Dayan was indignant: "All of this pocket doesn't count?" Meir chimed in: "He went to war; we didn't go to war." Kissinger responded that if he went back with the same Israeli map, they would be out of business. Since he had already conceded the hills to Israel, he focused on Assad's request for three villages in the south and Majdal Shams in the north. Unlike Quneitra and the other villages, which were deserted, Majdal Shams was a town inhabited by Druze, many of whom preferred to remain under Israeli rule. That provoked Meir, who said, "These were two wars in which we were attacked . . . and he is looking for villages?"

There ensued another epic battle of words between Meir and Kissinger. "Is it a crime to want a Syrian village back?" Kissinger asked provocatively. "Yes, after a war, a Syrian president . . . who has attacked people twice in seven years can't have what he wants," said Meir. "It's as simple as that!" Kissinger warned her again of the dire consequences of a breakdown in the negotiations. If the Soviets were clever, he said, "I believe that the succeeding diplomacy can present extraordinary dangers, and we will look back with nostalgia to the point where we were talking about a few hundred yards here and there."

Kissinger set a Tuesday deadline for agreeing on the line and recommended that she go back to the cabinet and see what could be done to move it. "We have gone over the line three times already!" Dayan said. "Where do we go from here? Where's the limit?" Dinitz asked.

Kissinger reminded them that they had offered something unpalatable from the beginning and that he had moved the Syrians to much less than Assad had originally demanded. The cabinet now only had to decide whether they would give up some uninhabited villages and ease the regime around Quneitra or "run the risk of liquidation of the whole strategy that has pretty well insulated you from the total impact of the consequences of the war."

"I doubt that made much of an impression," Kissinger reported to Nixon on May 13. But he decided to try one more time with Meir and Dayan the next morning before the cabinet met. He warned them that if they entered another period of "stalemate diplomacy" it would not be acceptable to the United States to be told, "Here is a hill; we won't leave it." That set her off again. She said sarcastically she would report to the cabinet that "when we say that this is important for security, it is not relevant, and [when Assad] says a village where there will be 300 settlers, this he must have, that's important." Kissinger took umbrage.

Then Dayan intervened with a way forward. He read from an intelligence intercept of a Syrian report to other Arab leaders on Kissinger's last meeting with Assad. It accurately summarized what Kissinger had reported to the Israelis about Assad's requirements for the hills around Quneitra but added that the agreement would include the resettlement of tens of thousands of displaced Syrian villagers. Dayan saw that as encouraging. Perhaps Assad's intentions were more peaceful than they had given him credit for. He asked Kissinger to show him on a map what a straightened line would look like. The two of them, with help from Sisco and Saunders, who had just visited Quneitra with General Gur, then engaged in a line-drawing exercise on the map that had been placed on the table.

When the cabinet met, however, it rejected the straightening of the line. Nevertheless, it was willing to concede the whole of Quneitra to Syrian control if the hills west of the town remained behind the Israeli military line. It was also willing to have UN observers on some of the hills inside Israel's zone, give up two hills north of Quneitra and the southern village of Ahmadiya, and keep Israel's main forces two kilometers west of Quneitra.

The cabinet, however, wanted the fields in between, up to the outskirts of Quneitra, to remain in Israel's hands so that the settlers could continue to cultivate them. Dayan added that there would have to be barbed wire and trenches dug on the outskirts of the town to separate the Israeli farmers from the Syrian townspeople.

"To go from the preposterous to the impossible is not a concession," Kissinger retorted. He wanted to know where the military would be deployed on the hills. Dayan and Gur hesitated to answer, provoking Kissinger to lose control: "You know, if you don't want an agreement, I can save the trouble.

Then I don't have to sit here dragging every bloody thing out of you!" Dayan tersely explained his position on the line again. Kissinger was incredulous: "Do you believe that any Syrian president can accept the proposition that not even one field can possibly be abandoned without being driven into a frenzy immediately?"

Dayan tried to explain that all he was doing was sticking to his concept of maintaining the Israeli line of defense while making some face-saving gestures. Kissinger made clear it would not stand, saying, "We will just have to go back to Washington and assess the situation." For the first time, Kissinger was introducing the idea of a "reassessment" of relations between the United States and Israel, a threat he would reintroduce when he faced a real breakdown in subsequent Israeli-Egyptian negotiations.

Dinitz understood the gravity of Kissinger's threat immediately. He pointed out that Israel was now in fact offering all of Quneitra, and Ahmadiya in the south, and two hills in the north. One could not say that Israel had made no effort. Kissinger allowed that there had been an effort, but all he was asking for were some minor adjustments, and the rejection of his requests was bound to have profound consequences.

Dayan again tried to save the day. He suggested that Kissinger see whether Assad would give up the hills if Israel were willing to have only "little forces" there. If it was then a matter of moving the line a little around Quneitra, Kissinger should come back and discuss it. Kissinger allowed that there was a slight chance Assad might accept this proposal.

In his memoirs, Dayan explains why he had turned from acting as Kissinger's partner to a principal opponent of his appeal for concessions. "The difficulty with this bargaining," he observes, "was not simply that we viewed it as undignified, but that it put us in an invidious position vis-à-vis the Israeli public." Since there were no secrets in Israel, "we would be accused of political surrender."

Dayan was feeling particularly vulnerable to such criticism. The Golan negotiations had become highly politicized because of the government's weakened condition and the opposition's greater confidence now that Ariel Sharon had joined the ranks of Menachem Begin's Likud Party. Unlike Dayan, Sharon had emerged a war hero for leading the IDF's crossing of the canal.

Kissinger returned to the King David Hotel and fired off an angry cable to Scowcroft reporting on Israel's intransigence. He ordered him to have Haig call Schlesinger and get him to put a hold on all new arms commitments and all items in the pipeline for Israel. When Scowcroft briefed the president on Kissinger's report, Nixon ordered a cutoff of *all* Israeli aid unless it softened its negotiating position, calling Scowcroft twice that night to ensure that his order had been implemented.

Tuesday, May 14, 1974, Damascus. The next morning Kissinger resolved to fashion the Israeli concessions into a package to which Assad, with his own penchant for small dispensations, might relate.

He began his presentation to Assad with a woe-is-me preamble: the Israelis were demonstrating against him, calling him "Killinger," and American Jews were undermining détente and opposing aid to Arab states. Against these formidable odds, he said, he was laboring mightily to get a better deal for Syria than he had secured for Egypt. Sadat had to accept a large UN buffer zone; Syria's would be small and its administration would go all the way up to the Israeli line, enabling forty to fifty thousand Syrians to return. He promised to improve U.S.-Syrian relations. Regardless of what happened, Kissinger assured Assad, the United States would say that "Syria was not unreasonable." Kissinger was using honey with Assad in contrast to the vinegar he had dispensed to the Israelis.

Finally, Kissinger unveiled "the few changes" he brought from Jerusalem. He explained that the UN would be out of Quneitra and Israel would be out of the hills to the north and Ahmadiya in the south. There could also be a substantial demilitarization of the hills to the west, but they would remain under Israeli control. President Nixon would be ready to provide an assurance to Assad that Israel would not be allowed to interfere with the return of civilian life to Quneitra.

"The situation you described leaves me at a loss for words. . . . There is no real change," said Assad. Kissinger urged Assad to see it as the start of a process in which he regained thirty kilometers of Syrian territory and engaged the United States. Assad noted that he would not be able to send anybody back to Quneitra under this arrangement because they would be at Israel's mercy, their fields would be gone, and a few shots from either side could ignite the area. But then, to Kissinger's amazement, Assad acknowledged that "the entry of the United States into the arena with a new mentality requires us to take your views into serious consideration."

Instead of rejecting the Israeli offer out of hand, as Kissinger had expected, Assad made a creative counterproposal. Let the hills around Quneitra be divided so that the line runs along their peaks; Syria would get the east slopes and Israel the west slopes. UN observers could be on the ridgeline, and the hills in the south could be under UN supervision. He also wanted the post on the peak of Mount Hermon that the Israelis had taken after the October 22 cease-fire. He warned, however, that he would not resettle Quneitra if it remained a pocket surrounded by Israeli-controlled hills.

Assad repeated his proposals in front of his advisers, and drew a red line:

"We will go as far as I have indicated but not a hair beyond." He then surprised Kissinger again by saying he should tell the press that "there has been progress on some fronts."

In the car ride returning to the airport, Khaddam and Shihabi characterized their leader's approach as "leaving a window open." Khaddam was particularly enthusiastic about the potential to build a bridge between the United States and Syria. Noting that Assad was the first Syrian leader to talk of peace, he pleaded with Kissinger to continue. "We can't reach the final step without the first one. . . . No matter how arduous we find it, we must reach step number one," argued this normally hard-bitten, cynical Ba'ath Party functionary.

Kissinger pondered his dilemma: With a little more pressure on both sides, could he resolve the issue of the hills, achieve agreement on the line, and then resolve the security issues? Or was he better off going home? Assad had shown some flexibility, "not asking for the removal of Israeli settlements, just breathing room for his own," as Kissinger would later characterize Assad's position. That evening he reported to Nixon that he had made "major progress" with Syria; later he would term Assad's drawing of a line on the top of the hills as "an extraordinary concession" although he surely knew the Israelis were unlikely to see it that way.

He had been on the road for seventeen days, and the Israelis had made it unmistakably clear that they were reaching the limits of their willingness to compromise. To move them further would take a bloody battle. As "a senior official" told the traveling press en route from Damascus to Jerusalem, "the talks could go either way."

Wednesday, May 15, 1974, Jerusalem. Just as Kissinger was weighing his options in the early morning of May 15, three Democratic Front for the Liberation of Palestine (DFLP) terrorists dressed in IDF fatigues crossed from Lebanon into the Israeli border town of Ma'alot, where they murdered an Israeli Arab woman and a Jewish family of three. They then seized a school, taking some one hundred Israeli students and four teachers hostage, and demanded the release of some twenty Palestinian prisoners.

This calamitous event naturally diverted the attention of Meir and her ministers. The cabinet went into continuous crisis session. Dayan was dispatched to the north to assess the situation. The meeting with Kissinger was postponed. At 5:30 p.m. that day, after great confusion surrounding the hostage negotiations, IDF commandos stormed the school and killed the three terrorists, but not before one of them had opened fire on the Israeli children, killing sixteen of them and wounding another seventy. That night, a haggard Meir speaking in a firm voice addressed the Israeli nation and explained the tragic chain of events and the shocking number of casualties, swearing to "cut off the hands that want to harm a child."

Meir also thanked Kissinger, "who is at present here with us." She knew that it would reassure the Israeli public that the secretary of state of Israel's great protector was present. I experienced a similar phenomenon on the night Yitzhak Rabin was assassinated in November 1995. While Israelis awaited news of the fate of their prime minister, I was surprised to hear on the radio that the U.S. ambassador was at the hospital where Rabin was fighting for his life. In fact, I was forty minutes away, and nobody knew that I was on my way there.

Sadat responded to the Ma'alot terrorist attack by writing a letter to Meir, which she considered "a revolution," in which he urged her to continue with the negotiations and promised that if they succeeded, he would have Kissinger develop "a joint procedure [between Egypt and Israel] to cope with and prevent such incidents in the future." Here lies the origin of the intense counterterrorism cooperation between Israel and Egypt that prevails today.

Perhaps in part responding to this noble gesture from Sadat, Meir devoted a late-night session of the cabinet on this traumatic day to discussing its next steps with Syria. Rather than arresting the peace process, it seems that the death of so many children was propelling the Israelis forward.

Following that meeting, Meir sent Dinitz to meet with Kissinger in his hotel suite. She wanted him to explain to Kissinger why Israel was so adamant about retaining the hills around Quneitra. Dinitz found Kissinger surrounded by piles of telexes coming out of a machine that contained the transcripts of the Nixon tapes that the White House had just released to Congress. Dinitz explained that the IDF was dependent on topography because it could not afford to keep the army mobilized on the Golan. That made movement beyond the hills very difficult. It was not a matter of defending the settlements; the hills represented the last line of natural defense on the Golan. Israel simply could not give up its entire defensive position on the Golan for a disengagement agreement.

Even though this rationale had been mentioned before by Gur and Dayan, they had tended to focus on the need to defend the settlements. Now Kissinger understood for the first time that retaining the hills had more to do with Israel's line of defense. "We would have saved ourselves a lot of tensions had somebody explained matters that clearly earlier," he told Dinitz. He responded by asking for "an act of grace" that would address Syrian pride, which amounted to widening the territory that Israel would cede in the fields around Quneitra at the expense of the settlements. In return, he would insist with Assad, as he had from the beginning, that Israel keep the hills.

Living through the Ma'alot trauma with the Israelis had touched Kissinger's heart. After the conciliatory meeting with Dinitz, he undertook his own act of grace by explaining to Nixon why it would be counterproductive to his efforts to follow through on the president's order to cut off all aid to Israel at this time of tragedy and mourning. He noted that the Syrians had moderated their position but were far from being helpful, while "it would be a grotesque error" and "unjust and contrary to facts" to put all the blame on Israel, something he had done repeatedly in his reporting to Nixon. Kissinger still wanted to preserve the leverage of a cutoff in aid in his diplomatic arsenal but, as he explained to Nixon, he did not want to use it now.

The next morning, Kissinger met with the Israeli team. Allon, as deputy prime minister, stood in for the prime minister who was too exhausted to participate. Kissinger reported on his latest discussions in Damascus, concluding that, in his judgment, Assad wanted an agreement and they were now as close as they were ever going to get. Reflecting his discussions with Dinitz the night before, he vowed that Israel would not have to keep making concessions. Then he asked for two more: room around Quneitra and a new line drawn as close as possible to the crest of the hills, with a UN presence on top and limitations on Israeli arms deployed there.

Allon said Israel would agree to a little more if Kissinger made it clear to Assad that it was the best he could do. But he insisted that Israeli settlers be able to cultivate the fields on the outskirts of Quneitra. Knowing now that the fields were not essential for Israel's security, Kissinger stood his ground: he could get Israel the hillcrests, but it would have to give up the slopes and the fields.

Slowly but surely, the Israelis were beginning to shift. This was confirmed by Meir when Kissinger paid a visit to her Balfour Street residence. She was willing to take it upon herself to tell the settlers that they had to give up some of the fields, but there was a limit. To the north and south of Quneitra the line could be moved west by some two hundred meters. Dayan was ready to accept a military line at the foot of the hills, but only if it led to an agreement. And then the prime minister essentially put Israel's fate in Kissinger's hands: "We all believe you can do it. . . . You have accomplished with us something nobody else could."

Thursday, May 16, 1974, Damascus. With the two sides getting closer, Kissinger decided to test the idea of an American bridging proposal with Khaddam on their long ride from the airport to Assad's office. The Syrian foreign

Syrian foreign minister Abdel Halim Khaddam escorts Henry Kissinger from his
plane at Damascus Airport on May 16, 1974. Like Fahmy and Eban, Khaddam met
Kissinger every time he landed in Damascus and rode with him to the palace to meet
President Assad. A cynical Ba'ath Party ideologue, Khaddam nevertheless became
committed to helping Kissinger succeed with the Israeli-Syrian disengagement
negotiations.

minister was open to the idea but said an American proposal would have to
talk about what happens after the first step—i.e., the 1967 borders. Kissinger
quickly responded that to talk about the final step now would be an obstacle
to resolving the first. But he provided a reassurance to Khaddam: "Before the
end of the year, ideally after our elections, we [will] begin a very determined
diplomacy for a substantial advance into the Golan." He had told the Israelis
just the opposite to reassure them. In fact, by year's end he would be focused
on regaining more territory in the Sinai for Sadat.

An eight-hour session with Assad ensued in which Kissinger put forward a
U.S. proposal based on his estimate of what the Israelis would accept if Assad
were prepared to accept it too.* Assad eventually conceded that the western
side of the hills could be under Israeli control with the eastern slopes under
UN control, and neither side would cultivate the fields. He also conceded the
Druze villages in the north. And he added a message to the Israelis: "If we get

---

* The line around Quneitra would move two hundred meters westward with the area beyond, up
to the hills (about 1.5 kilometers), under UN supervision. The hills would remain under Israeli
control with strict limitations on their military dispositions, guaranteed by the United States. The
Israeli line would be moved one kilometer west in the areas north and south of Quneitra.

a satisfactory settlement . . . we can have a long stamina there." If it were an unsatisfactory settlement, he added, "we will be constantly pressing to go on."

Assad was offering the Israelis a long respite from pressure to concede more territory on the Golan. That was very much what Meir—and Kissinger— wanted. But for Assad to offer such an inducement for a slight adjustment in the line of withdrawal was surprising. It was a Syrian version of territory for time and suggested that regaining the Golan was much less of a priority for him than other pressing issues at home and in Lebanon. Looking back now, that may well provide the best explanation of why the Golan is still in Israel's hands.

Friday, May 17, 1974, Jerusalem. Kissinger arrived back in Israel at 2:15 a.m. He slept in and met the Israeli team, this time with the prime minister in attendance, for a more relaxed end-of-week luncheon at Abba Eban's residence. Kissinger tried to lighten the mood by announcing that his team had decided to hand out awards to the Israelis for their consumption of food during their long meetings. He saved the highest award for Peres for his table manners, since he always passed the nuts and fruit to the Americans before partaking.

Kissinger believed the negotiations were reaching a climax. He had discussed recessing his mission with Assad, even going over the statement he would make. Assad had responded that it pained him to end the negotiation and had urged Kissinger to make one more effort. He recounted that exchange to his Israeli interlocutors as the prelude to his explaining what he had offered Assad as the American proposal. Meir adjourned the meeting for a private consultation with her team. When they came back, she offered to move the line a few hundred meters west of Quneitra, extend the UN buffer zone to the slope of the hills, maintain only light arms on the hills, and, to the north and south of Quneitra, move the line one kilometer west. Without pressure from Kissinger to make another concession, the Israelis had decided to reveal their bottom line.

Kissinger was satisfied that he had extracted as much as he could, though he added his usual caveat that he doubted Assad would accept it. Meir had learned by now not to take those assessments seriously. He went over what he would say when, after his next meeting with Assad, he announced the recessing of the talks while referring to the significant progress that had been made. Then he warned them one more time, now more in sorrow than in anger, of the likely consequences of the unsuccessful end of his mission. He foresaw "a period of extreme trial."

Saturday, May 18, 1974, Damascus. When Kissinger briefed the traveling press en route to Damascus he set low expectations for this climactic meeting with Assad. While he assessed that they were "as close to an agreement as one can be without having an agreement," he let them know that he was not expecting a breakthrough and planned to return to Washington after the meeting.

Kissinger was therefore surprised when Assad said, "We're not going to quibble about one kilometer," even though that was exactly what he had been doing for the last twenty days. "I have come to the conclusion we should be positive to the maximum," said Assad. "I am convinced that you are trying your utmost. I have convinced my colleagues too. If this serves the cause of peace, *we would forgo the question of the hills* in spite of our lack of optimism on how the Israelis behave [emphasis added]." Suddenly, unexpectedly, with a few simple words, Assad had executed an about-face on the very issue that had made a breakthrough impossible.

When an Arab autocrat changes his mind, one can never really know why. Assad had done the same to us in December 1998. Then, as in this earlier instance, his foreign minister was in shock. And then, as now, after dragging out the negotiations as if he had all the time in the world, he told the secretary of state he wanted to finish them quickly.

Notwithstanding Assad's newfound urgency, Kissinger's first reaction was to extend the meeting, which had lasted less than thirty minutes, to three hours. He explained to Assad this dilatory tactic was designed to show the Israelis that he was fighting hard to drag a dispensation out of the Syrian leader. He was deploying the same tactic he had used, albeit in more elaborate form, to convince Sadat that he was dragging a proposal for Sinai withdrawal out of the Israeli cabinet. When Assad tried to take advantage of the time to add conditions to his concession, Kissinger focused him instead on process and timetable, proposing they aim to wrap up the agreement by May 27, his birthday, nine days hence.

With the outline of the disengagement agreement now in view, Assad wanted a U.S. commitment to full Israeli withdrawal as the next step. Kissinger parried with his now familiar argument about the brawl it would generate back home with American Jews and again countered with the offer of a rapid improvement in bilateral relations. Strangely, Assad seemed satisfied with this. If he had known what promises Kissinger was making to Meir on the question of a further Golan withdrawal, he would not have been so reasonable.

That same evening, at Abba Eban's Jerusalem residence, Kissinger debriefed Meir and her large team of advisers and ministers. Assad "has decided to do it, for his own reasons, but to do it fast," he said. That night he wrote to Nixon that, with the issue of the hills decided in Israel's favor, an agreement was now in sight. Nixon was delighted, sending Kissinger an unusual paean on May 20, extolling his efforts as "one of the greatest diplomatic negotiations of all time" and an example of service to the country "far beyond the call of duty." The president's enthusiasm was partly motivated by the fact that he could now plan in earnest for his own trip to the Middle East, a ride on Kissinger's coattails designed to distract the American public from his Watergate agonies.

"In the course of every negotiation," Kissinger would subsequently write in his memoirs, "a point is reached when the parties either conclude that they will eventually come together or that they are hopelessly deadlocked. In the former case, the negotiation gathers steam." Kissinger had made five shuttle trips to Damascus and back to Jerusalem to secure agreement on the line of Israeli withdrawal. Even though it would still take him another eight trips to secure agreement on all the other issues, he was over the hump. The size of the limited-forces zones, the number and type of forces and equipment deployed there, the nature and size of the UN force, and the width of the buffer zone where it would operate would all lend themselves to amenable solutions. Consequently, the negotiations did gather steam. Nevertheless, it was by no means clear until the last moment whether he would achieve the final breakthrough.

There were times when both sides dug in their heels. For example, when Kissinger told Dayan that Assad would never accept that two of his divisions would have to be withdrawn from the forward line, Dayan exploded: "If they don't want to move their forces, there won't be any reduction and there won't be an agreement. If they are there, then we are there. That's it!"

When Kissinger relayed that the Israelis wanted to keep some positions on Mount Hermon, Assad's response was similar. He said dispassionately that Syria would then just keep on fighting. "We all vacate the mountain, or we all stay there," Assad insisted. "We believe we're right; they know they're wrong."

Back and forth, back and forth the intrepid secretary of state would go, painstakingly, patiently cajoling both sides ever closer to agreement. He saved his threats for the Israelis, his flattery for Assad. At times, he would express his frustration. "I am not going to travel back and forth between Damascus and Jerusalem like a rug merchant. It is incompatible to the dignity of the United States to go on in such sort of discussion day after day," he announced to Meir and Dayan on May 21. And yet that's what he continued to do, American amour propre notwithstanding.

At other times, he would threaten to go home, telling Assad on May 21 that "I cannot neglect my duties in Washington any longer." Yet that's exactly what he did. On May 23, in a candid moment, he admitted to the Israelis that he was stuck. Resorting to self-deprecation, he asked them, "Do you think my credibility will be undermined if for the fiftieth time I say I'm leaving?"

In his memoirs, Dayan describes Kissinger in these negotiations as a *yekke*. The term is used to describe German Jewish immigrants to Israel who brought a neat and sober fastidiousness to the chaotic, emotion-laden environment of a fledgling state struggling to survive in the Middle East. Dayan also noted how Kissinger leavened his seriousness and prodigious capacity for hard work with a keen wit and a highly developed sense of humor. "Occasionally he would pause in the middle of a conversation, withdraw into silence, stretch his legs, plunge into concentrated thought and seemingly consult with himself," Dayan observed. "These sudden spells of meditation would be preceded by a warning signal—he would start to chew on his yellow pencil like a child in kindergarten." Dayan noted that "after intense study, he registers maps he has never seen before and terrain with which he is unfamiliar and has them fixed in his mind."

With the Israelis, Kissinger would continue to portray the dark consequences of their failure to make further concessions, describing again, on May 22, the way in which the United States would be forced by the Europeans and another Arab oil embargo to impose the 1967 lines on Israel. Invoking the

Henry Kissinger with President al-Assad on May 27, 1974, when the Israel-Syria negotiations were about to break down. Assad walked Kissinger to the door to bid him farewell which was when Kissinger let slip that he still had an idea about the line of withdrawal. Assad said if he could get another kilometer, he would be satisfied. Since Meir had given that to Kissinger as her last, best offer, Kissinger was able to achieve a breakthrough instead.

specter of the sacrifice of Czechoslovakia to Hitler on the altar of appeasement, he noted, "Then we have a 1938 situation. This is my nightmare. . . .
Like many cancers, it may not be visible until it's fatal."

He would also rustle up, when necessary, the presidential missive. Nixon
predicted in a dispatch to Meir on May 22, for example, that public opinion
would hold Israel responsible if the talks broke down. Not only would congressional support deteriorate, but he would come under "massive pressure for
a reassessment of United States policy toward Israel," and that would jeopardize his ability "to continue to assist in meeting Israel's needs."

These threats, even from a severely weakened president, combined with
Meir's and Dayan's desire to bring the reservists home, enabled Kissinger to
get just enough from the Israelis to wheedle some more movement out of
Assad that justified him going back to the Israelis for a little more. Dayan, as
usual, provided the conceptual breakthroughs that Kissinger hungrily seized
and converted into talking points that persuaded Assad to accept them as a
defeat for Israel and therefore a victory for Syria.

Motta Gur too, for all of Kissinger's mocking of him to others, came up
with the simple idea that cut the Gordian knot on limiting forces. Assad had
been adamant that he keep three armored divisions along the front line. Gur
proposed that instead of demanding Assad withdraw two of the divisions,
Israel could accept one brigade of each of the three divisions in the forward
zone. It was the kind of simple, face-saving military reconceptualization that
diplomats depend on to finesse differences that are seemingly unbridgeable. In
this case, it enabled Kissinger to persuade Assad to withdraw his main battle
forces behind Damascus while keeping elements of all three of his divisions at
the front.

By nighttime on May 23, Kissinger reported to Nixon that he had reached
an understanding of a concept of limitations on armament behind the disengagement lines, and progress on handling the Israeli positions on Mount Hermon (they would be handed over to the UN observer force). There were still
a host of details to be resolved, but they were essentially technical.* Kissinger
decided to bring the negotiations to a close.

To facilitate that, he asked for a further Israeli concession on the red line
that marked the extent of Syrian forward movement. Instead of engaging in
histrionics, Meir found a way to reduce the size of the UN buffer zone on its
eastern side. That translated into the movement of the Syrian red line west-

---

* In the forward ten-kilometer disengagement zone, Israel was insisting on no artillery; Assad
wanted fifty-four short-range pieces. Behind that, in the twenty-five-kilometer zone, Assad was
refusing any limitation on military personnel or tanks, but there was agreement that all SAMs and
long-range artillery would be beyond that area. Assad insisted on moving his defense line farther
west; Israel insisted on a more robust UN observer force, both in numbers and mandate. See
Memo from Scowcroft to Nixon, May 25, 1974, FRUS 1969-1976:26, Doc. 72.

ward by one kilometer. Kissinger put that in his pocket. It would prove to be the deal clincher.

Sunday, May 26, 1974, Jerusalem–Damascus. This time, Kissinger was so determined to fold his tent and go home, with either a breakthrough or a breakdown, that he bid farewell to Meir and the Israeli team at a semi-public luncheon which she hosted at the King David Hotel, an event that signaled to Assad that his time was up too.

In front of all the members of her outgoing cabinet, with the ancient walls of Jerusalem visible through the high, arched windows, she became emotional as she toasted Kissinger. Raising her glass in his direction, she paid him a great compliment. She said that he had taught her that being right was not enough; that she also had to learn to live with her neighbors, "not to accept things that are not right, but at least to understand them."

Kissinger responded with his own toast to her. "We join you in the hope for a peace that will last, in which children can guard their innocence and all the men can turn to tasks of reconstruction," he said as he raised his glass. Shimon Peres later told the press at the King David that by the following night, "we may have reached the end of one of the most extraordinary and unique experiences in diplomatic life."

That evening Kissinger dined at the presidential palace in Damascus with Assad and his team. It was the twenty-fifth day of the Israel–Syria shuttle and the twelfth time he had visited Damascus during this negotiation. Over dinner, they got into a horrendous argument about the red line marking Syria's advance. Then Assad brought in his generals, who complained about their inability to explain to the Syrian public why there should be a demilitarized zone in Syrian territory, why Syrian villages had to be abandoned in this zone, and why they should be responsible for preventing Palestinian terrorist attacks from their territory.

At midnight, Assad dismissed them and met with Kissinger alone. Just like Meir, with the negotiations coming to an end, he wanted to see what he could get by way of side assurances from the United States. Kissinger had rejected Meir's demand for a letter saying that in any future negotiation, the United States would not expect Israel to come down from the Golan Heights. Now Assad wanted an American commitment that within one year the occupation of the Golan would end. Kissinger suggested that Assad could reach "a rather satisfactory understanding about the second phase" with Nixon when he came to Damascus to visit. And after the midterm elections, he promised the United States would engage in a sustained effort, involving "active pressure," to implement UNSC Resolution 338 (the October 1973 cease-fire resolution that incorporated UNSC Resolution 242).

Assad cast doubt on the whole exercise, arguing with considerable acuity that disengagement was just a process of "deflating various balloons," taking away the readiness of Arab armies, the unity of Arab states, and the will of the people to fight. He said he felt uneasy. Kissinger recognized the nervousness of a first-time buyer as he contemplated the final deal. He tried to reassure him by arguing that the war was a strategic setback for Israel and created an opportunity for peace. American attitudes were changing too. This all represented a defeat for extreme Zionism, he argued.

Assad agreed with him. Did Kissinger believe, he asked now, that Israel's withdrawal should be limited by 338's reference to "secure borders"? Kissinger answered him obliquely: "I do not know of any Arab state that would settle for less than full withdrawal to the 1967 lines." Assad asked for a U.S. commitment to full implementation of 338 within a year. Kissinger refused to budge. He wanted Assad to understand that the cupboard was bare and there was nothing to be gained by insisting on more.

Frustrated, Assad told Kissinger now what he had warned about earlier: Syrian families would not return to Quneitra because he had agreed to withdraw his guns and could not protect them. And they never did. Instead, Quneitra remains a ghost town, its flattened concrete edifices serving as a tourist site that regime tour guides use as evidence of Israeli brutality.

Nevertheless, Assad was still willing to move forward. His only real demand at this late stage was to move Syria's red line—the forward line of its armed forces—farther westward. Since Meir had already given Kissinger some leeway on that and he had managed to whittle down Assad's list of desiderata to this one item, he nonchalantly let slip "I could probably get another kilometer in here." Assad pretended he didn't hear him and repeated all the reasons why he couldn't possibly accept the current line.

It was after 2:00 a.m. Kissinger had decided he would stay the night in an effort to conclude the deal in the morning, so there was still some time left for the final haggle. "Let us sleep on it," said Assad.

Monday, May 27, 1974, Damascus. Neither leader went to bed. Instead, they met with their teams to go over the details of the deal once again. Sisco reported that they were hung up on every point. Assad's team was fixated on the red line. In the early hours of the morning, both sides went to bed exhausted, assuming that the negotiations were over, with no result.

When the two leaders met at 10:00 a.m. at the presidential palace, Kissinger told Assad that in his judgment there was "really no basis at this time to conclude the relatively few things that remain to be done." Assad agreed. Kissinger pulled out what he told me was his "best weapon," his departure statement. As they finalized what Kissinger would tell the press, Assad then commented: "The question of the red line is the basic thing." All the other issues could be sorted out, he averred.

Kissinger had already resolved in his own mind that, since the negotiations were going into recess, it made no sense for him to play his last card of the one kilometer that Meir had given him for the westward movement of the Syrian defense red line. He was exhausted. He felt he had repeated all his best arguments five hundred times. If he offered Israel's last concession now, he had to be ready for the negotiations to collapse or produce another round of haggling. He knew he could not go back to Israel and ask for more. Better, he calculated, to keep that card for the follow-up negotiations. "If I had done it then under the emotion of the moment and Assad rejected it," he told me, "we'd be stuck forever."

Instead, he suggested that it was best to recess the talks for a few weeks and then perhaps Nixon could pick it up when he visited. He expressed great disappointment but promised not to blame Assad, just as he had promised Meir. Assad reciprocated by promising to praise Kissinger and keep his media "pragmatic and objective." It would probably be better if the president came at a more auspicious time, Assad added. Kissinger suggested the alternative of sending a personal emissary to Washington to continue the negotiations. Assad said that wouldn't be useful.

Kissinger knew Nixon would be sorely disappointed. And he would have no next step in a process he still needed to keep alive for Sadat's sake. He also knew that once a negotiation fails, it is very hard to resurrect it. So, as Assad walked him to the door, Kissinger changed his mind and decided to dangle the carrot: "I have some ideas on the red line, but there is no sense negotiating with you, going back to Israel and having a three-day cabinet crisis." And then he gently waved the stick: "When we start again, we will start from a different position."

At the door now, clasping hands, Assad said he appreciated the "nice human, personal contact." He said he had grown fond of his American friend; out of loyalty, he was particularly keen to do him no harm. And then he asked tentatively, "In your view, how far could the red line be moved?" He was rising to the bait.

Kissinger said he had been thinking about it. He claimed to have no authority to offer it and didn't want to cause complications for his good Syrian friend. Assad said that he appreciated Kissinger's sincerity. And then, finally, like the Damascus bazaar merchant who calls the American tourist back into his shop after he realizes he is about to lose the deal, Assad suggested the distance between the red line (the Syrian army's forward line) and the blue line (the IDF's forward line) be cut in half, which would narrow the UN buffer zone between them by a kilometer in Syria's favor without moving the Israeli line. Bingo! Assad had proposed what Kissinger knew Meir would accept.

Making sure he had heard correctly, Kissinger asked whether Assad would accept that change. Yes, Assad said, if the red line could go around the three Syrian villages in the buffer zone. They returned to the map. Kissinger picked up his yellow pencil with the eraser on top and drew a new line that skirted the three villages.* Assad was satisfied: "If the red line could be as you pointed out, I will myself take the responsibility. We'll find a justification for why the red line has to be where it is."

The other outstanding issue was what Assad would do to prevent Palestinian terror attacks from Syrian territory. He had been reluctant to take on any commitment in writing that would look like he was defending Israel from Palestinian attacks. Now he responded to Kissinger's concern by promising to keep the cease-fire with Israel "scrupulously." Knowing this would be inadequate for the Israelis, Kissinger raised the idea of an American statement expressing understanding of Israel's need to protect itself should it come under Palestinian terror attack. As far as Assad was concerned, the United States could say what it wanted as long as there was no connection to Syria in the statement. However, he recognized that Israel had a right to defend itself against Palestinian attacks and he would not object to their actions provided they did not involve Syria in their response.

Tuesday, May 28, 1974, Jerusalem–Damascus. Notwithstanding this breakthrough, it took Kissinger yet one more Jerusalem–Damascus shuttle—the thirteenth—to finalize the deal. At first, he thought he would secure Meir's agreement to the changes in the map and send Sisco back to Damascus with it. But since the changes were coming on the heels of the devastating attacks in Kiryat Shmona and Ma'alot, the cabinet ministers felt they needed a more tangible commitment from Assad to prevent Palestinian terrorism if they were to defend the Golan withdrawal to their people. That was especially because Menachem Begin and other members of the opposition were claiming the agreement left the settlers there vulnerable to terrorist attack.

Kissinger captured the paradox in the discussion with Meir and her advisers: "The real problem is that [Assad] can act without admitting it, and for you the admission is the most important part." The only way to bridge the gap was

---

* The three villages were Hadar, Khan Arnabah, and Umm Batinah (see map page 410).

to make a final effort to seek clarity from Assad that he could report back to the Israeli cabinet and complement it with an American guarantee. Yet again, the U.S. role became essential.

So Kissinger made one last trek to Damascus, meeting Assad in his palace at 8:15 p.m. Satisfied with the map and the other arrangements, Assad tried to be as forthcoming as he could with Kissinger. He said again that Syria would "scrupulously" observe the cease-fire, there would be no firing by anyone across the front line into Israeli-held territory, the front would not be used as a launching site, and no armed bands would cross from there into Israel. But he refused to commit any of that to writing.

For more than forty years Assad, and subsequently his son Bashar, kept almost all the verbal commitments he made that day to Kissinger, preventing all but two Palestinian attacks on Israeli-held territory from the Syrian side of the Golan.* Until the civil war broke out in Syria in 2011, the Golan was the quietest of Israel's borders. Even in 2019, with IAF jets striking Iranian targets in Syria at will, there was only one incident in which an Iranian missile entered Israeli-controlled airspace on the Golan. In Lebanon, though, which Assad took effective control of in 1976, he did little to restrain Palestinian terror groups and, subsequently, Hezbollah, from attacking towns and kibbutzim across the border in northern Israel. He had never made a commitment in that regard, and he found such attacks quite useful as a disavowable reminder to Israel of the costs of retaining the Golan.

What happened to the Soviet role? Since they had been sidelined with Assad's willful cooperation, there was no useful role they could play. Kissinger's challenge was simply to prevent them from becoming a nuisance that could confound an already complex negotiation. Since his meeting with Gromyko in Cyprus almost three weeks earlier, Kissinger had ignored them. That had been possible only because Brezhnev and Gromyko had seemed satisfied to sit quietly on the sidelines and leave Kissinger to fail on his own. However, as the expectations of a breakthrough rose, Gromyko suddenly announced that he would fly into Damascus on Monday, May 27. Kissinger saw this as a transparent ploy to make it look as if the agreement were a product of superpower cooperation. He was determined to avoid being in Damascus at the same time as Gromyko.

Assad was happy to cooperate in this diplomatic disengagement, postpon-

---

* The two terrorist attacks occurred in October and November 1975. In the first attempt, there were no casualties. In the second, three yeshiva students in the Golan settlement of Ramat Magshimim were murdered by Palestinian infiltrators from Syria who escaped back across the border.

ing the Soviet foreign minister's arrival until late in the evening on the assumption that Kissinger would be long gone by then. However, nailing down the details of the agreement and side letters took longer than expected. Kissinger was only able to finalize the deal late in the evening, around the same time as Gromyko was landing. Over dinner, he apologized to Assad for the awkwardness of the situation. Assad laughed and said, "It is all right. You are eating his dinner."

Kissinger was concerned that the media would photograph Gromyko's Ilyushin jet alongside his USAF Boeing on the tarmac at Damascus International Airport. Assad obligingly had the Soviet plane towed to a dark corner of the airport. Gromyko's motorcade passed Kissinger's, like two ships passing in the night, as the American secretary of state sped toward the airport, heading for Jerusalem. As the headlights of Gromyko's motorcade appeared on the dark highway, Khaddam, who as usual was escorting Kissinger, said, "Here is your friend!"

"Should I wave?" Kissinger asked.

Since Gromyko was still in Damascus when Kissinger returned the next evening, a meeting was unavoidable. To Kissinger's surprise, Assad had not informed Gromyko that he had struck an agreement with Israel. Remembering the Soviets' reaction to their exclusion from the signing of the Israeli-Egyptian disengagement agreement, Kissinger agreed with Gromyko that this time the Soviet and American ambassadors to the Geneva Conference would attend the signing in Geneva on May 30.

A week later, in Washington, Kissinger tried to apply more balm to the wound his diplomacy had inflicted. At a press conference previewing Nixon's upcoming summit with Brezhnev in Moscow, he noted that the Soviet Union was a superpower with global interests, including in the Middle East. "Therefore, we have no intention, indeed we have no capability, of expelling Soviet influence from the Middle East," he said with a straight face. Five years earlier, he had articulated that very objective to the media standing by Nixon's swimming pool in San Clemente. Having now achieved it, he used the same vocabulary to deny that it was ever his objective. The diplomat in chief had mastered the art of speaking out of both sides of his mouth.

Wednesday, May 29, 1974, Jerusalem. Kissinger returned to Israel after midnight on this final leg of the shuttle and began a session with Meir that concluded at 4:00 a.m. Soon after that, the cabinet approved the Israeli-Syrian disengagement agreement, dropping its demand for a written Syrian commitment in exchange for Assad's verbal assurances buttressed by Kissinger's written word that the United States would support Israel's right to defend itself and retaliate if necessary.* To this day, whenever Israel is subjected to a terrorist attack across its borders, U.S. spokesmen will assert that Israel has a right to defend itself, even though they are rarely aware of the origins of that talking point in the Israeli-Syrian disengagement agreement.

One piece of unfinished business the Israelis surprisingly did not insist upon was the U.S.-Israeli memorandum of understanding that was supposed to commit the United States to a long-term arms supply relationship with Israel and provide assurance that the United States would not expect Israel to withdraw from the Golan Heights. In the rush to complete the agreement and the preoccupation with the Palestinian terrorism issue, neither Meir nor Kissinger had the energy to deal with the document. Instead, they settled for vague language in the MOU that committed the United States to be "fully responsive on a continuing and long-term basis to Israel's military requirements" and a supportive letter from Nixon to Meir suggesting that Israel send a team to Washington to discuss Israel's long-term needs, with particular regard to advanced aircraft and missiles (see Appendix B).† There was no mention of the Golan. The incoming Rabin government would be saddled with the responsibility of pinning Kissinger down on both issues. It would prove to be a source of considerable contention that soured relations between Kissinger and Rabin from the outset of his term as prime minister.

At 5:00 p.m. in Jerusalem and Damascus, 10:00 a.m. in Washington, on May 29, 1974, President Nixon announced from the White House that an agreement had been reached between Israel and Syria. He gave "enormous credit" to his secretary of state for his dogged determination to resolve the great differences between the parties. He also paid tribute to Meir's and Assad's statesmanship. The United States had, he asserted, removed a major roadblock on the way to a permanent peace in the Middle East.

Kissinger was, as usual, more cautious. In his toast at the prime minister's office, he expressed the hope that the agreement would "speed the day when a lasting peace comes to the area." Meir had the last word. As Kissinger embraced

---

* Beyond this assurance, Kissinger provided a series of other written assurances to both sides. To Assad, there was a presidential assurance that the United States would help rehabilitate Quneitra and consider the agreement as "only the first step toward a just and durable peace," based on the "full implementation of Security Council Resolution 338 in all of its parts," a settlement that "should take fully into account the legitimate interests of the Palestinian people." There was also a letter from Nixon to Assad conveying Israeli assurances that it would scrupulously observe the cease-fire, place no weapons on the eastern slopes of the two hills that surrounded Quneitra, and place no weapons on top of the hills that could fire into Quneitra. See Appendix B, page 580.
† The U.S.-Israeli memorandum of understanding also provided for a U.S. veto of any attempt to change the mandate or composition of the UN observer force that would operate in the buffer zone (the United Nations Disengagement Observer Force—UNDOF). It noted that Egypt had informed the United States that it supported the agreement and would not participate militarily if Syria breached the agreement. It committed the United States to doing its best to ensure the Geneva Conference proceeded "at a pace agreed upon by Israel and the United States," and to consult about supporting Israel should Syria violate the agreement. See Appendix B, page 579.

her and kissed her on the cheek, she said, alluding to the fact that he had so often been photographed kissing Sadat, "I didn't know you kissed women." *The New York Times* captured them on its front page laughing uproariously.

It was an exhilarating end to an exhausting negotiation. Although this would only become clear in retrospect, Kissinger had made major progress in taking Syria as well as Egypt out of the conflict with Israel. Henceforth each would seek to regain its territory from Israel only through American-led diplomacy. And from now on, no Arab state could contemplate making war on Israel. It was a milestone in the history of the Arab-Israeli conflict.

In the process, Kissinger had achieved all his objectives: a stable cease-fire on the Golan that relieved pressure on Israel to make further withdrawals there, Syrian cover for Sadat's pursuit of what would eventually emerge as a separate peace with Israel, a high-profile victory for American diplomacy at a time of deep political crisis for the U.S. president, and a second cornerstone laid for Kissinger's American-led Middle Eastern order.*

Yet again, Kissinger's wielding of the influence of the American superpower, combined with his talent for cajoling and manipulating the two sides, had won the day. It had required an immense degree of patience, energy, ingenuity, tactical finesse, and strategic clarity, but in the end the results spoke for themselves. Unlike the Vietnam peace accords, which were coming apart at the same time as he was poring over the maps of the Golan, the Israeli-Syrian disengagement agreement continues to be adhered to by both sides, notwithstanding the decline of Syria into a state of prolonged civil war, part of it playing out on the Golan. Neither Syria nor Israel has complained of a serious violation of the Golan accord.

The continued utility of the forty-five-year-old agreement was underscored at President Donald Trump's Helsinki summit with Russian president Vladimir Putin in July 2018, when Putin called for the upholding of the 1974 Israeli-Syrian disengagement agreement as the way to maintain peace on the Golan and stabilize Israeli-Syrian relations. When I pointed this out to the nonagenarian Kissinger, he said with a smile, "It gives me some satisfaction."

---

* The terms of the agreement provided for Israeli withdrawal from the three hundred square miles it had occupied in the Yom Kippur War, as well as a sliver of territory it had taken in 1967. A UN buffer zone would be established that would include Quneitra but not the hills around it. A UN force of 1,250 armed troops, supplied by countries not permanent members of the UN Security Council, would police the zone. Within ten kilometers on either side of the buffer zone, both sides would be allowed to deploy only six thousand soldiers with light weapons in two brigades of armed forces, along with seventy-five tanks and thirty-six artillery pieces with ranges of less than twelve miles. Beyond that, a second zone of ten kilometers' width on both sides would contain no more than 450 tanks and medium-range artillery but no long-range guns. No SAMs would be allowed closer than fifteen miles on either side of the UN buffer zone. (See map, page 410.)

Henry Kissinger and Golda Meir share a joke after toasting the conclusion
of the Israel-Syria disengagement agreement, Jerusalem, May 29, 1974. After
Kissinger embraced and kissed Meir on the cheek, she said, alluding to the
fact that he had so often been photographed kissing Sadat, "I didn't know you
kissed women." Israeli ambassador to the United States Simcha Dinitz is on
Meir's left.

It would be the last negotiation Kissinger conducted with Golda Meir. Yitzhak
Rabin's government was sworn in a few days later. Neither would surely mourn
the end of their epic battles. But Kissinger soon realized the value of this stubborn leader, and began to miss her sorely. For she was that rare kind of Israeli
prime minister—matched only by David Ben-Gurion, Menachem Begin, Ariel
Sharon, and, in a later incarnation, Yitzhak Rabin—who could commit Israel
to a painful territorial compromise and deliver the cabinet and the Knesset.

It would also be Kissinger's last negotiation with Dayan, and it would not
take long for Kissinger to sorely miss him too. Dayan's ability to conceptualize
both the purpose of an agreement and its necessary security components, and
bring Meir along with him, were indispensable elements in Kissinger's success.
Time and again, though, the unsung heroes of Kissinger's negotiations would
prove to be Israeli generals. Arele Yariv, Dado Elazar, and Motta Gur, as well
as Dayan, provided Kissinger with the security ideas and arrangements that
underpinned the breakthroughs he was able to achieve. When Israel's generals were allowed to determine Israel's security needs, territorial concessions
became much easier to secure. That applies today, when Israel's security needs
in the West Bank are more easily resolved than its political and ideological
demands to hold on to the territory.

It would also be the last direct negotiation Kissinger would conduct with Hafez al-Assad. He had grown fond of Assad, finding him "proud, tough, shrewd, cordial." And Assad had grown fond of him too, appreciating his broad experience and deep knowledge of international relations, and recognizing that Kissinger's guile made him a worthy sparring partner. Kissinger described Assad's unique style as that of "someone who negotiated at the edge of a precipice and who, in order to increase his bargaining position, jumped into the abyss hoping that something on the way down would break his fall." In fact, Assad was far too calculating to take that sort of risk. He never jumped before knowing that Kissinger would be there to provide the hand he could grasp to help him back up. And Kissinger was usually willing to go back to the Israelis for one more concession that would justify Assad's confidence in him and enable him to inform his generals and Ba'ath Party apparatchiks that he had secured the best possible deal.

Assad was no Sadat, whom Kissinger considered "far-seeing and determined to move towards peace, and who considered everything else trivial compared to that overriding objective." The avuncular Egyptian peasant and the Syrian bazaar merchant could not have been more different in temperament and personality. One was unconstrained by his military; the other would not move forward without securing its support. One was predisposed to grand gestures; the other gave nothing without getting in return. And yet for all their differences, they both were willing to put their trust in the American-Jewish diplomat whose sympathies, they correctly assumed, lay with their Israeli adversary. What mattered to them more was Kissinger's ability to move the Israelis, to secure for each of them through diplomatic means at least some of the occupied territories they had been unable to liberate by force.

Kissinger started the negotiations with Assad hoping they would somehow end in a Sadat-like moment when he would turn against the Soviet Union and move fully into the American camp. But he never really worked for that outcome or believed it necessary. It was enough for his new Middle Eastern order that Assad would henceforth calculate that it was in Syria's interest to avoid conflict with Israel.

Kissinger was quite proud of the agreement. It had started as a localized issue to bring Syria along with the peace process, but it grew to have greater purpose because he had managed to avoid the question of legitimacy; the agreement only said where the forces would be deployed but not why. "The reason the disengagement agreement lasted so long was because each party could carry out its provisions without giving away their principles," Kissinger said long afterward.

Forty-five years later, President Trump would devalue this effort to preserve running room for American diplomacy by formally recognizing Israel's sovereignty on the Golan Heights to help secure the reelection of Benjamin Netanyahu in Israel's April 2019 elections. Kissinger was upset by Trump's decision. He described the agreement as a "perfect situation": Israel could continue to occupy the Golan; Syria could continue to claim sovereignty over it. But the key to the longevity of this arrangement was to avoid making the Golan part of Eretz Yisrael, the land of Israel—to avoid an attempt to legitimize Israel's hold on the heights, because that was something Syria and the Arabs could never accept. As Kissinger lamented to me, Trump came along and upended it all for a momentary political advantage. Ironically, when Iranian-backed Syrian irregulars placed mines on the Israeli side of the disengagement line in November 2020, it was Netanyahu who called on Syria to enforce the disengagement agreement.

Friday, May 31, 1974, Geneva. At 11:00 a.m. members of the Egyptian-Israeli military working group, accompanied by U.S. ambassador Ellsworth Bunker, Soviet ambassador Vladimir Vinogradov, and UNEF commander Ensio Siilasvuo, filed into the high-ceilinged Council Chamber at the Palais des Nations. It had been five months since Arab and Israeli diplomats had first convened there under the auspices of Kissinger and Gromyko. Although they could not have foreseen it, this would be the last time they would assemble in that hallowed hall.

As Assad had notified Kissinger at the outset of their engagement, Syria was only willing to participate as part of the Egyptian delegation, thereby maintaining the fiction that they were not dealing directly with Israel. Whereas Israel was represented by Major General Herzl Shafir, at the last moment Assad had switched out his intelligence chief, General Shihabi, for a lower-ranking brigadier general, Adnan Tayara, who was clearly subordinate to Major General Taha el-Magdoub, the Egyptian head of delegation. Israel's delegation was seated between the UN and the United States, and the Egyptian and Syrian delegates were seated between the Soviet Union and the UN.

The ceremony lasted thirty minutes, time enough for the sole speech of General Siilasvuo and the signing of the disengagement agreement, the protocol on the role and size of the UN Disengagement Observer Force (UNDOF), and the map showing the UN buffer zone. The ceremony was prolonged by General Tayara's insistence that the press be cleared from the balcony so that they could not witness or photograph his signing of the documents. Even then, Assad was still keen to avoid any public manifestation of the agreement he had struck with the Israelis.

In his speech, Siilasvuo hailed the agreement as "an exceptional feat of diplomacy, unparalleled in the annals of international relations." Kissinger had become so famous for his diplomacy that it wasn't necessary for the general to mention his name, though Kissinger would have liked it. Siilasvuo also expressed his strong conviction that the agreement would turn out to be "that giant and courageous step that brought us to the threshold of a new era of trust, justice and peace in the Middle East." As he was speaking, the guns finally fell silent on the Golan Heights.

Fifty-four Israelis and hundreds of Syrians had been killed in the war of attrition that followed Kissinger's negotiation of the cease-fire that ended the 1973 Yom Kippur War. In the eerie quiet that now prevailed, Israeli settlers doggedly farmed the potato fields and apple orchards around Quneitra that they would soon have to relinquish, while Druze villagers collected discarded ammunition cases for firewood. A day later, the International Committee of the Red Cross arranged for the exchange of twelve Israeli and twenty-five Syrian wounded prisoners. Five days later the rest of the Israeli prisoners on the list that Kissinger had extracted from Assad came home to a tumultuous welcome. The Israeli-Syrian disengagement agreement did not bring the peace that Siilasvuo imagined, but it did ensure quiet on the Golan for decades to come. Not peace, but the absence of war, which is what Kissinger had aimed for, and what his determined diplomacy had now secured.

ISRAEL-SYRIA DISENGAGEMENT

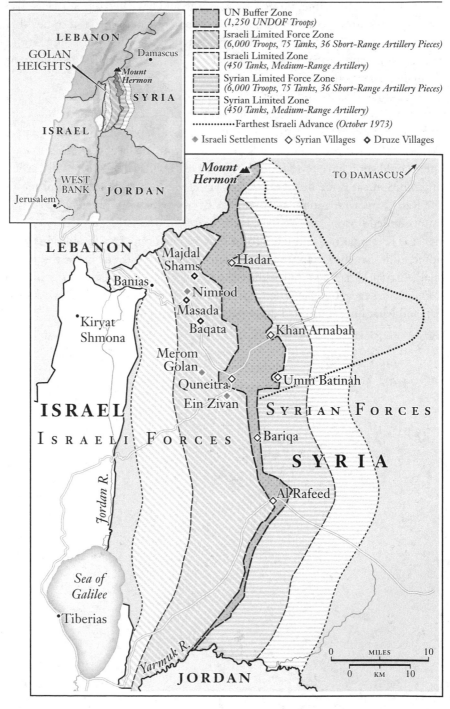

UN Buffer Zone
(1,250 UNDOF Troops)

Israeli Limited Force Zone
(6,000 Troops, 75 Tanks, 36 Short-Range Artillery Pieces)

Israeli Limited Zone
(450 Tanks, Medium-Range Artillery)

Syrian Limited Force Zone
(6,000 Troops, 75 Tanks, 36 Short-Range Artillery Pieces)

Syrian Limited Zone
(450 Tanks, Medium-Range Artillery)

............Farthest Israeli Advance *(October 1973)*

◆ Israeli Settlements   ◇ Syrian Villages   ◈ Druze Villages

LEBANON
GOLAN HEIGHTS
Damascus
Mount Hermon
SYRIA
ISRAEL
WEST BANK
Jerusalem
JORDAN

Mount Hermon
TO DAMASCUS

LEBANON

Majdal Shams
Hadar
Banias
Nimrod
Kiryat Shmona
Masada
Baqata
Khan Arnabah
Merom Golan
Quneitra
Umm Batinah
Ein Zivan
ISRAEL
ISRAELI FORCES
SYRIAN FORCES
Bariqa
SYRIA
Al-Rafeed

Jordan R.

Sea of Galilee
Tiberias

Yarmuk R.

JORDAN

0 MILES 10
0 KM 10

PART V

The Third Step

14

The Step Not Taken

The art of politics is to make a concession before you're forced to, to do today what would be less than you will have to do tomorrow.

—Henry Kissinger to King Hussein, December 1973

Much work remained to be done, but Kissinger took a moment to bask in the accolades and tributes. *Newsweek*'s cover featured him in a Superman suit; *Time* put a photograph of an ebullient Kissinger on its cover with the words "Mideast Miracle" printed across his forehead and ran an article effusively praising his accomplishment as "barely short of magnificent." He was even more satisfied by a *New York Times* analysis which pointed out that the United States had now displaced the Soviet Union as the major outside influence in the Arab world. The esteemed *Times* columnist C. L. Sulzberger argued that he should receive another Nobel Prize, likening him to Hercules lopping off the serpent heads of the Middle East's Hydra. The *Times* editorial board, which had questioned that award for his Vietnam peace negotiations, now opined that "with his tireless diligence and unswerving devotion to the cause of peace, Secretary Kissinger has without question earned the honor now." Eighty-five percent of Americans, according to a Harris poll, believed he was doing a "good to excellent job." Kissinger notes in his memoirs, "There is no record indicating that I resisted the hyperbole."

The moment was short-lived. Just as he had feared when he had resolved to linger on the Middle East's diplomatic highways, once he returned to Washington he was swept into the Watergate vortex. Within a week both *The Washington Post* and *The New York Times* were accusing him of dissembling at best and committing perjury at worst about his role in the FBI's wiretapping of his staff five years earlier, implying that legal proceedings might be necessary. Kissinger decided to confront the press in a daring effort to use the prestige he had acquired from Middle East peacemaking to counteract the feeding frenzy that was developing. He chose an unusual time and place for this dramatic event.

Monday, June 10, 1974, Salzburg. President Nixon's victory-lap tour of the Middle East began in Salzburg because he was suffering from painful phlebitis in his leg and had decided to make a rest stop there en route to Cairo. Against the advice of Haig, Kissinger decided to fill the downtime with a full-blown press conference in which he repeatedly threatened to resign unless his honor "was not at issue." Likened by some commentators to a temper tantrum, it nevertheless had the desired effect. By the next day, a bipartisan Senate resolution expressing support for the secretary of state had picked up fifty-two sponsors. He had cauterized the bleeding, but at a price. In the press, he was accused of being hypersensitive. Still, he preferred that to being accused of perjury and hauled before congressional investigative committees.

The higher price Kissinger paid was with Nixon, who did not appreciate being upstaged on the eve of what was supposed to be a triumphal presidential trip to the Middle East. They barely spoke during the journey, and Kissinger was reported by one aide to have sulked in the background for most of the time. He notes in his memoirs, "Had Watergate not soon over-

President Nixon and President Sadat are greeted by millions of Egyptians as they ride in a motorcade from Cairo International Airport to Qubba Palace on June 12, 1974. Nixon was in the throes of Watergate and would resign two months later. In his meeting with Sadat, Nixon led the Egyptian president to believe that the United States would support Israel's full withdrawal from the Sinai. Kissinger had done his best to dissuade Nixon from endorsing the 1967 lines.

whelmed [Nixon], I doubt whether I could have maintained my position in his Administration."*

Nixon's Middle East trip was intended as a flag-waving exercise to demonstrate the newly placed faith of Arabs and Israelis in the role of the United States as the midwife of a more hopeful future for their region. Millions of emotional Egyptians lined the routes from the airport through Heliopolis to Qubba Palace, as Nixon and Sadat waved to them from an open-roofed limousine. The same performance was repeated the next day as the two presidents rode in an open railway carriage from Cairo to Alexandria, greeted by hundreds of thousands of apparently adoring peasants and villagers along the way.

Kissinger's greatest concern was that Nixon, overwhelmed by the adulation, would make a commitment to Sadat to secure Israel's return to the 1967 lines. In Nixon's briefing papers, Kissinger had urged him to "neither endorse total Israeli withdrawal nor refuse to endorse it." But Sadat eventually secured

---

* Kissinger records that he found it disconcerting and painful "to be relegated . . . to a subsidiary role," conceding that this was "not to [his] credit." See Henry Kissinger, *Years of Upheaval* (Boston: Little, Brown, 1982), 1125.

something from Nixon that satisfied him while enabling Kissinger to argue that it did not represent a presidential commitment.

Sunday, June 16, 1974, Damascus. Nixon came under a more determined barrage of questions from Assad on the ultimate objective of America's peacemaking diplomacy. As we've seen, in the final days of the disengagement negotiations, Kissinger had deferred Assad's efforts to secure a U.S. commitment to Israel's full withdrawal from the Golan until this meeting with Nixon. Now, as Assad pressed Nixon, Kissinger realized his talking points on the necessity of keeping American objectives vague were insufficient for Nixon.* As Kissinger would later concede, Assad "would not have been far off the mark if he distilled from the conversation the idea that Nixon, in his own elliptical way, was agreeing to total Israeli withdrawal from the Golan."

In Israel, Nixon was less accommodating to Prime Minister Rabin's efforts to secure a commitment to a five-year, large-scale military assistance package. In response, he made clear that the United States expected Israel to make further territorial concessions. Its willingness to do so would determine America's readiness to underwrite new arms commitments subsidized by American taxpayers, Nixon told Rabin. This laid the foundation for a fundamental misunderstanding that would plague subsequent negotiations: Rabin felt that the commitment was owed Israel for its previous withdrawals, as Nixon and Kissinger had promised, not for future withdrawals.

When it came to the specifics of American expectations, Nixon talked at some length about the importance of making a deal with King Hussein next. Notwithstanding the placing of this marker, Kissinger did not travel with Nixon to Jordan, pleading the need to attend the signing of the new Atlantic Charter that he had concluded with his NATO counterparts.

Kissinger wanted some breathing room to consider his next move. The Syrian disengagement agreement was barely two weeks old, there was a new government in Israel that needed to find its sea legs, and Nixon's presidency was being consumed by Watergate.

Only in retrospect are history's turning points illuminated. The summer of 1974 was one of those hinges of history when the course of U.S. peacemak-

---

* In the president's briefing book, Kissinger counseled Nixon that he should say "the US understands the Syrian position and is committed to further negotiations in which these points will be addressed."

ing diplomacy in the Middle East and the destiny of Israel's relations with the Palestinians were determined. It would turn out to be the last moment when the Palestinian problem might have been handled in a state-to-state negotiation between Israel and Jordan. The Hashemite Kingdom of Jordan, with its British-built governmental institutions, its British-trained army and intelligence organization, and its special relationship with the West Bank Palestinians, who were at that time citizens of Jordan, might then have taken responsibility for the Palestinians and given expression to their right of self-determination while ensuring the implementation of any agreement reached with Israel.

Unlike Israel's other Arab neighbors, the Palestinians were then, and remain at this writing, stateless. At the time, they lacked the institutions of a state; they were led instead by a ragtag group of would-be liberation fighters, otherwise known as terrorists for the techniques they pioneered for killing innocent civilians to promote their cause. Even today, although the international community has put a great deal of effort and funding into building the institutions of statehood, the Palestinians still lack the status and capabilities of an independent state. That abiding reality has plagued both the Israeli-Palestinian negotiations and the PLO's ability to implement the agreements it entered into with Israel.

At the time, as he mulled his options, Kissinger well understood that he was at a crossroads. Israel, the Arab states, and the United States faced a choice between the king of Jordan and the PLO as Israel's eastern interlocutor in Kissinger's new order. He warned the Israeli leadership repeatedly—just as Nixon had during his visit to Jerusalem—that if they didn't negotiate an agreement with King Hussein, they would be left to deal with the PLO. Already, in December 1973, the Algiers Arab League summit had made a secret decision to recognize the PLO as the sole representative of the Palestinians and to demand their "full *national* rights [emphasis added]." In a forlorn attempt to preserve its role in the West Bank, Jordan was the only dissenting voice on that resolution. Subsequently, as we have seen, Kissinger had to finesse the issue of who would represent the Palestinians at Geneva by securing Egyptian agreement to postpone the decision until after the opening session. With its own seat at the table, Jordan was happy to concur.

Kissinger himself had recognized the salience of the PLO when, at the outset of his diplomatic mission in November 1973, he had authorized Vernon Walters to meet Yasir Arafat's representatives in Rabat. In that meeting, Khalid al-Hassan, a senior adviser to Arafat, made quite clear that the Palestinians could never live with a Hashemite state instead of their own, and that King Hussein would have to be overthrown. From that point on Kissinger felt the PLO was certain to be irredentist; it would turn on Jordan first and then on

Henry Kissinger meets with King Hussein at the Rabda Palace in Amman, Jordan, on December 16, 1973, to discuss an Israeli-Jordanian disengagement negotiation. Behind the king are photos of his great-grandfather Hussein bin Ali, Sharif of Mecca; his grandfather King Abdullah, who was assassinated in 1951 in Jerusalem; and his father, King Talal, who abdicated the throne in 1952 in favor of Hussein.

Israel. "Our aim," Kissinger said, "should be to strengthen [King Hussein's] position, not to encourage a group that avowed its determination to overthrow him."

To undertake a diplomatic initiative focused on an Israeli-Jordanian disengagement agreement, however, was complicated. It was the logical next step after the Egyptian and Syrian disengagement agreements, to be sure. But Jordan had avoided opening its own front with Israel during the Yom Kippur War, sending only two tank battalions and one infantry battalion to fight in Syria, which limited its engagement with the IDF. Since there was no fighting on the Israeli-Jordanian front, there were no forces to separate and no sense of urgency to stabilize the situation. Nor were the Arab oil producers conditioning the lifting of their oil embargo on an agreement with Jordan.

Kissinger had a sentimental attachment to the king, which led him repeatedly to articulate the high-minded principle "that friends of the United States should not be penalized." He understood the advantage of introducing a Jordanian presence on the West Bank as the best way to ensure that the Palestinian population there looked to Amman. In this way, he hoped the Palestinian issue could be resolved in a Jordanian context, making it an internal Jordanian problem rather than an American or Israeli problem. As he told the king in December 1973, "If we could design a settlement ourselves, we would favor the closest relationship between the West Bank and Jordan."

Yet whenever Kissinger contemplated undertaking an Israeli-Jordanian initiative, he came up against problematic realities. He knew that the West Bank had a great deal more political salience in Israel than the Sinai or the Golan Heights. The National Religious Party (NRP), which would play a significant role in Rabin's coalition, vehemently opposed any territorial concessions in the West Bank, which it viewed as Judea and Samaria, the land God had promised the Israelites, according to the Bible. Meir had promised the NRP that any West Bank territorial concessions would require new elections. Rabin had no choice but to honor that commitment. Kissinger faced a government in Israel that, for its own survival, would be reluctant to concede West Bank territory. Should he succeed, nevertheless, in brokering a Jordanian deal, he would have to subject it to the vagaries of an Israeli election.

Kissinger's second problem was Egypt. As we have seen, Sadat was determined not to let any other Arab leader hold him back from pursuing peace with Israel, particularly not King Hussein, for whom he had little respect. Where it suited his strategic objective, Sadat would play with the Palestinian issue, just like other Arab leaders. But he was wary of touching the third rail of inter-Arab politics in a way that could distract him from his own purposes.

Sadat had urged Kissinger to pursue the Syrian disengagement to help reduce opposition from the Arab radical camp. Once that was achieved, he wanted the United States to return its focus to Egypt and persuade Israel to relinquish more territory in the Sinai. Kissinger understood that his new order depended on taking the strong regional power of Egypt out of a potential Arab war coalition against Israel. Jordan was already in America's pocket and added little weight to the regional power balance either way.

Kissinger also had his doubts, reinforced by his advisers, that the king would be able to sustain a return of his authority to the West Bank in the face of certain opposition from the PLO. His reservations were confirmed in early January 1974 by Dayan, who told him on his visit to Washington to discuss the Syrian disengagement that he had spent time talking to West Bank Palestinians (something Kissinger never had the opportunity to do) and they had made clear that they would never accept King Hussein as their leader.

Negotiating over Israel's eastern border would be complex. Israel's security concerns would be particularly acute since the West Bank was like a soft underbelly, protruding into Israel and narrowing its waist to a mere eight to twelve kilometers. Beyond the security issues, and the questions of who represented the Palestinians and how to resolve their aspirations for statehood, lay

Jerusalem with all its religious sensitivities and irresolvable competing claims. (Israel had captured East Jerusalem and the West Bank from Jordan during the 1967 war.) Kissinger was well aware of the millennial conflicts over the Holy City and had resolved, long before assuming the mantle of peacemaker, that the issue of Jerusalem had to be left until last. Yet pursuing an Israeli-Jordanian negotiation would bring him dangerously close to it, given King Hussein's personal desire to regain the Hashemite foothold in Jerusalem that he lost in the Six-Day War.

The sentimentalist in Kissinger wanted to reward King Hussein for his friendship, but the realist in Kissinger understood the limits of U.S. noblesse oblige in the prevailing circumstances. As he told Dayan in June 1974, in his judgment it was in the American interest to make Egypt next while it was in Israel's long-term interest to make Jordan next.

Because of these concerns and calculations, Kissinger was never willing to put the weight of the United States behind the Jordanian option. Instead, he would repeatedly urge Israel's leaders to engage the king through their own direct channel, to make him a generous offer, and to act before it was too late because the alternative was to deal with the PLO. But he would always add that he was not pressuring them to do so, and that there was "no reason for us to be an intermediary." In his memoirs, he says that he could see the train coming but he was tied to the tracks, a strange metaphor for the all-powerful American secretary of state. Kissinger chose to be a passive player in a drama whose bad ending he could clearly foresee. Indeed, in a candid self-critique of his behavior in the summer of 1974, he would subsequently note that "a statesman who cannot shape events will soon be engulfed by them; he will be thrown on the defensive, wrestling with tactics instead of advancing his purpose."[*]

Could Kissinger have shaped events differently? After all, he was at that time the "president for foreign policy" of the most powerful nation in the world, and both Israel and Jordan were heavily dependent on the United States. With the benefit of hindsight and a close examination of the official declassified record, it is possible to discern two moments when Kissinger may well have been able to alter the course of history. That is conjecture, as Kissinger would be the first to point out. But it is nevertheless plausible to assert that had he committed himself, and the superpower he represented, to the effort, he could have better stabilized and legitimized the order he sought to build and thereby enhanced its duration.

––––––––

[*] Already, by the summer of 1975, Kissinger was admitting to Dinitz, "On Jordan, we made a big mistake last summer by not trying to get an interim agreement." See Memcon between Kissinger and Dinitz, July 1, 1975, FRUS 1969–1976:26, Doc. 202.

The first moment was in the winter and spring of 1973–74. On the margins of the Geneva Conference in December 1973, King Hussein's national security adviser, Zaid al-Rifai, had briefed Kissinger on Jordan's concept of a disengagement agreement with Israel. Physically, Rifai was similar to Ismail Fahmy. Short, balding, mustachioed, with a large cigar hovering between hand and mouth, he also had the same wiliness. Little wonder they disliked each other.

Rifai had first befriended the king in Alexandria when they were classmates at Victoria College, an English public school established to educate the children of the Arab world's elite. Rifai went on to study political science at Harvard, where he first met Kissinger. He was the epitome of the king's fiercely loyal advisers, and Hussein used him like a pit bull to defend Jordan's interests while the king adopted a more aloof, and always studiously polite, visage. In meetings, the king would sit ramrod straight, his feet planted together on the floor in front of him, speaking in flawless, British-accented English, with a voice so quiet his audience had to strain to hear him, always appending "sir" as he concluded his interventions. Rifai, conversely, would lounge around puffing on his cigar. For two decades after the 1967 war, Rifai was the king's point person for all his secret engagements with Israel, serving as organizer, negotiator, and note taker.

Sunday, December 16, 1973, Amman–Jerusalem. The idea Rifai proposed to Kissinger at Geneva was for Israel to make a small, four-kilometer withdrawal from the Jordan River to higher ground in the West Bank. Jordanian forces would not move across the river, but the king would assume administrative responsibility for the Palestinians in the area that Israel vacated, primarily in the biblical city of Jericho. Kissinger told the king on December 16 in Amman that he doubted this kind of disengagement was possible and suggested instead that the Israelis might be persuaded "to ease a few categories of control" over the West Bank Palestinians. Perhaps they would agree to thin out their forces and give the king a more visible role there, he tentatively suggested, a kind of virtual disengagement.

By the time he discussed it with the prime minister in Jerusalem that evening, however, he was dismissing the idea of a disengagement in the Jordan Valley. Meir was more positive than Kissinger, noting that her government had formally authorized her to negotiate with the king and in her last discussion with him he had seemed open to an interim arrangement. "I think we can work something out because I believe Hussein doesn't want another war," she told him.

In the larger meeting with Meir and her team, Dayan laid out his ideas for enhancing King Hussein's role in the West Bank, including access for West

Bank municipalities to Jordanian banks, appointment of West Bank administrators by the king, and the return of West Bank Palestinian refugees, most of whom had fled to the East Bank after the Six-Day War. Kissinger encouraged Dayan to make a dramatic move and suggested combining it with some movement of Israeli forces to reduce their visibility. Meir reiterated that she was ready to give the king "entrée" to the West Bank. Reflecting his view that this was an Israeli rather than an American interest, Kissinger responded, "We really have no interest in whether you make [an offer] or not," but if she were inclined to do it, then he preferred that it be done as part of the disengagement process.

The next day, Kissinger reported to the king on these discussions, noting that he "found the Israeli leaders already thinking of possible ways to discuss with Jordan in January steps that might be taken on the West Bank designed to strengthen Your Majesty's role there." He added, "I do not have anything specific to suggest along these lines because I am not close enough to the situation on the West Bank." He told the king that the Israelis did not seem to appreciate the opportunity and the danger they faced in dealing with the West Bank. "The art of politics is to make a concession before you're forced to," he explained, "to do today what would be less than you will have to do tomorrow." Yet he did not apply this wisdom to his own actions when it came to the Jordanian option.

Saturday, January 19, 1974, Aqaba. Kissinger warmed up a little to the idea of being an intermediary on a stop-off in Aqaba on January 19, 1974, after the successful conclusion of the Sinai disengagement negotiations. The king had built a flat-roofed, modern bungalow there, adjacent to the Israeli-Jordanian border with Eilat, which was clearly visible across the bay. It served as his weekend and winter retreat. To welcome Kissinger at the Aqaba Airport, the king conducted some aerobatics with his helicopter before transporting Kissinger to the royal bungalow. The king enjoyed extending these personal courtesies to visiting dignitaries.

The king's effort to extend the same courtesy to President Clinton produced an embarrassing incident on the occasion of Clinton's trip to Jordan to witness the signing of the Israeli-Jordanian peace treaty in the Wadi Arava on October 26, 1994. This was the first Middle East trip that Clinton's Secret Service detail had to deal with. They had transported his armored presidential limousine to the desert for the occasion and insisted that he ride in it. However, en route, we received word on Air Force One that the king would like to pick up the president at the airport and drive him personally to the signing ceremony in his Mercedes 600. The head of the president's security detail was adamant that the president could only ride in his own limousine. I instructed our ambassador in Jordan to decline the invitation and instead invite the king to ride with the president. Our ambassador, unfortunately, was too timid to deliver the bad news to the king.

When we landed, I looked out the window to see a red carpet extending from the aircraft stairs to the king's Mercedes lined up nose to nose with the president's armored Cadillac. When Clinton, escorted by the king, reached the end of the red carpet, Clinton invited him into the Cadillac, and the king gestured back, inviting the president to ride in his Mercedes. Then, in front of the world's cameras, they separated into their respective limousines and sped off, the heavy Cadillac doing its best to keep up with the supercharged Mercedes. An inauspicious beginning to a vital tour.

Within minutes, Saudi ambassador Bandar bin Sultan was on the phone, asking me what had happened. He had been watching the arrival ceremony on CNN. He warned that if the episode were repeated when Clinton arrived in Riyadh, it would be a major embarrassment for King Fahd. When I explained to him the strictures placed on the logistics by the Secret Service, he came up with a typically Saudi diplomatic solution: he would arrange to have King Fahd's license plates put on Clinton's limousine so that they could ride together in the American vehicle but the television audience would think it was the Saudi royal carriage.

Once settled in the king's bungalow, Kissinger said that the Israelis were negative about Rifai's four-kilometer withdrawal idea but suggested that limited Israeli forces remain there. Rifai countered by suggesting the establishment of an Israeli-Jordanian working group, akin to the Egyptian-Israeli military working group meeting in Geneva, to negotiate the issues. Kissinger promised to take it up with the Israelis but depicted them as being in such internal turmoil that it might take some time to get a response. He ended the meeting by saying, "We will support disengagement talks. . . . The basic objective has to be to introduce a Jordanian presence on the West Bank so that the population there will look to Amman."

The next day, Kissinger met with Allon and Eban at Ben Gurion Airport in Israel and asked them to agree to announce an Israeli-Jordanian working group. They seemed quite open to the idea but Kissinger did not lock it down.

Saturday, January 26, 1974, Wadi Arava. A week later, Meir and Dayan met with King Hussein and Rifai in an air-conditioned caravan on the border between Israel and Jordan, north of Eilat and Aqaba. The king laid out a clearer proposal for an Israeli withdrawal of four to six kilometers along the West Bank of the Jordan River, this time offering a parallel Jordanian troop withdrawal on the East Bank. Meir responded with an offer of Jordanian control over Jericho and a corridor to the heavily populated areas at the center of the West Bank. In the Jordanian proposal the IDF would withdraw from the Jordan Valley together with the settlements, and in the Israeli proposal both would stay, except in the Jericho–Ramallah corridor. The meeting ended with agreement to continue the dialogue.

That was the moment when Kissinger might have intervened. The differences between the Israeli and Jordanian approaches were no more unbridgeable than the opening positions of the two sides that Kissinger faced on the Egyptian and Syrian fronts. Kissinger subsequently told the king, "I know that Dayan is in favor of your plan." That was a stretch, since Dayan was in fact in favor of his own plan, which did not exactly accord with the king's vision. Nevertheless, Dayan was sufficiently interested in a Jordanian deal that Kissinger could have worked with him to establish a common approach and then bring Meir around, just as he did on the other negotiating tracks.

Kissinger, however, had a more urgent priority at that moment because of the need to launch negotiations on the Syrian track to relieve pressure on Sadat. Indeed, Dinitz records in his memoirs that Kissinger did not think it the right time to enter into meaningful negotiations with Jordan: "His mind was set on concluding an agreement with the Syrians." The Israelis too had a greater sense of urgency about the Syrians because they were losing soldiers in the war of attrition that had broken out on the Golan. By contrast, the border with Jordan was quiet.

But that did not preclude Kissinger from engaging in two negotiations simultaneously. Indeed, there were considerable tactical advantages in doing so, for he could play one track off against the other, probing for which one held more promise while fostering competition between the two.

This is precisely the tactic that Rabin followed in 1993, after Secretary of State James Baker had succeeded in launching simultaneous negotiations between Israel and Syria, and Israel and a Jordanian-Palestinian delegation following the Madrid Peace Conference. Rabin offered Assad full withdrawal from the Golan via Clinton's secretary of state, Warren Christopher, at the same time as he authorized Shimon Peres, his foreign minister, to negotiate an interim agreement with the PLO behind Clinton's back. Rabin found Arafat keen, even desperate, to move and willing to accept all of Rabin's red lines. Assad, on the other hand, was slow to respond to Christopher's efforts, so Rabin decided to go for the Oslo deal. At the last moment, when Arafat adopted his usual approach of demanding more, Rabin threatened to abandon him for a Syrian deal, which then generated the breakthrough with the Palestinians. Rabin in his second term as prime minister was certainly no better a tactician than Kissinger during his first. Yet there is no indication that Kissinger seriously contemplated playing this game at that moment.

In early February, when Dinitz briefed Kissinger on Meir's late January rendezvous with the king in the Wadi Arava, Kissinger maintained his arm's-length approach, noting that he was not pushing a Jordanian disengagement. But he warned Dinitz that if Israel didn't do something with the king, "within a year, Arafat will be spokesman for the West Bank." He could clearly see the consequences of inaction, yet he was determined to put the onus on Israel, rather than act himself.[*]

Sunday, March 3, 1974, Amman. This reticence bought Kissinger a rare rebuke from King Hussein when he next visited him at Basman Palace. The Hashemite court is unique among the palaces of Arab royalty. Its architecture and interior design were heavily influenced by the royal court of Windsor, expressed in an understated elegance, in contrast with the gaudy gold decoration of Saudi palaces. Instead of the red tunics and black bearskin headwear of the Queen's Guard at Buckingham Palace, the Hashemite kings are protected by fearsome-looking Circassian soldiers wearing full-length black tunics with red cuffs, bandoliers, and swords. They guard the palace entrances and the large oak doors outside the king's reception rooms. They also serve the ritual cardamom coffee in small cups at the commencement of meetings with His Majesty, intimidating guests into consuming the bitter brew.

King Hussein was clearly upset by rumors he had picked up from the Egyptians that Kissinger was engaging with the PLO, which was close enough to the truth to put Kissinger on the defensive.[†] The king then explained why he had rejected Meir's offer of what he viewed as Jordanian civil administration under Israeli occupation. Instead of exploring a more acceptable approach, Kissinger applauded him. Then the king reminded Kissinger that he had proposed the idea of an Israeli-Jordanian working group in Aqaba seven weeks

---

[*] Kissinger went through a similar exercise with Dinitz one month later. He first complained that Meir had not shown him what she had in mind with Jordan, then he urged her to give Hussein part of the West Bank, and then he warned that Sadat would soon back Arafat. But he concluded the conversation by declaring that "this is not now an American-Israeli issue." See Memcon between Kissinger and Dinitz, February 19, 1974, KT01033, NSA.

[†] Sadat had been urging Kissinger to engage with Arafat, and Kissinger had, by the time of the meeting with Hussein, authorized Walters to have another meeting with Arafat's aides in Rabat. The meeting took place on March 7, 1974.

earlier. "You promised us an answer in two weeks. We hoped to hear from you," said the king. "We would like to know once and for all what the United States is willing to do to obtain Israeli withdrawal from the West Bank," he added with uncharacteristic impatience.

Kissinger responded with what the members of Clinton's peace team would later label "the diplomatic yada yada." He admitted that it was "a slip-up," caused by the repeated postponement of the king's visit to Washington. He advised the king to meet with the Israelis before his next visit to Washington and give them an ultimatum: "Either they come up with a reasonable negotiation . . . or you dissociate yourself in some way." The threat to dissociate should be combined with a four-week deadline, he suggested, saying the United States would "support it strongly."

In short, lots of excuses, free advice, and encouragement for the king, but no direct U.S. engagement, which was the only thing that could have made a difference.

Four days later, the king met Meir and Dayan again in the Wadi Arava. Hussein followed Kissinger's advice, threatening to withdraw in favor of the PLO. Meir pleaded with the king to accept a step-by-step approach without an Israeli commitment to full withdrawal, just like Kissinger had persuaded Sadat and Assad to do. Because the plea came from the Israeli prime minister rather than the American secretary of state, it was easy for the king to reject it. "The reasons are psychological," he explained; Meir's offer of a corridor sounded too much like the first step of the Allon Plan, which would result in Israel's annexation of the Jordan Valley.* Dayan proposed an arrangement in which Jordan would become the ruling government in the West Bank, Palestinians would have Jordanian passports, and Jordan could have a military installation on the Israeli coast in exchange for Israeli early warning stations in the West Bank. The king repeated his concern that if Israeli forces did not withdraw, it would look like he was facilitating the occupation.

In reviewing these exchanges, one can imagine how Kissinger would have addressed the king's psychological concerns, arguing for a step-by-step approach, expanding the Israeli corridor, reducing the Jordanian zone, working his way around the settlements and military outposts, and picking up the elements of Dayan's approach and molding them into an American proposal. Whether this would have been sufficient to overcome the king's existential

* The Allon Plan, as it became known when Yigal Allon floated it after the 1967 war, provided for a peace agreement with Jordan in which Israel would annex the Jordan Valley from the Jordan River to the eastern slopes of the West Bank ridgeline. The rest of the West Bank would be returned to Jordan connected by a corridor through Jericho. This is the reason King Hussein saw Meir's corridor proposal for a disengagement agreement as a stalking horse for the Allon Plan. His position at the time was that peace with Israel would require Israel's full withdrawal from the West Bank and East Jerusalem.

concerns about his place in history, or Meir's reluctance to countenance a physical withdrawal from part of the West Bank, is conjecture because Kissinger never tested the proposition.

In his memoirs, Kissinger claims that it was futile to discuss the Jordanian option while Israel was in the process of government formation. That was certainly true in January and February 1974, but it did not stop Meir from engaging with Kissinger on the Syrian disengagement when he visited Jerusalem at the end of February. And, by early March, as noted earlier, Meir told Kissinger that she had secured a mandate from her new government to negotiate a Jordanian disengagement and had then set up her own meeting with King Hussein to pursue it.

After that meeting, Dinitz did convey her concern that her new government needed to establish itself before she could pursue the Jordanian disengagement in earnest, but Kissinger was fine with that because he was not pressing Israel to enter into serious negotiations with Jordan anyway. During that period, Kissinger was working assiduously with Sadat and Dinitz to launch the Syrian disengagement negotiations and browbeating the Saudis to lift the oil embargo if he succeeded. But he did not start the substantive negotiations with the Syrians until May. Clearly, the Israelis were willing to engage with the Syrians and Jordanians simultaneously. Kissinger in that period had the bandwidth to do both too.

Friday, March 15, 1974, Washington, DC. By the time King Hussein came to Washington, Kissinger had resolved to do the Syrian deal first and then, perhaps, focus on Jordan. As he told Eban, who happened to be in town at the same time, he expected the Syrian deal to be done by June and then, if Israel wanted a "Hussein-oriented solution," it should look toward opening some Kilometer 101–style forum "as soon as the Syrian thing is completed." In other words, the same Kissinger who had torpedoed the Egyptian-Israeli talks at Kilometer 101 because they were making progress without the presence of the United States was now advocating a similar Israeli-Jordanian negotiation in the absence of the United States. Eban expressed concern over whether Jordan could be held in suspense until the Syrian deal was concluded. Kissinger thought it could, but then warned that the next step after Syria might have to be with Egypt. If Israel were so concerned about Jordan, they should give the king some reassurance, but then he added for the umpteenth time, "There will be no American pressure."

When the king met Kissinger at Blair House, he told him he was "most pessimistic" after his last meeting with Meir. Kissinger urged him to stay the course, assuring him that "we will strongly support disengagement with Jordan," which contradicted what he had said to Eban a few hours earlier. Then he suggested that the king meet with Dayan, who had an idea for withdrawing the IDF from the Jordan Valley to the West Bank hills. Kissinger added that he would not participate in such a meeting because he could more easily take the king's side with Dayan if he wasn't present. Hussein understood that as yet another signal of Kissinger's unwillingness to engage. Sure enough, when Dayan came to Washington two weeks later, Kissinger never mentioned the king in their meetings.*

During his Syria–Israel shuttle in May, when he paid thirteen visits to Damascus, three visits to Cairo, and two visits to Riyadh, Kissinger paid only one visit to Amman. On that occasion, he promised the king to put before the Israelis a direct choice: deal with King Hussein now or deal with the PLO later. He explained the necessity of getting the Syrian disengagement done, but promised he would then "support" Jordan. He didn't return to Jordan during his shuttle and didn't think it necessary to accompany Nixon there on his June visit. It symbolized, he readily admitted, "their relegation to a secondary role."

The second moment when Kissinger might have pursued the Jordanian option came in the summer of 1974, with the Syrian disengagement behind him and the new Rabin government sworn in. At that point, he had to choose between a return to Geneva for a comprehensive negotiation, a second disengagement agreement in Sinai, a negotiation with Jordan over the West Bank, or both simultaneously. The idea of a comprehensive negotiation about Israel's withdrawal to the 1967 lines in which the Soviet Union and Syria would have a say, even a veto, was anathema to Kissinger. It was so antithetical to his strategy for remaking the Middle Eastern order that it is unlikely he gave it more than a moment's consideration.† But choosing between Jordan or Egypt next presented him with a real dilemma. Rather than confronting it, Kissinger chose to prevaricate while urging the new Rabin government "to begin to think about" a strategy for negotiations with Jordan after another step with Egypt.

Kissinger had ample reason at that moment for not deciding. Nixon's Middle East tour, a summit in Moscow, and a Greek-Turkish crisis over Cyprus

---

* Dayan did meet with King Hussein in London, but, not surprisingly, they made no progress. When Kissinger met with Dayan in Washington in June, after Dayan had left government, he briefed Kissinger on that meeting. Kissinger volunteered that he hadn't talked with the king lately and wouldn't be going to Amman with the president. See Memcon between Kissinger and Dayan, June 8, 1974, KT01218, NSA.
† When Allon raised the Geneva idea with Kissinger in his July 30 meeting, Kissinger immediately dismissed it: "Going to Geneva is suicidal, especially if it's not cooked in advance. The Russians will wreak havoc." See Memcon between Kissinger and Allon, July 30, 1974, FRUS 1969–1976:26, Doc. 93.

all demanded his attention during the summer of 1974. Then there was the turmoil unfolding in Washington at the same time, which led, on August 8, to Nixon's resignation.

Kissinger's very ability to conduct a coherent foreign policy was now in jeopardy. Just the same, he felt he owed it to Nixon to remain loyal to him to the end. On July 26, he concluded that for the good of the country Nixon had to go, but he waited until August 6 to suggest resignation to Nixon directly, after a cabinet secretaries' meeting in which he had been the only one to defend the president.

Nixon had earlier approved a military assistance package for Israel. However, on the evening of August 6, the president told Kissinger that he had changed his mind. He ordered him to cut off all military assistance to Israel until it agreed to a comprehensive peace and expressed regret that he hadn't done it sooner. It was one of Nixon's last decisions, an intemperate move that Kissinger believed was personal retaliation for his having dared to recommend Nixon resign earlier in the day.* Even in his last hours in office, it seems, Nixon couldn't resist acting on his oft-expressed view of Kissinger as more loyal to the Jewish state than to him.

In the end, though, it was Kissinger's Jewish faith to which Nixon finally appealed. On August 7, his last night in office, he asked Kissinger to join him in the residence to reminisce about their foreign policy triumphs. For two hours, they talked, cried, and drowned Nixon's sorrows in Courvoisier cognac left over from the evening, three years earlier, when they had toasted their breakthrough with China. As Kissinger got up to leave, Nixon took him into the Lincoln Bedroom and asked him to kneel with him in prayer.

It is not natural for Jews to kneel in prayer; it happens only on Yom Kippur, the Day of Atonement, when rabbis prostrate themselves in front of God.[†] Kissinger had abandoned prayer during the Second World War. Not surprisingly, as he knelt with Nixon he could not find the words of supplication to comfort his president at his moment of greatest anguish. It was an ironic end to a relationship between an instinctively anti-Semitic president and his Jewish foreign policy adviser. It had been a partnership that nevertheless had done much to

---

* Kissinger arranged for President Ford to reverse the order four days later. Kissinger told Dinitz on August 9 that Nixon had become increasingly hostile toward Jews and Israel in his final days because he believed they had not stood by him at his moment of need. Again, on August 20, he told Dinitz that at the end of Nixon's presidency it had become impossible to go to him with requests related to Israel because it would trigger an outburst against Israel and the Jews. See Kissinger, *Years of Upheaval*, 1205.

† Isaacson records that Kissinger remembered from his childhood, when he practiced Orthodox Judaism, that Jewish prayer did not involve kneeling. See Walter Isaacson, *Kissinger* (New York: Simon & Schuster, 1992), 599.

Israeli prime minister Yitzhak Rabin and Foreign Minister Yigal Allon waiting for a helicopter on the beach near Gaza on April 19, 1977. Allon and Rabin had been comrades in arms, but when Rabin became prime minister and appointed Allon as his foreign minister the relationship became strained. Allon was a friend of Kissinger's from the days of the Harvard International Seminar, which Allon had attended.

preserve and sustain Israel through a period of grave national peril and lay the foundations for Arab-Israeli peace.

Tuesday, July 30, 1974, Washington, DC. While this national and personal trauma unfolded, Kissinger still had to manage the foreign policy of the United States and maintain the appearance of normalcy at State even though the White House was in meltdown. During Nixon's final days, Yigal Allon, in his new position as Rabin's foreign minister, arrived in Washington for consultations with Kissinger, ahead of a scheduled visit by Rabin in September. They met three times over three days, the last session at Camp David as a personal gesture to Kissinger's old friend from summer camp at Harvard. Allon was comfortable in his seasoned relationship with the secretary of state but uncomfortable in his new role as Rabin's foreign minister. He had been Rabin's commanding officer during the War of Independence, from which they had both emerged as war heroes. They were good friends but that was not sufficient to overcome the resentment that Allon now felt serving as Rabin's subordinate.

This tension was typical of Rabin's first cabinet. It found expression in the rivalry between Rabin and his defense minister, Shimon Peres, too. Peres was closely affiliated with Dayan and a member of his party, Rafi. In 1965, under Ben-Gurion, Rafi had split from the Labor Party. The faction subsequently rejoined Labor but maintained its identity and supporters within the party. Rabin narrowly defeated Peres for the party leadership in 1974 and from that point on they became bitter rivals, with Rabin operating on the correct assumption that Peres was constantly seeking to undermine him. As Itamar Rabinovich, Rabin's biographer, notes, "This was the first round of a joint journey by two political Siamese twins . . . who both disliked and appreciated each other, competed and partnered, eventually realizing that they were joined at the hip and bound to collaborate with each other."* It was a partnership that would last twenty-one years, ending tragically when Rabin was assassinated in 1995, but it was a particularly uneasy one.

Instead of an Israeli government dominated by Golda Meir, Kissinger now faced a coalition, which at its outset only had a one-seat Knesset majority and was essentially ruled by the triumvirate of Rabin, Peres, and Allon, each representing a faction and each often pulling in a different direction.

When it came to Jordan, they had three distinct approaches. Consistent with his plan for a final settlement, Allon saw the first step as a withdrawal from Jericho and its environs with a road connection for Jordan to the main West Bank city of Ramallah. Peres, under the influence of Dayan, believed the Palestinians should run their own affairs under a joint Israeli-Jordanian condominium. This allowed for a disengagement in the Jordan Valley because Peres, like Dayan, believed Israel only needed to control the ridgeline that ran down the center of the West Bank, not the valley or the river below.

Rabin's approach was dictated by his political circumstances: he needed to bring the NRP into his coalition to stabilize his government. The NRP would not countenance any withdrawal from the West Bank. To this day, its successor—the Yamina Party, led by Naftali Bennett, who became prime minister in June 2021—is the strongest opponent of withdrawal and the greatest advocate for annexation of the West Bank. It took Rabin until October to bring the NRP into his government. From his point of view, in the critical period of the summer of 1974, any discussion of withdrawal from the West Bank simply needed to be postponed.

These tensions between Israeli personalities and their policies inevitably jaundiced Kissinger's already skeptical view of a Jordanian option. Nevertheless, in their July 30 meeting, Allon informed him of a formal decision by the new government "to do its best to open negotiations with Jordan on a peace

---

* Avi Gil, Peres's longtime aide and confidant, describes the contrast between the two personalities: "Rabin was seen as the ultimate *tzabar*—a native Israeli. A soldier from the Palmach, a warrior . . . emotionally restrained, straight talking, no funny business. Peres, in contrast, never shook off the specter of the Diaspora—in his accent, his cultural richness and his intellectual complexity." See Avi Gil, *Shimon Peres: An Insider's Account of the Man and the Struggle for a New Middle East* (London, UK: I.B. Tauris, 2020), 134.

agreement." That gave Allon license to discuss those negotiations with Kissinger even though he knew a full-fledged peace agreement with Jordan was unrealistic at this stage of American-led diplomacy.

The next day, Allon reiterated Meir's earlier commitment that, in the event of an agreement with Jordan, there would be a new election before it could be ratified. Far from using this as an excuse, Allon expressed confidence they would win that election on the basis of a pending agreement. He indicated that Israeli forces did not need to be concentrated in the Jordan Valley. They could be withdrawn from the river to the ridgeline and "if we don't have to withdraw from the river, at least not on the entire length, maybe we can embark on a negotiation," he said. That aligned with the position of Peres and Dayan.*

For the first time, Kissinger appeared to warm to the idea of a Jordanian disengagement. He suggested exploring a split between the people and the land in the West Bank. King Hussein would have control of the people; Israel would have control over the land but would acknowledge Jordanian sovereignty there. At the prompting of Harold Saunders, he suggested a two-track approach, starting with Jordan and then taking on Egypt, "but with the understanding between us that the Jordanian one will be concluded after the Egyptian one." In that way, the need for elections for a Jordanian deal would not hold up the conclusion of an Egyptian deal.

That two-track approach was a clever idea. If Jordan were negotiating with Israel under American auspices, the king could forestall an Arab move to anoint the PLO as the Arab negotiator for the West Bank. Such a negotiation would also reduce the isolation of Egypt, which was inherent in the Egypt-first approach.

Tuesday, August 6, 1974, Washington, DC. When Sisco met Zaid al-Rifai a few days later, he reported to the Jordanian that Kissinger had come away from his meetings with Allon feeling that the Israelis had shifted from "Egypt first" to being disposed to talk about the Jordan option. Sisco relayed that his boss was therefore open to a discussion about it in his own meeting with the king's adviser later the same day.

In that meeting, Rifai was upbeat. He had just come from a meeting in Cairo with Sadat and King Hussein in which they had reached agreement that it was Jordan's responsibility to recover the West Bank. Rifai said Sadat had agreed to this because he needed a Jordanian agreement to give him cover for

---

* During this visit, Allon and Kissinger had a detailed discussion about Israel's final borders, a second Sinai disengagement, and of course arms supplies. Kissinger recommended against discussing final borders with Jordan "because [Israel was] not ready to discuss Jerusalem." See Memcon between Kissinger and Allon, August 1, 1974, FRUS 1969–1976:26, Doc. 94.

a second Egyptian-Israeli agreement. That meant, he said, that the Egyptians were willing to have Jordan go first.

For a moment, Kissinger became excited. If the Egyptians were willing to wait, he said, "then I think we have a chance, Zaid."

"It's not a question of if, Henry, because Egypt can't move without Jordan," Rifai confidently asserted.

Kissinger then did something he had strongly resisted in the earlier consideration of the Jordanian option: he put forward his own idea of a "wide corridor" under Jordanian administration that would include Jericho and a substantial slice of the populated areas. Rifai was open to the idea but wanted a commitment from Kissinger to engage in the negotiation. Kissinger's ambivalence resurfaced. "*If* the Egyptians support this, *and* you're willing to accept Jericho, a corridor and a part of the West Bank, *then* it's possible [emphasis added]," he said. But he would also have to get the Israelis on board. He agreed to discuss it with Sadat during his trip in September.

"Is this disengagement on or not?" Rifai demanded to know.

"It is on," said Kissinger, but he added, "Timing is all in these things." And he warned that it would be "murderously difficult" with the Israelis.

At that moment "senior government officials" in Israel were telling Terence Smith, the Jerusalem bureau chief of *The New York Times*, that Israel was ready to negotiate some degree of military withdrawal from the Jordan River and a limited return of Jordanian civil administration to the West Bank. The Israeli sources (identified elsewhere in the story as "people close to Dayan") indicated a preference for a negotiation with Jordan as the next step rather than moving to a second stage with Egypt. They also claimed that Rabin was ready to go to elections if he secured an agreement with Jordan because it would strengthen his one-seat majority. Given the rivalries and resentments rife in Jerusalem at that time, Peres was most likely the source for Smith, which indicated that Peres, as well as Allon, was keen for a negotiation with Jordan.

But that was not Rabin's position. When he read the transcripts of Allon's three meetings in Washington, he instructed Allon to clarify for Kissinger that his government had not agreed to withdrawal on the West Bank and that any such withdrawal would require an election. When he received the message, Kissinger concluded, "that meant that [Rabin] did not want to proceed with the Jordanian option." Nevertheless, had Peres and Allon gained the backing of Kissinger, it is possible that Rabin would have gone along with the opening of a negotiation with Jordan. He was in no position at that stage to defy Peres any more than he was able to resist Peres's insistence on negotiating with the PLO, twenty years later.

———

The rivalry between Rabin and Peres over Jordan reached its peak in 1993–94, during Rabin's second term as prime minister when Peres was his foreign minister. After the signing of the Oslo Accords in September 1993, they agreed, in contrast with twenty years earlier, that Jordan should be next. They assumed, correctly as it would turn out, that with the cover of an Israeli-Palestinian agreement, the king could now make his own separate peace with Israel. Peres was determined to add another notch to his peace process belt after initiating the Oslo Accords. Rabin was equally determined that this time the achievement would be his, and his alone, and that it would be a better deal than Peres had negotiated with Arafat. When it came to getting the better deal, the rivalry between Rabin and Peres was not that much different than the rivalry between Assad and Sadat.

On November 2, 1993, Peres crossed the Jordan River in secret and traveled to Amman. There, in overnight negotiations with King Hussein and his brother, Crown Prince Hassan, they agreed quickly to conclude a Jordanian-Israeli peace agreement and settled on principles to govern their negotiations.* Peres could not contain his excitement, telling an Israeli TV interviewer in an off-camera remark a day later that he should "remember the third of November." It didn't take the Israeli media long to uncover that Peres had been in Amman, and to speculate that he had already achieved a peace agreement. The king was furious. Henceforth, he banned Peres from participating in the secret negotiations that then began in earnest with Rabin's confidants.† Rabin was more than content to let the king take responsibility for Peres's exclusion, which suited him well.

In mid-April 1994, the negotiators achieved a breakthrough that was sealed in a secret meeting between Rabin and the king on May 28, in London. This led to Hussein's agreeing to meet publicly with the Israeli prime minister at the White House on July 25, to announce the termination of the state of belligerency between Jordan and Israel.‡

For this ceremony, hosted by President Clinton on the South Lawn, just

* Peres and King Hussein agreed to accelerate negotiations for a peace agreement; Jordan would assume an immediate role in the Palestinian economy with Jordanian banks permitted to operate in the West Bank (this offer, which Dayan made the king twenty years earlier, was now acceptable); Israel would not agree to the establishment of an independent Palestinian state and would uphold Jordan's control of the *Waqf* in Jerusalem, which had responsibility for the Al-Aqsa Mosque. See Martin Indyk, *Innocent Abroad: An Intimate Account of American Peace Diplomacy in the Middle East* (New York: Simon & Schuster, 2009), 102–103.
† Cabinet secretary Elyakim Rubinstein and Mossad chief Efraim Halevy were Rabin's negotiators. The small Jordanian team was headed by Fayez Tarawneh and reported to Crown Prince Hassan.
‡ In his speech in front of Clinton and Rabin, the king noted that in Arabic and Hebrew there was no word for the concept of non-belligerency that appeared in the English version of the Washington Declaration they had just signed. Instead, he proposed clearer wording: "What we have accomplished and what we are committed to is *the end of the state of war* between Jordan and Israel [emphasis added]." See "Remarks by President Clinton, King Hussein, and Prime Minister Rabin at the Signing Ceremony of the Washington Declaration," July 25, 1994, Israeli

like the signing of the Oslo Accords, Rabin and Hussein had negotiated what came to be known as the Washington Declaration. So determined was Rabin to keep this pronouncement from Peres that he was only shown the text in the pre-meeting with Clinton and the king in the White House ten minutes before the ceremony took place. Peres felt humiliated, especially after Rabin bragged to the Israeli press that his foreign minister had not been involved in the negotiations and mocked him as "the prophet." Before boarding the plane to return to Israel, Peres told an Israeli journalist, "I will not let him assail my dignity or my credibility ever again."

The summer of 1974 was probably the last moment when the Jordanian option might have been pursued. All this sunny talk between Kissinger and Rifai was taking place while Nixon was deciding on the fate of his presidency. Immediately after his second meeting with Rifai on August 7, Kissinger was summoned to the Oval Office, where in an emotional encounter, Nixon informed him of his decision to resign. He urged Kissinger to stay on to help Gerald Ford, who would be the new president, to ensure foreign policy continuity. That was the night Nixon prayed with Kissinger. In these fraught circumstances, it took an extraordinary feat of compartmentalization for Kissinger to be able to discuss coherently the diplomatic options with his Middle Eastern interlocutors. It would not be surprising, at that moment, that he lacked the energy or concentration to commit himself to taking an initiative with Jordan. And yet, for one bright moment, Rifai and Kissinger had dared to dream of an Israeli-Jordanian disengagement agreement.

Tuesday, August 13, 1974, Washington, DC. A week later, Egypt's foreign minister, Ismail Fahmy, came to town and scoffed at the idea that Egypt needed Jordan. He agreed that Sadat had told Hussein he would support his negotiating a West Bank disengagement, establishing military outposts there, and bringing the UN into the process. However, according to Fahmy, Sadat did not agree on Jordan first. Sadat wanted another Sinai disengagement before October. "Believe me," Fahmy told Kissinger, "he cannot wait." Fahmy then asked what Kissinger had heard from Allon. "They prefer Egypt first," Kissinger responded, which was not an accurate depiction of Allon's position. But it was a fair description of Rabin's position and Kissinger's preference.

Fahmy was the first Middle Eastern official to meet with the new president.

Ministry of Foreign Affairs, https://mfa.gov.il/MFA/ForeignPolicy/MFADocuments/Yearbook9 /Pages/212%20Remarks%20by%20President%20Clinton-%20King%20Hussein%20and.aspx.

Ford had asked Kissinger to stay on and had arranged for him to provide daily briefings to bring him up to speed. Ford, a novice in international affairs, was totally dependent on Kissinger, but there was only so much Kissinger could do. In his memoirs, Fahmy describes meetings with Ford in which Kissinger would do almost all the talking in the name of the president and Ford would simply nod his head.

For Kissinger, the respite from the challenges of handling Nixon's complex personality and maneuvering for influence in a shark-infested, anti-Semitic West Wing was welcome indeed. His newfound sense of security was reinforced by the appointment of Nelson Rockefeller, his patron and good friend, as vice president. All that, however, could not substitute for the fact that the awesome authority of the Oval Office had been severely undermined by Nixon's demise. Kissinger believed it would inevitably affect his own ability to influence the course of international events. Six months later, in a moment of candor, he told the Israelis that the days were now gone when he and Nixon could rely on "a reputation for ruthlessness, decisiveness, rapidity of movement, and a touch of irrationality."

In a preparatory briefing on August 13 for the meeting with Fahmy, Kissinger showed Ford a map to illustrate the Jordanian proposal for a ten-kilometer withdrawal on both sides of the Jordan River. "Jordan says Egypt agreed that Jordan should go first, but Fahmy says Egypt has to go next," Kissinger explained. "While I love the king, Egypt is more important." He then described his concept of another Sinai disengagement, which would "take Egypt out of the war. Then we could deal with Jordan and then only Syria would be left."

It was the kind of simple, logical sequencing that a new president could easily embrace. Reading the transcript of this conversation reminded me of the moment when I first briefed President Clinton, explaining that with the collapse of the Soviet Union, the election of Rabin with a mandate to make peace, and all Israel's neighbors already in direct negotiations with it, he could achieve peace with Syria, the Palestinians, and Jordan and end the Arab-Israeli conflict. Clinton looked up from the lunch he was devouring and said, "I want to do that." We recommended that he focus on Syria first, rather than try for a deal with the Palestinians, which was more complicated and of less strategic value. Clinton embraced the idea.

Ford had a similar reaction: he was in no position to challenge his secretary of state, so he went along with Egypt first. In a meeting with Kissinger the next day, Fahmy sought to lock in the approach. "[The Israelis] should know that any Jordanian disengagement is impossible to support if there is no further Egyptian withdrawal," he said.

Kissinger said that he had just told Ford, "If we have to choose between Jordan and Egypt there is no question which we'll choose." He said the president would tell Fahmy that when he met him the next day. "Sadat is the man on whom we are counting in the Middle East," said Kissinger. To add credibility to this reassurance, he began plotting out the next steps with Fahmy: develop an agreed strategy, then get Rabin over to Washington in September, and then be ready to move. He planned to start formal talks in October and wrap up the deal by December. Underscoring Sadat's sense of urgency, Fahmy insisted that Kissinger launch his efforts a month earlier. As Kissinger records in his memoirs, "The upshot of Fahmy's visit was that a separate agreement between Israel and Egypt emerged as the most probable next step in the peace process."

Friday, August 16, 1974, Washington, DC. Two days later, King Hussein met with the new president. Unfamiliar with the sensitive issues involved, Ford was circumspect. When Hussein asked Ford what he thought Jordan should do next, Kissinger interrupted and said he would discuss it with the king over lunch at the State Department. "We are according a very high priority to Jordan," he emphasized. But Kissinger explained to the king and the president that he couldn't make rapid progress with the Israelis, and things were easier for them to do with Egypt, so a deal could be made more quickly there. "For Jordan, we are prepared to move ahead in a very active way," he said, but it was a question of timing.

Over lunch, Kissinger continued his effort to convince King Hussein of the wisdom of pursuing Egypt first. He did not mention that he had already made that commitment to Egypt's foreign minister a few days before. He showed mock interest in the Jordanian option by raising Allon's idea for a disengagement. The king said it would be very difficult, but Rifai thought they could accept Israeli military positions as enclaves. That was an interesting opening. Indeed, in a November 1974 postmortem of the Jordanian option, Kissinger told Dayan, "In my experience, in August, [King Hussein] would have accepted the principle of the Allon Plan."

But rather than probe, Kissinger confessed that the United States would go with Egypt first but "with an absolute condition that they support Jordan as the next step." The king argued that Egypt first would provoke Syria to oppose Jordan next, and then he wouldn't even be able to agree to a partial Israeli withdrawal from the Jordan River. It would be better for Egypt, he countered, if there were "progress" with Jordan first. Then he raised the idea of Israeli settlements staying on Jordanian territory as a temporary arrangement after

Israel withdrew (a principle that was applied to farmland that Israel ceded to Jordan in their peace treaty). Clearly, the king and Rifai were ready to show flexibility on substance and timing if only Kissinger would engage.

The king made one more attempt to argue that Egypt first would isolate Egypt and weaken Jordan in the Arab world. But Kissinger had stopped listening. Instead, he proposed a toast: "We are your friend, and we will make progress on the Jordanian front." He explained that Rabin would be coming to Washington and he would travel to the region in September and continue the discussion with the king then. He promised there would be a disengagement with Jordan "within a matter of months." The king should not be discouraged: "We want his authority reestablished on the West Bank. It is just a matter of the timeframe."

Their lunch concluded at 2:30 p.m. At 4:15 p.m., Kissinger was on the phone with Dinitz, reporting on Rifai's flexibility but telling the Israeli ambassador that after his trip in September they would do Egypt first, then Jordan, then Israeli elections. Kissinger had made up his mind to postpone the Jordanian option until later, which turned out to be never.

That was not, however, good enough for Rabin. In the bland communiqué Kissinger planned to issue after King Hussein's visit, he had included reference to continuing consultations on "an Israeli-Jordanian agreement for a disengagement of forces." Skittish about anything that could disrupt his negotiations with the NRP, Rabin demanded that the reference to a disengagement agreement be removed. That left Kissinger in no doubt that Rabin would not be a party even to a discussion of disengagement on the eastern front.

The unraveling of the Jordanian option proceeded from there. A week later, on August 24, Hussein met with Rabin, Allon, and Peres at the Wadi Arava caravan site. He again put forward his disengagement plan. Rabin, who was still focused on bringing the NRP into his coalition, rejected the idea in his characteristically brusque way. Peres proposed his idea of a joint Israeli-Jordanian condominium over the West Bank, which the king dismissed, insisting that there had to be some Israeli withdrawal. Allon responded by offering his Jericho-first idea with the corridor to Ramallah. The king insisted on withdrawal along the entire front. They could find common ground on only one issue: as Rabin described the encounter to Ford and Kissinger, "We both see the same way on the PLO and on having no third state between us."

At this stage, inter-Arab dynamics began to shift decisively against the Jordanian option as the PLO embarked on a series of diplomatic initiatives designed to make it a player in the peace process. On September 1, Arab foreign ministers meeting in Cairo set October 26 for an Arab summit in Rabat, Morocco, and resolved to support the PLO's request that "the question of Pal-

Prime Minister Rabin speaks at a White House press conference with President Ford on September 10, 1974, on the occasion of his first visit to Washington as prime minister. The visit did not go well. Ford expected Rabin to be grateful for the $700 million military assistance package that he had approved; Rabin believed that the United States owed Israel a lot more for the Israeli-Syrian disengagement agreement and vowed to make sure Israel was paid in full on the conclusion of the Sinai II Agreement.

estine" be treated for the first time as a separate agenda item at the upcoming UN General Assembly. On September 21, Egypt, Syria, and the PLO issued a tripartite communiqué in Cairo affirming that "an independent Palestinian authority" would be established in any territory liberated from Israel. Sadat was in effect contradicting the commitment he made to King Hussein that Jordan was responsible for the West Bank Palestinians.

Tuesday, September 10, 1974, Washington, DC. Rabin arrived in Washington with one objective: to secure the long-term arms commitment he believed was Israel's due for concluding the Israeli-Syrian disengagement agreement. Ford pressed him to make progress with both Egypt and Jordan. Rabin explained that he viewed Egypt as the leader, so it was better to go there first. That was especially because he wanted the next agreement to contain a political component of non-belligerency, which he did not believe the king could agree to ahead of the other Arabs. Taking Egypt out of the war was far more consequential than doing so with Jordan, which had no military option against Israel. "But Egypt can't be alone," Rabin conceded, "and we understand that it would be immediately followed by Jordan." In Kissinger's meeting with Rabin at Blair House, they agreed that when he came to Israel on his next trip, Rabin would provide him with a detailed proposal on what Israel could do with Egypt; Jordan was off the table for the time being. With Fahmy pressing Kissinger again to get moving, he finally embarked on an exploratory trip to the region in mid-October.*

Thursday, October 10, 1974, Cairo. After meeting with Sadat, Kissinger reported excitedly to Ford that Sadat had agreed to start negotiations with Israel on a second Sinai disengagement agreement that would contain elements of non-belligerency that Rabin was insisting on in return for a substantial Israeli withdrawal. Sadat was ready to go ahead regardless of Arab reaction. They had agreed to keep this understanding secret before the upcoming Arab League summit in Rabat on October 26 and only announce it when Kissinger returned to the region in the beginning of November.

When King Hussein met Kissinger two days later in Aqaba, the king warned him, "[W]e have reached a critical moment." He complained of being abandoned by Sadat and Assad, whom he knew were siding with the PLO. He confided that at Rabat he intended to force the Arab leaders to take a stand. If they did not support him, then he would focus his efforts on consolidating the East Bank and see how the PLO fared trying to wrest the West Bank from Israel without him.

Kissinger responded by blaming Israel. If only the king's proposal for disengagement had been accepted by the Israelis, he said, "we'd be in a completely different situation today." He allowed that "we had an impossible domestic situation over the summer for a showdown with Israel so it's partly our fault." As consolation, he offered the king reassurance that he would make U.S. opposition to the PLO clear to all the Arab leaders before they departed for Rabat. The king had been hesitating to attend the Rabat summit, but according to Rifai, he was so reassured by Kissinger that he would have the backing of Egypt, Saudi Arabia, and Morocco in Rabat that he resolved to go.

Kissinger's next stop was Jerusalem, where he succeeded in securing personal commitments from Rabin, Peres, and Allon that they would agree to the negotiation with Egypt—they could not take it to the cabinet for a decision because of Sadat's insistence on secrecy. Although they discussed the various ideas for a Jordanian disengagement, Kissinger concluded it was a hopeless endeavor.†

In a private meeting, Rabin offered Kissinger a thirty-to-forty-kilometer

---

* Fahmy visited Washington after Rabin's trip to lock down the Egypt-first approach. He insisted on concrete progress in two months and assured Ford that if the United States made the effort, Sadat was ready to proceed alone.

† According to an Israeli account, Kissinger told his aides in Jerusalem, "This team is incapable of doing anything. . . . There sits a prime minister shivering in fear every time I mention the word 'Jordan.' It is a lost cause." See Matti Golan, *The Secret Conversations of Henry Kissinger: Step-by-Step Diplomacy in the Middle East* (Chicago: Quadrangle, 1976), 226.

withdrawal in the Sinai, including the oil fields, in return for an Egyptian commitment to non-belligerency and a respite from further withdrawals for five years. Although the gaps were wide between Israel and Egypt, particularly on non-belligerency, when Rabin threw in the Sinai oil fields, Kissinger felt he had what he needed to work on an agreement. Thus, he reported to Ford on October 13, "We achieved what we came for."

Strangely, in his memoirs Kissinger says that his trip "failed to produce an agreement to open negotiations." But he had in fact reached agreement with Sadat and Rabin to do just that.

As the countdown to Rabat approached, Rabin again met with King Hussein in Wadi Arava on October 19. The king expressed deep concern about the growing support for the PLO among Arab leaders. Rabin said his first priority was a negotiation with Egypt. But he reassured him that he would not deal with the PLO and that Israel would have only one partner in the West Bank. This gave the king the confidence to take a stand in Rabat, knowing that even if he couldn't wrest any West Bank territory from Israel, the PLO would certainly not be able to do so.

The king's course, and his conscience, were now clear. At Rabat, he gave a passionate speech about Jordan's historic responsibility for the West Bank. He explained that his strategy had been to recover the West Bank and then let the Palestinians determine their own future. But if the Arabs decided to give that responsibility to the PLO, then he would withdraw and leave it to Arafat. When Sadat, King Faisal, and King Hassan then supported the resolution that declared the PLO "the sole legitimate representative of the Palestinian people" and affirmed its right to establish a national authority on any part of liberated Palestine, the king voted for the resolution and received a standing ovation.

Instead of persuading Israel to disengage from the West Bank, the king had been forced to do so himself. He could no longer claim responsibility for the Palestinians there. Henceforth, if there were to be negotiations with Israel over the West Bank, the PLO would take part in them. The Jordanian option was never to be resurrected, notwithstanding repeated efforts over the years, primarily by Shimon Peres.

Kissinger's prediction had proven correct. Failing to pursue an Israeli-Jordanian disengagement agreement in 1974 led to the PLO's control of the issue from that point on. Thirteen years later, Rabin as defense minister had to suppress a prolonged Palestinian uprising in the West Bank and Gaza. When he became prime minister again in 1992, he concluded Israel had no choice but to deal directly with the PLO. Ironically, in the Oslo Accords, Rabin would offer Yasir Arafat the very same proposal that Meir and Allon had offered King Hussein in 1974: an enclave in Jericho followed by a second stage in which

Arafat would gain control of the populated cities and villages of the West Bank. Whereas in 1974, the king did not accept that Israeli offer, nineteen years later Arafat had the legitimacy and the full support of the United States to do so.

Taking advantage of the political cover provided by Arafat's signing of the Oslo Accords in September 1993, Rabin and Hussein then entered into secret peace negotiations. That culminated in their signing of the Israeli-Jordanian peace treaty in Wadi Arava on October 26, 1994, twenty years to the day after the Rabat summit. While that peace treaty helped secure the longevity of Hashemite rule on the East Bank, PLO control of the populated areas of the West Bank proved disastrous for Palestinians and Israelis alike. A second Palestinian uprising in 2000, which Arafat did nothing to stop and Israel did everything to suppress, claimed the lives of thousands on both sides and, together with Israeli settlement activity, destroyed the trust so necessary for Israeli-Palestinian reconciliation.

Could history's course have been altered had Kissinger pursued the Jordanian option seriously in 1974? Simcha Dinitz certainly thought so. In his unpublished memoirs, he criticizes Kissinger for failing to push Israel to work with Jordan as the representative of the Palestinians, an unusual statement for the Israeli ambassador to the United States, whose responsibility was to fend off American pressure. But Dinitz recognized that only the United States could break Israel's domestic political deadlock on a matter of such strategic consequence to the Jewish state.

There is no doubt that political circumstances in Israel and the United States at the time would have complicated the task. Palestinian animus toward the king because of his banishing of the PLO to Lebanon after Arafat launched a rebellion against his rule in 1970 would have made the challenge of extending his control to the West Bank population difficult. Kissinger would have had to resist Sadat's siren song had he attempted to focus his efforts on the Jordanian king. He would also have had to overcome Hussein's need for reassurance about the final disposition of the West Bank. The king would have sought a U.S. guarantee that Israel would eventually withdraw from the West Bank and Arab East Jerusalem, which Kissinger would have resisted providing.

And yet, as I've shown, the opportunity presented itself twice in 1974. On both occasions, the Israelis were willing to engage and even showed some flexibility, and the Jordanians were all but begging Kissinger to get involved. He could have easily parried King Hussein's desire to know the final outcome as he had done with Assad and Sadat. King Hussein had far less leverage than they did. He could have managed Sadat's impatience by pursuing a two-track strategy, probing to see which one offered the better opening, playing all sides off against each other, using movement on one track to generate progress on the other. In short, he could have done what Kissinger did best, and certainly better than anybody else. Perhaps King Hussein's moderation and deep-seated commitment to peace with Israel, as well as the reintroduction of his state-based governing institutions in the West Bank, could have produced a better outcome for Palestinians and Israelis with far less loss of life.

Given the potential advantages of acting, and Kissinger's prescient awareness of the adverse consequences of not doing so, how can we make sense of his reluctance and passivity? Part of the explanation may lie in his exhaustion following the conclusion of the Israeli-Syrian shuttle and Nixon's subsequent demise. As he admitted at the time, and again in his memoirs, he was not on his game in the summer of 1974.

That does not explain, however, his reluctance to engage in the spring, when Meir and Dayan showed a readiness and Watergate had not yet reached its climax and denouement. Instead of involving himself, he repeatedly encouraged the Israelis to take the lead directly with the king. Contrast this with the way he short-circuited the Kilometer 101 talks between Yariv and el-Gamasy because he was not involved. While it's true that Kissinger was busy attempting to jump-start the Israeli-Syrian negotiations in the first quarter of 1974, that did not preclude him from other diplomatic gambits. On no other Arab-Israeli issue was he willing to subcontract to the Israelis and forswear pressuring them.

The more likely explanation is simply that, as Kissinger observed multiple times, he liked the king but he didn't value him. Jordan, simply put, lacked the weight in the Middle East power balance that would have made his diplomatic exertions necessary. Removing Egypt from the conflict with Israel was the strategic objective. The disengagement deal with Syria was critical to that mission and, as we shall see, a second Sinai agreement would go a long way to cementing the new American-led order. He feared that pursuing a Jordanian option would only interfere with his main endeavor, possibly provoke conflict between Jordan and the PLO, and bring up the question of Jerusalem, which he sought to avoid at all costs. He regarded the West Bank and Jerusalem as Israel's problem rather than America's, which is why he tried repeatedly to warn them of the consequences but always forswore pressure on them.

Pressing the Israelis to pursue the Jordanian option would have involved tension, perhaps even confrontation. We have seen time and again how carefully Kissinger picked his battles with Israel and its American supporters. He knew how much energy they would take, especially because, given his Jewish identity and his notoriously thin skin, he was exceptionally sensitive to criticism from Jewish quarters. Moreover, as I mentioned earlier, he was already engaged with the American Jewish leadership in an emotional confrontation over securing most-favored-nation treatment for the Soviet Union, a critical element in his design for détente that they were linking to exit visas for Soviet Jews. He was not reluctant to pressure Israel, but he did not want to start a fight that, from his point of view, was not worth engaging in. He preferred to save himself for more achievable and consequential outcomes.

Kissinger also had a plan B, which made it easier for him to keep the Jordanian option at arm's length. His Middle Eastern order could absorb a stalemate in which Jordan abandoned the West Bank to the PLO and Israel refused to deal with it. Jordan's and Israel's common interest in maintaining stability there, lest Palestinian violence spill over to Israel proper or to the East Bank, meant that he could safely focus elsewhere without fear of a crisis. It appeared to be a low-cost element in his new design.

To this day, his decision does not sit comfortably with him. Already by the summer of 1975 Kissinger was admitting to Dinitz that they had made "a big mistake" by not trying for an interim agreement with Jordan. He spends several pages of his memoirs accepting responsibility. And he records the king's bitter observation that Jordan, America's most constant friend in the Arab world, stood alone among Israel's neighbors without territorial gain as a result of American diplomacy.

Containing rather than resolving the Palestinian problem was an imperfect component of the new American-led order, but it was a design that lasted, more or less, for fourteen years. Given Kissinger's view of the temporary nature of any international equilibrium, especially in the Middle East, that was a reasonable outcome, even though during this hiatus the Israelis started settling the West Bank in earnest, seriously complicating the prospects for achieving peace in the future. And when the order broke down, as it eventually did in 1987, when the West Bank and Gaza Palestinians rose up against the status quo in anger, it resulted in a conflict that raged for four years, killing more than a thousand Palestinians and some 160 Israelis as well as wounding thousands on both sides. Yet even then the conflict remained contained to the West Bank and Gaza and did not disrupt the broader order that Kissinger had built.

Certainly, during Kissinger's time it appeared to be good enough, and much better than the stability he thought he had purchased before the Yom Kippur War by relying on Israel's deterrent power to maintain the equilibrium. That arrangement lasted barely three years. As we have seen, back then as well as in the summer of 1974, Kissinger was presented with the opportunity to pursue a process for resolving the conflict and chose a containment strategy to manage it instead. That was the cautious nature of his approach to the Middle East's discontents.

15

Breakdown

In the course of every negotiation, a point is reached when the parties
either conclude that they will eventually come together or that they
are hopelessly deadlocked.... In the latter instance... the negotiation
is doomed because, from then on, the parties concentrate on shifting
the blame for failure to each other.

—Henry Kissinger, *Years of Renewal*

W*ednesday, November 6, 1974, Cairo.* The Rabat summit impeded Kissinger's efforts to prepare for the pursuit of the Sinai II Agreement
(formally referred to as the Interim Agreement between Egypt and Israel) that
Sadat and Rabin had now agreed to negotiate. The Arab leaders had not only
anointed Yasir Arafat in place of King Hussein, they had also vowed to adopt
a united front in a deliberate Syrian-led effort to constrain Sadat's go-it-alone
instincts.

Kissinger had hoped to apply the successful negotiating methodology he
had developed during the last two disengagement agreements, but he quickly
discovered in a hastily organized post-Rabat trip to Middle Eastern capitals
that nothing would be the same this time around.

Sadat was suffering from a bad cold and conducted the conversation with
Kissinger from his sickbed at his home on the Nile corniche in downtown
Cairo. Kissinger found him discouraged by the results of Rabat, which now
appeared to put Assad in a position to veto Israeli-Egyptian negotiations.
Instead of forging ahead in his usual way, Sadat suggested simultaneous Israeli-
Syrian and Israeli-Egyptian negotiations. Kissinger was having enough trouble
getting Rabin to pursue negotiations with Egypt and was therefore unwill-
ing to countenance a Golan negotiation that he believed had no prospects.
Instead, he suggested pursuing talks discreetly through diplomatic channels.

Sadat then put down an unmistakable marker: "I need to get the oil and I need to have the passes. This is the minimum, Henry." Kissinger responded by noting that Rabin's last offer was so bad that he did not bother to transmit it to him. Sadat urged him to put the squeeze on Israel.

The Gidi and Mitla mountain passes to which Sadat was referring are located in central Sinai, on the western side of the mountain range, some 30 to 40 miles east of the Suez Canal and some 120 miles west of the international border between Israel and Egypt. Twenty miles long, they represent the only routes that armies could take to traverse the mountain range in either direction. To the north are impassable desert sands and to the south soaring mountains. Israel maintained an early warning station at the western edge of the Gidi Pass at Um Hashiba, equipped with state-of-the-art sensors and radars that gave it the ability to monitor the Egyptian air bases across the canal and the four roads leading from the canal to the passes. To the northeast of the Gidi Pass at Bir Gifgafa, Israel had built its forward Rephidim Air Base. The early warning station, the passes, and the air base were critical to the forward defense of Israel from an advancing Egyptian army.

The oil fields were located at Abu Rudeis, halfway down the Sinai coast of the Gulf of Suez. Because the steep mountains in southern Sinai descend to the edge of the gulf, land access to the oil fields from Suez city was limited to one narrow road along a thin coastline. Israel captured the oil fields in 1967 and immediately began pumping the oil and transporting it by tankers around Sharm el-Sheikh and up the Gulf of Aqaba to Eilat, where it was then pumped to oil refineries in Ashdod and Haifa. By 1974, Israel was pumping some seventy-five thousand to a hundred thousand barrels per day, meeting some 50 to 60 percent of its oil requirements. In those days, Israel imported the rest of its requirements from the shah's Iran. At the time, the Israelis estimated that the existing Egyptian wells had an eight-to-ten-year life span. The replacement cost of the oil was estimated to be as much as $400 million annually.

Kissinger needed no encouragement from Sadat to press the Israelis. His relationship with Rabin in his new role as prime minister had deteriorated rapidly. Despite the tight bond they had forged during Rabin's time as Israel's ambassador in Washington, the relationship was different now. As prime minister, Rabin viewed President Ford, not his secretary of state, as his counterpart. In his new role, he faced a complex political reality at home whose requirements didn't quite jibe with Kissinger's diplomatic agenda. And Rabin was all too familiar with Kissinger's manipulative ploys, particularly his use of the press.

From his time in Washington, Rabin knew well how to mobilize the American Jewish community and enlist influential congresspeople in Israel's cause, and he had developed close relationships with the Washington press corps, complemented by Dinitz.

The Labor Party, which Rabin had inherited, was struggling to maintain its dominance against a newly invigorated opposition, led by Menachem Begin, which, as I said earlier, stridently opposed any further withdrawals. The Israeli public had just been through the trauma of a war for the Jewish state's existence, followed in short order by two withdrawals from Arab territory. In these circumstances, Rabin needed time to consolidate his position. What he did not need when he first came into office was a new negotiation that would involve ceding more territory. So he stalled.

Kissinger, conversely, could not afford stasis in his Middle East diplomacy. The stable equilibrium he had been striving so hard to establish required additional steps if another war was to be averted and the Soviet Union kept at bay. As he knew from his study of nineteenth-century Europe, the balance of power needed constant tending to prevent it from tilting back in the wrong direction. Moreover, the oil embargo and price hike had plunged the American economy into a recession that was fast becoming the most serious since World War II; by February 1975, unemployment had surged to 8.2 percent with 7.5 million Americans out of work. The last thing the United States could afford was a new oil crisis provoked by a return to war between Israel and its Arab neighbors.

Kissinger's successful brokering of the disengagement deals had enhanced America's reputation. But the new Ford administration looked weak and ineffective in other regions and at home. Another quick Arab-Israeli agreement could provide just the fillip the administration needed. Kissinger put its purpose concisely to Ford on September 6: "We have to push [the Israelis] to give up half of what they have in Egypt. That would take Egypt out of the game for five years. . . . Then only Syria would be left."

As Kissinger's troubles multiplied, he increasingly identified Rabin's prevaricating as the source of his problems. It started in September with Rabin's first visit to Washington as prime minister. He had delayed his visit as long as possible to postpone American pressure for concessions to the Arabs. Kissinger's frustration at the delay was compounded by Rabin's outsized military assistance expectations and his ingratitude to Ford when the president agreed to meet the most urgent of them.* Kissinger took umbrage even though he was at the same time holding up responses to the big-ticket items, such as F-15s

---

* Rabin had submitted a huge laundry list of arms requests. Titled "Matmon" (the Hebrew for "treasure"), the master list was compiled from the wish lists of all the services of the IDF to "arm ourselves with everything we could get from the Americans." It was divided into three sections:

and M60 tanks, until Rabin demonstrated a willingness to move. By October, Kissinger was expressing doubt about Rabin's leadership. When the press said the Rabat summit represented a major setback for Kissinger's Middle East diplomacy, he was quick to blame Rabin.

At the same time, Kissinger was coming under attack from Jewish intellectuals, led by Walter Laqueur, who was highly respected among the nascent but voluble American neoconservatives. They had begun mounting a sustained critique of Kissinger's policy of détente.[*] In September 1974, at the time of Rabin's visit to Washington, Laqueur launched a broadside against Kissinger's approach to Israel's urgent resupply needs in the Yom Kippur War. Accusing Kissinger of an elaborate manipulation, Laqueur argued that during the war "the main obstacle to a rapid flow of military supplies to Israel . . . could only have been Kissinger."[†] As the record shows, the picture was more complicated, and Kissinger had in fact acted more in Israel's interests than he has been given credit for. But Laqueur's attack sparked a controversy that raged for years. Even today, many Israelis wrongly believe that Kissinger sacrificed Jewish blood for anti-Israel objectives.

Hypersensitive to criticism from Jewish intellectuals whom he considered his peers, Kissinger assumed Rabin was behind the campaign, particularly because of its timing and the fact that it was matched by negative articles in the Israeli press about the way he was treating Israel.

Rabin believed Nixon and Kissinger had taken on a moral commitment to meet Israel's long-term security needs as part of the Israeli-Syrian disengagement agreement. He objected to Kissinger's linking the supply of arms to a new political move. "You are trying to sell us the same item, not two but three times. . . . This is unacceptable in principle," said Rabin in a meeting with Kissinger in his State Department office on September 11.[‡]

When Arafat appeared before the UN General Assembly on November 13, 1974, pistol by his side and olive branch in hand, Rabin instructed Allon to complain about the inadequacy of U.S. efforts to prevent it. Kissinger was furious. He ordered Larry Eagleburger, his executive assistant at State, to call Dinitz and "with some heat" tell him that he was not prepared "to put up with

---

immediate need, intermediate requests, and long-term requirements. On Kissinger's advice, Ford had agreed to fulfill those in the first section and deferred consideration of the other two.

[*] Like Kissinger, Laqueur had fled Germany as a teenager; his parents had perished in the Holocaust. He too was a distinguished historian, the founding editor of *The Journal of Contemporary History* and a professor at Georgetown University.

[†] Laqueur published his attack in *Commentary*, the Jewish intellectual magazine edited by Norman Podhoretz, one of the founders of neoconservatism. His co-author was Edward Luttwak, a defense intellectual with close ties to Schlesinger's office. See Walter Z. Laqueur and Edward N. Luttwak, "Kissinger and the Yom Kippur War," *Commentary*, September 1974.

[‡] Rabin was also upset that Kissinger had still not produced a presidential letter assuring Israel that it would not have to come down from the Golan, a commitment Rabin believed Kissinger made to Meir in the context of the Israeli-Syrian disengagement agreement.

this kind of ingratitude and shortsightedness any longer." Rabin should know, Kissinger told Eagleburger, "that our foreign policy is made in Washington not Jerusalem and I do not appreciate his government's constant harassment!"

As Kissinger was en route to Israel for his November 6 visit, he put Ford up to calling in Dinitz to convey a personal message of presidential dissatisfaction to Rabin at his failure to move forward in the negotiations. We have seen how Kissinger repeatedly used Nixon for this purpose with Mrs. Meir, but it came naturally to Nixon to play the tough guy. Accordingly, it was never quite clear to the Israelis whether Kissinger was putting Nixon up to it or, as Kissinger would often claim, restraining him from pursuing his worst instincts. In Ford's case, however, Kissinger's role was not even thinly disguised.*

Thursday, November 7, 1974, Jerusalem. Kissinger was more circumspect in his meeting with Rabin the next day, but when he tried to lay the blame on Israel for the Rabat decision, Rabin would have none of it. As long as the United States didn't embrace the PLO, Rabin argued, King Hussein would be back in a year as representative of the Palestinians. When Kissinger sought to warn about the dangers of Europe's now embracing the PLO, Rabin lambasted him for exaggerating its importance, and criticized the United States for allowing Arab extremists to prevail.

The bickering continued until Kissinger had had enough. "One prediction that is always true," he told his negotiating team sardonically in front of Rabin and his advisers, "is that one hour after I sit down with the Israelis, they will have me on the defensive for a stalemate that is due to their intransigence."

They adjourned to a one-on-one meeting in which Kissinger told Rabin that Sadat was ready to negotiate a second Sinai deal but needed it to be in secret for the time being. Sadat also wanted him to know that Egypt would not intervene if Syria attacked Israel. Rabin reciprocated by confiding to Kissinger his position on a Sinai withdrawal: Israel needed to hold on to the Um Hashiba early warning station at the western end of the Gidi Pass, but on either side of that position he would be willing to withdraw 50 kilometers, and up to 120 kilometers south from Suez city, which would include the oil fields. He agreed to send Allon to Washington in December with a detailed Israeli proposal, which Kissinger could then convey to Sadat.

Kissinger thought he was back in business. As he later told Ford, he hoped

---

* In this case, Dinitz had already left town to be in Israel when Kissinger arrived, so the president of the United States, following Kissinger's script, delivered the reprimand to the Israeli chargé d'affaires, Mordechai Shalev, who pushed back. Scowcroft had to intercede to reinforce the president's weakly delivered message of American impatience. See Scowcroft's Report to Kissinger of Ford's Meeting with Shalev, November 7, 1974, FRUS 1969–1976:26, Doc. 117.

Henry Kissinger, Joe Sisco, and others on the U.S. negotiating team meet
across the cabinet table with Israeli foreign minister Yigal Allon, Prime
Minister Yitzhak Rabin, and Defense Minister Shimon Peres during the
Sinai II disengagement negotiations in Rabin's office in 1975 in Jerusalem.
The map on the wall had whet Kissinger's appetite. He thought the Israelis
were going to show him their proposed line of withdrawal in the Sinai but
that did not happen until after the talks had broken down.

to have the whole thing wrapped up by February 15. That was wishful thinking. Rabin records in his memoirs that he had told Kissinger on that visit that
he had two other requirements for the withdrawal: an Egyptian commitment
to non-belligerency and the passes remaining in Israel's hands. He also told
Kissinger, according to his account, that it was too early for Israel to delineate
a line of withdrawal.

Here lie the origins of the misunderstanding between Kissinger and Rabin
that would soon lead to a major U.S.-Israel crisis. Kissinger said he told Rabin
that Sadat would never agree to non-belligerency and Rabin responded, "I
know we can't get it." Unusually for Kissinger, he seems to have missed the
nuance in Rabin's position: non-belligerency was a demand that he would only
relinquish in return for giving less territory or getting other political concessions. He never intended to give it up for nothing, and could not do so, since
he had repeatedly told the Israeli public and the American media that it was a
basic requirement for any deal involving Israeli withdrawal in Sinai.

Kissinger assumed that because he told Rabin to forget about it, that was
the end of the matter. He seems to have been distracted by his concern that
the world—starting with the Israelis and the Arabs—no longer believed the

United States could deliver on its commitments following Nixon's resignation and the collapse of the Vietnam peace agreement. He was also the target of sustained criticism from Democratic presidential aspirants.[*] The Israelis seem to have gotten under his skin and he had become hypercritical of them.

In debriefing Ford, he depicted them as "villains" and "bastards." "The question is whether a nation of three million Jews can hold the security of the United States and the world in their hands," he said. Ford agreed and then asked whether the Israelis thought they could control the United States through their lobby. Kissinger responded in a way that was bound to upset his new boss: "The Israelis assess that you aren't strong enough."

But Kissinger was. When Schlesinger reported in mid-November that the Pentagon was ready to send a letter of offer to Israel for the purchase of F-15s, something Rabin dearly wanted, Kissinger was categorical. "They must come across in the negotiations before they get anything else. The only way they will make concessions," he averred, "is to give them less than what they need."

Monday, December 9, 1974, Washington, DC. In advance of Allon's arrival for consultations, Kissinger and Rabin agreed that he should not bring a cabinet-endorsed proposal, contrary to their earlier understanding. Brezhnev was scheduled to visit Cairo in mid-January. Kissinger did not want the Soviet leader to claim credit for any concession that Israel might make in the run-up to his visit. (Brezhnev subsequently canceled his trip because of ill health.) That suited Rabin fine, since he was happy not to have to pass something through his divided cabinet until absolutely necessary.

Nevertheless, Kissinger still thought Ford needed to keep the pressure on by expressing his impatience with Israel. In a letter the president sent the prime minister on November 26 in preparation for Allon's visit, Ford stressed that it was "absolutely essential that another step be taken soon," otherwise the United States risked losing all control over the situation.

Before Allon's departure, the Israeli triumvirate had been briefed by two of Israel's preeminent legal minds on the implications of their insistence on an Egyptian commitment to non-belligerency. According to Attorney General Meir Shamgar and the foreign ministry's legal adviser, Meir Rosenne, non-belligerency had no standing in international law. They recommended to demand its component parts instead.

Kissinger was unaware of these deliberations, but he took note of a Rabin interview that *Haaretz* published on December 3, in which Rabin said it was

---

[*] By February 1975, he had come under attack from Senators Lloyd Bentsen, Scoop Jackson, and Adlai Stevenson III.

unrealistic to expect Egypt to publicly commit to non-belligerency because of its obligations to the other Arab states. He concluded that the Israelis were softening their position. But from Rabin's point of view, giving up on non-belligerency was tantamount to reducing Israel's requirements for a political component in the agreement, which meant Israel would give less on the military side. Kissinger appears to have missed this less-for-less trade-off.

In his meeting with Kissinger on December 9, Allon tried on the idea of Egypt's committing to an "end of acts of belligerency." Kissinger asked Allon to define the acts of belligerency from which they wanted Egypt to desist. Allon provided a shopping list of twelve requirements, none of them particularly problematic in Kissinger's view.*

Allon made clear that he was only authorized to convey that the withdrawal would be from thirty to fifty kilometers and Israel would keep the oil fields and the passes. However, in an adaptation of Kissinger's own concept of trading territory for time, Allon then offered to withdraw to the eastern end of the passes and possibly throw in the oil fields for an agreement that would remain in force for ten years.

Kissinger decided to convey Allon's proposals to Sadat through Hermann Eilts, the highly professional U.S. ambassador in Cairo. Eilts met with Kissinger in Brussels on December 11 and 12 to receive the list of Israel's twelve requirements and the offer of a partial withdrawal. Kissinger instructed Eilts to tell Sadat that Ford promised him a settlement by March, with 80 percent by February 15; Sadat would possibly get all the oil fields, but he could not "get both those and the passes."

As sweeteners, Eilts was to tell Sadat that once an agreement was reached, the United States would provide directly to Egypt all the arms that had been on the list that Kissinger had given him during the Israeli-Syrian disengagement negotiations. Ford was also ready to proceed with Nixon's promise of the sale of a civilian nuclear reactor to Egypt that he had made during his visit to Cairo. That was a highly controversial commitment given Israel's sensitivity to any Arab country's acquiring nuclear capabilities.

Sadat's response was "vehemently and bitterly negative," according to Eilts's report of their meeting. He expressed disappointment in Kissinger for transmitting such "arrogant and impertinent ideas." The Israeli proposals were so unacceptable that Sadat would not respond to them. He denounced Israel for expecting him to concede both territory and sovereignty; for good measure, he also dismissed the arms and nuclear reactor sweeteners. What

---

* These requirements included that every area Israel withdrew from should be demilitarized. In addition, Egypt should commit not to join in any war against Israel or promote the boycott against Israel, and should end its arms supply relationship with the Soviet Union, stop its anti-Israel propaganda, and allow Israeli shipping through the canal.

he had hoped to do, he told Eilts with evident disappointment, was develop a U.S.-Egyptian strategy for the region. He now realized that was not possible because of American obligations to Israel, as the Syrians and Soviets had warned him. Threatening to abandon Kissinger's step-by-step stratagem, Sadat concluded that it seemed there was "no alternative but to go to Geneva" and negotiate a comprehensive peace.

Sadat did leave a slight opening, however. He proposed that the next Israeli withdrawal be a large one—well beyond the passes to the El-Arish–Ras Muhammed line (see map on page 527). The concessions Allon was demanding couldn't be made for anything less, he said. And he was ready to send Fahmy to Washington "to reexamine the basic strategy."

Sadat's response led Kissinger to tell Dinitz on December 17 that "we're running up against the end of the step-by-step approach." Israel was to blame for stalling for months, for offering King Hussein nothing, and now for insulting Sadat by presenting such a long list of demands with so little in return. The strategy of isolating Syria required larger Israeli concessions to Egypt, he argued. Absent that, he said, "we are without a strategy."

Kissinger wrote Sadat that Geneva was not an option because every problem Egypt had now would become even bigger there. Standing up to Sadat, he told him bluntly that he could deny Israel's proposals, but he had to make a counterproposal if he expected to achieve his objectives. Sadat responded by asking Kissinger to formulate an American proposal. To do that, Kissinger wrote back, he first had to know Sadat's ideas.

Sadat was not prepared to confide in Eilts. But for Kissinger to embark on another Middle Eastern shuttle, which Sadat clearly wanted him to do, was also high-risk. America's position in Indochina was collapsing, détente was fraying, the American economy was struggling through a recession, and after Rabat it looked like Kissinger's Middle East diplomacy was also faltering.

Thursday, January 16, 1975, Washington, DC. When Allon came to town again, he too argued for an "exploratory" shuttle. "That way it's riskless," he reassured Kissinger. But Kissinger was not convinced. If it failed, he responded, "we [will] have a monumental problem." When Kissinger and Ford tried to tie Allon down on what they could expect Israel to offer, Allon explained that he wasn't authorized to say anything beyond what he had conveyed on his last visit. Kissinger wanted at least to be able to ask Sadat what he was prepared to give up if Israel gave up the passes and the oil fields. But the most that Ford and Kissinger could extract from Allon was a caveat that Kissinger would have done well to heed: "There is a direct relation between what we can give and what we can get," he said. Allon spoke of Israel's need for a long duration for the agreement and a stable UN Emergency Force for that period. When Ford asked whether that would be enough for Israel to relinquish the oil fields and the passes, Allon would not commit.

Kissinger sought greater reassurance from Dinitz, who had let him know that he thought most of Allon's proposals were frivolous. Dinitz said Israel was now only looking for Sadat to agree to "surrender something of belligerency." Dinitz strongly recommended Kissinger persuade Egypt to accept a term of three years for the agreement, during which there should be no pressure on Israel from the United States to make further withdrawals.

Kissinger was right to worry. In the best case, the deal was going to look like an unequal bargain: Israel would be giving back tangible Egyptian assets for little visible recompense. The United States would be regaining some authority and Israel acquiring some time, but that was hardly going to satisfy critics either inside or outside the Israeli cabinet. He had to know Rabin's bottom line: "What is the maximum Israel can give in return for the minimum Egyptian position?" He asked Dinitz to find out.

To strengthen his hand, Kissinger also sought leverage over Israel. He knew Rabin was consumed by concern about Israel's arms requests, confirmed by an undiplomatic letter from the prime minister to the president complaining about Pentagon foot-dragging on Israel's military requests.

Before his departure, Kissinger told Schlesinger, "We must bring Israel to move by whatever means necessary."

"Just tell me what to do," said Schlesinger.

Kissinger repeated his instructions to hold up all of Israel's new arms requests until there was an agreement.

Kissinger asked the president whether he could inform Rabin that "we are not ready to move ahead on aid if there is no progress."

"Tell him cold" was Ford's response.

Tuesday, February 11, 1975, Jerusalem. As the American team filed into the Israeli cabinet room where they had spent so many hours with Golda Meir and her advisers, they noticed a change in the seating arrangements.* Rabin, Allon, Peres, Gur, and all their aides were facing the windows; the Americans were now facing the wall on which a large topographical map showing the Egyptian and Syrian disengagement lines had been hung. This raised their expectations

---

* Kissinger's team for this shuttle negotiation comprised: Joe Sisco, who had been elevated to under secretary of state for political affairs; Roy Atherton, who had taken his place as assistant secretary for Near Eastern and South Asian affairs; Harold Saunders, deputy assistant secretary for Near Eastern and South Asian Affairs; Peter Rodman, still Kissinger's special assistant; Kenneth Keating, the U.S. ambassador to Israel; and Hermann Eilts, the U.S. ambassador to Egypt.

that they were about to see a new Israeli proposal for a line of withdrawal in Sinai. Their appetite had been whetted by an ABC News interview Rabin had given a few days before their arrival in which he had publicly put the oil fields and passes in play, indicating that Israel was willing to withdraw from them but wanted in exchange that Egypt "effectively [be] taken out of the war."

They would be sorely disappointed.

As usual, Kissinger began the meeting with a detailed exegesis on the state of the world. But his jeremiad had changed. This time, he focused on an effort to justify his step-by-step diplomacy in the face of what he presented as a Jewish-led campaign against it in the United States. This was an echo of a public discussion that had broken out in Israel, with Ariel Sharon on the right and Abba Eban on the left both arguing that it was time to go to Geneva and negotiate a final peace deal rather than give up more territory without achieving peace. To an audience that should have needed no explanation of the dangers of a return to the Geneva Conference, he gave a detailed account of the gang-up by the Arabs and their Soviet patron against Israel and the United States that would occur there.

Kissinger argued that it was important to negotiate another Israeli-Egyptian agreement because the United States now faced a crisis of executive authority and a breakdown in cooperation between the executive and legislative branches of government over foreign policy. If there should be a major Middle East crisis, these tensions would generate division rather than a rallying around the president. American action would not be as decisive, Soviet action would be less risk averse, and the Europeans would be blocking energy cooperation and urging pressure on Israel. However, successful American diplomacy, as manifested in a new agreement between Israel and Egypt, could avert this doomsday scenario.

The alternative was to go to Geneva in an atmosphere of crisis in which the focus would be on imposing the 1967 borders. Israel had to choose. He downplayed the political dividend the Israelis could expect from Egypt, but then Israel would not be expected to give up territory of vital significance. The return for Israel lay in keeping the Arabs divided and preventing international forces from coalescing.

It was a powerful pitch, interspersed as usual with jokes at the expense of Sisco, Gromyko, and King Faisal. "Kissinger's graphic storytelling had us weeping with laughter," Peres would later say of the typical scene. "Amid his predictions of imminent regional or global catastrophe and his whimsical accounts of his own virtuoso diplomacy, the shape would slowly but unmistakably emerge of the concessions the secretary had actually come to squeeze out of us."

However, in this presentation an admission of American weakness had been added to the mix, undermining its usual effectiveness. And this time he was up against Rabin rather than Meir. His new sparring partner was as analytical as she had been emotional. Step by step, Rabin took Kissinger's argument apart.

He made clear that peace was Israel's strategic objective and that practical steps leading in that direction were needed. He wanted to move toward an interim settlement with Egypt, but it should be toward peace—"not just to give but to get something in return." Gaining time was worthwhile, especially if it strengthened those in Egypt who didn't want war. But there was no point in making concessions for a step with Egypt if two months later Israel had to go to Geneva in a much weaker position "because we gave territory to start a certain process and got the process we tried to avoid."

Kissinger avowed that of course there should be a quid pro quo for Israel, but all the ones he could think of were reversible, "so the real quid pro quo is in a process, not what's on paper." What should worry Israel, he argued, was a Geneva process in which Arab demands were backed by the United States. His step-by-step process would prevent that. He would also commit the United States to not linking the interim agreement with Egypt to any other track, even though he confided that he would have to pretend that he was contemplating another step with Syria.

In this exchange, we can see the gap that was opening between American and Israeli conceptions. Kissinger was still in the business of swapping territory for time; Rabin was intent on swapping territory for peace, or at least meaningful movement toward it. For the moment, they would paper over their differences. Rabin said fine, put Israel's requirements to Sadat.* But the gap would soon open again and prove to be unbridgeable.

Peres objected: "I would like to express my sincere doubts about the policy we are now conducting." If it was a matter of giving up land, Israel could do that at Geneva; the justification for the step-by-step approach was to get something in return. "We won't take the avoidance of Geneva as compensation for sacrificing," Peres said. If Sadat were ready to give a little, Israel would too, but "what we would be against is to give a long step and be met by a very short one."

Kissinger warned Peres that support for Israel in Congress and the American foreign policy establishment was eroding. The prevailing view there was that the United States was sacrificing its interests for Israel. "It is inconceivable," he said, "that the United States will stand still, in a stalemate, faced with requests for large demands for arms and not make diplomatic moves."

---

* Israel's requirements as outlined by Allon included: no linkage to any other agreement, no expectation that Israel would come down from the Golan, and no reconvening of Geneva before agreement with Egypt. In addition, the agreement needed to take Egypt out of the war as well as buy Israel three to ten years, and the area Israel withdrew from would need to be demilitarized.

Peres would not be denied: "The major point is we want American support for some return from Egypt." Offended at the implication that he wasn't supporting Israel, Kissinger raised his voice: "Who carried out the confrontation policy toward Europe last year?" Rabin brought the conversation to a close.

This Israeli fear of giving without getting, expressed repeatedly by each of the Israeli triumvirate in their exchanges with Kissinger, is a fundamental part of the Israeli psyche. In the hardscrabble struggle for existence that characterized the era of state building that Rabin, Allon, and Peres had experienced in Israel's formative decades, a fear of being taken advantage of grew in the minds of Israelis. It found expression in the Hebrew word *freier*.

A *freier* is a sucker, a person whose gullibility, naivete, and weakness are easily exploited. It is politically fatal for an Israeli politician to appear to be a *freier*. In 1996, Benjamin Netanyahu would use the pejorative in his campaign against the Oslo Accords, in which he asserted, "We are not *freier*s. We won't agree to give without receiving anything." It helped win him the election against Peres and became the fundamental underpinning of his tightfisted approach to the Palestinians.

Kissinger understood the psychological implication of the word. Fear of being seen as a *freier* was baked into the structure of his step-by-step approach to peacemaking. He was asking his Israeli interlocutors to give up tangible security assets for intangible Arab commitments, for a postponement of conflict rather than its end. Given this Israeli psychological predisposition, Kissinger's dire threats of future consequences were bound to be counterproductive. Tangible security assets were more, not less, essential if Israel were to become isolated and embattled, abandoned by its only ally.

After lunch with the Israeli cabinet, during which Kissinger was grilled for two hours about all its members' fears, Rabin and his negotiating team focused on the give and the get. There was no point, Kissinger said, in talking about anything other than giving up the passes and oil fields and what was possible in return. Rabin made clear that there was no cabinet decision to give up more than thirty-fifty kilometers. And no Israeli would give up the passes without an assurance, however expressed, "that there will be no more war."

Kissinger tried over and again to explain that Sadat could not agree to a de facto peace while a significant part of Sinai remained occupied. How was he then supposed to get the rest back? Through peaceful means, the Israelis responded, unwilling to accept that Sadat had constraints on how far he could get out ahead of the other Arabs to whom Israel was not ready, at that point, to make any concessions. They tried again to promote Allon's idea of a ten-year time commitment as a substitute. Kissinger didn't see how Sadat could justify that to his Arab brothers if Israel refused to countenance withdrawal on any other front.

Kissinger was exasperated. "For one-third of the Sinai they are supposed to make a permanent peace?" he objected.

"Let them say it should be half of the Sinai," said Rabin, attempting to persuade Kissinger to pursue his territory for peace trade.

They were clearly talking past each other. "I don't see why we should continue this discussion further," Kissinger said.

Kissinger seemed to have missed Rabin's offer. In a private meeting at the end of this visit, Rabin tried again. According to Dinitz, he told Kissinger that for an end to belligerency Israel would be willing to withdraw to the El-Arish–Ras Muhammed line, well to the east of the passes (see map on page 527). This was the same deep Israeli withdrawal that Sadat had raised earlier in his exchange with Ambassador Eilts, for which he had seemed willing to consider at least some of Allon's political requirements. If Kissinger had pressed, he might have discovered that Rabin was even ready for full withdrawal if Sadat were willing to commit to full peace—a bargain that Menachem Begin struck with Sadat three years later, and a bargain that Rabin was even prepared to offer Assad in 1993 when he told Clinton he was willing to withdraw fully from the Golan Heights in return for security arrangements and full peace.

Instead, Kissinger took it as a sign of Rabin's willingness to withdraw from the passes, without any political commitment from Sadat, missing Rabin's point that if Kissinger could persuade Sadat to accept his peace requirements, he would be willing to withdraw even farther than the passes. He reported to Ford that he believed Rabin wanted an agreement although he was struggling with a divided cabinet. He thought some of his requirements were achievable but depicted him as intent on extracting the highest possible price from Sadat, and that raised the serious question of whether Sadat could meet his expectations. To this day, Kissinger maintains that in private Rabin promised to give up the passes but then failed to deliver cabinet support. From Rabin's point of view, it was Kissinger who failed to deliver an Egyptian commitment to end the state of belligerency, and therefore he was not willing to try to convince his cabinet to give up the passes.

Wednesday, February 12, 1975, Al Qanater Al Khairiya. This time Sadat received Kissinger at his weekend retreat at the barrages north of Cairo. The halcyon environment had done little to relax Sadat. Kissinger found him worried, tense, and preoccupied with the pressure he was under from Syria not to make another separate deal with Israel. He had Fahmy respond to Kissinger's list of Israeli requirements, explaining why most of them were impossible, especially non-belligerency.

After lunch with Nancy and Sadat's wife, Jehan, the two men met alone in Sadat's study. Instead of exploring Rabin's idea of a larger deal, Kissinger suggested a smaller deal. Sadat rejected the idea, arguing that the reaction to any deal in the Arab world would be so adverse that the risk would only be worthwhile for a big deal. For that he needed the passes and the oil fields, but he was willing to have implementation of the withdrawal over several months if he received the oil fields up front. He rejected non-belligerency again, as Kissinger had expected, but was willing to make a commitment not to attack Israel provided the United States guaranteed that Israel would not attack any other Arab state. He expressed his frustration with the Israelis: "When I said I would make war, they didn't believe it. Now, when I say I will make peace, they don't believe me." Actually, Rabin was prepared to believe him; Kissinger was the one who was unwilling to test the proposition.

They resumed their conversation over a dinner that Fahmy hosted at his home in the tony district of Zamalek, located on Gezira Island in the heart of Cairo. As the other guests mingled, Fahmy took Kissinger off to a corner, where they sat with Sadat and Sisco. Sadat insisted that if they were going to do the deal, it had to be done quickly to avoid Syrian interference. That meant Kissinger should come out in March and finish it through his shuttle diplomacy. Kissinger made it clear that were he to do that, there had to be a quid pro quo for the Israeli withdrawal that Sadat was seeking. Sadat expressed a willingness to accept many of the elements that the Israelis had raised. He ordered Fahmy to provide Kissinger with a document that outlined Egypt's position on what they termed non-resort to force, a step back from non-belligerency.

Kissinger decided not to share the document with the Israelis at that stage, claiming that Sadat had refused to be specific for fear that it would leak and set off a firestorm in the Arab world. Instead, he reported to Rabin, "It was left that they would try to see what they can think up by the time I come back." He added a caveat about the bind Sadat felt he was in: "He seems like a man who wants to do it but wants to be able to tell his Arab friends he hasn't done it."

Just how much Sadat had to fear became clear the next day, when Kissinger traveled to Damascus to see Assad. The Syrian president was happy to see Kissinger but left him in no doubt that if Egypt did a separate deal, he would vehemently oppose it and paint the United States as the enemy of the Arabs. He obliquely threatened to cause instability in Egypt and warned there would be an explosion between them. However, recognizing that he might not be able to stop Sadat and revealing his own fear of isolation, Assad then made clear that if Egypt concluded another disengagement with Israel, he wanted one for Syria too.

Kissinger felt that he had met with enough encouragement to commit to another exercise in shuttle diplomacy beginning on March 8, in Egypt. It appeared to him that Egypt and Israel were now in the zone of a possible agreement: Rabin and Allon at least understood that an agreement would require Israeli withdrawal from the oil fields and the passes, while Sadat seemed willing to entertain meaningful concessions in return. However, the vagueness of the deal troubled him. Unlike in the earlier negotiations, Israel had not yet given him a proposed line of withdrawal in the Sinai. His concern was compounded by the clear constraints operating on both Rabin and Sadat from a fractious cabinet and raucous opposition in Israel, and from a recalcitrant and suspicious Arab world.

Kissinger would have done well to listen to Meir, whom he consulted at her home in Ramat Aviv en route to Ben Gurion Airport on February 14. When he explained to her what the deal would have to look like, she told him bluntly that Rabin was too weak to pass it through his cabinet. Based on his private discussions with Rabin, he dismissed her warnings. He remembers telling Sisco and Atherton afterward that even though she had only been out of office for nine months, she was already out of touch.

He did take note, however, of a speech Rabin gave in the Knesset on February 12, while Kissinger was in Cairo meeting with Sadat. In what appeared to be ad lib remarks, Rabin declared, "Failing abrogation of the state of war, the passes and the oil fields will remain in the hands of the State of Israel." He was immediately applauded by Israel's right-wing opposition for toughening his stance. Rabin's statement therefore should have raised the question in Kissinger's mind whether another shuttle could bridge the gap between Rabin's end-of-war requirement and Sadat's need to avoid looking like he was abandoning the Arab world. But he had worked a miracle with Assad and Meir; surely, he could do it with Rabin and Sadat too.

Saturday, March 8, 1975, Aswan. Kissinger launched the shuttle at Sadat's winter retreat. It was a brilliant day, with the fragrant jasmine trees blooming in the president's garden. This time Sadat was more relaxed and ready to do business. He had decided to return to Aswan, the site of his successful negotiation of the first Sinai agreement, because he felt its mystic atmosphere would positively influence the negotiations. He greeted Kissinger with words that were a tonic to his troubled soul: "I hope your visit will be fruitful and decisive." He seemed determined to reach an agreement.

It had been a difficult three weeks for Kissinger. Cambodia was teetering on the edge of collapse as communist insurgents advanced on the capital and Congress held up military assistance. North Vietnam began a new offensive against the South that would soon prove decisive. The shah of Iran betrayed the Kurds by signing an agreement to end his border dispute with Iraq, and Saddam Hussein wasted no time in assaulting Iraqi Kurdistan. At home, *The New York Times* reported that Kissinger had "fallen from political grace" on Capitol Hill, where he was being charged with "one-man authoritarianism" for his supposed role in the Greek overthrow of Cyprus's president, Archbishop Makarios, in July 1974, and the Turkish invasion that followed. The *Times* predicted "a hard year for Mr. Kissinger and his diplomacy."

The launching of this shuttle had begun inauspiciously with a PLO seaborne terrorist attack in the heart of Tel Aviv on March 5, in which eleven Israelis were killed. Kissinger read it as a signal from Assad of his ability to disrupt the American juggernaut. He prevailed on Rabin not to retaliate for fear it would disrupt his diplomacy.

The mood was also negatively impacted by the way Israel and Egypt had begun to emulate Kissinger's use of the media to promote their positions in the negotiations. Peres had told the *Times* on March 2 that only a direct pledge of "an end to belligerency" would suffice, warning that "Israel won't pay dearly and be repaid cheaply." Sadat meanwhile was reported to have reassured the Arabs that any agreement would be purely military. In Kissinger's presence at Aswan, he told the press that he would not sign a pledge of non-belligerence while a single Israeli soldier was occupying any of the Arab territories seized in 1967.

In private, however, Sadat told Kissinger he was willing to commit to a "no-war pledge." He also agreed to avoid any linkage to a Syrian deal. Then he brought General el-Gamasy, now his minister of defense, into the meeting to brief Kissinger on the military requirements of the deal.[*] At last, a map was now on the table. Predictably, all three lines on the map presented by el-Gamasy moved Egyptian forces east of the passes. At this point, Kissinger could have recounted Rabin's private offer of a withdrawal to the El-Arish–Ras Muhammed line in return for an Egyptian declaration of non-belligerency. Instead, Kissinger told Sadat, after the general had left, that the Israelis could never accept such a line. Sadat accepted this negative assessment, explaining that he had to let the military make its pitch, but he would agree that the limit of his army's advance would be to the line Israeli forces were presently hold-

---

[*] El-Gamasy outlined six principles: the lines on both sides should be secure from the other side's forces; no side should have a military advantage; the deployments of both sides in Sinai should be balanced; the new line should be sufficiently east not to threaten the canal cities or navigation through the canal; the buffer zone needed to be wide enough to avoid clashes; and an open canal would require more Egyptian forces in Sinai because it presented an obstacle to Egyptian military action.

ing, west of the passes, as long as Israel withdrew to the east of the passes. As Kissinger reported to Ford, Sadat had given him enough "at least to get the negotiations started in a serious way." But in the process, Kissinger had now conceded the one thing that Rabin required.

Sunday, March 9, 1975, Damascus–Jerusalem. Assad was in a feisty mood when he received Kissinger again in Damascus. He argued that he now had the backing of the Arab world, even Iraq, to oppose a separate deal, and would do so with force if necessary. When Kissinger responded that the United States would not allow it, Assad noted that Washington had already abandoned Taiwan, Cambodia, Vietnam, Turkey, and Portugal, implying it was just a matter of time before the United States abandoned Israel too. Nevertheless, Assad showed no interest in going to Geneva and made clear, in an unusual photo op with the press at the beginning of their meeting, that he was not opposed to partial agreements as long as they were on all fronts.

In private, Assad proposed Kissinger start a simultaneous negotiation with Syria alongside Egypt. Kissinger had already discussed that possibility with Ford and secured his agreement to tell Assad privately that the United States would make a good-faith effort as soon as the Egyptian-Israeli deal was finished. He told Ford that such an effort was bound to fail since the Israelis wouldn't countenance it. He was stringing Assad along in the hope that he could at least delay Syrian opposition to the Israeli-Egyptian deal until it was too late to undo it. In that context, Kissinger told Assad that there was no Egyptian proposal, even though that's exactly what he was carrying from Sadat to Rabin.

At a late dinner that night with the Israeli team at the prime minister's Jerusalem residence, Kissinger gave Rabin the headlines of his engagement with Sadat, while Rabin laid out precisely Israel's seven requirements for the agreement.[*] The Israelis were willing to discuss something short of non-belligerency as long as it was "a step toward peace," but Rabin continued to insist that the extent of withdrawal would be determined by the extent of peace.

The next morning, at Rabin's office, Kissinger presented el-Gamasy's map and principles, but made clear that even though Israel would have to relinquish the passes, Sadat knew that it was impossible for Egypt to gain control of them. He then responded to Rabin's seven points, arguing that most were

---

[*] The requirements were: (1) a separate agreement with Egypt "that stands on its own feet"; (2) a "step towards peace"; (3) a declared, public commitment to "end the use of force"; (4) arrangements to prevent a surprise attack including buffer zones; (5) an indefinite duration for the agreement; (6) the relationship between the agreement and reconvening the Geneva Conference; (7) a new line to be determined by the other six points. See Appendix to Memcon between Kissinger, Rabin, et al., March 9, 1975, KT01523, NSA.

attainable, including some declaration of non-use of force and an indefinite duration for the agreement. Sadat would be flexible about the Egyptian line; what he would insist upon, however, was that the Israeli line be east of the passes.

"We can't change the line without a different situation," Peres said. Israel would be abandoning an excellent line of defense to a country that had just attacked it. Siding with Peres, Rabin concluded that the gap between the sides was still very wide.

Reading these exchanges with the benefit of hindsight, it is again clear that Kissinger and his Israeli interlocutors were talking past each other. Kissinger was focused on the nuts and bolts of withdrawal, an approach he had perfected in the two previous disengagement agreements. The Israeli team—and there appears to have been little difference between Rabin and Peres on this score—was treating the deal as something more significant than another military separation of forces. They wanted an "interim agreement" rather than a "disengagement agreement." They were looking to change the political situation by persuading Sadat to make a significant move toward peace.

Kissinger acknowledged their aspiration. Indeed, in an attempt to move Israel out of its give-get, *freier* mentality, he now borrowed a play from Sadat's book. Why, he asked, didn't Rabin write Sadat a letter expressing the fears that Peres had raised? If Rabin put his demands in a way that would be psychologically acceptable to Sadat, it might put him in a frame of mind in which he felt he was working with Israel as a partner and didn't feel he had to outdo every Israeli move.

They met again the next night, after Kissinger returned from a quick trip to Turkey. Rabin had used the time to consult with his colleagues and presented Kissinger with an elaborated version of his seven requirements, which Kissinger patiently commented on. On the third point, non-use of force, he noted that the Israelis had reinserted non-belligerency language. Kissinger told the trio that Sadat was "as firmly committed not to renounce belligerency as you are to ask him to do it because to him it's equivalent to making peace." Rabin urged him, "Try your best then."

Kissinger wanted the Israelis to understand that Sadat's situation was complicated too: "Once the Syrians see it's a negotiation, we've got a problem." And there was the danger that Sadat would lose patience and move back to a hard line. He was also uneasy about the Russians, who had just dispatched Vinogradov, their ambassador to the Geneva Conference, to Arab capitals without informing Kissinger, presumably to consult about reconvening Geneva.

Kissinger was beginning to have doubts about where things were headed. "I frankly don't have any idea how to get it from here to there," he confessed to the Israelis.

He inquired about the letter he had suggested Rabin write Sadat. Rabin handed over a draft. Kissinger liked the tone. He thought Sadat would like it too and it would ease the discussion of all of Israel's requirements. But he was going to have to show soon that this effort was going somewhere.

"With all frankness, I'm not saying an agreement is attainable," cautioned Rabin.

"That's a general statement; we need to get from the realm of philosophy to some practical steps," said Kissinger.

They met yet again the next morning, March 12, before Kissinger departed for Aswan. They tinkered with Israel's proposal, and again Kissinger told them "an undertaking of the renunciation of belligerency . . . is clearly unattainable."

Kissinger suggested that if he could get reasonable responses from Sadat, the Israelis should then draft a formal paper with American assistance. That would necessarily trigger a cabinet deliberation. Rabin made clear he would do that only if he saw something from Sadat that made it worthwhile to make an agreement. No matter how many times Kissinger shut the door on non-belligerency, the Israelis would keep trying to open it again.

Rabin then revealed that, notwithstanding Kissinger's dire warnings, he was now quite satisfied with his situation. He explained that he had succeeded through his public statements in making clear to all that the issue was not about Israel's willingness to concede territory; it was rather about an Arab willingness to move toward peace.

Kissinger tried to challenge Rabin's sangfroid by noting that his comfort level would be fleeting. Within a few months of a breakdown, the pressures on Israel would build again. In the meantime, the step-by-step process would be discredited, and America's ability to support Israel would be eroded. "Even if you have achieved a good tactical position for failing," Kissinger warned, the strategic logic still made an agreement highly desirable.

Rabin was unmistakably signaling that he could walk away from these negotiations and come out stronger, at least domestically; Kissinger could not. But, at that moment, Kissinger preferred to look at the glass as half full. He reported to Ford that he felt he had forged a negotiating partnership with Rabin, and he thought even Peres was coming around. Rabin, he wrote, was handling his delicate domestic situation in a way that "*when* he recommends Israeli withdrawal from passes and the oil fields [emphasis added]," he will have enough from Sadat to pass it through his cabinet and the Knesset. Kissinger was intent on ignoring Rabin's condition for those concessions—he had told Kissinger time and again he would not recommend giving up the passes and oil fields to the cabinet unless Sadat agreed to non-belligerency.

———

Wednesday, March 12, 1975, Aswan. Kissinger found Sadat ready to get down to business. He included Fahmy in the meeting and later brought el-Gamasy in too. Kissinger reported that when he returned to Jerusalem with Sadat's responses to the Israeli "non-paper," Rabin would be ready to take the issues to the cabinet, including the geographic requirements.* But to win over the cabinet, Kissinger explained, Rabin would need the maximum quid pro quos from Sadat.

He then raised the idea of non-resort to use of force instead of non-belligerency. Sadat had been amenable to that all along. He repeated in front of his aides the offer he had previously made Kissinger in private: he would only move the Egyptian military line forward to the present Israeli line at the western approaches to the passes.

To Kissinger's surprise, Sadat opined that the Israeli positions were "very mild." He accepted that the UN Emergency Force (UNEF) mandate could be renewed annually for as long as the peace process continued. So far so good, except Kissinger was proceeding on the false assumption that he could persuade Rabin to trade the passes for an Egyptian commitment to "non-resort to use of force," whereas Rabin had made clear he was also seeking an Egyptian "step towards peace."

Sadat and Kissinger adjourned to Sadat's study for a private conversation before dinner. There Kissinger handed him the personal letter from Rabin. In it, Rabin expressed the hope "that Providence will extricate us from the vortex of warfare and enmity." He said that he was doing his best to put himself in Sadat's shoes. "I, on my part, am determined to make all efforts to promote a peace between us," Rabin wrote. But he had to be able to convince his people that by giving up strategic positions, "we will not be exposing ourselves to increased hardships." This would only be possible, Rabin wrote, "if it is visibly shown that the act of withdrawal marks *the real beginning of progress towards peace by deeds and words that demonstrate the intention of peace* [emphasis added]."

Kissinger reported to Ford that night that Sadat had been moved to tears. Privately the next day, Sadat dictated to Kissinger an oral response for Rabin in which he gave him four personal assurances: "Power will never again play a role in the relations of our two peoples"; "my determination is to bring about the ultimate withdrawal to agreed lines by peaceful means only"; "if a Geneva conference is assembled after this agreement is signed, I will not touch this agreement or change anything between us at Geneva"; and "whatever the problems, *I will not use force* [emphasis added]."

In his memoirs, Kissinger writes that the Israelis seemed unaffected by

---

* In diplomatic terms, a "non-paper" is a discussion paper that has no official status and therefore does not bind the government involved in drafting it.

Sadat's reply. Strangely, in Rabin's memoirs, he recalls Kissinger reporting that Sadat was deeply moved by his letter, but "be that as it may, I never received an answer." In his memoirs, Dinitz criticizes Kissinger for making "a cardinal mistake" in not insisting that Sadat reply in writing, which is why Rabin claimed he never received a response.

Kissinger does not recall what happened back then, but he agrees with Dinitz that Sadat's oral response had zero impact on the Israeli negotiating team. Kissinger should have been able to develop this private channel as a means of lubricating his diplomacy, as he had managed to do earlier with Sadat and Meir. It was not beyond his considerable diplomatic skills to encourage a dialogue about peacemaking that might have led Sadat, with his spirit of generosity, to go further toward peace, and Rabin, with his insistence on reciprocal steps, to modify his requirements. Preoccupied with the way things were falling apart in Indochina and the assault on him at home, his heart just didn't seem to be in this negotiation. But there was a conceptual problem as well. For Kissinger peace was the absence of war, so Sadat's offer of a non-resort to use of force was a meaningful concession. For Rabin an absence of war had little worth compared to a political commitment to end the state of war and make peace.

Friday, March 14, 1975, Jerusalem. Kissinger briefed Rabin, Peres, Allon, and Gur on Sadat's formal responses to their demands, especially the substitutes he had offered instead of a declaration of non-belligerency.* Rabin's reaction was affected by his anger at Kissinger for telling the press that morning in Aswan, at a joint press conference with Sadat, that he was returning to Israel with "new ideas" and that he expected the Israelis to respond with "concrete ideas" of their own. Rabin saw this as a deliberate attempt to paint Sadat as moderate and forthcoming and Israel as intransigent. Just as he had done with Sadat's peace initiative before the war, Rabin now discounted and belittled what Kissinger had brought from Sadat. All Sadat's proposed elements of non-belligerency were meaningless because they could be revoked at any time, he

---

* Egypt was prepared to offer the following: the interim agreement would be a step toward peace, all differences would be resolved by peaceful means, there would be no use of force against Israel even if Syria reignited the war, and the agreement would remain valid until superseded by another agreement. In addition, Egypt agreed to automatic annual review of UNEF, a wide buffer zone between Israeli and Egyptian forces and significant limitations on Egyptian forces in Sinai, and free passage for Israeli-bound cargoes through the canal. Egypt was willing to reduce hostile propaganda emanating from Egyptian-controlled media and would allow free passage through the Strait of Bab al-Mandeb. It was willing to undertake quietly and informally, particularly in relation to selected American firms, ways to ease Arab economic boycott practices. See Memo from Scowcroft to Ford, March 14, 1975, FRUS 1969–1976:26, Doc. 145.

argued. Undaunted, Kissinger told the Israelis that he wanted to return to Egypt with concrete proposals "sufficiently forthcoming to make it possible to move quickly to conclude the negotiations." Rabin agreed to take Sadat's responses to the cabinet on Sunday morning.

The mood had soured. After Kissinger met with Rabin, Dan Patir, Rabin's press spokesman, told the traveling press at the King David that while a "few" Egyptian responses were acceptable, others were "inadequate and insufficient." Overall, he said, "we did not feel we had the concrete answers we're looking for."

Kissinger opened their next meeting, two nights later after a trip to Amman, by registering a formal complaint. The impression was being created in the Israeli press "that the United States and Egypt are working in collusion, by clever maneuvers, to extort things from Israel," he said. Rabin brushed that aside. In the meantime, he had met with the cabinet and wanted to present its formal response to the Egyptian ideas. On the three issues crucial to Israel—non-use of force, a real move toward peace, and the duration of the agreement—"basically very little has been achieved," Rabin said. None of the answers were satisfactory. Unless Sadat moved on all three issues, he stated, "I don't see what can be done."

Searching for a way to proceed, Kissinger asked whether he could go back to Sadat with a line of withdrawal. Allon, who should have been the most sympathetic, said, "We're not in a position with these Egyptian ideas to ask for a definite line from the cabinet." He wanted Kissinger to ask Sadat for something more concrete on the three major points.

Kissinger thought that was absurd. "Tell me the scenario of my first fifteen minutes with Sadat: 'Israel may or may not give up the passes and fields. Please give more,'" Kissinger said sarcastically.

As the argument continued, it became clear to Kissinger that the problem was more than just an unwillingness to draw the line of withdrawal. Rabin told him, "We are not entitled by the cabinet to discuss anything other than non-belligerency." If all Sadat was prepared to offer was non-use of force, then Israel would not be willing to concede either the passes or the oil fields, said Rabin.

Grasping for leverage, Kissinger summoned his "Chicken Little" argument that the sky was certain to fall if they continued on this course. He predicted the failure of this shuttle and with it the end of the step-by-step process. He quoted King Hussein, whom he had just met, as predicting that Arab radicalism would be strengthened, there would be a turn to war, and all the pressure would be directed at the United States because of its support for Israel. "The reality will be that America can't produce even a minimal withdrawal . . . and only a radical course will work," he said. And he warned ominously that a breakdown would produce a parting of the ways between Israel and the United States.

Kissinger gave the Israelis time to think about it overnight, but all that produced was a reformulation of the non-belligerency requirement: Egypt would not only have to undertake not to resort to the use of force and resolve all disputes by peaceful means, it would also have "to refrain from permitting, encouraging, assisting or participating in" any kind of hostile or warlike activity against Israel anywhere.[*]

Monday, March 17, 1975, Aswan. Sadat was at first willing to consider this Israeli language, but then Fahmy pointed out that by referring to the settlement of all disputes "by peaceful means," the Israeli language went beyond non-belligerency to introduce elements of peace. This turned Sadat around. When he came to understand that Kissinger still did not have a line of withdrawal from the Israelis, Sadat rejected the formulation as an insult that would require him to make peace while his territory was still occupied. Kissinger managed to convince him to make the best offer he could, and he would make a last-ditch effort to get the Israelis to accept it. He was now staring into the diplomatic abyss.

But an hour after he left Sadat's villa, he received an urgent visit from Fahmy while he was dining with his team at the New Cataract Hotel, in the same room where el-Gamasy had choked up during the Sinai I negotiations. Fahmy reported that he had left Sadat in an agitated state and feared he would say something to the press the next day, after his meeting with Kissinger, that would derail the whole effort.

To head him off, Fahmy gave Kissinger a new Egyptian non-paper with formulations that Kissinger felt went a long way toward meeting Israeli concerns.[†] Had Kissinger succeeded in softening up the Israelis on non-belligerency, this paper would have given him a lot to work with, and he was appreciative of the Egyptian effort. But he feared it would fall short.

---

[*] The full Israeli formula was: "Egypt and Israel hereby undertake in the relations between themselves not to resort to the use of force and to resolve all disputes between them by negotiations and other peaceful means. They will refrain from permitting, encouraging, assisting, or participating in any military, paramilitary, or hostile actions, from any warlike or hostile acts and any other form of warfare or hostile activity against the other party anywhere." See Memo from Scowcroft to Ford, March 18, 1975, FRUS 1969–1976:26, Doc. 149.

[†] Fahmy's paper contained the following points: the Middle East crisis would not be solved "by military force but rather by peaceful means," Egypt would renounce the use of force *unconditionally*, the agreement would last *indefinitely* (i.e., until superseded by another agreement), UNEF would be extended *automatically* every year, Geneva would not interfere with the agreement, there would be no linkage to any other agreement, and Sadat would give a formal written assurance to the United States not to resort to the use of force.

When they met again the next morning, Sadat endorsed the Fahmy paper, adding that the passes should be in the UN buffer zone with each side's forces at the entrances, equidistant from the center of the passes. He made it clear that he was only going this far to avoid letting Kissinger down. More in sorrow than in anger, he expressed his deep disappointment in the Israelis, an attitude that Kissinger wholeheartedly endorsed. For the first time, they discussed how to handle the collapse of the talks, with Kissinger suggesting the need to develop a common U.S.-Egyptian strategy via a summit with President Ford, something he knew Sadat would relish.

After Kissinger departed for Israel, Sadat wrote an unusual letter to Ford expressing his indignation at Israel's demands and its intransigence and making clear that Israel would bear full responsibility if the situation in the region deteriorated. Having moved all his chips to the American side of the table, he was attempting to make sure U.S.-Egyptian relations didn't suffer because of the breakdown. But the ever-sensitive Kissinger interpreted it as an attempt to go over his head—an indication that Sadat had lost faith in him. This sense of his own fall from grace was reinforced by a complaint he received that evening from Fahmy, via Eilts, questioning how he could have embarked on the shuttle in the first place given the Israeli positions.

That report coincided with news from Saigon that North Vietnamese forces had taken over the Central Highlands of South Vietnam, precipitating the abandonment by the Diem regime of two-thirds of the country and a massive refugee flow south. Little wonder the traveling press reported from Kissinger's plane that a sense of gloom had gripped the secretary of state and his aides. Like Icarus, he had flown too close to the sun and now seemed to be falling to earth.

Tuesday, March 18, 1975, Jerusalem. In advance of his meeting with Rabin and the Israeli team on Tuesday evening at the prime minister's office, Kissinger had received an angry message from Ford telling him that the United States could not be expected to isolate itself in the world "in order to stand behind the intransigence of Israel," and giving him full backing to lower the boom on them. Even the congenial Ford had grown frustrated with Israeli tactics. Kissinger, however, wasn't yet ready to give up the game.

He told the Israelis that what he brought from Sadat was the maximum Egypt could agree to; if they could not accept it, Sadat would break off the talks on Thursday and then Israel would face a dangerous situation. Rabin indicated to Kissinger in private, after the meeting, that he would do his best to convince the cabinet. But his ability to deliver was circumscribed by Peres, who had argued in the larger meeting that, contrary to Kissinger's assessment, he believed Israel would be in a stronger strategic position if it did not accept Sadat's last, best offer.

They met again on Wednesday morning before Rabin took Sadat's offer to the cabinet. Kissinger read Sadat's letter to Ford out loud. Allon took umbrage at the idea that Sadat should blame Israel. He had been given a negative assessment by Israel's lawyers of Sadat's formula on non-use of force and he now dismissed it as worthless, as even less than the Egyptians had already agreed to in the Sinai I Agreement. Rabin turned negative too. "What he wants is the passes and the oil fields for practically nothing, with no commitment beyond one year and automatic renewal of the UN."

Kissinger was nonplussed. He had been under the impression that an Egyptian commitment to non-use of force was important to the Israelis; it may not have been non-belligerency, but to dismiss it as "practically nothing" was denigrating Kissinger's efforts, not just Sadat's offer. To have invested American prestige in the pursuit of something that the Israelis could so easily dismiss was a humiliation. He warned them again that Israel might enjoy a propaganda victory for a few months, but the pressures from the international community would grow and the United States would not be able to help. "If you think you can score points with the difference between non-belligerency and non-use of force, you're smoking pot!" he said in exasperation. He forecast a massive loss of American influence in the region. Israel, he feared, had talked itself into a position in which anything short of non-belligerency would be viewed as a defeat.

Rabin protested, saying that was not true, but Kissinger had had enough. He said he had to leave.

While Kissinger flew to Riyadh to consult with King Faisal, the Israeli cabinet deliberated for ten hours. It decided to stick with Allon's formula on non-use of force and reject Sadat's counterproposal. Even though Sadat had committed to remove any time element from the duration of the agreement, the cabinet still wanted an Egyptian commitment to a specific number of years. In return, however, the cabinet made what it regarded as a concession: Israel would withdraw to the middle of the passes, Egyptian forces would move to Israel's current line, and the area between there and the new Israeli line would be a demilitarized UN zone; Egypt would control the oil fields, but it would be in an enclave surrounded by Israeli forces. For half non-belligerency (i.e., non-use of force), Israel was now offering half the passes.

Rabin and his team reported all this to Kissinger the next morning, Thursday, March 20. Kissinger asked for a five-minute break to consult with his team. When he returned thirty minutes later, a clinical coolness masked his white-hot anger. He asked all the Israeli aides to leave the room. He spoke gravely to the seven Israeli principals that remained.* He said he considered the cabinet's pronouncements as a deliberate, strategic decision "probably to go to war this year, to have a confrontation with the Arab states . . . and with the United States." He pointed out that there was not the slightest attempt to deal with any of the points he had made over many months. It was obvious that Egypt would reject the counteroffer and that the cabinet knew this. He reviewed the history of the negotiations and delivered a harsh conclusion: "The objective result is that we were misled."

He then took up a paper that contained talking points cleared by Ford and read them out slowly. They repeated all the terrible things that would now befall the United States and Israel, and not just in the Middle East. "We are being asked to finance a stalemate threatening our interests in all parts of the world," it concluded.

Then came the hammer: "Failure of these negotiations will require an overall *reassessment* of the policies of the United States that have brought us to this point [emphasis added]." Kissinger had introduced the R-word. His tone now changed from anger to sorrow. He enumerated all the positive elements in the Egyptian offer, concluding that "we will look back with nostalgia on the period when Egypt was willing to make these concessions and Saudi Arabia was offering to support our efforts." He tried to convince the Israelis again that the quid pro quo was not in the details they were endlessly obsessing about, but rather in "the process," in the willingness of the Arabs to let the United States run it, and "in our ability to shield you from international pressures."

He warned them that the United States would not relinquish its relations with the Arab states because that was an American interest. But he promised them that he would not say anything critical: "There will be no public confrontation." Referring to himself as a friend "who has carried out meticulously every commitment to you," he complained that Israel had not fulfilled its part of their joint strategy, saying, "Israel has taken a decision of a grave nature, and there will be serious consequences."

As far as I am aware, this unvarnished exchange is unique in the annals of the U.S.-Israeli relationship. Whatever the Israeli press and the protesters might say about Kissinger, he had proved himself time and again to be a good friend

---

* Rabin, Allon, Peres, Gur, Dinitz, Rabin's director general Mordechai Gazit, and the director general of the foreign ministry, Avraham Kidron.

of Israel. To him, Israel's leadership had now crossed a red line, acting in a way that would damage not just Israel's interests but the interests of the United States. As secretary of state, he would not countenance it.

Was Kissinger threatening "serious consequences" to jolt the Israelis out of their preoccupation with their domestic politics in a last-minute attempt to generate concessions from them that would help him rescue a breakthrough from the jaws of failure? Rabin and Allon thought so. Rabin conceded that Kissinger had always said non-belligerency could not be achieved and now offered to try to resolve the formula in Sadat's favor. But Kissinger had in fact given up. "The formulation is impossible, the line is impossible, the duration is impossible," he said.

Allon said it was still possible to improve the wording. Kissinger was exasperated: "Yigal, you're talking about a negotiation and I'm talking about a termination." Allon ignored him and spoke again about the duration of the agreement and then suggested they talk about the line "so we can see what we can get." Kissinger wasn't interested.

Nor was Rabin. He said he was willing to give on the political requirements but "on the line, very little." Kissinger had convinced him that it was over. He had been prepared to withdraw to the middle of the passes and relinquish the oil fields, he said, but he didn't feel he was getting enough in return to go any further than that. Nevertheless, since Rabin had already called for another cabinet meeting, Kissinger decided to wait around for it.

And then something strange happened. Claiming the Israelis had offered it all along, Gur suggested that in return for keeping the Israeli early warning station at Um Hashiba, just west of the Gidi Pass, Egypt could have a similar station on a ridge at the western end of the passes in what would be the UN buffer zone. This piqued Kissinger's interest. Reversing course, he asked Allon for his new formula on non-use of force, and together they started tinkering with the language. Since the cabinet members were waiting outside, Rabin adjourned the meeting and delegated Gazit and Dinitz to work with Sisco and Saunders on the language.

Notwithstanding everything Kissinger had just said about ending the negotiations, he had shown a willingness to reopen them. He was repeating the edge-of-precipice ploy he had used successfully in the Israeli-Syrian negotiations.

The wielding of his sledgehammer had only limited impact on the cabinet, however. The Israelis dropped any reference to what might look like non-belligerency, but they did not change their offer of a vague withdrawal to the middle of the passes, nor the arrangements for the oil fields in which the Egyptians would have to operate an enclave within Israeli lines. Allon was convinced that Sadat would accept the line in the middle of the passes "because it's really a great concession." Kissinger thought he was on another planet and told him so. "It's a great Israeli concession in terms of the Israeli domestic debate!" he said.

Thursday, March 20, 1975, Aswan. Kissinger reported to Ford en route to Aswan that he had made modest progress with the Israelis, but he doubted Sadat would see enough in it to continue the negotiations. Yet he had not given up. Nor had Sadat. Although his patience for more concessions to the Israelis who "want everything" was clearly limited, he said he wanted to help Kissinger. Accordingly, he was willing to work with Israel's changes on the non-use of force language, but that concession made him more adamant about the line of withdrawal. He rejected the idea that the Israelis would remain in the middle of the passes, insisting that nothing short of Israel's evacuation of the passes in favor of the UN would suffice. He also rejected the Israeli proposal for Egyptian and Israeli warning stations in the UN buffer zone unless Israel withdrew entirely from the passes.*

Kissinger told Sadat that he now thought he had the bare outlines of an agreement, but the critical issue that remained was Sadat's requirement that Israel evacuate the passes. If he could move the Israelis on that, he told Sadat, "an agreement could be written quite quickly." It was a mirage. Kissinger should have known by then that he could not get Sadat the passes without an Egyptian commitment to non-belligerency, and no amount of wishful thinking was going to change that.

Friday, March 21, 1975, Jerusalem. Up to this point, Kissinger had viewed Rabin as his partner in the effort to move the Israeli cabinet. After the last go-around, he reported to Ford that Rabin "has acted extremely well, and he himself wants an agreement." He had underestimated Rabin's determination to stick to his requirements and overestimated his willingness to persuade his cabinet. Having conceded on non-belligerency, he was not about to give up all the passes; halfway was his limit, since he believed Sadat had only met him halfway by agreeing to non-use of force. It was the mirror image of the Egyptian position: having conceded non-use of force, Sadat was not willing to give up half the passes. It was an unbridgeable gap, and Rabin told Kissinger so when he arrived back in Israel.

---

* Sadat also wanted the Egyptian line moved beyond the existing Israeli line, and clear access to the oil fields by putting the road from Suez under UN control. He was willing to accede to Kissinger's request that he assure Israel in strict secrecy that in the event Syria attacked Israel, Egypt would not support Syria.

Perhaps it was because he had just spent eight hours with the Knesset Foreign Affairs and Defense Committee, during which the members had grilled him on how he could have conceded even half the passes, but Rabin told Kissinger he was losing his credibility. Moving to the large map on the wall, he pointed out the Egyptian advance that Sadat was now proposing, which went well beyond the Israeli line that he had been willing to concede. Then, turning to Kissinger, he said, "To me, it is totally unacceptable, and I will do my best not to recommend it to the cabinet because I believe that Israel cannot, in present circumstances, in return for what is offered, withdraw from the passes, and the oil fields, and accept movement forward of [the Egyptian forces'] line."

"We will not participate in any further negotiations between Egypt and Israel," Kissinger said glumly.

In a bizarre twist, Rabin then asked Gur to show Kissinger the map they had prepared of the line of Israeli withdrawal.* Kissinger had been waiting six months for such a map. Had he received it earlier in these negotiations, he could have tried to work his magic in a concrete way, just as he had done with the earlier disengagement agreements. But Rabin's purpose was not to restart the negotiations; rather, he wanted to show how far he had been prepared to go. He was laying the groundwork for the blame game to come. Indeed, immediately after this meeting, he instructed Dinitz to fly to Washington to get there no later than Kissinger "in order to counter his forthcoming criticism of Israel."

Even though it was Friday evening—the beginning of the Sabbath, during which God commanded no work be done—Rabin convened his cabinet in an extraordinary session. Toward the end of another marathon sitting, a letter arrived for Rabin from President Ford. When he drafted this letter for the president, Kissinger had not expected the cabinet to meet on Shabbat. As soon as he found out, he tried first to get Scowcroft, and then Dinitz, to intercept it. Too late. Rabin received it while he was sitting with his cabinet colleagues and immediately read it aloud to them:

> I am writing to convey my deep disappointment over the position taken by Israel during the course of the negotiations. . . . Secretary Kissinger's mission, which your government strongly encouraged, involved the vital interests of the United States in the area. The failure to achieve an agreement is bound to have far-reaching effects in the area and on our relations.
>
> I have directed an immediate reassessment of U.S. policy in the area,

---

* The line went from Bardawil on the Mediterranean to Ras Sudar on the Red Sea, cutting the Gidi and Mitla Passes in half. It was approximately forty kilometers east of the current Israeli line.

including our relations with Israel, with a view to assuring that the overall interests of America in the Middle East and globally will be protected.

You will be informed of our decisions.

The peremptory tone and the threat of a "reassessment" of relations with Israel shook the cabinet ministers. There was no doubt that Ford and Kissinger intended to blame Israel for the breakdown and that relations with the United States, Israel's only defender in international forums and the underwriter of the Jewish state's security, were about to deteriorate, perhaps dramatically. But that specter was not enough to moderate any of the cabinet members' positions. Indeed, it had the opposite effect, convincing most of the ministers to dig in their heels—the default reaction of a small power when faced with a threat to what it perceives as its vital interests by its superpower patron.

That was a blind spot for Kissinger, who was steeped in the hierarchy of power in which, historically, smaller states had no choice but to give way to the demands of the great powers. He had underestimated Israel's will to resist. Later, he would admit that the timing of the letter was unfortunate because it looked like a crude act of pressure.

Kissinger reported to Ford that all three of the triumvirate, shaken by his letter, seemed now to want an agreement but could not find a way out of the domestic hole they had dug for themselves. By convincing Israeli public opinion of the vital necessity of non-belligerency if the passes and oil fields were to be ceded back to Egypt, he explained, they had painted themselves into a corner.

Saturday, March 22, 1975, Masada. Since it was Shabbat, Kissinger gave Rabin the day to think it over before they met again in the evening. In the meantime, he took Nancy to the Dead Sea redoubt of Masada, the symbol of Israeli martyrdom, for a guided tour by Yigael Yadin, Israel's preeminent archaeologist. He also canvassed Sadat by cable to see if he had any new suggestions to break the deadlock, but he knew from his earlier experience that there was no chance Sadat would make more concessions in the face of none from Israel. A reflection of Kissinger's mood can be seen in the concluding, melodramatic sentence of that day's report to Ford. "We may be witnessing the twilight of democracy," wrote Kissinger.

Sadat's response, dictated to Fahmy, was that there was no change in the Egyptian position and therefore if Kissinger felt there was no chance of progress, he should return directly to Washington. He added that the failure would have a deleterious impact in the Arab world and would strike an "irrevocable

While the Israeli cabinet debated Sadat's last, best offer in a rare Shabbat session on March 22, 1975, Kissinger toured Masada with Yigael Yadin, Israel's foremost archaeologist. When Kissinger heard from Rabin that the cabinet had rejected his requirements, he likened it to what had happened at Masada 1,900 years earlier, noting that it was tragic "to see a people dooming themselves to a course of unbelievable peril for reasons that are heroic, stubborn—and disastrous." Israel's leaders were unmoved.

and fatal blow to the step-by-step process." Egypt's new course would be a return to Geneva, a position Fahmy reiterated publicly a day later.

The American and Israeli core teams assembled for the last time at 10:35 p.m. in Rabin's office. The mood was somber as they coordinated the announcement of the shuttle's suspension. Each side solemnly committed not to start a public dispute even though they all knew there was no real prospect of containing the fallout once the press caught on to a crisis in U.S-Israeli relations. Indeed, while they were meeting, someone on the Israeli side was already leaking the president's letter to the Israeli press, a move that would enrage Ford. Someone else, probably in Peres's office, was preparing a dossier of the minutes of all the meetings with Kissinger to hand over to Matti Golan, the diplomatic correspondent for the Israeli daily *Haaretz*.

Allon wanted to talk about how to restart the process after a hiatus. "There will not be another American initiative in the area in the near future, and I think your planning should assume this," said Kissinger. "You have effectively destroyed by this decision a year and a half of American policy, from which certain consequences will flow," he threatened, adding for good measure: "We will not oppose resumption of the Geneva Conference."

Rabin said he understood.

Kissinger wanted them to know that they had let him down as partners in a strategy he had designed overwhelmingly to favor Israel. The quid pro quo for them was not in Egyptian political concessions; it was rather "in enabling us to control the diplomacy and exhaust all the participants." Compared to that, he claimed, the location of the line didn't matter. Plus, in any case, he had gotten all the military elements of non-belligerency they had demanded from the Egyptians. From his point of view, the risks they would have run compared to the ones they would now run from a gang-up at Geneva constituted "a real tragedy."

Rabin, as a strategic thinker, wasn't prepared to concede the point. He argued that the Yom Kippur War had changed the strategy they had agreed on when they worked together in Washington. Then the purpose was to show the Arabs they could only attain their political objectives through Washington. Now the Egyptians had concluded that by turning to Washington they could use the United States to extract concessions from Israel, that in effect Israel had to pay for America's relationship with Egypt and the Arab world. Yes, Israel had an obligation to assist the United States, but for Israel to sacrifice security assets for the sake of that strategy was too much to ask.

Kissinger acknowledged his point. "Your position is not unreasonable. It is disastrous, but not unreasonable."

Nobody laughed.

He said that before the war his strategy had been to frustrate the Arabs, and that served Israel well. But frustrating the Arabs now would only advantage the Soviet Union. U.S. influence with them would diminish and, worst of all, events were "now out of American control." The United States could not go to Geneva without a plan, and the pressure would be inexorable to promote a plan that called for Israel to withdraw to the 1967 borders. "This is my nightmare, what I see now marching towards you. And compared to that, ten kilometers in the Sinai is trivial."

And then he delivered what he must have thought was the coup de grâce: "It is tragic to see a people dooming themselves to a course of unbelievable peril for reasons that are heroic, stubborn—and disastrous." Rabin understood that Kissinger was referring to his visit to Masada earlier in the day, the site where in 73 CE nearly a thousand Jewish Zealots chose to kill each other rather than surrender to the Romans. He was unmoved by the analogy.

They discussed what each would say to the press. Kissinger promised he would make a conciliatory departure statement at the airport. Rabin assured him they would praise his efforts. All the Israelis nodded in unison as Rabin allowed that they were sad about how things had developed. "There is no doubt about your intentions, about what you sought to achieve, and we are very grateful to you," said Rabin as he gracefully concluded the meeting.

Peres escorted Kissinger down to his motorcade and the awaiting press. On the landing, choking back tears, Peres sought to assure him that this out-

A dejected Henry Kissinger announces the failure of his shuttle diplomacy in farewell remarks at Tel Aviv's Ben Gurion Airport on March 23, 1975. As he declared that "we have no other goal except to enable the young people in this area to grow up without the fear of war," he choked up. So too did members of the traveling press.

come was not what he had intended. Kissinger said he believed him, but to this day he holds Peres responsible for thwarting the deal.

There were quite a few tears shed in the next twenty-four hours. To avoid the appearance of a rupture in relations, Rabin bid farewell to Kissinger at the airport the next morning. They had an emotional meeting there as Rabin explained how deeply he regretted the failure of Kissinger's mission and reassured him that the journey was not over. He wanted Kissinger to understand that he had not taken the decision lightly. He felt a responsibility for every soldier in the IDF; he had both a son and a son-in-law serving on the front lines in Sinai. Yet he felt Israel had no choice but to reject the agreement in its current form, knowing the consequences for U.S.-Israeli relations.

They both spoke to the press on the tarmac next to Kissinger's plane. As Kissinger declared that "we have no other goal except to enable the young people in this area to grow up without the fear of war," he choked up. Rabin notes in his memoir that he observed at that moment the inner turmoil that Kissinger was experiencing "as an American and a Jew." Marvin Kalb recalls that he and others in the traveling press were also crying.

Kissinger had reassured Rabin and his colleagues that there would be no blame game and that he would remain positive in his remarks to the press. However, while Rabin watched Air Force Two become a tiny speck in the sky, "this remarkable man," as he referred to Kissinger, wasted little time backgrounding the traveling press. He told them that there was no choice now but to go to Geneva and decried the shortsightedness of Israel's leaders. He was reported in the Israeli press to have disparaged Rabin as a small man, intimidated by Peres; Allon as lacking strength and imagination; and Peres as a pseudo-hawk who lived in Dayan's shadow. Rabin heard that Kissinger had also told the press that his hard line had caused Israel once again to miss an opportunity. Ford's letter to Rabin announcing the "reassessment" appeared in the Israeli press on the same day. The battle for American public opinion had already begun.

This time, Kissinger's tried-and-true tactics failed him. Part of the explanation lies in the lack of urgency felt by Rabin and Sadat, especially in comparison to Kissinger's own almost desperate need for a breakthrough. He was a victim of his own success in separating the armies in Sinai and on the Golan, which had relieved the pressure on Israel and the Arabs alike to bring the troops home. Now facing a severe backlash in the Arab world if he broke with them, Sadat hesitated to make the political concessions that Rabin regarded as the sine qua non for relinquishing strategic assets.

Rabin too was a reluctant partner to the deal, refusing to make the territorial concessions that Sadat required, fearing the collapse of his government and a leadership challenge from Peres if he conceded. A modest second agreement in Sinai therefore held little attraction for the leaders on either side. It is a maxim of any negotiation that the United States cannot succeed if it wants the deal more than the parties themselves, and that has especially been the case in the Middle East. That was the reality Kissinger now confronted, and it robbed him of that precious diplomatic commodity, leverage.

The Israelis had become inured to his doomsday threats too. Those seemed now to have more to do with America's standing in the world than with Israel's immediate situation. The collapse of South Vietnam and the apparent weakness of the American presidency had rendered the United States a less credible guarantor of Israel's security, which made it less necessary to take its concerns into account.

The threat of recourse to Geneva also had little impact on the Israelis. They believed they could tie everybody up in procedural arguments over Palestinian participation and exploit inter-Arab tensions and superpower rivalries to avoid the imposed settlement Kissinger thought would be the ultimate result. Rabin knew Kissinger well enough to be certain that he had zero interest in going to Geneva anyway because it would advantage the Soviet Union at America's expense. In Jerusalem, his threat was therefore viewed as an empty one.

It's unclear whether Kissinger's deployment of threatening letters from Nixon in the earlier negotiations had any measurable impact on Israeli calculations, but those from Ford were clearly counterproductive. The Israelis believed that Kissinger was the author and the president was merely affixing his signature. They underestimated Ford's personal interest in a successful outcome, and the intensity of his feelings when he believed he was being played with, or worse, ignored. But in this negotiation, his threats would only serve to encourage Israeli obduracy.

Withholding arms supplies was the one source of leverage that should have worked, especially on Rabin, who was preoccupied with rebuilding Israel's military capabilities and making sure Israel was never again as vulnerable as it had been in the early stages of the Yom Kippur War. However, at that particular moment, Israel's arsenal was full because of Kissinger's resupply largesse and Ford's agreement to fulfill Rabin's emergency list. All the other arms requests involved longer-term requirements that could wait. Besides, Israel had its not-so-secret weapon of broad, bipartisan congressional support that it could deploy in a crunch—and was now preparing to do so.

Kissinger's influence on Sadat was also more limited this time around. He had been unable to deliver on his promise of arms supplies to the point where his renewed promises had lost their credibility. Although he made three side trips to Damascus on this shuttle, Kissinger could not alleviate Sadat's Syrian problem because he could not offer Assad the one thing he required to acquiesce in Sadat's deal with Israel: a second agreement of his own.

With Syria, however, Kissinger underestimated Assad's interest in making a second agreement with Israel. He was focused on what he considered the impossibility of persuading Israel to make another limited withdrawal on what was left of the Israeli-controlled Golan Heights, especially because it would have involved uprooting settlements. He was having enough difficulty extracting territory from the Israelis in the vast Sinai Peninsula, where the only settlers were nomadic Bedouin tribesmen. His decision to avoid compounding his problems was understandable if unhelpful to his immediate objective.

And yet, each time he turned up in Damascus on this shuttle, he was surprised by Assad's responses to his purposeful prevarications. The man was no fool. He knew Sadat intended to go his own way and America's interest lay in helping him get there. He lacked the ability to block the Egyptians, but he could use his ability to impede their agreement to secure his own deal and, like Sadat, build Syria's relations with the United States. Assad repeatedly made it clear that he was ready to follow Sadat into the American camp, to the point where he was even willing to state that if peace with Israel was the price, Syria was ready to pay it.

What Kissinger revealed in these negotiations was his innate caution. Time and again, when he would explain to Rabin that Sadat would not agree to nonbelligerency in exchange for the passes and oil fields, Rabin or Peres would contemplate taking "the big step." But Kissinger was always quick to dismiss the idea. El-Gamasy too gave him an opening when he laid out Egypt's map of its preferred military lines at the start of these negotiations. The Egyptian general conceded that the 1967 lines were not an ideal defense line for Israel and that it would be better off with the El-Arish–Ras Muhammed line that he was proposing. At that moment, Kissinger might have resurrected the concept that he and Nixon had floated in their ill-fated conversations with Hafez Ismail, Sadat's national security adviser, in February 1973: the idea of Israel conceding Egyptian sovereignty over all of Sinai in return for Egypt accepting Israeli security positions there. Recall that Ismail had been ready to accept that idea before the war; el-Gamasy was offering it again, in Sadat's presence, after the war.

Perhaps Kissinger judged that Rabin was in too weak a position politically to sustain such a sweeping withdrawal in the Sinai, which Rabin repeatedly raised. It was the same Rabin, however, in March 1993, on his first visit to Clinton's White House, who offered to withdraw fully from the Golan Heights if Israel's peace and security requirements were met.

In both cases, Rabin was willing to take calculated risks for peace as long as he received real commitments to peace from his Arab interlocutors in return. Kissinger was not. His caution and skepticism had created a design problem with his step-by-step diplomacy. His gradualist approach was well suited to the military disengagements that had been so necessary after the war. But for such diplomacy to succeed beyond that, it needed to address the political dimensions of the conflict too. Otherwise, the Israelis would rightly conclude that all it involved was "salami tactics" in which Israel gave up more slices of territory in return for a weakening of its defense lines. The original bargain in UNSC Resolution 242 was "territory for peace," but because Kissinger looked at peace with a jaundiced eye, he underestimated its value to the Israelis and its ability to inspire even the most cynical of Arab leaders.

16

Reassessment

In our foreign involvement, we have oscillated between exuberance
and exhaustion, between crusading and retreats into self-doubt.

—Henry Kissinger, speech to the American Society
of Newspaper Editors, April 1975

The crestfallen diplomat returned to a disconsolate Washington, his concern about the stability of the order he was striving so hard to consolidate
heightened by the assassination on March 25, 1975, of King Faisal, one of its
pillars.

The sources of gloom were cataloged by James "Scotty" Reston, the highly
respected *New York Times* columnist: "South Vietnam has collapsed . . . ;
Henry Kissinger's latest peace mission to the Middle East has failed; one of
the most moderate and powerful figures in the Arab world, King Faisal of
Saudi Arabia, has been murdered; and Europe . . . has found its Mediterranean
flank, from Portugal to Greece and Turkey, in disarray." *Newsweek*, in contrast
to its Henry as Superman cover only ten months earlier, now portrayed him as
a hapless Gulliver in Lilliput, "bedeviled by foreign policy crises on all sides."
A White House cabal, led by Chief of Staff Donald Rumsfeld, was doing its
best to undermine him. For the first time since entering the White House in
1969, there were calls for his resignation. Kissinger remembers it as "a very
painful time."

Notwithstanding his melancholy mood, Kissinger moved furiously to put
the pieces in place to do battle with Israel and the American Jewish community.
He was encouraged in his purpose by President Ford, who took the setback
to his foreign policy personally. Ford's approach to Israel was not weighed
down by the complexity of Kissinger's diplomatic calculations. He was, in Kis-

singer's view, "a straight-laced midwesterner." Although he admired Israel and had long supported it in Congress, as president he viewed the relationship in straightforward terms: "If we gave Israel an ample supply of economic aid and weapons, she would feel strong and confident, more flexible and more willing to discuss a lasting peace."

Following that transactional logic, Ford had provided Rabin with a generous down payment of arms during Rabin's first meeting with him in September 1974; the president had expected reciprocation and believed Rabin had promised it. Now he was convinced he had been misled. In his memoirs he remembers being "mad as hell." In an interview with Hearst Newspapers on March 27, 1975, he depicted Israel as "inflexible."* Subsequently, he would commit to Israel's "survival" but purposely avoid the usual commitment to its "security," since he did not want to imply that the United States supported Israel's territorial conquests. All of that fueled a furor in the pro-Israel community.

Kissinger reinforced Ford's instincts. The day after his return, he told Ford that the Israelis had behaved outrageously. "To have received a letter from you and not to change one iota is an indignity to the United States," he said. He did it again two days later, during Ford's morning briefing, decrying a situation in which "three million Israelis" were running American foreign policy and ruining trade relations with the Soviet Union. He praised Ford's interview but warned him, "They will attack you." Ford said he expected it but, he admitted, "I kind of enjoy a fight when I know I'm right."

Both Ford and Kissinger were surprised and encouraged in their confrontational approach by the response from the congressional leadership when they briefed them on March 24. Kissinger explained that he had designed the process to benefit Israel and yet its leadership had been unwilling to concede "a few kilometers" to help the United States manage that process. He emphasized that he had told the Israelis on twenty-four occasions that nonbelligerency was unachievable.† On leaving the White House, the leadership praised Kissinger's diplomacy to the press gaggle outside.‡ Returning to Capi-

---

* Ford's public remarks were made less than twenty-four hours after Kissinger returned from Israel. In an interview with William Randolph Hearst Jr. for the Hearst Newspapers he said, "If [the Israelis] had been a bit more flexible . . . I think in the longer run it would have been the best insurance for peace." His remarks ended up as a banner headline on the front page above the fold of *The New York Times*. See Bernard Gwertzman, "Ford Says Israel Lacked Flexibility in the Negotiations," *New York Times*, March 28, 1975.

† Kissinger knew it was twenty-four times because, in preparation for the public relations battle, he had Peter Rodman compile a list of the occasions from his notes.

‡ Mike Mansfield, the venerable Democratic Senate majority leader, and John C. Stennis, the Democratic chairman of the Senate Armed Services Committee, both expressed strong support for the reassessment. Carl Albert, the Democratic Speaker of the House, and Hugh Scott, the Republican Senate minority leader, went along too, though less vociferously. In the meeting, Mansfield criticized the extreme rigidity of the Israelis and wondered whether they had a death

tol Hill, they quickly introduced a Senate resolution that fully endorsed the administration's policy, which passed unanimously by voice vote.

Ford and Kissinger read this as a green light to proceed with their confrontation. But they would soon discover that while the congressional leadership might have been momentarily with them, the rank and file were not. That was partly a function of effective advocacy by AIPAC—the Israel lobby—which tapped Senator Jacob Javits to lead the effort. Javits was a well-respected liberal Jewish Republican from New York who had crossed the aisle to co-sponsor the 1973 War Powers Act and vote against aid to Cambodia and Vietnam. He was joined in his opposition to the reassessment by pro-Israel stalwart Scoop Jackson, whose chief aide, Richard Perle, orchestrated a network of like-minded staffers.[*]

AIPAC's efforts in this fight were aided by overwhelming public support for Israel, which had come to be seen as the underdog in the wake of the deeply unpopular Arab oil embargo. In early April, pollster Lou Harris found that support for Israel had surged from 39 percent in 1973 to 52 percent at the time of the reassessment; only 7 percent sided with the Arabs. A strong majority of 66 percent of Americans favored sending Israel what it needed by way of military hardware. And a similarly strong majority of 64 percent opposed stopping military aid to Israel in order to secure oil supplies.

That did not deter Kissinger. He wasted no time in outlining to Ford the next steps: issue immediately a National Security Study Memorandum ordering the reassessment;[†] cancel upcoming visits to Washington by Peres, as well as an Israeli military delegation that was supposed to discuss a timeline for F-15 deliveries; delay the delivery of Lance missiles and laser-guided bombs (LGBs); and instruct each government department to curtail the privileged access that Israeli officials had come to enjoy.

On the afternoon of March 28, Ford conveyed these steps to Secretary of Defense James Schlesinger, CIA director William Colby, Treasury Secretary William Simon, and Joint Chiefs chairman George S. Brown at a National Security Council meeting. The reassessment was to be concluded by early May, the president directed. It was explicitly to include a review of Israel's

---

wish. Stennis remarked that "the trouble is the Israelis just assume we will be supporting them no matter what." See Memo for the Files, Ford's Meeting with Kissinger and Congressional Leadership, March 24, 1975, FRUS 1969–1976:26, Doc. 160.

[*] The network included R. James Woolsey from the Senate Armed Services Committee, Richard Gilmore from Senator Hubert Humphrey's staff, Alan Platt from Senator Edmund Muskie's staff, and Tom Dine from Senator Frank Church's staff.

[†] National Security Study Memorandum 220 was issued on March 26, 1975, calling for "a study of U.S. interests, objectives, strategy and policy in the Middle East in the light of recent developments." It was to address bilateral relations with the principal countries in the region and "the diplomacy of settlement of the Arab-Israeli conflict." Joe Sisco was appointed chairman of an NSC Ad Hoc Group, which was expected to report within three weeks. See National Security Study Memorandum 220, March 26, 1975, FRUS 1969–1975:26, Doc. 163.

request for $1.8 billion in military assistance and $700 million in economic assistance for the fiscal year beginning on October 1, 1975.

Schlesinger suggested the new policy be defined as one of "dignified aloofness." The Israelis had to understand that there were consequences for their behavior. Taking a sideswipe at Kissinger, he said, "There should not be full policy coordination with Israel as in the past." The Pentagon, he argued, had badly overestimated the number of Soviet arms that had been shipped to Egypt after the war. "The military balance from the Israeli standpoint is much better," he noted, and therefore it was unnecessary to be concerned that delaying arms deliveries would tip the balance against Israel.

Ford liked the concept of aloofness. He ordered Simon to apply it to the Joint Economic Committee (JEC) the Treasury secretary had recently established with his Israeli counterpart, Finance Minister Yehoshua Rabinowitz, to assess Israel's need for additional economic assistance. Agreeing with Schlesinger, Ford wanted to restrict the points of contact with Israeli officials in government departments. "Channelize them," he ordered. "The proper relationship," Ford explained, "should be business-like but arms-length and aloof."

Kissinger's punitive list was swiftly implemented. Even intelligence cooperation was attenuated. Kissinger added a personal element by ordering the removal of the direct hotline between Dinitz's office and his own; henceforth Dinitz was told to conduct his business through Larry Eagleburger, the executive assistant to the secretary of state. Dinitz remembers this act as akin to "school children carrying a grudge at each other." Kissinger recalled the U.S. ambassadors to Israel, Egypt, Syria, and Jordan for consultations and convoked a meeting with outside experts—the "wise men"—among them George Ball, a former under secretary of state and Vietnam war critic who had become the most high-profile advocate of an imposed solution on Israel.[*]

Dinitz wasted no time in rallying his troops to make the case that Israel had been flexible but the Egyptians weren't willing to make peace. An emergency meeting was called in New York City, attended by seven hundred Jewish leaders. The Jewish Labor Committee mobilized the American unions that were staunch supporters of Israel. The union giant George Meany, head of the AFL-CIO, declared that the American labor movement was with Israel in its efforts to resist "extermination." Jewish war veterans addressed gatherings of the American Legion. Jewish students were mobilized on campus.

---

[*] The experts included Dean Rusk, Cyrus Vance, George Shultz, Averell Harriman, Robert McNamara, David Rockefeller, and Bill Scranton (who had famously called for a more "even-handed" policy as envoy to the Middle East at the outset of the Nixon administration). That consultation led to a rare rebuke by Max Fisher, who reported that the Jewish community was up in arms because the experts were all "pro-Arab." Kissinger tried to make up for that by meeting subsequently with Arthur Goldberg and Eugene Rostow, but the damage was done.

Rabin dispatched Dayan, Eban, and Chaim Herzog, Israel's most articulate spokesmen, to make the case to UJA meetings, Jewish Federation gatherings, and AIPAC audiences, as well as at twenty-one campus rallies across the country.*

At first, fearing a head-on confrontation with the president, the Jewish leadership tried to play down the rift. AIPAC called it "temporary differences of opinion" and promoted Kissinger's public statement of support for Israel's survival and his assertion that "punishment of a friend cannot be the purpose of national policy."

On March 27, Max Fisher, still the doyen of the American Jewish community and a longtime Republican friend of the president's from his home state of Michigan, met with Ford and Kissinger in the Oval Office. Ford repeated his charge that Rabin and Allon had misled him, and said that "if Israel has no respect for our interests, then we must act alone." He had expected Israel to show more understanding for America's difficulties and be more willing to facilitate its policy goals. Military aid would now be measured in terms of American self-interest, said the president. Fisher promised to take his message privately to Rabin.

Fisher returned with a conciliatory message from Rabin. He met again with Ford and Kissinger on April 9. Rabin, he reported, was contrite. He admitted to Fisher that he might have been too confident in expressing a willingness to be flexible, and too public early on in his offer of the passes and oil fields. He had not intended to mislead Ford and he was not insensitive to America's wider interests. While Rabin did not want to proceed into negotiations with the reassessment hanging over Israel's head, he believed he had more room for movement now because his domestic position had been strengthened. He said he was ready to go to Geneva, but he preferred that Kissinger resume his step-by-step diplomacy and was working with Peres and Allon to develop more concrete steps.

This conciliatory message from Rabin had been complemented a week earlier by Sadat's surprise announcement that he planned to go ahead with the reopening of the Suez Canal on June 5, the eighth anniversary of the Six-Day War.

Here were the first positive indications that, contrary to Kissinger's worst fears, Sadat and Rabin were still looking to Washington to take the lead

---

* Eban delivered a typically loquacious speech to the annual AIPAC Policy Conference in April in which he argued that since Israel had experienced the "solitude of sacrifice" in putting its soldiers' lives on the line, it should have sole responsibility for deciding its security requirements. He called on the audience of pro-Israel activists "to bring your influence in massive strength to bear to mend the injured texture of the American-Israel dialogue." See "The Mysterious Texture of U.S.-Israel Relations," *Near East Report* 19, no. 17 (April 23, 1975): 75.

Max Fisher, a leader of the American Jewish community and a confidant of Republican presidents, meets President Ford in the Oval Office on March 27, 1975, in the midst of the "reassessment."

in peacemaking. Kissinger understood the signals, but he was in no hurry, because his softening-up process had just begun.

He had not included in his calculus the political fallout for Ford. But Max Fisher did. In a coda to the message he carried from Israel, Fisher warned Ford of the negative political consequences for his reelection bid if he were perceived in the Jewish community to be separating the United States from Israel. That should have indicated to Kissinger that the longer he dragged out the reassessment, the more politically exposed his president would become.

When whipped up by Israeli spokesmen and American politicians, the organized American Jewish community becomes like a car with an accelerator and no brakes. For example, in a March 31 meeting with Jewish intellectuals, Kissinger invoked his experience in the Holocaust to explain to American Jews that he could not possibly be anti-Israel. This was ferociously thrown back in his face through full-page press advertisements on Holocaust Memorial Day (April 8, 1975), paid for by the UJA. Appearing in *The New York Times* and the *New York Post*, they called on Jews to speak out against Kissinger's reassessment as if it threatened another Holocaust: "The price of silence was the Warsaw Ghetto. Bergen Belsen. Auschwitz. Dachau. Speak now, so that we never again pay the price of silence."

On Capitol Hill, a bipartisan chorus that included House Majority Leader

Tip O'Neill, Hubert Humphrey, Birch Bayh, Claude Pepper, Edward Kennedy, Frank Church, and Dale Bumpers joined Javits and Jackson. Senate Minority Leader Hugh Scott, who had supported Kissinger and Ford at the outset of this donnybrook, quickly buckled under the pressure. Jesse Helms, then a Republican congressman, called for Kissinger's resignation. A bevy of influential pro-Israel columnists joined these critics of reassessment, including William Safire in *The New York Times*, George Will in *The Washington Post*, and Mary McGrory in *The Washington Star*.

Nevertheless, Kissinger was not willing to back down. His anger was fueled by his conviction that the Israelis had intentionally humiliated him. The backing of his president boosted his confidence, and he mistakenly believed he was untouchable because he was Jewish. At one point in April, Sisco began to get cold feet as the wrath of the Jewish community grew; he recommended that Kissinger bring the Israelis into the reassessment process. Kissinger rejected that suggestion.

As the battle grew more intense, Kissinger enlisted the help of some influential Jews. Elie Wiesel, the world's post-Holocaust Jewish conscience, offered to interview Sadat and then write an article attesting to his peaceful intentions. Nahum Goldmann, the head of the World Jewish Congress and an exponent of quiet diplomacy for Jewish causes, organized a support group of Jewish luminaries.

In his public statements, Kissinger was careful to avoid criticizing Israel directly, but that only served to buttress the charge that he was speaking out of both sides of his mouth because, in his private statements, he did not hold back. For example, in his meeting with Jewish intellectuals, who were likely to report back to Dinitz, he termed Israel's decision to reject his diplomacy "a historic disaster." He said that he and his aides had lost confidence in Israel; "we simply cannot get over it." In a closed-door meeting with the Senate Foreign Relations Committee, he accused Israel of reneging on a commitment to the success of his negotiating efforts. At the meeting of the "wise men," he said he regretted giving the Israelis so much military equipment, noted that they had shown total contempt for Ford's domestic position, and complained that they had treated him with disdain. Speaking to his State Department advisers, he charged the Israelis with a campaign of deception.

Russell Baker, the longtime satirist for *The New York Times*, captured in his "Observer" column the popular American Jewish perception of Kissinger at the time as blaming Israel for his failings. "In the Middle East, we wanted to hear that a peace agreement could be miraculously wrung out of two intractably opposed enemies, so Mr. Kissinger told us it might be possible. When the inevitable failure occurred, we did not want to hear that no miracles are possible in diplomacy, so Kissinger blamed the Israelis."

William Safire, the Nixon speechwriter turned *New York Times* columnist, accused Kissinger of being two-faced. In a scathing column, he interpreted the reassessment to mean: "Israel, not having obeyed our orders, had better watch out."

Both sides now dug in their heels. Ahead of Foreign Minister Allon's trip to Washington for consultations in mid-April, Rabin told the *Times* that Israel had no intention of softening its position or considering a new negotiating strategy until the Ford administration resumed talks on Israel's pending arms requests. This further infuriated Ford, who had already instituted the opposite linkage (i.e., there would be no talk of military assistance until Israel softened its position). His anger was compounded by an interview Rabin gave to an Israeli newspaper that appeared on the same day, in which he explained that Allon's trip to the United States was designed to rally public support for a confrontation with the administration.

"There is no country in the world . . . that has the right to send its foreign minister to engage in a public campaign of propaganda against the administration," Kissinger told Allon when they met on April 21. "It is absolutely inappropriate," he said, noting that the president "took violent exception." He warned Allon there would be long-lasting consequences. The exchange became acrimonious. Allon tried repeatedly to find a way forward, but he had nothing new to offer on the substance of Israel's positions, only on a process of U.S.-Israeli talks to send the public signal that the relationship was back on track. Kissinger insisted that the relationship would only improve when the Israelis came forward with new ideas that could advance the negotiations.

Despite his bravura performance, Kissinger was beginning to have doubts. The reassessment was unleashing the very forces he had repeatedly warned Israel about. For example, former governor John B. Connally, a Texas politician, told him that if he were advising somebody how to sweep the Midwest and Southwest, he would recommend an anti-Semitic campaign.

Sisco, Kissinger's closest Middle East policy adviser, had written him an extraordinary eyes-only, private memo recommending a strategy for isolating Israel in the United Nations and imposing a settlement on it through Security Council and General Assembly resolutions initiated by the United States. Kissinger saw that as indicative of what the Washington bureaucracy would do if he allowed it to have its way.

Nevertheless, at Kissinger's direction, the State Department initiated the reassessment process, preparing three memos under Sisco's supervision that analyzed the options that lay before them. Sisco authored the paper on a "Small Transitional Agreement"; Eilts, the U.S. ambassador in Cairo, wrote a memo on the "Outline of a Possible Medium Agreement"; and the team drafted a paper on the comprehensive solution, detailing the blueprint for a final Arab-Israeli settlement. It is clear from these memos that the State Department bureaucrats had already made up their minds that the only viable option was to reconvene Geneva, lay down an American plan for a final settlement, and impose it on Israel.

For the option of returning to the small interim agreement, Sisco proposed that Israel would give up the passes entirely and in return gain "a bit more verbally and practically from the Egyptian non-belligerency and non-use of force." However, Sisco concluded, "I do not believe we have come up with any fresh sweeteners that are sufficient to move the negotiations off dead center."

Eilts dismissed the idea of going bigger—which might have appealed to Rabin since it would give him the commitment to non-belligerency he was seeking—because Israel would have to withdraw farther east, to the El-Arish–Ras Muhammed line (he clearly was unaware of the private offer Rabin had made to Kissinger to do just that). Eilts concluded that non-belligerency would be too much for Sadat and offered little hope for the "semi-permanency" of an end to the conflict that Rabin sought. Rather than expend the energy required to secure an intermediate agreement, Eilts argued that it was preferable to go for an all-out peace agreement.

On April 3, and then again on April 8, Kissinger convened meetings with his advisers and the ambassadors he had recalled from the Middle East to discuss the options. Given the consensus that was forming in favor of Geneva and an imposed solution, both inside the State Department and among outside experts, Kissinger proceeded cautiously. Intellectually, he could not have disagreed more strongly with this approach. He had always had an aversion to Geneva as a negotiating forum because it would inevitably lead to a gang-up on Israel. The United States would then be forced either to join the consensus and beat up on a vulnerable ally or to isolate itself. In either case, the Soviets would gain the credit with the Arabs for any U.S. success in delivering Israeli concessions, while the United States would bear the blame for any lack of progress.

There was also a more personal element that was bothering Kissinger. He was filled with self-doubt and self-recrimination over the collapse of the governments in Cambodia and South Vietnam that was taking place as they deliberated the Arab-Israeli options. He feared that an attempt to impose a solution on Israel would break its back psychologically. As he confides in his memoirs, "I was haunted by the specter that I might once again be, with the best of intentions, the driving force behind another peace process that would end with the collapse of an ally . . . especially vis-à -vis an ally so closely linked with my family's fate in the Holocaust." He had imposed the Vietnam peace agreement on Saigon and now it was coming apart. Kissinger swore to himself that "if the step-by-step approach had to be abandoned and the U.S. was driven to state terms for a settlement, [he] would resign."

As we have seen, Kissinger frequently threatened to resign, but his record of resisting an imposed solution on the 1967 lines is well established. Either way, he dared not share this conviction, driven by concern for the fate of the Jewish state, with his colleagues or the president. Instead, he applied his guile and agility to the challenge of shifting the consensus back to his much-preferred step-by-step approach, which would also be more manageable for Israel.

To obfuscate his intentions, he made it appear to both Ford and his State Department advisers that he preferred the Geneva route. In the April 3 discussion, he dismissed the idea of a bigger interim agreement. Kenneth Keating, the U.S. ambassador to Israel, tried to lend credibility to that option by reporting that Allon had told him that Israel was ready to go well beyond the passes for non-belligerency. This is what Rabin and Peres had previously suggested Kissinger should explore, but Kissinger had ignored them. To his aides now, Kissinger was scornful. He questioned the Israelis' sanity. "If they blew up the talks for six kilometers and then go back eighty kilometers for something that's not quite non-belligerency, they must be nuts," he said.

Kissinger outlined his own version of the three options: "We can try to start the talks again, or we can go to Geneva and let nature take its course, or we can go to Geneva with an American plan." Sisco, now chary about confronting the American Jewish community, argued for a fourth option: going to Geneva only after they had secured an interim agreement.

While Sisco's option was consistent with his own thinking, Kissinger wanted to show them he was made of tougher stuff. Privately he may have been in turmoil about the fate of the Jewish state, but in this State Department forum he argued that they had an opportunity to show that the United States really stood for something. He knew the Jewish community would harass him, but that was "just the price we pay," he assured them. He ordered up further studies.

When they convened again, five days later, they dismissed the idea of resuming the effort to achieve a small interim agreement: in the consensus view, the Israelis would still demand more for the passes than Sadat could give. Additional concessions would be difficult for both sides to make because they were now publicly dug in. And there was the ever-present Syrian problem: if Kissinger pursued an interim agreement with Egypt, he would have to do one with Syria too, or risk heightening tensions that could lead to war.

When the State Department team reviewed this with Ford on April 14, Kissinger, with an assist from Eilts, then killed the idea of a larger interim agreement because Israel would insist on non-belligerency and Sadat would only give that for a total, or almost total, withdrawal.

That left the Geneva option. They all agreed that going to Geneva would be problematic unless the United States presented a comprehensive plan for peace beforehand. Kissinger had studied the State Department plan and pretended to be quite comfortable with its call for Israel to withdraw to the 1967 lines with minor border rectifications in the West Bank; his only caveat was to leave Jerusalem out of the plan for the time being.

The president enthusiastically embraced this idea. Ford acknowledged it would lead to a confrontation with the American Jewish community, but since that battle was already joined, he didn't feel he had much more to lose and judged that Congress would be with him in the last resort. On one issue, the president was adamant. "Until we get progress there will be no [administration] request for Israeli aid," he told his advisers. "If Congress tries to force it, I will veto it." Ford was proving to be much tougher in private than his mild-mannered public demeanor led people to believe.

Having put the president up to an imposed solution, however, Kissinger did not proceed with the option of developing a comprehensive plan. Instead, he substituted process for policy: he instructed Eilts and Keating to return to Cairo and Jerusalem and inform Sadat and Rabin that he was looking to them to come up with new ideas.

He gave expression to this approach in a meeting with Dinitz. He had been boycotting the Israeli ambassador, but Fisher had warned him that this was negatively impacting Kissinger's standing in the American Jewish community. In an April 8 meeting, Dinitz tried to convince him that he should resume the negotiations on an interim step. Kissinger dismissed that idea as "playing games." He outlined the three options, warning Dinitz that if Ford chose to go for the comprehensive approach, the United States would have to lay out its position on final borders, something Israel should want to avoid. With the stick now out on the table, Kissinger subtly offered a hint of the way out: if Israel were to come with a proposal for something less than non-belligerency in exchange for the passes and a narrow Egyptian connection to the oil fields, then he would be willing to consider it. But he added, nonchalantly, that he wasn't that interested because of the price Israel would demand from the United States, including tying its hands for years to come.

By now, Dinitz was all too familiar with Kissinger's methods. Notwithstanding all the talk about proceeding to Geneva with a comprehensive plan, Kissinger was actually indicating a readiness to return to the "small" interim agreement if Israel were willing to offer a little more and take a little less and seek compensation instead from the United States in terms of long-term commitments.

Kissinger tried to plant a similar seed in his conversation with Allon a week later. After the rancorous exchange in his office recounted earlier, he hosted the Israeli visitor for lunch upstairs in his dining room. There he told Allon that he believed an interim agreement was still possible if Israel left the passes and provided an unbroken link to the oil fields. He was willing to put forward an American proposal, but he needed to hear what the Israelis would require in return, other than non-belligerency, which was off the table. He insisted that new ideas needed to come from Jerusalem.

For this approach to germinate, he would have to keep the Soviets at bay, and Sadat engaged, while the Israeli ideas incubated. He arranged to meet with Gromyko on May 20 in Geneva. Ford would meet with Sadat on June 1 in Salzburg. Then Rabin would be invited to Washington on June 11. Kissinger calculated that the process would require another two months. In the meantime, he told Ford and Rockefeller, "we must maintain coolness and discipline." Though nobody seemed to notice, Kissinger was quietly shelving the reassessment.

President Ford, meanwhile, was heading in the opposite direction. On May 7, for example, he told Kissinger, "I think we would look bad if after the reassessment we kept the status quo and went back to step-by-step." Instead, Ford wanted to start "getting our ducks in line for the comprehensive approach."

Kissinger discusses the reassessment options with President Ford, Vice President Nelson Rockefeller, and Deputy National Security Adviser Brent Scowcroft on March 24, 1975, in the Oval Office. Kissinger quietly shelved the reassessment by asking Rabin and Sadat to come up with ideas that could restart the negotiations from the point where they had left off.

Having encouraged the president to move in this direction, Kissinger now had to find a way to walk him back. The meetings with Sadat and Rabin provided the means. At a National Security Council meeting on May 15, the president agreed to defer a final decision until he had conferred with them.

As Kissinger and the president prepared for their trip to Austria, the Jewish community's lobbying efforts were peaking. Kissinger had tried to lower the temperature by green-lighting the JEC meeting that Treasury Secretary Simon had wanted to convene back in March. On May 12, Simon and his Israeli counterpart, Finance Minister Rabinowitz, issued a joint statement announcing a package of economic agreements and their opposition to the Arab boycott of American companies doing business with Israel.

It was too little, too late. With AIPAC's backing, Javits and Birch Bayh, a Democrat from Indiana, had been circulating in the Senate the draft of a letter to the president. In it, they argued that any Israeli withdrawal "must be accompanied by meaningful steps towards peace with its Arab neighbors." They also called for "a level of military and economic support adequate to deter a renewal of war by Israel's neighbors" and warned that "withholding military equipment from Israel would be dangerous." The letter arrived on the White House doorstep on May 21, signed by seventy-five senators: fifty Democrats and twenty-five Republicans.[*]

The number of signatories indicated that if the president recommended a lower level of aid than Israel wanted, there were enough votes to increase the appropriation. Separately, Senator Hubert Humphrey warned that if the president did not submit his request for assistance to Israel in a timely fashion, "we will prepare one of our own." Publicly, the White House welcomed the letter as just another input into the reassessment process. Privately, however, the letter "really bugged" him, Ford admits in his memoirs. It undermined the squeeze play he and Kissinger were orchestrating to persuade Rabin to come up with "new ideas." In the president's view, it was Israel's way of showing him "who's boss."

Ford was determined not to capitulate to the pressure. But with his reelection campaign looming in 1976, both he and Kissinger knew that time was no longer on their side. Accordingly, Ford agreed to use the meetings with Sadat and Rabin to try to resurrect the option of an interim Israeli-Egyptian agreement and keep the Geneva option in his back pocket. As Kissinger remarks in his memoirs, "The reassessment had brought us back to our original judgments." In fact, Kissinger had never left them.

Ironically, the Syrians and Russians became the enablers of this decision

---

[*] An additional Democrat, Senator J. Bennett Johnston from Louisiana, signed the letter after it was transmitted, bringing the total to seventy-six senators.

because they signaled that they too were in no hurry to pursue alternatives. On the same day the letter from the seventy-six senators was sent to the White House, Assad informed the UN secretary-general that he would renew the UNDOF mandate on the Golan for another six months, relieving any military pressure on Israel. When Kissinger met with Gromyko in Geneva, they deadlocked over the question of inviting the PLO to the Geneva Conference. Nevertheless, Gromyko was content to announce after the meeting that they would meet again in July to continue their consultations. It seemed that the Russians had concluded, just like Kissinger, that Geneva was a trap in which their inability to deliver progress would be exposed. They preferred the United States take all the risks and so agreed to await the outcome of Ford's meetings with Sadat and Rabin.

Sunday, June 1, 1975, Salzburg. Ford's first meeting with Sadat took place over a lunch that Sadat hosted at Schloss Fuschl, a fifteenth-century castle built for the prince-archbishops of Salzburg on a peninsula at one end of a serene glacier lake hemmed by snowcapped mountains. During the Second World War, Hitler's foreign minister, Joachim von Ribbentrop, had appropriated the castle for his summer residence and used it for diplomatic receptions for allies of the Nazis. The irony was not lost on Kissinger.

It was President Ford's first opportunity to bathe in the limelight that Kissinger had generated by his high-flying Arab-Israeli diplomacy. Unfortunately for Ford, as he descended the ramp of Air Force One, he stumbled and fell down the last few rain-slicked steps, losing a heel from his shoe in the process. The photo of Bruno Kreisky, the Austrian chancellor, and a military aide picking him up off the tarmac went viral and became the unintended symbol of his presidency.* He stumbled again as he and Sadat emerged from their meeting at the schloss; this time he was saved from falling down a steep flight of stairs by Sadat.

In three separate conversations, Sadat gave Ford and Kissinger the "ideas" they had hoped for to restart the step-by-step process. Ford opened their first meeting by saying, "The impact of the [senators'] letter is negligible." He then expressed his disappointment in the Israelis. This was music to Sadat's ears. He viewed Ford as a weak president because he had been appointed in the wake of Watergate without a mandate in his own right (the same was true of Sadat when he succeeded Nasser). Sadat nevertheless made clear that in his view the

---

* Ford had developed a trick knee as the result of a football injury that tended to give out when he was tired. Ford notes in his memoirs that the way the late-night comedians made fun of him over this incident "helped create the public perception of me as a stumbler." See Gerald Ford, *A Time to Heal* (New York: Harper & Row, 1979), 289.

United States held all the cards because Washington gave everything to Israel, "from a loaf of bread to Phantom fighter-bombers." He said he looked to Ford to play those cards by delivering Israel.

Sadat then surprised Ford by denouncing the idea of reconvening Geneva. As if he were channeling Kissinger, he explained that the United States would have to defend Israel in that forum, and Sadat would have to insist on the PLO's inclusion, which would be opposed by Israel. It was just a recipe for further stagnation. "I want us to make progress, to make a complete peace. And I want the United States to achieve it, not the Soviet Union." As Kissinger observes in his memoirs, "Any other Middle Eastern leader would at this point have introduced some element of blackmail by threatening us with his Soviet option." But Sadat was not just any Arab leader. He made clear to Ford that he had broken irrevocably with Moscow.[*]

Ford argued that they needed to maintain the Geneva option publicly to pressure Israel to make an interim agreement possible. Sadat agreed. Sensing that they were on the same page, he reached for what he had long sought from the United States, a joint strategy that could "save the Arab world from Soviet infiltration" and "convince those idiots in Israel to come to their senses." Ford responded emphatically, "We can work together; we will work together."

Kissinger proposed resuming the negotiations from where they had left off.[†] To jump-start the process, he needed Sadat to offer more on the UNEF renewal period, on a warning station in the passes, and on the Egyptian boycott of American firms doing business with Israel. If Sadat would indicate movement on these issues, Ford could present an American proposal to the Israelis. In return, Egypt would get Israeli withdrawal to a line drawn east of the passes and land access to the oil fields. He assessed that the deal could be wrapped up in a month if these conditions were met.

They met again on the afternoon of June 2 in the Residenz, the palace of the prince-archbishops of Salzburg, which had been built in the sixteenth century, when the city had functioned as an independent religious state. Two hundred years later, Wolfgang Amadeus Mozart premiered his opera *Il Re Pastore* in its magnificent conference room.

---

[*] Sadat told Ford he was no longer interested in the Soviets' support because they had refused to supply him with replacements for the arms he expended during the war, they were encouraging the Syrians and the Palestinians to act against him, they were squeezing him economically, and now they were trying to outflank him by providing arms to Qaddafi in neighboring Libya.

[†] Sadat later revealed in a speech to the Egyptian National Assembly that at Salzburg the Americans had offered him "the whole of Sinai" for non-belligerency, but he claimed he had turned it down because he did not want to leave his Arab brothers stranded. From the transcript of the meeting, it's clear that Kissinger raised the idea but did not give Sadat a chance to turn it down—he turned it down for him. See "Excerpts from Sadat Speech on the Pact and Its Critics," *New York Times*, September 5, 1975, and Henry Tanner, "Sadat Says Soviet Is Trying to Split Arabs over Sinai," *New York Times*, September 5, 1975.

Like the envoys of old, Ford and Kissinger traversed the grand state rooms to meet Sadat in one of the high-ceilinged baroque private chambers. Surrounded by portraits of earlier inhabitants, Sadat went straight to the heart of the matter. He would agree to renew the UNEF mandate annually and commit to another year in writing. Kissinger reminded him that he had offered that in the previous negotiations and the Israelis would not see it as new. Gingerly now, he asked whether Sadat could agree to a two-year period and a one-year renewal commitment, which would provide a three-year assurance to the Israelis that the agreement would not be challenged by Egypt.

Sadat worried that Israel would insist on postponing Geneva for that period, making it difficult to manage Arab reaction. Kissinger reassured him that the United States would begin preparations for Geneva by the end of the year, regardless of Israeli objections, but implementation would have to wait until 1977, after the presidential elections in the United States. Sadat was always easily satisfied by American promises. He said that he could not put an additional two-year renewal in writing, "but we don't differ practically." He ordered Fahmy: "Work out the language with Henry."

As for the early warning station in the passes, Sadat proposed that it be

After their second meeting in Salzburg, Austria, on June 2, 1975, President Ford and President Sadat address the press who had been waiting in the rain singing "We Shall Overcome." Ford purposely put Rabin on notice by asserting that the reassessment process would come to an end with the presentation of "an American plan." In fact, there was no intention by that stage to present a plan. Instead, Kissinger was preparing to relaunch his shuttle negotiations after Sadat had given him two new cards to play.

manned by Americans, noting that this would give the Israelis a stronger guarantee against Egyptian attack than if he left Israelis there to man it themselves.
Kissinger, impressed, believed the Israelis would view this as an even better
assurance than a three-year commitment.

He suggested presenting Sadat's concessions to the Israelis as an American
proposal. He urged Sadat not to look too eager in the meantime; rather, he
should say that he was going home to think about what they had discussed.
Meanwhile, Kissinger would "get tough with Rabin."

Sadat loved the idea of conspiring with the United States. "President Ford
could adopt the posture of putting pressure on me. He could say [to the Israe-
lis] he has insisted that I modify my position," he suggested in an attempt to
be helpful. This was precisely the tactic that Kissinger had repeatedly urged
on the Israelis in earlier negotiations. Unlike them, Sadat needed no tutoring.

The meeting lasted for all of twenty minutes, including a discussion of economic aid for Egypt in which Ford committed to seeking $800 million from
Congress once the agreement was struck. Ford and Sadat went out together to
brief the rain-soaked press, who had been waiting for them patiently in the castle's courtyard, singing "We Shall Overcome" to lift their spirits. To put Rabin
on notice, Ford answered a question about the Senate letter by saying his reassessment would come to an end with the submission of "an American plan."

Wednesday, June 11, 1975, Washington, DC. Ford was now eager for the encounter with Rabin. Kissinger had told him on June 9 that his hanging tough had
produced the momentum; "I rather enjoy it," Ford responded. Kissinger
advised him to be hard on Rabin, saying, "He is smart and shy, but not all
that tough." If Rabin came across, Ford should keep him on a tight aid leash
by agreeing to only $1 billion of Israel's $2.5 billion suspended aid request. If
Rabin didn't bend, "Keep them to the level of this year," said Ford, completing
Kissinger's sentence.

Earlier, Ford had briefed the congressional leadership on his meeting with
Sadat. He told them that if he did not succeed in getting Israel to move, he
would be off to Geneva. He expected his words would get back to Rabin.

Kissinger and Rabin prepared for their first meeting since the breakdown
of negotiations eleven weeks earlier like two knights arming for a joust. To signal to Rabin that his lance was sharp, Kissinger summoned Dinitz to a debrief
on the day he returned to Washington from the Salzburg meetings. Restoring
the channel to Rabin, Kissinger confided to Dinitz that Sadat had agreed to
a UNEF extension of more than a year and put Dinitz on notice that Ford
expected Rabin to come with new ideas too.

Dinitz proposed that Kissinger help Rabin with the Israeli cabinet, which would meet in advance of Rabin's departure for Washington, by agreeing to move on the three big arms issues that had been held in abeyance (the F-15s, the Lance missiles, and the LGBs). Not interested in providing sweeteners in advance, Kissinger told Dinitz that if Rabin and Ford found a way to move ahead, "it's a soluble problem."

Rabin felt his armor and lance were strong too. He was happy about the Senate letter and felt confident that American public opinion and the press were on Israel's side. But he recognized that Sadat posed a threat to Israel's primacy in the American arena. This charming, urbane, pipe-smoking Egyptian leader with a genial smile was winning over American TV audiences by talking about peace with Israel.

On June 5, a week before Rabin arrived in Washington, Sadat opened the Suez Canal with all the pomp and ceremony that Americans so admire. As the Egyptian destroyer the *Sixth of October*, with Sadat on its bridge resplendent in a white admiral's uniform, led a flotilla down the canal from Port Said to Ismailia, the cruiser USS *Little Rock*, the flagship of the U.S. Sixth Fleet, was noticeable as the third in line. Meanwhile, an uninvited Soviet destroyer languished in Port Said harbor.

Anticipating the public relations windfall for Egypt in the United States, Rabin launched a preemptive strike, a tactic he had implemented with devastating effect as IDF chief of staff at the outset of the Six-Day War. Three days before the canal ceremony, Rabin announced the unilateral withdrawal of half the IDF troops and tanks deployed along the Sinai front line near the canal, as well as the pullback of artillery and missiles that could threaten passage through the canal. A senior Israeli official told *The New York Times*, "We wanted to demonstrate that there is no Egyptian monopoly on peace-seeking."

Kissinger was at planeside to greet Rabin when he landed at Andrews Air Force Base, a gesture that protocol did not require. Rabin was unimpressed. He told Peres and Allon later that Kissinger had met him with "a sour face on." As they rode together to Blair House in Kissinger's black Cadillac, he told Rabin that the president was mad at him and he too was upset about leaks. "He tried to scare me the whole way," reported Rabin, "but I knew this was just his tactic and part of the game."

The "game" began in earnest the next morning when Kissinger paid a call on Rabin at Blair House ahead of their meeting with President Ford. It was as if the two knights were circling each other, looking for chinks in the other's armor. Kissinger jabbed with a complaint about the senators' letter; Rabin parried with a demand to know whether Israel would be subjected to another reassessment if the talks broke down again. Kissinger took offense; Rabin said he too was offended by the charge that he had misled Ford. Kissinger probed for an opening by hinting that he could produce concessions from Sadat on early warning, the duration of the agreement, and the boycott of U.S. companies that did business with Israel. But in return Israel would have to withdraw from the passes. "The rest of the line doesn't make any difference," Kissinger said. "It makes all the difference in the world," Rabin responded, explaining that an IDF withdrawal from its current line would require a massive rebuilding of its defense infrastructure in Sinai that could take two to three years. At that, Kissinger observed gravely, "We made a mistake getting into this negotiation." Rabin showed a little flexibility by suggesting that Israel could settle for defensive positions "at the eastern part" of the passes. But then he insisted that before there could be any interim agreement with Egypt, the United States and Israel had to have an agreement on the overall settlement, an understanding about how to deal with Syria's demand for an interim agreement on the Golan, and a resolution of Israel's aid requirements.

As he hastened across Pennsylvania Avenue to brief Ford before his meeting with Rabin, Kissinger realized that moving the Israelis was going to be a lot more complicated than he had thought. He was going to need the president's intervention to weaken Rabin's resolve. Ford required little coaching in that regard. Rabin's behavior had been gnawing at him, and he had decided to get his grievances off his chest in his straightforward way.

Once the photographers had been cleared from the Oval Office, Ford unburdened himself: "I want to say to you that I am disillusioned, I am disappointed, and disturbed." He listed his grievances: Israel's inflexibility in the negotiations, the leaking of his reassessment letter, the Israeli embassy's political efforts to pressure him at home. "This is not at all helpful," the president chided Rabin.

Ford reviewed the three months of "agonizing reassessment." He noted that, though it was not a final conclusion, he was in favor of the option of "moving to an overall settlement to Geneva, to try to achieve a peace . . . that would include agreement on borders."

Covering his customary bluntness with politesse, Rabin expressed appreciation for Ford's generosity and admiration for his efforts to achieve Middle East peace. He blamed Israel's inflexibility on its public opinion and promised to do everything to prevent further leaks.

Rabin told Ford that he knew military means would not solve Israel's problems, but his country had to have the ability to defend itself. The overall settlement that Ford preferred had three requirements from Israel's perspective that had never been bridged by diplomacy: the nature of peace, the borders of peace, and the Palestinian issue. For peace, Israel needed normalization of relations with its Arab neighbors, not just non-belligerency. If it were to withdraw to the vulnerable 1967 borders without real peace, Israel would have to mobilize every time the Arabs moved their armies forward, threatening Israel's economic survival. Consequently, Israel could not withdraw fully from the Sinai or go down from the Golan Heights unless there was a fundamental change in Arab attitudes, which would take at least a decade. In this incisive analysis, Rabin seemed to be giving precise expression to Kissinger's own views.

As for the Palestinian issue, the Arabs wanted to create "an Arafat state" in the West Bank, from where Palestinian missiles could shoot down planes landing at Israel's only international airport. He pointed out that the PLO advocated for a secular state in place of the Jewish state, requiring the elimination of all Jews who arrived since 1923. "Therefore, as we see it, a return to the 1967 borders and the establishment of a Palestinian state means that Israel cannot survive." Israel was ready to go to a Geneva Conference and consider an overall peace if that was what Ford preferred, he said, "but we cannot budge from the positions which I have described."

However, Rabin continued, there was another way: together they should resume the effort to achieve an interim agreement with Egypt that could help produce an overall peace in phases. At this point, Rabin unfurled a large map of the Sinai Peninsula and pointed to three strategic considerations:

1. Israel needed to be at Sharm el-Sheikh, at Sinai's southern tip, until Egypt had demonstrated a "solid" commitment to peace;
2. Sixty percent of Israel's oil came from the Abu Rudeis oil fields, halfway down Sinai's west coast, at a savings of $400 million a year, making the Jewish state almost energy independent. If Israel were to cede the oil fields it would need a reliable replacement.
3. The strategic Gidi and Mitla Passes were the gateways to western Sinai on one side, and Israel on the other. Withdrawal from there would require Israel to establish a very long defensive line.

Rabin said there were two other considerations. First, what would be the relationship between an interim agreement with Egypt and a Syrian deal? Israel could only make "cosmetic" changes on the Golan for an interim agreement. An overall agreement would be different, but then if the United States pushed for a final peace agreement with Syria, Egypt would want the same. And that raised the second concern: What would be the relationship between an interim agreement with Egypt and the Geneva Conference? As Rabin put it bluntly, "Why should we give up the passes for nothing and end up negotiating an overall settlement in six months from a weaker position?" From his perspective, there needed to be several years between the interim agreement and the overall one to allow time to change the environment for peace.

Kissinger was impressed. He passed a note to Sisco in which he wrote, "Why didn't they raise all this last year?" But Kissinger had to focus on more practical matters. He homed in on the passes, because they remained the key to the interim agreement. Would Rabin consider moving his forces one kilometer out of the passes? That would mean the total disruption of Israel's defense system, Rabin answered. What about Egyptian forces in one end of the passes and Israel's in the other? That would be complicated, Rabin responded. "There would be an argument as to where the western and the eastern end of the passes are," he said, accurately forecasting what was in store for the two of them. For now, Kissinger was content to put down a clear marker: "I don't know if an interim solution is possible on the passes with you remaining there." Rabin felt he had put down a marker too, noting in his memoirs that he had explained why it was out of the question for Israel to give up the passes.

Ford suggested that Kissinger and Rabin try to sort through all these complexities. Rabin gave his shy smile and shrugged, "I'll try." Ford warned him that because the situation was volatile, he was only prepared to give the interim negotiation two to three weeks. If they couldn't reach an agreement in that time, then he "would have no alternative but to go to an overall settlement," which he emphasized would be quite specific in its details.

This made little impression on Rabin. He knew Geneva would lead to a stalemate, which would only help the Soviet Union regain regional primacy. Kissinger should have known he could not bluff Rabin. After all, they had worked together to torpedo the Rogers Plan for a comprehensive settlement. Yet he would continue to depend on this ploy, partly because the president liked the idea of a "Ford plan for Middle East Peace," and partly because he had no better alternative.

That night, Ford hosted a small, black-tie "working dinner" for Rabin at the White House to which he invited some ten senators and congressmen. Rabin seemed to deliberately avoid referring to Kissinger in his toast and then, in the after-dinner discussion, made disparaging comments about the U.S. role at the end of the Yom Kippur War. Kissinger was furious. He called Dinitz late that night and read him the riot act. On Thursday morning, he was still fuming, telling Ford, "These guys are the world's worst shits. [Rabin's] performance last night was a disgrace."

Kissinger's anger was assuaged by Rabin's willingness to get down to business when they had breakfast the next morning at Blair House. Rabin was surprised to discover that Kissinger was enthusiastic about an interim agreement with Egypt. He stipulated Israel's requirements, all of which now seemed feasible to Kissinger. Instead of non-belligerency, Rabin said he would accept the formula for non-resort to use of force that Kissinger had persuaded Sadat

Rabin addresses a small dinner at the White House in the State Dining Room hosted by President Ford on June 11, 1975. Earlier, Ford began the meeting in the Oval Office by complaining to Rabin that he was "disillusioned . . . disappointed, and disturbed." In his toast Rabin offended Kissinger by failing to mention him and then infuriated him by complaining about the way that the United States had treated Israel at the end of the Yom Kippur War. Kissinger's body language captures his attitude.

to offer before the negotiations had broken down in March. Rabin needed six to nine months for implementation of the Israeli withdrawal, but he would hand over the oil fields within the first two months. Kissinger thought that was workable too. He wanted the agreement to last for four years, regardless of what happened with Syria or Geneva. Kissinger thought he could get three years from Sadat (he already had that in his pocket from Salzburg), plus nine months for implementation. Rabin wanted to retain the Israeli early warning station at Um Hashiba beyond Israeli lines. Kissinger told him Sadat would accept this.

That left the passes. To Kissinger's evident satisfaction, Rabin said he would agree to withdraw to a new defense line "based on the eastern end of the passes." It was reasonable for Kissinger to conclude from this conversation that Rabin had agreed to move his forces to the eastern end of the passes. And that is what he reported to Ford, adding, "I think they're cracking."

Rabin confirmed this assessment when he was ushered back into the Oval Office. He cataloged the Israeli positions Ford could present to Sadat: UNEF in place for four years, uninterrupted Egyptian access to the oil fields, *and a new Israeli defense line at the eastern end of the passes.* Encouraged by Kissinger, Ford expressed satisfaction, providing the opening for Rabin to present his shopping list that would make his offer palatable to the Israeli cabinet: $2.5 billion in additional military assistance, $700 million in economic assistance, and an Israeli veto over any proposals the United States might put forth at Geneva. Ford responded positively, in general terms.

This sense of easing tensions carried on into the evening, when Kissinger attended a dinner in Rabin's honor at Dinitz's residence. In his toast, Kissinger dismissed the friction of the last three months as "merely a family quarrel." He declared that the reassessment period was drawing to a close and that they were moving toward new momentum in Middle East diplomacy. Rabin, no doubt tutored by Dinitz, reciprocated by speaking of his long friendship with Kissinger and his deep appreciation for his support.

The bonhomie quickly dissipated at midnight, however, when they adjourned for coffee in Dinitz's lounge. After the morning meetings, the American team had formulated a paper that cataloged the areas of consensus using language that approximated a draft agreement. Kissinger reviewed this with Rabin. They agreed on the first five points, but when Kissinger read out loud that the Israeli line would be at the eastern end of the passes, Rabin said this translated "as the entrance to the passes" but meant the "eastern ridge." He emphasized that Israel would have to be on top of the ridgeline, which was actually in the middle of the passes.

Kissinger was stunned: "Then we're back where we started." Rabin said no, Israeli forces would be farther back than the line he had insisted upon in March. Since Rabin had never shown him that line on a map, Kissinger had no way of judging the extent of the movement, if there was any. Smelling a rat, Kissinger said he wanted to go over the map when he met Rabin the next day, before Rabin departed Washington to spend the weekend in New York. He warned Rabin that to be acceptable to Sadat, the IDF presence in the passes needed to be minimal.

Then Kissinger raised the idea of limited-forces zones, which he had assumed was a natural application of the principles of the earlier Sinai disengagement arrangements to the new interim agreement. Now it was Rabin's turn to blow a fuse: "You are pushing us back and pushing us back." He had not previously explained that if the IDF withdrew to the eastern end of the passes, he could not afford to also thin out its forces beyond there without jeopardizing Israel's security.

They moved on to discuss a Syrian interim agreement. Kissinger summarized their earlier discussion on this subject by suggesting that Rabin propose a limited withdrawal, which Assad was bound to reject. Then the Israelis would consider a unilateral withdrawal. Rabin said he had never agreed to that and would not be able to explain to his cabinet why Israel would have to agree to even a minimal withdrawal on the Golan in addition to the Sinai withdrawal.

Now Kissinger raged: "Your cabinet will have to understand you are not an island. If you don't want to do serious work at Geneva, you have to help us with what is needed to have no serious work at Geneva!" Rabin, trying to calm things down, suggested he would think about a unilateral withdrawal on the Golan. Kissinger said okay, "but then you can't say you decided not to do it." He warned him that Ford was "not as complicated as you are"; the president would not agree to go down a road that would lead to an impasse. If that was the case, Rabin said, then Kissinger should stop threatening Geneva, because Israel would resist any step that endangered its security there and that too would lead to an impasse. Sisco intervened to end the meeting before things deteriorated further.

Given their almost identical conceptual approaches to negotiations with the Arabs, it is puzzling that Kissinger and Rabin would now find it so difficult to develop a common strategy. Yet the confrontation of the last three months had taken its toll on their friendship. Rabin, who placed great store on his personal integrity, believed that Kissinger had misunderstood him and was trying to manipulate him. Kissinger believed Rabin had tricked him into telling Ford to go easy on him even though he wasn't willing to concede the passes.

Exacerbating matters, Dinitz had informed Kissinger just before Rabin's visit that Matti Golan, the chief diplomatic correspondent for the Israeli newspaper *Haaretz*, was about to publish a book that recounted many of Kissinger's confidential, highly sensitive conversations with his Israeli interlocutors. Kissinger was sure that a senior Israeli official, perhaps Peres or even Rabin himself, had leaked the protocols of their meetings to embarrass and defame him and even force his resignation. Although Rabin had intervened with Israel's military censor to prevent the publication of the book, Kissinger believed *The New York Times* and the Egyptians already had copies of the draft.[*] He had expected Rabin to apologize during this visit, but Rabin didn't believe he had anything to apologize for given the way that Kissinger leaked whenever it suited him. Mistrust and a sense of betrayal had infected their relationship.

---

[*] *The Secret Conversations of Henry Kissinger* was not published until 1976, even though Golan submitted the manuscript to the censor on March 25, 1975. On May 7, it was officially banned on the grounds that it would severely damage relations with the United States "and could cause the cutting off of military aid." In banning the book, the military censor told Golan that the material he proposed to publish "can only come from very senior personalities." That same day, Rabin had convened a cabinet meeting and told the ministers that if the book were published, Kissinger would have to resign and relations with the United States would be damaged irrevocably. Rabin also tried to censor reporting about the book's existence. On May 13, 1975, however, the details of the censorship were published in *The New York Times*. See Matti Golan, prologue to *The Secret Conversations of Henry Kissinger: Step-by-Step Diplomacy in the Middle East* (Chicago: Quadrangle, 1976), and Terence Smith, "Israel Bars Publication of a Manuscript Disclosing Secret Remarks of Kissinger," *New York Times*, May 13, 1975.

Behind his back, Kissinger now referred to Rabin as a "chiseler" and a "trickster," a dishonorable man engaged in "a clear pattern of deception." For his part, Rabin objected to the way Kissinger used Ford "as his battering ram." When Rabin wondered in one of their Washington meetings why there were suddenly so many misunderstandings between them since they had success-fully worked together for years, Kissinger said that "we never used to have misunderstandings with the Israeli government" (i.e., before Rabin became prime minister).

In another of their meetings, he interrogated Rabin about U.S. intelli-gence reports that a clandestine meeting had taken place between Allon and Soviet officials in Bucharest. Rabin said it never happened; Kissinger didn't believe him. "So there were no meetings with members of Allon's party? Allon didn't meet with the Soviets, or travel somewhere to meet with the Soviets? I want to make sure that I don't fail to ask the right question," Kissinger said with disdain-tinged sarcasm. Things did not improve when they convened again on Friday evening, June 13, before Rabin departed for New York. This time Rabin produced a map, which he had not cleared with his colleagues, that showed Kissinger how the IDF could make deeper withdrawals north and south of the passes while still holding the eastern ridgeline in the passes.

In response, Kissinger arranged for the president to call Rabin that night. Ford was blunt: "I must tell you in all frankness that you have not moved far enough to make me feel that we have made any progress. . . . I am disap-pointed." He was willing to have Kissinger present Rabin's offer to Sadat, but the United States would not endorse or support it. Rabin understood that meant Sadat would reject it. He told Ford in no uncertain terms that he was not willing to change his position: "We shall hold on to the eastern ridge of the passes."

Ford wasn't ready to give up. He asked Scowcroft to call Dinitz with a mes-sage for Rabin: he should consider Ford's phone call as a personal, presidential request for a modification in Israel's position.

Kissinger took another run at Rabin on Saturday, when they met in New York in Rabin's Waldorf Astoria suite. He suggested that the Israeli defense line should be moved from the mountaintops to the eastern slopes, an idea he had used to good effect in the Syrian disengagement negotiations. Rabin rejected the notion. "No!" he shouted. "I am making myself perfectly clear. In March we proposed that Israel retain the central portion of the passes. After-ward we agreed to move a little bit eastward. Now we are proposing that Israel retain no more than the last ridge on the eastern end of the passes," he said, implying that he had made a series of concessions. Kissinger was unpersuaded.

They met one more time at the Waldorf, on Sunday, before Rabin returned to Israel.* The meeting began with mutual recriminations. When they focused on substance, Kissinger was dismissive. How could he ask the Egyptians to pay an additional price now "for nothing more than this nebulous road [to the oil fields] which will take a year's work to make passable?" Rabin pointed out that he had also agreed to Egyptian army companies at the western end of the passes. Kissinger dismissed that as "cosmetic."

Rabin said he would return to Israel, discuss the president's request for reconsideration with his cabinet, and then send an emissary back to Kissinger by the end of the week with a map that he could convey to Sadat. Kissinger repeated that he would transmit it without comment, recommendation, or U.S. support. He said Sadat might be desperate enough to accept it, but he feared it would drive Sadat back into Soviet arms, pushing the United States out of the Middle East.

If the negotiations then failed, he added, "we will wash our hands of interim agreements." He used the cold language of a diplomatic threat: "You said you would protect your interests, so will we protect ours." Emphasizing that those words reflected the president's views, he repeated that if Sadat rejected Rabin's offer, "we won't support your position if this breaks down." But if they could reach an interim agreement with Sadat, then they could play with the Syrians and Soviets in "a battle of movement." In that case, Rabin asked, would there be no overall Ford plan? The question indicated he was more worried about Ford's threat than he would subsequently allow in his memoirs.

"If we had a joint strategy, we could keep the process going and negotiate for a substantial length of time," Kissinger responded, holding out a carrot that Rabin immediately recognized from their Washington days.

Why not then harmonize U.S. and Israeli positions for the overall agreement and avoid a future confrontation? Dinitz asked. Kissinger reminded them of his approach: "I am trying to avoid formulating anything; I thought that would be helpful to you."

His message was not lost on Rabin. The interim agreement with Egypt was a "territory for time" deal. If Rabin would offer a little more territory in the passes, Kissinger could help him better achieve his objective of exhausting the Arabs so that they would eventually make their deals with Israel short of the 1967 lines and leave the Palestinians "high and dry." But if Rabin persisted

* That morning, Kissinger had been greeted when he awoke in his suite at the Pierre with the State Department press clips that highlighted an interview Rabin had given to *U.S. News & World Report* in which he had staked out his old demand for non-belligerency from Egypt if Israel were to cede its defense line in the Sinai passes. Rabin said, "If the state of war is unchanged and Egypt claims all the rights of a belligerent power, we cannot give up our defense line on the Mitla and Gidi Passes in the Sinai." See Bernard Gwertzman, "U.S. Still Unsure of a Sinai Accord After Rabin Talk," *New York Times*, June 15, 1975.

in "a posture of rigidity," as Kissinger put it, then it would lead to a public line being drawn between the United States and Israel, and once that happened, he said, "you will be facing a quite different America." Kissinger reminded Rabin, "That is what I have long tried to avoid." Carrot and stick. To sweeten the carrot, Kissinger added that, if they reached an interim agreement, he would want to move quickly on Israel's assistance request so that it could be explained to the Arabs as the U.S. contribution to the agreement. While he thought $2.5 billion was high, he said, "we can take care of the weapons you need."

As the meeting broke up, Kissinger took Rabin aside and told him, in strictest confidence, that if Israel proposed American-manned early warning stations in the passes, he thought Congress would accept this. Rabin liked the idea, believing that an American presence would deter Egypt from contemplating breaking the agreement, and it took the issue out of UN hands, adding an element of stability to the arrangement. Kissinger did not tell Rabin that this was Sadat's idea.

This was vintage Kissinger. Notwithstanding the personal umbrage, he had found a way to walk Rabin back from the brink of a confrontation neither of them could afford. And he had provided Rabin with the key to solving the problem of the passes. He had made sure to conceal that it was an Egyptian idea, convincing Rabin to present it as an Israeli idea.

Demonstrating his confidence in the outcome, he told the press outside the Waldorf after the meeting that there was a possibility of new shuttle diplomacy.

Kissinger, however, still had a problem with the president. Ford was just as offended as he was by Rabin's obduracy but, as he had pointed out to Rabin, "the man from Grand Rapids," as Kissinger would refer to the president, was not as complicated as the two of them. When Kissinger reported to him on their last meeting, Ford told him he was determined to be very tough. He said he should have been stronger when he met with Rabin on Thursday. He told Kissinger he was now determined to proceed with his overall peace plan. Kissinger, again, had to find a way to turn Ford around.

He apologized for misleading the president when he had reported that Rabin was ready to cede the passes. Then he said that Rabin had clearly been shaken by the president's call and had talked in conciliatory terms (not exactly an accurate portrayal of their confrontation). Since Ford had asked him to moderate his position, Rabin had promised to go back and try to move his ministers on the passes. They needed to wait for the game to play itself out.

The president was willing to moderate his feelings and let Kissinger handle the diplomatic maneuvering but, he said, "the orders are we have got to prepare for the overall." Kissinger warned him that "if you put us behind anything you must make them do it." Then he added a little flattery by reporting that

John Chancellor, the highly respected anchor of the *NBC Nightly News*, had told him that Ford enjoyed strong support around the country for his honesty and decency. Ford was assuaged, but he wanted to keep the pressure on the Israelis. "Make them feel like I'm a SOB," said the president as he hung up.

Wednesday, June 18, 1975, Jerusalem. Poor Rabin. When he reported to Peres and Allon that he had shown a map to Kissinger with the line drawn on the eastern ridge, Peres reminded him that the cabinet had not authorized him to do so and criticized him for moving it too far back. Rabin said that while he had insisted on holding on to the eastern ridge in the passes, Kissinger rejected this proposal and threatened to put "all the necessary pressure on us." In addition, Ford was threatening to go for a comprehensive plan that would look like the Rogers Plan. And many in the American Jewish community would support the call for an Israeli withdrawal to the 1967 lines. He said Dinitz was not confident Israel could win a confrontation with the president in these circumstances.

When Rabin reported this dire news to the cabinet, the ministers decided to overrule Peres's objections and approve the line Rabin had offered. Rabin's military secretary, Brigadier General Ephraim Poran, brought Kissinger the map a few days later. "The line is no better than it was," he said in disbelief. Dinitz confirmed that but added, "At least [Rabin] succeeded in getting it approved!"

Poran's report of the deliberations in Jerusalem made clear that while the cabinet was not yet ready to move the line out of the passes, it was now focused on the terms for doing so, dropping its demand for non-belligerency and, like Rabin, looking instead for compensation from Washington. Kissinger was guiding Rabin in an awkward, slow dance toward relinquishing the passes. And Rabin was using his dance partner to convince his ministers that they could get a good price for them.

At last, Kissinger had an Israeli cabinet–approved line of withdrawal to convey to the Egyptians. Hermann Eilts, the U.S. ambassador in Cairo, who had returned to Washington to pick up the map, predicted accurately that Sadat would reject it. Since neither Ford nor Kissinger was willing to put America's weight behind the Israeli proposal, Sadat risked nothing by doing so. What he would not understand, Eilts explained to Ford, was why the United States, "which provides Israel with everything, cannot move them."

Monday, June 23, 1975, Alexandria. Fahmy met Eilts at Cairo Airport and drove with him to Alexandria, where Eilts delivered the map to Sadat. With

Vice President Hosni Mubarak and el-Gamasy by his side, Sadat rejected it as "totally unacceptable." He countered with the map el-Gamasy had presented to Kissinger in March. Fahmy explained that if Israel could present an unacceptable line, Egypt could too.

On June 25, Sadat sent a letter to Ford stating that at Salzburg he had reached the limits of his concessions. Blaming Israeli intransigence on American "pampering," he wrote that the time had come for "an American map reflecting its proposals." If that failed to produce Israeli movement, then Sadat too threatened Geneva, "to which all parties should be invited, including the PLO."

Sadat's request for an American proposal landed on the president's desk around the same time as a seventeen-page memo from Kissinger outlining the hard choice that Ford now needed to make. He warned that if the United States were unable to produce movement, the Arabs would start preparations for war and another oil embargo, which could be launched in 1976, an election year in the United States. To head this off, the president needed to decide whether to put forward an American plan for the interim agreement, as Sadat was now requesting, or a comprehensive plan for Geneva. In either case, he would face a confrontation with Israel's supporters in Congress and the American Jewish community that he could not afford to lose.

The choice was an invidious one, Kissinger explained. An interim agreement would require him to press Israel to give up the strategic passes for something short of non-belligerency. On the other hand, promoting a comprehensive plan might put the U.S. in a better position with the Arabs and precipitate a debate in Israel, but the result could be paralysis.

Always preferring the more cautious, incremental approach, Kissinger recommended that Ford make one last effort to pressure the Israelis to move out of the passes. The president agreed to write a letter to Rabin formally requesting a reconsideration of Israel's position. The purpose, as Kissinger defined it in a memo to Ford, was "to shock the Israelis" and force the cabinet to choose between relations with the United States and holding on to the eastern ridge of the passes.

Friday, June 27, 1975, Washington, DC. Dinitz was summoned to the Oval Office, where the president presented him with the letter. In it, Ford first reminded Rabin of all the military assistance he had provided Israel since becoming president and the way he had produced movement in Egypt's positions, including lately at Salzburg. Yet Israel had not moved to accept "the minimum requirements of an interim agreement." Now, with Sadat's rejection of Rabin's latest inadequate offer, the negotiations were at a crossroads.

"Our judgment," Ford wrote, "is that Israel's position is forcing the evolution of the negotiations to an outcome which runs counter to the interests of the United States and the world." The very core of the U.S.-Israeli relationship was at stake, he continued. It could only be salvaged by Israel's acceptance of the parameters of the interim deal. And in case some of Rabin's ministers might consider an end run again to Congress, Ford expressed confidence that "Congress will support my conclusions as to the national interest."

Handing the letter to Dinitz, Ford added two points. First, Kissinger would be meeting with his Soviet counterpart on July 11 to discuss reconvening Geneva; the U.S. position in that meeting would depend on Israel's response. Second, Ford warned against mobilizing the American Jewish community again. "Any political activity would be very, very unhealthy."*

Dinitz was shown out of the Oval Office without any discussion. Adding to the sense of crisis, the White House informed the press that the meeting had lasted only ten minutes.

In his memoirs, Kissinger notes that "not since Eisenhower . . . had an American President addressed an Israeli government in so abrupt a manner." Nearly twenty years earlier, President Eisenhower had issued an ultimatum to Prime Minister Ben-Gurion to leave the Sinai Peninsula; now President Ford was issuing an ultimatum—albeit disguised as a formal request—to Prime Minister Rabin to leave the Sinai passes.

If Dinitz were now to fulfill his role as one of the custodians of the U.S.-Israeli relationship, he needed clarity about what Ford was asking of Israel. He hastened to Kissinger's office at the State Department to inquire, "Do I say to the prime minister that the President expects Israel to . . . withdraw from the passes or do I say the President says the Israeli positions have not come far enough?"

The letter had been purposely vague on that point; Kissinger's answer was not clear-cut either. With so much at stake, and the Geneva alternative so unpromising, he was trying to get the Israeli cabinet to bend; he had no desire to break the relationship. So he answered by wrapping the president's fist in a diplomat's glove: "The President hopes the former."

From early on in the crisis, Dinitz had been quietly urging Rabin to find a way to restart the negotiations.† Sensing that the moment was ripe, he now

---

* The talking points Kissinger had prepared for Ford for this meeting were far blunter: "You are an Ambassador accredited to the president of the United States. It is not proper for you or your embassy to conduct or organize domestic lobbying against the office to which you are accredited. . . . Trying to set Americans against their government on an issue that could seriously affect the national interest could have the most unhappy consequences for Israel and its friends here." See Memo to the President, June 27, 1975, Records of Joseph Sisco, 1951–76, RG 59, General Records of the Department of State, NARA.
† At the end of March, for example, even as Dinitz was rallying support on Capitol Hill, he warned Rabin that they might win over public opinion, and Kissinger might even resign, but they

moved into overdrive. He asked Kissinger, on Rabin's behalf, whether it would be acceptable to the president if the cabinet's initial response to his letter was that discussions on the interim agreement would remain open. Kissinger said yes; it was essential that the cabinet avoid a rejection.

Dinitz informed Rabin that Kissinger did not want him to respond to the president's letter until Kissinger had returned from a short vacation he was taking over the July 4 weekend at Nelson Rockefeller's retreat at Caneel Bay in the Virgin Islands. In the meantime, Kissinger had suggested that Rabin "put an offer on the table that retains a symbolic sliver of the passes for Israel." This should be an informal offer that would enable Kissinger to explore whether it might be acceptable to Sadat.

Dinitz informed Kissinger that Rabin was trying to create a situation "which will get us out of the passes and yet can bring an agreement." Having been burned once before, Kissinger expressed doubt that Rabin could deliver, but Dinitz was determined to try. Kissinger told Dinitz he could reach him through the White House switchboard.

While Kissinger tried to relax in the humid heat of the Caribbean summer, the drama now shifted to Jerusalem. After his meeting with Kissinger, Dinitz transmitted the president's letter and his assessment to the Israeli negotiating team. He repeated Rabin's earlier warning to Peres and Allon that a failure to show flexibility on the line of withdrawal now would result in an end to the interim negotiations and the publication of an American comprehensive plan. On the other hand, he noted that Rabin had succeeded in convincing Kissinger during his visit that Israel would need to retain a presence in the eastern end of the passes rather than vacate them completely. Dinitz therefore proposed that Israel show some flexibility on the line of withdrawal from the passes in exchange for U.S. commitments on negotiations with Syria, a coordinated strategy on Geneva, and military and economic assistance.

Saturday, June 28, 1975, Jerusalem. On this evening in Jerusalem, Shimon Peres decided to surrender. In the cabinet deliberations that left the response to Ford's letter open, Finance Minister Rabinowitz had sounded the alarm about the Israeli economy. It was heading for disaster, he said, if they could not secure the economic assistance and funding for Israel's arms requirements

---

would be left with Ford and probably a secretary of state who would be worse than Kissinger. He recommended that Rabin instead take a diplomatic initiative to jump-start negotiations.

from the United States.* As defense minister, Peres had responsibility for pro-curing Israel's arms, but he had been stymied since February by the hold Ford had put on Israel's requests for the sophisticated weapons that would consti-tute the backbone of Israel's longer-term defense, and the military assistance needed to pay for them. He also wasn't welcome in Washington to make his case. In the meantime, Rabin's approval rating among Israelis had risen dra-matically, to 70 percent, as a result of his standing up to the Americans, while Peres's had languished as a consequence of his inability to deliver.

When the cabinet met on the evening of June 28 to consider its response to the president's ultimatum, a new consensus emerged in favor of exiting the passes while finding a way to maintain the IDF's defense system in Sinai. Peres ordered the chief of staff to draw up deployment options for the IDF if it had to evacuate the passes.

Then Peres seized on Kissinger's idea, which Rabin had brought back from Washington, of American-manned early warning stations in the passes. He proposed the creation of a rectangular zone stretching from the western to the eastern end of the passes that would be manned by a joint American-Soviet military force that would operate the early warning sites there and substi-tute for an IDF presence. To break out of the personal boycott Kissinger had imposed on him, Peres proposed that he should be the one to fly secretly to the Virgin Islands to present the plan to Kissinger. Peres explained to Rabin and Dinitz that he wanted to have a "heart to heart" with Kissinger to avoid what he called a Greek tragedy. He described it as "a last ditch, nearly desper-ate effort."

Rabin erupted. For six months, Peres had second-guessed him, undercut him, and constrained his ability to move on the interim deal. Now, when he had decided to end the crisis with the United States, he felt Peres was trying to steal the kudos from him by volunteering himself to negotiate the break-through with Kissinger. He was happy that Peres had now accepted the idea of an American presence in the passes as a substitute for an Israeli presence there. But knowing that Kissinger would never agree to insert Soviet forces into the Sinai as well, he used that issue to kill Peres's proposal.

Four years later, when Rabin published his memoirs, he was still using it to denigrate his archrival. "I was flabbergasted," he recalled. "Had I not, with my own ears, heard a senior Israeli minister propose that Israel take the initiative

---

* After the Yom Kippur War, Israel's military expenditures had grown enormously, consuming 37 percent of the budget in 1975 and representing almost 30 percent of GDP. The oil crisis had led to a dramatic rise in oil and commodity import prices. That combination fueled inflation and generated a ballooning deficit in the balance of payments. Growth slowed from 11 percent before the war to 3 percent afterward. See Amos Shifris, *The First Rabin Government, 1974–1977* [in Hebrew] (Tel Aviv, Israel: Havatzelet, 2013), 128–31.

in inviting Soviet troops into the Sinai I would have sworn that the defense minister's enemies were slandering him."*

Rabin now instructed Dinitz to report that Kissinger judged there was insufficient time for an envoy to fly all the way from Israel. According to Dinitz's report, Kissinger preferred that Dinitz travel to Caneel Bay from Washington to brief him on the new Israeli proposal.

Time did nothing to lessen the Peres-Rabin rivalry. Seventeen years later, when Rabin was again elected prime minister and Peres became his foreign minister, it flared again. Peres was determined to pursue a breakthrough with the Palestinians; Rabin preferred the strategic advantages of a peace deal with Syria. But Rabin had to respect Peres's weight in the party and, after the Palestinian intifada, he too wanted to test whether progress could be achieved with the PLO. Rabin therefore acquiesced in Peres's dispatch of Uri Savir, his director general at the Israeli foreign ministry, to Oslo to negotiate with Arafat's advisers. Because the PLO was facing bankruptcy at that moment, and Peres was able to make more progress with Arafat than Secretary of State Warren Christopher was able to with Syria's Assad, the deal was done with the Palestinians first, behind the back of the United States.

In contrast to the Caneel Bay episode, Rabin wanted Peres to brief Christopher on the Oslo Accords. He preferred that his rival take responsibility for the politically dangerous decision to reconcile with Arafat. And when Clinton offered to host the signing ceremony at the White House, Rabin decided that Peres should represent Israel.

When I reported this to Clinton, he was surprised. As an experienced politician, he understood instinctively that if Rabin stayed away, Israelis would see that he was not fully committed to the highly controversial deal, likely sinking its chances for survival. Clinton called Rabin and invited him to come. Rabin said he didn't want to create difficulties for the president. Clinton understood that the difficulty he was referring to was Arafat, for if Rabin came, Arafat would have to be invited. But Clinton thought Arafat should be there too. From the president's perspective, this was a historic breakthrough; it was essential that both leaders publicly embrace the agreement, shaking hands to symbolize that the Israeli-Palestinian conflict was over. He told Rabin he needed to be there and that he shouldn't worry about embarrassing the United States. Rabin demurred again but with less resolve.

---

* Peres responds in his own memoirs, labeling Rabin's account as "tendentious." He claims that it was his "fresh idea" that broke the logjam in the negotiations. While he admits that he proposed a U.S.-Soviet presence, it was to be a small, technical team rather than a military deployment. See Shimon Peres, *Battling for Peace* (New York: Random House, 1995), 144–46.

Clinton hung up and then turned to me, red-faced. "You may be the Middle East expert," he said angrily, "but I'm telling you Rabin wants to come!" He called Christopher and told him to make sure Rabin understood that the president was personally inviting him and would take care of any "difficulties." Rabin reconsidered. If this was going to be as big a deal as Clinton portrayed, he couldn't let Peres steal his thunder. He told Christopher he would come. He explained to his aides that he could not refuse the personal invitation of the president of the United States. However, it was in the nature of his dysfunctional relationship with Peres that he was too embarrassed by his volteface to inform him. Peres found out the next morning when he turned on his radio to listen to the 5:00 a.m. news. Humiliated yet again, Peres tendered his resignation.

Rabin could not afford to lose Peres at this risky political juncture, so he insisted that we make arrangements that would salve Peres's wounded ego. After the signing ceremony, Christopher hosted a large diplomatic luncheon in honor of Peres in the State Department's grand ballroom on the eighth floor. The guest list included most of the Arab ambassadors as well as Abu Mazen, who was Peres's Palestinian counterpart at the time. Meanwhile, the president ate alone with Rabin in his private dining room at the White House, where they drowned their sorrows with too much wine. In the preceding ceremony on the White House lawn, Rabin had given Peres the honor of signing the Oslo Accords on behalf of the Israeli government. But Rabin had the last word. With the whole world watching, he shook Arafat's hand. Then he turned to Peres and said, "Now it's your turn."

17

Denouement

> The art of statesmanship is to make necessities look desirable, and to arrange it.
>
> —Henry Kissinger to Moshe Dayan, April 1975

Tuesday, July 1, 1975, Caneel Bay, St. John, U.S. Virgin Islands. Dinitz flew in on an unmarked U.S. Air Force jet, accompanied by Larry Eagleburger. They landed at St. Thomas because there was no airport on St. John. A twenty-minute boat ride deposited them at the pier in a small, picturesque bay with crystal-clear, azure water framed by a white sand beach. The Caneel Bay resort, if you could call it that, comprised a series of small bungalows on the beach. They arrived as the sun was setting. Dinitz was intrigued by the wooden hut lit by lanterns where Henry and Nancy were staying. He noted that one of the fly screens was torn. "I guess one must be very rich to live so very poor," he remarked to Kissinger as they greeted each other.

Their meeting began after dinner and carried on until sunrise. Dinitz presented a message from Rabin which emphasized that the Israeli cabinet wanted to avoid a crisis with the United States. Rabin asked for clarifications that would enable him to gain approval from the cabinet for a line of withdrawal that Kissinger would find acceptable.*

Now that Rabin had finally agreed to yield, Kissinger praised him to

---

* Rabin's questions included: Was it a withdrawal to the eastern slope of the passes? Would the line south of the passes that he had previously shown Kissinger be acceptable? If Israel withdrew from the passes, could it be compensated in the north to preserve its air base at Rephidim? What changes would be necessary in the corridor to the oil fields? Could Israelis be present in the American-controlled early warning positions? Would the Egyptian line advance only to the current UN buffer zone? What does "easing of the boycott" mean? What does "easing of diplomatic conflict" mean?

Dinitz as "by far the best available man to run Israel." Gracious in victory, he explained that he had only come to understand in his last meeting with Rabin that his concerns were strategic. He conceded that Israel was going to be worse off because there could be no real quid pro quo for yielding territory. That was why he had recommended his "time-wasting strategy" as alternative compensation.

Dinitz pressed him for answers to Rabin's questions. Kissinger was not explicit for fear that he would not be able to deliver Sadat's agreement. Dinitz persisted, and Kissinger finally clarified his position: "It looks to me that wherever you put yourself *on the eastern slope* can be presented as substantially out of the passes [emphasis added]." In other words, the line would need to be "well back from the summit," something that could be presented to Sadat as an exit from the passes "even if it isn't." If Israel offered that, Kissinger said, "we would try to look at it with sympathy."

Dinitz was relieved. Would Kissinger object if the line to the north of the passes that Rabin had shown him in Washington was moved westward to protect the logistical bases there? As long as it wasn't too visible, some minor adjustments could be handled, Kissinger responded, resorting to his penchant for obfuscation.

The rest of the issues were similarly resolved.* In addition, Rabin wanted an assurance that there would be no attempt to move with Jordan or the PLO next, and that for the duration of the agreement with Egypt (i.e., three to four years), the United States would not submit a plan for an overall settlement unless there was prior coordination with Israel. Kissinger had never embraced the Jordanian option, let alone the PLO, so he had no problem assuring Rabin on that count. On a comprehensive plan, he couldn't commit the next administration, but if he were still there, he said, "my basic strategy [would be] to exhaust the parties so that we can move toward . . . non-belligerency." He added, indiscreetly, that he disagreed with Ford as to the wisdom of putting forward an overall plan and he was not interested in rushing to Geneva.

Dinitz again raised Rabin's request that the United States commit not to press Israel "to get off the Golan." Kissinger again prevaricated. Dinitz moved on to Israel's requests for military and economic assistance and compensation

* The Egyptian road to the oil fields at Abu Rudeis presented a problem because there was not enough room on the thin strip of flat land between the Red Sea coast and the soaring Sinai mountains to separate it sufficiently from an Israeli road that provided the IDF with a connection to its position at Sharm el-Sheikh. Kissinger said he would look into it. On the manning of the early warning stations, Kissinger said he thought Israelis could be present in one of them, knowing that Sadat had already agreed to that. On future negotiations with the Syrians, they agreed that Kissinger would only expect Rabin to make cosmetic changes on the Golan, and in return Rabin would consider a unilateral move there to ease the pressure for progress.

for the Abu Rudeis oil fields. Kissinger was generally supportive but caviled at the $2.5 billion price tag, indicating that $1.5 billion to $2 billion was "about right."

Dinitz was satisfied. As Kissinger walked him to the door, he said there was no chance Ford would approve the package they had just agreed on. Dinitz was unfazed. As he notes in his memoirs, "You had to understand Kissinger's vocabulary." If he had refused to take it to the president, then it would really have no chance. But for Kissinger to say "there is no chance" meant there was a fairly good chance that it would be approved.

They met again the next morning to summarize their understandings. Kissinger reemphasized that "the minimum the Egyptians might accept is the eastern slopes." If Israel were ready to leave the summit in the passes, then the specific line could be resolved later. They discussed the idea of a follow-up meeting between Rabin and Kissinger in Europe to resolve the line of withdrawal, the American presence in the passes, and the broader issues of a coordinated strategy. At last, U.S.-Israeli relations appeared to be back on track.

When Dinitz flew to Jerusalem to brief the cabinet ministers on his Caribbean jaunt, they assailed him with their doubts and demands. Nonetheless, upon his return to Washington a week later, Dinitz told Kissinger that the negotiating team—Rabin, Allon, and Peres—was prepared to recommend to the cabinet an offer to move the IDF "to the eastern slope of the passes to an agreed line taking into account the military requirements." They wanted an American presence in four early warning sites in the four entrances to the passes, in addition to the two Israeli and Egyptian sites already agreed on. At last, the Israelis had decided to relinquish the passes.

Rabin had authorized Dinitz to show Kissinger the new map that the IDF had drawn up. Kissinger had opened the door to minor adjustments in the line at Caneel Bay, but the IDF now proposed a line to the north and south of the passes that was ten kilometers west of where a straight line would have been. This had the effect of turning the passes into an eastern bulge, or "belly," inside a line to the west of them. Kissinger told Dinitz the new Israeli line was "a noose around the passes" and predicted that he would have "a massive problem" persuading Sadat to accept it.* Nevertheless, he told Ford that he believed "the Israelis are getting ready to cave." He calculated that as long as he could show Sadat that the IDF had withdrawn from the passes, he could persuade him to be flexible about the rest of the line.

---

* Dinitz also explained the difficulty in separating the Egyptian and Israeli roads along the southern coast to the Abu Rudeis oil fields. Because there were two points where the mountains made two separate roads impossible, Rabin proposed use of the road on alternate days.

Saturday, July 12, 1975, Erftstadt, Germany. With a cabinet decision looming, Rabin wanted to discuss the new line and the accompanying assurances with Kissinger directly. He was due to make a four-day visit to Germany, the first Israeli prime minister to do so. They arranged to meet at Schloss Gymnich, the German government's guesthouse in Erftstadt, outside Bonn, where Rabin was staying. This medieval castle, moat and all, made little impression on Rabin. Kissinger was more impressed by the noise machine the Secret Service had installed to prevent the Germans from listening in on their conversation.

Despite the din, Kissinger and Rabin were able to have their first substantive strategic discussion since their Washington days. The last year of acrimony had strained their friendship but Kissinger, at heart a sentimentalist, was touched by Rabin's acknowledgment that he had always acted "in the framework of the strategy" that they had agreed upon back in 1970.

They did not find it easy, however, to agree on a strategy to suit the new circumstances. They first perused every detail of the new line on Rabin's map, considered alternative approaches to the difficulty of giving Egypt unimpeded access to the oil fields, and discussed the arrangements for and location of the early warning stations. Then Kissinger analyzed Rabin's conceptual approach, explaining that only in their June meetings in Washington had he come to understand that Rabin sought to ensure that the IDF dominated Sinai even as it withdrew, so that no Egyptian threat could emerge there.

Kissinger, on the other hand, saw the interim agreement as an opportunity to address the psychological dimensions of the conflict and create a new atmosphere of comity between Egypt and Israel. Kissinger's approach was to provide Sadat with a face-saving arrangement that would separate Egypt from the radical Arab camp, reduce Soviet influence, and buy Israel time. In his view, the Sinai passes were a small price to pay. He encouraged Rabin to recognize the strategic advantage to Israel (and the United States) of removing Egypt from the conflict and therefore the wisdom of showing greater flexibility on the line of withdrawal.

The irony was palpable. Rabin had embarked on these negotiations with the objective of removing Egypt from the conflict through a non-belligerency pact. Kissinger had convinced him that was unachievable. Now that Rabin was focused on a military disengagement, Kissinger was trying to convince him that he should make concessions to achieve a political objective. Since they could not reconcile these two approaches other than through negotiating an agreement, they went back to focusing on the details.

Kissinger explained to Rabin that in the post-Vietnam era, Ford would not agree to a large American troop presence in the Sinai.* Instead, Kissinger proposed that the main early warning stations be under American command but staffed mostly by Israelis and Egyptians respectively. The four smaller ones in the passes could be manned by fifteen to twenty Americans each.

As for the proposed line, Kissinger accepted the concept of Israeli retention of control over the eastern end of the passes through its positions to the north and south of them. He agreed to try to sell the idea to Sadat by emphasizing Israeli withdrawal from the passes themselves.

Kissinger had succeeded in moving the Israelis, but Rabin had succeeded in dragging Kissinger down into the weeds. To prevent the Israelis from getting the better of him, he asked the CIA to produce a detailed, three-dimensional topographical map of the Sinai, which his aides would henceforth lug around in a huge case to his meetings with Rabin and Sadat.

Now that he had Rabin in the zone of a possible agreement, Kissinger needed to make sure that Sadat was still there. He did this by a series of familiar maneuvers. On his way back to Washington, he sent a message from his plane to Fahmy emphasizing that "after much discussion and firm insistence on our part, Rabin agreed to take into account the considerations which we outlined."

Then he summoned Eilts to Washington to pick up a new map that Dinitz brought from Israel. On it, Kissinger had marked in yellow the "fallback line," which represented Kissinger's view of what he could get out of Rabin with more effort but was, in fact, what Rabin had already agreed to at Schloss Gymnich. "Don't say it's agreed to yet," he cautioned Eilts. "Then [Sadat] can still get something out of us."

Eilts wanted to tell Sadat that the Israelis would be out of the passes. When Kissinger affirmed that, Eilts said, "I think we're getting into the range." Kissinger instructed Eilts "to lead Sadat to know" that he could get slight improvements on the line, but that to go beyond this would require "an effort of the magnitude not distinguishable from that needed for an overall agreement." He instructed Sisco to send another cable to Fahmy, telling him that he was holding Eilts back in Washington because he was pressing the Israelis for more concessions and awaiting their response. "I think that given their epic minds this will help," he explained to his advisers. He didn't realize that Fahmy was just as aware of his games as Dinitz.

Here was Kissinger's tactic of obfuscation elevated to an art form. He understood that what mattered at this stage was to get both sides into the zone

---

* In preparation for the meeting, Harold Saunders had done a study of the personnel requirements of the six early warning stations the Israelis were proposing. His conclusion was that it was impractical: it would take too long to train the hundreds of American technicians needed. See Harold H. Saunders, "U.S. Manning of Intelligence Facilities in Sinai," Memo, Department of State, July 8, 1975, Records of Joseph Sisco, 1951–76, RG 59, General Records of the Department of State, NARA.

and make them grateful to him for the Herculean effort involved. To do that he had to tell Sadat that Israel would be out of the passes and tell Rabin that he could stay on their eastern slopes. How he would reconcile those positions would remain a mystery until the endgame. But now he had assembled the elements—including variations to the lines, introduction of an American presence, and U.S. assurances and aid—that he would manipulate to satisfy both sides' minimum requirements.

Eilts met with Sadat on July 20 to brief him. The next day he was summoned by Sadat to receive his counterproposal and, in typical fashion, his fallback position, which he expected Kissinger to use to manipulate Rabin just as Kissinger was using Rabin's fallback position to maneuver Sadat. The good news was that even though Sadat didn't care much for the bulge, as long as Israel was out of the passes, he was willing to accept it if that was the best Kissinger could do. In return, he wanted to be able to move the Egyptian line forward by a couple of kilometers beyond the existing UN buffer zone, which Kissinger knew Rabin was willing to consider.

"I think I can now see a way this can go to a conclusion," an excited Kissinger told his staff on July 23. The only sticking points appeared to be the road in the south and Rabin's insistence on six early warning positions in the passes, versus Sadat's preference for only two. With the onset of Ramadan and the Jewish high holidays in September, he moved up the date of the shuttle to mid-August and asked Rabin to cancel a trip he had planned to Austria.

On August 4, Kissinger briefed Ford: "This negotiation is done unless Rabin is setting us up for a fall." He estimated he could wrap it up by the end of August.

"No one else could have done it," said the president.

Thursday, August 21, 1975, Jerusalem. As he flew into Ben Gurion Airport, Kissinger reviewed the short list of issues that he would have to resolve with Rabin and Sadat on this shuttle. The gaps were no longer wide and none were irresolvable. The line of Israeli withdrawal was more or less agreed upon. The one sticking point was in the Gidi Pass, where the Israeli line was on the eastern slope, as Kissinger had allowed, but still inside the pass; Kissinger would have to persuade Rabin to make a one-kilometer adjustment there.[*]

The line of Egyptian advance was still at issue. Peres was objecting to any movement beyond the UN line. The number of American-manned early warning stations in the passes remained to be agreed upon, and there were

---

[*] In the Mitla Pass, the Israeli line was farther east. At Rabin's suggestion, Kissinger had sent Sam Hoskinson, a CIA expert, to walk the passes with IDF officers. They set the line in the Mitla Pass at the Parker Memorial, a slab of stone marking the place where a British officer had died.

some issues in the text of the agreement that had to be resolved.* This time, it would take Kissinger only ten days to achieve agreement, shuttling back and forth between the cabinet room in Jerusalem and Sadat's beach villa in Alexandria, with only one side trip to Damascus to try to keep Assad sweet.

Less than two years earlier, at the end of the Yom Kippur War, Kissinger had been welcomed in Israel as the savior of the Jewish state. Not so anymore. The change in the image of the super-statesman had begun with the U.S. vote to condemn Israel in the Security Council over its retaliation for the Kiryat Shmona massacre of Israeli children. For Israelis, the first two disengagement agreements had served a useful purpose in terms of separating the warring armies, returning the POWs, and enabling Israel's reservists to demobilize. But the prolonged argument with the United States over the second withdrawal in the Sinai had become bitter and personal. Rabin had insisted on an Egyptian commitment to non-belligerency because the Israeli public wanted to believe that they were getting some peace in return for yielding strategic assets in Sinai. When Kissinger rejected this requirement and Ford criticized Israel for inflexibility, the Israeli public turned on them. Holding back security assistance only increased their unpopularity.

Kissinger's reassessment of the U.S.-Israeli relationship had prompted an Israeli reassessment of Kissinger himself, particularly his role in the Yom Kippur War. Many Israelis now believed that he had played with their fate by preventing Meir from launching a preemptive strike, holding up the vital arms resupply, and then robbing the IDF of victory. None of this was accurate, but it fast became Israeli folklore and created fertile ground for a newly invigorated opposition led by Menachem Begin, a fiery orator, and fueled by the ideological vigor of the Gush Emunim religious nationalists, who opposed any territorial concessions.

A foretaste of the anger in the Israeli street took place on July 14, 1975, when fifteen thousand demonstrators turned out to protest U.S. pressure for a Sinai withdrawal in Tel Aviv's main square at City Hall (the same square, now renamed Kikar Rabin, where Rabin would be assassinated twenty years later). A group broke away from the main crowd and marched to the U.S. embassy, where they proceeded to stone the building.

Kissinger's arrival served as a rallying point. Demonstrations took place in major cities across the country. In Jerusalem, mobs outside the King David Hotel made it difficult for Kissinger's motorcade to proceed to the Knesset, where Rabin had decided to host him for a festive welcome dinner. Throngs of demonstrators stormed through the streets of Jerusalem and laid siege to

---

* For example, Fahmy was insisting on a reference to Article 51 of the UN Charter that provided for the right of self-defense; Allon feared this diluted the Egyptian commitment to non-resort to use of force.

Demonstrators outside the Knesset on August 21, 1975, where Kissinger was being hosted for a dinner by Prime Minister Rabin at the beginning of his shuttle. Police had to use clubs and water cannons to clear the streets so that Kissinger could return to his hotel. As well as this sign that called him a liar, cheat, and traitor, there were signs that called him a "Jewboy," a "Kapo," and "the husband of the gentile woman."

the Knesset. By 10:00 p.m., when the guest of honor was ready to return to the hotel, the police had to use clubs and water cannons to clear the streets. An hour later, Kissinger was led out a back entrance of the Knesset and beat a furtive retreat to the King David. But he had seen the demonstrators' signs: "Jewboy," "Kapo," "Hitler Spared You to Finish the Job." They implied that Kissinger, as a Jew, had betrayed his people by pressing Israel to give up territory. To add insult to injury, Rabbi Zvi Yehuda Kook, the spiritual mentor of Gush Emunim, branded him as *ba'al hagoya,* "husband of the goy [i.e., a gentile woman]," in other words, a Jew who deserved to be shunned as someone who had left the tribe.

Even in the most intense phases of subsequent negotiations, when Warren Christopher, Madeleine Albright, or John Kerry pressed Israel to yield territory, the demonstrations paled in comparison to Kissinger's experience this time. The worst the protesters would do is carry signs that said, "Dennis Don't Menace" and "Ross Go Home, Indyk Too." A hard-line cabinet minister in Netanyahu's government, Rehavam "Gandhi" Ze'evi, had called me a "Jewboy" when I was ambassador to Israel, but he had been roundly denounced by his fellow ministers, although Prime Minister Netanyahu remained notably silent.*

---

* Ze'evi was head of the ultra-right-wing Moledet Party. The racist slur he used to taunt me at the ceremony commemorating the laying of the cornerstone of the Rabin Center in Tel Aviv was *yehudon.*

At the dining room in the prime minister's residence in Jerusalem on August 22, 1975, Henry Kissinger negotiates with Yitzhak Rabin, Shimon Peres, and Yigal Allon. Kissinger had little tolerance for their tactics. He told his team afterward, "This group is in the grocery business. They're selling bags of potatoes."

Rabin, however, was embarrassed, appalled, and furious at the anti-Semitic spectacle. He told the press the demonstrators had "struck a blow to the very soul of our way of life." Here lie the origins of his animus toward the settler movement, a member of which eventually took Rabin's life. Taking it in stride, Kissinger affected bemusement, but as a Holocaust survivor he was deeply hurt.

Kissinger had expected that things would go more easily this time with the Israeli triumvirate of Rabin, Allon, and Peres. In fact, the engagement was particularly vexing. They were no longer interested in Kissinger's usual efforts to persuade them of the strategic costs of not going forward. The merchandise—the passes and the oil fields—had been agreed upon. For them, it was now a question of settling on the price.

Ahead of the trip, Rabin had dispatched Mordechai Gazit, his director general, and Meir Rosenne, the foreign ministry's legal adviser, to Washington to negotiate a twenty-four-page draft memorandum of understanding with Sisco and Atherton, the assistant secretary of state for Near Eastern affairs, that detailed Rabin's list of required assurances. Kissinger had managed to get Ford to sign off on the less controversial items and had green-lighted Rabin's entire arms list. Rabin had requested $2.5 billion in assistance; Ford told Kissinger he could not exceed a generous $2.1 billion.

In the cabinet room in Jerusalem, Kissinger tried to remind the trio that his step-by-step approach was designed to help Israel. They should see it as a victory, yet it seemed all they wanted to do was wrangle. As he noted to Sisco and Saunders, "This group is in the grocery business. They're selling bags of potatoes." In one of his nightly reports to Ford, he complained that the talks had taken on "more the character of exchanges between adversaries than between friends." He described the mood in the endless hours of negotiations as "grudging not generous, more concerned with finding a scapegoat than a common strategy." The bitter taste remained with him for some time. He told Ford after he returned to Washington with the agreement in hand that the Israelis were "treacherous, petty, deceitful—they didn't treat us like allies."

At Schloss Gymnich, Rabin had indicated a willingness to accept an Egyptian advance of a few kilometers beyond the previous UN buffer zone. Now he explained that his public would not accept it. Kissinger said if he could persuade Sadat to forgo his demand for movement of his forces beyond the UN line, perhaps Rabin would give him an extra kilometer in the Gidi Pass. Sadat was willing to make the concession, but Rabin responded with a sliver of two hundred meters in exchange for Sadat's allowance of several kilometers. Kissinger flew into a rage. "This negative, grudging, piddling way in which this agreement is being presented and discussed between us isn't worthy of what we are trying to do," he said. To no avail.

Kissinger fared better with the Egyptians because he could rely on Sadat's innate generosity of spirit. Fahmy would nitpick over the wording of the text; el-Gamasy would defend the amour propre of the Egyptian army. When

Henry Kissinger negotiates with President Sadat in the garden of his summer villa at Mamoura, Alexandria, August 25, 1975. Kissinger appealed to him to stop his aides from haggling. Always the man of grand gestures, Sadat agreed.

things reached an impasse, Kissinger would ask to see Sadat alone and appeal to his better angels.

In a meeting with Sadat in Alexandria on August 25, Fahmy and el-Gamasy objected yet again to the Israeli line in the passes. Kissinger sat with Sadat alone and, as usual, gave him his analysis of the situation. Someone had to stop the haggling, he said: "We either make an arrangement this week or we are going to have a prolonged stalemate." Sadat threw up his hands in resignation and agreed to conclude the deal, issuing the appropriate instructions to Fahmy and el-Gamasy, including his acceptance of Rabin's two-hundred-meter offer in the Gidi Pass.

The lines had now been agreed upon, and Kissinger could report to Ford that both sides were caught up in the momentum of the negotiations. Neither side, though, was particularly happy with the deal. El-Gamasy complained that his troops in Sinai would be under Israel's guns.* Fahmy said the document looked like a set of unilateral Egyptian concessions. Sadat long ago had pocketed the passes and the oil fields. When he looked at the map now, he could see that two-thirds of Sinai would remain in Israel's hands. He complained to Kissinger that the Israeli strategy was to sell his land to the United States for arms "which they will use to prevent giving up any more of any land." Kissinger had no answer to that.

Peres was upset that Kissinger would not support his demand for six American-manned early warning stations. He had used this idea as a ladder to climb down from his insistence that the passes had to remain in Israel's hands. Kissinger admitted that Ford had originally agreed to six but had changed his mind when he found out that hundreds of American technicians would be required. In the post-Vietnam environment, even a pro-Israel Congress was reluctant to commit American advisers abroad. Kissinger responded to Peres, "You had better be able to justify this in terms of what it does for America" not what it does for Israel.

In the end, they settled on an American-supervised system involving some two hundred American technicians overseeing one strategic early warning station each for Israel and Egypt, and three American-manned tactical radar stations complemented by three unmanned sensor fields to monitor movement in the passes that would provide early warning to both sides.

There was one part of the agreement that remained to be finalized—the compensation that Rabin was determined to secure from the United States in

---

* Kissinger assuaged el-Gamasy's dignity by persuading the Israelis to increase the number of Egyptian troops in the Sinai from seven thousand to eight thousand.

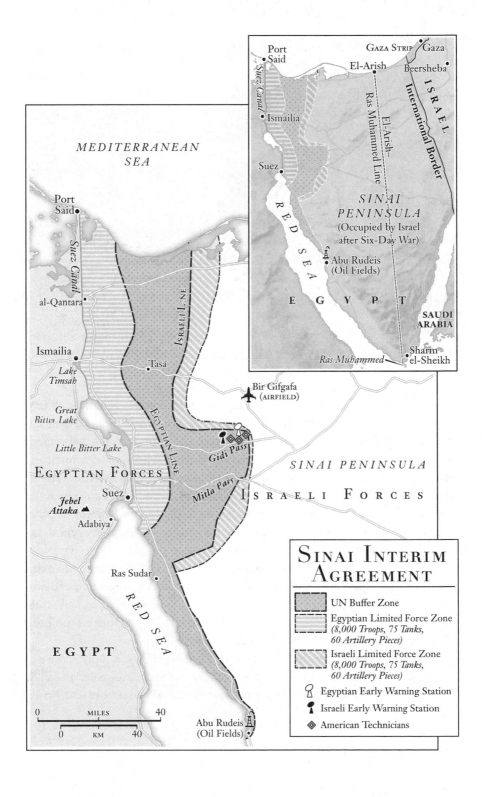

MEDITERRANEAN
SEA

Port
Said•

Suez Canal

al-Qantara•

Ismailia•

Lake
Timsah

Great
Bitter Lake

Little Bitter Lake

EGYPTIAN FORCES

Jebel
Attaka ▲

Suez•

Adabiya•

Ras Sudar•

RED SEA

EGYPT

ISRAELI LINE

Tasa•

EGYPTIAN LINE

Gidi Pass

Mitla Pass

Bir Gifgafa
(AIRFIELD)

SINAI PENINSULA

ISRAELI FORCES

Abu Rudeis
(Oil Fields)•

0   MILES   40
0   KM   40

Port
Said•

Suez Canal

Ismailia•

Suez•

RED SEA

GAZA STRIP •Gaza

El-Arish•   Beersheba•

Ras Muhammed Line

El-Arish–

ISRAEL
International Border

SINAI
PENINSULA
(Occupied by Israel
after Six-Day War)

Abu Rudeis
(Oil Fields)

EGYPT

SAUDI
ARABIA

Ras Muhammed

Sharm
el-Sheikh•

SINAI INTERIM AGREEMENT

- ▰ UN Buffer Zone
- ▱ Egyptian Limited Force Zone
  (8,000 Troops, 75 Tanks, 60 Artillery Pieces)
- ▱ Israeli Limited Force Zone
  (8,000 Troops, 75 Tanks, 60 Artillery Pieces)
- ♀ Egyptian Early Warning Station
- ♟ Israeli Early Warning Station
- ◈ American Technicians

The Israelis argued about every little detail and Kissinger got down into the weeds with them. Scrutinizing the disengagement map (from left to right) are IDF chief of staff Motta Gur, Harold Saunders (crouching), Simcha Dinitz, Henry Kissinger, Shimon Peres, and Joe Sisco (pointing).

return for the concessions he was making to Egypt. He was mindful of Meir's failure to lock down those commitments at the end of the Golan disengagement negotiations, fifteen months earlier. Had she done so then, Rabin might have been in a stronger position to resist American pressure for territorial concessions now. Kissinger had repeatedly emphasized that the U.S. position in the region had come to depend on additional Israeli withdrawals. Rabin wanted to ensure that the next time Israel was called upon to yield territory, his country would be able to negotiate from a position of greater strength and would not be as vulnerable to American suspension of aid.

Notwithstanding their exhaustion, Kissinger and Rabin went at it in marathon negotiating sessions with their teams that began on August 29 and concluded at 5:30 a.m. on September 1. At one point, as dawn approached on the final day, the two of them paused their exchange to notice that all the other members of the two negotiating teams were fast asleep.

The result was a striking series of documents that not only gave new meaning to the term "assurances" but also laid the foundations for the U.S.-Israeli relationship as we have come to know it.[*] As Kissinger observed at the

---

[*] The documents included a U.S.-Israeli memorandum of agreement (MOA), letters of commitment from President Ford to Sadat and Rabin, and a secret letter from Ford to Rabin. See Appendix C.

The weather in Alexandria was so pleasant that the Egyptians set up the negotiations outside in the garden, where Fahmy and el-Gamasy complained about the arrangements in Sinai. In the end, Kissinger took Sadat aside and appealed to his better angels. From left to right: Eilts, Kissinger, Sisco, Fahmy, Sadat, Mubarak, el-Gamasy.

time, "Never has a government achieved so many unreciprocated things from another government for an agreement which is basically in its favor."

As with everything else he did, there was purpose behind his largesse. Kissinger had long been preoccupied with Israel's strategic vulnerability as a small Jewish state surrounded by larger, more powerful Arab states. Now that he had bent Israel's leaders to his will, he was intent on making it up to them, not as a reward, or even as compensation, but rather as a way of stabilizing the order he was creating. An Israel that was capable of defending itself by itself would also be capable of deterring war for as long as it took for its neighbors to accept it and live in peace with it. On its own, that would never be enough to ensure stability, as the Yom Kippur War had demonstrated. But it was an essential cornerstone for the infrastructure of his new Middle Eastern order.

According to Kissinger's calculus, the more territory Israel gave up, the more it needed to be strengthened to defend itself and play its role. By the same token, he believed the stronger it became, the more capable it would be of giving up territory to lubricate the peace process and thereby help legitimize the order. Of course the opposite would prove to be true too: the stronger Israel became, the more capable it would be of resisting U.S. pressure to yield territory. But that did not appear to be part of Kissinger's reasoning.

First came the military commitments. In 1973, before the Yom Kippur War, Israel received less than $500 million annually in military and economic assistance from the United States. To help pay for the war, Nixon had approved a one-time supplementary appropriation of $3.3 billion in grants and loans, of which $2.8 billion was for military assistance. In the judgment of the U.S. intelligence community, that military assistance had already given the IDF the capability to fight a four-week war at the same level of intensity as the Yom Kippur War and to destroy the combined Egyptian and Syrian offensive capabilities within two weeks.

Now Rabin was seeking a U.S. commitment to fund a *ten-year* military buildup that would double the number of Israeli combat forces, provide Israel with the most sophisticated weapons systems available, and ensure an effective deterrent against air or missile attacks on Israeli population centers.[*]

In September 1974, Ford had agreed to provide Rabin with the most urgent requirements on his list. Kissinger knew from a detailed intelligence estimate that Rabin's entire list of arms requirements in the second tranche, as detailed in "Matmon B," could be met with an additional $1.7 billion in military assistance. In advance of these negotiations, Kissinger had already secured Ford's agreement to an overall level of $2.1 billion, including economic assistance. According to the intelligence estimate, that would provide sufficient foreign exchange reserves and balance of payments support to enable Israel to continue its massive military import program and most of its civilian imports, "a luxury the United States does not enjoy." Kissinger therefore stuck with the $2.1 billion and Rabin grudgingly accepted it.

Kissinger touted this to Ford as standing firm, but it was in fact a huge gift to Israel, one that would have long-lasting consequences.[†] As the intelligence community warned, this was but the first of an expected series of ten annual lists. Ford's response would provide the floor for future Israeli aid levels.

Beyond the levels of military assistance, Rabin also sought access to the most sophisticated weapons systems the United States was then developing. This included the F-16, Lance missiles, forward-looking infrared devices, and Pershing missiles.

---

[*] This massive buildup was designed to meet a worst-case scenario of a 50 percent increase in Arab ground forces, a doubling of Arab air forces, and a tripling of Arab air-defense missile forces, even though the CIA and DIA seriously doubted the Arabs' ability to absorb such arms acquisitions and organize and train their forces on the scale that Israel projected.

[†] According to Rabin, from November 1973 to June 1977, during Kissinger's tenure as secretary of state, the IDF doubled its overall strength, the number of planes increased by 30 percent, the tank force by more than 50 percent, and the number of APCs by 700 percent. All that equipment came from the United States. See Yitzhak Rabin, *The Rabin Memoirs* (Berkeley, CA: University of California Press, 1996), 290.

The Pershing was particularly sensitive since it was a solid-fueled ballistic missile that served as the U.S. Army's primary *nuclear-capable* theater-level weapon. Its development had only been completed in 1974. Since Israel was believed by then to have produced its own nuclear arsenal, the Pershing could be used as a highly effective delivery vehicle. Indeed, notwithstanding Israel's denials to the contrary, the request to acquire Pershings, "as far as we were concerned, was purely strategic," noted Uzi Eilam, the head of the IDF's Research and Development Directorate at the time. Even with a conventional warhead, its precise homing capabilities and 450-mile range would provide the IDF with an ability to strike Cairo from Israel and the Aswan Dam from Sinai.

In a secret letter from Ford to Rabin that accompanied the Israeli-Egyptian agreement, the president committed the United States to an early joint study of the high technology and sophisticated items that Rabin had requested "with a view to giving a positive response." That commitment specifically applied to the Pershing missile, albeit with a conventional warhead. See Appendix C, pages 593–94.

To compensate Israel for relinquishing the Abu Rudeis oil fields, the United States would backstop Israel's energy requirements in the event Israel was unable to satisfy its needs on its own and would seek five-year funding from Congress to cover the costs of purchasing the oil and stockpiling a year's reserves in Israel.*

Rabin had early on registered his concern that after completing this agreement Israel would be presented with U.S. demands to make additional withdrawals from Sinai, the West Bank, and the Golan. Even though that was the logic of Kissinger's step-by-step diplomacy, Rabin now persuaded Kissinger to agree, in the MOA, that the next negotiation with Egypt should be for a final peace agreement. Why Kissinger agreed to this when he had already told Rabin that the next step was to pursue a non-belligerency agreement with Egypt remains a mystery.

Similarly, "under existing political circumstances," the MOA ruled out the idea of an interim agreement with Jordan. Kissinger registered his discomfort with this commitment even though he saw no prospect for such a deal. Rabin said he needed the assurance for domestic reasons—the opposition to ceding West Bank territory had grown stronger in the context of the Sinai withdrawal. Kissinger repeated what he had said when the Jordanian option was under serious consideration: We won't press you.

The MOA was silent on what would happen on the Syrian front. Out of

---

* The MOA also committed the United States to ensuring that Egypt fulfilled its pledge to permit all Israeli cargoes passage through the Suez Canal. And it committed U.S. support for Israel's right to free and unimpeded passage through the Bab el-Mandeb and Gibraltar Straits, as well as overflight rights there and over the Red Sea.

concern to minimize any adverse reaction to the agreement from Damascus, Kissinger had promised Assad and Sadat that he would next seek another Israeli-Syrian agreement. That promise was expressed in a presidential letter from Ford to Sadat that also accompanied the Israeli-Egyptian agreement. Rabin was willing to play along with this ruse as long as Kissinger understood that Israel could make only a very limited move on the Golan and would not, under any circumstances, be expected to come down from there.

The latter understanding had been a long-standing Israeli objective, beginning with Meir's repeated request to Kissinger in the context of the Golan disengagement agreement. Kissinger had managed to parry that petition, just as he had resisted the demand from Assad for an American commitment to full Israeli withdrawal from the Golan. However, Nixon had given Assad the verbal assurance of U.S. support for a full withdrawal from the Golan on his visit to Damascus in June 1974. And in September 1974, Ford had given Rabin a verbal commitment that Israel could stay there.

Now Kissinger acceded partially to Rabin's demand for a written assurance. In the secret letter that also detailed the sensitive military commitments, the president noted, as Kissinger had repeatedly stated, that the United States had not developed a final position on the borders. "Should it do so," Ford wrote Rabin, "it will give great weight to Israel's position that any peace agreement with Syria must be predicated on Israel remaining on the Golan Heights."

In reporting to Ford on these negotiations, Kissinger argued that none of these political commitments changed U.S. policy. Giving "great weight" to an Israeli position did not require the United States to accept it. And did a letter from one president bind the next one? It was hardly the same as legislation passed by both houses of Congress and signed into law.

Israelis, however, place great store on such presidential letters. In the context of Israel's unilateral withdrawal from Gaza, President George W. Bush wrote Prime Minister Ariel Sharon on April 14, 2004, stating that "in light of *new realities on the ground*, including already existing major Israeli population centers, it is unrealistic to expect . . . a full and complete return to the armistice lines of 1949 [emphasis added]." That wording was interpreted by Israel as an official assurance that the United States would not ask Israel to return to the 1967 borders in the West Bank and that the large settlement blocs (the "new realities on the ground") would be incorporated into Israel in any final agreement with the Palestinians.

However, when Prime Minister Netanyahu tried to use the Bush letter to bind the Obama administration, Secretary of State Hillary Clinton declared that "in looking at the history of the Bush administration, there were no informal or enforceable agreements." Obama subsequently declared that "the borders of Israel and Palestine should be based on the 1967 lines with mutually agreed swaps," thereby returning U.S. policy more or less to where it had been before the Bush letter.

The point was moot for Kissinger since he had no intention of pursuing a final Israeli-Syrian peace agreement. It turned out to be moot for Rabin too. When he came around to negotiating again with the Syrians, eighteen years later, he offered to withdraw completely from the Golan Heights.*

Why then did Rabin, and other Israeli leaders, labor so hard to secure these commitments if they do not bind the U.S. government? In part, they serve a useful domestic political purpose at the moment of decision for the Israeli cabinet when it is considering withdrawal. Its ministers are bound to fear the next demand for territorial concessions and seek a U.S. commitment as insurance against it.

These assurances also reflect the dependent relationship between Israel and the United States. Because Israeli leaders know that Sadat was right in saying that only the United States can deliver Israeli territorial concessions, they will always seek to constrain Washington's ability to do so. The optimal moment to do that is when Israel is in fact conceding to American pressure.

While he was at it, Rabin also made sure to eliminate the threat that Ford had wielded during the negotiations to put forward an American plan for a comprehensive settlement. In Ford's secret letter to Rabin, he wrote that given the new Israeli-Egyptian interim agreement, there was no need for the United States "to put forward proposals of its own." Ford promised Rabin that should the United States desire to do so in the future, it would "make every effort to coordinate with Israel . . . with a view to refraining from putting forth proposals that Israel would consider unsatisfactory." That commitment became standard operating procedure for all future administrations, encapsulated in the formula of "no surprises," meaning that Israel would always be consulted before the United States put forward a peace initiative.

At times, as Kissinger demonstrated, close consultation can be a useful device for moving Israel forward. But President Trump's peace plan was a good example of how this process could go haywire. Trump's peace team—comprising his son-in-law, Jared Kushner; his bankruptcy lawyer and ambassador to Israel, David Friedman; and his real estate lawyer, Jason Greenblatt—spent two years

---

* Rabin was not the only Israeli prime minister to offer full Israeli withdrawal from the Golan. He was followed by Peres, Netanyahu, Barak, and Olmert. Sharon, an infantryman who prized the high ground, was the only prime minister since Rabin not to offer it before the prolonged civil war in Syria rendered the issue moot.

in secret consultations with Netanyahu, Ron Dermer, his ambassador in Washington, and Dore Gold, a close adviser. They then took all of Netanyahu's ideas for a Palestinian "state minus" (i.e., minus sovereignty, territorial contiguity, and a capital in East Jerusalem) and presented them as a fait accompli to the Palestinians, ensuring that they would be rejected. Kissinger would never have accepted U.S. policy being subordinated to Israel's desires, nor would he have allowed American credibility as a mediator to be damaged in the process.

Rabin also wanted to lock down the arrangements for reconvening the Geneva Peace Conference, since it was the most likely next step once the Sinai agreement was implemented. These were codified in a separate six-point U.S.-Israeli MOA (see Appendix C, pages 589–90). The United States in that document undertook not to recognize or negotiate with the PLO as long as it did not recognize Israel's right to exist and accept UNSC Resolutions 242 and 338, with their requirements for direct negotiations and allowance for Israeli withdrawal to "secure and recognized borders." The United States also confirmed that Israel would have a veto over any additional "state, group or organization" participating in the conference.*

Although not engaging with the PLO was existing U.S. policy, that had not stopped Kissinger from talking to the PLO through intelligence channels. But now he agreed to have the ban spelled out in a formal agreement. In subsequent years, AIPAC arranged for Israel's friends in Congress to codify this commitment in U.S. law, creating a situation in which even a casual handshake between a U.S. diplomat and a PLO official became forbidden. President Carter's UN ambassador, Andrew Young, had to resign after lying about an encounter with a PLO official at the United Nations. The absurdity was highlighted in 1993, when Rabin himself decided to deal directly with the PLO behind the back of the United States after Secretary of State James Baker had gone to extraordinary lengths to exclude the PLO from the 1991 Madrid Peace Conference, the successor to the Geneva Conference, on Israel's insistence. Rabin said he didn't inform us of his direct, official engagement with the PLO because he knew it was against the law for U.S. officials to do so!

Kissinger's willingness to indulge Rabin in these ways stands in contrast with the brutal pressure he had applied to secure the territorial concessions he needed to enable the agreement with Sadat. But throughout he had maintained strict limits on how far he was prepared to go. For all his apparent

---

* The other points included U.S. commitments to coordinate the timing of any reconvening of the Geneva Conference, ensure that negotiations there took place on a bilateral basis, and oppose any UNSC effort to alter the terms of reference or change Resolutions 242 and 338.

accommodation of his president's penchant for imposing a comprehensive solution on Israel, he repeatedly undermined that option in favor of a much smaller step that he correctly assessed Israel's body politic could absorb. Once he had succeeded, he pivoted immediately to repairing the relationship and restructuring it in a way that had a profound and enduring impact on Israel's survival and well-being.

When I asked Kissinger, some forty-five years later, whether that was his intention, he paused for a long time, and silently nodded his head in affirmation. Then, after another long, pregnant silence, he pointed to the joint study of Israel's high-technology requests that the MOA with Rabin had also mandated. "You know," he said, "that study resulted in Israel gaining access to American military technology which laid the foundation for its high-tech industries today."[*]

The moment of truth for Rabin came on August 27, after the line of withdrawal had been finalized. "The method of negotiation in which we negotiated the territorial issue without relation to what we will get in return [from Egypt] . . . has produced a kind of result that I am really worried about," he said to Kissinger, claiming it put him in an awkward position before his cabinet and his people.

"I must say frankly, Mr. Prime Minister," said an incredulous Kissinger, "I didn't believe it was possible that we could within the space of five months twice wind up in the same place for substantially the same reasons."

Sisco pointed out the advantages to Israel: Egypt was committed to non-resort to the use of force in the settlement of the conflict, there would be a joint Egyptian-Israeli commission to resolve disputes arising from the agreement, non-strategic Israeli cargoes could transit through the canal, and UNEF would be renewed for three years. Kissinger added that the agreement was open-ended, there would be no militarization of the territory Israel gave up, and it would retain a lot more territory to bargain with for a final agreement.

Rabin seemed to be pining after the non-belligerency commitment that Kissinger had never been prepared to pursue. Kissinger tried to console him by pointing to the strategic advantage of separating Egypt from the other Arabs and buying time. Territory was worth more than promises, he conceded. That would always be Israel's predicament. But it would be even worse with a final peace agreement, even if it were signed in blood, Kissinger argued. From

---

[*] Uzi Eilam, the father of Israel's missile defense development, confirms that the beginning of Israel's path to technological independence began in the 1970s, "based primarily on what we could learn from the Americans." See Uzi Eilam, *Eilam's Arc: How Israel Became a Military Technology Powerhouse* (East Sussex, UK: Sussex Academic Press, 2011), 83.

his perspective, this deal was actually better for Israel than a peace agreement because Israel had to give up less territory for a greater strategic gain.

Then he added something that revealed more about his jaundiced attitude toward peace than Rabin's unrequited hopes for that Garden of Eden. "This will be your problem throughout the peace process," Kissinger said, "which is one of the reasons I have never participated with any enthusiasm . . . in efforts to push you to a final peace." Nevertheless, he tried to console Rabin with the promise that the next step would be "real non-belligerency." That must have been cold comfort for Rabin.

Peres interrupted the melancholy moment by suggesting that they insert into the text of the agreement that "the parties hereby undertake not to resort to the threat or use of peace!"

"That's the worst threat you could utter," Kissinger retorted. And he meant it.

Wednesday, April 23, 2014, Ben Gurion Airport, Israel. My wife Gahl's flight had just landed. The Israeli-Palestinian final-status negotiations over which I was presiding would soon break for Passover and Easter, which we planned to spend in the Galilee. I too was the husband of a gentile woman. As we waited for her bags to be disgorged onto the carousel in the cavernous arrival hall, my cell phone rang. The duty officer at the U.S. embassy in Tel Aviv wanted to alert me to an announcement by Wafa, the Palestinian news agency, that Palestinian president Mahmoud Abbas had reached a reconciliation agreement with the Hamas leadership stipulating that they would set up a joint unity government in five weeks and hold presidential and parliamentary elections in six months.

As we climbed into a black, armored SUV and headed out of the airport toward Jerusalem, I urgently dialed Saeb Erekat, the chief Palestinian negotiator. He was clearly just waking up after the previous night's lengthy negotiating session. We had been working furiously to reconcile Israeli and Palestinian requirements for extending the negotiations. In one week, the nine-month deadline for the final-status negotiations that Secretary of State John Kerry had orchestrated would expire. The mistrust that had characterized these negotiations from the outset had become even more intense in the last week as yet again both sides failed to live up to their commitments. Netanyahu had not released the last tranche of prisoners on time and Abu Mazen, losing patience, had abrogated his promise not to join UN conventions, particularly the Rome Statute of the International Criminal Court, which would allow the Palestinians to press for indicting Israel for war crimes.

The sticking point in our negotiations was settlements: Abu Mazen wanted a three-month settlements freeze everywhere, including in East Jerusalem, during which the negotiators would define the borders of the Palestinian state. After that the Israelis could build wherever they wanted on their side of the border. Netanyahu was willing to countenance a freeze in the West Bank, but not in East Jerusalem.

The previous night, the Israeli team, Tzipi Livni and Yitzhak Molho, had offered to their Palestinian counterparts, Saeb Erekat and Majed Faraj, to hand over "tens of thousands of dunams" of land in Area C to the Palestinian Authority for expansion of Palestinian towns and cities (Area C was the 60 percent of the West Bank still under complete Israeli control).* This would differ from the existing arrangements, where any Palestinian land use in Area C required permits from the IDF, which were rarely forthcoming. Under the arrangement that Livni and Molho had proposed on Netanyahu's behalf, planning, zoning, and building would be under the sole aegis of the Palestinian Authority.

The Palestinian negotiators knew only too well how their cities and towns had been hemmed in by their inability to expand into Area C. They asked to be consulted about the location of the land assigned for Palestinian development, urged the Israelis not to be influenced by Palestinian "land sharks" in making their decisions about what land would be handed over, and said they needed to consult with their leadership. As the sun rose over the Judean Hills, I had gone to bed thinking that at last there was some hope.

Now, as the embassy's SUV raced up the highway from Ben Gurion Airport to Jerusalem, past the British fort at Latrun and through the Bab el-Wad, it began to dawn on me what Abu Mazen's move would mean for the negotiations. Bringing Hamas into his government would give Netanyahu an easy way out by enabling him to blame Abu Mazen for the breakdown of the negotiations. After all, Israel could not be expected to negotiate with a Palestinian government that included an organization committed to its destruction, an organization that was, for good reason, also on the State Department's terrorism list.

"What the fuck? We're trying to negotiate with you in good faith and you go and do this?" I shouted through the phone at Saeb. He had no idea what I was talking about. He had not had time to brief Abu Mazen on the previous night's more hopeful negotiations. When I recounted what the Palestinian news agency was reporting, he appeared thunderstruck. Erekat hated Hamas, as he had told me many times. He did not want his grandchildren growing up under Islamic rule. The last thing he wanted was a unity government with an organization that sought to overthrow the Palestinian Authority.

---

* Livni told me later that the amount of land was actually 35,000 dunams, the equivalent of 8,650 acres. Concerned that the Palestinians would pocket the offer and ask for more, Molho had insisted that they not inform them of the exact amount Netanyahu had approved.

We didn't have to wait long for Netanyahu's reaction. If the pact with Hamas moved forward, he told NBC News, "it means peace moves backward." He canceled Israel's participation in the negotiating session that evening. Final-status negotiations were never resumed.

True to form, Netanyahu blamed the Palestinians for the breakdown. I was authorized by the White House to set the record straight in a background interview with Nahum Barnea, a leading Israeli journalist. This "senior U.S. official" made clear that both sides were to blame, noting that Israel's announcement of thousands of new settlement units during the negotiations had seriously complicated our efforts. This sparked a Netanyahu-inspired uproar in Israel and the American pro-Israel community, somewhat akin to the furor Ford and Kissinger had generated by charging that Israel had been inflexible.

When I arrived back in Washington, I received a phone call from Kissinger in which, based on his experience in 1975, he urged me, "Don't fall on your sword." I thanked him for the sage advice but told him it was too late.

Kerry and I agreed that it was time for a reassessment of our whole approach. I announced that review in a speech on May 8, in which I summa-

The opening luncheon of the last Israeli-Palestinian final-status negotiations, in the secretary of state's dining room, July 29, 2013. Nine months later, when Prime Minister Netanyahu called off the negotiations, the two sides were farther apart than they had been at the beginning. On the American side of the table is Secretary of State John Kerry with the author on his right; on the other side of the table are Tzipi Livni (head of the Israeli delegation) with Saeb Erekat (head of the Palestinian delegation) on her left.

rized the Obama administration's judgment of why the negotiations had failed, comparing the moment to Kissinger's announcement of the reassessment in March 1975. Heeding Kissinger's admonition, I praised Netanyahu for the "flexibility" he had shown in the negotiations. I also criticized both sides for the unilateral steps they had taken: the Israeli settlement announcements and the Palestinian signing of UN conventions had both been unhelpful. I pointed out to the predominantly Jewish audience that there was one important difference between Kissinger's reassessment and the one we were about to embark upon. Obama and Kerry "would never suspend U.S.-Israel military relations as their predecessors did back then."

Kissinger's suspension of new arms sales to Israel had been effective in achieving the agreement with Egypt that served both the United States and Israel so well. But Obama categorically refused to consider linking military assistance to Israel to any peace process moves. His priority was a nuclear deal with Iran. In that context, he didn't want anybody questioning his commitment to Israel's security.

Two weeks after my return from Israel, I convened the staff of the special envoy's office for a review of our policy options. Ilan Goldenberg, then my chief of staff, had written a paper which argued for presenting an American plan that would outline the principles for a two-state solution. He titled the paper "Go Big or Go Home." It was similar in concept to the plan for a comprehensive solution that Kissinger's staff had prepared during the 1975 reassessment. It took our bridging ideas on the five core final settlement issues—borders, security, Jerusalem, refugees, and mutual recognition—and packaged them in a speech that Obama or Kerry would make. It called upon the two sides, when they were ready, to resume negotiations based on the principles. One version of this option had the United States seeking to enshrine the principles in a new UN Security Council resolution that would update UNSC Resolutions 242 and 338 as the basis for negotiating Israeli-Palestinian peace.

A second option, attempting to restart the final-status negotiations, held little attraction because the parties were now farther apart than ever. Netanyahu's offer to transfer territory in Area C in a way that did not require cabinet approval was a promising idea. Perhaps in better times it could serve as a basis for a new process focused on a return to an interim agreement, another incremental Kissingerian step. But not now. Abu Mazen's reconciliation with Hamas gave Netanyahu an ironclad excuse for not engaging in negotiations, and Abu Mazen was focused on trying to maneuver Hamas into agreeing to elections. They were both happy to be relieved of the pressure to continue the negotiations.

Kerry took the idea of a "Go Big" speech to a meeting at the White House with President Obama and his aides soon after. In his phlegmatic way, Obama listened to Kerry's presentation, but instead of first asking all the other people in the room what they thought, as he usually did, he spoke himself. He recalled that he had been surprised by Kerry's success in bringing the Israelis and Palestinians back to the negotiating table. He had therefore been willing to give him an opportunity to try to move the parties toward an agreement even though he had been deeply skeptical that either Netanyahu or Abu Mazen had the will or ability to compromise. Unfortunately, through no lack of effort on Kerry's part, his assessment had proven correct. Now he told Kerry he needed him to focus on the Iran nuclear negotiations.

Unlike Ford, Obama wasn't interested in having his name on a Middle East peace plan. Kerry, though, was not ready to give up on peacemaking. He explained to Obama how he could quietly shop his principles around in the Arab world, gin up the support of Egypt, Jordan, and Saudi Arabia, and then, perhaps after an Iran deal was concluded, he could relaunch publicly.

Obama looked at him with an indulgent smile as he issued a direct order: "John, don't go chasing butterflies."*

---

* Kerry was eventually allowed to give the "Go Big" speech in December 2016, at the end of the Obama administration, when it was too late to do anything with the principles for an Israeli-Palestinian settlement which he outlined there. He had also floated the idea of a UNSC resolution that would formalize the principles he expressed in the speech. Obama decided against that too. See "Remarks on Middle East Peace," State Department, December 28, 2016, https://2009-2017 .state.gov/secretary/remarks/2016/12/266119.htm.

Epilogue

We might not be the leaders who made the final peace, but we would always take satisfaction if someday it could be truly said, it all started here.

—Henry Kissinger, *Years of Upheaval*

Thursday, September 4, 1975, Geneva. For the third time in less than two years, the high representatives of Middle Eastern states assembled in the Council Chamber of the Palais des Nations. This time, there were only three tables set for the delegates, each with copies of the two-page "Interim Agreement between Egypt and Israel" and its accompanying annexes and maps, awaiting their signatures.* As the delegates took their places, the Egyptian and Israeli representatives shook hands with General Siilasvuo, the head of UNEF, who would preside over the ceremony from his middle table. They did not shake hands with each other.

Notably absent were the American and Soviet co-chairmen of the Geneva Conference. Kissinger had dispatched Roy Atherton, his assistant secretary of state for Near Eastern and South Asian Affairs, to represent the United States. When Atherton arrived in Geneva the night before, he learned that the Soviet Union had decided to boycott the ceremony. Brezhnev and Gromyko were offended by the lack of consultation on the agreement and the insertion of an

---

* The documents were the "Interim Agreement Between Egypt and Israel" setting forth the basic scope of the accord; an annex that provided detailed guidelines for the implementation of the accord by military working groups in Geneva; a third document, called simply a "proposal," outlining the role of the American technicians in the passes; and a map showing the new Egyptian and Israeli lines and the UN buffer zone between them. Separate from the documents signed at Geneva, there were private letters from President Ford to Prime Minister Rabin and President Sadat and two memorandums of agreement between Israel and the United States. See Appendix C.

Kissinger with Rabin, Peres, and Allon initialing the Sinai II Agreement in Jerusalem on September 1, 1975. In his toast afterward, Kissinger said that reaching an agreement had been challenging, "because it is so hard to compare the tangible quality of territory against the intangible quality of political trust."

American-only team of technicians in the Sinai passes. Gromyko would later dismiss the agreement as an approach based on "momentary considerations and publicity." Kissinger, not wanting to highlight the Soviet absence, ordered Atherton to stay away too.

In an attempt to emphasize the political element in this agreement, Rabin had appointed Mordechai Gazit, then Israel's ambassador designate to France, instead of a general, to head the Israeli delegation. The Egyptians did not reciprocate. Their delegation was headed, as usual, by Major General Taha el-Magdoub. Not surprisingly, Syria boycotted as well.

After the delegates had signed all the documents, General Siilasvuo asked, "Are there any points to be raised at this meeting?" There were none. The Egyptian and Israeli representatives filed out of the Council Chamber through separate doors. They would never return.

Three days earlier, Kissinger and Rabin had initialed the agreement at a ceremony in the cabinet room of Rabin's office, where they had concluded their seemingly interminable negotiations. As they sat for the first time on the same side of the cabinet table, raising glasses of champagne, Rabin half joked that Kissinger could save himself a lot of trouble next time if he promoted direct

Arab-Israeli negotiations. In his toast, Kissinger said that reaching an agreement had been challenging, "because it is so hard to compare the tangible quality of territory against the intangible quality of political trust."

Still, as Sadat noted at the initialing ceremony in Alexandria, the agreement was a turning point in the Arab-Israeli conflict. As Article I declared, the Israeli and Egyptian governments had agreed that "the conflict between them and in the Middle East shall not be resolved by military force but by peaceful means." Article II committed both parties "not to resort to the threat or use of force or military blockade against each other." For countries that had gone to war three times in less than three decades, those commitments represented a sea change in their relationship.

To compensate for the lack of political trust, an elaborate, American-supervised early warning system would be established in the Sinai, buttressed by UN monitors, and there would be limitations on force deployments on both sides of the UN buffer zone. This system would serve as a security template for future Israeli withdrawals in Sinai, as well as those contemplated but never implemented on the Golan Heights and in the West Bank.

The concept of normal peaceful relations found expression for the first time in an Egyptian commitment to allow non-strategic cargoes bound for Israeli ports to transit the Suez Canal. American businesses would now be able to operate freely in Egypt even if they also did business in Israel. This was the first breach of the Arab boycott of Israel, which was only formally abandoned eighteen years later, after the signing of the Oslo Accords.

For over four decades since, through assassinations, revolution, and counterrevolution, there has never been a resort to force in Egyptian-Israeli relations. Kissinger's removal of Egypt from any potential Arab war coalition against Israel also eliminated the possibility of another Yom Kippur War–like state-to-state conflict, since without Egypt no other combination of Arab states could take on Israel and hope to defeat it. Henceforth the clashes on Israel's borders would only be with irregular forces—the PLO, Hamas, and Hezbollah. True to Sadat's private commitment conveyed by Kissinger to Rabin, Egypt never joined in. By contrast, since 2015, Egypt and Israel have taken coordinated military action against al-Qaeda-affiliated terrorist elements in the Sinai and concerted their policies to contain Hamas in Gaza.

The Sinai II Agreement also represented a turning point in Egyptian-American relations. In his remarks at the initialing ceremony in Alexandria, Sadat noted that the agreement demonstrated what he had always asserted, "that the United States holds all the cards." This conviction was at the heart of Sadat's realignment of Egyptian foreign policy from Moscow to Washington, which began with the eviction of Soviet military advisers in July 1972. It would culminate in March 1976, in Sadat's abrogation of the Soviet-Egyptian Friendship Treaty, as he had promised Ford in Salzburg.

Sadat had not wavered, even in March 1975 when the negotiations had broken down. Instead, as we have seen, under the table at Salzburg Sadat gave Kissinger two new cards—a three-year agreement and American monitors in the Sinai passes—to facilitate the role he needed the United States to play.

He would do the same with Jimmy Carter in 1977, when Carter lost his way in his determination to reconvene the Geneva Conference. Sadat announced instead that he was ready to travel "to the ends of the earth," even to Jerusalem, to make peace. His purpose was to reshuffle the deck and deal the United States the high cards it needed to conclude the Israeli-Egyptian peace treaty. At Camp David in September 1978, try as he might, Carter was unable to move Israeli prime minister Menachem Begin beyond his narrow definition of Palestinian autonomy. Sadat threw up his hands once again and accepted the best that Carter could do, which was a separate peace with Israel in return for the rest of Sinai. As Kissinger would later observe, it was "the Sadat way." His unique statesmanship lay in his ability "to state a great objective and not haggle over every detail . . . not to look good to your subordinates but to look good to history."

For Sadat's troubles in negotiating the Sinai II Agreement, Ford would reward him with the first official visit of an Egyptian president to Washington. It took place in October 1975 and was followed by a congressional vote of $750 million in vital economic assistance to Egypt. A year later, the first significant U.S. security assistance to Egypt was provided in the form of six C-130 military transport planes.

Although this aid seems paltry in comparison with the largesse heaped on Israel as a corollary to the Sinai Agreement, Sadat understood that he was establishing a precedent. After he signed the peace treaty with Israel in 1979, the United States rewarded Egypt with $1.3 billion in military assistance and $250 million in economic aid annually. Four decades later, Egypt is still receiving $1.3 billion in military aid annually and $100 million a year in economic assistance. In total, Egypt has received more than $80 billion since 1975, making it the second-largest U.S. aid recipient behind Israel.

Sadat paid a steep price, however, in Egypt's relations with the Arab world. Kissinger's efforts had secured him Saudi support, but his attempt to keep Assad mollified only made the Syrian leader more bitter. In a congratulatory phone call from President Ford, who was at Camp David at the time of the initialing of the agreement, Sadat urged him to pursue an Israeli-Syrian agreement next. But that was hardly enough to moderate Assad's anger at Sadat's forswearing of the use of force against Israel. From Assad's point of view, Egypt's role as a combatant in the Arab cause was over. He also felt betrayed by Kissinger, who had outwitted him after all. He launched a campaign to isolate Egypt in the Arab world, abetted by Libya, Iraq, and the PLO, and supported by the Soviet Union.

Sadat returned the favor. In a speech to the National Assembly soon after signing the agreement, he lambasted the Syrians for their ingratitude, their anti-Egyptian demonstrations, and their snub of Vice President Mubarak, whom Sadat had dispatched to Damascus to brief Assad on the agreement. He also excoriated the Soviet Union, accusing Moscow of flagrant incitement and an attempt to split Arab ranks. Sadat warned them both that had he really wanted to go his own way, he could have made peace with Israel and regained all of Sinai. Two years later, he would do just that.

Rabin fared better. Although Israelis were not enthusiastic about the agreement, he secured overwhelming backing in the Labor Party, which endorsed it by a vote of 370 to 4—in part due to his bringing Peres on board. Golda Meir summed up the general Israeli attitude when she argued that the agreement should be greeted "not with fanfare, but also not with a feeling of mourning." Rabin had hardly secured the peace that Israelis longed for, but he had succeeded in laying the groundwork for it. In the process, he had taken the U.S.-Israeli relationship to a new level of strategic cooperation in the pursuit of a more stable Middle East. And he had enlisted U.S. support for a massive strengthening of the IDF. In the end, Rabin bent to Kissinger's will, but he made sure Israel was well rewarded for doing so.

Rabin came under withering criticism from Menachem Begin. But that was easily tolerated because he had managed to co-opt Sharon during the reassessment period by appointing him as his military adviser, thereby robbing Begin of his most credible spokesman. Rabin was learning on the job.

In a surprise move, however, Moshe Dayan broke with Rabin and Peres. He denounced the agreement for its failure to gain an Egyptian commitment to non-belligerency in return for Israel's giving up strategic assets. He even criticized Peres's idea of American monitors in the passes, a proposal he had initially encouraged Peres to make. Dayan was laying the groundwork for his rehabilitation, not in the Labor Party, where he would remain damaged goods, but rather with the Likud opposition, which valued the credibility he could still lend them. Two years later, in a move that Kissinger would have recognized as straight out of Talleyrand's playbook, Dayan became Begin's foreign

President Ford welcoming Kissinger home from the Middle East at Andrews Air Force Base on September 3, 1975. Ford had taken the unprecedented step of traveling out to the airport with Vice President Rockefeller to express his appreciation to the conquering hero. Nancy Maginnes and Joe Sisco, who had both been by Kissinger's side throughout this last Arab-Israeli shuttle, look on with pride.

minister and was instrumental in negotiating the breakthrough to peace with Egypt.[*] As Rabin noted resentfully, Dayan reaped the fruits of Rabin's labor.

Kissinger reaped little but grief for his labors. Ford greatly appreciated his efforts and demonstrated it in the unprecedented gesture of traveling to Andrews Air Force Base with Vice President Rockefeller to hail his return. At the airport, Ford congratulated Kissinger on "a great achievement, one of the most historic certainly of this decade and perhaps of this century."

The American press, however, treated the agreement with skepticism. *The New York Times* editorial board viewed it only as a potentially historic step, pointing to the opposition in the Arab world, Israel, and Washington as indicative of the fragile equilibrium it had produced. *Time* featured on its cover a caricature of a dismayed and disheveled Kissinger trying to force the reluctant, child-sized figures of Sadat and Rabin to shake hands. On Kissinger's shoulder, a scrawny dove looked heavenward for salvation.

In Washington, Kissinger was quickly engulfed in a battle with Congress

---

* Charles-Maurice de Talleyrand-Périgord served as Napoleon's foreign minister, switching sides to become Louis XVIII's foreign minister to negotiate peace on behalf of France at the Congress of Vienna.

to secure its support for deploying the two hundred American technicians to the Sinai passes.* As Kissinger had warned Peres, Congress was skeptical, fearing a new Vietnam-like commitment. Senator Mike Mansfield, the longtime Democratic majority leader in the Senate, led the opposition, supported by a freshman senator from Delaware named Joe Biden. They were both opposed to foreign entanglements.

Eventually, on October 9, 1975, after deliberating for five weeks, Congress voted overwhelmingly for the agreement. But not before the Senate Foreign Relations Committee had insisted on reviewing all the secret assurances the administration had provided to the parties. This created a problem for Kissinger. The memoranda of agreements had already been leaked to the *Times*, including an "addendum on arms," which excerpted the paragraph on the F-16s and Pershing missiles from the secret Ford letter to Rabin. The State Department appears to have leaked the addendum to avoid revealing the other element in the secret letter: Ford's Golan commitment to Rabin.

The publication of the arms commitments to Israel generated anger and bitterness in Cairo. Kissinger had not informed Sadat about the Pershing mis-

---

* The resolution endorsing the U.S. commitment of two hundred American technicians to the Sinai mission passed 341 to 69 in the House and 70 to 18 in the Senate.

sile provision. Had Kissinger also revealed to Congress the secret assurance from Ford to Rabin about not expecting Israel to withdraw from the Golan, it would have further embarrassed Sadat and lent credibility to Syria's claim that he had betrayed the Arab cause.

To avoid that, in another act of obfuscation, Kissinger told the Senate Foreign Relations Committee that he had revealed "all undertakings, commitments and assurances that the United States regarded as legally binding and upon which Israel and Egypt could legally rely."[*] It seems the State Department legal counsel had resolved that Ford's Golan commitment was not legally binding and therefore did not need to be revealed to the senators.[†] Kissinger's skill at muddying the waters was also evident in the way both the Israelis and the Egyptians now asserted paternity for the idea of the American technicians in Sinai. Kissinger knew that it had originated in Salzburg as a Sadat proposal, which he had cleverly sold to Rabin, who repackaged it as an Israeli proposal put forward by Peres, which Kissinger then resold to Sadat. But the magician was not about to reveal his secret.

In the last of many appearances on the Hill defending the Sinai II Agreement, Kissinger told Senator George McGovern that "we're coming to the end of the step-by-step process" in the Middle East. Kissinger didn't quite mean it. During the Sinai negotiations, he had told his Israeli interlocutors that the next step with Egypt should be a non-belligerency deal. That is what he pursued during the last year of his occupancy of the seventh-floor suite at the State Department.

He had persuaded Sadat, Rabin, and even Assad of the necessity of taking a breather from the burdens of peacemaking during 1976, an American presidential election year. But Kissinger understood that the Middle East balance of power needed constant tending to stabilize his newly established order in the face of Soviet-backed radical Arab challenges. That would require a new diplomatic initiative in 1977 if Ford was reelected and he asked Kissinger to stay on. In the meantime, consistent with his step-by-step approach, he looked for another step.

---

* In a closed-door session with the Senate Foreign Relations Committee, Kissinger is reported to have said that the assurances were not binding on the United States as state-to-state documents but were more in the nature of statements of diplomatic intent or of putting on paper what already was existing practice. See Bernard Gwertzman, "A Senator Warns of Sinai Impasse," *New York Times*, September 30, 1975, 17; Gwertzman, "House Unit to Back Civilians for Sinai," *New York Times*, October 3, 1975, 1; "U.S. Participation in Sinai Accord Approved," *Congressional Quarterly*, in *CQ Almanac 1975*, 31st ed. (Washington, DC: Congressional Quarterly, 1976), 344–49.
† Amazingly, the Israelis only leaked the existence of Ford's letter six years later, in the context of a controversy over Prime Minister Begin's extension of Israeli law to the Golan Heights. See Mel Laytner, "Israelis Say Ford Made Secret Promise on Golan," UPI, December 23, 1981.

This time he appropriated the concept of land for non-belligerency that Rabin had advocated in their Sinai negotiations and Kissinger had repeatedly dismissed as unachievable. The idea he put to Sadat and Rabin was a yearlong preparation for a three-track negotiation—an even more complicated version of the method he had rejected a year earlier when considering the Jordanian option. He wanted Israel to begin the process by offering partial withdrawals on the Egyptian, Syrian, and Jordanian fronts in return for their commitments to non-belligerency.

Lo and behold, when Sadat came to Washington a month after the signing of the Sinai II Agreement, he responded to Kissinger's idea by offering non-belligerency in return for an Israeli withdrawal in the Sinai to the El-Arish–Ras Muhammed line. That was the very proposal that Rabin had put to Kissinger six months earlier, at the outset of the just-completed negotiations—a proposal that Kissinger had dismissed on the grounds that Sadat would never accept it.

This time, according to Kissinger, Sadat was prepared to go beyond non-belligerency and offer Israel "land for peace" if it would withdraw to a line twenty-five kilometers from the international border. This was consistent with the Sadat initiative that Hafez Ismail had brought Kissinger in February 1973, before the Yom Kippur War.

Kissinger did not present Sadat's more fulsome offer to Rabin when he visited Washington in January 1976, instead sticking to his own, more cautious, non-belligerency initiative. In principle, Rabin was willing to go along with the withdrawal offers to Egypt and Syria that Kissinger sought, even offering to remove Golan settlements to enable a more significant withdrawal on the Syrian front. Unsurprisingly, he would not commit to a significant West Bank withdrawal. However, in February 1976, Rabin even managed to persuade his cabinet to agree to that, at least in theory.

Despite this promising start, the initiative never gained traction. It was quickly eclipsed by the eruption of civil war in Lebanon that same month. This presented a serious challenge to Kissinger's regional order. With so many outside players intervening to support one or another Lebanese faction, and the PLO operating there as a state within a state, the escalation of the Lebanese conflict risked a wider war. Kissinger feared that Israel and Syria, Lebanon's neighbors, would be dragged into confrontation there, threatening his whole enterprise. This time Sadat could not be relied on to help because he was siding with the PLO against the Syrian-backed Christian forces as retribution for the grief that Assad had been causing him for the Sinai II Agreement.

In the midst of this chaos, Kissinger was surprised to receive a message from General Shihabi, now the chief of staff of the Syrian army. He inquired whether Israel would be willing to accept a Syrian "peacekeeping" force in

Lebanon that would intervene in support of the Christian-dominated status quo. Kissinger understood from Shihabi's question that Assad was proposing "an agreement on spheres of interest with Israel via American mediation." He notes in his memoirs that "it was almost a caricature of classic balance-of-power diplomacy," in which the United States could now play the role of the "indispensable balance wheel."

To have Syria assume responsibility for protecting the Lebanese Christians and curbing the PLO was a godsend for Israel. Rabin, though, insisted the Syrian deployment in Lebanon could be no larger than a brigade, and that the forces should not deploy more than ten kilometers south of the Damascus–Beirut highway, keeping them a safe distance from the Israeli border. Once Kissinger had confirmed this understanding with the Syrians, Rabin promptly agreed to green-light Assad's intervention.

The PLO and the irregular Druze and Muslim militias were no match for the Syrian army. Consequently, the civil war abated. Assad was so pleased with the result that he suggested to Kissinger that the United States and Syria had now developed parallel interests in combatting radical forces across the Arab world. Kissinger had managed to enlist Syria in the ranks of the status quo powers. As he observed with some pride, "The radical coalition against the peace process was in tatters." In his view, the "delicate equilibrium which emerged preserved the prospects for an overall peace."

There was a flaw in Kissinger's design for stabilizing Lebanon, however, though it took years to surface. By preventing the Syrian army from moving south of the Litani River, Rabin had created a vacuum in southern Lebanon that the PLO quickly filled, the better to launch terrorist attacks against Israel's northern border towns. This eventually provoked a full-scale Israeli military intervention in 1982 to drive the PLO north to Beirut and thence out of Lebanon to distant Tunisia.

Subsequently, Israel occupied Lebanon's south for eighteen years, while Syria occupied the north for five years beyond that. Prolonged occupations inevitably breed resistance. Eventually, with the backing of Iran, Hezbollah took over the south and then gained effective control of the government in Beirut. Kissinger's objective in Lebanon had been to prevent another radical state from emerging there, but in the end that is what happened, provoking two more wars with Israel in Lebanon until a new equilibrium was established. Nevertheless, with the exception of some minor skirmishes during the 1982 invasion, Israel and Syria avoided conflict in Lebanon and preserved their disengagement agreement on the Golan, while Egypt made and kept its peace with Israel.

Kissinger's diplomacy had succeeded in creating a more or less stable regional Middle Eastern order. It had taken three years of constant exertion to build; its maintenance would require continued efforts to move the peace process forward. According to Kissinger's design, that should be in small, incremental steps.

In all the years that have passed since Kissinger's glory days, he has never wavered in his belief in the gradualist, step-by-step approach that became his leitmotif. Yet as Jimmy Carter demonstrated two years after Kissinger left office, Israel and Egypt were ripe for peace, in good measure because of Kissinger's diplomacy. And, as the record shows, Sadat and Rabin gave him clear signals that they were ready for "the big step." Why did Kissinger never reach for a final peace agreement? Or, when he was given the opportunity, at the outset of the Sinai II negotiations, why did he dismiss the idea of pursuing a non-belligerency agreement?

Kissinger's commitment to his design stemmed from his understanding of the Arab refusal to recognize Israel. Although his skepticism had been there all along, he would only give written expression to it in his book *World Order*, which he published in 2014. European-style secular states like Israel had no precedent in Arab history, he argues there. The shaping of the Middle Eastern system was informed by the sacred Muslim obligation to expand the "dar al-Islam"—the region where the Muslim faith prevailed—to the "dar al-Harb," the provinces of the non-believers. The faith was to be spread, by force, where necessary.

From Kissinger's perspective, this limited the prospects for a stable order in which the Islamic states operated on equal terms with non-Muslim states. And this became the source of his skepticism about peace between the Arabs and Israel, a Western-style secular democracy established in the heart of the Muslim, Arab world. The level of coexistence that Israel expected of its neighbors, in Kissinger's view, "could not possibly arise from a single formal [peace] document but only at the end of a lengthy period of peacefully living side by side."

Kissinger derived this concept of gradualism from Immanuel Kant's essay on "Perpetual Peace." Kant argued that conflict between states would eventually lead to the exhaustion of their powers. Only at that point, Kissinger believed, would the Arab states prefer peace to the misery of war. That "would in time oblige men to contemplate an alternative . . . peace by reasoned design," Kissinger noted.

For Kissinger, the reasoned design was more important than the peace it might eventually produce because it could generate something that he considered more valuable—stability. His purpose was to exhaust the Arabs by keeping the process going long enough "until the point would eventually be reached where one Arab state would say, 'This is enough. It simply is not worth fighting every six months for every 20 kilometers.'"

For Kissinger, as we have seen, the cornerstone of his design was Egypt. His strategic objective was to remove Egypt from the arena of conflict by integrating it, like France after the Napoleonic Wars, into the new Middle Eastern order. In Metternich's design, France became the equipoise to Russia. In Kissinger's design, Egypt backed by the United States would become the equipoise to the radical Arab states backed by the Soviet Union. That would stabilize the order because Kissinger understood that without Egypt, the largest and militarily most powerful Arab state, the Arabs could not go back to war with Israel. In that way it would also advance the process of exhausting them to the point where they would eventually be ready to live in peace with Israel.

Accordingly, at the end of the 1973 war, Kissinger ensured the survival of the Egyptian Third Army after his own hubris and guilt had enabled the IDF to besiege it. Had he allowed the Israelis to force its surrender instead, Sadat would have been humiliated by a triumphant Israel. Neither would have been malleable enough to be molded into the roles Kissinger needed them to play. The hard-won Egypt-Israel agreements that followed vindicated Kissinger's conception and his judgment, creating the mainstays of his grand design.

Kissinger was so committed to this strategy of gradualism, however, that he failed to recognize that by 1975 Sadat had reached the point of exhaustion. It would take a dramatic, unilateral act by Sadat—in this case his decision to travel to Jerusalem two years later—to demonstrate that he was ready for peace. By then, Kissinger was out of office. Nevertheless, Sadat's journey to Jerusalem vindicated Kissinger's approach.

Four decades later, in signing the Abraham Accords, the United Arab Emirates and Bahrain justified their normalization of relations with Israel on the grounds that they had grown tired of the conflict. That provided further confirmation of Kissinger's conception, but on a timetable that conformed more to his expectations.

At the time, Kissinger knew that, on its own, removing Egypt from the radical Arab camp would not be sufficient to legitimize and stabilize the system. Syria, as one of the leaders of that camp, had to be incorporated into the design too. Again, Kissinger's purpose was to give Syria a stake in maintaining the order, not to promote peace between Israel and Syria. Thus, when Assad gave him the opening to make peace, he did not pursue it.

That moment came in the midst of his negotiations with Sadat and Rabin for the Sinai II Agreement. In an unusual interview with *Newsweek*'s Arnaud de Borchgrave, published on March 3, 1975, in advance of a visit to Damascus by Kissinger, Assad expressed his willingness to enter into a long-term peace treaty with Israel. "This is not propaganda," he told de Borchgrave. "We mean it—seriously and explicitly. . . . It is our fundamental position, decided by party leaders." As if he were speaking to Israelis at a time when Rabin was trying to persuade Kissinger to pursue non-belligerency with Sadat, Assad said there needed to be an end to the state of belligerency, "and the end of belligerency will mean the beginning of a stage of real peace." Of course, Assad was also explicit about the price of full peace—full Israeli withdrawal from the Golan Heights and a state for the Palestinians. That was the standard Syrian position; "real peace" was not, and yet that is what Assad said he was prepared to offer Rabin.

On March 15, 1975, Kissinger discussed this idea with Assad in Damascus. The exchange is instructive. He admitted that after his discussions with Rabin he could see for the first time "just a glimmer" of how peace could come, but quickly added, "We're not at that point yet." Assad responded by repeating his commitment to peace. He swore that it was not a maneuver because his people wouldn't stand for it. "We want peace," he said. "It is my conviction that it is in Syria's interest. My talk of peace is for our people—not for Israel. Peace would be our gain." Contrast this with Assad's earlier statements in his first engagement with Kissinger in which he justified Syria's absence from the Geneva Conference because his people were opposed to Syrian officials even appearing in the same room with their Israeli counterparts.

Kissinger responded by defining peace as "the atmosphere in which people feel no injustice is being done to them." That, he said, could not be achieved by a few kilometers in Sinai or the Golan. The reason to start with those "unsatisfactory steps," however, was to get people on both sides used to "the process of peace." In other words, the *objective* of peace was a bridge too far for Kissinger. The best that he could offer was a gradual peace process consisting of steps that were admittedly unsatisfactory because they could not quench the desire for justice but might eventually reconcile the demands and expectations of both sides. It was a bizarre exchange: a pan-Arab nationalist leader was avowing his desire for peace with Israel and an American secretary of state was telling him the Arabs weren't ready.

In the meantime, Kissinger's model of order required a stable arrangement on the Golan and sufficient Syrian engagement in the peace process to provide cover for Sadat to proceed separately, ahead of the other Arab states. Hence his frequent visits to Damascus, even when he had nothing substantial to offer Assad.

Kissinger rightly worried that the Golan disengagement agreement that he had negotiated would be insufficient to keep Assad from disrupting the status quo, especially after he secured the Sinai II Agreement with Egypt. However, he did not believe he could negotiate another partial Israeli retreat on the Golan because it would require the evacuation of Israeli settlements. He never contemplated negotiating the full Israeli withdrawal from the Golan that Rabin might have been willing to offer had he known that Assad was ready to reciprocate with real peace. Eighteen years later, when Rabin became prime minister again, one of the first things he did was to offer President Clinton a full Israeli withdrawal from the Golan, including the settlements, if Assad were willing to end the conflict.

Instead, something else turned up, as it often does in the Middle East. Events in Lebanon provided Kissinger with the opportunity to plus-up the return on Assad's investment in his new Middle Eastern order. The U.S. and Israeli willingness to acknowledge Assad's sphere of influence in Lebanon provided the necessary compensation for his maintenance of calm in the Levant.

Jordan and the PLO were relegated to minor roles in Kissinger's design because their limited power denied them the ability to disrupt the new order. Therefore, by his calculation, their grievances did not need to be satisfied. Jordan was already in the American camp when Kissinger began to engage in Middle Eastern diplomacy, and King Hussein was effectively dependent for his regime's survival on the United States and Israel. That was demonstrated in the 1970 Jordan crisis when they acted effectively together to pressure Syria to end its intervention there.

Because of that assessment, Kissinger missed the role Jordan might have played in containing and eventually resolving the Palestinian problem in the framework of an existing, functioning state. His initial unfamiliarity with the ways of the Arab world had led him to underestimate the importance of the Palestinian issue in the legitimation of his American-led order. That judgment was reinforced by his initial encounters with Sadat and Assad, which led him to conclude, correctly, that they were not prepared to condition their involvement in the peace process on dealing with the Palestinian issue. And since Israel was unwilling to countenance any dealings with the PLO, Kissinger assumed he could easily sideline the organization with nothing more than an occasional clandestine meeting.

Thus, he was unpleasantly surprised by the decision of the Arab leaders at Rabat in 1974 to anoint the PLO as the sole, legitimate representative of the Palestinians, and to demand a role for them in the peace process. It forced him to recognize that the United States would eventually need to address the Palestinian dimension of the conflict too. But, consistent with his time-buying approach, he believed that it should be put off for as long as possible.

Kissinger's critics viewed this as "a blind spot," but it was actually a realist's clear-eyed view that distinguished between those actors who contributed to the regional order and those who did not. During his tenure, the PLO, with its call for the destruction of Israel and the overthrow of King Hussein, clearly fit into the latter category. Bringing the PLO into the negotiations before it was ready to come to terms with Israel's existence, he believed, would only stall progress. The Israelis would object strenuously, and the PLO would demand more than the Arabs would support, or Israel could concede.[*]

President Carter's failed efforts to bring the PLO into the negotiations proved Kissinger's point. It was not until near the end of the Reagan administration, in November 1988, that the PLO finally accepted UNSC Resolution 242 and disavowed terrorism. That led to a short-lived U.S.-PLO dialogue.[†] Only when Rabin and Peres negotiated directly with the PLO in Oslo, in 1993, behind Clinton's back, did the United States finally incorporate this non-state actor into the American-led peace process.

Kissinger's preference had always been for Jordan to serve as the custodian of the Palestinians, via a confederation under the king's rule, rather than an independent Palestinian state. He believed that was the only way to contain the radical, irredentist impulses of the Palestinian national movement. Still, when he had the chance to promote his conception, he did not try to achieve it. That was where his blind spot actually lay—his belief in a hierarchy of power meant that he paid too little attention to the way less powerful states and even non-state actors could disrupt the prevailing equilibrium and destabilize his hard-won order if their demands for justice were not in some way assuaged.

Kissinger was naturally much more sensitive to the disruptive role the Soviet Union, with its immense power, could play. He had relied on détente between the superpowers to stabilize the prewar order but was misled by his assump-

---

[*] After the Sinai II Agreement, Kissinger's aides pushed for PLO inclusion in the next stage of the process. Bowing to their pressure, Kissinger allowed Harold Saunders to announce a slightly modified U.S. approach to the Palestinian issue. In November 1975, in testimony before Congress, Saunders recognized that the Palestinian issue was at "the heart" of the conflict and that Palestinian "legitimate interests" would have to be considered in negotiating peace. However, when that limited opening generated concern in Jerusalem that the administration was backsliding, Kissinger was quick to disavow his aide. He told a Senate committee that if there were to be a change in policy, "it would not be announced by a deputy assistant secretary of state before a subcommittee of Congress." See Bernard Gwertzman, "U.S. Seeks Talks on PLO, Denies a Change in Policy," *New York Times*, December 31, 1975, and U.S. House of Representatives Committee on Foreign Affairs, *Search for Peace in the Middle East Documents and Statements, 1967–1979*, Report Prepared for Subcommittee on Europe and the Middle East of the Committee on Foreign Affairs (Washington, DC: U.S. Government Printing Office, 1979), 305–307.

[†] The dialogue was launched in 1988, at the end of the Reagan administration after the PLO renounced terrorism and accepted UNSC Resolution 242. It was canceled in May 1990, after a terrorist raid by Ahmed Jibril's Palestine Liberation Front (PLF) on an Israeli beach. The PLF was a member organization of the PLO but Arafat refused to condemn the raid.

tion that lesser powers would be unable to disrupt this arrangement. It was one of the reasons he did not take seriously Sadat's expulsion of the Soviet advisers in 1972. When Sadat's decision forced Moscow to choose between maintaining stability and protecting its regional position of influence, Kissinger did not believe the Kremlin would respond by providing the arms necessary for Egypt and Syria to launch war. When Moscow proved him wrong, it reinforced Kissinger's judgment that he needed to diminish the Soviet role in the Middle East by demonstrating to the Arabs that the United States would never allow Soviet arms to prevail.

The Yom Kippur War gave him the opportunity to drive that lesson home through the massive American airlift of arms to Israel, and his encouragement of Israel to increase the battlefield pressure on the Arab armies. But reducing Soviet influence also required him to demonstrate that the Arabs could profit by turning to Washington for a diplomatic solution. When they did, the United States had to produce Israeli withdrawals. Kissinger's hard-won diplomatic successes in this regard on the Egyptian and Syrian fronts led to the diminishment of the Soviet role in the Middle East heartland and its relegation to the peripheral Arab states of Iraq, Libya, and Yemen, from where its capacity for troublemaking became heavily circumscribed.

Kissinger discovered first in the 1970 Jordan crisis, then again in the confrontation with Moscow over the cease-fire in the Yom Kippur War, and yet again when the Kremlin failed to take advantage of his stumble during the Sinai II negotiations, that the Soviets were lacking the will to confront the United States in the Middle East, and the skill to exploit his misstep.

Kissinger claimed that he "took pains not to humiliate the Soviet Union" in the process. At times, however, his competitive instincts got the better of him. As we have seen, he unnecessarily embarrassed the Soviets by excluding them from even a ceremonial role in the Sinai disengagement agreement. He then literally ate Gromyko's dinner in Damascus while concluding the Golan disengagement agreement with Assad. The fact that these petty humiliations resulted in nothing more than Soviet griping reinforced Kissinger's conviction that he had the upper hand, and he did not hesitate to press his advantage. By doing so, he reinforced American dominance in the Middle East and helped ensure that his American-led order would no longer be challenged by an external power.

By 1979, Moscow's focus shifted even further to the Middle East's periphery as it became sucked into a decade-long, futile war in Afghanistan. When the Soviet Union collapsed in 1992, in the wake of the American eviction of its Iraqi client from Kuwait, the Russians vacated the Middle East entirely. They would return only in 2015, when Russian forces intervened in the Syrian civil war to bolster the regime of Hafez al-Assad's son, Bashar. Ironically, President

Vladimir Putin justified the Russian intervention as an effort to stabilize Kissinger's state-based order against the rebel forces, many of them aligned with al-Qaeda and its affiliates, whose purpose was to overthrow the existing order.

Above all, for Kissinger's design to work, he had to convince Israel to give up territory. This is the most interesting element of his diplomatic artistry and why I have dwelled on his many arguments with his Israeli interlocutors. They provide a unique insight into how he succeeded in moving the Israelis on four separate occasions when so many American diplomats who came after him failed, and his success laid the groundwork for the few who later managed to prevail.

Jimmy Carter's negotiation of the Israeli-Egyptian peace treaty, for example, would not have been possible without Kissinger's diplomacy, which established the principle and practice of Israeli withdrawal from occupied territory, built trust between the two sides, and habituated the leaders to view each other as partners in peacemaking.

Kissinger's ability to move Israel, as with every other one of his diplomatic endeavors, began with a concept. Israel was, to him, a prototypical Westphalian state created by the United Nations and protected by the United States, the custodian and principal defender of the liberal international order.* But it was a highly vulnerable state. He viewed its pre-1967 borders as indefensible. The sea of Arab hostility that surrounded it created an existential predicament: How could such a small, weak state survive in a region in which Arabs outnumbered Israelis by a ratio of ten to one?

Kissinger's concern reminds me of Hedley Bull, one of the other great theorists of international order and the hierarchy of states, who was my doctoral dissertation supervisor at the Australian National University. When I told him I wanted to write my thesis on U.S.-Israeli relations, he looked at me quizzically and said, "Why would you waste your time on that topic? It's clear that Israel cannot survive."

Unlike Bull, Kissinger cared whether Israel survived. His Jewish identity gave him a special sensibility toward the Jewish state, and a distinct sense of responsibility. He felt uncomfortable talking about that responsibility, beyond acknowledging that "one cannot live the life I've led without feeling a common destiny with the Jewish people."

He believed, however, that the relationship between Israel and the United States needed to transcend such personal considerations. As he told an Ameri-

---

* The Peace of Westphalia of 1648 created the modern-day international system of states by recognizing the sovereignty and equality of states in the European system at the time.

can Jewish audience in January 1977, just after he left office, "The support for a free and democratic Israel in the Middle East is a moral necessity . . . to be pursued by every administration." His aspiration had been and would remain "an Israel that is secure, that is accepted, that is at peace."

Few Israelis would recognize this portrait of Kissinger's Jewishness, seeing him more as a "court Jew," or worse, a self-hating Jew, because of his attempts to curry favor in the anti-Semitic environment of Nixon's White House. But as the historical record recounted here shows, at critical moments he acted to ensure Israel's survival and well-being when it was far from what others in Washington, or the international community, wanted to do.

Israel's survival, in Kissinger's view, needed to be based on a balance of power sufficiently tipped in its favor to deter Arab attacks, and a legitimacy that came from the recognition of the international community. The United States, as Israel's protector, could help ensure the balance of power, but Israel's legitimacy required the recognition of the other regional powers, its Arab neighbors.

Because Kissinger was so convinced that the Arabs were not ready for peace, he developed the mechanism of a peace process instead, and lubricated it with successive Israeli withdrawals that gave credibility to the legitimizing principle of land-for-peace. As we have seen, that was no easy sell to skeptical Israeli leaders and an even more distrustful Israeli public. Accordingly, Kissinger tailored his efforts to make them palatable to Israel, both politically and psychologically.

Because of his own insecurities, he was particularly sensitive to Israel's. As Max Fisher, the American Jewish leader, once told Ford, "You know how [the Israelis] are—like Henry is as a person." Kissinger understood that Israeli anxieties were a product of both Jewish history and particular circumstances, given the vulnerability of Israel's borders and the hostility of its neighborhood. His step-by-step approach was designed in part to avoid breaking Israel psychologically by forcing it to withdraw in one step to what he regarded as the vulnerable 1967 borders. Eisenhower had done that in Sinai in 1957, after the Suez crisis. Kissinger did not believe that exercise could be repeated without undermining Israel's survival. That is one of the reasons why he was so determined to avoid Nixon's and Ford's preference for a comprehensive solution that would have required the imposition of the 1967 borders with minor rectifications.

Kissinger was generally indulgent of the particular negotiating style that Israel's insecurity produced. He was bemused more often than infuriated by the excessively legalistic and Talmudic approach to every word in the agreements, the exaggerated definitions of Israel's security requirements, and the seemingly endless need for political, economic, and military assurances from the United States. By the end of the negotiations with Rabin and his colleagues, however, he had become exasperated with Israel's neediness. The wonder is that it took him so long.

In bringing the Israelis around to adopting his approach or persuading them to respond to the best offer that he was willing to secure from the Arabs, Kissinger recognized the need for leverage. And while he was willing to accommodate Israeli fears and insecurities and tailor his approach to what he thought they could handle, as we have seen, he was not averse to using the lever of military assistance. Once Nixon gave him control of the Israeli arms spigot in 1970, he did not hesitate to calibrate its flow to achieve the political malleability his strategy required. The most effective exercise of this leverage was during the reassessment in 1975, when Kissinger, with Ford's backing, held up arms supplies in the face of a political onslaught by Israel and its supporters in the United States until Israel's leaders eventually bent to his will.

Kissinger's approach was always carefully calibrated to ensure that Israel's security was not undermined in the process. That would have defeated his aim of ensuring a balance of power tilted in Israel's favor to deter war, maintain stability, and ensure Israel's survival. Rather, his method was to make sure Israel had what it needed to defend itself in the short term before putting longer-term requests on hold. As we saw in the case of the 1975 reassessment, once his leverage achieved its purpose, he was quick to overcompensate by providing a cornucopia of arms to meet all of Israel's longer-term requirements.

Many accuse him of holding up urgently needed arms supplies to Israel during the first week of the Yom Kippur War to keep the country on a short leash. In fact, as Israel's postwar assessments showed, there had been no shortage of materiel during the war. The problem was an inability to transport the munitions to the frontline units, something for which Kissinger could not be blamed. Nevertheless, as the documentary record reveals, before Kissinger became aware of Israel's military setbacks, he secured a presidential commitment to replace all the weapons and materiel the IDF used up in the war. Once he understood Israel's difficulties, he attempted to provide for Israel's immediate needs, albeit in a low-profile way to avoid an Arab oil embargo, a not unreasonable concern given the consequences for the U.S. economy when it was actually imposed.

During that time, far from restraining Israel, Kissinger was urging the IDF to advance on Damascus. When he thought Israel lacked the military materiel to prosecute its offensives on the Golan and in the Sinai, he went to Nixon to seek a more direct, if still low-profile, resupply effort. Once Nixon ordered a full-fledged airlift, Kissinger rode herd on the Pentagon to ensure it continued apace. He understood that in a crisis, Israel's dependence on the United States obviated the need for arms supply leverage. On the contrary, as he explained to Nixon at the outset of the war, "we must be on their side now so that they have something to lose afterwards. . . . If we kick them in the teeth, they have nothing to lose."

Over time, Kissinger's principal source of leverage would diminish as assistance for Israel's long-term military requirements became institutionalized in the U.S.-Israeli relationship. This found its ultimate expression in 2016, when President Obama signed a ten-year memorandum of understanding with the Israeli government that provided for $38 billion in military assistance, making it difficult to control the arms spigot in the way that Kissinger was able to do in the 1970s. Still, arms in the pipeline can be placed on hold, and other military-related means can be developed to signal to the Israeli government the need to respect the interests of its American ally.[*]

At the same time as Kissinger used military assistance as a lever to induce Israeli flexibility, he also undertook a painstaking effort to educate the Israeli leadership about the negotiating game he needed them to play. Convincing Meir, in particular, of the need to yield even a minimum amount of territory was painful, difficult, and frustrating, yet he was indefatigable. Hour after hour, he would muster every argument in his arsenal and deploy each one at times with a sense of humor that charmed his stiff-necked Israeli audience, at other times with threats that only reinforced their resistance. Handicapped by his jaundiced view of the rewards for Israel's concessions, believing there was little of lasting value the Arabs would offer Israel for the return of their territory, he would dwell instead on the dangers of Israeli inaction. Eventually, they tired of his threats, even when they were delivered in the name of the president of the United States.

Because Kissinger was skeptical of the trade of territory for peace, he did his best, as we've seen, to convince Israel's leaders of the virtue of trading territory for time: time for Israel to get over the trauma of the Yom Kippur War; time to reduce Soviet influence in the region; time to build Israel's military and economic strength, assisted by the United States; and time for the Arabs to finally accept Israel. This approach worked better than his attempts at intimidation, and, ironically, became the foundational principle of Israeli negotiating strategy.

---

[*] In 2020 for example, Senator Chris Van Hollen and twelve other Senate Democrats filed an amendment to the Fiscal Year 2021 National Defense Authorization Act to prohibit Israel from using U.S. security assistance to unilaterally annex Palestinian territory in the West Bank. Others have suggested that the amount that Israel spends on West Bank settlements should be deducted from the military assistance it receives from the United States.

Ariel Sharon depicted this approach for me in graphic terms when I was U.S. ambassador to Israel and he had become prime minister. In the winter of 2001, I visited him on his Cypress Ranch in southern Israel near Gaza. In front of a crackling fire as I savored, and he devoured, his wife Lily's legendary cherry strudel, he told me how he would watch his cows at the abattoir being pushed into what he called the *corrales* (i.e., the holding pens). He described how they would be forced by the cows behind them to move from the larger to the smaller pens until, bellowing at their fate, they would be pushed inexorably into the chute where slaughter awaited them.

Sharon told me that he identified the fate of Israel with those cows, imagining his country being forced inevitably toward "the chute" of the 1967 borders. His role, he explained to me between mouthfuls of strudel, was to prolong the time before Israel was pushed into the chute by shutting the gates on each of the corrals and making it as difficult as possible for the Arabs and the international community to open them. Later, when he withdrew Israel unilaterally from Gaza, I understood that Sharon, ever the tactician, had opened a smaller gate there in order to shut what he considered the more important gate to territorial concessions in the West Bank.

Kissinger's agreements with Egypt bought Israel five years before it had to deal with a full withdrawal from Sinai. The Israeli-Egyptian peace treaty, signed in 1979, bought Israel another fourteen years of continued control of the West Bank and the Golan Heights. The Oslo Accords, signed in 1993, with its interim agreements and undefined endpoint for Israeli withdrawal, enabled Israel to cede only 40 percent of the West Bank. Those Israeli-Palestinian agreements, together with Sharon's unilateral withdrawal from Gaza, bought Israel another twenty-five years to consolidate its hold on East Jerusalem and the rest of the West Bank.

In the interim, with American assistance, Israel used time to build its military, economic, and technological capabilities to the point where it became the strongest power in the Middle East, with one of the most powerful armies in the world. Israel today is no longer the small, vulnerable state that Kissinger worried about.

Meanwhile, over time, the Arab states gradually came to tire of the conflict, accept the Jewish state in their midst, and recognize the benefit of cooperating with it, from security assistance in Sinai, to water for Jordan, to strategic cooperation with Saudi Arabia and the UAE against Iran, and help in Washington for all four. It was just as Kant and Kissinger had predicted.

To be sure, time buying did not end the conflict with the stateless Palestinians in Israel's midst, but it has steadily lowered their expectations of what their state would look like and increased their willingness to accept Israel's security concerns (from accepting a state in 30 percent of historic Palestine, to agreeing to its demilitarization, to engaging in ever more effective security cooperation with the IDF and the Shin Bet).

There lay a cruel irony, however, in Kissinger's concept of using territory to buy time as a way of increasing Israel's sense of security. It would also have the unintended consequence of solidifying Israel's grip on the territory remaining in its control, as settlers continued to build and expand their communities in the West Bank and on the Golan, with government support. By the end of Kissinger's tenure as secretary of state, the number of settlers in the West Bank was a mere 1,900; by 2020, the number had swelled to more than 466,000 in some 131 settlements. That made it all the more difficult politically to relinquish the territory even as Israel's strength grew, until now, more than four decades later, it has become almost unimaginable.

During the Trump administration the settlers and their friends made a deliberate attempt to do away with the principle of territory for peace altogether, and almost succeeded. Their efforts included President Trump's recognition of Israeli sovereignty on the Golan Heights, an attempt in the Security Council to pronounce UNSC Resolution 242 obsolete, and the green-lighting of Israel's annexation of some 30 percent of the West Bank, including the Jordan Valley and all of the settlements. It was only the UAE's offer of full normalization with Israel in exchange for canceling the annexation that salvaged the principle of territory for peace for the time being.

Kissinger could not have foreseen in January 1974 that the right wing in Israel, with its nationalist and religious commitment to retaining as much of the West Bank as possible, would so effectively exploit his time-buying concept to serve their aims. But he did understand the consequences for his legitimizing principle if they succeeded. He writes in his memoirs that he believed Israel had no choice in the end but to cede territory for peace: "It could not risk not making the experiment, for the Jewish state would consume its moral substance if it sought to rest its existence on naked force."

Ironically, when it came to dealing with the Palestinians, Kissinger produced a surprising Israeli convert to his strategic design—Yitzhak Rabin. Notwithstanding their epic confrontation over peacemaking in 1975, when Rabin returned to the prime minister's office in 1992 he adopted Kissinger's step-by-step methodology. Five years earlier, as defense minister in the Likud-led government of Yitzhak Shamir, Rabin was confronted by an unexpected Palestinian effort to disrupt the order that Kissinger had so effectively established with his grudging cooperation. This first intifada, which originated spontaneously in Gaza and the West Bank, convinced Rabin that he could no longer preserve stability by maintaining the Israeli occupation there, much as Kissinger concluded when the Yom Kippur War broke out in 1973 that he could not preserve stability merely by supporting the Israeli occupation of Sinai and the Golan.

Rabin believed that the Palestinians were not yet willing to come to terms with Israel's existence and that Israelis were not yet ready to accommodate Palestinian demands for a state on the 1967 borders with East Jerusalem as its capital. Like Kissinger, therefore, he introduced the idea of a step-by-step process—he called it "phase-by-phase"—in which the Palestinians would gradually assume control of more territory previously occupied by Israel. The process would begin with Palestinian rule in Gaza and Jericho, the very idea that the Israelis had suggested to King Hussein back in 1974. That would be followed by three further IDF withdrawals in the West Bank over a five-year period, toward the end of which the two sides would engage in final-status negotiations to resolve all outstanding issues. In the meantime, Rabin insisted, just like Kissinger would have done, that the end state when it came to borders, Jerusalem, refugees, and statehood would be left undefined.

The Oslo Accords that resulted were certainly Peres's idea, but Rabin infused them with Kissinger's concept of a gradual process designed to allow the Palestinians to govern themselves while habituating them and Israelis to a compromise deal for coexistence. By the end of five years, the two sides were supposed to conclude a final peace agreement. But Rabin was quick to announce that there were "no sacred dates," and that he would not be held to that notional timetable unless both sides were ready.

Because Rabin was dealing with the PLO, rather than a state with established institutions, like Egypt and Syria, and because Jordan had been excluded from playing a role, the process fared badly. Rabin had to rely on Arafat to curb a terrorist onslaught by Hamas and Palestine Islamic Jihad aimed at undermining the peace process. Instead of confronting them, Arafat preferred to co-opt them. Meanwhile, Israeli settlers used the time to expand their presence in the West Bank. A peace process designed to test peaceful intentions and generate trust was serving only to convince both sides that the other side wasn't really committed to coexistence. Yet on the eve of Rabin's assassination, in November 1995, Arafat had begun to respond to Rabin's pressure to do more to foil terrorist attacks and Rabin was adjusting his own vision of a final settlement to embrace the idea of an independent Palestinian entity, albeit in some undefined relationship with Jordan.*

* In a little-remembered speech on the occasion of the signing of the Oslo II Agreement, five weeks before he was assassinated, Rabin outlined this vision of a separation from the Palestinians "not because of hatred but because of respect." He spoke of a political arrangement between "a Palestinian entity in which they rule themselves by themselves, Israel as a Jewish, independent

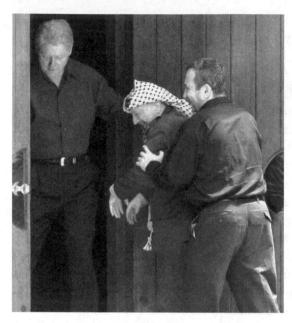

President Bill Clinton assists Prime Minister Ehud Barak in bundling Chairman Yasir Arafat into a meeting at Laurel Lodge at Camp David on July 11, 2000, to try to reach an end to the Israeli-Palestinian conflict. Arafat had resisted Clinton's invitation to the Camp David II summit because he was not in a position to compromise on final-status issues. He preferred Kissinger's step-by-step approach that Yitzhak Rabin had adopted in the Oslo Accords.

Perhaps if Rabin had not been assassinated, his adaptation of Kissinger's step-by-step process might have eventually produced a peaceful resolution. Unfortunately, Kissinger was in no position to tutor Rabin's successors, who set about ignoring the basic principles of his peacemaking strategy. And try as he might, Bill Clinton was unable to convince them to stick with Rabin's gradualist approach. Benjamin Netanyahu stalled the process while expanding the settlements; it took Clinton almost two years to convince him to relinquish a mere 13 percent of the West Bank. Then in Clinton's last year in office, Ehud Barak as prime minister insisted on abandoning the process entirely in pursuit of a conflict-ending agreement that Arafat resisted at Camp David II in July 2000. The failure to achieve a final agreement generated a second Palestinian intifada, which consumed the Oslo step-by-step process in a paroxysm of violence and generated a conflict that lasted five years and left thousands of casualties on both sides, destroying all trust between them.

From the outset, Kissinger's construction of the American-led Middle Eastern order did not depend on a resolution of the Israeli-Palestinian conflict. He did not believe that the question of who controlled the West Bank and Gaza was of strategic consequence to the United States, which is why he kept the PLO on the sidelines and did not pursue the Jordanian option when he had the opportunity. Kissinger told Dayan at the time that Egypt was an

---

state, and Jordan." See Yitzhak Rabin, Remarks at Reception for Heads of State at the Corcoran Museum, September 28, 1995, https://www.youtube.com/watch?v=X-cEFbtW5vo&feature=youtube.

American interest; the West Bank was an Israeli interest. So too today, who rules in Ramallah is a local issue—a vital interest for Israel, Jordan, and the Palestinians to be sure, but not for the United States, and increasingly not for the other Arab states either. Nevertheless, as Kissinger knew, any order depends for its legitimacy on a sense of justice, and as long as the Palestinians are unable to realize their aspirations to live free in their own land, the Middle Eastern order will not be stable and Israel's "moral substance," as Kissinger put it, will erode.

The more profound challenges to Kissinger's Middle Eastern order, however, emerged from events unrelated to the Arab-Israeli conflict. A few years after Kissinger left office, the revolution in Iran removed the shah, who had served as one of the pillars of the new order, policing security in the Gulf. That presaged the rise of revolutionary and messianic movements, first in Shiite Iran and then across the Sunni Arab world, that were intent on overthrowing Kissinger's order, especially because it was American led.

The peace process could not serve as an adequate mechanism for containing them, though for a while that was not evident. The Oslo Accords afforded cover for the Israel-Jordan peace treaty that secured Israel's eastern flank and ensured the longevity of the Hashemite kings. That progress in the early years of the Clinton administration advantaged the effort to contain the challenges to the order from Saddam Hussein's Iraq and the ayatollahs' Iran.

But then it all unraveled. An Israeli-Syrian peace deal miscarried in March 2000 because of bad timing. The failure of the Camp David II summit in July 2000 led to the outbreak of the Palestinian intifada in October of that year. Then al-Qaeda's 9/11 attack on the American-led order a year later precipitated Bush's toppling of Saddam Hussein and the growth of Iranian revolutionary influence in Baghdad. The United States became bogged down in wars in Afghanistan and Iraq. Revolutions in the Arab world led to the overthrow of Hosni Mubarak, Sadat's successor, driving Egypt into strategic hibernation and precipitating a civil war in Syria. And the Iranians seized the opportunity to make their bid for hegemony across the Sunni Arab world.

How would Kissinger have attempted to re-create order out of this landscape of Middle Eastern chaos? In his book *World Order*, he provides some clues. The messianic revolutionaries who sought to establish their own "divinely-inspired system" through violent intimidation of secular states would have to be vanquished. In the case of ISIS and al-Qaeda, that task is all but complete. Iran, on the other hand, had been "a great nation legitimately lodged in the Westphalian system of states." The challenge, he argues, was to persuade Iran to abandon its revolution and return to more stately behavior.

He does not advocate the overthrow of the regime. Rather, in classic balance-of-power terms, he suggests that once Iran has again decided to play by the rules, the United States needs to act as the balancer, positioning itself as closer to all the contending powers than they are to each other.

In the meantime, a new equilibrium would have to be created to balance Iran. He suggests it would need to be produced by an alliance of Sunni states. But with Egypt preoccupied with its internal challenges and problems in its immediate neighborhood, Syria in chaos, Iraq under Iran's influence, and the Gulf Arab states fighting among themselves, that is a challenging proposition. The Trump administration tried to put together a Middle East Strategic Alliance of Sunni Arab states—dubbed the "Arab NATO"—to counter Iran. It never got off the ground because most of the Arab states, especially Egypt, were not interested in being dragged into a confrontation with Iran.

Kissinger's redesign could not take account of another factor that he would have nevertheless recognized from America's retrenchment from Southeast Asia during his time in office. By the time of the Obama administration, the United States had begun to retrench from its forlorn engagements in the Middle East's wars, a process that continued under the Trump and Biden administrations. With its dramatically reduced dependence on Middle Eastern oil, and with the rise of China requiring a reassignment of military assets and high-level attention back to Asia, the U.S. role in stabilizing the Middle East would have to change. The redesign now requires the United States to change roles from dominating the regional order to supporting America's regional allies and partners as they increasingly take the lead.

Israel, Saudi Arabia, and the UAE are the principal regional players allied to the United States capable of playing that role. They share a common perception of the Iranian threat and are concerting their policies for countering it. Given their strength and oil wealth, respectively, they could, in theory, provide the pillars of a new Israeli-Sunni alliance—supported by the United States—that could serve as the equipoise to Iran and, with the support of Egypt and Jordan, provide the foundations of a new regional order.

Saudi Arabia, however, is a problematic pillar in this redesigned American-supported order. Its ambitious, headstrong, and ruthless young leader, Crown Prince Mohammed bin Salman, respects few of Kissinger's rules of the game. His aggressive campaign to suppress Iranian-backed Houthi rebels in Yemen was a high-cost, no-gain proposition for Saudi Arabia that only advantaged Iran. His decision to increase oil production dramatically at a time when demand was cratering because of the coronavirus pandemic caused a collapse in oil prices, devastating the U.S. shale oil industry. His siege of neighboring Qatar only succeeded in making that small state more dependent on Iran. A product of homeschooling, he clearly could benefit from a Kissingerian education in how better to maintain the regional order.

Israel is more capable and reliable in balancing Iran, and Arab states are increasingly willing to make common cause with the Jewish state either under the table or, in the case of the UAE, Bahrain, Morocco, and Sudan, above the table too. As Kissinger predicted, they have grown exhausted by the conflict and are ready to normalize relations with Israel without requiring a resolution of the conflict with the Palestinians. But, as Kissinger could tell them, and as the outbreak of conflict between Israel and Hamas in 2021 underscored, a stable order requires at least a degree of justice for the Palestinians.

That brings us full circle to the need for a peace process the better to promote the regional order, and the need for a stable regional order the better to promote peace. Kissinger continues to hold a pessimistic view of the chances for genuine reconciliation between Israel and the Palestinians, so he comes back to the idea of "some interim arrangement . . . to enhance the possibility of practical coexistence" between Israel and a Palestinian state in part of the West Bank "granted the attributes of sovereignty pending a final agreement." Not a "state minus," in Netanyahu's humiliating formulation, but rather a state-in-the-making, gradually reconciling with Israel as it builds the capabilities to assume its responsibilities within a stable Middle Eastern order. For that step-by-step process to work, however, a useful first step would be for Israel to recognize the Palestinian state with the final border between them to be negotiated in the future. In the meantime, Palestinians would gradually need to gain greater control over West Bank territory, while Israel would need to stop expanding settlements there.

Here is the kernel of an idea that is worth developing in the aftermath of the successive failures of Secretary of State John Kerry's efforts to devise acceptable principles for a final status agreement and Special Envoy Jared Kushner's attempt to impose a solution on the Palestinians. It would involve resisting the siren song of comprehensive peace in favor of a return to Kissingerian gradualism, a step-by-step process that aimed to rekindle trust by both sides in the intentions of the other and faith in Israel that it can once again become more secure not less by ceding territory. The first step could be another Israeli withdrawal from West Bank territory—i.e., the third further redeployment of the IDF from parts of Area C as provided for under the Oslo agreement. In that process, as Kissinger suggests, the Palestinians could gain U.S. and Israeli recognition of their state-in-the-making. It would be a state with undefined final borders, just as Israel has been for much of its existence. But its recognition could come with a commitment from the United States and other international powers to support an eventual negotiation of its final borders based on the 1967 lines with border rectifications involving mutually agreed swaps of territory.

A critical element, not mentioned by Kissinger but a lesson from his failure to value Jordan's role, should be an effort to reengage the Hashemite Kingdom in settling the Palestinian problem. Once the interim Palestinian state is recognized, for example, it could be encouraged to enter into a confederation with Jordan that would facilitate its economic development and enable final status issues to be resolved in an Israeli-Jordanian-Palestinian context, perhaps resulting in a trilateral confederation. Egypt should be encouraged to play a similar custodial role in neighboring Gaza, encouraging Hamas to reconcile with the Palestinian Authority and eventually with Israel. Meanwhile, normalization of relations between Israel and a widening circle of Arab states can contribute to this process by providing Israel with the recognition it has too long been denied in return for forgoing its West Bank territorial ambitions in favor of a contiguous Palestinian state living alongside it in peace.

In my last interview with Kissinger, when he was ninety-seven, I asked him whether he regretted never reaching for the ultimate deal of a final peace agreement. He confirmed that if he had stayed on as secretary of state, he

Egyptian president Anwar Sadat, President Jimmy Carter, and Israeli prime minister Menachem Begin at the signing of the Camp David Accords in the East Room of the White House on September 18, 1978. Kissinger was content to have laid the foundations for this breakthrough to Egyptian-Israeli peace. His caution and skepticism had led him to avoid pushing the parties to achieve a final peace agreement.

would have aimed for non-belligerency agreements rather than peace treaties because he did not believe the Arabs were ready to recognize and live in peace with Israel. But then he added, "I never tried to push the parties for a final peace agreement because I was afraid that, if I did, I would break the process." That innate caution led him to miss the chance to be the American diplomat who negotiated the peace treaty between Egypt and Israel. Jimmy Carter achieved that in his stead, though Kissinger seemed to have no regrets on that score. Rather, he had a deeper concern with the determinants of American foreign policy.

As he detailed in his monumental book *Diplomacy*, American statesmen rarely understand or respect the rules of the game that his conception of international order required. Their idealism is often driven by a sense of divine providence. That is especially so when it comes to making peace in the Holy Land. They imagine that pursuing peace there is not only desirable but achievable; the only challenge is to come up with the right formula for a solution and apply it. That was as true for Nixon and Ford as it was for Carter, Clinton, Obama, Kerry, and Trump.

Those American leaders who have come after Kissinger tended to pursue the Holy Grail of Middle East peace with too little concern for maintaining the regional order he had established. As he notes in his first book, *A World Restored*, "It is not balance which inspires men but universality, not security but immortality." Kissinger's successors certainly shared little of the skepticism that had generated his cautious approach to remaking the region. Consequently, Clinton acceded to Israeli prime minister Ehud Barak's insistence on an attempt to achieve a final Israeli-Palestinian agreement in 2000, which had such disastrous results. Since then, American presidents trying for a final peace have been unable to put the peace process, like Humpty Dumpty, back together again.

Was it better to try for less the Kissingerian way and limit the consequences of failure? When I was an adviser to President Clinton, I thought it was better to try for more. But at the end of this journey, I have come to appreciate Kissinger's point. Failing to pursue peace when the opportunity arose, as Kissinger did before the Yom Kippur War, and in the case of Jordan after the war, had its appalling, unintended consequences. But pursuing peace with too much enthusiasm and too little Kissingerian skepticism and guile has also had horrific results. That is the tragic aspect of Middle East peacemaking, as Kissinger would be the first to point out. We will never know what would have happened if Kissinger's more cautious way had been pursued.

Herein lies the dilemma at the heart of Middle East peacemaking diplomacy. As Kissinger understood, the maintenance of order required a credible peace process, but the scale of the diplomat's ambition could end up destabilizing that order. As he had pointed out on the first page of *A World Restored*, "Those ages which in retrospect seem most peaceful were least in search of peace." His study of history married to his own experience led him to fear overreaching for peace. That is why he was so committed to gradualism. If he were to make a mistake, it would be to err on the side of caution rather than ambition. As we have seen, that led him to miss opportunities, but it also enabled him to shape a Middle Eastern order that resulted in the avoidance of major wars and the possibility of peace.

Having repeatedly tried the alternative of an end-of-conflict Israeli-Palestinian peace agreement and failed, it is time for U.S. policymakers to return to Kissinger's step-by-step approach as part of a broader strategy for building a new American-supported Middle Eastern order.

This is not to suggest that all Kissinger's stratagems should be emulated. As this account has revealed, his attempt to promote a European-style, hierarchical order for the Middle East had its shortcomings, primarily in his underestimation of the ability of lesser regional actors to disrupt the will of the superpowers. And his preference for order and skepticism about peace meant that he missed the chance to create conditions that might have helped secure its ultimate achievement with regard to the Palestinians. His day-to-day Middle Eastern maneuverings at times looked like improvisation rather than the implementation of a grand strategic design. They led to major missteps essentially because, as he would often point out, they were based on judgments that he could not prove true when he made them. And, as Kissinger would be the first to concede, a significant amount of his success was due to the statesmanship of his interlocutors, particularly Anwar Sadat, rather than his own brilliance alone.

Nevertheless, the art in his Middle East diplomacy lay in his conception and achievement of an American-led regional order in which the pursuit of peace was an essential mechanism. As Kissinger once observed, "The statesman . . . will be judged by history on the basis of how wisely he managed the inevitable change and, above all, by how well he preserves the peace." In the end, when it came to managing violent Middle Eastern passions and preserving peace, history's judgment should surely be that Henry Kissinger did well. Future statesmen would do well too by learning from his experience in their pursuit of Middle East peace.

Acknowledgments

The idea for this book was conceived in long conversations with Jonathan Segal, my editor at Knopf. He was intrigued by what diplomats did behind closed doors in their efforts to negotiate peace in the Middle East. Out of my attempt to explain it to him came the idea of writing a book about Henry Kissinger's Middle East diplomacy, illuminated by my own experiences negotiating Middle East peace twenty years later. Throughout this eight-year journey, with its long hiatuses, Jonathan has patiently nurtured and painstakingly edited the manuscript, and taught me to write along the way.

This book would not have been possible without the extensive cooperation of its subject, Henry Kissinger. He granted me access to his papers, but far more important, through many hours of conversation, he gave me access to his thinking. In his nineties, he remains a formidable intellect. I expect he will feel that the generosity and friendship he has shown me have not been reciprocated by some of my criticisms in these pages. I hope he will understand that, taken in full, this book reflects my deep respect for him and my appreciation of his statesmanship.

I began writing this book at the Brookings Institution in Washington and completed it at the Council on Foreign Relations in New York. I am particularly indebted to my friends at both these institutions for the unstinting support they have provided. In particular, Richard Haass, the president of CFR, and Strobe Talbott, the president of Brookings at the time, inspired and encouraged me throughout this long journey.

I am deeply grateful to the many research and administrative associates who were indispensable to the completion of this project. Nicki Alam and Charlotte Baldwin at Brookings and Amy Baker and Shira Schwartz at CFR supported me tirelessly. Nadav Greenberg and Yael Mizrahi-Arnaud did the lion's share of the work of tracking down documents in the archives and libraries in both the United States and Israel, including translating them from Hebrew. I will cherish those moments of delight when they would burst into my office to share with me their latest discovery. Roni Kipnis complemented their labors in the Israeli archives. Basia Rosenbaum checked all the references, tracked down the photos, and took care of the myriad details involved in shepherding the manuscript to publication, all with amazing ingenuity and persistence. This book is as much a reflection of their efforts as my own.

I also depended on a number of interns to supplement the work of these research associates. In particular, Matthew Eady, Kitaneh Fitzpatrick, Andrea Kemmerle, Connor McCune, Michael Reeves, and Daniel Waqar contributed their energy and talent.

A host of librarians helped in locating documents and photographs. In particular, I would like to express my appreciation to Louise Fischer and Yaacov Lozowick at the Israel State Archives; Ernest Emrich and Margaret McAleer at the Library of Congress; Joshua Cochran, who handles the Kissinger Papers at Yale University Library; Melissa Heddon at the Richard Nixon Presidential Library; and Elizabeth Druga at the Gerald R. Ford Presidential Library.

William Burr and the National Security Archive at George Washington University deserve special praise for the remarkable job they have done in securing the declassification of many of the documents used in this study. Similarly, Erich Stein and the researchers at the State Department's Office of the Historian made an invaluable contribution to this study through their expert curation of the Foreign Relations of the United States documentary compendiums.

The wonderful professionals at Knopf did an excellent job shepherding the manuscript to publication. I am deeply grateful to Chip Kidd, Cassandra Pappas, Nicole Pedersen, Sarah Perrin, Erin Sellers, Nicholas Latimer, and mapmaker David Lindroth.

Special thanks to Vivian Dinitz, who shared the unpublished memoirs of her husband, Ambassador Simcha Dinitz, whose role in this drama has gone unrecognized for too long.

Liaquat Ahamed, Nahum Barnea, Ivor Indyk, James Lindsay, Shannon O'Neill, Itamar Rabinovich, Robert Satloff, Asher Susser, and Ehud Ya'ari, as well as two anonymous peer reviewers, read the manuscript, providing me with sage advice and correcting the record where they could. Winston Lord, William Quandt, Harold Saunders, and Brent Scowcroft, all members of Kissinger's team, provided crucial insights. Nabil Fahmy and Ahmed Aboul Gheit shared their invaluable understanding of Egyptian policymaking at the time. Amos Eran, Efraim Halevy, Dalia Rabin, and Moshe Raviv provided fascinating perspectives on the Israeli side. The other people I interviewed for this book are too numerous to name but I am deeply grateful to all of them. The remaining shortcomings are my responsibility.

Writing a book requires the sustenance and encouragement of friends and family. Charles Bronfman, Ronnie Cohen, Hirsh Goodman, Jacob Indyk, Sarah Indyk, Ben Jacobs, Frank Lowy, Jeffrey Skoll, Harry Solomon, and most important, Haim Saban, have been generous and genuine in their friendship and support.

Special thanks to the Friedman Family Foundation Strategic Innovation Fund, the Lowy Institute for International Policy, and the Skoll Foundation for their support for this project.

My wife, Gahl Hodges Burt, has been my constant companion, inspiration, and gentle critic. Reading the manuscript together on balmy days in Central Park is my fondest memory of the miserable pandemic. We began this journey with Henry Kissinger separately, forty-seven years ago. I am so grateful that we are ending it together.

I have dedicated this book to my grandchildren in the hope that they too, with the guidance of their wonderful parents, will pursue peace in their lifetimes, following the teaching of the Torah sages that it is not up to us to finish the job, "but neither can we desist from it."

Appendix A

EGYPTIAN-ISRAELI AGREEMENT ON DISENGAGEMENT
OF FORCES IN PURSUANCE OF THE GENEVA PEACE CONFERENCE

January 18, 1974

A. Egypt and Israel will scrupulously observe the cease-fire on land, sea, and air called for by the UN Security Council and will refrain from the time of the signing of this document from all military or para-military actions against each other.

B. The military forces of Egypt and Israel will be separated in accordance with the following principles:

1. All Egyptian forces on the east side of the Canal will be deployed west of the line designated as Line A on the attached map. All Israeli forces, including those west of the Suez Canal and the Bitter Lakes, will be deployed east of the line designated as Line B on the attached map.
2. The area between the Egyptian and Israeli lines will be a zone of disengagement in which the United Nations Emergency Force (UNEF) will be stationed. The UNEF will continue to consist of units from countries that are not permanent members of the Security Council.
3. The area between the Egyptian line and the Suez Canal will be limited in armament and forces.
4. The area between the Israeli line (Line B on the attached map) and the line designated as Line C on the attached map, which runs along the western base of the mountains where the Gidi and Mitla Passes are located, will be limited in armament and forces.
5. The limitations referred to in paragraphs 3 and 4 will be inspected by UNEF. Existing procedures of the UNEF, including the attaching of Egyptian and Israeli liaison officers to UNEF, will be continued.
6. Air forces of the two sides will be permitted to operate up to their respective lines without interference from the other side.

C. The detailed implementation of the disengagement of forces will be worked out by military representatives of Egypt and Israel, who will agree on the stages of this process. These representatives will meet no later than 48 hours after the signature of this agreement at Kilometer 101 under the aegis of the United Nations for this purpose. They will complete this task within five days. Disengagement will begin within 48 hours after the completion of the work of the military representatives and in no event later than seven days after the signature of this agreement. The process of disengagement will be completed not later than 40 days after it begins.

D. This agreement is not regarded by Egypt and Israel as a final peace agreement. It constitutes a first step toward a final, just and durable peace according to the provisions of Security Council Resolution 338 and within the framework of the Geneva Conference.

For Egypt:
General Abdul Ghani el-Gamasy

For Israel:
David Elazar, Lt. Gen., Chief of Staff of I.D.F.

MEMORANDUM OF UNDERSTANDING BETWEEN THE UNITED STATES GOVERNMENT AND THE GOVERNMENT OF ISRAEL

January 18, 1974

1. The United States informs Israel that Egypt's intentions are to clear and open the Suez Canal for normal operations, and to rehabilitate the cities and towns along the Canal and resume normal peacetime economic activities in that area, beginning as quickly as possible after the Disengagement Agreement is implemented.

2. The United States has received assurances from Egypt of its intention, upon completion of the implementation of the Agreement, to start reducing significantly its forces under mobilization if Israel gives a like indication to Egypt through the United States.

3. It is the policy of the United States that implementation of the Disengagement Agreement and substantial steps by Egypt to implement its intentions in Paragraph 1 above should take precedence over the undertaking of new commitments by the parties related to subsequent phases of the Geneva Conference. The United States will do its best to help facilitate the Conference proceeding at a pace commensurate with this view.

4. The United States position is that withdrawal of United Nations Emergency Forces during the duration of the Disengagement Agreement requires the consent of both sides. Should the matter of the withdrawal come before the United Nations Security Council without the consent of Israel, the United States will vote against such withdrawal.

5. The United States will oppose supervision of Israeli-held areas by United Nations Observers from the Soviet Union, from other communist countries or from other countries which have no diplomatic relations with Israel. With respect to the deployment of forces in the United Nations Emergency Forces zone, the United States will approach the United Nations Secretary General with a view to working out arrangements whereby no units or personnel of nations which do not have diplomatic relations with Israel will (a) be deployed adjacent to the Israeli line, or (b) participate in the inspection of the Israeli area of limited forces and armaments.

6. The United States has informed the Governments of Israel and Egypt that it will perform aerial reconnaissance missions over the areas covered by the Disengagement

Agreement at a frequency of about one mission every ten days or two weeks and will make the photographs available to both Israel and Egypt.

7. The United States regards the Straits of Bab el-Mandeb as an international waterway and will support and join with others to secure general recognition of the right of free and innocent passage through those Straits. The United States will strongly support free passage of Israeli ships and cargoes through the Straits. In the event of interference with such passage, the United States will consult with Israel on how best to assure the maintenance and exercise of such rights.

8. With regard to the Egyptian undertaking not to interfere with the free passage of Israeli ships or cargoes through the Straits of Bab el-Mandeb, the United States informs the Government of Israel that it is the United States position that no notification in advance of the names of vessels passing through the Straits or any other prior communication to Egypt is required. The United States will immediately seek confirmation that this is also the Egyptian position.

9. Recognizing the defense responsibilities of the Government of Israel following redeployment of its forces under the Disengagement Agreement, the United States will make every effort to be fully responsive on a continuing and long-term basis to Israel's military equipment requirements.

10. In case of an Egyptian violation of any of the provisions of the Agreement or any of its attachments, the United States Government and the Government of Israel will consult regarding the necessary reaction.

SINAI I ASSURANCES

Letter from President Nixon to Egyptian President Sadat

Washington, January 17, 1974

Dear Mr. President:

I am transmitting the attached proposal as part of the agreement between Egypt and Israel on the disengagement of their forces. I am also transmitting the attached proposal to the Prime Minister of Israel.

Receipt of your signature on the attached proposal will constitute acceptance, subject to the signature of the same proposal by the Prime Minister of Israel.

Sincerely,
Richard Nixon
Attachment

In order to facilitate agreement between Egypt and Israel and as part of that agreement, and to assist in maintaining scrupulous observance of the ceasefire on land, air, and sea the United States proposes the following:

1. That within the areas of limited armament and forces described in the agreement there will be: (a) no more than eight reinforced battalions of armed forces and 30 tanks; (b) no artillery except anti-tank guns, anti-tank missiles, mortars and 6 batteries of howitzers of a caliber up to 122 mm (M–3) with a range not to exceed 12 kilometers; (c) no weapons capable of interfering with the other party's flights over its own forces; (d) no permanent, fixed installations for missile sites. The entire force of each party shall not exceed 7,000 men.

2. That to a distance 30 kilometers west of the Egyptian line and east of the Israeli line, there will be no weapons in areas from which they can reach the other line.

3. That to a distance 30 kilometers west of the Egyptian line and east of the Israeli line, there will be no surface-to-air missiles.

4. That the above limitations will apply as from the time the agreement on disengagement between Egypt and Israel is signed by the parties and will be implemented in accordance with the schedule of the basic agreement.

Letter from President Nixon to Israeli Prime Minister Meir

Washington, January 17, 1974

Dear Madam Prime Minister:

I want to inform you that the Government of the United States has received from the Government of Egypt assurances to the effect that, in connection with the agreement on the disengagement of Egyptian and Israeli forces, the Government of Egypt confirms that it regards the Straits of Bab el-Mandeb as an international waterway for ships of all flags and that it will not interfere with the free passage of Israeli ships or cargoes.

Further assurances have been received from Egypt that upon the opening of the Suez Canal, the principle of free passage will likewise be observed and that principle will be extended to Israel when the state of belligerency between Egypt and Israel has ended. As a first step, all cargoes destined for and coming from Israel will be permitted through the Canal from the time of its opening.

Sincerely,
Richard Nixon

Letter from President Nixon to Egyptian President Sadat

Washington, January 17, 1974

Dear Mr. President:

I understand that once the agreement between Egypt and Israel on disengagement of forces is in effect, you intend to begin work looking toward an early return of the Suez Canal to full operation and toward the rehabilitation of the cities and towns along the Canal and the resumption of normal economic activities in that area. I want you to know that if you proceed in this way the United States gives you its assurance that Israel will refrain from taking any military action against those civilian centers, installations and populations.

Sincerely,
Richard Nixon

Appendix B

SEPARATION OF FORCES AGREEMENT
BETWEEN ISRAEL AND SYRIA

May 31, 1974

A. Israel and Syria will scrupulously observe the cease-fire on land, sea and air and will refrain from all military actions against each other, from the time of the signing of the document, in implementation of United Nations Security Council resolution 338 dated October 22, 1973.

B. The military forces of Israel and Syria will be separated in accordance with the following principles:

1. All Israeli military forces will be west of the line designated as Line A on the map attached hereto, except in the Kuneitra area, where they will be west of line A 1.
2. All territory east of Line A will be under Syrian administration, and the Syrian civilians will return to this territory.
3. The area between Line A and the Line designated as Line B on the attached map will be an area of separation. In this area will be stationed the United Nations Disengagement Observer Force established in accordance with the accompanying protocol.
4. All Syrian military forces will be east of the line designated as Line B on the attached map.
5. There will be two equal areas of limitation in armament and forces, one west of Line A and one east of Line B as agreed upon.
6. Air forces of the two sides will be permitted to operate up to their respective lines without interference from the other side.

C. In the area between Line A and Line A-1 on the attached map there shall be no military forces.

D. This agreement and the attached map will be signed by the military representatives of Israel and Syria in Geneva not later than May 31, 1974, in the Egyptian-Israeli military working group of the Geneva Peace Conference under the aegis of the United

Nations, after that group has been joined by a Syrian military representative, and with the participation of representatives of the United States and the Soviet Union. The precise delineation of a detailed map and a plan for the implementation of the disengagement of forces will be worked by military representatives of Israel and Syria in the Egyptian-Israeli military working group, who will agree on the stages of this process. The military working group described above will state their work for this purpose in Geneva under the aegis of the United Nations within 24 hours after the signing of this agreement. They will complete this task within five days. Disengagement will begin within 24 hours after the completion of the task of the military working group. The process of disengagement will be completed not later than twenty days after it begins.

E. The provisions of paragraph A, B, and C shall be inspected by personnel of the United Nations Disengagement Observer Force under this agreement.

F. Within 24 hours after the signing of this agreement in Geneva all wounded prisoners of war which each side holds of the other as certified by the ICRC will be repatriated. The morning after the completion of the task of the military working group, all remaining prisoners of war will be repatriated.

G. The bodies of all dead soldiers held by either side will be returned for burial in their respective countries within 10 days after the signing of this agreement.

H. This agreement is not a peace agreement. It is a step toward a just and durable peace on the basis of Security Council Resolution 338 dated October 22, 1973.

Protocol Concerning the United Nations Disengagement Observer Force

Israel and Syria agree that:

The function of the United Nations Disengagement Observer Force (UNDOF) under that agreement will be to use its best efforts to maintain the cease-fire and to see that it is scrupulously observed. It will supervise the agreement and protocol thereto with regard to the area of separation and limitation. In carrying out its mission, it will comply with generally applicable Syrian laws and regulations and still not hamper the functioning of local civil administration. It will enjoy freedom of movement and communication and other facilities that are necessary for its mission. It will be mobile and provided with personal weapons of a defensive character and shall use such weapons only in self-defense. The number of the UNDOF shall be about 1,200, who will be selected by the Secretary-General of the United Nations in consultation with the parties from members of the United Nations who are not permanent members of the Security Council.

The UNDOF will be under the command of the United Nations, vested in the Security Council.

The UNDOF shall carry out inspections under the agreement, and report thereon to the parties, on a regular basis, not less often than once every fifteen days, and, in addition, when requested by either party. It shall mark on the ground the respective lines shown on the map attached to the agreement.

Israel and Syria will support a resolution of the United Nations Security Council which will provide for the UNDOF contemplated by the agreement. The initial authorization will be for six months subject to renewal by further resolution of the Security Council.

*Memorandum of Understanding between the United States Government
and the Government of Israel*

(1) The United States position is that withdrawal of the United Nations Disengagement Observer Forces agreed upon under the Israeli-Syrian Disengagement Agreement will require the consent of both sides. Should the matter of the withdrawal of the United Nations Disengagement Observer Forces or a change in its mandate be proposed before the United Nations Security Council without the consent of Israel or the United States, the United States will vote against such withdrawal or any change of mandate which would, in our mutual judgment, affect adversely the present operation of the Force.

(2) The United States will oppose supervision of Israeli held areas by U.N. personnel from the Soviet Union, from other communist countries, or from countries which have no diplomatic relations with Israel. With respect to the deployment of forces in the area of separation, the United States will approach the United Nations Secretary General or directly Syria with a view to working out arrangements whereunder no units or personnel of nations which do not have diplomatic relations with Israel will (a) be deployed adjacent to the Israeli line, or (b) participate in the inspection of the Israeli area of limited forces and armaments.

(3) The United States has informed the Governments of Israel and Syria that it will perform aerial reconnaissance missions over the areas covered by the Disengagement Agreement at a frequency of about one mission every ten days or two weeks, including special missions on request, and will forward the photographs to both Israel and Syria as soon as they are ready. In the event aerial reconnaissance detects violations, the United States will take this up diplomatically with Syria to bring about a rectification.

(4) The United States informs Israel that Egypt has informed the United States that it will support the disengagement agreement with Syria and that it is a fair agreement. It is the United States' understanding, from its discussions with Egypt, that Egypt has not committed itself to participate militarily in support of Syria if Syria violates the agreement by reopening hostilities or beginning a war against Israel.

(5) Recognizing the defense responsibilities of the Government of Israel following redeployment of its forces under the Disengagement Agreement the United States reaffirms that it will make every effort to be fully responsive on a continuing and long-term basis to Israel's military equipment requirements.

(6) It is the policy of the United States that implementation of the Disengagement Agreement should take precedence over the undertaking of new commitments by the parties related to subsequent phases of the Geneva Conference. The United States will do its best to help facilitate the Conference proceeding at a pace agreed upon by Israel and the United States.

(7) In case of a meaningful Syrian violation of any of the provisions of the Disengagement Agreement, or any of its attachments, the United States Government will immediately consult Israel regarding the necessary reaction and with a view to giving appropriate diplomatic support to Israel.

SYRIA DISENGAGEMENT ASSURANCES

Letter from Secretary of State Kissinger to Syrian President Asad

Washington, May 30, 1974

Dear Mr. President:

I have the honor to transmit the text of a letter from President Nixon. The signed original will be forwarded to you.

Dear Mr. President:

In connection with the agreement between Syria and Israel on the disengagement of their forces, the Government of the United States has received the assurances below from the Government of Israel with respect to the Israeli presence on Tell abou Nida and Tell el Aaram, the two hills just to the west of Quneitra.

First, Israel will scrupulously observe the ceasefire, including observance with respect to the people and city of Quneitra.

Second, there will be no Israeli forces or weapons on the eastern slopes of the two hills.

Third, there will be no weapons on top of these hills which can fire into Quneitra.

I want to assure you, Mr. President, that the United States will do its utmost to assure that these conditions are scrupulously observed.

As you begin to rebuild and repopulate Quneitra, I want you to know also that the United States is prepared to consider how it might assist in the rehabilitation of that area.

Sincerely,
(Richard Nixon)

Sincerely,
Henry A. Kissinger

Letter from Secretary of State Kissinger to Prime Minister Meir

Washington, May 30, 1974

Dear Madame Prime Minister:

This is to inform you that the assurances with respect to guerilla action from Syria conveyed to the Israeli Government have the following characteristics:

1. They were made to the Secretary of State by President Asad on the condition that there would be no publicity whatsoever.

2. President Asad emphasized that any publicity would force him to make a public statement contradicting the assurances and perhaps make it impossible for him to maintain them.

Best wishes,
Henry A. Kissinger

Letter from President Nixon to Israeli Prime Minister Meir

Washington, May 31, 1974

Dear Madame Prime Minister:

The Secretary of State has brought to my attention your letter dated May 12, 1974, in which you have outlined your country's major concerns. Let me assure you, Madame Prime Minister, that I read it with great attention and understanding, for you know that during my entire Administration I have given concrete evidence of my own feelings for and commitment to Israel's continued survival in peace and security. I would like now to refer to those items which you raised.

With regard to your request to enter with the United States into a long-range military arrangement which will assure Israel the supply of the necessary military equipment for the next ten years, you have my full backing. I have noted the figures that you have quoted, and I understand your basic needs. With respect to modern aircraft, I understand that preliminary talks have already been held with Secretary Schlesinger, and I recognize your need to move into the new generation of aircraft. With respect to ground-to-ground missiles, I agree that Israel should be equipped with weapons similar to those supplied by the Russians to both the Egyptians and the Syrians. I assure you of my support in this program.

I suggest that a mission from your country come to Washington in the month of June to work out all concrete details. This will give me the opportunity to review the specifics sympathetically and within the framework of the aforementioned principles.

I realize that such a long-range military program will entail a heavy financial burden. I was mindful of this fact when I proposed special emergency assistance of $2.2 billion subsequent to the October war. I fully realize that substantial U.S. financial assistance will be needed to support this program, and I intend to ask Congress to provide such support.

I fully understand your concern for working out a contingency plan to provide Israel with military supplies, both ammunition and replacement of major equipment, in case of emergency. I have authorized our appropriate agencies to work with your officials to devise such a plan.

I noted your particular concern with regard to the continued supply of oil to Israel, in case any interruption occurs resulting from change of circumstances or other development. I suggest that appropriate representatives of our two countries meet in order to devise a plan whose objective would be to assure uninterrupted oil supply to Israel.

Madame Prime Minister, as you leave office, I want to pay tribute to the strong and effective leadership which you have given to Israel and its people.

Warmest regards,
Richard Nixon

Appendix C

INTERIM AGREEMENT BETWEEN EGYPT AND ISRAEL

September 1, 1975

The Government of the Arab Republic of Egypt and the Government of Israel have agreed that:

ARTICLE I

The conflict between them and in the Middle East shall not be resolved by military force but by peaceful means.

The Agreement concluded by the parties on 18 January 1974, within the framework of the Geneva Peace Conference, constituted a first step towards a just and durable peace according to the provisions of Security Council Resolution 338 of 22 October 1973.

They are determined to reach a final and just peace settlement by means of negotiations called for by Security Council Resolution 338, this Agreement being a significant step towards that end.

ARTICLE II

The parties hereby undertake not to resort to the threat or use of force or military blockade against each other.

ARTICLE III

The parties shall continue scrupulously to observe the cease-fire on land, sea and air and to refrain from all military or para-military actions against each other. The parties also confirm that the obligations contained in the annex and, when concluded, the Protocol shall be an integral part of this Agreement.

ARTICLE IV

A. The military forces of the parties shall be deployed in accordance with the following principles:

(1) All Israeli forces shall be deployed east of the lines designated as lines J and M on the attached map.

(2) All Egyptian forces shall be deployed west of the line designated as line E on the attached map.

(3) The area between the lines designated on the attached map as lines E and F and the area between the lines designated on the attached map as lines J and K shall be limited in armament and forces.

(4) The limitations on armament and forces in the areas described by paragraph (3) above shall be agreed as described in the attached annex.

(5) The zone between the lines designated on the attached map as lines E and J will be a buffer zone. In this zone the United Nations Emergency Force will continue to perform its functions as under the Egyptian-Israeli Agreement of 18 January 1974.

(6) In the area south from line E and west from line M, as defined on the attached map, there will be no military forces, as specified in the attached annex.

B. The details concerning the new lines, the redeployment of the forces and its timing, the limitation on armaments and forces, aerial reconnaissance, the operation of the early warning and surveillance installations and the use of the roads, the United Nations functions and other arrangements will all be in accordance with the provisions of the annex and map which are an integral part of this Agreement and of the protocol which is to result from negotiations pursuant to the annex and which, when concluded, shall become an integral part of this Agreement.

ARTICLE V

The United Nations Emergency Force is essential and shall continue its functions and its mandate shall be extended annually.

ARTICLE VI

The parties hereby establish a joint commission for the duration of this Agreement. It will function under the aegis of the chief coordinator of the United Nations peace-keeping missions in the Middle East in order to consider any problem arising from this Agreement and to assist the United Nations Emergency Force in the execution of its mandate. The joint commission shall function in accordance with procedures established in the Protocol.

ARTICLE VII

Non-military cargoes destined for or coming from Israel shall be permitted through the Suez Canal.

ARTICLE VIII

This Agreement is regarded by the parties as a significant step toward a just and lasting peace. It is not a final peace agreement.

The parties shall continue their efforts to negotiate a final peace agreement within the framework of the Geneva peace conference in accordance with Security Council Resolution 338.

ARTICLE IX

This Agreement shall enter into force upon signature of the Protocol and remain in force until superseded by a new agreement.

ANNEX TO THE EGYPT-ISRAEL AGREEMENT

Within five days after the signature of the Egypt-Israel Agreement, representatives of the two parties shall meet in the military working group of the Middle East peace conference at Geneva to begin preparation of a detailed Protocol for the implementation of the Agreement. The working group will complete the Protocol within two weeks. In order to facilitate preparation of the Protocol and implementation of the agreement, and to assist in maintaining the scrupulous observance of the cease-fire and other elements of the Agreement, the two parties have agreed on the following principles, which are an integral part of the Agreement, as guidelines for the working group.

1. Definitions of Lines and Areas

The deployment lines, areas of limited forces and armaments, buffer zones, the area south from line E and west from line M, other designated areas, road sections for common use and other features referred to in article IV of the Agreement shall be as indicated on the attached map (1:100,000—United States edition).

2. Buffer Zones

(A) Access to the buffer zones will be controlled by the United Nations Emergency Force, according to procedures to be worked out by the working group and the United Nations Emergency Force.

(B) Aircraft of either party will be permitted to fly freely up to the forward line of that party. Reconnaissance aircraft of either party may fly up to the middle line of the buffer zone between E and J on an agreed schedule.

(C) In the buffer zone, between lines E and J, there will be established under article IV of the Agreement an early warning system entrusted to United States civilian personnel as detailed in a separate proposal, which is a part of this Agreement.

(D) Authorized personnel shall have access to the buffer zone for transit to and from the early warning system; the manner in which this is carried out shall be worked out by the working group and the United Nations Emergency Force.

3. Area South of Line E and West of Line M

(A) In this area, the United Nations Emergency Force will assure that there are no military or para-military forces of any kind, military fortifications and military installations; it will establish checkpoints and have the freedom of movement necessary to perform this function.

(B) Egyptian civilians and third country civilian oil field personnel shall have the right to enter, exit from, work and live in the above indicated area, except for buffer zones 2A, 2B and the United Nations posts. Egyptian civilian police shall be allowed in the area to perform normal civil police functions among the civilian population in such number and with such weapons and equipment as shall be provided for in the Protocol.

(C) Entry to and exit from the area, by land, by air or by sea, shall be only through United Nations Emergency Force checkpoints. The United Nations Emergency Force shall also establish checkpoints along the road, the dividing line and at either points, with the precise locations and number to be included in the Protocol.

(D) Access to the airspace and the coastal area shall be limited to unarmed Egyptian civilian vessels and unarmed civilian helicopters and transport planes involved in the civilian activities of the area as agreed by the working group.

(E) Israel undertakes to leave intact all currently existing civilian installations and infrastructures.

(F) Procedures for use of the common sections of the coastal road along the Gulf of Suez shall be determined by the working group and detailed in the Protocol.

4. Aerial Surveillance

There shall be a continuation of aerial reconnaissance missions by the United States over the areas covered by the Agreement (the area between lines F and K), following the same procedures already in practice. The missions will ordinarily be carried out at a frequency of one mission every 7–10 days, with either party or the United Nations Emergency Force empowered to request an earlier mission. The United States Government will make the mission results available expeditiously to Israel, Egypt and the chief coordinator of the United Nations peace-keeping missions in the Middle East.

5. Limitation of Forces and Armaments

(A) Within the areas of limited forces and armaments (the areas between lines J and K and lines E and F) the major limitations shall be as follows:

(1) Eight (8) standard infantry battalions.
(2) Seventy-five (75) tanks.
(3) Seventy-two (72) artillery pieces, including heavy mortars (i.e. with caliber larger than 120 mm), whose range shall not exceed twelve (12) km.
(4) The total number of personnel shall not exceed eight thousand (8,000).
(5) Both parties agree not to station or locate in the area weapons which can reach the line of the other side.
(6) Both parties agree that in the areas between line A (of the disengagement agreement of 18 January 1974) and line E they will construct no new fortifications or installations for forces of a size greater than that agreed herein.

(B) The major limitations beyond the areas of limited forces and armament will be:

(1) Neither side will station nor locate any weapon in areas from which they can reach the other line.
(2) The parties will not place anti-aircraft missiles within an area of ten (10) kilometres east of line K and west of line F, respectively.

(C) The United Nations Emergency Force will conduct inspections in order to ensure the maintenance of the agreed limitations within these areas.

6. Process of Implementation

The detailed implementation and timing of the redeployment of forces, turnover of oil fields, and other arrangements called for by the Agreement, annex and Protocol shall be determined by the working group, which will agree on the stages of this process, including the phased movement of Egyptian troops to line E and Israeli troops to line J. The first phase will be the transfer of the oil fields and installations to Egypt. This process will begin within two weeks from the signature of the Protocol with the introduction of the necessary technicians, and it will be completed no later than eight weeks after it begins. The details of the phasing will be worked out in the military working group.

Implementation of the redeployment shall be completed within five months after signature of the Protocol.

Proposal

In connection with the early warning system referred to in article IV of the Agreement between Egypt and Israel concluded on this date and as an integral part of that Agreement (hereafter referred to as the basic Agreement), the United States proposes the following:

1. The early warning system to be established in accordance with article IV in the area shown on the map attached to the basic agreement will be entrusted to the United States. It shall have the following elements:

    A. There shall be two surveillance stations to provide strategic early warning, one operated by Egyptian and one operated by Israeli personnel. Their locations are shown on the map attached to the basic Agreement. Each station shall be manned by not more than 250 technical and administrative personnel. They shall perform the functions of visual and electronic surveillance only within their stations.

    B. In support of these stations, to provide tactical early warning and to verify access to them, three watch stations shall be established by the United States in the Mitla and Giddi Passes as will be shown on the map attached to the basic Agreement. These stations shall be operated by United States civilian personnel. In support of these stations, there shall be established three unmanned electronic sensor fields at both ends of each Pass and in the general vicinity of each station and the roads leading to and from those stations.

2. The United States civilian personnel shall perform the following duties in connexion with the operation and maintenance of these stations.

    A. At the two surveillance stations described in paragraph 1 A. above, United States civilian personnel will verify the nature of the operations of the stations and all movement into and out of each station and will immediately report any detected divergency from its authorized role of visual and electronic surveillance to the parties to the basic Agreement and to the United Nations Emergency Force.

    B. At each watch station described in paragraph 1 B. above, the United States civilian personnel will immediately report to the parties to the basic Agreement and to the United Nations Emergency Force any movement of armed forces, other than the United Nations Emergency Force, into either Pass and any observed preparations for such movement.

    C. The total number of United States civilian personnel assigned to functions under this proposal shall not exceed 200. Only civilian personnel shall be assigned to functions under this proposal.

3. No arms shall be maintained at the stations and other facilities covered by this proposal, except for small arms required for their protection.

4. The United States personnel serving the early warning system shall be allowed to move freely within the area of the system.

5. The United States and its personnel shall be entitled to have such support facilities as are reasonably necessary to perform their functions provided for in the United Nations Emergency Force Agreement of 13 February 1957.

6. The United States personnel shall be immune from local criminal, civil, tax and customs jurisdiction and may be accorded any other specific privileges and immunities provided for in the United Nations Emergency Force Agreement of 13 February 1957.

7. The United States affirms that it will continue to perform the functions described above for the duration of the basic Agreement.

8. Notwithstanding any other provision of this proposal, the United States may withdraw its personnel only if it concludes that their safety is jeopardized or that continuation of their role is no longer necessary. In the latter case the parties to the basic Agreement will be informed in advance in order to give them the opportunity to make alternative arrangements. If both parties to the basic Agreement request the United States to conclude its role under this proposal, the United States will consider such requests conclusive.

9. Technical problems including the location of the watch stations will be worked out through consultation with the United States.

SINAI II ASSURANCES

Memorandum of Agreement between the Governments of Israel and the United States

The United States recognizes that the Egypt-Israel Agreement initialed on Sept. 1, 1975 (hereinafter referred to as the agreement), entailing the withdrawal from vital areas in Sinai, constitutes an act of great significance on Israel's part in the pursuit of final peace. That agreement has full United States support.

[1] The United States Government will make every effort to be fully responsive, within the limits of its resources and Congressional authorization and appropriation, on an on-going and long-term basis, to Israel's military equipment and other defense requirements, to its energy requirements and to its economic needs. The needs specified in paragraphs 2, 3 and 4 below shall be deemed eligible for inclusion within the annual total to be requested in FY '76 and later fiscal years.

[2] Israel's long-term military supply needs from the United States shall be the subject of periodic consultations between representatives of the U.S. and Israeli defense establishments, with agreement reached on specific items to be included in a separate U.S.-Israeli memorandum. To this end, a joint study by military experts will be undertaken within three weeks. In conducting this study, which will include Israel's 1976 needs, the United States will view Israel's requests sympathetically, including its request for advanced and sophisticated weapons.

[3] Israel will make its own independent arrangements for oil supply to meet its requirements through normal procedures. In the event Israel is unable to secure its needs in this way, the United States Government, upon notification of this fact by the Government of Israel, will act as follows for five years, at the end of which period either side can terminate this arrangement on one year's notice.

(a) If the oil Israel needs to meet all its normal requirements for domestic consumption is unavailable for purchase in circumstances where no quantitative restrictions exist on the ability of the United States to procure oil to meet its normal requirements, the United States Government will promptly make oil available for purchase by Israel to meet all of the aforementioned normal requirements of Israel. If Israel is unable to secure the necessary means to transport such oil to Israel the United States Government will make every effort to help Israel secure the necessary means of transport.

(b) If the oil Israel needs to meet all of its normal requirements for domestic consumption is unavailable for purchase in circumstances where quantitative restrictions through embargo or otherwise also prevent the United States from procuring oil to meet its normal requirements, the United States Government will promptly make oil available for purchase by Israel in accordance with the International Energy Agency conservation and allocation formula as applied by the United States Government, in order to meet Israel's essential requirements. If Israel is unable to secure the necessary means to transport such oil to Israel, the United States Government will make every effort to help Israel secure the necessary mean of transport.

Israeli and U.S. experts will meet annually or more frequently at the request of either party, to review Israel's continuing oil requirement.

[4] In order to help Israel meet its energy needs, and as part of the over-all annual figure in paragraph 1 above, the United States agrees:

(a) In determining the overall annual figure which will be requested from Congress, the United States Government will give special attention to Israel's oil import requirements and, for a period as determined by Article 3 above, will take into account in calculating that figure Israel's additional expenditures for the import of oil to replace that which would have ordinarily come from Abu Rudeis and Ras Sudar (4.5 million tons in 1975).

(b) To ask Congress to make available funds, the amount to be determined by mutual agreement, to the Government of Israel necessary for a project for the construction and stocking of the oil reserves to be stored in Israel, bringing storage reserve capacity and reserve stocks, now standing at approximately six months, up to one year's need at the time of the completion of the project. The project will be implemented within four years. The construction. operation and financing and other relevant questions of the project will be the subject of early and detailed talks between the two Governments.

[5] The United States Government will not expect Israel to begin to implement the agreement before Egypt fulfills its undertaking under the January 1974, disengagement agreement to permit passage of all Israeli cargoes to and from Israeli ports through the Suez Canal.

[6] The United States Government agrees with Israel that the next agreement with Egypt should be a final peace agreement.

[7] In case of an Egyptian violation of any of the provisions of the agreement, the United States Government is prepared to consult with Israel as to the significance of the violation and possible remedial action by the United States Government.

[8] The United States Government will vote against any Security Council resolution which in its judgment affects or alters adversely the agreement.

[9] The United States Government will not join in and will seek to prevent efforts by others to bring about consideration of proposals which it and Israel agree are detrimental to the interests of Israel.

[10] In view of the long-standing U.S. commitment to the survival and security of Israel, the United States Government will view with particular gravity threats to Israel's security or sovereignty by a world power. In support of this objective, the United States Government will in the event of such threat consult promptly with the Government of Israel with respect to what support diplomatic or otherwise, or assistance it can lend to Israel in accordance with its constitutional practices.

[11] The United States Government and the Government of Israel will, at the earliest possible time, and if possible within two months after the signature of this document, conclude the contingency plan for a military supply operation to Israel in an emergency situation.

[12] It is the United States Government's position that Egyptian commitments under the Egypt-Israel agreement, its implementation, validity and duration are not conditional upon any act or developments between the other Arab states and Israel. The United States Government regards the agreement as standing on its own.

[13] The United States Government shares the Israeli position that under existing political circumstances negotiations with Jordan will be directed toward an over-all peace settlement.

[14] In accordance with the principle of freedom of navigation on the high seas and free and unimpeded passage through and over straits connecting international waters, the United States Government regards the Straits of Babel Mandeb and the Strait of Gibraltar as international waterways. It will support Israel's right to free and unimpeded passage through such straits. Similarly, the United States Government recognizes Israel's right to freedom of flights over the Red Sea and such straits and will support diplomatically the exercise of that right.

In the event that the United Nations Emergency Force or any other United Nations organ is withdrawn without the prior agreement of both parties to the Egypt-Israel agreement and the United States before this agreement is superseded by another agreement, it is the United States view that the agreement shall remain binding in all its parts.

The United States and Israel agree that signature of the protocol of the Egypt-Israel agreement and its full entry into effect shall not take place before approval by the United States Congress of the U.S. role in connection with the surveillance and observation functions described in the agreement and its annex. The United States has informed the Government of Israel that it has obtained the Government of Egypt agreement to the above.

Memorandum of Agreement between the Governments of Israel and the United States on the Geneva Peace Conference

1. The Geneva peace conference will be reconvened at a time coordinated between the United States and Israel.

2. The United States will continue to adhere to its present policy with respect to the Palestine Liberation Organization, whereby it will not recognize or negotiate with the Palestine Liberation Organization so long as the Palestine Liberation Organization does not recognize Israel's right to exist and does not accept Security Council Resolutions 242 and 338. The United States Government will consult fully and seek

to concert its position and strategy at the Geneva peace conference on this issue with the Government of Israel. Similarly, the United States will consult fully and seek to concert its position and strategy with Israel with regard to the participation of any other additional states. It is understood that the participation at a subsequent phase of the conference of any possible additional state, group or organization will require the agreement of all the initial participants.

3. The United States will make every effort to insure at the conference that all the substantive negotiations will be on a bilateral basis.

4. The United States will oppose and, if necessary, vote against any initiative in the Security Council to alter adversely the terms of reference of the Geneva peace conference or to change Resolutions 242 and 338 in ways which are incompatible with their original purpose.

5. The United States will seek to insure that the role of the co-sponsors will be consistent with what was agreed in the memorandum of understanding between the United States Government and the Government of Israel of Dec. 20, 1973.

6. The United States and Israel will concert action to assure that the conference will be conducted in a manner consonant with the objectives of this document and with the declared purpose of the conference, namely the advancement of a negotiated peace between Israel and its neighbors.

Letter from Secretary of State Kissinger to Israeli Foreign Minister Allon

Jerusalem, September 1, 1975

Dear Mr. Minister:

In connection with the Agreement initialed on September 1, 1975, between the Governments of Egypt and Israel, I hereby convey the following to you:

1. The United States Government has received an assurance from Egypt that it will not use lack of progress at the Geneva Conference as a pretext for not fulfilling its obligations under the Agreement.

2. The United States Government will transmit a letter to Israel conveying Egypt's undertaking on annual renewals of UNEF's mandate.

3. The United States Government has received from Egypt an expression of its intention to reduce hostile propaganda in its government-controlled media.

4. The United States Government has received an assurance from Egypt of its willingness to ease the boycott of American companies on a selective basis and that it will not discriminate against any American company that wants to do business in Egypt, regardless of whether this company is on the boycott list. The United States will encourage the Government of Egypt to expand the above to include European and other companies.

5. It is the understanding of the United States Government that Egypt intends to avoid active diplomatic efforts to discourage selected other states from resuming diplomatic relations with Israel.

6. The United States Government will seek to ascertain whether Egypt is willing that ships, aircraft, passengers and crews of either Party in distress will be given assistance by the other and will be permitted to continue on their route.

7. The United States informs Israel that Egypt has informed us that it will maintain the assurances, written and oral, undertaken at the time of the Egyptian-Israeli Agreement on Disengagement of Forces in January 1974 in addition to the provisions of the Agreement.

8. The United States informs Israel that Egypt will not interfere with the flights of any civilian Israeli aircraft in the airspace above the Straits of Bab el-Mandeb leading into the Red Sea.

9. With respect to the reference to "para-military forces" in paragraph 3a of the Annex, the United States understanding of the view of the Government of Egypt is that this phrase includes irregular forces as well.

Respectfully,
Henry A. Kissinger

Letter from Secretary of State Kissinger to Egyptian Deputy Prime Minister and Foreign Minister Fahmy

Jerusalem, September 1, 1975

Dear Ismail:

This is to inform you that with respect to Syria, we have an Israeli assurance that Israel will not initiate military action against Syria.

Warm regards,
Henry A. Kissinger

Letter from Secretary of State Kissinger to Israeli Prime Minister Rabin

Washington, undated

Dear Mr. Prime Minister:

I have the honor to transmit to you the text which follows of a letter to Your Excellency from the President of the United States:

"Dear Mr. Prime Minister:

I am writing you this letter to inform you of the statement I have received of the position of Egypt on the question of the duration of the second Egyptian-Israeli agreement on the Sinai. The agreement includes language that the agreement shall 'remain in force until superseded by a new agreement.'

With respect to the duration of UNEF, I have been informed of Egypt's undertaking to make every effort to extend the United Nations Emergency Force annually for the duration of the agreement. However, should the Security Council, because of the action of a third state, fail to renew the UNEF mandate to assure continuous operation, I am informed that Egypt undertakes to concert actively with the U.S. to have the General Assembly take appropriate action to bring about annual renewals for at least two renewals after the first annual mandate goes into effect.

In the event such affirmative General Assembly action did not prove possible, I am informed that Egypt will request an augmented UNTSO to continue the supervision responsibilities, and to have the joint Egyptian-Israeli Commission cooperate with it.

This letter is for the United States and should not be passed to another government or publicized.

Sincerely,
Gerald R. Ford"

The signed original of this letter will be forwarded to you.

Sincerely,
Henry A. Kissinger

Letter from Secretary of State Kissinger to Egyptian President Sadat
Washington, undated

Dear Mr. President:

I have the honor to transmit to you the text which follows of a letter to Your Excellency from the President of the United States:

"Dear Mr. President:

In connection with Article VII of the Agreement between Egypt and Israel, the United States' understanding of the word non-military is that it excludes all types of weapons, weapons systems, ammunition, missiles and armor. It does not exclude economic items such as raw materials, oil and other civilian cargo. The Government of Israel has assured me that it will carry out this Article in accordance with the above definition.

Sincerely,
Gerald R. Ford"

The signed original of this letter will be forwarded to Your Excellency.

Sincerely,
Henry A. Kissinger

Letter from President Ford to Egyptian President Sadat
Washington, undated

Dear Mr. President:

I am writing to you to give you some indication as to our intentions with respect to a number of questions on which Secretary Kissinger was asked to ascertain my views.

The United States intends to make a serious effort to help bring about further negotiations between Syria and Israel, in the first instance through diplomatic channels.

In connection with the peace negotiations, I can reaffirm the intention of the United States to promote a solution of the key issues of a just and lasting peace in the Middle East on the basis of UN Security Council Resolution 338, taking into account the legitimate interests of all the peoples of the area, including the Palestinian people, and respect for the right to independent existence of all states in the area.

As I indicated to you in my recent letter the U.S. recognizes the situation following Israeli withdrawal from the passes and the oil fields will not be an acceptable permanent solution. You will recall also what I said to you at Salzburg about moving toward a comprehensive, just and lasting peace in the Middle East and the importance of permitting the realities in the area and internationally to mature to the point where an all-out effort to achieve final peace can be made in circumstances that seem most promising for success and in a deliberate and systematic way. The United States will remain active in the peacemaking process. We recognize that a final peace is importantly a matter to be negotiated by the parties. Nevertheless, we would be prepared to put forward ideas of our own when and if it becomes necessary to do so. We have brought these views to the attention of Israeli leaders.

In the event of an Israeli violation of the Agreement, the United States is prepared to consult with Egypt as to the significance of the violation and possible remedial action by the United States.

The United States will provide technical assistance to Egypt for the Egyptian Early Warning Station.

Sincerely,
Gerald R. Ford

Undisclosed Letter from President Ford to Israeli Prime Minister Rabin

Washington, undated

Dear Mr. Prime Minister:

I wish to inform you that the U.S. recognizes that the Israeli-Egyptian Interim Agreement entailing withdrawal from vital areas in the Sinai constitutes an act of great significance on Israel's part in the pursuit of final peace and imposes additional heavy military and economic burdens on Israel.

I want to assure you that the U.S. will make every effort to be fully responsive within the limits of its resources and Congressional authorization and appropriation on an ongoing and long-term basis to Israel's military equipment and other defense requirements as well as to Israel's economic aid needs, all of this based on the requests submitted by Israel, joint studies and previous U.S. Presidential undertakings.

Further to those undertakings, it is my resolve to continue to maintain Israel's defensive strength through the supply of advanced types of equipment, such as the F-16 aircraft. The United States Government agrees to an early meeting to undertake a joint study of high technology and sophisticated items, including the Pershing ground-to-ground missiles with conventional warheads, with the view to giving a positive response. The U.S. Administration will submit annually for approval by the U.S. Congress a request for military and economic assistance in order to help meet Israel's economic and military needs. Realizing as I do the importance of the Interim Agreement to the Middle Eastern situation as a whole, the U.S. will make every possible effort to assist in the establishment of conditions in which the Agreement will be observed without being subjected to pressures or deadlines.

In the spirit of the special relationship existing between the United States and Israel and in light of the determination of both sides to avoid a situation in which the U.S. and Israel would pursue divergent courses in peace negotiations, the U.S. will take the position that these are negotiations between the parties. As I indicated to you in our conversation on 12 June 1975, the situation in the aftermath of the Israeli-Egyptian interim agreement will be one in which the overall settlement can be pursued in a systematic and deliberate way and does not require the U.S. to put forward an overall proposal of its own in such circumstances. Should the U.S. desire in the future to put forward proposals of its own, it will make every effort to coordinate with Israel its proposals with a view to refraining from putting forth proposals that Israel would consider unsatisfactory.

The U.S. will support the position that an overall settlement with Syria in the framework of a peace agreement must assure Israel's security from attack from the Golan Heights. The U.S. further supports the position that a just and lasting peace, which remains our objective, must be acceptable to both sides. The U.S. has not developed a final position on the borders. Should it do so it will give great weight to Israel's position that any peace agreement with Syria must be predicated on Israel remaining on the Golan Heights. My view in this regard was stated in our conversation of September 13, 1974.

Sincerely,
Gerald R. Ford

Notes

A NOTE ON SOURCES

Accessing the official papers of Henry Kissinger's time in government is almost as challenging as making peace in the Middle East. Researchers are fortunate that Kissinger, as a historian, understood the importance of thoroughly documenting his conversations and written communications. For years, however, the declassification process was put on hold because of a dispute between Kissinger and the State Department about the disposition of the documents. Thankfully, most have now been declassified, but they are spread in a number of different places. Most are available in the National Archives and the Library of Congress, and copies are in the Yale Library collection of Kissinger's papers. Others can be found in the Richard Nixon and Gerald R. Ford Presidential Libraries.

The State Department Office of the Historian has done a thorough and highly professional job of curating these documents in the volumes of the Foreign Relations of the United States (FRUS).*

The National Security Archive (NSA) at George Washington University has made effective use of the Freedom of Information Act (FOIA) to achieve declassification of additional documents, including Kissinger's telephone conversations and the memoranda of conversations of his two meetings with Egyptian national security adviser Hafez Ismail, which would otherwise have remained unavailable for public use.[†]

The Israel State Archives (ISA) has opened its files for the period under investigation for this book, although many documents remain classified. Like the State Department Office of the Historian, ISA has produced a number of curated volumes. However, the editors have not reproduced the actual documents but rather summarized and quoted from them to generate the narrative.[‡] Some of the transcripts of Kissinger's

---

* Volumes used include: FRUS 1969–1976:15 (Soviet Union, June 1972–August 1974); FRUS 1969–1976:23 (Arab-Israeli Dispute, 1969–1972); FRUS 1969–1976:24 (Middle East Region and Arabian Peninsula, 1969–1972; Jordan, September 1970); FRUS 1969–1976:25 (Arab-Israeli Crisis and War, 1973); FRUS 1969–1976:26 (Arab-Israeli Dispute, 1974–1976); FRUS 1969–1976:36 (Energy Crisis).
† The Digital National Security Archive can be accessed at: https://nsarchive.gwu.edu/.
‡ Amos Shifris, *The First Rabin Government, 1974–1977* [in Hebrew]; Hagai Tzoref, ed., *Golda Meir: The Fourth Prime Minister, Selected Documents (1898–1978)* [in Hebrew]; and Shimon Golan, *War on Yom Kippur* [in Hebrew].

conversations with Israeli leaders were leaked to the Israeli journalist Matti Golan, who paraphrased them in his book.[*]

The enormous caches of American and Israeli documents constitute the basic sources for my historical account of Kissinger's Middle East diplomacy. They have been supplemented by Kissinger's own biographic volumes that draw upon the same documents[†] and the many books written by journalists whom he briefed in detail on his diplomatic excursions in the Middle East.[‡] I have also drawn on the many biographies of his Arab and Israeli interlocutors, although all of these are subject to the drawbacks of selective memory, self-justification, and other biases.[§]

Unfortunately, Arab archives for the period are not accessible, if they exist at all. I have had to rely on the public record and personal biographies. In some cases, these are based on documentary evidence, but its presentation is necessarily selective.[¶]

Two historical accounts of the period have been particularly important. One, by William Quandt, covers the entire period in U.S. policy and is based on inside knowledge of what transpired; the other, by Yigal Kipnis, is based on detailed analysis of the Israeli and American documents of the period leading up to the outbreak of war in 1973.[**]

Where possible, I have sought to supplement this rich and voluminous material with interviews with those Americans, Arabs, and Israelis who were involved in the events of the time. Unfortunately, many have long since passed away, and others no longer remember the details of what occurred then.

There is one notable exception: Henry Kissinger, who turned ninety-eight as this book was being sent to the printer. I was fortunate to have eight formal interviews with him and many informal conversations over the years. Some events, such as the 1973 Yom Kippur War, he remembers in great detail; others he has long since forgotten. With access to so many primary documents, however, I did not need to rely on him for an account of what happened. Instead, I focused the interviews on gaining an understanding of his thinking, conceptualizations, strategies, and perceptions of the leaders with whom he interacted.

In this way, I have sought to triangulate the many sources of information to present the reader with as accurate an account as possible of what transpired when Henry Kissinger brought his diplomatic skills to bear in the forging of an American-led peace process in the Middle East.

---

[*] Matti Golan, *The Secret Conversations of Henry Kissinger: Step-by-Step Diplomacy in the Middle East* (Chicago: Quadrangle, 1976).

[†] These volumes are: *White House Years, Years of Upheaval, Years of Renewal,* and *Crisis: The Anatomy of Two Major Foreign Policy Crises.*

[‡] For example, Walter Isaacson, *Kissinger,* and Marvin Kalb and Bernard Kalb, *Kissinger.*

[§] Anwar Sadat, *In Search of Identity;* Ismail Fahmy, *Negotiating for Peace in the Middle East;* Mohamed Abdel Ghani El-Gamasy, *The October War: Memoirs of Field Marshal El-Gamasy of Egypt* [in Arabic]; Mohammed Hafez Ismail, *Egyptian National Security in an Era of Challenges* [in Arabic]; Yitzhak Rabin, *The Rabin Memoirs;* Moshe Dayan, *Moshe Dayan: Story of My Life;* Shimon Peres, *Battling for Peace;* Simcha Dinitz, "Diplomatic Memoirs" (unpublished, in possession of the author); and Patrick Seale, *Asad: The Struggle for the Middle East.*

[¶] Notable are the accounts of the time presented by Bouthaina Shaaban in *The Edge of the Precipice: Hafez al-Assad, Henry Kissinger, and the Remaking of the Modern Middle East* (based on Syrian presidential archives), and Ahmed Aboul Gheit, *Witness to War and Peace, Egypt, the October War and Beyond* (based on Egyptian Foreign Ministry documents). Sadat's many public statements and interviews have been curated by Raphael Israeli in the three volumes of *The Public Diary of President Sadat.*

[**] William B. Quandt, *Peace Process: American Diplomacy and the Arab-Israeli Conflict Since 1967,* and Yigal Kipnis, *1973: The Road to War.*

In the notes, the sources have been abbreviated. The following is a list of the main sources and their abbreviations.

KEY TO ABBREVIATIONS

FRUS: Foreign Relations of the United States. These documents are all accessible online through the Office of the Historian at https://history.state.gov/historicaldocuments.

ISA: Israel State Archives

NARA: National Archives and Record Administration

NSA: National Security Archive. Declassified documents are available online through a subscription to the Digital National Security Archive at https://nsarchive.gwu.edu/digital -national-security-archive.

Memcon: Memorandum of Conversation

Telcon: Telephone Conversation

PROLOGUE

3 *The New York Times* put it: David Binder, "Kissinger Sworn, Praised by Nixon," *New York Times*, September 23, 1973.

4 He no longer believed in: Niall Ferguson, *Kissinger, 1923–1968: The Idealist* (New York: Penguin, 2015), 202.

4 German Jewish past: Indyk interview with Guido Goldman, June 21, 2017.

5 "a Middle East war going on today": Henry Kissinger, *Crisis: The Anatomy of Two Major Foreign Policy Crises* (New York: Simon & Schuster, 2003), 27.

13 "The Middle East": "King Faisal: Oil, Wealth, and Power," *Time*, April 7, 1975. Kissinger made this comment at the time of King Faisal's death.

13 "Men become myths": Henry Kissinger, *A World Restored: Metternich, Castlereagh and the Problems of Peace, 1812–1822* (Brattleboro, VT: Echo Point Books and Media, 2013), 322.

14 opening to China: See, for example, Jussi Hanhimäki, *The Flawed Architect, Henry Kissinger and American Foreign Policy* (Oxford: Oxford University Press, 2004), Christopher Hitchens, *The Trial of Henry Kissinger* (London: Verso, 2001), and William Shawcross, *Sideshow: Kissinger, Nixon and the Destruction of Cambodia* (New York: Simon & Schuster, 1979).

14 By his own count: Ferguson, *Kissinger*, 80–81.

14 "a traumatic experience": Edward Luce, "Henry Kissinger: 'We Are in a Very, Very Grave Period,'" *Financial Times*, July 20, 2018.

14 Although he rejected the idea: Ferguson, *Kissinger*, 80–81, and Indyk interview with Henry Kissinger, January 15, 2016.

14 Arab leaders believed: Jeremi Suri, *Henry Kissinger and the American Century* (Cambridge, MA: Harvard University Press, 2009), 262.

18 compounding the turmoil: Philip Gordon, *Losing the Long Game: The False Promise of Regime Change in the Middle East* (New York: St. Martin's Press, 2020).

18 a stable Middle Eastern order: See Martin Indyk, "Disaster in the Desert: Why Trump's Middle East Plan Can't Work," *Foreign Affairs* 98.6, (November/December 2019).

18 "when vision overcame reality": Henry Kissinger, *World Order* (New York: Penguin, 2014), 171.

I. THE STRATEGY

23 the obvious choice: Hedrick Smith, "Foreign Policy: Kissinger at Hub," *New York Times*, January 19, 1971.

23 nuclear strategists: Jeremi Suri, *Henry Kissinger and the American Century* (Cambridge, MA: Harvard University Press, 2009), 142–43.

24 the most widely read text: Suri, *Henry Kissinger*, 145.

24 study group: Walter Isaacson, *Kissinger* (New York: Simon & Schuster, 1992), 84–86.

24 Serving in Germany: "Letters of recommendation, 1945–1951," Box 116, Folder 14, Henry A. Kissinger Papers, Part II (MS 1981), Manuscripts and Archives, Yale University Library.

24 His personification: Suri, *Henry Kissinger*, 70–71.

24 "psychological warfare": Niall Ferguson, *Kissinger, 1923–1968: The Idealist* (New York: Penguin, 2015), 269.

24 International Seminar: Ferguson, *Kissinger*, 267, 275, and Robin B. Wright, "International Seminar Introduces Foreign Dignitaries to United States," *Harvard Crimson*, August 12, 1969.

24 American policymakers: Isaacson, *Kissinger*, 72–73. Among the contributors were: McGeorge Bundy, Reinhold Niebuhr, Walt Rostow, John Kenneth Galbraith, Hannah Arendt, Raymond Aron, Sidney Hook, Hans Morgenthau, and Paul Nitze.

25 Defense Studies Program: Isaacson, *Kissinger*, 99. Guests included Michigan congressman Gerald Ford.

25 he learned: Isaacson, *Kissinger*, 90–92.

26 "the best and the brightest": David Halberstam, *The Best and the Brightest* (New York: Random House, 1972).

26 the frustrating experience: Henry Kissinger, *White House Years* (Boston: Little, Brown, 1979), 8–9.

26 "telling him": *The Dick Cavett Show*, PBS, December 7, 1979.

26 The Pulitzer Prize–winning: Henry Kissinger, "Eulogy for Arthur M. Schlesinger," April 23, 2007, https://www.henryakissinger.com/remembrances/eulogy-for-arthur-m-schlesinger-jr/.

26 However, Kennedy's muted: Isaacson, *Kissinger*, 113.

27 At the end of: Isaacson, *Kissinger*, 122.

27 "behind the scenes": Isaacson, *Kissinger*, 129.

27 "that there is a better": Richard Nixon, *RN: The Memoirs of Richard Nixon* (New York: Grosset & Dunlap, 1978), 324.

27 Kissinger's information: George Packer, *Our Man: Richard Holbrooke and the End of the American Century* (New York: Alfred A. Knopf, 2019), 135. Holbrooke later said of this episode that he had trusted Kissinger. "It is not stretching the truth to say that the Nixon campaign had a secret source within the U.S. negotiating team," he admitted.

27 Both treated him: Nixon, *RN*, 340, and Ferguson, *Kissinger*, 791.

27 national security adviser: Isaacson, *Kissinger*, 133, and "Humphrey Discloses Plan to Name Kissinger," *New York Times*, March 12, 1973.

27 "High office": Kissinger, *White House Years*, 27.

28 his attention: Ferguson, *Kissinger*, 380–81, and Kissinger, *White House Years*, 347.

28 Intellectually, he also questioned: Ferguson, *Kissinger*, 71.

28 be assured: Indyk interview with Henry Kissinger, December 19, 2019.

28 "the besetting difficulty": Minutes of Kissinger's Staff Meeting, January 21, 1974, KT01007, NSA.

29 Kissinger made five trips: Henry Kissinger, *Years of Renewal* (New York: Touchstone, 1999), 360.

29 "splinter" of territory: Henry Kissinger, "Tribute to Shimon Peres," Peres Center for Peace and Innovation, September 13, 2017.

29 building nuclear weapons: Memcon with Henry Kissinger, February 1, 1965, in William Burr and Avner Cohen, "Duplicity and Self-Deception: Israel, the United States, and the Dimona Inspections, 1964–65," National Security Archive Briefing Book #732, and Avner Cohen, "Israel's Nuclear Secrets That Peres Shared with Kissinger in 1965," *Haaretz*, December 14, 2020.

29 January 1968: Yitzhak Rabin, *The Rabin Memoirs* (Berkeley, CA: University of California Press, 1996), 124–25.

29 "join the struggle for it": Kissinger, *White House Years*, 342.

30 "overthrow the order": Henry Kissinger, *A World Restored: Metternich, Castlereagh and the Problems of Peace, 1812–1822* (Brattleboro, VT: Echo Point Books and Media, 2013), 145.

30   "moral consensus is essential": Henry Kissinger, "The White Revolutionary: Reflections on Bismarck," *Daedalus* 97.3 (Summer 1968): 899–900.
30   limit its scope: Kissinger, *A World Restored*, 1.
31   conquering of Europe: Henry Kissinger, *Diplomacy* (New York: Simon and Schuster, 1994), 316.
31   "a precarious state": Henry Kissinger, *Years of Upheaval* (Boston: Little, Brown, 1982), 1085.
32   an absence of war: Kissinger, *A World Restored*, 1.
32   "the root dilemma": Kissinger, *White House Years*, 70.
33   Kissinger had bad-mouthed him: Isaacson, *Kissinger*, 134–35.
33   problem for Nixon: Robert Dallek, *Nixon and Kissinger, Partners in Power* (New York: HarperCollins, 2007), 170.
33   "unlikely": Isaacson, *Kissinger*, 139.
34   "destiny of our nation": Kissinger, *White House Years*, 7.
34   could aspire to in Germany: *The Dick Cavett Show*, PBS, December 6, 1979.
34   Kissinger also recounts that he and Nixon: Kissinger, *White House Years*, 11–12, and Ferguson, *Kissinger*, 852.
34   "both were hypersensitive": Ferguson, *Kissinger*, 438.
34   "little he could do without me": Indyk interview with Henry Kissinger, December 19, 2019.
34   "tearing the country apart": Henry Kissinger, "Remarks at American Academy of Diplomacy Fifteenth Annual Diplomatic Awards Luncheon Honoring the Late Joseph Sisco," December 9, 2004.
35   active diplomacy: Stephen Sestanovich, *Maximalist: America in the World from Truman to Obama* (New York: Vintage Books, 2014), 7.
35   "complete ignorance of foreign policy": Kissinger, *White House Years*, 54–55.
36   "Japan and Europe": Nixon, *RN*, 477.
36   disavow any involvement: Leonard Garment, *Crazy Rhythm: From Brooklyn and Jazz to Nixon's White House, Watergate, and Beyond* (New York: Times Books, 1997), 185.
36   "Kissinger's Jewish background": Nixon, *RN*, 477.
36   "had his doubts": Kissinger, *White House Years*, 559.
37   "shed his Jewishness": Suri, *Henry Kissinger*, 209.
37   And Kissinger distinguished: Indyk interview with Henry Kissinger, May 17, 2016.
37   shield himself from the charge: Isaacson, *Kissinger*, 212–27.
38   a harder line: Gal Beckerman, "Why Kissinger Said U.S. Jews Acted 'Traitorously,'" *Forward*, December 14, 2010.
38   "The emigration of": Douglas Brinkley and Luke A. Nichter, *The Nixon Tapes: 1971–1972* (Boston: Mariner Books, 2014), 148.
38   "Israel's security could be": Kissinger, *Years of Upheaval*, 204.

2. GAINING CONTROL

41   "powder keg, very explosive": Richard Nixon, "President's News Conference," January 27, 1969, quoted in Chris Barber, "Israel and the Nuclear Weapons Issue," January 13, 2016, https://www.nixonfoundation.org/2016/01/israel-and-the-nuclear-weapons-issue-1970/.
41   In one of his early memos: Henry Kissinger, *White House Years* (Boston: Little, Brown, 1979), 358.
41   "It meant that": Kissinger, *White House Years*, 351.
41   attempt at slow-rolling: Kissinger, *White House Years*, 353.
41   "minimal changes": Kissinger, *White House Years*, 357.
43   from Israel via the United States: Kissinger, *White House Years*, 364, and William B. Quandt, *Peace Process: American Diplomacy and the Arab-Israeli Conflict Since 1967* (Berkeley, CA: University of California Press, 1995), 72–73.
43   "linkage": Walter Isaacson, *Kissinger* (New York: Simon & Schuster, 1992), 167–68.
44   Four years later: Martin Indyk, *Innocent Abroad: An Intimate Account of American Peace Diplomacy in the Middle East* (New York: Simon & Schuster, 2009), 14.

44   He had come: Indyk correspondence with Efraim Halevy, April 1, 2020.

45   at the height of the crisis: Michael Brecher, *Decisions in Israel's Foreign Policy* (Oxford: Oxford University Press, 1974), 391–92.

46   "negotiations can only begin": Yitzhak Rabin, *The Rabin Memoirs* (Berkeley, CA: University of California Press, 1996), 133.

46   "We were finished": Rabin, *Memoirs*, 145.

46   "his integrity": Kissinger, *White House Years*, 355.

47   And Kissinger's focus: Indyk correspondence with Efraim Halevy, April 12, 2020.

48   The breakthrough with China: Kissinger, *White House Years*, 29–30.

48   "nurtured them": Kissinger, *White House Years*, 589.

48   "Rabin understands": Indyk interview with Henry Kissinger, January 15, 2016.

50   "extreme warmth": Richard Nixon, *RN: The Memoirs of Richard Nixon* (New York: Grosset & Dunlap, 1978), 478.

50   In fact, she knew: Kissinger, *White House Years*, 370.

51   "than reducing it": Rabin, *Memoirs*, 151–52.

51   As with the bombing of North Vietnam: Henry Kissinger, *Years of Upheaval* (Boston: Little, Brown, 1982), 200–201.

52   President Kennedy: Warren Bass, *Support Any Friend: Kennedy's Middle East and the Making of the U.S.-Israel Alliance* (Oxford: Oxford University Press, 2003), 186–87.

52   In return: "Israel Crosses the Threshold," Document 22, Kissinger to the President, "Discussions with the Israelis on Nuclear Matters," October 7, 1969, NSA, https://nsarchive2 .gwu.edu/NSAEBB/NSAEBB189/index.htm.

53   nuclear Non-Proliferation Treaty: Avner Cohen and William Burr, "The Untold Story of Israel's Bomb," *Washington Post*, April 30, 2006.

53   "weak militarily": Rabin, *Memoirs*, 154.

53   "qualitative military edge": William Wunderle and Andre Briere, "U.S. Foreign Policy and Israel's Qualitative Military Edge: The Need for a Common Vision," Washington Institute for Near East Policy, Policy Focus 80, January 2008.

53   "prime importance": Rabin, *Memoirs*, 261.

53   public address: Secretary Rogers, "A Lasting Peace in the Middle East," *Department of State Bulletin*, vol. 62, January 5, 1970, 7–11.

54   Israeli-Jordanian peace agreement: Memo from Kissinger to Nixon, December 17, 1969, FRUS 1969–1976:23, Doc. 76, fn. 2.

54   "Israel will not be sacrificed": Quandt, *Peace Process*, 68.

54   "the Rogers Plan": Kissinger, *White House Years*, 29–30.

54   "wherever she goes": Leonard Garment, *Crazy Rhythm: From Brooklyn and Jazz to Nixon's White House, Watergate, and Beyond* (New York: Times Books, 1997), 192.

54   "arms supplies": Rabin, *Memoirs*, 163.

56   "dominant position": Kissinger, *White House Years*, 567.

56   "The moment Israel": Rabin, *Memoirs*, 171.

56   "firmly established": Kissinger, *White House Years*, 579–80.

57   comfortable with the concept: Indyk interview with Henry Kissinger, January 15, 2016.

57   "one colonialism for another": Kissinger, *White House Years*, 580, and "Background Briefing," June 26, 1970, Box 393, Folder 7, Henry A. Kissinger Papers, Part II (MS 1981), Manuscripts and Archives, Yale University Library.

57   "maintain Israel's strength": Kissinger, *White House Years*, 580.

58   but on the walls: Marvin Kalb and Bernard Kalb, *Kissinger* (New York: Little, Brown, 1974), 8.

58   he had been astonished: Memcon between Kissinger and Dayan, December 11, 1970, HZ-3/9352, ISA.

3. THE JORDAN CRISIS

62   The king barely escaped: Nigel Ashton, *King Hussein of Jordan: A Political Life* (New Haven, CT: Yale University Press, 2008), 144–45.

63 in case an evacuation: Memo from Kissinger to Nixon, September 9, 1970, FRUS 1969–1976:24, Doc. 213, and Minutes of Combined WSAG and Review Group Meeting, September 9, 1970, FRUS 1969–1976:24, Doc. 214.

63 from "any quarter": Telegram from Embassy in Jordan to Department of State, September 21, 1970, FRUS 1969–1976:24, Doc. 284.

63 from the aircraft carrier: Telcon between Nixon and Kissinger, undated, FRUS 1969–1976:24, Doc. 286.

64 on using Israeli forces: Minutes of a Combined WSAG and Review Group Meeting, September 9, 1970, FRUS 1969–1976:24, Doc. 214.

64 He preferred to use: Telcon between Nixon and Kissinger, September 17, 1970, FRUS 1969–1976:24, Doc. 256.

64 "U.S. *and Israeli* assistance": Memo from Kissinger to Nixon, September 15, 1970, FRUS 1969–1976:24, Doc. 246.

64 When Kissinger conveyed this: Henry Kissinger, *White House Years* (Boston: Little, Brown, 1979), 612.

65 Nixon warned her against: Telcon between Nixon and Kissinger, September 17, 1970, FRUS 1969–1976:24, Doc. 262.

65 position off Crete: Minutes of WSAG Meeting, September 18, 1970, FRUS 1969–1976:24, Doc. 264.

65 In a phone call: Telcon between Nixon and Kissinger, September 17, 1970, FRUS 1969–1976:24, Doc. 256.

65 "tougher policy in the Middle East": Telcon between Kissinger and Director of U.S. Information Agency, Shakespeare, September 17, 1970, FRUS 1969–1976:24, Doc. 261.

65 "Those fools at State": Telcon between Kissinger and Director of U.S. Information Agency, Shakespeare, September 17, 1970, FRUS 1969–1976:24, Doc. 261.

66 "Also, what if we failed": Telcon between Kissinger and Rogers, September 17, 1970, FRUS 1969–1976:24, Doc. 257.

66 "even from Israelis": Minutes of WSAG Meeting, September 17, 1970, FRUS 1969–1976:24, Doc. 254, and Telcon between Kissinger, Rogers, and Sisco, September 20, 1970, FRUS 1969–1976:24, Doc. 285, fn. 4.

67 "and clean them out": Telcon between Nixon and Kissinger, September 20, 1970, FRUS 1969–1976:24, Doc. 286.

68 "Situation deteriorating dangerously": Telegram from Embassy in Jordan to Department of State, September 21, 1970, FRUS 1969–1976:24, Doc. 284.

68 "at the right time": Telcon between Kissinger, Rogers, and Sisco, September 20, 1970, FRUS 1969–1976:24, Doc. 285.

69 "We would look favorably": Telcons between Kissinger and Rabin, September 20, 1970, FRUS 1969–1976:24, Docs. 287 and 289.

69 As Rabin would describe it: "The Principles of the U.S.-Israel Relationship," *Strategy and Defense in the Eastern Mediterranean: An American-Israeli Dialogue*, Washington Institute for Near East Policy, July 1986, 8.

69 withdraw from Jordanian territory: Telcon between Nixon, Kissinger, and Haig, September 21, 1970, FRUS 1969–1976:24, Doc. 297.

70 "Tell [Rabin], Go!": Telcon between Nixon, Kissinger, and Haig, September 21, 1970, FRUS 1969–1976:24, Doc. 292.

70 withholding information from the president: H. R. Haldeman, *The Haldeman Diaries: Inside the Nixon White House* (New York: G. P. Putnam, 1994), 196.

70 "the interest of everybody": Telcon between Kissinger and Rabin, September 21, 1970, FRUS 1969–1976:24, Doc. 301.

71 "*not* . . . in Jordan": Telcon between Kissinger and Sisco, September 21, 1970, FRUS 1969–1976:24, Doc. 309.

72 "Did I understand you correctly": Telcon between Kissinger and Rabin, September 21, 1970, FRUS 1969–1976:24, Doc. 308.

72 "present positioning": Memo from Kissinger to Nixon, September 23, 1970, FRUS 1969–1976:24, Doc. 316.

72   the American force buildup: Memo from Kissinger to Nixon, September 22, 1970, FRUS 1969–1976:24, Doc. 315.

73   "Then you would win either way": Minutes of WSAG Meeting, September 23, 1970, FRUS 1969–1976:24, Doc. 317, and Kissinger, *White House Years*, 629.

73   mechanical breakdown: Minutes of NSC Meeting, September 22, 1970, FRUS 1969–1976:24, Doc. 313.

73   take the president at his word: Rabin–Dinitz Cable on Kissinger Meeting, September 21, 1970, HZ-9/9341, ISA.

73   Decades later: Indyk interview with Henry Kissinger, January 15, 2016.

73   As Saunders explained it: Indyk interview with Harold Saunders, October 23, 2015.

74   who the superpower was: Dennis Ross, *The Missing Peace: The Inside Story of the Fight for Middle East Peace* (New York: Farrar, Straus and Giroux, 2004), 261.

74   "obsessive and messianic": Barak Ravid, "Ya'alon Raises U.S. Ire Calling Kerry 'Obsessive and Messianic,'" *Haaretz*, January 14, 2014.

74   Syrian side of the border: Minutes of NSC Meeting on Jordan and Cuba, September 23, 1970, FRUS 1969–1976:24, Doc. 318.

74   The day before: Haldeman, *Haldeman Diaries*, 196.

75   "grateful for Israeli cooperation": Minutes of NSC Meeting on Jordan and Cuba, September 23, 1970, FRUS 1969–1976:24, Doc. 318.

75   "monumental head of steam": Haldeman, *Haldeman Diaries*, 197.

75   "The President will never forget": Yitzhak Rabin, *The Rabin Memoirs* (Berkeley, CA: University of California Press, 1996), 189.

75   "the most far-reaching statement": Rabin, *Memoirs*, 189.

76   "You remember the Jordanian crisis?": Memcon between Kissinger and Dinitz, September 10, 1973, FRUS 1969–1976:25, Doc. 88.

4. A FAILURE OF IMAGINATION

78   "as a weak man": "Remarks by the Honorable Henry A. Kissinger," Anwar Sadat Chair for Peace and Development, University of Maryland, College Park, MD, May 4, 2000, https://sadat.umd.edu/events/remarks-honorable-henry-kissinger, and Jon B. Alterman, ed., *Sadat and His Legacy*, Washington Institute for Near East Policy, 1998, x.

78   Elliot Richardson described him: Interview with U.S. ambassador to Egypt Hermann Eilts in Deborah Hart Strober and Gerald S. Strober, *The Nixon Presidency: An Oral History of the Era* (New York: HarperCollins, 1994), 124.

78   talentless boor: Uri Bar-Joseph, *The Angel: The Egyptian Spy Who Saved Israel* (New York: HarperCollins, 2016), 82–83.

78   "For all we knew": Amir Oren, "Kissinger Wants Israel to Know: The U.S. Saved You During the 1973 War," *Haaretz*, November 2, 2013.

78   prompt withdrawal: Nigel Ashton, *King Hussein of Jordan: A Political Life* (New Haven, CT: Yale University Press, 2008), 148.

78   undisputed ruler: Patrick Seale, *Asad: The Struggle for the Middle East* (Berkeley, CA: University of California Press, 1989), 154–56.

79   "through Washington": Henry Kissinger, *White House Years* (Boston: Little, Brown, 1979), 1279.

79   "framework of the strategy": Henry Kissinger, *Years of Renewal* (New York: Touchstone, 1999), 458.

79   Kissinger recounted: Memcon between Kissinger, Meir, Rabin, Allon, Eban, et al., May 2, 1974, KT00129, NSA.

80   "creating the illusion": Yitzhak Rabin, *The Rabin Memoirs* (Berkeley, CA: University of California Press, 1996), 202.

80   speech Sadat had made in February 1971: "Address to the Nation's Council," Radio Cairo, February 4, 1971, reprinted in Raphael Israeli, ed., *The Public Diary of President Sadat*, vol. 1 (Leiden, Netherlands: Brill, 1978), 30–32.

81   "launch a process": Kissinger, *White House Years*, 1281.

81   "protracted and inconclusive negotiations": Kissinger, *White House Years*, 1285.

81   "to give the Soviets": Kissinger, *White House Years*, 1288–89.

81   To lubricate this initiative: Rabin, *Memoirs*, 209, and Kissinger, *White House Years*, 1289.

82   The implications for the Arab-Israeli conflict: "Texts of Nixon-Brezhnev Declaration and of Joint Communique at End of Visit," *New York Times*, May 30, 1972.

82   "Middle East on ice": Kissinger, *White House Years*, 1246.

82   "justice" and "fairness": Henry Kissinger, "The White Revolutionary: Reflections on Bismarck," *Daedalus* 97.3 (Summer 1968): 899.

83   Kissinger understood these signals: Kissinger, *White House Years*, 1285.

83   "military relaxation": "Sadat's Alexandria Speech," *Summary of World Broadcasts—Middle East*, BBC, April 3, 1974, 4569.

83   wrote at the time: Mohamed Heikal, *The Road to Ramadan* (London: Collins, 1975), 165–72.

83   "military action": Kissinger, *Years of Renewal*, 354.

83   Egyptian army's achievements: Memcon between Kissinger and Meir, May 10, 1974, KT01156, NSA. Kissinger subsequently recounted to Meir and Dayan what Sadat had told him.

84   "major American initiative": Henry Kissinger, *Years of Upheaval* (Boston: Little, Brown, 1982), 202.

84   "But now I've got it all for nothing": The version of Kissinger's reaction to the expulsion that found its way back to Cairo was recounted in Heikal, *The Road to Ramadan*, 184. See also Kissinger, *White House Years*, 1296, and Kissinger, *Years of Renewal*, 353.

85   On July 29: The account of the exchanges leading up to the Ismail-Kissinger meetings comes from Kissinger, *White House Years*, 1295–98. See also Mohammed Hafez Ismail, *Egyptian National Security in an Era of Challenges* [in Arabic] (Cairo: Ahram Center for Translation and Publishing, 1987).

85   "My strategy": Memcon between Kissinger and Rabin, February 22, 1973, FRUS 1969–1976:25, Doc. 23.

86   "take any position": Yigal Kipnis, *1973: The Road to War* (Washington, DC: Just World Books, 2013), 59.

86   "Sadat could not escape": Kissinger, *Years of Upheaval*, 206.

86   "get them more arms": Conversation between Nixon and Haig, January 23, 1973, FRUS 1969–1976:25, Doc. 6. When this conversation took place, Haig was vice chief of staff of the U.S. Army. Nixon appointed Haig White House chief of staff on May 4, 1973

87   "get a total settlement later". Editorial Note, undated, FRUS 1969–1976:25, Doc. 11.

87   Kissinger would subsequently joke: Kissinger, *White House Years*, 418.

87   The third option: Memo from Kissinger to Nixon, February 23, 1973, FRUS 1969–1976:25, Doc. 25.

88   "We are now Israel's only major friend": Kissinger, *Years of Upheaval*, 211–12.

88   He recommended that: Memo for the President's Files, February 23, 1973, FRUS 1969–1976:25, Doc. 26.

90   "Sadat's Henry Kissinger": Henry Fairlie, "Egyptian to Visit US to Give View," *New York Times*, February 18, 1973.

90   Sadat gave him one objective: Indyk interview with Ahmed Aboul Gheit, November 17, 2018. Aboul Gheit served on Ismail's staff.

92   "standard Arab fare": Kissinger, *Years of Upheaval*, 213, and Kissinger, *Years of Renewal*, 354.

93   "The big part": Memcon between Kissinger and Hafiz Ismail in New York, February 25 and 26, 1973, KT00681 and KT00682, NSA.

94   "military clash": Memcon between Kissinger and Hafiz Ismail in New York, February 26, 1973, KT00682, NSA.

95   first subheading: Memo from Kissinger to Nixon, February 25–26, 1973, FRUS 1969–1976:25, Doc. 28.

96   "little reason for optimism": Kissinger, *Years of Upheaval*, 215–16.

96   "diplomatic progress": Kissinger, *White House Years*, 559.

97   "Why do we need a new strategy?": Memcon between Kissinger and Rabin, February 27, 1973, FRUS 1969–1976:25, Doc. 31, and Rabin, *Memoirs*, 215.

97 "to get us back": Francine Klagsbrun, *Lioness: Golda Meir and the Nation of Israel* (New York: Schocken Books, 2017), 602–603.

98 she worried: Memcon between Nixon, Kissinger, and Meir, March 1, 1973, FRUS 1969–1976:25, Doc. 35.

98 "Israel would have to accept": Rabin, *Memoirs*, 216.

98 "knowing damn well we will": Conversation between Nixon and Kissinger, March 1, 1973, FRUS 1969–1976:25, Doc. 36.

99 "might be worked out": Memo from Kissinger to Nixon, March 12, 1973, FRUS 1969–1976:25, Doc. 40.

99 negative response: Kipnis, *1973*, 96.

100 *The New York Times* reported: William Beecher, "Israelis Will Buy More Jets in U.S., Total Put at 48," *New York Times*, March 14, 1973.

100 "preclude any progress towards": Back-Channel Message from Ismail to Kissinger, March 20, 1973, FRUS 1969–1976:25, Doc. 41.

100 "We have to tell the world": Radio Cairo, March 26, 1973, reprinted in Israeli, *Public Diary of President Sadat*, 322–42.

100 Arnaud de Borchgrave: Arnaud de Borchgrave, "Anwar Sadat's Uncertain Trumpet," *Newsweek*, April 9, 1973.

100 "peace process": De Borchgrave tells the story in Strober and Strober, *Nixon Presidency*, 127.

101 "clobbered": Conversation between Nixon, Kissinger, and Sisco, April 13, 1973, FRUS 1969–1976:25, Doc 49.

101 CIA's assessment as well: Memo from CIA Director to Kissinger, April 16, 1973, FRUS 1969–1976:25, Doc. 50.

101 "The trouble with you": Simcha Dinitz, "Diplomatic Memoirs" (Unpublished manuscript, in author's possession: 2003), 68.

102 "troubled America": Dinitz, "Diplomatic Memoirs," 69.

102 "Nobel Prize on the Middle East": Memcon between Kissinger and Dinitz, March 30, 1973, FRUS 1969–1976:25, Doc. 43.

102 "There's no Nobel Peace Prize": Martin Indyk, *Innocent Abroad: An Intimate Account of American Peace Diplomacy in the Middle East* (New York: Simon & Schuster, 2009), 379.

102 a highly placed agent: Indyk interview with William B. Quandt, January 13, 2016.

102 "gain more time": Memcon between Kissinger and Dinitz, April 11, 1973, KT00698, NSA.

103 border with Egypt: Kipnis, *1973*, 140.

103 "after the battle": De Borchgrave, "Anwar Sadat's Uncertain Trumpet."

103 Kissinger described it: Kissinger, *Years of Upheaval*, 227.

103 "in a very innocent way": Seymour Hersh, "Broad Role Cited," *New York Times*, May 17, 1973.

106 sitting by a stream beyond the garden: Kissinger, *Years of Upheaval*, 227, and Jack O'Connell, *King's Counsel: A Memoir of War, Espionage, and Diplomacy in the Middle East* (New York: W. W. Norton, 2011), 116–17, 120–21. Trone's account is retold by his CIA colleague Jack O'Connell, who was at the time the station chief in Amman. Kissinger also recounts Trone's description of Ismail as "visibly dispirited and glum" after their meeting.

106 "This whole exercise": Kipnis, *1973*, 134–35. Kissinger reported to Dinitz that, in contrast to the meeting in February, he now felt a lack of interest on the part of the Egyptians and added, "It seems as though they think there is no chance of political progress."

107 Libya and Iraq: Abraham Rabinovich, *The Yom Kippur War: The Epic Encounter That Transformed the Middle East* (New York: Schocken Books, 2017), 23.

107 Cline's memo: Richard Parker, *The October War: A Retrospective* (Gainesville, FL: University Press of Florida, 2001), 113–25.

107 *"most imminent"*: Editorial Note, undated, FRUS 1969–1976:25, Doc. 68.

107 "You would prefer no document": Memcon between Kissinger and Dinitz, June 15, 1973, KT00757, NSA.

108 "situation from flaring up": Memo for Nixon's Files by Kissinger, June 23, 1973, FRUS 1969–1976:25, Doc. 73.

108 "Unless the Israelis do withdraw": "Excerpts from the Second Segment of Frost's Television Interview with Nixon," *New York Times,* May 13, 1977.

108 "diplomatic keys to a settlement": Kissinger, *Years of Upheaval,* 298.

108 Nixon had Haig turn it off immediately: Memorandum for the Record, Next Steps on the Middle East, June 29, 1973, NSA, https://nsarchive2.gwu.edu//NSAEBB/NSAEBB98/octwar-04.pdf.

108 "as still corpses": "Sadat's Alexandria Speech," April 3, 1974; Henry Tanner, "Sadat Says War Made Egypt Truly Free," *New York Times,* April 3, 1974; Martin Indyk, "Détente and the Politics of Patronage," *Australian Outlook* 30 (August 1976): 171–96.

109 "step-by-step": Dinitz's report to Golda Meir, Kipnis, *1973,* 195.

109 with a positive response: Kipnis, *1973,* 46.

109 "exhaust the Arabs": Memcon between Kissinger and Dinitz, September 10, 1973, FRUS 1969–1976:25, Doc. 88.

109 "in a reasonable period after elections": Kipnis, *1973,* 204.

109 As the Syrians and Egyptians: Memo from Cline to Kissinger, September 30, 1973, FRUS 1969–1976:25, Doc. 93.

110 "Israelis do not perceive": Telegram from Embassy in Israel to Department of State, October 1, 1973, FRUS 1969–1976:25, Doc. 94.

110 "revolutionary": Kissinger, "White Revolutionary," 901.

110 "tragic aspect of policymaking": Henry Kissinger, "Domestic Structure and Foreign Policy," *Daedalus* 95.2 (1966): 503–29, cited in Ferguson, *Kissinger,* 727.

110 whom he viewed as "a buffoon": Matti Golan, *The Secret Conversations of Henry Kissinger: Step-by-Step Diplomacy in the Middle East* (Chicago: Quadrangle, 1976), 144–46. Golan's book is based on leaked Israeli transcripts of Kissinger's meetings with Israelis. There is no record of this conversation in the American archives. However, when I checked with Kissinger, he accepted the accuracy of the quotations, noting that it was true that he had not taken Sadat seriously before he launched the war.

111 toyed with him: Memcon between Kissinger and Meir, May 10, 1974, KT01156, NSA, and Golan, *Secret Conversations of Henry Kissinger,* 144–46. Kissinger told Meir that he looked at Sadat as a "nuisance," not as a strategic opportunity, saying, "[W]henever I talked to the Egyptians, I played with them."

112 only war would trigger: Memcon between Kissinger and Assad, February 26, 1974, KT01039, NSA.

112 "We couldn't have done better": Memcon between Ford and Kissinger, August 12, 1974, FRUS 1969–1976:26, Doc. 95.

112 "some conception of the future": Kissinger, "Domestic Structure and Foreign Policy," 505.

5. RESUPPLY

116 a moment to flirt: Telcon with Liza Minnelli, October 19, 1973, Series IV: Telephone Conversation Transcript Copies, Box 195, Folder 4, Henry A. Kissinger Papers, Part III (MS 2004), Manuscripts and Archives, Yale University Library.

118 At Scowcroft's suggestion: Indyk interviews with Brent Scowcroft and Gahl Hodges Burt, October 20, 2015, and December 16, 2020.

118 fired him in 1975: Gerald Ford, *A Time to Heal* (New York: Harper & Row, 1979), 324.

119 "wanton sneak attack": Adm. Thomas H. Moorer to AMEU, Memorandum, "Attack on USS *Liberty* June 8, 1967," June 8, 1997, http://www.la.utexas.edu/users/chenry/usme/moorer.html.

119 "The basic problem": Minutes of WSAG Meeting, October 6, 1973, FRUS 1969–1976:25, Doc. 103.

119 "we have to come down hard": Telcon between Kissinger and Haig, October 6, 1973, FRUS 1969–1976:25, Doc. 106.

119 To keep the Israelis content: Henry Kissinger, *Crisis: The Anatomy of Two Major Foreign Policy Crises* (New York: Simon & Schuster, 2003), 50–51.

120   "any reply to the Israeli request": Minutes of WSAG Meeting, October 6, 1973, FRUS
       1969–1976:25, Doc. 112.

120   "We will need the assistance": Simcha Dinitz, "Diplomatic Memoirs" (Unpublished manu-
       script, in author's possession: 2003), 76.

120   "Don't ever preempt!": Marvin Kalb and Bernard Kalb, *Kissinger* (New York: Little, Brown,
       1974), 460.

121   tough to do: Memcon between Kissinger and Shalev, October 7, 1973, FRUS 1969–
       1976:25, Doc. 115.

121   Mount Hermon had fallen: Kissinger, *Crisis*, 87–88.

121   "we must be on their side": Telcon between Kissinger and Haig, October 7, 1973, FRUS
       1969–1976:25, Doc. 116.

121   "in the back of our minds": Telcon between Nixon and Kissinger, October 7, 1973, FRUS
       1969–1976:25, Doc. 117.

121   "widen the confrontation": Back-Channel Message from Ismail to Kissinger, October 7,
       1973, FRUS 1969–1976:25, Doc. 118.

122   "unless things were stirred up": Minutes of WSAG Meeting, October 7, 1973, FRUS
       1969–1976:25, Doc. 121.

122   first day of the war: Telcon between Kissinger and Dobrynin, October 6, 1973, FRUS
       1969–1976:25, Doc. 105.

122   "to give back territory": Telcon between Kissinger and Dobrynin, October 6, 1973, FRUS
       1969–1976:25, Doc. 111.

122   In the meantime: Telcon between Kissinger and Eban, October 7, 1973, FRUS 1969–
       1976:25, Doc. 119.

123   until after the fighting had ended: Minutes of WSAG Meetings, October 8 and 9, 1973,
       FRUS 1969–1976:25, Docs. 131 and 135.

123   advance beyond the current lines: Cable from Dinitz to Gazit, October 8, 1973, A-3/4996,
       ISA.

124   in helping resolve the conflict: Message from Kissinger to Ismail, October 8, 1973, FRUS
       1969–1976:25, Doc. 125.

124   "we are well-positioned": Minutes of WSAG Meeting, October 8, 1973, FRUS 1969–
       1976:25, Doc. 131.

124   "They can't do that to us again": Telcon between Nixon and Kissinger, October 8, 1973,
       FRUS 1969–1976:25, Doc. 132.

124   "expected a quick victory": Memcon between Kissinger, Dinitz, et al., October 9, 1973,
       FRUS 1969–1976:25, Doc. 134.

125   send a terrible signal: Henry Kissinger, *Years of Upheaval* (Boston: Little, Brown, 1982),
       493.

125   "the depth of his despair": Abraham Rabinovich, *The Yom Kippur War: The Epic Encoun-
       ter That Transformed the Middle East* (New York: Schocken Books, 2017), 218–19, and
       Moshe Dayan, *Moshe Dayan: Story of My Life* (London: Weidenfeld and Nicolson, 1976),
       390–91.

125   of suicide: Francine Klagsbrun, *Lioness: Golda Meir and the Nation of Israel* (New York:
       Schocken Books, 2017), 626.

126   before Iraqi and Jordanian forces joined in: Rabinovich, *Yom Kippur War,* 261.

127   "a costly victory": Memcon between Kissinger, Schlesinger, Rush, Moorer, and Colby,
       October 9, 1973, FRUS 1969–1976:25, Doc. 135.

127   "If it gets hairy": Memcon between Nixon, Kissinger, Haig, and Scowcroft, October 9,
       1973, FRUS 1969–1976:25, Doc. 140.

127   "let them be destroyed": Peter Golden, *Quiet Diplomat: A Biography of Max M. Fisher* (New
       York: Cornwall Books, 1992), 289.

127   "We want to stick by Israel": Memcon between Nixon, Kissinger, Haig, and Scowcroft,
       October 9, 1973, FRUS 1969–1976:25, Doc. 140.

128   "If it should go very badly": Memcon between Kissinger, Dinitz, and Shalev, October 9,
       1973, FRUS 1969–1976:25, Doc. 141.

128   "won't abandon Israel": Cable from Dinitz to Gazit, October 9, 1973, A-3/4996, ISA.

131 "easy and elegant victories": Henry Kamm, "War of 'Attrition,'" *New York Times*, October 10, 1973.

131 "sense of inferiority": Memcon between Nixon, Kissinger, Haig, and Scowcroft, October 9, 1973, FRUS 1969–1976:25, Doc. 140.

131 "a profoundly shocking experience": Minutes of Kissinger's Staff Meeting, October 10, 1973, FRUS 1969–1976:25, Doc. 148.

132 partly because of its dependence: Kissinger, *Years of Upheaval*, 561–62.

132 "four days of juggling to do": Minutes of Kissinger's Staff Meeting, October 10, 1973, FRUS 1969–1976:25, Doc. 148.

132 difficult discussions: Kissinger, *Crisis*, 162.

133 massive Soviet airlift: Telcon between Schlesinger and Moorer, October 10, 1973, FRUS 1969–1976:25, Doc. 144.

134 The main sitting room: Kalb and Kalb, *Kissinger*, 8–9.

134 "the entire administration": Cable from Dinitz to Gazit, October 10, 1973, A-3/4996, ISA.

134 faced with a choice: Telcon between Kissinger and Haig, 9:14 p.m., October 10, 1973, KA11143, NSA, and Telcon between Kissinger and Scowcroft, 8:59 p.m., October 10, 1973, KA11142, NSA.

134 complained about the substantial airlift: Telcon between Kissinger and Dobrynin, October 10, 1973, KA11128, NSA.

134 "to teach the Syrians": Terence Smith, "Israelis Push Six Miles into Syria, Wrecking Dozens of Foe's Tanks," *New York Times*, October 12, 1973.

135 "If we hear any more": Telcon between Nixon and Kissinger, October 11, 1973, FRUS 1969–1976:25, Doc. 153.

135 "beside himself": Telcon between Kissinger and Shalev, October 11, 1973, FRUS 1969–1976:25, Doc. 154.

136 "standstill" resolution: Kissinger, *Crisis*, 185–86.

136 "when I talked to the President": Telcon between Kissinger and Scowcroft, October 11, 1973, FRUS 1969–1976:25, Doc. 156.

136 "or lesser uncertainty": Carl von Clausewitz, *On War* (Princeton, NJ: Princeton University Press, 1984), 101.

137 the peninsula: Rabinovich, *Yom Kippur War*, 343–45.

137 heavier casualties: Shimon Golan, *War on Yom Kippur* [in Hebrew] (Jerusalem: Modan Publishing, 2013), 753–61.

138 cease fire anyway: Rabinovich, *Yom Kippur War*, 384.

139 These were fresh Iraqi forces: Rabinovich, *Yom Kippur War*, 314, and Uzi Eilam, *Eilam's Arc: How Israel Became a Military Technology Powerhouse* (East Sussex, UK: Sussex Academic Press, 2011), 106–107.

139 international pressure: Telcon between Nixon and Kissinger, October 12, 1973, FRUS 1969–1976:25, Doc. 159.

139 "For us to have gone in": Memcon between Kissinger, Schlesinger, Rush, Clements, Moorer, and Colby, October 13, 1973, FRUS 1969–1976:25, Doc. 173.

139 "with understanding and good will": Back-Channel Message from Kissinger to Ismail, undated, FRUS 1969–1976:25, Doc. 160.

140 "would threaten détente": Bernard Gwertzman, "Kissinger Says U.S. and Soviet Have Acted to Keep War Restricted to Mideast," *New York Times*, October 13, 1973.

140 a day later: Tim O'Brien, "Jackson Hits Kissinger on Aid to Israel," *Washington Post*, October 15, 1973.

140 Although there is no record: Kissinger, *Years of Upheaval*, 508.

140 if any Soviet aircraft: Kissinger, *Years of Upheaval*, 509–10.

140 "Once you have been threatened": Kissinger, *Crisis*, 207.

141 in the next two days: Cable between Dinitz and Gazit, October 12, 1973, A-4/4996, ISA.

142 "fear of God into him": Memcon between Kissinger, Dinitz, Shalev, and Scowcroft, October 12, 1973, FRUS 1969–1976:25, Doc. 166.

142 "out of it": Telcon between Kissinger and Schlesinger, October 13, 1973, FRUS 1969–1976:25, Doc. 167

142 freedom of operations: Knesset Foreign Affairs and Defense Committee Meeting, October 12, 1973, A-2/8163, ISA.

143 "forced charters": Kissinger, *Crisis*, 219.

143 "is not above the law's commands": Lesley Oelsner, "Judges Rule 5–2," *New York Times*, October 13, 1973.

143 *"make it work"*: "Excerpts from the Second Segment of Frost's Television Interview with Nixon," *New York Times*, May 13, 1977, and Richard Nixon, *RN: The Memoirs of Richard Nixon* (New York: Grosset & Dunlap, 1978), 926–27.

144 "it was urgent": Memcon between Kissinger, Schlesinger, Rush, Clements, Moorer, and Colby, October 13, 1973, FRUS 1969–1976:25, Doc. 173.

144 Kissinger had coordinated closely: Minutes of Kissinger's Staff Meeting, October 23, 1973, FRUS 1969–1976:25, Doc. 250.

144 "diplomacy to work": Memcon between Kissinger, Schlesinger, Rush, Clements, Moorer, and Colby, October 13, 1973, FRUS 1969–1976:25, Doc. 173.

144 "The Israelis are slackening off": Telcon between Kissinger and Haig, 9:35 a.m., October 13, 1973, KA11202, NSA.

144 "If the Arabs see that": Memcon between Kissinger, Schlesinger, Rush, Clements, Moorer, and Colby, October 13, 1973, FRUS 1969–1976:25, Doc. 173.

145 As long as the Syrians: Memcon between Kissinger and Fahmy, October 29, 1973, FRUS 1969–1976:25, Doc. 298.

145 "a gross political and strategic blunder": Anatoly Dobrynin, *In Confidence: Moscow's Ambassador to Six Cold War Presidents* (New York: Crown, 1995), 289.

145 "We went to the Soviets": Memcon between Kissinger and Assad, March 1, 1974, FRUS 1969–1976:26, Doc. 29.

146 He concluded that the Soviets: Telcon between Nixon and Kissinger, October 14, 1973, FRUS 1969–1976:25, Doc. 180.

146 "only understand brutality": Telcons between Kissinger and Scowcroft, October 13, 1973, 2:25 p.m. and 4:05 p.m., KA11212 and KA11216, NSA.

146 "The President is extremely": Kissinger, *Crisis*, 241–46.

147 "would accept nothing more": Dobrynin, *In Confidence*, 291.

147 "We are working to link": Memcon of Middle East WSAG Meeting, October 14, 1973, FRUS 1969–1976:25, Doc. 181.

147 that the American airlift: Telcon between Kissinger and Dobrynin, October 14, 1973, FRUS 1969–1976:25: Doc. 183.

148 "I don't see": Memcon of Middle East WSAG Meeting, October 14, 1973, FRUS 1969–1976:25, Doc. 181, and Telcon between Moorer and Goodpaster, October 15, 1973, FRUS 1969–1976:25, Doc. 185.

148 "We are trying to force": Minutes of Kissinger's Staff Meeting, October 15, 1973, FRUS 1969–1976:25, Doc. 187.

148 "if I contribute anything": Telcon between Nixon and Kissinger, October 14, 1973, FRUS 1969–1976:25, Doc. 182.

148 "important superpower": Eilam, *Eilam's Arc*, 109.

148 "they were hit": Rabinovich, *Yom Kippur War*, 356.

149 "The repair shops": Rabinovich, *Yom Kippur War*, 352.

149 was now moot: Abba Eban, *Abba Eban: An Autobiography* (Jerusalem, Israel: Steinmatzky's Agency, 1977), 520.

6. CEASE-FIRE

151 "that we could put in things faster": Minutes of Kissinger's Staff Meeting, October 15, 1973, FRUS 1969–1976:25, Doc. 187, and Minutes of WSAG Meeting, October 15, 1973, FRUS 1969–1976:25, Doc. 186.

152 "peace to the Middle East": Henry Kissinger, *Years of Upheaval* (Boston: Little, Brown, 1982), 522–23.

152 Kissinger to Cairo: Henry Kissinger, *Crisis: The Anatomy of Two Major Foreign Policy Crises* (New York: Simon & Schuster, 2003), 259–60.

152 *"including withdrawal of forces"*: Kissinger, *Years of Upheaval*, 530–31.

153 "to finally expel the Israelis": Victor Israelyan, *Inside the Kremlin During the Yom Kippur War* (University Park, PA: Pennsylvania State University Press, 1995), 96.

153 "Egypt was not ready to accept": Telegram 3136 from Cairo, October 16, 1973, in Back-Channel Message from Kissinger to Ismail, October 16, 1973, FRUS 1969–1976:25, Doc. 190, fn. 3.

154 IDF's canal crossing: Israelyan, *Inside the Kremlin*, 105, and Anwar Sadat, *In Search of Identity* (New York: Harper & Row, 1978), 309.

154 WSAG meeting on Tuesday morning: Minutes of WSAG Meeting, October 16, 1973, FRUS 1969–1976:25, Doc. 191.

155 than of what he'd accomplished in Vietnam: Kissinger, *Years of Upheaval*, 370.

155 assured the president: Memcon between Nixon, Kissinger, Saqqaf, and Bouteflika, October 17, 1973, FRUS 1969–1976:25, Doc. 195.

156 "I think we're going to get": Telcon between Nixon and Kissinger, October 17, 1973, FRUS 1969–1976:25, Doc. 197.

156 "Saudi Foreign Minister": Minutes of WSAG Meeting, October 17, 1973, FRUS 1969–1976:25, Doc. 198.

156 10 percent: "Saudis Cut Oil Output 10% to Put Pressure on U.S.," *New York Times*, October 19, 1973.

156 given interviews: "Faisal Interview," *Washington Post*, November 23, 1973, and John Cooley, "Interview with King Faisal," *Christian Science Monitor*, September 4, 1973.

156 The experts: Rachel Bronson, *Thicker Than Oil: America's Uneasy Partnership with Saudi Arabia* (Oxford: Oxford University Press, 2006), 116; Nicholas C. Proffitt, "An Arab Blend of Oil and Politics: Faisal's Threat," *Newsweek*, September 10, 1973; Jim Hoagland, "Faisal Seen Backing Cairo by Using Oil to Press U.S.," *Washington Post*, September 2, 1973; "Faisal Interview," *Washington Post*, November 23, 1973; John Cooley, "Interview with King Faisal," *Christian Science Monitor*, September 4, 1973.

157 the letter offended the king: Editorial Note, October 15, 1973, FRUS 1969–1976:36, Doc. 216.

157 "We have had no indication": Minutes of WSAG Meeting, October 15, 1973, FRUS 1969–1976:25, Doc. 186.

157 "blow off emotionally": Minutes of WSAG Meeting, October 16, 1973, FRUS 1969–1976:25 Doc. 191.

157 answered affirmatively: Note from Scowcroft to Kissinger, October 17, 1973, FRUS 1969–1976:25, Doc. 196.

157 "very hard to refuse": Kissinger, *Crisis*, 281–82.

157 conceded this point to the Soviet Union: Abba Eban, *Abba Eban: An Autobiography* (Jerusalem, Israel: Steinmatzky's Agency, 1977), 523.

158 quickly in the Security Council: Minutes of WSAG Meeting, October 17, 1973, FRUS 1969–1976:25 Doc. 198.

158 "a small episode": Israelyan, *Inside the Kremlin*, 107.

158 "stubborn, persistent, adamant, and irresponsible": Israelyan, *Inside the Kremlin*, 112, and Sadat, *In Search of Identity*, 309.

158 cabled Assad: Sadat, *In Search of Identity*, 309.

159 "they are moving in our direction": Kissinger, *Crisis*, 288, 290.

159 "highly acceptable": Telcon between Kissinger and Scowcroft, October 18, 1973, FRUS 1969–1976:25, Doc. 205.

159 "fundamental settlement": Kissinger, *Years of Upheaval*, 541.

160 Revealing how little: Message from Dinitz to Kissinger, October 18, 1973, FRUS 1969–1976:25, Doc. 206.

160 "it would be good": Telcon between Kissinger and Dobrynin, October 19, 1973, FRUS 1969–1976:25, Doc. 209.

160 Kissinger discussed the issue with Nixon: Kissinger, *Crisis,* 293.
160 in one day: Telcons between Kissinger and Dobrynin, October 19, 1973, FRUS 1969–1976:25, Docs. 210 and 211.
160 "the outcome cannot be": Kissinger, *Crisis,* 301.
161 "the embargo on oil": Message from Fahd to Kissinger, October 23, 1973, FRUS 1969–1976:25, Doc. 224.
161 "The negotiations I am about to undertake": Telegram from Kissinger to Scowcroft, October 20, 1973, FRUS 1969–1976:25, Doc. 215.
162 "my complete support": Message from Nixon to Brezhnev, October 20, 1973, FRUS 1969–1976:25, Doc. 217.
162 Kissinger "was horrified": Kissinger, *Years of Upheaval,* 547.
162 "respective friends": Telegram from Scowcroft to Kissinger, October 20, 1973, FRUS 1969–1976:25, Doc. 218.
162 "will be incalculable": Telegram from Kissinger to Scowcroft, October 21, 1973, FRUS 1969–1976:25, Doc. 220.
163 "live out his fantasies": Kissinger, *Years of Upheaval,* 1182.
163 "medium-sized organ": Kissinger, *Years of Upheaval,* 549.
164 linking the cease-fire to Israeli withdrawal: Memo from Scowcroft to Nixon, October 21, 1973, FRUS 1969–1976:25, Doc. 219.
164 even chance of a breakthrough: Memo from Scowcroft to Nixon, October 21, 1973, FRUS 1969–1976:25, Doc. 219.
164 had been achieved: Back-Channel Message from Kissinger to Ismail, undated, FRUS 1969–1976:25, Doc. 214, fn. 2.
164 ambassador Vladimir Vinogradov: Israelyan, *Inside the Kremlin,* 129.
166 "the solution of all the key issues": Memcon between Brezhnev, Gromyko, Kissinger, et al., October 21, 1973, FRUS 1969–1976:25, Doc. 221.
167 "especially Dinitz": Telegram from Kissinger to Scowcroft, October 21, 1973, FRUS 1969–1976:25, Doc. 222.
167 language of the resolution: Letter from Nixon to Meir, October 21, 1973, FRUS 1969–1976:25, Doc. 228, fn. 2.
167 "I looked up to find": Kissinger, *Years of Upheaval,* 557.
167 Kirya in Tel Aviv: Call between Meir and Dinitz, October 21, 1973, A-3/7792, ISA.
167 accept the cease-fire resolution: Letter from Nixon to Meir, October 21, 1973, FRUS 1969–1976:25, Doc. 228.
168 out of the negotiations: Shimon Golan, *War on Yom Kippur* [in Hebrew] (Jerusalem, Modan Publishing, 2013), 1130.
168 "reject the cease-fire": Golan, *War on Yom Kippur,* 1130.
168 "contrary to most UN ceasefire resolutions": Eban, *Abba Eban,* 529–31.

7. DEFCON 3

170 "one of the most moving": Henry Kissinger, *Years of Upheaval* (Boston: Little, Brown, 1982), 560.
170 "mad at me": Abba Eban, *Abba Eban: An Autobiography* (Jerusalem, Israel: Steinmatzky's Agency, 1977), 532.
171 overcome her chagrin: Eban, *Abba Eban,* 532.
171 "She was heartbroken": Kissinger, *Years of Upheaval,* 562.
172 "Even if they do": Memcon between Kissinger, Meir, et al., October 22, 1973, FRUS 1969–1976:25, Doc. 230.
172 "within a day or two": Eban, *Abba Eban,* 532.
173 Kissinger changed the subject: Memcon between Kissinger, Meir, Allon, and Eban, October 22, 1973, FRUS 1969–1976:25, Doc. 232.
173 military situation: Protocol of Kissinger Meeting with the Israeli Cabinet, October 22, 1973, A-15/7047, ISA.

173 As Kissinger would subsequently recall: Kissinger, *Years of Upheaval*, 565.

173 "we'll respond": Abraham Rabinovich, *The Yom Kippur War: The Epic Encounter That Transformed the Middle East* (New York: Schocken Books, 2017), 461.

174 General Kalman Magen's division: Rabinovich, *Yom Kippur War*, 462–64.

174 the four hours lost: Kissinger, *Years of Upheaval*, 569.

174 agreed to the cease-fire: Eban, *Abba Eban*, 530.

174 "entire Third Army": Indyk interview with Henry Kissinger, October 17, 2017.

174 "were decisive": Memcon between Kissinger, Meir, Shalev, and Dinitz, November 1, 1973, FRUS 1969–1976:25, Doc. 305.

174 Kissinger added, defensively: Summary of Calls and Conversations at Israeli Embassy, October 24, 1973, A-3/7792, ISA.

176 "somehow it works out": Hagai Tzoref, ed., *Golda Meir: The Fourth Prime Minister, Selected Documents (1898–1978)* [in Hebrew] (Jerusalem: Israel State Archives, 2016), Doc. 164, 576.

176 "a few miles in the desert": Henry Kissinger, *Crisis: The Anatomy of Two Major Foreign Policy Crises* (New York: Simon & Schuster, 2003), 321.

176 She could not tolerate: Kissinger, *Crisis*, 314.

177 after an Arab attack: Telcon between Kissinger and Dinitz, October 23, 1973, FRUS 1969–1976:25, Doc. 245.

177 letter to Nixon: Back-Channel Message from Sadat to Nixon, October 23, 1973, FRUS 1969–1976:25, Doc. 248.

177 commitment from Meir: Hotline Message from Brezhnev to Nixon, October 23, 1973, FRUS 1969–1976:25, Doc. 246; Hotline Message from Brezhnev to Nixon, October 23, 1973, FRUS 1969–1976:25, Doc. 247; Kissinger, *Crisis*, 322.

177 "the events of the last two weeks": Minutes of Kissinger's Staff Meeting, October 23, 1973, FRUS 1969–1976:25, Doc. 250.

178 "concrete proposal": Minutes of WSAG Meeting, October 24, 1973, FRUS 1969–1976:25, Doc. 259.

178 "By December we will turn on them": Memcon between Kissinger, Schlesinger, Moorer, and Scowcroft, October 24, 1973, FRUS 1969–1976:25, Doc. 261.

179 "forces" to the Middle East: Back-Channel Message from Kissinger to Ismail, October 24, 1973, FRUS 1969–1976:25, Doc. 260, fn. 2.

179 "UN resolution": Kissinger, *Years of Upheaval*, 579.

179 "If you want [a] confrontation": Kissinger, *Crisis*, 337.

179 "much better off": Kissinger, *Crisis*, 340.

179 "pisswisher" of a message: Memo for the Record, October 24–25, 1973, FRUS 1969–1976:25, Doc. 269.

179 "immediate and clear reply": Message from Brezhnev to Nixon, undated, FRUS 1969–1976:25, Doc. 267.

180 Moscow should be prepared: Victor Israelyan, *Inside the Kremlin During the Yom Kippur War* (University Park, PA: Pennsylvania State University Press, 1995), 166.

180 "anybody's guess": Anatoly Dobrynin, *In Confidence: Moscow's Ambassador to Six Cold War Presidents* (New York: Crown, 1995), 293.

180 how the prime minister would have him respond: Kissinger, *Crisis*, 344.

180 Kissinger answered no: Telcon between Kissinger and Haig, October 24, 1973, KA11413, NSA.

180 "too distraught": Kissinger, *Years of Upheaval*, 585.

181 unmistakable threat: Memo for the Record, October 24–25, 1973, FRUS 1969–1976:25, Doc. 269.

181 "Either we would be the tail": Kissinger, *Years of Upheaval*, 584.

181 "the most serious consequences": Memo for the Record, October 24–25, 1973, FRUS 1969–1976:25, Doc. 269.

181 reciprocal withdrawal: Telcon between Kissinger and Dinitz, October 24, 1973, FRUS 1969–1976:25, Doc. 270.

182   "one of the more thoughtful discussions": Kissinger, *Crisis*, 349.
182   nuclear strike force: Memo for the Record, October 24–25, 1973, FRUS 1969–1976:25, Doc. 269.
182   Kissinger to visit Cairo: Kissinger, *Years of Upheaval*, 588.
183   "hard to achieve": Message from Nixon to Brezhnev, October 25, 1973, FRUS 1969–1976:25, Doc. 274.
183   "be honest with me!": Telcon between Kissinger and Dinitz, October 25, 1973, FRUS 1969–1976:25, Doc. 272.
184   "profoundly heartened and impressed": Eban, *Abba Eban*, 535. Eban records that "no Israeli minister who took part in the all-night meeting on October 25 will ever forget the tension that gripped us."
184   Dinitz believed this was achievable: Rabinovich, *Yom Kippur War*, 337.
184   "the $64,000 question": Memo for the Record, October 24–25, 1973, FRUS 1969–1976:25, Doc. 269.
185   saving the Egyptian Third Army: Indyk interview with Henry Kissinger, October 17, 2017.
185   "no functional President": Memo for the Record, October 24–25, 1973, FRUS 1969–1976:25, Doc. 269.
185   "They find a cripple": Kissinger, *Crisis*, 346–47.
185   "charging around": Telcon between Kissinger and Haig, October 24, 1973, KA11416, NSA.
185   "approaching nightmare": Kissinger, *Years of Upheaval*, 581.
185   "early hours of the morning": Kissinger, *Years of Upheaval*, 593.
186   "strange period": Indyk interview with Henry Kissinger, October 17, 2017, and Kissinger, *Years of Upheaval*, 593.
186   decisions in solitude: Alexander Haig, *Inner Circles: How America Changed the World* (New York: Grand Central Publishing, 1992), 415–16.
187   At Arafat's invitation: Deborah Sontag, "Clinton Watches as Palestinians Drop Call for Israel's Destruction," *New York Times*, December 15, 1998.
187   He was in an ebullient mood: "Event at the Main Terminal of Gaza Int'l Airport in Gaza City," Gaza, William J. Clinton Presidential Library, December 14, 1998, https://www.youtube.com/watch?v=tBht5QeKHaA.
188   "forward together": "Remarks by President Clinton to the Palestinian National Council," Israeli Ministry of Foreign Affairs, December 14, 1998, https://mfa.gov.il/MFA/Foreign Policy/MFADocuments/Yearbook12/Pages/119%20Remarks%20by%20President%20Clinton%20to%20the%20Palestinia.aspx.
188   "Focus on your job": Dennis Ross, *The Missing Peace: The Inside Story of the Fight for Middle East Peace* (New York: Farrar, Straus and Giroux, 2004), 489.
189   "in the essential national interest": "Secretary Kissinger's News Conference," October 25, 1973, *Department of State Bulletin*, vol. 69, November 12, 1973, 585–94.
189   "forces around the world": "President Nixon's News Conference," October 26, 1973, *Department of State Bulletin*, vol. 69, November 12, 1973, 581–84.
190   "sounded like it": Kissinger, *Crisis*, 383.
190   "mostly determined by domestic considerations": Dobrynin, *In Confidence*, 295.
191   "appropriate measures with Israel": Israelyan, *Inside the Kremlin*, 168–69.
191   USS *John F. Kennedy*: Rabinovich, *Yom Kippur War*, 482.
191   the Politburo was satisfied: Israelyan, *Inside the Kremlin*, 185–86.
191   forgo his request: Kissinger, *Crisis*, 354.
191   "Sadat was staking his future": Kissinger, *Crisis*, 355.
192   Watergate woes?: "Mideast Crisis: The Watergate Connection," *Washington Post*, October 26, 1973, A26, and Joseph Kraft, "Combined Crisis," *Washington Post*, October 28, 1973, C7.
192   "We are attempting to conduct": "Secretary Kissinger's News Conference," October 25, 1973, *Department of State Bulletin*, vol. 69, November 12, 1973, 585–94.
192   "final peace settlement": Kissinger, *Crisis*, 370.

192 threatening "desperate measures": Telcon between Kissinger and Dinitz, October 26, 1973, FRUS 1969–1976:25, Doc. 284.

193 either break the Israeli siege: Telcon between Kissinger and Schlesinger, October 27, 1973, KA11501, NSA.

193 Kissinger was not interested in confronting: Kissinger, *Crisis*, 371.

193 Israelis "strongly": Telcon between Nixon and Kissinger, October 26, 1973, KA11454, NSA.

193 "since the Cuban missile crisis": "Transcript of President Nixon's News Conference on Domestic and Foreign Affairs," *New York Times*, October 27, 1973.

193 "made a mess with the Russians": Telcon between Kissinger and Haig, October 26, 1973, FRUS 1969–1976:25, Doc. 285.

193 "say something you will regret": Telcons between Kissinger and Dinitz, October 26, 1973, FRUS 1969–1976:25, Docs. 281 and 284.

194 "You play your game": Telcon between Kissinger and Dinitz, October 26, 1973, FRUS 1969–1976:25, Doc. 284.

194 "get a condemnation on you": Telcon between Kissinger and Dinitz, October 26, 1973, FRUS 1969–1976:25, Doc. 284.

194 "neither surrender nor humiliation": Back-Channel Message from Kissinger to Ismail, October 26, 1973, FRUS 1969–1976:25, Doc. 286.

194 not recommending Egypt accept it: Back-Channel Message from Kissinger to Ismail, October 26, 1973, FRUS 1969–1976:25, Doc. 286.

195 Leonard Garment: Tzoref, *Golda Meir*, Doc. 164, 576.

195 Kissinger's purpose: Tzoref, *Golda Meir*, Doc. 164, 576.

195 "jeopardize the interests": Hotline Message from Brezhnev to Nixon, October 26, 1973, FRUS 1969–1976:25, Doc. 288.

196 "prefer being coerced": Kissinger, *Crisis*, 393.

196 Third Army go free: Telcon between Kissinger and Dinitz, October 26, 1973, FRUS 1969–1976:25, Doc. 289.

196 "sitting under Brezhnev's and Sadat's threats": Tzoref, *Golda Meir*, Doc. 165, 577.

197 "on its own": Kissinger, *Crisis*, 398.

197 The quid pro quo: Back-Channel Message from Ismail to Kissinger, October 27, 1973, FRUS 1969–1976:25, Doc. 291.

197 Describing it as a miracle: Tzoref, *Golda Meir*, Doc. 165, 577.

198 "domestic crisis of a century": Kissinger, *Crisis*, 302.

8. GOLDA'S INFERNO

203 foreign minister Andrei Gromyko: Memcon between Kissinger and Gromyko, December 22, 1973, FRUS 1969–1976:15, Doc. 155.

204 "resolute in the substance": Amos Gilboa, *Mar Modi'in: Arale Yariv* [in Hebrew] (Tel Aviv: Yedioth Ahronot, 2013), 638.

205 the humanity of the moment: Mohamed Abdel Ghani El-Gamasy, trans. Gillian Potter, Nadra Morcos, and Rosette Frances, *The October War: Memoirs of Field Marshal El-Gamasy of Egypt* (Cairo: American University in Cairo Press, 1993), 322.

206 "wants peace": Memcon between Nixon, Kissinger, and Meir, November 1, 1973, FRUS 1969–1976:25, Doc. 306.

206 Dayan especially angered: Gilboa, *Mar Modi'in*, 645.

207 generals had already reached: Gilboa, *Mar Modi'in*, 650, and El-Gamasy, *October War*, 335.

208 "The statesman must weigh": Henry Kissinger, *Years of Upheaval* (Boston: Little, Brown, 1982), 615.

208 "further steps easier": Kissinger, *Years of Upheaval*, 616.

209 "the master of the insinuating innuendo": Henry Kissinger, *Years of Renewal* (New York: Touchstone, 1999), 366–67.

210   burn a hole: Indyk interview with Ismail Fahmy, November 4, 2018.

210   "behalf of Israel": Ismail Fahmy, *Negotiating for Peace in the Middle East* (Abingdon, UK: Routledge, 1983), 32.

210   "extremist, fanatic Jews": Fahmy, *Negotiating for Peace*, 32. Fahmy cites no greater authority than Kissinger himself for this assertion, although it is highly unlikely that Kissinger would have described his parents in this way.

210   Nor would Sadat accept: Memcon between Kissinger and Fahmy, October 29, 1973, FRUS 1969–1976:25, Doc. 298.

211   between Egypt and the United States: Memcon between Kissinger and Fahmy, October 30, 1973, FRUS 1969–1976:25, Doc. 300.

211   west bank of the canal: Memcon between Kissinger and Fahmy, October 31, 1973, FRUS 1969–1976:25, Doc. 303.

211   consolidate the cease-fire first: Memcon between Nixon and Fahmy, November 1, 1973, FRUS 1969–1976:25, Doc. 307.

213   "We had no choice": "Dayan Says U.S. Threat Forced Relief Convoys," *New York Times*, October 31, 1973.

213   "We cannot appear": Uzi Eilam, *Eilam's Arc: How Israel Became a Military Technology Powerhouse* (East Sussex, UK: Sussex Academic Press, 2011), 129.

213   "to integrate": Henry Kissinger, *A World Restored: Metternich, Castlereagh and the Problems of Peace, 1812–22* (Brattleboro, VT: Echo Point Books and Media, 2013), 140–42.

214   In his view: Kissinger, *Years of Upheaval*, 620–23.

214   "the son-in-law": Uri Bar-Joseph, *The Angel: The Egyptian Spy Who Saved Israel* (New York, HarperCollins, 2016), 4.

215   the anti-Israel tsunami: Memcon between Kissinger and Meir, November 1, 1973, FRUS 1969–1976:25, Doc. 305.

216   sole protector: Kissinger, *Years of Upheaval*, 620.

217   "It would be better if you made": Memcon between Kissinger and Meir, November 1, 1973, FRUS 1969–1976:25, Doc. 305.

217   "She's going to find": Telcon between Nixon and Kissinger, October 30, 1973, KA11453, NSA.

219   "where the line is": Memcon between Nixon, Kissinger, and Meir, November 1, 1973, FRUS 1969–1976:25, Doc. 306.

220   "there will be consequences": Minutes of WSAG Meeting, November 2, 1973, FRUS 1969–1976:25, Doc. 308.

220   "national policy": Minutes of WSAG Meeting, November 2, 1973, FRUS 1969–1976:25, Doc. 308, fn. 5.

220   "accomplish anything": Memcon between Kissinger and Fahmy, November 1, 1973, FRUS 1969–1976:25, Doc. 307.

221   "the bigger problem?": Memcon between Kissinger and Fahmy, November 2, 1973, FRUS 1969–1976:25, Doc. 311.

221   his most important achievement: Fahmy, *Negotiating for Peace*, 48.

223   they sleep on it: Memcon between Kissinger and Meir, November 2, 1973, FRUS 1969–1976:25, Doc. 312.

225   "with conviction": Memcon between Kissinger and Meir, November 3, 1973, KT00886, NSA.

225   Zvi Zamir: Indyk interview with Efraim Halevy, January 29, 2020.

9. HENRY OF ARABIA

228   Accompanying Kissinger: Marvin Kalb and Bernard Kalb, *Kissinger* (New York: Little, Brown, 1974), 506, and Walter Isaacson, *Kissinger* (New York: Simon & Schuster, 1992), 550–51.

229   They were ready to indulge him: Indyk interviews with Marvin Kalb and Bernard Gwertzman, March 18, 2016, and April 12, 2016. Gwertzman coined the term "shuttle diplomacy." See Gwertzman, "Kissinger Hoping to Speed Accord," *New York Times*, January

12, 1974; Gwertzman, "A Kissinger Seminar," *New York Times*, December 25, 1973; and Marvin Kalb and Bernard Kalb, "Twenty Days in October: Kissinger's Triumph Began in Trauma," *New York Times*, June 23, 1974.

230 "moral support": Henry Kissinger, *Years of Upheaval* (Boston: Little, Brown, 1982), 821.

231 give Kissinger a chance: Kissinger, *Years of Upheaval*, 631.

231 "We wanted it to be": Kissinger, *Years of Upheaval*, 627.

232 "early peace process": Back-Channel Message from Walters to Kissinger, November 4, 1973, FRUS 1969–1976:25, Doc. 318, and Kissinger, *Years of Upheaval*, 628–29.

233 "quintessential 1950s Cairo": "A Taste of America: The Former Nile Hilton Hotel," *Cairo Observer*, September 14, 2011.

233 "prove fatal": Kissinger, *Years of Upheaval*, 634.

235 "they are mastering events": Kissinger, *Years of Upheaval*, 638.

235 "reach it": Jon B. Alterman, ed., *Sadat and His Legacy*, Washington Institute for Near East Policy, 1998, 4.

237 "great man": Kissinger, *Years of Upheaval*, 646.

238 "He spoke logically": Mousa Sabri, *Documents of the October War* [in Arabic] (Alexandria, Egypt: al-Maktab al-Misri al-Hadith, 1974), 32.

238 the beginning of a beautiful friendship: Anwar Sadat, *In Search of Identity* (New York: Harper & Row, 1978), 267, 291, and Mohamed Abdel Ghani El-Gamasy, trans. Gillian Potter, Nadra Morcos, and Rosette Frances, *The October War: Memoirs of Field Marshal El-Gamasy of Egypt* (Cairo: American University in Cairo Press, 1993), 360.

238 "It proved": Kissinger, *Years of Upheaval*, 643.

238 Heikal's view: "Henry Kissinger Meets Muhammad Hassanain Haikal," *al-Anwar*, November 16, 1973, in "Kissinger Meets Heikal," *Journal of Palestine Studies* 3.2 (Winter 1974): 210–26, and Martin Indyk, "Détente and the Politics of Patronage," *Australian Outlook* 30 (August 1976): 171–96.

239 once observed: Kissinger, *Years of Upheaval*, 652.

239 "a *fantastic* achievement": Memcon between Sisco and Meir, November 7, 1973, KT00891, NSA.

240 "the first step along": Henry Kamm, "Israel and Egypt Sign Agreement for a Cease-Fire," *New York Times*, November 12, 1973.

240 soldiers were greeted: Terence Smith, "Israel and Egypt Exchange POWs," *New York Times*, November 16, 1973.

240 "the President is elated": Telegram from Haig to Kissinger in Amman, November 8, 1973, FRUS 1969–1976:25, Doc. 325.

240 "Never take your eyes off him": Terence Smith, "3-Day Negotiations Leave the Israelis Breathless, Wary," *New York Times*, November 12, 1973.

241 "the embargo on oil": Message from Fahd to Kissinger, October 23, 1973, FRUS 1969–1976:36, Doc. 224.

241 "We will break it": Minutes of Kissinger's Staff Meeting, October 23, 1973, FRUS 1969–1976:25, Doc. 250.

242 "I am not a prophet": Memcon of Meeting with Oil Executives, October 26, 1973, FRUS 1969–1976:36: Doc. 230.

242 "If we once get on the wicket": Minutes of Kissinger's Staff Meeting, November 19, 1973, KT00913, NSA.

242 impervious to pressure: Kissinger, *Years of Upheaval*, 875.

242 address before Congress: "Address to the Nation About Policies to Deal with the Energy Shortage," in *Public Papers: Nixon, 1973* (Washington, DC: United States Government Printing Office, 1975), 916–22.

242 "after your return": Telegram from Haig to Kissinger in Amman, November 8, 1973, FRUS 1969–1976:25, Doc. 325.

243 Faisal was no stranger: Bruce Riedel, *Kings and Presidents: Saudi Arabia and the United States Since FDR* (Washington, DC: Brookings Institution Press, 2017), 39–47.

243 Nasser's defeat in Yemen: Riedel, *Kings and Presidents*, 48.

245 "We warily circled": Kissinger, *Years of Upheaval*, 663.

245 Those Jews who weren't killed: Haggai Mazuz, *The Religious and Spiritual Life of the Jews of Medina* (Leiden, Netherlands: Brill, 2014), and F. E. Peters, *The Arabs and Arabia on the Eve of Islam* (London: Routledge, 2014).

246 slight mark: Michael Lecker, *The Jews and Pagans: Studies on Early Islamic Medina* (Leiden, Netherlands: Brill, 1995), and Marina Rustow, "Jews and Muslims in the Eastern Islamic World," in Abdelwahab Meddeb and Benjamin Stora, eds., *A History of Jewish-Muslim Relations: From the Origins to the Present Day* (Princeton, NJ: Princeton University Press, 2013), 75–98.

246 after-dinner conversation: Memcon between Kissinger, Faisal, et al., November 8, 1973, KT00894, NSA.

248 "proven ability and wisdom": Kissinger, *Years of Upheaval*, 665.

248 Faisal was blessing: Memcon between Kissinger, Faisal, et al., November 8, 1973, KT00894, NSA.

248 Kissinger's lack of success: Juan de Onis, "Kissinger Fails to Sway Saudis from Oil Embargo," *New York Times*, November 10, 1973.

248 "the thread of a solution": Memcon between Kissinger, Fahd, et al., November 8, 1973, FRUS 1973–1976: E-9, Part 2, Doc. 96.

248 walked him hand in hand: Memo from Scowcroft to Nixon, November 9, 1973, HAK Office Files, Country Files, Middle East, Nixon Presidential Materials Project, NARA, and Kissinger, *Years of Upheaval*, 665–66.

249 "The Geneva Conference": Kissinger, *Years of Upheaval*, 747.

250 to lift their embargo?: Telegram from Department of State to U.S. Interests Section, Cairo, November 18, 1973, FRUS 1969–1976:25, Doc. 347. As Kissinger explained it in a polite but insistent response to Fahmy, "[P]ressing the disengagement question prematurely or seeking some agreement on it as a prerequisite to the conference could result in little progress in achieving disengagement and fail to bring about a conference."

250 "Geneva to be completed": Kissinger, *Years of Upheaval*, 750.

251 "I fear it will limit": Back-Channel Message from Kissinger to Ismail, November 20, 1973, FRUS 1969–1976:25, Doc. 349.

251 "some meaningful progress": Telegram from the U.S. Interests Section in Cairo to Department of State, November 22, 1973, FRUS 1969–1976:25, Doc. 351.

251 peace conference: Back-Channel Message from Kissinger to Eilts, undated, FRUS 1969–1976:25, Doc. 352.

252 King Salman was infuriated: "Saudi King Salman Concludes 'Jerusalem Summit' in Dhahran," *Al Arabiya English*, April 15, 2018, http://english.alarabiya.net/en/News/gulf/2018/04/15/Saudi-King-Salman-inaugurates-Jerusalem-Summit-in-Dhahran.html.

253 moved to Geneva: Memo from Saunders and Quandt to Kissinger, December 3, 1973, FRUS 1969–1976:25, Doc. 371.

253 Sadat ordered the Kilometer 101 talks suspended: Henry Tanner, "No New Date Set," *New York Times*, November 30, 1973.

254 "our central role": Kissinger, *Years of Upheaval*, 752.

254 "the Israelis find ways to keep the talks": Summary of Kissinger-Dinitz Meeting, November 20, 1973, A-7/7061, ISA; Summary of Kissinger-Eban Meeting, November 22, 1973, A-10/7024, ISA; Telcon between Scowcroft and Dinitz, November 25, 1973, A-7/7061, ISA; Memcon between Scowcroft and Dinitz, November 26, 1973, FRUS 1969–1976:25, Doc. 357.

254 "wanted all major political moves": Simcha Dinitz, "Diplomatic Memoirs" (Unpublished manuscript, in author's possession: 2003), 102.

254 "We have accepted your suggestion": Memcon between Kissinger and Dinitz, November 26, 1973, FRUS 1969–1976:25, Doc. 359.

254 while he was still negotiating: Amos Gilboa, *Mar Modi'in: Arale Yariv* [in Hebrew] (Tel Aviv: Yedioth Ahronot, 2013), 677.

255 "unmindful of his achievements": Moshe Dayan, *Moshe Dayan: Story of My Life* (London: Weidenfeld and Nicholson, 1976), 451.

255 "We have to discuss a strategy": Memcon between Kissinger and Dayan, December 7, 1973, KT00942, NSA.

256 "springing some things": Minutes of WSAG Meeting, November 29, 1973, FRUS 1969–1976:25, Doc. 364.

256 "a political decision": Memcon between Kissinger and Dayan, December 7, 1973, KT00093, NSA.

256 "Any time you have any wild ideas": Memcon between Kissinger and Dayan, December 7, 1973, KT00943, NSA.

256 "a brilliant manipulator": Kissinger, *Years of Upheaval*, 1042.

257 "hotheads": Kissinger, *Years of Upheaval*, 754.

257 "our constructive influence": Telegram from Department of State to U.S. Interests Section in Cairo, December 1, 1973, FRUS 1969–1976:25, Doc. 369.

257 Sadat was losing face: Telegram from Eilts, U.S. Interests Section in Cairo to Mission to NATO, December 10, 1973, FRUS 1969–1976:25, Doc. 382.

258 November 30: Kissinger, *Years of Upheaval*, 752–53.

258 in a letter: Sadat's response to Nixon was summarized in Memo from Kissinger to Nixon, December 10, 1973, FRUS 1969–1976:25, Doc. 384.

258 detailed the considerable progress: Memo from Saunders and Quandt to Kissinger, December 3, 1973, FRUS 1969–1976:25, Doc. 371.

260 "the road to American mediation": Kissinger, *Years of Upheaval*, 755.

10. "A TIME FOR PEACE"

261 the Madrid Peace Conference: Peter Baker and Susan Glasser, *The Man Who Ran Washington: The Life and Times of James A. Baker III* (New York: Doubleday, 2020), chap. 24.

262 Prime Minister Meir was unwilling to accept: Back-Channel Message from Scowcroft to Kissinger, December 10, 1973, FRUS 1969–1976:25, Doc. 383.

262 restricting the UN auspices: Telegram from U.S. Interests Section in Cairo to Department of State, December 11, 1973, FRUS 1969-1976:25, Doc. 385.

263 "while she had accepted": Memo from Scowcroft to Nixon, December 13, 1973, FRUS 1969–1976:25, Doc. 387.

263 "transmit promptly your favorable reply": Letter from Nixon to Meir, December 13, 1973, FRUS 1969–1976:25, Doc. 388.

263 get in touch directly: Simcha Dinitz, "Diplomatic Memoirs" (Unpublished manuscript, in author's possession: 2003), 99.

263 "I urge you not to underestimate": Back-Channel Message from Kissinger to Scowcroft, December 14, 1973, FRUS 1969–1976:25, Doc. 389.

264 "to indulge Israel's nationalist sentiments": Anatoly Dobrynin, *In Confidence: Moscow's Ambassador to Six Cold War Presidents* (New York: Crown, 1995), 302.

266 U.S. resupply of Israel: Galia Golan, *Yom Kippur and After: The Soviet Union and the Middle East Crisis* (Cambridge, UK: Cambridge University Press, 1977), 135–36.

267 three elements: Editorial Note, undated, FRUS 1969–1976:25, Doc. 390.

268 "as a last resort": Lizette Alvarez, "Britain Says U.S. Planned to Seize Oil in '73 Crisis," *New York Times*, January 2, 2004, A4.

268 When he raised this: Memcon between Kissinger, Schlesinger, et al., November 29, 1973, FRUS 1969–1976:25, Doc. 363.

268 most of the king's advisers: Message from Adham to Kissinger, December 2, 1973, FRUS 1969–1976:36, Doc. 257.

269 "total personal commitment": Letter from Nixon to Faisal, December 3, 1973, FRUS 1969–1976:36, Doc. 258.

269 back-channel response from Prince Fahd: Message from Prince Fahd to Kissinger, December 3, 1973, FRUS 1969–1976:36, Doc. 259.

269 Algerian insisted: Memcon of Meeting with Saudi and Algerian Oil Ministers, December 5, 1973, FRUS 1969–1976:36, Doc. 263.

269   "radical Algerian": Henry Kissinger, *Years of Upheaval* (Boston: Little, Brown, 1982), 883. There is no archival record of this meeting.

270   lifting of the oil embargo: Kissinger, *Years of Upheaval*, 894.

271   "more explicit than that": Memcon between Kissinger, Faisal, et al., December 14, 1973, KT00951.

272   "where two adversaries": Memcon between Kissinger, Faisal, Fahd, et al., December 14, 1973, FRUS 1969–1976:36, Doc. 267.

272   "crumble to ruin": Mark Twain, *The Innocents Abroad* (London: Collins, 1869), 263.

273   with more than 99 percent of the vote: Bouthaina Shaaban, *The Edge of the Precipice: Hafez al-Assad, Henry Kissinger, and the Remaking of the Modern Middle East* (Beirut: Dar Bissan, 2017), 35–36.

273   As Kissinger described it to Meir: Memcon between Kissinger and Meir, May 22, 1974, KT01185, NSA.

274   "wicked sense of humor": Kissinger, *Years of Upheaval*, 781.

275   "the toughest and least conciliatory": Memo from Scowcroft to Nixon, December 16, 1973, FRUS 1969–1976:25, Doc. 396.

277   "a major breakthrough": Kissinger, *Years of Upheaval*, 784–85.

278   "frank and useful talk": Memcon between Kissinger and Assad, December 15, 1973, FRUS 1969–1976:25, Doc. 393.

278   "somewhat more than we had hoped for": Kissinger, *Years of Upheaval*, 785.

278   "under all circumstances": Telegram 4043 from Cairo, December 16, 1973, in Telegram from Kissinger to U.S. Interests Section in Cairo, December 16, 1973, FRUS 1969–1976:25, Doc. 395, fn. 7.

279   their placards expressing: Marvin Kalb and Bernard Kalb, *Kissinger* (New York: Little, Brown, 1974), 526.

279   concerns in person: Letter from Nixon to Meir, December 14, 1973, FRUS 1969–1976:25, Doc. 391.

280   '67 lines: Memcon between Kissinger and Meir, December 16, 1973, FRUS 1969–1976:25, Doc. 398.

281   The dinner concluded at: Memcon between Kissinger and Meir, December 16, 1973, FRUS 1969–1976:25, Doc. 399.

281   approved the letter of invitation: Kissinger, *Years of Upheaval*, 791, and Kalb and Kalb, *Kissinger*, 526.

282   Carter was deaf to their concerns: Stuart E. Eizenstat, *President Carter: The White House Years* (New York: St. Martin's, 2018), 454–56.

282   of the Geneva Conference: William B. Quandt, *Camp David: Peacemaking and Politics* (Washington, DC: Brookings Institution Press, 1982), 125–31.

283   he arrived in Israel: Martin Indyk, "To the Ends of the Earth: Sadat's Jerusalem Initiative," Middle East Monograph, Center for Middle Eastern Studies, Harvard University, 1984.

283   Even that stunning, historic initiative: Eizenstat, *President Carter*, 474.

283   "a comprehensive consultation at Geneva": Quandt, *Camp David*, 150.

284   "preserve the cease-fire": Papers Prepared in the Bureau of Near Eastern and South Asian Affairs, December 22, 1973, FRUS 1969–1976:25, Doc. 417.

284   "hope our inspiration": "Middle East Peace Conference Opens in Geneva," *Department of State Bulletin*, vol. 70, January 14, 1974, 21.

286   to resolve the problem: Kissinger, *Years of Upheaval*, 795–96, and *Switzerland Peace Conference*, SYND 20 12 73, "Delegates Arrive in Geneva for Middle East Peace Conference," AP Television, https://www.youtube.com/watch?v=06_081Tkw7I.

11. THE SINAI DISENGAGEMENT

291   "a healthy thing": "Laird Quits, Urges Speed on Impeachment Question," *New York Times*, December 20, 1973, 34.

291   eighty-six thousand workers: Agis Salpukas, "G.M. to Lay off 86,000 Workers; Sales Lag Cited," *New York Times*, December 29, 1973.

291 hike the price of oil: Bernard Weinraub, "Oil Price Doubled by Big Producers on Persian Gulf," *New York Times*, December 24, 1973.

291 "collapse of Nixon's mental balance": Robert Dallek, *Nixon and Kissinger: Partners in Power* (New York: HarperCollins, 2007), 545.

292 "Israelis would have to do it alone": Cable from Dinitz to Gazit, January 5, 1974, A-10/7025, ISA.

292 Nixon's anti-Israel initiative: Memcon between Kissinger and Dinitz, January 21, 1974, A-7/7060, ISA.

292 Leslie Gelb: Leslie Gelb, "Nixon's Role in Foreign Policy Is Altered; Some Assert Kissinger Is Now in Charge," *New York Times*, December 24, 1973.

292 *Time*'s headline: "Diplomacy: The Superstar on His Own," *Time*, December 24, 1973.

292 "beginning to wonder": Telcon between Kissinger and Haig, January 4, 1974, KA11789, NSA.

294 she had agreed with him: Memcon between Kissinger, Meir, Dayan, et al., December 17, 1973, FRUS 1969–1976:25, Doc. 401.

294 memorandum to Nixon: Memo from Kissinger to Nixon, January 6, 1974, FRUS 1969–1976:26, Doc. 1.

295 a more stable arms supply: Memcon between Kissinger, Dayan, Dinitz, et al., January 4, 1974, KT00979, NSA.

295 "general concepts": Kissinger and Dayan Press Conference Following Meeting in Memcon between Kissinger, Dayan, Dinitz, et al., January 4, 1974, KT00979, NSA.

296 "demands for reciprocity": Memo from Kissinger to Nixon, January 6, 1974, FRUS 1969–1976:26, Doc. 1.

296 "propensity for the sudden stroke": Henry Kissinger, *Years of Upheaval* (Boston: Little, Brown, 1982), 803.

296 "an element of vanity": Kissinger, *Years of Upheaval*, 803.

299 Israel had made no proposal: Memcon between Kissinger, Dayan, Dinitz, et al., January 5, 1974, KT00980, NSA.

299 "to form concrete proposals": Unofficial Transcript of Remarks to Press in Memcon between Kissinger, Dayan, Dinitz, et al., January 5, 1974, KT00980, NSA.

300 to get the oil embargo lifted: Memo from Kissinger to Nixon, January 6, 1974, FRUS 1969–1976:26, Doc. 1.

300 drive Nixon "into orbit": Telcon between Kissinger and Haig, January 4, 1974, KA11789, NSA.

300 the weather in San Clemente: Telcon between Nixon and Kissinger, January 4, 1974, KA11797, NSA.

300 "terminal date for my tenure": Telcon between Haig and Kissinger, January 8, 1974, KA11812, NSA.

300 "I will certainly resign": Telcon between Scowcroft and Kissinger, January 8, 1974, KA11817, NSA.

300 "I think you ought to leave": Telcon between Haig and Kissinger, January 8, 1974, KA11818, NSA.

300 to destroy subpoenaed evidence: Lesley Oelsner, "Tape Experts Tell Sirica That Gap in 18-Minute Watergate Recording Was Due to at Least Five Erasures," *New York Times*, January 16, 1974.

300 whole effort would be jeopardized: Kissinger, *Years of Upheaval*, 830, 833.

301 no concrete proposal: Cable between Dinitz and Gazit, January 8, 1974, A-7/7060, ISA.

301 getting her cabinet to approve it: Memcon between Kissinger and Dinitz, January 9, 1974, KT00986, NSA.

301 "to confront the Israelis": Memcon between Kissinger and Ghorbal, January 10, 1974, KT00987, NSA.

301 to talk to the Israeli cabinet: Bernard Gwertzman, "Kissinger Hoping to Speed Accord," *New York Times*, January 12, 1974.

301 the basis for the negotiations: Bernard Gwertzman, "Suez Arms Pact Emerges from American Proposal," *New York Times*, January 18, 1974.

302   failed to fool: Mohamed Abdel Ghani El-Gamasy, trans. Gillian Potter, Nadra Morcos,
       and Rosette Frances, *The October War: Memoirs of Field Marshal El-Gamasy of Egypt* (Cairo:
       American University in Cairo Press, 1993), 336, and Ismail Fahmy, *Negotiating for Peace in
       the Middle East* (Abingdon, UK: Routledge, 1983), 59.

303   pharaohs of ancient Egypt: Fahmy, *Negotiating for Peace in the Middle East*, 55, 126.

304   In that conversation: Telcon between Kissinger and Sisco, January 8, 1974, KA11835,
       NSA.

304   "caught in a vise": Telcon between Kissinger and Haig, January 4, 1974, KA11789, NSA.

306   return in a month: Fahmy, *Negotiating for Peace in the Middle East*, 57–58.

307   transiting through Bab-el Mandeb: Kissinger, *Years of Upheaval*, 814.

307   "no doubt in my mind": Memcon between Kissinger, Meir, Allon, Eban, Dayan, et al.,
       January 13, 1974, FRUS 1969–1976:26, Doc. 4.

309   underestimated Sadat before: Memcon between Kissinger and Meir, January 12, 1974,
       KT00989, NSA.

309   did not believe in haggling: Matti Golan, *The Secret Conversations of Henry Kissinger: Step-
       by-Step Diplomacy in the Middle East* (Chicago: Quadrangle, 1976), 159–60. There is no
       memorandum of the dinner with the Israeli cabinet ministers on the evening of January 12.

310   bring back Sadat's counteroffer: Memcon between Kissinger, Meir, Allon, Eban, Dayan, et
       al., January 13, 1974, FRUS 1969–1976:26, Doc. 4.

310   "domestic situation": Memcon between Kissinger, Meir, Allon, Eban, Dayan, et al., Janu-
       ary 13, 1974, FRUS 1969–1976:26, Doc. 4.

312   alienating most of them as well: Martin Indyk, Kenneth Lieberthal, and Michael O'Hanlon,
       Bending History: Barack Obama's Foreign Policy (Washington, DC: Brookings Institution
       Press, 2012), 113–19.

312   "confidence is a precious commodity": Kissinger, *Years of Upheaval*, 853.

313   "even our doves say they will": Memcon between Kissinger and Eban, January 13, 1974,
       KT00991, NSA.

313   he looked pleased: Marvin Kalb and Bernard Kalb, *Kissinger* (New York: Little, Brown,
       1974), 533.

314   "political issues": Memcon between Kissinger, Sadat, Fahmy, et al., January 14, 1974,
       FRUS 1969–1976:26, Doc. 5.

315   Israel would agree to vacate: Kissinger, *Years of Upheaval*, 823–25.

315   "I cannot accept everything": Memcon between Kissinger, Allon, Dayan, et al., January 15,
       1974, KT00994, NSA.

315   "vintage Sadat": Kissinger, *Years of Upheaval*, 824.

316   "we can do better": Memcon between Kissinger, Fahmy, et al., January 14, 1974, FRUS
       1969–1976:26, Doc. 5.

316   draw up the documents: Memcon between Kissinger, Sadat, Fahmy, et al., January 14,
       1974, KT00993, NSA.

316   "the basic Arab position": Fahmy, *Negotiating for Peace*, 58–60.

317   "will sign it!": Kissinger, *Years of Upheaval*, 825.

317   promoting him to minister of war: El-Gamasy, *October War*, 335–36.

318   "end of belligerency": Fahmy, *Negotiating for Peace*, 59.

318   walked out in a huff: Memcon between Kissinger, Fahmy, et al., January 14, 1974,
       KT00993, NSA.

319   "luring America into pressing Israel": Kissinger, *Years of Upheaval*, 829.

319   Sadat had insisted: Kissinger, *Years of Upheaval*, 829.

321   "You didn't waste your time": Memcon between Kissinger, Allon, Dayan, et al., January 15,
       1974, KT00994, NSA.

321   "everything fell into place": Kissinger, *Years of Upheaval*, 832.

321   in the Knesset: Memcon between Kissinger, Allon, Dayan, et al., January 15, 1974, FRUS
       1969–1976:26, Doc. 6.

323   Despite her shingles: Memcon between Kissinger and Meir, January 15, 1974, KT00996,
       NSA.

324 returned home with an agreement: Memcon between Kissinger, Allon, Dayan, et al., January 16, 1974, FRUS 1969–1976:26, Doc. 7.

325 in eight battalions: Kissinger, *Years of Upheaval*, 834.

327 "I left the meeting room angry": El-Gamasy, *October War*, 336.

327 "We sign with the United States": Memcon between Kissinger, Fahmy, and el-Gamasy, January 16, 1974, KT00998, NSA.

328 "through him": Kissinger, *Years of Upheaval*, 836.

328 "on the verge of an agreement": Memo from Scowcroft to Nixon, January 16, 1974, FRUS 1969–1976:26, Doc. 8.

329 "He never raised the question": Memcon between Kissinger, Allon, Dayan, et al., January 17, 1974, FRUS 1969–1976:26, Doc. 9.

330 "Why is he doing this?": Memcon between Kissinger and Meir, January 17, 1974, KT01000, NSA.

331 "far from jubilant": Gwertzman, "Suez Arms Pact Emerges."

331 "both physically and emotionally drained": *The Dick Cavett Show*, PBS, December 6, 1979.

331 "I want to tell you": Kissinger, *Years of Upheaval*, 841.

332 "all her instincts rebelled": Kissinger, *Years of Upheaval*, 840–42.

332 "It is indeed extremely fortunate": Kissinger, *Years of Upheaval*, 844.

332 "taking off my military uniform": Kissinger, *Years of Upheaval*, 844.

333 better future: Telegram from Kissinger to Department of State, January 19, 1974, FRUS 1969–1976:26, Doc. 16.

334 Brezhnev wrote to Nixon: Kissinger, *Years of Upheaval*, 843.

335 Ellsworth Bunker: Kissinger, *Years of Upheaval*, 843–44.

335 "to keep the Soviet Union": Minutes of Kissinger's Staff Meeting, January 21, 1974, KT01007, NSA. That was his explanation to the State Department senior staff in a subsequent review of his disengagement diplomacy.

335 "I think it was a mistake": Memcon between Kissinger and Eban, March 15, 1974, KT01068, NSA.

336 happy to be going home: Henry Tanner, "Sadat, on Tour, Asks for Arab Unity," *New York Times*, January 20, 1974.

336 The most hopeful aspect: Terence Smith, "Outlook in Israel: A Good Deal with Chances of More," *New York Times*, January 19, 1974.

336 the Israeli public began to soften: Terence Smith, "Eban Terms Agreement with Syria Now Possible," *New York Times*, January 18, 1974, and Bernard Gwertzman, "Reporter's Notebook: Middle East Shuttle," *New York Times*, January 16, 1974.

336 "Rightly or wrongly": Smith, "Outlook in Israel."

336 "Kissinger's coming!": Kalb and Kalb, *Kissinger*, 611, and "Kissinger's Coming" [in Hebrew], *National Library of Israel*, January 11, 1974, https://www.nli.org.il/en/archives/NNL_ARCHIVE_AL003569826/NLI.

12. "PLOUGHING THE OCEAN"

340 "Unless something happens with Syria": Memcon between Kissinger and Meir, February 27, 1974, KT01041, NSA.

341 Assad was bitterly disappointed: Patrick Seale, *Asad: The Struggle for the Middle East* (Berkeley, CA: University of California Press, 1989), 224.

341 "It means Israel will move": Bouthaina Shaaban, *The Edge of the Precipice: Hafez al-Assad, Henry Kissinger, and the Remaking of the Modern Middle East* (Beirut: Dar Bissan, 2017), 57–58.

341 he might as well explore: Indyk interview with Henry Kissinger, July 23, 2019.

341 willing at least to test: Seale, *Asad*, 239.

341 a challenge that the professor: Seale, *Asad*, 244–46.

342 "a man of superb intelligence": Telcon between Kissinger and Kraft, May 31, 1974, KA12384, NSA.

342 identifying Kissinger as part: Shaaban, *Edge of the Precipice*, 62, and Seale, *Asad*, 239.

343 Assad no longer believed him: Seale, *Asad*, 238, and Shaaban, *Edge of the Precipice*, 60.

343 "that pimp into Damascus!": Kissinger related this story to Golda Meir and her negotiating team in Memcon between Kissinger, Meir, et al., February 27, 1974, KT01042, NSA.

343 Sadat had put the idea: Telcon between Kissinger and Dinitz, January 31, 1974, KA11945, NSA.

344 "giving a suitable number": Memcon between Kissinger and Assad, January 20, 1974, NSA, KT01003; Henry Kissinger, *Years of Upheaval* (Boston: Little, Brown, 1982), 850–51; Shaaban, *Edge of the Precipice*, 61–67.

344 "is that you have put yourself": Kissinger, *Years of Upheaval*, 849.

344 At a funeral ceremony: Matti Golan, *The Secret Conversations of Henry Kissinger: Step-by-Step Diplomacy in the Middle East* (Chicago: Quadrangle, 1976), 185.

346 to explain their backsliding: Seale, *Asad*, 240–41.

346 "every time we promise something": Telcon between Nixon and Kissinger, February 5, 1974, KA11980, NSA.

346 "the more we build it up": Telcon between Nixon and Kissinger, February 18, 1974, KA12050, NSA.

346 didn't even want to discuss it: Telegram from Department of State to Embassy in Lebanon, February 11, 1974, FRUS 1969–1976:26, Doc. 24, and Memcon between Nixon and Saudi Ambassador al-Sowayel, February 7, 1974, KC00271, NSA.

347 "This is what I wanted": Memcon between Nixon, Fahmy, and Saqqaf, February 19, 1974, KC00273, NSA.

347 "Golda will get": Memcon between Kissinger and Dinitz, February 17, 1974, KT01030, NSA.

348 "to start military action": Memcon between Kissinger and Meir, February 27, 1974, KT01041, NSA. Two months later, Kissinger repeated the explanation to Meir: "The Egyptians asked us to ask the Shah to put pressure on Iraq so Iraqi troops all leave Syria. That is why there was trouble in February between Iran and Iraq." See Memcon between Kissinger and Meir, May 7, 1974, FRUS 1969–1976:26, Doc. 47.

348 a threat to Assad's regime: Broadcast from February 12, 1974, *Radio Iran Courier*, Second Series ME/4488, *Summary of World Broadcasts*, British Broadcasting Corporation, 1974, and "Iran-Iraq Conflict Is Reported Ended," *New York Times*, March 20, 1974.

348 understood the game: Seale, *Asad*, 243. Seale notes that Kissinger worked with the shah to fan the Kurdish revolt against Saddam Hussein in the spring of 1974 to pin down the Iraqi army.

349 "by any failure": Memcon between Nixon and Gromyko, February 4, 1974, FRUS 1969–1976:15, Doc. 159.

349 Kissinger said, "All right": Memcon between Kissinger and Gromyko, February 5, 1974, FRUS 1969–1976:15, Doc. 160.

349 reciprocal steps to jump-start: Telegram from Department of State to U.S. Interests Section in Syria, February 6, 1974, FRUS 1969–1976:26, Doc. 22.

350 "we were overwhelmingly strong": Indyk interview with Henry Kissinger, July 23, 2019.

350 "the cowboy who rides all alone": Oriana Fallaci, *Interviews with History and Conversations with Power* (Milan, Italy: Rizzoli, 2011), 45–46.

351 "no more important event": Memcon between Kissinger and Assad, February 26, 1974, KT01039, NSA.

351 his pan-Arab credentials: Shaaban, *Edge of the Precipice*, 77.

352 "not more cause for them to worry": Memcon between Kissinger and Assad, February 27, 1974, KT01040, NSA.

353 at that moment: Dennis Ross, *The Missing Peace: The Inside Story of the Fight for Middle East Peace* (New York: Farrar, Straus and Giroux, 2004), 113, and Itamar Rabinovich, *Yitzhak Rabin: Soldier, Leader, Statesman* (New Haven, CT: Yale University Press, 2017), 193.

353 "as if she was embracing": Simcha Dinitz, "Diplomatic Memoirs" (Unpublished manuscript, in author's possession: 2003), 131.

353 he expressed his appreciation: Memcon between Kissinger and Meir, February 27, 1974, KT01041, NSA.

353 "To us it means more": Memcon between Kissinger, Meir, et al., February 28, 1974, KT01042, NSA. Kissinger does not record his feelings at that moment. In retrospect, he categorized it as "one of the moving occasions that ennoble public life." See Kissinger, *Years of Upheaval*, 960.

353 "under any circumstances": Memcon between Kissinger, Meir, Allon, Eban, Dayan, et al., January 13, 1974, FRUS 1969–1976:26, Doc. 4.

355 "Our strategy": Memcon between Kissinger, Meir, et al., February 27, 1974, KT01042, NSA.

356 Marwan's reports went directly: Uri Bar-Joseph, *The Angel: The Egyptian Spy Who Saved Israel* (New York: HarperCollins, 2016), 103–105.

356 Dayan revealed it to Kissinger: Memcon between Kissinger, Meir, Dayan, et al., May 18, 1974, KT01175, NSA.

357 protect Sadat's interests: Memcon between Kissinger and Sadat, February 28, 1974, KC00280, NSA. Some details of this discussion come from Kissinger's debrief to the Israelis. See Memcon between Kissinger and Israeli Cabinet, March 1, 1974, FRUS 1969–1976:26, Doc. 28.

357 anything beyond that: Memcon between Kissinger and Sadat, February 28, 1974, KC00280, NSA.

358 "dynamite": Memcon between Kissinger and Meir, March 1, 1974, KT01043, NSA. In order to give Kissinger's mission a further boost, Sadat also gave a press conference after he departed in which he spoke of Kissinger's good intentions, touted his new relationship with the United States, and explained that, like Egypt's negotiations with Israel, the disengagement negotiations between Israel and Syria would inevitably take some time.

358 "be forced into a war": Memcon between Kissinger, Meir, et al., March 1, 1974, FRUS 1969–1976:26, Doc. 28.

359 "I will make": Memcon between Kissinger and Assad, March 1, 1974, FRUS 1969–1976:26, Doc. 29.

359 "One of the maddening things": Memcon between Kissinger, Meir, et al., February 27, 1974, KT01042, NSA.

360 "for your success": Memcon between Kissinger and Faisal, March 2, 1974, FRUS 1969–1976:36, Doc. 332.

360 because the king committed: Kissinger told this story to King Hussein, in Memcon between Kissinger and Hussein, May 5, 1974, KT01138, NSA.

361 it would not be reimposed: Juan de Onis, "Most Arab Lands End Ban on Oil Shipments for U.S.," *New York Times*, March 19, 1974.

361 "dead duck tomorrow": Telcon between Kissinger and Dinitz, March 14, 1974, KA12148, NSA.

361 If the Syrians insisted: Memcon between Kissinger, Eban, and Dinitz, March 19, 1974, KT01074, NSA.

361 called on the president: Martin Tolchin, "Senator Buckley Bids Nixon Quit," *New York Times*, March 20, 1974.

362 "a permanent settlement": Telcon between Nixon and Kissinger, March 18, 1974, FRUS 1969–1976:26, Doc. 341.

362 "free to act": Memcon between Kissinger, Brezhnev, and Gromyko, March 26, 1974, FRUS 1969–1976:15, Doc. 167.

362 "had chosen to negotiate": Kissinger, *Years of Upheaval*, 1034.

362 "without us you get nothing": Memcon between Kissinger, Scowcroft, Dayan, Dinitz, et al., March 29, 1974, FRUS 1969–1976:26, Doc. 32.

363 Now he would discover: Moshe Dayan, *Moshe Dayan: Story of My Life* (London: Weidenfeld and Nicolson, 1976), 471–72.

363 stuck to his brief: Memcon between Kissinger, Scowcroft, Dayan, Dinitz, et al., March 29, 1974, FRUS 1969–1976:26, Doc. 32.

364 might look like blackmail: Memcon between Kissinger, Scowcroft, Dayan, Dinitz, et al., March 30, 1974, KT01094, NSA, and Telcon between Kissinger and Haig, March 30, 1974, KA12250, NSA.

364 a short honeymoon: Walter Isaacson, *Kissinger* (New York: Simon & Schuster, 1992), 587.

364 Kissinger agreed: Cable between Dinitz and Gazit, March 29, 1974, A-8/7060, ISA.

364 "some hope that we can expect": Letter from Kissinger to Meir, April 3, 1974, FRUS 1969–1976:26, Doc. 33.

365 "reflects the position": Letter from Meir to Kissinger, April 9, 1974, in Letter from Kissinger to Meir, April 3, 1974, FRUS 1969–1976:26, Doc. 33, fn. 4.

365 "in a confrontational mood": Kissinger, *Years of Upheaval*, 1044.

366 In his memoirs: Kissinger, *Years of Upheaval*, 1044.

367 "We will negotiate": Memcon between Kissinger and Shihabi, April 13, 1974, FRUS 1969–1976:26, Doc. 35.

367 When that attempt: Kathleen Teltsch, "U.S. Mideast Policy Shift Seen at UN," *New York Times*, April 26, 1974.

368 Israeli media: Barak Ravid, "Kerry in a Closed Conversation: Without Peace, Israel Is Liable to Become an Apartheid State" [in Hebrew], *Haaretz*, April 28, 2014.

368 "Wisdom most certainly": Kissinger, *Years of Upheaval*, 1049.

369 "regret this": Memcon between Kissinger, Meir, et al., May 2, 1974, KC00294, NSA.

371 consulted with Sadat: Memcon between Kissinger, Meir, et al., May 2, 1974, KT01129.

371 Reflecting on these meetings: Kissinger, *Years of Upheaval*, 1058.

371 secure agreement on the line: Memcon between Kissinger, Meir, et al., May 2, 1974, KT01128.

371 "sprightly as ever": Dayan, *Story of My Life*, 475.

372 "This is the first thing": Memcon between Kissinger and Dayan, May 2, 1974, KT01130, NSA.

372 Kissinger said he understood: Memcon between Kissinger and Meir, May 3, 1974, KT01132, NSA.

373 "insulting map": Memcon between Kissinger and Assad, May 3, 1974, KT01131, NSA.

373 "political destruction in America": Memcon between Kissinger and Sadat, May 4, 1974, KT01135, NSA.

374 he didn't believe a word of it: Ismail Fahmy, *Negotiating for Peace in the Middle East* (Abingdon, UK: Routledge, 1983), 123–24.

374 "I think you will have it": Memcon between Kissinger and Sadat, May 4, 1974, KT01135, NSA.

375 "in diplomacy": Kissinger, *Years of Upheaval*, 1063.

375 "*great* concession": Memcon between Kissinger, Meir, et al., May 6, 1974, KT01140, NSA.

376 Kissinger reported to Nixon: Memo from Scowcroft to Nixon, May 8, 1974, FRUS 1969–1976:15, Doc. 179.

376 "if you don't mind": Memcon between Kissinger, Meir, et al., May 7, 1974, FRUS 1969–1976:26, Doc. 47.

377 "time could be an ally": Kissinger, *Years of Upheaval*, 1063.

377 to buy off Assad: Memcon between Kissinger and Meir, May 6, 1974, FRUS 1969–1976:26, Doc. 46.

377 "I give you my personal": Memcon between Kissinger and Meir, May 8, 1974, KT01145.

378 "We would only agree": Memcon between Kissinger and Assad, May 8, 1974, FRUS 1969–1976:26, Doc. 48

379 "For the first time": Memcon between Kissinger and Meir, May 8, 1974, KT01149.

13. BREAKTHROUGH

380 Dayan had two basic principles: Moshe Dayan, *Moshe Dayan: Story of My Life* (London: Weidenfeld and Nicolson, 1976), 477.

381 "going home": Memcon between Kissinger, Meir, et al., May 8, 1974, FRUS 1969–1976:26, Doc. 49.

382 Bibi sent his staff: Dennis Ross, *The Missing Peace: The Inside Story of the Fight for Middle East Peace* (New York: Farrar, Straus and Giroux, 2004), 439–41.

382 criticism of his foreign policy: Henry Kissinger, *Years of Upheaval* (Boston: Little, Brown, 1982), 1115, and James Reston, "Where Are You Now, Henry?" *New York Times*, May 22, 1974. On May 21, while Kissinger was still threatening Assad with a return to Washington, he received an article from a left-wing magazine, *New Times*, which reported that trouble was brewing for him in Washington, where there was talk of indicting him for perjury over wiretapping.

383 would shake the very foundations: Walter Isaacson, *Kissinger* (New York: Simon & Schuster, 1992), 616.

383 get them to move further: Memcon between Kissinger, Sadat, and Fahmy, May 10, 1974, KT01155, NSA.

384 "terminal phase of his presidency": Kissinger, *Years of Upheaval*, 1071.

384 made him look duplicitous: Bouthaina Shaaban, *The Edge of the Precipice: Hafez al Assad, Henry Kissinger, and the Remaking of the Modern Middle East* (Beirut: Dar Bissan, 2017), 110.

384 Foreign Affairs and Defense Committee: Memcon between Kissinger, Meir, Rabin, et al., May 10, 1974, KT01156, NSA.

384 As he summarized: Telegram from Kissinger to Nixon, May 12, 1974, FRUS 1969–1976:26, Doc. 53.

385 "concrete issues": Memcon between Kissinger and Assad, May 12, 1974, KT01159, NSA.

386 "consequences of the war": Memcon between Kissinger, Meir, et al., May 12, 1974, KT01160, NSA.

386 "an impression": Telegram from Kissinger to Scowcroft, May 13, 1974, FRUS 1969–1976:26, Doc. 54.

386 on the map: Memcon between Kissinger, Meir, et al., May 13, 1974, KT01161, NSA.

387 Assad might accept this: Memcon between Kissinger, Meir, et al., May 13, 1974, KT01162, NSA.

387 "we would be accused": Dayan, *Story of My Life*, 472.

387 He ordered him to have: Telegram from Kissinger to Scowcroft, May 14, 1974, FRUS 1969–1976:26, Doc. 56.

387 When Scowcroft briefed: Kissinger, *Years of Upheaval*, 1078, and Memo from Scowcroft to Nixon, May 15, 1974, FRUS 1969–1976:26, Doc. 59.

389 "there has been progress": Memcon between Kissinger and Assad, May 14, 1974, KT01164, NSA.

389 "We can't reach the final": Memcon between Kissinger and Khaddam, May 14, 1974, KT01165, NSA.

389 "an extraordinary concession": Kissinger, *Years of Upheaval*, 1075, and Memo from Scowcroft to Nixon, May 14, 1974, FRUS 1969–1976:26, Doc. 57.

389 "the talks could go": Bernard Gwertzman, "Kissinger's Talks Show No Progress," *New York Times*, May 15, 1974.

389 Palestinian prisoners: Dayan, *Story of My Life*, 482.

390 "cut off the hands": Bernard Gwertzman, "Mrs. Meir Pledges Steps to Protect Israeli People," *New York Times*, May 16, 1974.

390 "such incidents in the future": The text of Sadat's message is in Memcon between Kissinger and Meir, May 16, 1974, KT01168, NSA.

390 "We would have saved ourselves": Simcha Dinitz, "Diplomatic Memoirs" (Unpublished manuscript, in author's possession: 2003), 132.

391 In return: Kissinger, *Years of Upheaval*, 1077. We only have Kissinger's and Dinitz's accounts of this conversation. There is no record in the archives.

391 Kissinger still wanted to preserve: Memo from Scowcroft to Nixon, May 15, 1974, FRUS 1969–1976:26, Doc. 59.

391 the slopes and the fields: Memcon between Kissinger, Allon, et al., May 16, 1974, KT01167, NSA.

391 "We all believe": Memcon between Kissinger and Meir, May 16, 1974, KT01168, NSA.

392 "substantial advance into the Golan": Memcon between Kissinger and Khaddam, May 16, 1974, KT01169, NSA.

393 "pressing to go on": Kissinger, *Years of Upheaval*, 1082–83.

393 "a period of extreme trial": Memcon between Kissinger, Meir, et al., May 17, 1974, KT01172, NSA.

394 "I have come to the conclusion": Memcon between Kissinger and Assad, May 18, 1974, KT01173, NSA.

394 If he had known: Memcon between Kissinger and Assad, May 18, 1974, KT01173, NSA.

395 "far beyond the call of duty": Telegram from Scowcroft to Kissinger, May 21, 1974, FRUS 1969–1976:26, Doc. 66.

395 "a point is reached": Henry Kissinger, *Years of Renewal* (New York: Touchstone, 1999), 406.

395 "If they don't want to move": Memcon between Kissinger, Meir, et al., May 21, 1974, KT01181, NSA.

395 "We all vacate the mountain": Memcon between Kissinger and Assad, May 21, 1974, KT01183, NSA.

395 "I am not going to travel": Memcon between Kissinger, Meir, et al., May 21, 1974, KT01181, NSA.

396 "Do you think my credibility": Memcon between Kissinger and Meir, May 23, 1974, KT01188, NSA.

396 "after intense study": Dayan, *Story of My Life*, 476.

397 "it's fatal": Memcon between Kissinger and Meir, May 22, 1974, KT01185, NSA.

397 "to continue to assist": Letter from Nixon to Meir, May 22, 1974, FRUS 1969–1976:26, Doc. 69.

397 Kissinger reported to Nixon: Memo from Scowcroft to Nixon, May 23, 1974, FRUS 1969–1976:26, Doc. 70.

397 movement of the Syrian red line: Memcon between Kissinger, Meir, et al., May 24, 1974, KT01193, NSA.

398 "we may have reached the end": Bernard Gwertzman, "Kissinger Makes Progress in Syria but Snags Arise," *New York Times*, May 27, 1974, and Kissinger, *Years of Upheaval*, 1095.

399 "Let us sleep on it": Memcon between Kissinger and Assad, May 27, 1974, FRUS 1969–1976:26, Doc. 74.

400 "we'd be stuck forever": Indyk interview with Henry Kissinger, July 23, 2019.

401 Israel had a right to defend: Memcon between Kissinger and Assad, May 27, 1974, FRUS 1969–1976:26, Doc. 75.

401 "The real problem": Memcon between Kissinger and Meir, May 28, 1974, KT01204, NSA.

402 refused to commit: Memcon between Kissinger and Assad, May 28, 1974, KT01206, NSA.

403 "his dinner": Kissinger, *Years of Upheaval*, 1104.

403 "Should I wave?": Memcon between Kissinger and Khaddam, May 27, 1974, KT01201, NSA.

403 "Therefore, we have no intention": Leslie Gelb, "Kissinger Reassures Soviet of Continued Mideast Role," *New York Times*, June 7, 1974.

405 captured them on its front page: Bernard Gwertzman, "Israel and Syria Accept Accord for Disengaging on Golan Front," *New York Times*, May 30, 1974.

405 called for the upholding: "Full Text: Trump and Putin's Press Conference Transcribed," *Politico*, July 16, 2018, https://www.politico.com/story/2018/07/16/full-text-trump-putin-meeting-transcript-724369.

405 "some satisfaction": Indyk interview with Henry Kissinger, July 23, 2019.

406 rare kind of Israeli prime minister: Dennis Ross and David Makovsky, *Be Strong and of Good Courage: How Israel's Most Important Leaders Shaped Its Destiny* (New York: PublicAffairs, 2019). The authors do not include Meir in their analysis of Israeli leaders, but they do detail the leadership of Ben-Gurion, Begin, Rabin, and Sharon.

407 "someone who negotiated": Kissinger, *Years of Upheaval*, 1098.

407 "overriding objective": Memcon between Kissinger, Meir, et al., May 23, 1974, KT01188, NSA.

407 "The reason the disengagement agreement": Indyk interview with Henry Kissinger, July 23, 2019.

408 for a momentary political advantage: Indyk interview with Henry Kissinger, July 23, 2019.

409 "that giant and courageous step": "Syria and Israel Sign Separation Pact in Geneva and Guns Fall Silent in Golan," *New York Times*, June 1, 1974.

409 In the eerie quiet: Charles Mohr, "At Last, All Quiet on the Golan Front," *New York Times*, June 1, 1974.

14. THE STEP NOT TAKEN

413 "barely short of magnificent": "Middle East: The Miracle Worker Does It Again," *Time*, June 10, 1974.

413 "good to excellent job": ". . . And of a Diplomat," *New York Times*, May 30, 1974; C. L. Sulzberger, "Henry Hercules and Hats," *New York Times*, June 1, 1974; "Middle East: The Miracle Worker Does It Again," *Time*, June 10, 1974.

413 "There is no record indicating": Henry Kissinger, *Years of Upheaval* (Boston: Little, Brown, 1982), 1111.

414 fifty-two sponsors: Walter Isaacson, *Kissinger* (New York: Simon & Schuster, 1992), 585–86; "Transcript of Kissinger Statement and Answers to Questions at News Conference," *New York Times*, June 12, 1974; Bernard Gwertzman, "Kissinger Backed by 52 Senators," *New York Times*, June 14, 1974.

414 Kissinger was reported by one aide: William B. Quandt, *Peace Process: American Diplomacy and the Arab-Israeli Conflict Since 1967* (Berkeley, CA: University of California Press, 1995), 215.

415 "Had Watergate not soon overwhelmed": Kissinger, *Years of Upheaval*, 1122.

415 to "neither endorse": Briefing Book, June 1974, Secretary Kissinger's Middle East Trip Memorandum of Conversations & Report, HAK Office Files, Nixon Presidential Materials, Nixon Presidential Library.

416 insufficient for Nixon: Patrick Seale, *Asad: The Struggle for the Middle East* (Berkeley, CA: University of California Press, 1989), 248–49.

416 "would not have been far off": Kissinger, *Years of Upheaval*, 1135.

416 Nixon talked at some length: Quandt, *Peace Process*, 217, and Matti Golan, *The Secret Conversations of Henry Kissinger: Step-by-Step Diplomacy in the Middle East* (Chicago: Quadrangle, 1976), 218.

417 He warned the Israeli leadership: Henry Kissinger, *Years of Renewal* (New York: Touchstone, 1999), 358–59; Kissinger, *Years of Upheaval*, 627–29; Memcon between Kissinger and Meir, December 16, 1973, FRUS 1969–1976:25, Doc. 399.

417 made quite clear: Vernon A. Walters, *Silent Missions* (New York: Doubleday, 1978), 426–27.

418 "should be to strengthen": Kissinger, *Years of Upheaval*, 626.

418 "friends of the United States": Memcon between Kissinger and Hussein, November 8, 1973, KT00893, NSA, and Kissinger, *Years of Upheaval*, 846.

419 an American or Israeli problem: Memcon between Kissinger and King Hussein, January 19, 1974, KT01002, NSA, and Minutes of Kissinger's Staff Meeting, January 21, 1974, KT01007, NSA.

419 "If we could design": Memcon between Kissinger and Hussein, December 16, 1973, KT00978, NSA.

419 in early January 1974: Memcon between Kissinger and Dayan, January 4, 1974, KT00979, NSA.

420 As he told Dayan: Memcon between Kissinger and Dayan, June 8, 1974, KT01218, NSA.

420 "no reason for us": Memcon between Kissinger and Dayan, January 4, 1974, KT00979, NSA.

420 "a statesman who cannot shape events": Kissinger, *Years of Upheaval*, 1141.

421 Rifai was the king's: Avi Shlaim, *Lion of Jordan: The Life of King Hussein in War and Peace* (New York: Vintage, 2009), 282. Shlaim was able to detail all the exchanges in the Israeli-Jordanian meetings based on the interviews he conducted with Rifai for his book. Some of these accounts were confirmed by Dinitz in his occasional briefings of Kissinger.

421 a kind of virtual disengagement: Memcon between Kissinger and Hussein, December 15, 1973, KT00953, NSA.

421 "I think we can work something out": Memcon between Kissinger and Meir, December 16, 1973, FRUS 1969–1976:25, Doc. 398.

422 "We really have no interest": Memcon between Kissinger, Meir, Dayan, et al., December 16, 1974, KT00959, NSA.

422 "I do not have anything specific": Telegram from Kissinger to U.S. Embassy Jordan, December 17, 1973, FRUS 1969–1976:25, Doc. 404.

422 "The art of politics": Memcon between Kissinger and Hussein, December 16, 1973, KT00978, NSA.

423 "We will support disengagement talks": Memcon between Kissinger, Hussein, and Rifai, January 19, 1974, KT01002, NSA.

423 They seemed quite open: Memcon between Kissinger, Allon, Eban, et al., January 20, 1974, KT01005, NSA.

424 The meeting ended with agreement: Shlaim, *Lion of Jordan*, 381, and Memcon between Kissinger and Dinitz, February 9, 1974, KT01024, NSA.

424 "His mind was set on": Simcha Dinitz, "Diplomatic Memoirs" (Unpublished manuscript, in author's possession: 2003), 126.

425 Oslo deal: Martin Indyk, *Innocent Abroad: An Intimate Account of American Peace Diplomacy in the Middle East* (New York: Simon & Schuster, 2009), 87.

425 "spokesman for the West Bank": Memcon between Kissinger and Dinitz, February 9, 1974, KT01024. Dinitz's instructions from Gazit requested him to explain to Kissinger that Meir wanted to wait to deal with the Jordanian-Palestinian issue until after the Syrian and Egyptian agreements were finalized because of political sensitivities in Israel. See Report on Hussein and Meir Meeting, February 4, 1974, A-9/7059, ISA.

426 The king repeated his concern: Shlaim, *Lion of Jordan*, 383.

427 futile to discuss: Kissinger, *Years of Upheaval*, 848.

427 Kissinger was fine with that: Cable between Gazit and Dinitz, March 11, 1974, A-9/7059, ISA.

427 "There will be no American": Memcon between Kissinger and Eban, March 14, 1974, KT01068, NSA.

428 He explained the necessity: Memcon between Kissinger and Hussein, May 5, 1974, KT01138, NSA.

428 "their relegation to a secondary role": Kissinger, *Years of Upheaval*, 1142, and Shlaim, *Lion of Jordan*, 384.

428 a moment's consideration: Memcon between Kissinger and Allon, July 30, 1974, FRUS 1969–1976:26, Doc. 93.

428 "to begin to think about": Dinitz's Report to Gazit of Private Meeting with Kissinger, July 12, 1974, HZ-3/6858.

429 for the good of the country: Kissinger, *Years of Upheaval*, 1196.

429 He ordered him to cut off: Isaacson, *Kissinger*, 596, and Meeting between Kissinger and Dinitz, August 20, 1974, A-5/7031, ISA.

429 more loyal to the Jewish state: Kissinger, *Years of Upheaval*, 1205.

429 for Jews to kneel in prayer: Isaacson, *Kissinger*, 599.

429 as he knelt with Nixon: Kissinger, *Years of Upheaval*, 1210; Isaacson, *Kissinger*, 599; Robert Dallek, *Nixon and Kissinger: Partners in Power* (New York: HarperCollins, 2007), 609–10.

431 "This was the first round": Itamar Rabinovich, *Yitzhak Rabin: Soldier, Leader, Statesman* (New Haven, CT: Yale University Press, 2017), 103.

431 or the river below: Shimon Peres, *Battling for Peace* (New York: Random House, 1995), 142–43.

432 "if we don't have to withdraw": Memcon between Kissinger and Allon, July 30, 1974, FRUS 1969–1976:26, Doc. 93, and Memcon between Kissinger and Allon, July 31, 1974, KT01267, NSA.

432 "but with the understanding": Memcon between Kissinger and Allon, July 31, 1974, KT01267, NSA.

433 "Timing is in all these things": Memcon between Kissinger and Rifai, August 6, 1974, KT01275, NSA.

433 Rabin was ready to go: Terence Smith, "Israelis Report Readiness for Jordan Compromise," *New York Times*, August 7, 1974.

433 instructed Allon to clarify: Memo from Rabin to Allon, August 2, 1974, A-5/7031, ISA.

433 "to proceed with the Jordanian option": Kissinger, *Years of Renewal*, 362.

434 between Jordan and Israel: Indyk, *Innocent Abroad*, 137.

435 "I will not let him assail": Indyk, *Innocent Abroad*, 137; Rabinovich, *Yitzhak Rabin*, 205–206, 218; Avi Gil, *Shimon Peres: An Insider's Account of the Man and the Struggle for a New Middle East* (London: I.B. Tauris, 2020), 124.

435 depiction of Allon's position: Memcon between Kissinger and Fahmy, August 12, 1974, KT01284, NSA.

436 simply nod his head: Ismail Fahmy, *Negotiating for Peace in the Middle East* (Abingdon, UK: Routledge, 1983), 123.

436 "a reputation for ruthlessness": Memcon between Kissinger, Rabin, et al., February 11, 1975, KT01493, NSA.

436 "only Syria would be left": Memcon between Kissinger and Ford, August 13, 1974, KC00322, NSA.

436 "I want to do that": Indyk, *Innocent Abroad*, 15–16.

437 "The upshot of Fahmy's visit": Memcon between Kissinger and Fahmy, August 13, 1974, KT01285, NSA, and Kissinger, *Years of Renewal*, 368.

437 a question of timing: Memcon between Ford, Kissinger, Hussein, and Rifai, August 16, 1974, National Security Adviser, Memoranda of Conversations, 1973–1977.

437 "would have accepted the principle": Memcon between Kissinger and Dayan, November 11, 1974, KT01411, NSA.

438 The king should not be discouraged: Memcon between Kissinger and Hussein, August 16, 1974, KT01292, NSA.

438 would not be a party: Golan, *Secret Conversations*, 224–25.

438 "We both see the same way": Memcon between Ford, Kissinger, and Rabin, September 10, 1974, FRUS 1969–1976:26, Doc. 99, and Shlaim, *Lion of Jordan*, 379.

439 "an independent Palestinian authority": "The Tripartite Palestinian-Egyptian-Syrian Communiqué," September 21, 1974, in "Documents on Palestine and the Arab-Israeli Conflict," *Journal of Palestine Studies* 4.2 (Winter 1975): 164.

439 "immediately followed by Jordan": Memcon between Ford and Rabin, September 13, 1974, FRUS 1969–1976:26, Doc. 100.

439 Rabin would provide him with a detailed proposal: Memcon between Kissinger and Rabin, September 13, 1974, KT01324, NSA.

440 an exploratory trip: Memcon between Ford, Kissinger, and Fahmy, October 5, 1974, FRUS 1969–1976:26, Doc. 102.

440 keep this understanding secret: Memo from Scowcroft to Ford, October 11, 1974, FRUS 1969–1976:26, Doc. 104.

440 "it's partly our fault": Memcon between Kissinger and Hussein, October 12, 1974, KC00354, NSA.

440 resolved to go: Shlaim, *Lion of Jordan*, 390.

440 a hopeless endeavor: Golan, *Secret Conversations*, 226, and Memo from Scowcroft to Ford, October 14, 1974, FRUS 1969–1976:26, Doc. 107.

441 he reported to Ford: Memo from Scowcroft to Ford, October 14, 1974, FRUS 1969–1976:26, Doc. 107.

441 agreement with Sadat and Rabin: Kissinger, *Years of Renewal*, 381–82.

441 he would not deal with the PLO: Shlaim, *Lion of Jordan*, 441–42.

442 an unusual statement: Dinitz, "Diplomatic Memoirs," 101.

444 "a big mistake": Memcon between Kissinger and Dinitz, July 1, 1975, FRUS 1969–1976:26, Doc. 202.

444 without territorial gain: Kissinger, *Years of Renewal*, 456.

15. BREAKDOWN

446 "This is the minimum": Memcon between Kissinger and Sadat, November 6, 1974, KT01401, NSA.

446 The early warning station: Drew Middleton, "Sinai's Passes Vital, Israeli Generals Say," *New York Times*, August 2, 1975.

446 land access to the oil fields: Terence Smith, "Israelis at Oil Wells in Sinai Believe Days There Are Numbered," *New York Times*, January 13, 1975.

447 into a recession: Eileen Shanahan, "Unemployment at 8.2 Percent; A January Rise of 930,000 Puts Total at 7.5 Million," *New York Times*, February 8, 1975.

447 "We have to push": Memcon between Ford, Rockefeller, and Kissinger, September 6, 1974, KC00334, NSA.

447 He had delayed his visit: Cable between Dinitz and Gazit, August 20, 1974, A-5/7031, ISA.

447 Kissinger took umbrage: Uzi Eilam, *Eilam's Arc: How Israel Became a Military Technology Powerhouse* (East Sussex, UK: Sussex Academic Press, 2011), 131–32, and Henry Kissinger, *Years of Renewal* (New York: Touchstone, 1999), 380–81.

448 quick to blame Rabin: Memo from Scowcroft to Ford, October 30, 1974, FRUS 1969–1976:26, Doc. 112.

448 "could only have been Kissinger": Walter Z. Laqueur and Edward N. Luttwak, "Kissinger and the Yom Kippur War," *Commentary* 58, September 1974.

448 Hypersensitive to criticism: Cable between Dinitz and Gazit, August 28, 1974, HZ-4/6858, ISA, and Dinitz Report on Private Conversation with Kissinger, October 22, 1974, A-7/6858, ISA.

448 "You are trying to sell us": Memcon between Kissinger and Rabin, September 11, 1974, KT01320, NSA.

449 "that our foreign policy": Telegram from Kissinger to Eagleburger, October 31, 1974, FRUS 1969–1976:26, Doc. 113.

449 presidential dissatisfaction: Telegram from Scowcroft to Kissinger, November 7, 1974, FRUS 1969–1976:26, Doc. 117.

449 "One prediction that is always true": Memcon between Kissinger and Rabin, November 7, 1974, KT01405, NSA.

450 the whole thing wrapped up: Memcon between Kissinger and Ford, November 10, 1974, National Security Adviser, Memoranda of Conversations, 1973–1977, Box 7, Ford Presidential Library. There is no record of this meeting with Rabin. This account comes from Kissinger's debrief of President Ford.

450 Rabin records in his memoirs: Yitzhak Rabin, *The Rabin Memoirs* (Berkeley, CA: University of California Press, 1996), 248–49.

450 "I know we can't get it": Memcon between Kissinger and Allon, December 9, 1974, KT01443, NSA. Kissinger related this conversation with Rabin to Allon when he came to Washington on December 9.

451 "The Israelis assess": Memcon between Ford and Kissinger, November 10, 1974, National Security Adviser, Memoranda of Conversations, 1973–1977, Box 7, Ford Presidential Library.

451 "The only way": Memcon between Kissinger and Schlesinger, November 14, 1974, KC00358, NSA.

451 That suited Rabin fine: Memcon between Kissinger and Dinitz, November 16, 1974, KT01417, NSA.

451 "absolutely essential": Letter from Ford to Rabin, November 26, 1974, FRUS 1969–1976:26, Doc. 120. In the letter, Ford told Rabin that Allon should come to Washington with "a proposal that can promptly become the basis for a realistic negotiation with Egypt." Lest he be misunderstood, he emphasized, "I am counting on substantial progress during the Foreign Minister's visit."

451 They recommended to demand: Matti Golan, *The Secret Conversations of Henry Kissinger: Step-by-Step Diplomacy in the Middle East* (Chicago: Quadrangle, 1976), 231.

452 Israel would give less: Rabin, *Memoirs*, 251.

452 "end of acts of belligerency": Memcon between Ford, Kissinger, and Allon, December 9, 1974, FRUS 1969–1976:26, Doc. 123.

452 remain in force for ten years: Memcon between Ford, Kissinger, and Allon, December 9, 1974, FRUS 1969–1976:26, Doc. 123.

452 "get both": Memcon between Kissinger and Eilts, December 11–12, 1974, KT01448, NSA.

452 a highly controversial commitment: Golan, *Secret Conversations*, 214. Nixon had made the commitment to provide Egypt with a nuclear reactor during his visit to Cairo in June 1974.

453 "to reexamine the basic strategy": Cable from Eilts to Kissinger in Memcon between Kissinger and Dinitz, December 17, 1974, KT01456, NSA.

453 "we are without a strategy": Memcon between Kissinger and Dinitz, December 17, 1974, KT01456, NSA.

453 Kissinger wrote back: Memcon between Kissinger and Dinitz, December 23, 1974, KT01463, NSA.

453 "There is a direct relation": Memcon between Ford, Kissinger, and Allon, January 16, 1975, FRUS 1969–1976:26, Doc. 127.

454 "What is the maximum": Memcon between Kissinger and Dinitz, January 27, 1975, KT01483, NSA.

454 complaining about Pentagon foot-dragging: Minutes of WSAG Meeting, January 14, 1975, FRUS 1969–1976:26, Doc. 126, fn. 7.

454 Kissinger repeated his instructions: Memcon between Kissinger, Schlesinger, et al., February 8, 1975, National Security Adviser, Memoranda of Conversations, 1973–1977, Box 9, Ford Presidential Library.

454 "Tell him cold": Memcon between Ford and Kissinger, February 7, 1975, FRUS 1969–1976:26, Doc. 130.

455 "effectively [be] taken out": Memo from Scowcroft to Ford, February 11, 1975, FRUS 1969–1976:26, Doc. 131.

455 "Amid his predictions". Shimon Peres, *Battling for Peace* (New York: Random House, 1995), 142.

456 contemplating another step: Memcon between Kissinger, Rabin, et al., February 11, 1975, KT01493, NSA

457 "Who carried out the confrontation": Memcon between Kissinger, Rabin, et al., February 11, 1975, KT01493, NSA.

458 "I don't see why": Memcon between Kissinger, Rabin, et al., February 11, 1975, KT01494, NSA.

458 According to Dinitz: Simcha Dinitz, "Diplomatic Memoirs" (Unpublished manuscript, in author's possession: 2003), 148.

458 intent on extracting the highest: Memo from Scowcroft to Ford, February 11, 1975, FRUS 1969–1976:26, Doc. 131.

459 "they don't believe me": Memcon between Kissinger and Rabin, February 13, 1975, KT01497, NSA.

459 outlined Egypt's position: Ismail Fahmy, *Negotiating for Peace in the Middle East* (Abingdon, UK: Routledge, 1983), 125–26.

459 "he hasn't done it": Memcon between Kissinger and Rabin, February 13, 1975, KT01497, NSA.

459 Assad then made clear: Memo from Scowcroft to Ford, February 16, 1975, FRUS 1969–1976:26, Doc. 135.

460 willing to entertain: Henry Tanner, "Cairo Describes Talks as Buoying," *New York Times*, February 14, 1975. Kissinger was encouraged by an upbeat account of his meetings with Sadat given by Egyptian officials to *The New York Times*.

460 compounded by the clear constraints: Memos from Scowcroft to Ford, February 14 and 16, 1975, FRUS 1969–1976:26, Docs. 134 and 135.

460 He remembers telling Sisco: Indyk interview with Henry Kissinger, December 19, 2019.

460 "hands of the State of Israel": "Reply in the Knesset by Prime Minister Rabin to a motion

for the agenda," Israel Ministry of Foreign Affairs, February 12, 1975, https://mfa.gov
.il/MFA/ForeignPolicy/MFADocuments/Yearbook2/Pages/63%20Reply%20in%20the
%20Knesset%20by%20Prime%20Minister%20Rabin%20to.aspx.

460 "fruitful and decisive": Memo from Scowcroft to Ford, March 9, 1975, FRUS 1969–
1976:26, Doc. 140.

461 "a hard year for Mr. Kissinger": Leslie Gelb, "Kissinger and Congress," *New York Times*,
February 22, 1975.

461 "be repaid cheaply": Henry Kamm, "Minister Reports Israelis Seek Direct Sadat Pledge,"
New York Times, March 3, 1975.

461 he told the press: Bernard Gwertzman, "Kissinger Meets Sadat in Aswan over a Sinai
Pact," *New York Times*, March 9, 1975.

462 "at least to get the negotiations": Memo from Scowcroft to Ford, March 9, 1975, FRUS
1969–1976:26, Doc. 140.

462 Assad showed no interest: Memo from Scowcroft to Ford, March 10, 1975, FRUS 1969–
1976:26, Doc. 141.

462 Kissinger had already discussed: Memcon between Kissinger and Ford, March 5, 1975,
KC00401, NSA.

463 in an attempt to move Israel: Memcon between Kissinger and Rabin, March 10, 1975,
KT01524, NSA.

464 "from the realm of philosophy": Memcon between Kissinger and Rabin, March 11, 1975,
KT01531, NSA.

464 "Even if you have achieved": Memcon between Kissinger, Rabin, et al., March 12, 1975,
Folder "March 7–22, 1975—Kissinger's Trip—Vol. I (6)," Box 3, National Security Adviser,
Kissinger Reports on USSR, China and Middle East Discussions, 1974–1977, Ford Presi-
dential Library.

464 "*when* he recommends Israeli withdrawal": Memos from Scowcroft to Ford, March 11,
1975, FRUS 1969–1976:26, Docs. 143 and 144.

465 "if it is visibly shown that the act": Memcon between Kissinger, Rabin, et al., March 12,
1975, Folder "March 7–22, 1975—Kissinger's Trip—Vol. I (6)," Box 3, National Security
Adviser, Kissinger Reports on USSR, China and Middle East Discussions, 1974–1977,
Ford Presidential Library.

466 "a cardinal mistake": Kissinger, *Years of Renewal*, 410; Rabin, *Memoirs*, 255; Dinitz, "Diplomatic Memoirs," 151.

466 "concrete ideas": Bernard Gwertzman, "Kissinger Gets New 'Ideas' from Sadat for Israelis," *New York Times*, March 14, 1975.

467 Rabin agreed to take: Memo from Scowcroft to Ford, March 14, 1975, FRUS 1969–
1976:26, Doc. 146.

467 "we did not feel we had": Bernard Gwertzman, "Israel Indicates Cool Reaction to Egypt's
Ideas," *New York Times*, March 15, 1975, and Golan, *Secret Conversations*, 236.

468 a parting of the ways: Memcon between Kissinger, Rabin, et al., March 16, 1975, Folder
"March 7–22, 1975—Kissinger's Trip—Vol. II (1)," Box 3, National Security Adviser, Kissinger Reports on USSR, China and Middle East Discussions, 1974–1977, Ford Presidential Library.

468 "assisting or participating in": Memo from Scowcroft to Ford, March 18, 1975, FRUS
1969–1976:26, Doc. 149.

468 Kissinger managed to convince him: Memcon between Kissinger and Sadat, March 17,
1975, KT01541, NSA.

468 a new Egyptian non-paper: Memo from Scowcroft to Ford, March 18, 1975, FRUS 1969–
1976:26, Doc. 149.

469 they discussed how to handle: Memcon between Kissinger and Sadat, March 18, 1975,
KT01542, NSA.

469 Sadat wrote an unusual letter: The text of Sadat's letter is in Memcon between Kissinger,
Rabin, et al., March 19, 1975, National Security Adviser, Kissinger Reports on USSR,
China and Middle East Discussions, 1974–1976, Box 4, Ford Presidential Library.

469 This sense of his own fall: Text of Fahmy's message contained in Memcon between Kissinger, Rabin, et al., March 22, 1975, FRUS 1969–1976:26, Doc. 158.

469 Little wonder the traveling press: Bernard Gwertzman, "U.S. Mideast Review," *New York Times*, June 18, 1975.

469 "in order to stand behind the intransigence": Telegram from Scowcroft to Kissinger, March 18, 1975, FRUS 1969–1976:26, Doc. 150.

469 But his ability to deliver: Memcon between Kissinger, Rabin, et al., March 18, 1975, National Security Adviser, Kissinger Reports on USSR, China and Middle East Discussions, 1974–1976, Box 4, Ford Presidential Library, and Memo from Scowcroft to Ford, March 19, 1975, FRUS 1969–1976:26, Doc. 152.

470 that was not true: Memcon between Rabin, Allon, Kissinger, et al., March 19, 1975, National Security Adviser, Kissinger Reports on USSR, China and Middle East Discussions, 1974–1976, Box 4, Ford Presidential Library.

471 "Israel has taken a decision": Memcon between Kissinger, Rabin, et al., March 20, 1975, National Security Adviser, Kissinger Reports on USSR, China and Middle East Discussions, 1974–1976, Box 4, Ford Presidential Library.

472 adjourned the meeting: Memcon between Kissinger, Rabin et al., March 20, 1975, 9:50 a.m., National Security Adviser, Kissinger Reports on USSR, China and Middle East Discussions, 1974–1976, Box 4, Ford Presidential Library.

473 "It's a great Israeli concession": Memcon between Kissinger, Rabin, et al., March 20, 1975, National Security Adviser, Kissinger Reports on USSR, China and Middle East Discussions, 1974–1976, Box 4, Ford Presidential Library.

473 "an agreement could be written": Memcon between Kissinger and Sadat, March 20, 1975, KT01544, NSA.

473 "has acted extremely well": Memo from Scowcroft to Ford, March 20, 1975, FRUS 1969–1976:26, Doc. 153

474 "in order to counter": Dinitz, "Diplomatic Memoirs," 152.

475 "our decisions": Letter from Ford to Rabin, March 21, 1975, FRUS 1969–1976:26, Doc. 156.

475 Later, he would admit: Bernard Gwertzman, "Failure of Kissinger's Mideast Mission Traced to Major Miscalculations," *New York Times*, April 7, 1975.

475 painted themselves into a corner: Memo from Scowcroft to Ford, March 22, 1975, FRUS 1969–1976:26, Doc. 157.

475 "We may be witnessing": Memo from Scowcroft to Ford, March 22, 1975, FRUS 1969–1976:26, Doc. 157.

475 "irrevocable and fatal blow": Memcon between Kissinger, Rabin, et al., March 22, 1975, FRUS 1969–1976:26, Doc. 158.

476 Fahmy reiterated: Henry Tanner, "Egyptians Place Blame on Israel," *New York Times*, March 23, 1975.

477 "There is no doubt about": Memcon between Kissinger, Rabin, Allon, et al., March 22, 1975, National Security Adviser, Memoranda of Conversations, 1973–1977, Box 10, Ford Presidential Library.

478 Kissinger said he believed him: Kissinger, *Years of Renewal*, 420.

478 "no other goal": Remarks by Prime Minister Rabin and Secretary of State Kissinger—Ben Gurion Airport, *Israeli Ministry of Foreign Affairs*, March 23, 1975, https://mfa.gov.il/MFA/ForeignPolicy/MFADocuments/Yearbook2/Pages/71%20Remarks%20by%20Prime%20Minister%20Rabin%20and%20Secretary%200.aspx.

478 Marvin Kalb recalls: Indyk interview with Marvin Kalb, March 18, 2016.

478 no choice now: Bernard Gwertzman, "Kissinger Home, Sees No Renewal of Mideast Role," *New York Times*, March 24, 1975.

479 Rabin heard that Kissinger: Golan, *Secret Conversations*, 241, and Rabin, *Memoirs*, 261.

479 avoid the imposed settlement: Arnaud de Borchgrave, "Voices Across the Fence," *Newsweek*, March 3, 1975. Dayan told *Newsweek*, "I am not afraid of Geneva. I don't believe it will become a forum for Arab extremism. We are strong and mature enough to run it our way."

479 Rabin knew Kissinger well enough: Memo from Scowcroft to Ford, February 11, 1975, FRUS 1969–1976:26, Doc. 131.

16. REASSESSMENT

482 "foreign policy crises on all sides": James Reston, "Dangers of Pessimism," *New York Times*, April 2, 1975.

482 calls for his resignation: "The Difficulty of Being Henry Kissinger," *Time*, April 28, 1975.

482 "a very painful time": Indyk interview with Henry Kissinger, May 17, 2016.

483 "discuss a lasting peace": Gerald Ford, *A Time to Heal* (New York: Harper & Row, 1979), 245.

483 "mad as hell": Ford, *A Time to Heal*, 247.

483 a furor in the pro-Israel community: Bernard Gwertzman, "Ford Says Israel Lacked Flexibility in the Negotiations," *New York Times*, March 28, 1975.

483 "when I know I'm right": Memcom between Ford, Rockefeller, and Kissinger, March 24, 1975, FRUS 1969–1976:26, Doc. 161, and Memcon between Ford and Kissinger, March 26, 1975, 1969–1976:26, Doc. 162.

483 On leaving the White House: President's Meeting with the Secretary and Congressional Leadership, March 24, 1975, FRUS 1969–1976:26, Doc. 160.

484 to secure oil supplies: Lou Harris, "Oil or Israel," *New York Times Magazine*, April 6, 1975.

484 had come to enjoy: Memcon between Ford and Kissinger, March 24, 1975, FRUS 1969–1976:26, Doc. 159.

485 beginning on October 1, 1975: National Security Study Memorandum 220, March 26, 1975, FRUS 1969–1976:26, Doc. 163.

485 "The proper relationship": Minutes of National Security Council Meeting, March 28, 1975, FRUS 1969–1976:26, Doc. 166.

485 intelligence cooperation was attenuated: Memcon between Dean Rusk, Cyrus Vance, et al., March 31, 1975, FRUS 1969–1976:26, Doc. 169. Kissinger revealed this in the meeting he held with outside experts (the "wise men") on March 31.

485 "carrying a grudge at each other": Simcha Dinitz, "Diplomatic Memoirs" (Unpublished manuscript, in author's possession: 2003), 157.

486 across the country: James Feron, "Israelis Taking Their Case to American Audiences," *New York Times*, April 27, 1975, and "The Mysterious Texture of U.S.-Israel Relations," *Near East Report* 19, no. 17 (April 23, 1975): 75.

486 "the purpose of national policy": "Israel's Case Will Prevail," *Near East Report* 19, no. 14 (April 2, 1975): 57.

486 Fisher promised: Cable from Dinitz to Allon, March 26, 1975, HZ-7/6859, ISA, and Peter Golden, *Quiet Diplomat: A Biography of Max M. Fisher* (New York: Cornwall Books, 1992), 314.

487 "The price of silence": Golden, *Quiet Diplomat*, 403.

488 because he was Jewish: Telcon between Kissinger and Ziffren, April 25, 1975, KA13558, NSA. At one point in early April, Kissinger told Max Fisher, "The Jewish community cannot be so insane as to believe that a Jewish secretary of state is against them." He later told Paul Ziffren, a Jewish Democratic leader from California, "In a confrontation between the President and the Jewish community, the Jews will lose the battle." See Telcon between Kissinger and Fisher, April 2, 1975, KA13429, NSA.

488 rejected that suggestion: Telcon between Kissinger and Sisco, April 9, 1975, KA13450, NSA.

488 "we simply cannot get over it": Memcon between Kissinger and Jewish Intellectuals, March 31, 1975, FRUS 1969–1976:26, Doc. 168.

488 a campaign of deception: Memcon between Kissinger, Sisco, et al., April 8, 1975, FRUS 1969–1976:26, Doc. 171.

488 "In the Middle East, we wanted to hear": Russell Baker, "Dr. Feelgood," *New York Times*, May 6, 1975.

489 "had better watch out": William Safire, "Henry's Two Faces," *New York Times*, March 27, 1975.

489 confrontation with the administration: Terence Smith, "Israel Says Balk on Arms Request Delays Sinai Talk," *New York Times*, April 21, 1975.

489 Kissinger insisted that the relationship: Memcon between Kissinger and Allon, April 21, 1975, KT01588, NSA.

489 an anti-Semitic campaign: Memcon between Kissinger and Jewish Intellectuals, March 31, 1975, FRUS 1969–1976:26, Doc. 168.

489 Kissinger saw that as indicative: Personal Memo, Subject: Israel, March 31, 1975, Records of Joseph Sisco, 1951–76, Box 25, RG 59, General Records of the Department of State, NARA, and Indyk interview with Henry Kissinger, December 19, 2019.

490 Arab-Israeli settlement: Joseph J. Sisco, "Arab-Israeli Peace Settlement," Memo from Under Secretary of State for Political Affairs, April 7, 1975, Records of Joseph Sisco, 1951–76, Box 25, RG 59, General Records of the Department of State, NARA.

490 "a bit more verbally and practically": Joseph J. Sisco, "Small Transitional Agreement," Memo from Under Secretary of State for Political Affairs, April 7, 1975, Records of Joseph Sisco, 1951–76, Box 25, RG 59, General Records of the Department of State, NARA.

490 all-out peace agreement: Ambassador Eilts, "Outline of a Possible Medium Agreement," Department of State Briefing Memorandum, undated, Records of Joseph Sisco, 1951–76, Box 25, RG 59, General Records of the Department of State, NARA.

491 "[he] would resign": Henry Kissinger, *Years of Renewal* (New York: Touchstone, 1999), 424, 428.

491 "just the price we pay": Memcon between Kissinger, Sisco, et al., April 3, 1975, FRUS 1969–1976:26, Doc. 170.

491 lead to war: Memcon between Kissinger, Sisco, et al., April 8, 1975, FRUS 1969–1976:26, Doc. 171.

492 "I will veto it": Memcon between Ford, Kissinger, et al., April 14, 1975, FRUS 1969–1976:26, Doc. 173.

492 he wasn't that interested: Memcon between Kissinger and Dinitz, April 8, 1975, KT01565, NSA.

493 come from Jerusalem: Memcon between Kissinger and Allon, April 21, 1975, KT01588, NSA.

493 "maintain coolness and discipline": Memcon between Ford and Kissinger, April 24, 1975, National Security Adviser, Memoranda of Conversations, 1973–1977, Box 11, Ford Presidential Library.

493 "for the comprehensive approach": Memcon between Ford and Kissinger, May 7, 1975, National Security Adviser, Memoranda of Conversations, 1973–1977, Box 11, Ford Presidential Library. Ford repeated this view again in a conversation with Kissinger on May 8: "For us to go back to the step-by-step when Israel is frozen just won't work." On each occasion, Kissinger did not respond; he simply changed the subject. See Memcon between Ford and Kissinger, May 8, 1975, National Security Adviser, Memoranda of Conversations, 1973–1977, Box 11, Ford Presidential Library.

494 At a National Security Council meeting: Minutes of National Security Council Meeting, May 15, 1975, FRUS 1969–1976:26, Doc. 174.

494 "withholding military equipment from Israel": Letter from 75 Senators to President Gerald Ford in Support of Israel, May 21, 1975, Collection GRF-0056: White House Central Files Subject Files (Ford Administration).

494 "we will prepare one of our own": "A Very Loud and Clear Position," *Near East Report* 19, no. 22 (May 28, 1975): 94; Bernard Gwertzman, "75 Senators Back Israel's Aid Bids," *New York Times*, May 22, 1975; Bernard Gwertzman, "White House Backs Israel, But It Avoids a Reply to 76 Senators," *New York Times*, May 23, 1975.

494 In the president's view: Ford, *A Time to Heal*, 287–88.

494 "our original judgments": Kissinger, *Years of Renewal*, 433.

495 Assad informed the UN secretary-general: Kathleen Teltsch, "Damascus Agrees to 6 More Months for Buffer Force," *New York Times*, May 22, 1975.

495 agreed to await the outcome: Leslie Gelb, "U.S.-Soviet Effort on Mideast Is Set," *New York*

Times, May 21, 1975, and Henry Kissinger, *Years of Upheaval* (Boston: Little, Brown, 1982), 433–34.

495　Sadat nevertheless made clear: Anwar Sadat, *In Search of Identity* (New York: Harper & Row, 1978), 351.

496　"not the Soviet Union": Memcon between Ford, Kissinger, and Sadat, June 1, 1975, FRUS 1969–1976:26, Doc. 177, and Kissinger, *Years of Renewal*, 436.

496　"Any other Middle Eastern leader": Kissinger, *Years of Renewal*, 435.

496　conditions were met: Memcon between Ford, Kissinger, and Sadat, June 1, 1975, FRUS 1969–1976:26, Doc. 177.

498　the agreement was struck: Memcon between Ford, Kissinger and Sadat, June 2, 1975, FRUS 1969–1976:26, Doc. 178.

498　Ford answered a question: Henry Tanner, "Ford and Sadat See Basis of Long-Term Friendship," *New York Times*, June 3, 1975.

498　"Keep them to the level of this year": Memcon between Ford, Kissinger, and Scowcroft, June 9, 1975, FRUS 1969–1976:26, Doc. 180.

498　off to Geneva: Kissinger, *Years of Renewal*, 438–39.

498　new ideas too: Memcon between Kissinger and Dinitz, June 4, 1975, KT01656, NSA.

499　"it's a soluble problem": Telcon between Kissinger and Dinitz, June 6, 1975, KA13708, NSA.

499　an uninvited Soviet destroyer: Henry Tanner, "Egyptians Reopen Canal Amid Pomp," *New York Times*, June 6, 1975.

499　"monopoly on peace-seeking": Terence Smith, "Israel to Thin Out Suez Line Force; Egypt Hails Step," *New York Times*, June 3, 1975.

499　"He tried to scare me": Israeli Cabinet Meeting, June 17, 1975, A-5/7025, ISA.

500　Israel's aid requirements: Memcon between Kissinger and Rabin, June 11, 1975, KT01663, NSA.

502　"all this last year?": Kissinger, *Years of Renewal*, 442.

502　Rabin felt he had put down a marker: Yitzhak Rabin, *The Rabin Memoirs* (Berkeley, CA: University of California Press, 1996), 263–64.

502　"would have no alternative": Memcon between Ford and Rabin, June 11, 1975, FRUS 1969–1976:26, Doc. 183.

502　Geneva would lead to a stalemate: Rabin, *Memoirs*, 263.

502　He called Dinitz late that night: Telcon between Kissinger and Dinitz, June 11, 1975, KA13728, NSA.

502　"was a disgrace": Memcon between Ford and Kissinger, June 12, 1975, FRUS 1969–1976:26, Doc. 184.

503　"based on the eastern end of the passes": Memcon between Kissinger, Rabin, et al., June 12, 1975, KT01666, NSA.

503　"I think they're cracking": Memcon between Ford and Kissinger, June 12, 1975, FRUS 1969–1976:26, Doc. 184.

503　Encouraged by Kissinger: Kissinger, *Years of Renewal*, 443.

504　tutored by Dinitz: Bernard Gwertzman, "Kissinger's Assurances Buoy Israel," *New York Times*, June 14, 1975.

505　Sisco intervened to end the meeting: Memcon between Kissinger and Rabin, June 12, 1975, KT01668, NSA.

506　"So there were no meetings with members": Memcon between Kissinger and Rabin, June 15, 1975, FRUS 1969–1976:26, Doc. 188.

506　"We shall hold on to the eastern ridge": Rabin, *Memoirs*, 265–66.

506　He asked Scowcroft to call Dinitz: Memcon between Kissinger, Sisco, et al., June 14, 1975, FRUS 1969–1976:26, Doc. 187. As recounted by Kissinger to his aides.

508　"the weapons you need": Memcon between Kissinger and Rabin, June 15, 1975, FRUS 1969–1976:26, Doc. 188.

508　this was Sadat's idea: Memcon between Ford and Kissinger, June 12, 1975, FRUS 1969–1976:26, Doc. 184, fn. 4. In reporting this idea to Allon and Peres, Rabin said that he did not believe Kissinger had discussed it with Sadat, but that Kissinger would not have suggested it "unless he had reason to believe Sadat would agree." See Rabin, *Memoirs*, 270.

508 he told the press outside the Waldorf: Terence Smith, "Israel Sees Pact on Sinai Nearing," *New York Times*, August 9, 1975.

508 "man from Grand Rapids": Memcon between Kissinger and Jewish Leaders, June 15, 1975, FRUS 1969–1976:26, Doc. 189.

509 "Make them feel like": Telcon between Ford and Kissinger, June 15, 1975, NSA, https://nsarchive2.gwu.edu/NSAEBB/NSAEBB526-Court-Ordered-Release-of-Kissinger-Telcons/documents/4B%206-15-75%20Ford.pdf.

509 He said Dinitz was not: Dinitz Assessment Cable, June 18, 1975, A-10/7099, ISA, and Israeli Cabinet Meeting, June 17, 1975, A-5/7025, ISA.

509 Rabin was using his dance partner: Memcon between Kissinger and Dinitz, June 20, 1975, KT01676, NSA.

510 Fahmy explained: Back-Channel Message from Kissinger to Eilts, June 27, 1975, FRUS 1969–1976:26, Doc. 199, fn. 2, and Memcon between Ford and Kissinger, June 25, 1975, FRUS 1969–1976:26, Doc. 197, fn. 4.

510 promoting a comprehensive plan: "Options for Advancing Arab-Israeli Negotiations," Memo for the President from Kissinger, undated, Records of Joseph Sisco, 1951–76, RG 59, General Records of the Department of State, NARA.

511 lasted only ten minutes: Memcon between Ford and Dinitz, June 27, 1975, FRUS 1969–1976:26, Doc. 200. Ford's letter to Rabin is at Tab A of this document.

511 now President Ford was issuing an ultimatum: Kissinger, *Years of Renewal*, 446.

511 So he answered by wrapping: Memcon between Kissinger and Dinitz, June 27, 1975, KT01686, NSA.

511 restart the negotiations: Cable from Dinitz to Allon, March 28, 1975, HZ-7/6859, ISA.

512 Kissinger told Dinitz: Telcon between Kissinger and Dinitz, June 27, 1975, KA13801, NSA, and Call between Rabin and Dinitz, June 27, 1975, A-9/7063, ISA.

512 military and economic assistance: Dinitz had originally proposed his idea of a package deal to Rabin and Peres on June 18. See Dinitz Assessment Cable, June 18, 1975, A-10/7099, ISA.

513 an IDF presence: This account is provided in the summary of the cabinet's deliberations. See Amos Shifris, *The First Rabin Government, 1974–1977* [in Hebrew] (Tel Aviv, Israel: Havatzelet, 2013), 54–55.

513 "a last ditch, nearly desperate": Telcon between Dinitz, Rabin, and Peres, June 30, 1975, A-9/7063, ISA.

513 "Had I not, with my own ears": Rabin, *Memoirs*, 267.

514 According to Dinitz's report: Telcon between Dinitz and Mizrachi, June 30, 1975, A-9/7063, ISA.

17. DENOUEMENT

516 "I guess one must be very rich": Simcha Dinitz, "Diplomatic Memoirs" (Unpublished manuscript, in author's possession: 2003), 156.

518 "about right": Memcon between Kissinger and Dinitz, July 1, 1975, FRUS 1969–1976:26, Doc. 202.

518 "there is no chance": Dinitz, "Diplomatic Memoirs," 158.

518 "the minimum the Egyptians might accept": Memcon between Kissinger and Dinitz, July 2, 1975, FRUS 1969–1976:26, Doc. 203.

518 "a noose around the passes": Memcon between Kissinger and Dinitz, July 7, 1975, KT01694, NSA.

518 "the Israelis are getting ready": Memcon between Ford and Kissinger, July 7, 1975, National Security Adviser, Memoranda of Conversations, 1973–1977, Box 13, Ford Presidential Library.

519 "in the framework": Henry Kissinger, *Years of Renewal* (New York: Touchstone, 1999), 458.

520 "after much discussion": Telegram from Kissinger to Embassy in Egypt, July 12, 1975, FRUS 1969–1976:26, Doc. 208.

520 "I think that given their epic minds": Memcon between Kissinger and Advisers, July 17, 1975, FRUS 1969–1976:26, Doc. 209.

521 move the Egyptian line: Memcon between Kissinger, Sisco, Atherton, and Saunders, July 23, 1975, FRUS 1969–1976:26, Doc. 211, fn. 2, and Telcon between Kissinger and Shalev, July 21, 1975, KA13858, NSA.

521 With the onset of Ramadan: Memcon between Kissinger, Sisco, Atherton, and Saunders, July 23, 1975, FRUS 1969–1976:26, Doc. 211, and Telcon between Kissinger and Dinitz, July 23, 1975, KA13880, NSA.

521 "could have done it": Memcon between Ford, Kissinger, and Scowcroft, August 4, 1975, FRUS 1969–1976:26, Doc. 213.

524 "blow to the very soul": Henry Kamm, "Rabin Reassures Israelis on Pact," *New York Times*, August 23, 1975.

524 Ford told Kissinger: Memcon between Ford and Kissinger, August 16, 1975, FRUS 1969–1975:26, Doc. 214.

525 "treacherous, petty, deceitful": Memcon between Kissinger, Rabin, Allon, et al., August 22, 1975, KT01752, NSA; Memo from Scowcroft to Ford, August 23, 1975, FRUS 1969–1976:26, Doc. 217; Memcon between Ford, Kissinger, and Scowcroft, September 4, 1975, FRUS 1969–1976:26, Doc. 235.

525 "This negative, grudging, piddling way": Memcon between Kissinger, Rabin, Allon, et al., August 22, 1975, KT01752, NSA.

526 Sadat threw up his hands: Memcon between Kissinger, Rabin, Allon, et al., August 25, 1975, KT01758, NSA.

526 "which they will use to prevent": Memcon between Ford and Kissinger, September 4, 1975, FRUS 1969–1976:26, Doc. 235.

529 "Never has a government achieved": Memcon between Kissinger and Rabin, August 31–September 1, 1975, KT01764, NSA.

530 "a luxury the United States": Kissinger for the President: "Economic and Military Assistance Levels for Israel," Department of State, June 6, 1975, Records of Joseph Sisco, 1951–76, Box 25, RG 59, General Records of the Department of State, NARA.

530 long-lasting consequences: Yitzhak Rabin, *The Rabin Memoirs* (Berkeley, CA: University of California Press, 1996), 290.

531 "as far as we were concerned": Uzi Eilam, *Eilam's Arc: How Israel Became a Military Technology Powerhouse* (East Sussex, UK: Sussex Academic Press, 2011), 132.

531 "with a view to giving": Memorandum of Agreement between the Governments of Israel and the United States, September 1, 1975, FRUS 1969–1969:26, Doc. 227, and Letter from Ford to Rabin, undated, FRUS 1969–1976:26, Doc. 234.

531 Kissinger repeated: Memcon between Rabin, Allon, Kissinger, et al., August 31–September 1, 1975, KT01764, NSA.

532 "it will give great weight": Letter from Ford to Rabin, undated, FRUS 1969–1976:26, Doc. 234.

532 *"new realities on the ground"*: Elliott Abrams, *Tested by Zion: The Bush Administration and the Israeli-Palestinian Conflict* (Cambridge, UK: Cambridge University Press, 2013), 108–109.

533 Obama subsequently declared: Martin Indyk, Kenneth Lieberthal, and Michael O'Hanlon, *Bending History: Barack Obama's Foreign Policy* (Washington, DC: Brookings Institution Press, 2012), 133–34.

533 from the Golan Heights: Itamar Rabinovich, *Yitzhak Rabin: Soldier, Leader, Statesman* (New Haven, CT: Yale University Press, 2017), 176–81, and Martin Indyk, *Innocent Abroad: An Intimate Account of American Peace Diplomacy in the Middle East* (New York: Simon & Schuster, 2009), 62.

534 These were codified: Memorandum of Agreement between the Governments of Israel and the United States, September 1, 1975, FRUS 1969–1976:26, Doc. 227.

535 "that study resulted": Indyk interview with Henry Kissinger, December 19, 2019, and Eilam, *Eilam's Arc*, 83.

536 "That's the worst threat you could utter": Memcon between Kissinger, Rabin, et al., August 27, 1975, KT01761, NSA.

538 "it means peace moves": "Israel Calls Off Peace Talks After Palestinian Deal," NBC News, April 24, 2014.

538 negotiations were never resumed: Anne Gearan and Ruth Eglash, "Israel Suspends Peace Talks with Palestinians," *Washington Post*, April 24, 2014.

538 that both sides were to blame: Nahum Barnea, "Inside the Talks' Failure: US Officials Open Up," *Ynet News*, May 2, 2014, https://www.ynetnews.com/articles/0,7340,L-4515821,00 .html.

539 "would never suspend U.S.-Israel military": "Ambassador Martin Indyk's Speech to The Washington Institute's Weinberg Conference," Washington Institute for Near East Policy, May 8, 2014, https://2009-2017.state.gov/p/nea/rls/rm/225840.htm.

EPILOGUE

542 "momentary considerations and publicity": Paul Hofmann, "Gromyko Urges Middle East Parley," *New York Times*, September 24, 1975, 1. Gromyko took this sideswipe at Kissinger in his UNGA speech three weeks later.

542 through separate doors: "Israel and Egypt Sign Their New Pact; Ceremony Is Shunned by Soviet and U.S.," *New York Times*, September 5, 1975.

543 "quality of political trust": Henry Kamm, "View of Israelis: Best Attainable," *New York Times*, September 2, 1975, 17.

543 coordinated military action: David D. Kirkpatrick, "Secret Alliance: Israel Carries Out Airstrikes in Egypt, with Cairo's O.K.," *New York Times*, February 3, 2018.

544 "to look good to history": "Remarks by the Honorable Henry A. Kissinger," Anwar Sadat Chair for Peace and Development, University of Maryland, College Park, MD, May 4, 2000, https://sadat.umd.edu/events/remarks-honorable-henry-kissinger.

545 outwitted him after all: Patrick Seale, *Asad: The Struggle for the Middle East* (Berkeley, CA: University of California Press, 1989), 260–61.

545 all of Sinai: Henry Tanner, "Sadat Says Soviet Is Trying to Split Arabs over Sinai," *New York Times*, September 5, 1975.

545 "a feeling of mourning": "Middle East Pact . . . ," *New York Times*, September 3, 1975, 36. A public opinion poll taken at the time showed 58 percent of Israelis supported the accord and only 28 percent opposed it.

545 encouraged Peres to make: Simcha Dinitz, "Diplomatic Memoirs" (Unpublished manuscript, in author's possession: 2003), 156.

546 fruits of Rabin's labor: Yitzhak Rabin, *The Rabin Memoirs* (Berkeley, CA: University of California Press, 1996), 275.

546 "of this century": James M. Naughton, "Ford Hails Step," *New York Times*, September 2, 1975.

546 heavenward for salvation: *Time*, August 25, 1975, and "Middle East Pact . . . ," *New York Times*, September 3, 1975, 36.

547 "addendum on arms": "US Documents Accompanying the Sinai Accord," *New York Times*, September 17, 1975, 16.

547 bitterness in Cairo: Henry Tanner, "Some in Cairo Now Feel Kissinger Misled Them," *New York Times*, September 27, 1975, 4.

548 in the Middle East: Bernard Gwertzman, "Senate Committee Backs 200 Technicians for Sinai," *New York Times*, October 8, 1975, 4.

549 the international border: Henry Kissinger, *Years of Renewal* (New York: Touchstone, 1999), 1034–35.

549 In principle: Kissinger, *Years of Renewal*, 1036–37.

550 "indispensable balance wheel": Kissinger, *Years of Renewal*, 1039, and 1043.

550 "an overall peace": Kissinger, *Years of Renewal*, 1050–51.

551 by force: Henry Kissinger, *World Order* (New York: Penguin, 2014), 39.

551 "side by side": Kissinger, *Years of Renewal*, 348.

551 "peace by reasoned design": Kissinger, *World Order*, 40.

552 "every 20 kilometers": Memcon between Kissinger and Jewish Intellectuals, March 31, 1975, FRUS 1969–1976:26, Doc. 168.

552 tired of the conflict: Abdullah bin Zayed Al Nahyan, "'Peace. Shalom. Salaam,'" *Wall Street Journal*, September 14, 2020.

553 "a stage of real peace": Arnaud de Borchgrave, "Voices Across the Fence," *Newsweek*, March 3, 1975.

553 the Arabs weren't ready: Memcon between Kissinger and Assad, March 15, 1975, KT01534, NSA.

554 willing to end the conflict: Indyk, *Innocent Abroad: An Intimate Account of American Peace Diplomacy in the Middle East* (New York: Simon & Schuster, 2009), 28–29.

554 "a blind spot": William B. Quandt, *Peace Process: American Diplomacy and the Arab-Israeli Conflict Since 1967* (Berkeley, CA: University of California Press, 1995), 251, and Khaled Elgindy, *Blind Spot: America and the Palestinians, from Balfour to Trump* (Washington, DC: Brookings Institution, 2019), 93–94.

555 the Palestinian national movement: Elgindy, *Blind Spot*, 83, and Kissinger, *Years of Renewal*, 370.

556 exploit his misstep: Kissinger, *Years of Renewal*, 753, and Henry Kissinger, *Diplomacy* (New York: Simon and Schuster, 1994), 737.

558 "an Israel that is secure": Kissinger's Address to the Conference of Presidents of Major American Jewish Organizations, January 11, 1977, cited in Jeremi Suri, *Henry Kissinger and the American Century* (Cambridge, MA: Harvard University Press, 2009), 269.

558 "like Henry is as a person": Memcon between Ford and Fisher, December 12, 1975, FRUS 1969–1976:26, Doc. 252.

558 legalistic and Talmudic: Kissinger, *World Order*, 131.

559 inability to transport: Uzi Eilam, *Eilam's Arc: How Israel Became a Military Technology Powerhouse* (East Sussex, UK: Sussex Academic Press, 2011), 131.

560 "nothing to lose": Telcon between Kissinger and Haig, October 7, 1973, FRUS 1969–1976:26, Doc. 116.

562 all of the settlements: "Proclamation on Recognizing the Golan Heights as Part of the State of Israel," *White House*, March 25, 2019, https://trumpwhitehouse.archives .gov/presidential-actions/proclamation-recognizing-golan-heights-part-state-israel/; Jason Greenblatt, "Remarks at a UN Security Council Open Debate on the Middle East," United States Mission to the United Nations, July 23, 2019, https://usun.usmission.gov /remarks-at-a-un-security-council-open-debate-on-the-middle-east-9/; "President Donald J. Trump's Vision for Peace, Prosperity, and a Brighter Future for Israel and the Palestinian People," *White House*, January 28, 2020, https://trumpwhitehouse.archives.gov /briefings-statements/president-donald-j-trumps-vision-peace-prosperity-brighter-future -israel-palestinian-people/.

562 "existence on naked force": Kissinger, Henry Kissinger, *Years of Upheaval* (Boston: Little, Brown, 1982), 842–43.

563 relationship with Jordan: Rabin's Speech, Remarks at Reception for Heads of State at the Corcoran Museum, September 28, 1995, https://www.youtube.com/watch?v=X-cEFbtW 5vo&feature=youtu.be.

567 "pending a final agreement": Kissinger, *World Order*, 133.

569 "break the process": Indyk interview with Henry Kissinger, December 19, 2019.

569 international order required: Kissinger, *Diplomacy*, chap. 2.

569 "which inspires men": Henry Kissinger, *A World Restored: Metternich, Castlereagh and the Problems of Peace, 1812–1822* (Brattleboro, VT: Echo Point Books and Media, 2013), 317.

570 "preserves the peace": Kissinger, *Diplomacy*, 27–28.

Index

Page numbers in *italics* refer to photo captions.

Photo Credits

285   AP Photo

296   AP Photo/Bob Daughtery

308   David Hume Kennerly White House Photographs/Photographs selected for possible use in Years of Renewal [4 of 5] - Image 19, Henry A. Kissinger Papers, Part III (MS 2004). Manuscripts and Archives, Yale University

317   AP Photo/Ahmed El Tayeb

334   UN Photo/Yutaka Nagata

356   Egypt trip with Richard Nixon - Image 30, Henry A. Kissinger Papers, Part II (MS 1981). Manuscripts and Archives, Yale University

392   AP Photo/Azad

396   AP Photo/Azad

406   Richard Melloul/Sygma/Sygma via Getty Images

414   *Newsweek*

415   Karl Schumacher/The Richard Nixon Presidential Library and Museum (National Archives and Records Administration)

418   David Hume Kennerly White House Photographs/Amman, Jordan-Image 25, Henry A. Kissinger Papers, Part III (MS 2004). Manuscripts and Archives, Yale University

430   Israeli Government Press Office, Saar Yaacov

439   Thomas/Gerald R. Ford Presidential Library

450   David Hume Kennerly/Getty Images

476   Peter Rodman/Photographs selected for possible use in *Years of Renewal* [4 of 5], 1974–1976. Henry A. Kissinger Papers, Part III (MS 2004). Manuscripts and Archives, Yale University.

478   AP Photo/Max Nash

487   Karl Schumacher/ Gerald R. Ford Presidential Library

493   David Hume Kennerly/Gerald R. Ford Presidential Library

497   Gerald R. Ford Presidential Library

503   Israeli Government Press Office, Saar Yaacov

523   William KAREL/Gamma-Rapho via Getty Images

524   David Hume Kennerly White House Photographs/State Department photographs, Volume 8 - Image 19, Henry A. Kissinger Papers, Part III (MS 2004). Manuscripts and Archives, Yale University.

525   David Hume Kennerly White House Photographs/Photographs selected for possible use in Years of Renewal [3 of 5] - Image 51, Henry A. Kissinger Papers, Part III (MS 2004). Manuscripts and Archives, Yale University.

528   David Hume Kennerly White House Photographs/State Department photographs, Volume 8 - Image 31, Henry A. Kissinger Papers, Part III (MS 2004). Manuscripts and Archives, Yale University

529   David Hume Kennerly White House Photographs/Photographs selected for possible use in Years of Renewal [4 of 5] - Image 27, Henry A. Kissinger Papers, Part III (MS 2004). Manuscripts and Archives, Yale University.

538   State Department

542   Israeli Government Press Office, Moshe Milner

546   Thomas/Gerald R. Ford Presidential Library

547   From TIME. © 1975 TIME USA LLC. All rights reserved. Used under license.

564   Stephen Jaffe/AFP via Getty Images

568   David Hume Kennerly/Getty Images

Grateful acknowledgment is made to the following for permission to reprint previously published material:

EnVeritas Group, Inc.: Excerpt from "Anwar Sadat's Uncertain Trumpet" by Arnaud De Borchgrave, originally published in *Newsweek* on April 9, 1973. Reprinted by permission of EnVeritas Group, Inc.

The Orion Publishing Group, London: Excerpt from *The Rabin Memoirs* by Dov Goldstein and Yitzhak Rabin. Originally published in Great Britain by Weidenfeld & Nicolson, a division of The Orion Publishing Group, London, in 1979. Copyright © 1979 by Yitzhak Rabin. Reprinted by permission of The Orion Publishing Group, London.

The Wylie Agency, LLC: Excerpts from *White House Years* (Little, Brown, 1979), *Years of Upheaval* (Little, Brown, 1982), *Years of Renewal* (Simon & Schuster, 1999), and *Crisis* (Simon & Schuster, 2003) by Henry Kissinger. Reprinted by permission of The Wylie Agency, LLC.

MARTIN INDYK was born in London, raised in Sydney, and edu-
cated at Sydney University and the Australian National University,
where he graduated with a PhD in international relations. He migrated
to the United States in 1982, founded the Washington Institute for
Near East Policy, and became an American citizen in 1993. During
President Clinton's two terms he served as senior director for Middle
East and South Asia on the National Security Council, assistant secretary of state for Near Eastern affairs, and twice as U.S. ambassador to
Israel. In 2001, he joined the Brookings Institution, establishing the
Saban Center for Middle East Policy there, and was then appointed
vice president and director of the Foreign Policy Program. He was
appointed special envoy for Israeli-Palestinian negotiations by President Obama in 2013, returning to Brookings in 2014 to become its
executive vice president. In 2018, he moved to New York to become
a distinguished fellow at the Council on Foreign Relations. He is the
author of *Innocent Abroad: An Intimate Account of American Peace Diplomacy in the Middle East* and the co-author, with Kenneth G. Lieberthal
and Michael E. O'Hanlon, of *Bending History: Barack Obama's Foreign
Policy*.

A NOTE ON THE TYPE

This book was set in Janson, a typeface long thought to have been made by the Dutchman Anton Janson, who was a practicing typefounder in Leipzig during the years 1668–1687. However, it has been conclusively demonstrated that these types are actually the work of Nicholas Kis (1650–1702), a Hungarian, who most probably learned his trade from the master Dutch typefounder Dirk Voskens. The type is an excellent example of the influential and sturdy Dutch types that prevailed in England up to the time William Caslon (1692–1766) developed his own incomparable designs from them.

Composed by North Market Street Graphics,
Lancaster, Pennsylvania

Printed and bound by Berryville Graphics,
Berryville, Virginia

Designed by Cassandra J. Pappas